SSM 510

Systems Management

Communications Theory

ORGANIZATIONAL COMMUNICATION

McGRAW-HILL SERIES IN MANAGEMENT
Keith Davis and Fred Luthans, Consulting Editors

Allen Management and Organization
Allen The Management Profession
Argyris Management and Organizational Development: The Path from XA to YB
Beckett Management Dynamics: The New Synthesis
Benton Supervision and Management
Bergen and Haney Organizational Relations and Management Action
Blough International Business: Environment and Adaptation
Bowman Management: Organization and Planning
Brown Judgment in Administration
Buchele The Management of Business and Public Organizations
Campbell, Dunnette, Lawler, and Weick Managerial Behavior, Performance, and Effectiveness
Cleland and King Management: A Systems Approach
Cleland and King Systems Analysis and Project Management
Cleland and King Systems, Organizations, Analysis, Management: A Book of Readings
Dale Management: Theory and Practice
Dale Readings in Management: Landmarks and New Frontiers
Davis Human Behavior at Work: Organizational Behavior
Davis Organizational Behavior: A Book of Readings
Davis and Blomstrom Business and Society: Environment and Responsibility
DeGreene Systems Psychology
Dunn and Rachel Wage and Salary Administration: Total Compensation Systems
Dunn and Stephens Management of Personnel: Manpower Management and Organizational Behavior
Edmunds and Letey Environmental Administration
Fiedler A Theory of Leadership Effectiveness
Finch, Jones, and Litterer Managing for Organizational Effectiveness: An Experiential Approach
Flippo Principles of Personnel Management
Glueck Business Policy: Strategy Formation and Management Action
Hampton Contemporary Management
Hicks and Gullett The Management of Organizations
Hicks and Gullett Modern Business Management: A Systems and Environmental Approach
Hicks and Gullett Organizations: Theory and Behavior
Johnson, Kast, and Rosenzweig The Theory and Management of Systems
Kast and Rosenzweig Experiential Exercises and Cases in Management
Kast and Rosenzweig Organization and Management: A Systems Approach
Knudson, Woodworth, and Bell Management: An Experiential Approach

Koontz Toward a Unified Theory of Management
Koontz and O'Donnell Essentials of Management
Koontz and O'Donnell Management: A Book of Readings
Koontz and O'Donnell Management: A Systems and Contingency Analysis of Managerial Functions
Lee and Dobler Purchasing and Materials Management: Text and Cases
Levin, McLaughlin, Lamone, and Kottas Production/Operations Management: Contemporary Policy for Managing Operating Systems
Luthans Contemporary Readings in Organizational Behavior
Luthans Introduction to Management: A Contingency Approach
Luthans Organizational Behavior
McNichols Policymaking and Executive Action
Maier Problem-solving Discussions and Conferences: Leadership Methods and Skills
Margulies and Raia Organizational Development: Values, Process, and Technology
Mayer Production and Operations Management
Miles Theories of Management: Implications for Organizational Behavior and Development
Monks Operations Management: Theory and Problems
Mundel A Conceptual Framework for the Management Sciences
Newstrom, Reif, and Monczka A Contingency Approach to Management: Readings
Petit The Moral Crisis in Management
Petrof, Carusone, and McDavid Small Business Management: Concepts and Techniques for Improving Decisions
Porter, Lawler, and Hackman Behavior in Organizations
Prasow and Peters Arbitration and Collective Bargaining: Conflict Resolution in Labor Relations
Ready The Administrator's Job
Reddin Managerial Effectiveness
Richman and Copen International Management and Economic Development
Sartain and Baker The Supervisor and His Job
Schrieber, Johnson, Meier, Fischer, and Newell Cases in Manufacturing Management
Shore Operations Management
Shull, Delbecq, and Cummings Organizational Decision Making
Steers and Porter Motivation and Work Behavior
Sutermeister People and Productivity
Tannenbaum, Weschler, and Massarik Leadership and Organization
Wofford, Gerloff, and Cummins Organizational Communication: The Keystone to Managerial Effectiveness

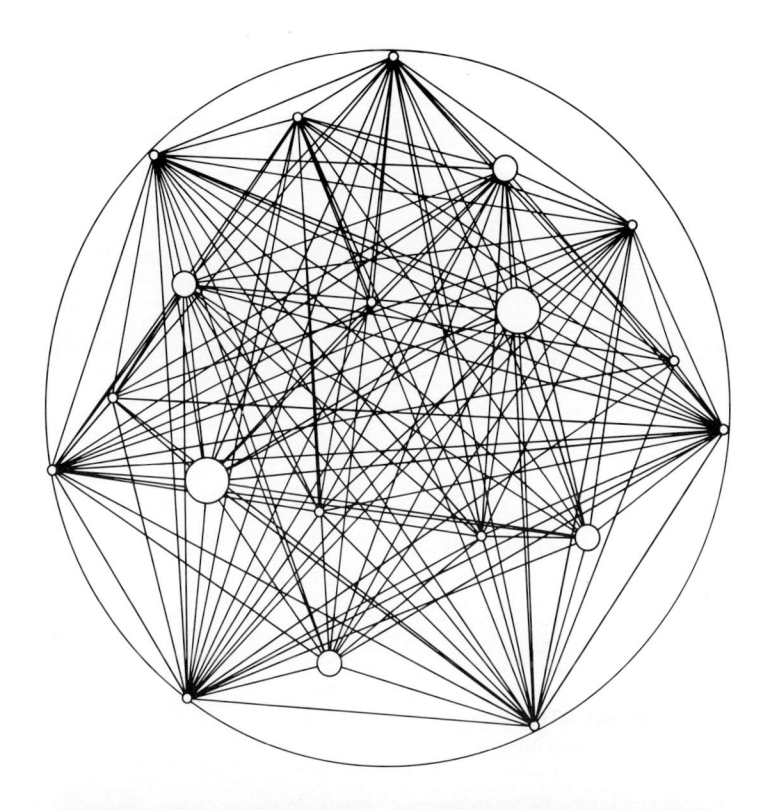

ORGANIZATIONAL COMMUNICATION

The Keystone to
Managerial Effectiveness

JERRY C. WOFFORD
College of Business Administration, University of Texas at Arlington

EDWIN A. GERLOFF
College of Business Administration, University of Texas at Arlington

ROBERT C. CUMMINS
Industrial Consultant

McGRAW-HILL BOOK COMPANY
New York   St. Louis   San Francisco   Auckland   Bogotá   Düsseldorf
Johannesburg   London   Madrid   Mexico   Montreal   New Delhi   Panama
Paris   São Paulo   Singapore   Sydney   Tokyo   Toronto

ORGANIZATIONAL COMMUNICATION
The Keystone to Managerial Effectiveness

Copyright © 1977 by McGraw-Hill, Inc. All rights reserved. Printed in the United States of America. No part of this publication may be reproduced, stored in a retrieval system, or transmitted, in any form or by any means, electronic, mechanical, photocopying, recording, or otherwise without the prior written permission of the publisher.

6789101112   KPKP   898765

Library of Congress Cataloging in Publication Data
Wofford, Jerry C

    Organizational communication.
    (McGraw-Hill series in management)
    Includes index.
    1. Communication in management.   2. Communication in organizations.   I. Gerloff, Edwin A., joint author.
II. Cummins, Robert C., joint author.   III. Title.
HF5718.W6   658.4′5   76-25065
ISBN 0-07-070230-6

This book was set in Janson by University Graphics, Inc. The editors were William J. Kane and Claudia A. Hepburn; the designer was Elliot Epstein; the production supervisor was Leroy A. Young. The drawings were done by J & R Services, Inc.
Kingsport Press, Inc. was printer and binder.

*To
Our
Families*

CONTENTS

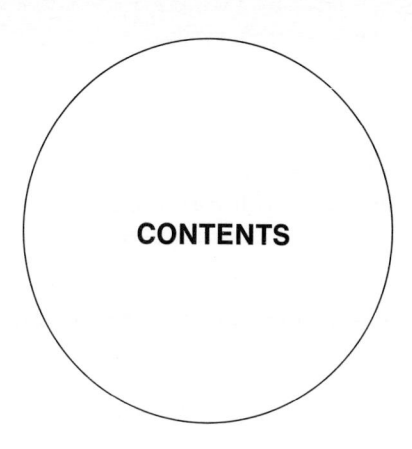

Preface xiii

PART ONE
An Introduction and Point of View for the Study of Organizational Communication

1. **Communication and Management** 3
   The Paradox of Human Communication / The Management Process and Communication / The Orientation of This Book

2. **Communication as a Process** 22
   The Dilemma of Modeling Communication / Communication as a Process / Some Important Considerations in Implementing the Communication Process

3. **Exploring the Nature of the Human Communication Process** 43
   Data and Information Distinguished / The Human Communication Process / Achieving Effectiveness in Human Communication

4. **The Communication Process and Organizations: A Framework for Managerial Analysis** 61
   Organization Goals: Interdependency and Structure / Communication in the Formally Structured Organization / An Analytical Approach to Communication Behavior in Organizations

PART TWO
Managing Organizational Communication: Intra- and Interpersonal Communication

5. **Management of Interpersonal Communication: An Introduction and Overview** 85
   The External-Internal System at the Interpersonal Level of Communication / The Primary Problem Areas in Interpersonal Communication

6. **Intrapersonal Foundations for Interpersonal Communication** 98
   Managing Motivation to Influence Interpersonal Communication / The Effects of Interpersonal Motivation upon Interpersonal Communication / Application of Interpersonal-Needs Concept to Organizational Relationships / Interpersonal Perception upon Communication / Interpersonal Perception and Superior-Subordinate Relations / The Role of Emotions in Interpersonal Communication

7. **Self-Confidence as an Essential Intrapersonal Variable for Effective Communication** 120
   Interpersonal Competence Requires Self-Confidence / Development of Self-Confidence / Developing Self-Confidence in Subordinates / Consequences of Building Self-Confidence

8. **Models for Understanding Interpersonal Relationships** 132
   Exchange Theory as a Model for Interpersonal Communication / Johari Window as a Model for Interpersonal Communication / Transactional Analysis as a Model for Interpersonal Communication

9. **Styles of Human Communication** 147
   Description of the Communication Styles / The Effects of Communication Styles

10. **Barriers to Communication** 169
    Power Differences as a Barrier to Communication / Language as a Barrier to Communication / Communication Which Provokes Defensiveness

11. **Gateways to Effective Interpersonal Communication** 183
    Interpersonal Trust as a Gateway to Communication / Listening as a Gateway to Communication / Feedback as a Gateway to Communication / Nonverbal Communication as a Gateway for the Manager / Nondirective Counseling as a Gateway for the Manager

12. **Communication for Interpersonal Influence**   207
    The Influence Process / Resistance to Change / The Process of Changing Attitudes and Behaviors / Organizational Limitations to Interpersonal Influence / The Attainment of Interpersonal Influence in Organizations / Interpersonal Influence by the Machiavellian Approach

13. **Resolving Interpersonal Conflict**   230
    The Importance of Conflict Resolution / Theory of Interpersonal Conflict / The Confrontation Meeting as an Approach to Conflict Resolution / Types of Possible Solutions in Conflict Resolution

PART THREE
Managing Organizational Communication: Communication within Organization Subsystems and Small Groups

14. **An External-Internal Systems Orientation to the Management of Communication within Small Groups**   245
    Analysis of the External System of the Group / The Group as an Organizational Subsystem / Analysis of the Internal System of the Group / The Impact of the External and Internal Systems upon the Communication Process

15. **Elements of Group Behavior and the Communication Process**   251
    Establishing the Group Identity through the Communication Process / The Relationship of Social Structure to the Communication Process / The Goals of the Group and the Communication Process / Group Cohesiveness and the Communication Process / Group Norms and Communication

16. **Group Communication Networks**   269
    The Nature of Communication Networks / Types of Communication Networks / Properties of Communication Networks / Effects of the Networks of Communication / Factors Which Determine the Nature of the Communication Networks

17. **Group Communication and Performance**   287
    Communication in Group Social Interaction / Groups Oriented toward Personal-Growth Objectives / Communication in the Group Decision-making Process / Communication in Groups Oriented toward Production Objectives

18. **The Relationship of Leadership Behavior with Communication**   317
    Comparison of the Emergent and the Formal Leaders / The Communication-Influence Functions of the Leader / Analysis of Leadership Influence and Power / The Process of Leadership / The Dimensions of Leadership Behavior / Situational Variables Which Influence Leadership Effectiveness / The Importance of the Follower for Leadership Communication

PART FOUR
Managing Total Organizational Communication: A Global Level of Analysis

19. **Formal Organizations and Communication**   337
    Nature of Communication within Formal Organizations / Matching Formal Organization and Communication to Environment / Managing the Formal Organization through Communication

20. **Management and Communication Problems of the Formal Organization**   366
    Problems, Conflicts, and Consequences of Formal Organization / Distortion and Filtering in the Formal Communication Channels / How Successful Organizations Provide Communication and Deal with Conflict

21. **Informal Communication Systems as Compensators**   388
    A High Level of Useful Communication Occurs in the Informal System / Factors Affecting the Formation of Informal Communication Networks / Operational Considerations: The Two-Step Flow of Informal Communication

22. **The External and Internal System Mix and Approaches to Organizational Communication**   422
    Considerations in Determining an External-Internal Mix / The Mechanistic-Organic Mix and Organizational Information Needs

23. **Managing Organizational Communication**   443
    Organizational Subsystems and Their Information and Communication Needs / The Manager's Influence on Organizational Communication / Organizations as Information Processors

Indexes   465
   Name Index
   Subject Index

PREFACE

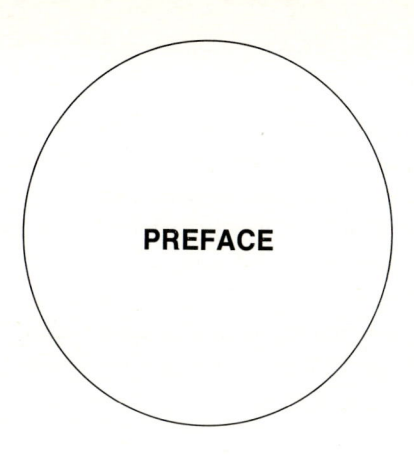

An important, developing field within business curricula is that of organizational communication. Communication is a required skill at every level of organizational functioning for organizations of all types. The effectiveness with which a person will be able to perform in almost any organization, whether social, governmental, or commercial, will depend in large measure upon the ability to communicate effectively.

This book is planned as a text to provide basic understanding of organizational communication at the undergraduate and graduate levels. The style and language of the book are designed to ensure readability and interest for undergraduate students, while the theory and research content provide a thorough coverage of the subject matter that will meet the needs of graduate students. The chapters contain many examples and incidents which illustrate the problems being discussed and which stimulate students to think about the topics being presented and to relate the concepts to their own experiences. Review questions, incidents, role-playing exercises, cases, and games at the end of each chapter are designed to generate interest and to improve the communication skills of the students.

The emerging discipline of organizational communication is not fully identifiable in previous books. In this text the theory and research of a number of diverse disciplines are distilled into a comprehensive and consistent conceptual framework. The intent is to present the essence of this new discipline in a concise, orderly, and applicable fashion for the student and the practitioner of management. Continuity of ideas and content is provided by starting with the individual communication processes and then expanding through the two-person relationships to groups and finally to the total organizational level. In using this approach we not only enhance continuity but also contribute to the learning process by building new concepts upon those presented for an earlier level of analysis.

We take a great deal of pleasure in acknowledging the help we have received from the many students who have critically reviewed the manuscript; from Mrs. Royce Dunn, Mrs. Fran Estill, Mrs. Barbara Dinsmore, Mrs. Golda King, Mrs. Irene Koby, and Mrs. Pam Cooley, who helped in the preparation of the manuscript; and from the many behavioral and social science theorists and researchers whose work provided resource material for the book. We are also grateful to the following persons for their helpful comments upon reading the manuscript: Jon M. Huegli, Eastern Michigan University; C. Don Porterfield, University of Texas at San Antonio; and Raymond E. Hill, University of Michigan.

Jerry C. Wofford
Edwin A. Gerloff
Robert C. Cummins

ORGANIZATIONAL COMMUNICATION

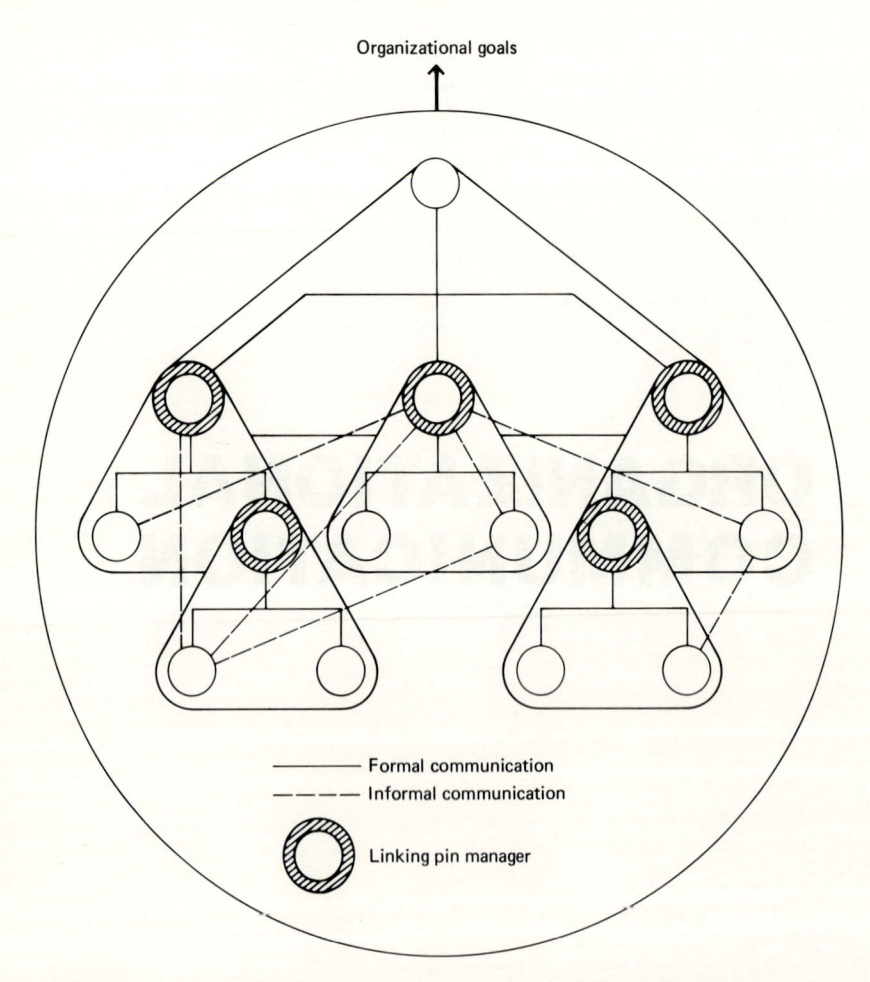

FIGURE 1 Linking organizational units together via linking pins and communication. [*After Rensis Likert*, New Patterns of Management *(New York: McGraw-Hill Book Company, 1961).*]

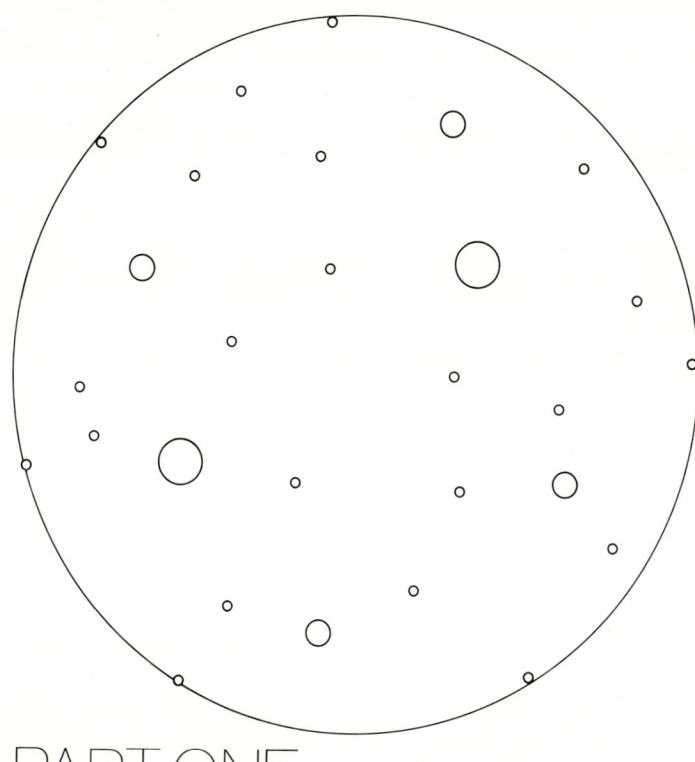

PART ONE

AN INTRODUCTION AND POINT OF VIEW FOR THE STUDY OF ORGANIZATIONAL COMMUNICATION

Terms such as "management" and "communication" are sufficiently broad that they mean almost anything to almost anybody. Accordingly, we shall begin this book by seeking to clarify what *we* mean when we say *organizational communication* and *management*. A second and related concern of this opening section is to provide the reader with a point of view and analytical framework which can be used in the remaining sections of the book. Chapter 1 discusses the nature of the management process and examines the importance of communication to the effective implementation of management. The nature of organizational communication is also described. Chapter 2 discusses communication as a general process which consists of certain critical elements. Certain determinants of the effectiveness of the communication process will also be discussed. In Chapter 3 the process model is adapted to the human-communication situation. Chapter 4 treats the organization as a hierarchy of goals which is highly dependent on managerial and communicative processes for its effectiveness. An analytical approach is presented.

1

COMMUNICATION AND MANAGEMENT

In this chapter we shall briefly examine the nature of the management process. Emphasis will be given to the dependency of each phase of the management process on effective communication. Three approaches to the study of communication for managers will be identified.

It can be shown that communication is the binding agent of all social systems and subsystems. The experience of many of us has been that success or failure in communication can often be identified as a major determinant of the outcome of any social episode. The observation seems to hold true regardless of the type of social event. Communication is instrumental in the outcome of games, international negotiations, and the management of organizations. Perhaps a few examples will drive this point home.

The outcome of a baseball game is partly dependent on the effectiveness of communication between teammates. The catcher and pitcher understand the importance of communication and usually establish a set of signals which will convey information concerning pitching tactics for a given opposing batter. We all are aware that football teams use special coding and communication systems for calling plays with the intention of confusing and baffling the players of the opposing team. We are all equally aware that such communication systems do not always work as intended. The pass receiver thought he was to "block" instead of "catch." The running back ran in the wrong direction. The center or some other lineman missed the count and blew the play. Communication failures are perhaps more frequent than communication successes in the lives of all of us. At least it always seems so.

THE PARADOX OF HUMAN COMMUNICATION

Communication between humans is clearly an essential element for all levels of human activity. It is one of the most pervasive forces of living itself. We all communicate or at least attempt to do so. However, something of a paradox exists in that the more we communicate, the more we seem to fail. One normally expects to become more skilled at activities performed frequently. Contrary to our personal assumptions about ourselves as well as prevailing popular opinion, most of us are pretty bad communicators. Perhaps we don't really understand what is involved in communicating. A few brief examples of some of the problems involved will help make the point.

Problems with Multiple Messages

One reason why the communication process is so difficult to understand is that a given communication episode may contain many types of messages. We are reminded of an incident that is said to have occurred in a football game once. The coach of one team was frantically shouting instructions to the players during a crucial part of the game (a message). An official saw this, threw the flag, and told the coach that the team was to be penalized 5 yards because the coach was "coaching from the sidelines" (a message). The coach protested that the rules of the game had not been violated, but that if they had, the rules called for a 15-yard penalty for that particular infraction. The official replied that the penalty assessed matched the seriousness of the infraction. There was a clear inference that the coach's ability did not justify the full penalty yardage (a message). It is clear that this incident involved at least three messages: coach to players, direct official to coach (flag and penalty), indirect official to coach (inference about coaching ability). Think of a specific personal experience of your own and try to enumerate the kinds of messages and types of communication channels which were involved, and you will find just how common and complex the communication process can be.

Problems with Differences in Language and Meaning

To further make our point concerning the ubiquity and complexity of the communication process, consider the arena of international negotiations. The representatives of the United States and North Vietnam met in Paris for approximately four years seeking to negotiate an end to the war in Southeast Asia. There was some evidence that an agreement had been reached in October 1972 and then the talks were suddenly halted. Without being drawn into the politics of what actually happened, consider the situation as described by *Time* (January 1, 1973, p. 25). Henry Kissinger (the chief United States negotiator) had displayed considerable optimism until, at the last minute, he received the exact protocol which Hanoi had in mind for the International Control Commission which was to keep the peace. Kissinger later said,

> To the U.S. the proposal was a joke; it called for a force of 250 men to handle a task the U.S. thought would require a force of some 5,000 men. (*Time*, January 1, 1973)
>
> The North Vietnamese perception of international machinery and our perception is at drastic variance. (*Time*, December 25, 1972)

The situation described by Kissinger is not really surprising. Research (Blake and Mouton, 1961) has shown that misunderstandings regarding the objective properties of solutions are directly related to one's membership affiliation. We comprehend *our* solution but not the opponent's, even where the two are similar.

Problems with the Effects of Situation and Individual Psychology

As an example that is more relevant to the management of organizations, consider the restaurant situation. Research in the industry suggested that an apparently simple communication situation requiring the transfer of the customer's order to the cook brought about considerable stress and frustration under certain circumstances. Whyte (1961) observed that the type of communication channel used, the status differences of users, and the pressures of workload and timing tended to cause a great deal of friction at certain interface points (see Figure 1-1) in the communications network. As a general rule, the cook resents having his work initiated by the waitress, who is of lower status, but the situation can become especially troublesome during rush hours when the increased workload forces errors in processing the customer's order. If he or she receives stew instead of soup, the irate customer is apt to convey displeasure to the waitress, who in turn must consult with the cook. Perhaps she will suggest that the cook was in error, and eventually the whole unhappy circumstance will be dumped on the manager (by three irate individuals). The insertion of a spindle in the communication network (a change in the channel) reduced the probability of error as well as the frequency of

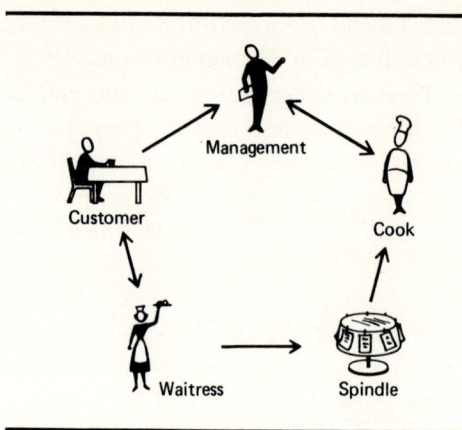

FIGURE 1-1 The spindle. The introduction of the spindle breaks up the face-to-face relation between the waitress and the cook. [*Source:* Elias H. Porter, Man-power Development *(New York: Harper & Row, Publishers, 1964), p. 5. Reproduced with permission.*]

direct contact between the waitress and the cook. The customer's check (with his or her order in writing) was simply placed on the spindle so that the cook could read it for himself. Thus there was a much less personal connection between the two, and the written record tended to reduce error or at least minimize arguments concerning who was to blame. Though the waitress still initiated the cook's work, there was a greater psychological distance and the opportunity for interpersonal friction was minimized. As in the case of one's personal-communication situation, the apparent simplicity of the organizational-communication situation can also disguise its complexity in terms of the multiplicity of messages and channels which actually exist.

Practice Does Not Always Make Perfect

Such examples as the preceding ones suggest that though we are all *users* of communication, we do not always seem to understand its complexity. Perhaps the following remark will bring the point into focus.

> A celebrated authority on Canon law and medieval universities, Dr. Hastings Rashdall, was one of those who could ride, but not understand a bicycle. One day, for example, having had a puncture in his front tire, he was found vigorously

pumping up the back one; when a passerby pointed this out to him, he remarked, "What? Do they not communicate?" I sometimes wonder whether, in our present-day eagerness to "put people in the picture," we do not behave rather like Dr. Rashdall, strenuously pumping in information at one end of a firm, in the hopeful expectation that it will somehow find its way to the other. Perhaps we too ride, but cannot understand. (Higham, 1957)

Indeed it is difficult to conceive of a human situation or activity which is not dependent in some fashion on the conveyance of meaning and information. Similarly, one is not hard-pressed to think of numerous personal experiences in which such a conveyance was not adequately achieved. The process of communicating is fundamental to life itself, it is a highly personal phenomenon for all persons, it is ubiquitous. Communication processes, communication successes, and communication failures can be detected in all walks and levels of life.

All this does not mean we are not trying to improve our understanding of communications. We would not have written this book and you would not be reading it unless there was a mutual interest in improving human communication. Actually, numerous and diverse groups are committed to expanding our knowledge of the subject. There is considerable effort and research on the subject of communication by engineers, scientists, psychologists, sociologists, management theorists, and information theorists, to name but a few. Schools of communication are emerging in the universities, there are at least two journals devoted exclusively to the subject, and untold numbers of articles and conferences have been concerned with some aspect of communication. Thayer (1967) noted that the participants in the Second International Symposium on Communication Theory and Research represented five different nations and twenty different disciplines.

Relative to such a diverse array of disciplines, the scope of this book is much more narrow. It is aimed at helping people in organizations to communicate more effectively with one another and will do so primarily by drawing from the literature and research in such fields as psychology, sociology, and management. In particular, the thrust of the book is aimed at meeting the needs of potential and practicing managers. The literature and research of a number of disciplinary areas will be utilized to provide a comprehensive overview of the nature of human communication and its intricate involvement with the management function. It is hoped that, armed with new-found *understanding*, the manager will then be a better *user* of communication. A brief discussion of the nature of managerial work and its dependency on communication is necessary before we leap further into our ambitious undertaking.

THE MANAGEMENT PROCESS AND COMMUNICATION

Beginning at least as early as 1900 with the work of Fayol and continuing into the present time, numerous authors have treated management as a function or process. The primary concern of such literature seems to have been to identify and analyze the nature of managerial work and to make recommendations regarding its implementation. Having specified the form and content of managerial work, the author(s) could then analyze the conditions, requirements, behaviors, and technology necessary for effective performance of the management process. Similarly, we wish to briefly examine the nature of the managerial process and establish the integral relationship of communication with managerial performance. The interdependency of management and communication then becomes a point of reference for an in-depth examination of communication, which is the central focus of this book. When the time is appropriate, of course, we will make our own recommendations concerning the implementation of both the management and the communication process.

Some variance exists among the many authors with respect to precisely which elements of the managerial function or process are identified and how they are

TABLE 1-1 The Process of Management as Viewed by Selected Authors

Management function or process element	Koontz and O'Donnell	Dale	Massie	Newman, Summer, and Warren	Hicks	Fayol
Planning	✓	✓	✓	✓	✓	✓
Organizing	✓	✓	✓	✓	✓	✓
Staffing	✓	✓	✓			
Directing/commanding	✓	✓	✓			✓
Controlling	✓	✓	✓	✓	✓	✓
Innovating/creating		✓			✓	
Decision making			✓			
Leading				✓		
Motivating					✓	
Communicating			✓		✓	
Coordinating						✓
Representation		✓				

labeled. Table 1-1 summarizes the elemental behaviors of management as viewed by several respected management authors.

For the purposes of this book, we need not be drawn into a controversy concerning which view of the management process is most appropriate. It should suffice to say that some combination of the listed elemental behaviors or others which are similar will be required in the performance of any managerial task.

Planning, organizing, directing, and *controlling* are all widely discussed in the literature as basic elements of the management process.[1] Because of their resulting widespread general familiarity, these same elements of managerial behavior have been selected for the discussion which follows. It will be shown that communication is interwoven with the performance of each of these elements of the management process. Lest the point be missed, it should be emphasized now that we contend that communication is the underpinning of all elements of the management process. We have isolated these particular ones merely for convenience of discussion. Indeed, it is suggested that the reader, as an additional exercise, try to expand on the role of communication for the balance of the managerial-process elements shown in Table 1-1.

Planning

Planning is, or at least should be, a dominant feature of any manager's job. Planning is aimed at determining what objectives and goals should be accomplished and, in a very general way, how they should be accomplished. Included under the planning category would be the development of strategy, policy, budgets, and the other general guides to action which we find in most organizations. We have all been involved with the process of planning or affected by its results. As examples, the legislative and executive branches of our government engage in the development of general plans to meet the nation's energy, economic, and employment needs. The head of a department in a university participates in the determination of a budget for the department and, subsequently, will surely find that operations are constrained by that budget. Indeed, each faculty member and student will be affected by such budgetary constraints. Any manager or employee finds that he or she must conform to the requirements of numerous policies and plans. Managers often participate directly in the formulation of such plans, and develop related plans and policies for those who are below them in the hierarchy. Such plans are instrumental in guiding the collective behavior of organization members toward the intended organizational goals. You can probably

---

[1]For an in-depth discussion of these together with other management-process elements, a number of fine texts are available including those listed in the Bibliography at the end of this chapter.

think of many examples in your own experiences which demonstrate the effect of planning in guiding and constraining the behavior of all of us.

Even on the basis of such a brief discussion of planning, it is possible to show a direct linkage and interdependency between planning and communication. The manager is unable to formulate plans in the absence of information, and it is through the process of communication that we move information to those who require it. Conversely, the results of planning (strategy, policy, etc.) will be of no value to the organization if not communicated to managers and other organizational participants.

The incident described earlier concerning Kissinger's problem in international negotiation can be used as an example of the interdependency of planning and communication. Kissinger and the North Vietnamese were surely attempting to formulate a set of plans and policies which would ensure the peace, but they were unable to do so when a breakdown in communication occurred. We have seen that Kissinger was later able to recognize that he and the North Vietnamese had not clearly communicated their respective positions concerning a control mechanism. As a result, other aspects of the overall plan for peace failed. Further, even the successful development of a set of policies by the negotiators would have been no guarantee of peace. There still would be the problem of communicating the policies to those individuals in the field who would actually implement them. Any manager faces similar problems which arise from the interdependency of planning and communication. Plans cannot be developed and they cannot be implemented without communication.

Organizing

Some writers include organizing as an integral part of planning. There is merit in doing so in the sense that many formal aspects of the organization are planned in advance. Organizing is a natural extension of the planning process and it does involve a planning phase. We prefer to distinguish organizing from planning because the two phases of the management process have somewhat different effects in terms of scope and degree of specificity. Planning tends to generate broad-gauge guides and constraints to action, whereas organizing is aimed at prescribing specific activities which are required to achieve goals and objectives. To a degree, we can think of planning as the process of defining goals or ends and of organizing as the process of establishing the means through which the ends or goals will be achieved.

In any event, the manager who is organizing will be determining the specific set of activities and interrelationships which are necessary to accomplish the objectives of his or her unit. In doing so, the manager is likely to group activities together in a meaningful fashion, structure individual roles, and determine the necessary authority-responsibility relationships. The manager is, in effect, designing his or her organization. It should be clear that, in some fashion, the manager will be dividing the total work of the unit among its various members. Such a subdivision will, in turn, necessitate that adequate communication be provided among the various subunits.

As was the case for planning, the manager's organizing function is heavily dependent on effective communication. Communication is needed so that a given manager can understand the overall organization goals and objectives (the partial results of planning as discussed previously). Using knowledge of overall goals as a basis, the manager and/or subordinates can then define lower-level subunit operations to be consistent with those of the overall organization. Where several individuals are engaged in the organizing activity, communication among them will clearly be required. Once the organizing plan is complete, it must be communicated to those who will implement it. Finally, as has already been suggested, communication is a necessary ingredient in the day-to-day operation of the plan. Managers in all types of organization have experienced the interdependency of organizing and communicating. Perhaps the reader can recall similar experiences of his or her own.

Directing

For many, though it is a misguided impression, directing epitomizes the manager's job. Perhaps the first mistake of the embryonic manager is to be obnoxiously directive and "bossy." We must hasten to add that when management writers discuss the directive aspect of the management function, they usually do not mean "giving orders" in the narrowest sense of the phrase. Still, the directive aspect of the management job is much more operational in nature and much less planning in nature than either planning or organizing. Directing is often what managers find themselves to be doing. *Directing* might be defined as the global set of behaviors which are used by the manager to encourage the organization members to perform as required by organization need, plan, and design. Directing, in this broader sense, probably includes leading, motivating, coordination, and communicating (see Table 1-1). The directing behavior of any two managers might be quite different for the same situation, and the results might be quite different. We shall have more to say about the subject when leadership is discussed in a subsequent chapter.

Perhaps an example will clarify the broader meaning we have in mind for directing. The director of a play cannot just "tell" the actors to display the emotion called for by the script. Directors may choose to demonstrate their intentions by "playing the part" themselves. They may tell personal stories which arouse the desired emotions in the actors, or they may place the actors in situations such that the necessary emotions are aroused. Some managers may appeal to the subordinate's sense of loyalty and fair play to encourage productivity, while others make obvious use of direct instructions, reward, and discipline to achieve the same purpose. Some managers will find ways of utilizing the ego and achievement drives of employees to accomplish organizational purposes. Perhaps there are still other managers who can make use of all three approaches or even some quite different approach in directing subordinates. Whatever the style of the manager in directing subordinates, some form of communication will be an integral part of the process.

In order for directing in any of its many possible forms to take place effectively, communication must occur. Directing is the initiation, the activation, the implementation of the organization plan. The minimum requirement in directing is that the manager must communicate to subordinates his or her expectations concerning their job performance. However, successful managers are often capable of going much beyond this minimum. They communicate to their subordinates concerning values, attitudes, sentiments, work technology, and an almost infinite array of topics which can support job performance. Thinking of your own job experiences, you can perhaps recall supervisors of each type—some who merely communicated job expectations and others who communicated concerning a rich array of topics. Depending on circumstances, either type of supervisor might quite effectively perform the directing function. The point for now is that no manager can direct in the absence of communication.

Controlling

Controlling can best be distinguished from planning, organizing, and directing by focusing on the relative time of occurrence of each function. Planning and organizing must precede the actual operative work of the organization. The manager plans goals and objectives and then organizes the work to accomplish the goals. Directing occurs on a day-to-day basis as the plans are put into operation. *Controlling* also occurs as plans are put into operation, but the emphasis is quite different. In the case of directing, the manager wishes to see that operatives perform their tasks as prescribed by plan and design. The focus is primarily on "how" the task is performed. When controlling, the manager is interested in how well the unit is accomplishing its objectives. In this case, the manager focuses on "what" is done. To accomplish this purpose, the manager must collect information concerning the actual performance or output of the unit and compare this with intended performance. Should there be an unacceptable discrepancy between the two measures, the manager then must ascertain the cause and ensure that the necessary corrective action is taken.

Controlling, like the other elements of the management function, can take many forms, and an extensive discussion is not possible in this text or consistent with its purposes. However, a few observations are in order to highlight the role of communication in implementing the managerial function of controlling. Depending on circumstances, the controlling function may be provided by one person (the manager), a number of persons (the manager and others), technology, or some combination of people and technology. If the shop supervisor sets production quotas for his or her people and checks their output against these quotas, he or she is controlling. If the plant superintendent in a dress factory establishes certain quality standards for tailors and then hires a number of inspectors to check the garments, he or she, too, is controlling. On the other hand, the computerized management information system may also be used for purposes of control. Printouts may inform purchasing agents (and their boss) that they have exceeded their budgets. Printouts may also warn the manager of a complex project that an important PERT milestone (deadline) has passed, or tell the personnel manager that additional machinists will be needed to complete a production contract. Controlling, too, is an important part of the management process, and it too is highly dependent on communication.

The essential elements of control as a process include measurement, comparison, decision making, and feedback or corrective action. Each of these elements, even for the simplest of control situations, involves communication or the flow of data and information. The measurement of actual performance together with the intended standard must be made available at the location where comparison and decision making will occur. Any corrective action or feedback must be communicated to those who can effectively initiate the required action. It is probably true that for most controlling situations, a number of individuals (in addition to the manager) are involved in the process. As a consequence, communication among them becomes crucial to success.

The literature of managerial control is rich with examples of controlling malfunctions which have resulted from communication difficulties. Perhaps budget-overrun information is communicated to a person who is not responsible for the controlled activity, and who is therefore unable to effect a change. During communication from the measurement point to the comparison point, the production schedule for an important component part is misstated. The effect is that the responsible manager believes he or she is ahead of schedule instead of dangerously behind schedule. Communication affects the control process in less direct fashion also. For example, through effective communication, standards may be updated or the control process itself may be changed to meet new needs and requirements. There is nothing so useless as an outmoded system of control. A review of your own experiences with the process of control will probably be quite enlightening. See how many examples you can count which reflect the interdependency of control and communication.

Interdependence of Management and Communication

In reality, communication is an integral process of the management function itself. Much of the previous discussion has viewed communication as a basic *input* and *output* for the managerial process, but it is also synonymous with the act of management as it occurs in the "real time" sense. As one manages, one is also simultaneously communicating. A number of writers (Melcher and Beller, 1967; Sigband, 1969; and Timbers, 1966, are examples) have treated the interdependence of managerial effectiveness and communication. Hicks (1972), in discussing his version of the six functions of management (see Table 1-1), observes that each functional element occurs within the other. When managers plan, they also create, organize, and so on. Hicks contends that all six functions are subfunctions of each other. Indeed, this line of reasoning can be extended to all the management-process elements shown in Table 1-1. Of course, our particular point in discussing the matter presently is simply that one cannot manage without communicating.

The interrelationship of communication and the management process can be summarized by modifying Albers's (1974) model of the management process as has been done in Figure 1-2. In carrying out the managerial process, definite but changing communication relationships must be established between the manager and subordinates. The forward communication described by Albers will be primarily of a directive nature. Such communication may flow vertically downward through the hierarchy, or it may spread horizontally through the organization along with the flow of work. In either case the intention is to communicate to subordinates the current expectations of management regarding job performance. The feedback path takes form as an upward flow of communication which informs

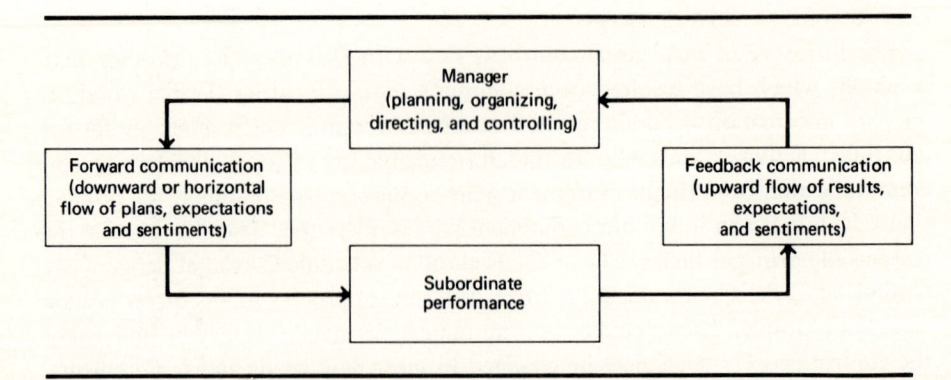

FIGURE 1-2 The management process and communication. [*Source:* Henry H. Albers, Principles of Management: A Modern Approach, *4th ed. (New York: John Wiley & Sons, Inc., 1974).*]

the manager concerning the subordinate's performance and any problems which might occur. Such feedback is clearly related to the manager's control function. It is important to emphasize that both kinds of communication are vital to the manager; his or her success and the success of the organization depend on both kinds of information. It is equally important to note that the process is dynamic—it changes with each new situation. Finally, we should point out that the precise nature of the communication channels involved is quite varied. Some channels will be formal ones and involve the written word while others may be informal and oral, or perhaps even nonverbal in nature. All channels will be influenced by the attitudes and values of the participants. For this reason we have included sentiments in Figure 1-2. Much remains to be said about such matters, and we will do so in the balance of this book. First, however, a word about the particular approach to management communication that we will use in this book.

THE ORIENTATION OF THIS BOOK

It is obvious from the preceding discussion that communication is of sweeping breadth and touches on every facet of life and social order, including management. Some concept of communication is treated in almost every disciplinary area of study, ranging from speech and drama to engineering and the sciences. For a book that is specifically concerned with organization and management, three general approaches to the study of communication seem especially relevant.

Information Theory

One possible approach is to take an *information theory* point of view to the study of communication and management. This approach involves the application of mathematical, scientific, and other forms of technical theory to the flow of data through an organization. Information theory is typically concerned with a systemic analysis of the problem of transmitting a mass of data in a distortion-free fashion to locations where it is needed. Pioneering work in the field of information theory has been performed by Shannon and Wiener.[2] The field of information theory falls mostly outside the scope of this book. However, some of the terminology and theory is directly transferable to the study of human communication, and where appropriate, we have made such transfers. In doing so, we will, of course, make an appropriate notation.

---

[2]See Norbert Wiener, *Cybernetics* (New York: John Wiley & Sons, Inc., 1948). Also see Claude E. Shannon, "The Mathematical Theory of Communication," *Bell System Technical Journal*, July–October 1948.

Individual Communication

A second approach to the study of communication is that of *individual* or *human communication*. This view is distinguished from information theory in that it draws heavily from the behavioral science literature rather than the mathematical and technical literature. Such an approach draws from the research and theory focusing on motivation, perception, and emotion to explain human communication. By *human communication* we mean the establishment of a relationship between two or more persons such that the actions, thoughts, feelings, and intentions of one person (the sender) evoke a response in others (targets or receivers). Ideally, the evoked response is one which the communicator *intended*. Human communications, for the purposes of this book, are contrived or *purposeful*; people communicate for a reason. We are concerned with communications in human organizations that, in large part, are planned to achieve some specific purpose or purposes. However, it is conceded that not all human communication in the organization is planned or contrived. Indeed the reader is cautioned that, to the contrary, much of the communication which occurs is unplanned by the sender and elicits unintended responses in the receiver. We will, then, be concerned with communication failures or how the wrong "meaning" is sometimes conveyed to the receiver. Such failures often involve human consideration, and for this reason, the behavioral science literature will be more important than is the literature of information theory.

Organizational Communication

A third approach to the study of communication has been called *organizational communication*. We have selected this approach as the most feasible one for examining the communication aspects of the management function. In a sense, organizational communication lies somewhere in between information theory and human communication. We will be concerned with the *flow* of data through the organization as are the information theorists. However, our emphasis will be on the flow of communication as it occurs between individuals in the network formed by the structure of the organization itself. In the global sense, the organizational-communication network will include downward, horizontal, and upward flows of communication between organization members. Such a continuously operating network of communication is superimposed on the organization structure and must be effectively used by its members in carrying through the organization's mission. Guetzkow (1965) refers to organizational communication as, "the matrix which links members together in organizations" and which "serves as the vehicle by which organizations are embedded in their environments." Such a view, of course, is quite distinct from the information theorist's concern with the effective movement of masses of data through the organization.

In addition to the structural influences on flow, the network will also be influenced by the psychosocial makeup of the participants. Accordingly, our study of organizational communication will be much more concerned with the concepts and literature of human communication than that of information theory. The emphasis is justified because in addition to a concern with the *flow* of messages in the organization's structural networks, we will be concerned with their *meaning*. What are the intended (by the sender) contents of a message and what are its contents according to the recipient? What factors influence the differences and how may they be controlled? These questions and other similar ones are very valid ones for the manager and other organizational participants to ask. To answer such questions (if this is at all possible), one must understand the complex and intricate interrelationships of organization structure and human behavior, especially as each affects the communication process.

Organization of the Book

This book is aimed at improving the reader's understanding of organizational communication. To do so, we shall use the balance of this part of the book to examine the nature of the communication process and to provide a sense of perspective as to how it fits into the structure of the organization. An analytical approach to organizations will also be introduced in this part. In subsequent parts of the book, the intrapersonal, interpersonal, and small-group factors and their impact on the communication process will be examined. The final part of the book will provide an overview of organizational communication by focusing on the interrelationship of intrapersonal, interpersonal, and group factors. The role of the manager in blending the three levels of factors into a climate for effective organizational communication will be stressed.

SUMMARY

In this opening chapter we have noted the ubiquitous nature of communication in all levels of life. We are all *users* of communication but indications are that we really do not understand communication as a process. The particular emphasis of this book is on communication as a major subset of the management process itself. Management subfunctions such as planning, organizing, directing, and controlling were shown to be intricately involved with and dependent on communication. Three general approaches to the study of communication for the manager were identified and described. Organizational communication was seen as the most balanced approach to the communication problems of the manager. Organizational communication is concerned with the network of communication flows as determined by the structure of the organization and the psychosocial behavior of the individuals who operate it.

REVIEW QUESTIONS

1. Drawing from your own experiences, describe some specific recent communication events which affected you personally. Did the events involve communication successes or failures? What sorts of channels were involved (verbal, nonverbal, written, oral, etc.)?
2. Imagine a world, a nation, a state, or an organization without communication. Describe and evaluate the effectiveness of such a system.
3. Describe the "work of the manager." How is management connected with communication? Can one manage without communicating? Why?
4. Think of the most stressing problem you have faced in some organization. Was communication involved in solving the problem? What sorts of communicative behavior were involved? Where did you get the needed information? What kinds of barriers did you encounter? Might the situation have been handled differently?
5. Referring to Table 1-1 and your own experiences, find as many examples as you can which reflect the dependence of each element of managerial behavior on communication.
6. Discuss three possible approaches to the study of communication and give examples of each.
7. Communication can be considered as a type of interface between the organization and the individual or the organization and its environment. Would you be willing to accept this statement as an accurate one? Why or why not?

INCIDENT 1: A WORLD WITHOUT COMMUNICATION

Suppose you are the single passenger of a spaceship that has landed on the planet Sarious. You find a population of people with whom you cannot communicate in any fashion. Further, you find they have developed no form of communication with one another.

1. How would such a lack of communication make their society different from our own?
2. How would you behave in such a society?
3. What could be substituted for communication?

INCIDENT 2: THE MANAGER'S LOG

The following events are typical of a day at the office for the chairperson of a large department in a large American university. The experiences of this manager are probably representative of those of many managers.

9:00 A.M.   On arrival, met for fifteen minutes with Professor X concerning budget for departmental computer accounts.

9:15 A.M.   Met for thirty minutes with Professor Y (assistant chairperson) concerning fall semester enrollment and registration problems requiring prompt action.

9:45 A.M.   Met for fifteen minutes with Professor Z (graduate advisor) concerning fall semester enrollment.

10:00 A.M. Met briefly with Professors Y and Z to discuss fall semester enrollment.

During the thirty-minute period, 10:05–10:35 A.M., composed a letter to the relative of a student regarding curriculum requirements. This was accomplished when not interrupted by miscellaneous telephone calls and other interruptions.

10:35 A.M. Professor A handed me a rather long and involved memo complaining about a space problem. He is a member of another department. Discussed the problem with Professor A for about ten minutes.

10:45 A.M. Spent fifteen minutes discussing the space problem and other matters with the dean.

11:15 A.M. After fifteen minutes discussing the space problem with the assistant dean and Professor B, attempted to call Professor A. Unable to contact him.

11:35 A.M. Completed twenty-minute conversation regarding service policy on office machine with secretary and service person. When this discussion was completed, used the next twenty-five minutes to return important telephone calls which had accumulated while I was in conference.

12:00 N   Went to lunch.

12:45 P.M. Spent thirty minutes discussing the service policy with the assistant chairperson. We agreed on the steps needed to solve the problem.

1:15 P.M.   Placed telephone call to sales representative of the office machine company.

1:30 P.M.   Spent ninety minutes at meeting of the executive committee discussing goals for the college.

3:00 P.M.   Discussed the space problem for sixteen minutes with Professors A and B. Told them I had already spent more time on the matter than it was worth, and that I was going to devote the balance of my time to work on course material, including this log. Will decide the issue later after seeing Professor C. Two hours required to review lecture notes and prepare for 5:30 P.M. class. This evening's subject is a topic in human communication.

1. Judging from this incident, what do managers do?
2. Can the management process occur in the absence of communication? Why or why not?

EXERCISE 1

Prepare a log of your activities for two weekdays. In groups of six, review your log. Discuss the following questions:

1. How much time were you involved in a form of communication?
2. What form of communication was used most often?
    a. Face to face
    b. Telephone
    c. Written
    d. Nonverbal
    e. Small group
3. How important was communication to the success of your activities?

BIBLIOGRAPHY

Albers, Henry H.: *Principles of Management: A Modern Approach,* 4th ed. (New York: John Wiley & Sons, Inc., 1974).

Blake, Robert R., and Jane S. Mouton: "Comprehension of Own and Outgroup Positions under Intergroup Competition," *Journal of Conflict Resolution,* vol. 5, no. 3, September 1961.

"Chronology: How Peace Went Off the Rails," *Time,* Jan. 1, 1973.

Dale, Ernest: *Management: Theory and Practice,* 3d ed. (New York: McGraw-Hill Book Company, New York, 1973).

Fayol, Henri: *General and Industrial Management* (London: Sir Isaac Pitman & Sons, Ltd., 1949).

Guetzkow, Harold: "Communication in Organizations," in James G. March (ed.), *Handbook of Organizations* (Chicago: Rand McNally & Company, 1965), pp. 534–573.

Hicks, Herbert G.: *The Management of Organizations: A Systems and Human Resources Approach,* 2d ed. (New York: McGraw-Hill Book Company, 1972).

Higham, T. M.: "Basic Psychological Factors in Communication," *Occupational Psychology,* vol. 31, National Institute of Industrial Psychology, London, 1957.

Koontz, H., and C. O'Donnell: *Principles of Management,* 5th ed. (New York: McGraw-Hill Book Company, 1972).

Likert, Rensis: *New Patterns of Management* (New York: McGraw-Hill Book Company, 1961).

Massie, Joseph L.: *Essentials of Management* (Englewood Cliffs, N.J.: Prentice-Hall, Inc., 1964).

Melcher, A. J., and R. Beller: "Toward a Theory of Organization Communication: Consideration in Channel Selection," *Academy of Management Journal,* March 1967.

Newman, William H., C. E. Summer, and E. K. Warren: *The Process of Management,* 3d ed. (Englewood Cliffs, N.J.: Prentice-Hall, Inc., 1972).

Porter, Elias H.: *Manpower Development* (New York: Harper & Row Publishers, Incorporated, 1964), p. 5.

Sigband, N. B.: "Needed: Corporate Policies on Communication," *Advanced Management Journal,* April 1969.

Thayer, Lee (ed.): *Communication Concepts and Perspectives* (Washington: Spartan Books, 1967).

Timbers, E.: "Strengthening Motivation through Communication," *Advanced Management Journal,* April 1966.

"The War: A Shattering," *Time,* Dec. 25, 1972.

Whyte, William Foote: *Men at Work* (Homewood, Ill.: Richard D. Irwin, Inc., 1961), pp. 125–135.

2

COMMUNICATION AS A PROCESS

In this chapter we will briefly examine the problem of developing a communication model and applying it to organizations and management. The communication-process model will be developed as a viable approach to the study of organizational communication. The critical elements of the communication process will be identified and some important observations will be made regarding the determinants of its effectiveness.

In Chapter 1 the notion was developed that the process of management is highly dependent on communication for its success. An argument was made that communication is an integral part of the management process itself. We now wish to look much more closely at this important basic element of management. Just what is communication and what do managers and others do when they communicate? To answer such questions, we must develop a model which adequately represents the communication situation. The process model of communication will be suggested to be generally applicable to the situations faced by the manager.

THE DILEMMA OF MODELING COMMUNICATION

Communication models can take many forms—for example, we may use arrow diagrams, graphic or pictorial representation, technological schematics, and mathematical models, to mention but a few. Thayer (1968, p. 23) indicates that one commonly used representation of communication is:

$$A \longrightarrow B = X$$

This model represents a very simple communicative relationship. A has communicated some message to B, and X is the resultant. Thayer goes on to suggest that the simplicity of the model belies the complexity of the reality which it represents. For example, the model does not convey the intricacies of encoding or decoding messages, nor does it remind us of the effects of differences in channels and languages.

A manager who is restricted to such a simple perspective of communication may be guilty of subscribing to what Berlo (BNA film) and others have labeled the "conveyor theory of communication." By this theory, communication is assumed to be essentially a transportation problem. Referring to the diagram, such a manager is concerned only that data be moved from A to B. According to the conveyor theory, communication has occurred when A sends an interoffice memo to B. We have all seen from our own experiences that this is a short-sighted or "heroic" assumption.

Many things can occur which will disrupt communication between A and B, but we will not take time to discuss them now. Let it suffice for now to say that perceptual differences between A and B will drastically affect their interpretations of the same message and thus impair communication. Accordingly, a serious limitation of the arrow diagram is that it simply does not alert us to the potential for such difficulties.

The arrow diagram, as presented, simply fails to tell us enough about the nature of communication. As a model, it is an oversimplification of reality. Oversimplification is one extreme of the dilemma faced by all modelers. At the other end of the modeling continuum, we find the highly complex model which is intended to reflect all the major variables and relationships that are found in reality. The risk here is that the model becomes so complex that ease of comprehension and manipulation are lost. The challenge to the modeler is to achieve a balance between the two extremes so that the model is acceptably representative, but at the same time lends itself to comprehension. In the paragraphs which follow, we will attempt to present a model of communication which satisfies this criterion.

COMMUNICATION AS A PROCESS

For the purposes of this book, the process model of communication seems most appropriate. Using the Shannon-Weaver mathematical model as a basis and blending his own extensive experiences with the available behavioral science research, Berlo (1960) developed a model of the communication process. The essential elements in Berlo's communication-process model are presented in the flow diagram at the top of page 24.

24 INTRODUCTION AND POINT OF VIEW FOR THE STUDY OF ORGANIZATIONAL COMMUNICATION

| Communication source | → | Encoder | → | Message | → | Channel | → | Decoder | → | Communication receiver |

Each element of the communication process will be discussed separately in the following paragraphs. However, readers are cautioned that while such a separation is necessary for discussion purposes, it does tend to mask the interrelated nature of the process element. Readers should not permit themselves to be lulled into thinking of each element as a separate entity. Just as a manager can simultaneously engage in several elements of the management process, so the communicator can simultaneously engage in several elements of the communication process. We are freezing the process of communication and discussing its elemental parts as a matter of literary convenience. In reality the process of communication is a dynamic and continuous experience for all of us. We are constantly emitting and receiving messages and thus are involved in all the elements of the communication process on a continuing basis.

A pictorial model such as Figure 2-1 can be used to open our discussion of the

FIGURE 2-1 Communication as a process.

communication process. Each element of the communication process is represented in the figure. Our Indian friend in the foreground seems to be the source-encoder. He is attempting to communicate to the Indian on the distant peak who is the decoder-receiver. The two are connected by the channel which carries the message in signal form. The message itself has been converted to signal form via a systematic arrangement of symbols which are produced by the encoder.

The reader is encouraged to think of this for a moment. In your communication experiences with others, can you think of a single communication system which does not include some form of source-encoder, message, channel, and decoder-receiver? It seems there is an obvious explanation of the need for such elemental processes. One human mind has no other known means for directly communicating with another one short of some form of mental telepathy (a subject beyond the scope of this book). We must provide reliable methods for transforming the message into the appropriate form for transmission through the channel and for converting the signal back into message form at the receiving terminal of the channel.

The Source-Encoder

Communication cannot occur where there is no originating source for the message. Nor can it occur in the absence of an adequate encoding process to prepare the message for transmission into the channel. The observations are valid ones for both technological and person-to-person communication situations. When data are to be "communicated" to a computer, the terminal equipment (and the operator, if any) is serving as a source-encoder for transmission into the computer. We have already noted that our Indian friend in Figure 2-1 is a source-encoder for that particular communication event. He has some message he wishes to send to the man on the distant peak, and he prepares it for transmission by converting it into a *signal*. The signal is composed of a systematic group of *symbols*, which in this case are puffs of smoke. Each symbol has its own prearranged meaning and conventional usage. Taken as a whole, the set of symbols used by these Indians and their friends is a type of code or language. In communicating to the computer, we must also use a language, a programming language.

Where the encoding process is defective or perhaps uses an incorrect language, serious distortion or a total breakdown in communication is likely to occur. Perhaps you have experienced the frustration of making a seemingly minor error, such as a simple transposition of characters, in programming a computer. The results are often disastrous. Similar communication breakdowns occur for the human situation and they have similar undesirable effects.

Suppose the Indian on the distant peak of Figure 2-1 has a different "meaning" in mind for a few of the important symbols the source Indian is using? Communication, in the sense intended by the source, is just not going to occur.

Another example of the encoding problem is found in a phrase commonly used in many offices. We use the expression "burn this" when asking that a copy be made. Suppose the boss requests a new employee to "burn this in a hurry." The new employee, eager to please the boss, rushes out to literally burn an important document.

We have all experienced many times the disruptive effects of faulty encoding. We have all been able to find humor in such experiences. Perhaps all too often, we have failed to grasp the significance of encoding and its sometimes tragic effects. Remember, two minds cannot communicate directly with one another without some intervening process. The intervening process is the systematic scheme of symbols which can be used to represent the intended information or meaning. Obviously, the symbols must be mutually acceptable to both transmitter and receiver and must be compatible with the channel, but there are no other particular constraints. *Symbols* can be pulses formed by the presence or absence of electrical current, puffs of smoke, sounds of the human voice, or most anything else imaginable. The English language is a general systematic code of symbols which has come to be used by a fairly large portion of the earth's population as one method of interpersonal communication. The main point of emphasis for now is that *some* code (English or otherwise) must be used if meaning is to be elicited at the receiver. We will return to the discussion of such problems later, but for now we turn to other elements of the communication process.

The Message

It is very important to remember that a message is like a coin: it has two sides. There is the *message* as seen by the source-encoder and the *message* as seen by the decoder-receiver. The two are not necessarily the same. The selection and interpretation of messages may differ dramatically because of differences in psychology and situation for the persons who are serving as transmitter and receiver. In part, such differences can be explained as encoding-decoding failures. However, we can better grasp the meaning of such failures by noting the effects of perception and the potential of sources for multiple meanings.

Information Sources Have Multiple Meanings. In the general case, the information source can be anything—for example, a computer, a television camera, the human mind, a portrait, or perhaps some particular situational context. The observation that the information source can be anything (animate or inanimate) seems strange at first but should not be too difficult to accept. With how many different information sources did you interact today? The traffic signal, as you drove to school? The cute girl or handsome guy at the bus stop? A poor score on your last math quiz? The list is lengthy, no doubt.

Our Indian friends shown in Figure 2-2 reacted to the mushroom-shaped cloud in a special fashion; they selected a special meaning from this source of information. Though it is useful to recognize that information sources are of infinite variety, it can be even more important to recognize that the nature of a particular information source can have a complex effect upon the communicator. It influences the form and content of the message and has implications for the choice of channel.

The relationship between a person and his or her situational environment often goes unnoticed, but it has important implications for human communication. The message the source person ultimately transmits is dramatically influenced by what that person "sees" in his or her situational environment. A person does not respond to all stimuli in his or her environment, but rather selects certain things and ignores others. One does so, of course, on the basis of one's own psychological makeup. Thus, the interaction of the source individual and the situational environment becomes a crucial determinant of just which message will actually be sent.

The complex and far-reaching effects of the information source can be better

FIGURE 2-2 *(Original cartoon by Anthony Gerloff, 1974.)*

understood if we examine more closely the nature of information sources. Indeed, closer study should reveal that many information sources involve multiple alternatives or meanings. The traffic signal along your route to school was green in your favor as you passed the intersection. What did this mean? Did it mean that no cars were coming from the other direction and your safe passage was assured? Did it mean that those traveling in the opposite direction were seeing red and therefore would stop? Did it mean you could proceed through the intersection with no fear of receiving a traffic citation? What about the cute girl or handsome guy at the bus stop as a source of information? Was the slight trace of a smile intended for you? Perhaps she or he was only smiling at the thought of a pleasant day? Perhaps she or he noticed a humorous bumper sticker on a passing car? The math quiz score? Does it mean you definitely should not be an engineer? That you should study harder? That the professor is a lousy teacher? It should be clear that for any of these situations, the choice of a given meaning is influenced by both the source and the nature of the individual.

Information sources can involve multiple meanings and alternative choices. It is often necessary to select one meaning from among many possible ones. One can argue that this phenomenon of choice can also be attributed to the peculiarities of perception in the beholder; but in making the general observation, we are not limiting ourselves to people as information sources. Further, we are not really concerned with the cause at this time, but we do wish to emphasize the existence of such multiple meanings in information sources.

Selection from Alternative Possible Meanings. The reason for our emphasis is that the existence of multiple meanings and alternatives has two important implications for the communication system: *selection* and *uncertainty*. Since many information sources will involve alternatives, the source-encoder will find it necessary to make a selection. A particular meaning and message must be chosen. We do not mean to say that the transmitter in every communication system always engages in selection activities, but we do intend to convey the notion that the need for selection is often present. Further, the choice may not be a conscious one. It may be the subconscious resultant of motivation, perception, emotion, or other effects and experiences. To the extent that a given information source includes multiple meanings, some selection is necessary if the proper message is to be transmitted.

Uncertainty about Messages. Having characterized the multiple information content of information sources and the consequent need for selection, we can make an important observation regarding the impact of uncertainty. A question can be raised concerning a dilemma faced by the designer of the communication system. In those situations where the information source has multiple meanings, which one will be transmitted? The form and content of the message will be an important determinant of the form and content of the communication system.

People send postcards to say that they are enjoying a vacation, but not to communicate a final financial and operational appraisal of a distant amusement park which the company is considering as an investment. Obviously, a much more complex communication system will be required in the latter case.

Where alternative courses of action exist, we can say there is some degree of uncertainty present. We cannot be positive as to which message will be sent. Our usual method for dealing with alternative courses of action and the consequent uncertainty is to make use of probability concepts in decision making.

In the general case of an information source with multiple meanings, we can assign (using the best information available) probability values to each possible meaning. Obviously, an examination of such probability relationships would be of benefit to those who design communication systems which are to be used by others. Some messages have a much higher probability of being transmitted than do others.[1] The system should be designed accordingly. We would wish our communication system, particularly its encoding-decoding processes and channels, to be compatible with the type of messages which are to be sent.

It is important for the manager to understand that the degree of certainty or uncertainty regarding messages can vary drastically depending on circumstances. One situation may be such that the information source has many possible meanings, all having nearly equal probabilities of being transmitted. The manager is uncertain as to just which message will be sent at any given instant. In this situation, the encoder-decoder systems and channels must be flexible enough to handle a variety of message forms and contents.

As an example, consider the manager of a group of scientists and engineers who are working on a complex research and development (R&D) project. The manager can hardly afford to restrict his or her people to the use of written memos or to limit the use of the telephone. Such individuals must be free to communicate face to face as determined by the situational needs of the project.

On the other hand, the supervisor of a production-line group can probably be much more certain about the kinds of messages required by subordinates. There are fewer possible messages than in the R&D case, and their form and content are relatively certain. Surprises, short of machine breakdowns and parts shortages, are much less likely to occur. Even the exceptional events are more predictable in this situation. Accordingly, the manager may be more restrictive in planning the communication system. Perhaps the manager will decide to provide employees

---

[1] It is not necessary to our purposes here to get into the mathematics, but the inquisitive reader is referred to the work of Shannon and Weaver as a valuable supplemental reading assignment.

with quotas and similar information, but otherwise he or she may severely restrict communication between individuals in the group.

The Influence of Perception. Perception and the perceptual mechanism also influence the way in which we encode and decode messages. Berlo (1960, p. 175) states that "meanings are in people." When the source person selects a specific message for encoding and transmission, he or she has a specific meaning in mind. The symbols used to encode the message as a signal also have specific meanings, *to the source person*. To the person who is the decoder-receiver, however, the meaning assigned to the message and symbols may be quite a different one.

Each of us learns meanings for all the events, objects, and symbols which we encounter in life. Over time, we form our own personal perceptual lens. We interact with the world around us through this lens. Two individuals who experience the same situation are likely to react quite differently because of differences in perception and previous background or experience. As an example, our two Indian friends in Figure 2-2 are interpreting the mushroom-shaped cloud based on their past experiences with smoke signals. Their inference as to the meaning of the cloud is likely to be at variance with the interpretation given by a Pentagon general.

Part of the difficulty stems from the variability of human behavior and the consequent difficulty of predicting how a given individual will react in a given communication situation. Motivational, perceptual, and emotional differences between two individuals may cause them to see different meanings in the same array of data, and consequently the reactions and communication behavior of each will be quite different. Consider the example of international negotiations mentioned previously. Surely Kissinger and the North Vietnamese negotiator were looking at the same data, but they were making different inferences and drawing different conclusions. As Kissinger later stated, their perceptions were at considerable variance. Research concerning the perceptual mechanism (Leavitt, 1964) suggests that the individual's needs are important determinants of his or her perceptions. The point of needs affecting perceptions is made quite vividly in a story once told by a professor to his psychology class.

As the story had it, during his days as an undergraduate the professor had enrolled for an afternoon laboratory section and his schedule was such that he missed lunch. This was bad enough but was made worse by the fact that the laboratory assignment often kept him well into the dinner hour. By the time he left the lab in the evening he was a very hungry man. His route home to the dormitory always took him past the Sigma Delta Tau ($\Sigma\Delta T$) fraternity house and at this time of the year it was rather dark. According to the professor, Sigma Delta Tau's neon sign always very clearly read, "EAT"! The drives which differentiated Kissinger's perception from those of his North Vietnamese counterpart were probably not hunger drives. Still, the point seems clear that needs affect perception.

Perceptual differences also affect the selectivity mechanism. Two individuals receiving the same message may perceive it to have entirely different meanings because of differences in experience, training, and education. For example, the research of Dearborn and Simon (1958) suggests that executives with sales and production backgrounds tended to see the same problem quite differently. Each group explained the problem in terms of their respective backgrounds.

In a sense, those with sales backgrounds are sensitized to sales-oriented problems while those with production backgrounds are oriented to production problems. Such selectivity results from the fact that the information content of our environment often exceeds our ability to deal with it, and we respond by choosing only a portion of the total information spectrum. Thus, the perceptual process serves as a filter as we ignore that type of information to which we are not sensitized. The sales-oriented executive tends to filter out the production information and vice versa. We have greatly oversimplified the perceptual mechanism for the purpose of making the point concerning the variability of the interpersonal dimension, but the subject will be discussed in depth in later sections of the book.

It should be clear from the preceding discussion that the *message* is a major element of the process of communication. It is intricately involved with and affected by the number of potential meanings in the information source and the perceptual mechanisms of those who are attempting to communicate. We turn our discussion now to the third major element of the communication process.

The Channel

In essence the communication *channel* is any medium which couples the source to the receiver. Communication channels occur in an almost infinite variety of types, and the communicator is often free to choose from among several channel types for a given situation. Some of the more common channels between persons would include: verbal, nonverbal, telephone, letter, memo, telegram, newspapers, and books. There are, of course, many other types of channels, and it might be useful for readers to develop their own lists. Under the proper circumstances, any of the many channel types can be effective.

The channel-choice decision is an important one. It has implications for the type of encoding-decoding required as well as the ultimate success of the communication effort. The channel-choice decision is not always the result of a rational, logical process. Indeed, it is not always a conscious decision. Channel choice and channel appropriateness will be important topics of discussion in subsequent portions of this book.

We commented earlier in this chapter concerning the interrelatedness of the communication-process elements and the danger of compartmentalizing each as a separate entity. It seems particularly appropriate to emphasize the point now in view of the interdependence of encoding-decoding and the type of channel. Consider again the situation reflected in Figures 2-1 and 2-2. In either case, the basic channel connecting the two Indians is the same, the atmosphere. However, the types of signals (coded messages) required for each are quite distinct. In the case of the two Indians who are sending smoke signals (Figure 2-1), the signals are puffs of smoke which vary according to some prearranged code and are carried aloft in the atmosphere. The receiver can then visually observe the signals and decode them. His *visual* senses and *mental* processes are the decoding mechanism.

Our two Indian friends in Figure 2-2 are also using the atmosphere as a channel. However, quite a different communication system is involved. The signals in this case are the verbal pulsations of airwaves controlled according to the rules and requirements of a commonly accepted language. The *hearing* and *mental* processes of the receiver are the decoding mechanism in this case. Taking each channel in conjunction with its matching encoding-decoding processes, we can see that they are quite distinct. Though a common basic transmission medium is shared by the two systems, they are not necessarily equivalents and interchangeable. Communication breakdowns often occur because a specific encoding-decoding system has not been matched to a specific channel. Our friends of Figure 2-2 seem to have made such an error in their interpretation of the mushroom-shaped cloud.

Channel Noise. Assuming that a correct choice has been made with respect to type of channel and the related encoding-decoding systems, we still must contend with the effects of channel noise. *Noise* is perhaps best defined as anything present in the perceived signal which was not present in the original message. It may consist of sounds (such as static, tone, or a buzz), distortions of image (such as a ghost on the television screen), or perhaps an error in transmission (such as sending the message to an unintended receiver). Berlo (1960, p. 41) comments that one of his students described noise as what you get when there is no communication.

Where noise is severe enough, communication will be completely disrupted. Perhaps the reader has experienced a long-distance telephone call in which the noise was so bad that another circuit (channel) had to be requested. Think of other personal situations in which some form of noise disrupted communication. Can you identify its source?

Noise is often inputted to the channel, but this is by no means always the case. Noise may also be introduced at either the source-encoder or the decoder-receiver, or at both points. Such noise is often the result of semantic and/or perceptual differences between persons at each terminal of the communication channel. We will defer any further discussion of the semantic topic until a later section of this book. Our focus for the balance of this discussion will be on the nature of channel noise and how we can deal with its effects.

The writer is acquainted with a rather high level official of a very successful American corporation. This particular executive enjoys explaining (often to students who are prospective employees) why his company has a rather stringent and conservative dress code. His explanation centers on the nature of the company's relationship to its customers. In essence the corporation provides a service which is of such a nature that its customers must entrust privileged information to the corporation. The executives of the client organizations are typically rather conservative businesspersons. It is felt that these executives will be reluctant to entrust privileged information to individuals who wear modern long hairstyles and brightly colored clothes.

Though at first glance such an approach may seem naive, it is entirely consistent with the concept of channel noise. The flashy clothes and mod hairstyles may very well be channel noise. Under the circumstances described, the style of dress attracts all the customer executive's attention and prevents his or her "hearing" any other message. The approach used by this company is one method for dealing with the problem of channel noise. In effect, we identify the cause of the noise and take corrective action. We have all had similar experiences with channel noise, and it may be beneficial for the reader to recall some personal experiences in dealing with the problem.

Channel Redundancy. Channel redundancy is another method for dealing with the problem of channel noise. For example, we have all redialed when a telephone conversation was disrupted by noise. In doing so, we sought a redundant or backup channel. Indeed, the Bell System maintains extensive backup systems to its major carrier networks for just such eventualities. We have all read or heard of the extensive redundancy provided in high-technology aerospace systems to ensure mission success. This latter example raises the major difficulty of using channel and equipment redundancy to avoid noise conditions: it is very expensive. Indeed, the costs are often prohibitive and such redundancy can be provided only where other circumstances necessitate that continuity take precedent over cost.

Language Redundancy. In addition to the identification and elimination of noise and the use of channel redundancy, there is one other general approach to the problem of channel noise. This final approach is based on the systematic nature of our languages. We will use the English language for our discussion, but other languages will involve similar relationships.

The requirement of grammar, syntax, and etymology statistically determine an order and arrangement for the symbols that constitute a message (at least, up to a point). For example, the probability is quite low that the letter "j" will follow the letter "k" in any given message or vice versa. On the other hand, the probability is higher that "j" or "k" will be followed by a vowel such as an "a" or an "e."

Similarly, many more words in the English language begin with the letter "s" than begin with the letter "z," and so we would expect our signals (coded messages) to vary according to the probabilities involved. Using such reasoning, one can say that to an extent the *rules* of coding limit our free choice in structuring the message into a signal. Some of the *form* of our signalized message results not from the information source, but from the statistical nature and systematic requirements of the coding system. We can refer to the portion of the signal which has been statistically determined in this fashion as a special form of redundancy. The term "redundant" seems appropriate because this fraction of the signal is not essential for the meaning of the message per se.

It is stated (Shannon and Weaver, 1949) that the English language is 50 percent redundant. Only one-half of the words and letters we use in communicating are freely selected by the transmitter in framing the signal. The other one-half are systematically determined by the coding rules and statistics. Though the proportions may be open to debate, surely the concept is a sound one if one thinks about it for a moment or two.

The language-caused redundancy does help combat noise for a reason which should be fairly obvious. Since a portion of the signal has been systematically determined, we can restructure that portion at the receiving terminal if we are familiar with the system. Further, if a reasonable portion of the free-choice symbols get through, we can replace them in the systematic portions and recover a substantial portion of the message. A similar process is used by technicians to restore portions of audio tapes which have somehow been partially erased or otherwise become inaudible. The process is somewhat analogous to the assembly of a jigsaw puzzle. Armed with a mental image of how the puzzle "should look," we are usually able to make rather rapid progress in placing the pieces in the correct position.

Problems with Redundancy. On the other hand, there are times when the redundancy of language is a burden to the process of communication. Individuals and groups sometimes find it convenient to eliminate some of the cumbersome redundancy. We see all about us the emergence of special slang, colloquialisms, and jargon which are simplifications of the general English language as a coding system. Recall the communications from the lunar lander back to earth during the first moon landing; surely this was a special jargon. Consider the research that has been conducted into special ghetto jargon which suggests that once the outsiders understand it, it is changed. Such special jargon will be discussed in subsequent chapters. The point for now is to consider why such languages work.

If one stops to think about it, the coding process must consume considerable time and this can be costly under some circumstances. Further, if the coding system is unnecessarily redundant in the sense described above, we will expend energy and time encoding material which is not required for the explicit message. This is perhaps one reason for the emergence of jargon; it seeks to reduce the redundancy and encode only the essence of the message for transmission. There is a caveat concerning the reduction of such redundancy and it concerns channel noise. As has been suggested, language redundancy can counteract the effects of noise, and it should be used this way if conditions warrant.

It should be obvious from our discussion of channels and channel noise in this section that each is intricately linked with the coding element of the communication process. Effective management and communication will depend on an adequate understanding of the relationships that are involved.

Receiver-Decoder

At this point our analysis of communication as a process is essentially complete. We have examined closely the subprocesses, relationships, and limitations involved in taking a message at some source, converting it to a signal via the process of encoding, and moving it along an appropriate channel which is subject to the effects of noise. Little can be gained by discussing the decoding-receiving process in similar detail. The processes at the receiving terminal are essentially the reverse of those at the transmitting terminal. Indeed, it should be pointed out that the total process is completely reversible. Under the proper conditions, the source person may become the receiver and the original receiver will become the source. This reversal will be discussed later under the concept of feedback.

At the receiving terminal of the channel, *decoding* is the transformation of the received signal back into a message using the appropriate systematic code. *Selection* again occurs in that we assume the possibility of multiple meanings and the need to select a particular one. Finally, the message becomes an output which is ready for use or storage by the target person as the situation and his or her own psychosocial makeup demand. Decoding and selection at the receiving terminal are subject to the same constraints and interrelationships as are encoding and selection at the transmitting terminal. As has been noted before, each process subelement is interrelated with the effectiveness of the others. The choice of a particular channel and method of encoding at the transmitter necessitates the choice of the same channel and a compatible decoding method at the receiving terminal if communication is to occur. Noise in the channel has implications for both the source and the receiver. Should the person at the receiver fail to select the intended (by the source) meaning from among the alternative possibilities, communication will not occur. These systemic interrelationships are inescapable.

SOME IMPORTANT CONSIDERATIONS IN IMPLEMENTING THE COMMUNICATION PROCESS

Briefly, we have attempted to view the general process of communication as a dynamic one which results from a blending of several interdependent subprocesses. The important subprocesses of communication were identified as follows: *source-encoder*, *message*, *channel*, and *receiver-decoder*. It should be emphasized that when communication occurs in any of its many possible forms, these essential subprocesses or functions are present. The observation holds true regardless of the type of communication involved. For example, both person-to-person communication (as in ordinary conversation) and machine-to-machine communication (perhaps terminal to computer) will involve all the basic subelements of the communication process. It will be a useful exercise for the reader to select a few different types of communication systems and identify the common elemental processes in each.

The General Communication Problem

As we have seen, the subelements of the communication process are detectable in all forms of communication. So too, it seems, the basic problem of communication is always the same regardless of the type of communication situation we are dealing with. Weaver (Shannon and Weaver, 1949) generalized that there are three levels of the communication problem.

Level A. The *technical problem* of achieving accuracy in the transmission of signals.

Level B. The *semantic problem* of assuring that the transmitted signals convey the desired meaning.

Level C. The *effectiveness problem* of assuring that the received meaning affects behavior in the desired way.

If communication in any of its many human and technological forms is to be effective, each level of the problem must be solved or its effects minimized. Clearly, such a categorization seems to adequately cover all imaginable types of communication problems for every conceivable communication system, human or otherwise. Kissinger in international negotiations, a telephone circuit, two Indians using smoke signals, two interconnected computers, or any other imaginable communication system is susceptible to these problems. Indeed, for the special case of human communication, it is an unfortunate circumstance that all three levels of the problem are frequently present.

An engineer designing an intercom system for a hospital would tend to be concerned with the technical problem of level A. The manager will typically begin at level A, but must not stop at this point. As we have seen, the transfer of data from one location to another does not mean that communication has occurred. Meanings are in people. The manager deals with people and so must go beyond level A.

Still, it should be emphasized that any effort to remedy semantic or effectiveness problems (levels B and C) can be accomplished only within the limits permitted by the available signal accuracies. Accurate signal transmission is a prerequisite to the solution of semantic and effectiveness problems. Thus, level A, or more specifically, technical capacity, is a fundamental constraint which limits the alternatives available to us in dealing with semantic or effectiveness problems. The three levels are inextricably interrelated, and an understanding of the technical-level relationships permits a more thorough analysis at the semantic and effectiveness levels. We shall discuss the matter in greater detail as we adapt the general-process model specifically to the human situation. For now, we wish to focus on the importance of coding.

Channel and Source Compatibility

In this section, an important point to be made is the *vital* function of the *code*. In the final analysis, one mind communicates with another through some form of encoding and decoding. This, after all, is what communication systems are all about: converting the thought message for transmission and then reconverting it to a thought message. In effect, we are connecting an information supply (the source) to an information demand (the receiver). The communication process is the connecting link, but it is not a static connection—it is a dynamic one. The physical link or channel may be fixed, but the other elements such as information sources, encoding-decoding, and messages tend to be in a state of continuous change. The nature of the coding-decoding system must be carefully selected to ensure it is an appropriate one with reference to the capacities of the information source and the channel.

We have already observed that each of us continuously interacts with the sources of information which surround us. Some sources of information and situations may involve a very high information content while others involve very low information content. In some cases, the information capacity of the source (or one's environment) is stable, and in other cases it is dynamic or changing. Thus, as we have noted, we get into the problem of selection of messages and uncertainty as to just what message is to be communicated at any specific point in time.

A rather complicated problem emerges from such dynamics. We must somehow match the information content or capacity of the source to the relatively fixed capacity of the channel. We refer to channel capacity as "relatively fixed" because it will be changed only if the manager or the source person chooses to change it. Yet, as we have seen, the source has a certain dynamic character which arises from selectivity and uncertainty. Should the channel capacity be considerably lower than that of the source to which it is connected, an information overload is likely to occur. The consequence of this, of course, is loss of the message or some distortion of its meaning. In dealing with the problem, one must give consideration to the nature of the information source and the type of channels and coding systems available. All are interrelated, and we will discuss the essentials of the interrelationship in the paragraphs which follow.[2]

The Role of Coding

The preceding discussion brings us directly to the importance of coding as a mediating device. By choosing the proper coding system, we can balance differences between the nature and capacities of information sources and channels. The problem we focus on here is somewhat analogous to threading a very small needle with very large thread: it is difficult if it can be done at all. As a further example, suppose you found it necessary to transfer some liquid from one container to another and the receiving container had a rather small opening. What would you do? Get a funnel, you say? Okay, and we will assume that the funnel has considerably less capacity than does either container. How will you proceed with actual process of transferral? Clearly, any attempt to move all the liquid *at once* through the funnel would be disastrous. At any given instant the capacity of the funnel is exceeded, liquid will be wasted. You would choose to meter the flow of liquid so as not to exceed the capacity of the funnel.

The funnel problem is not unlike the channel problem in the communication system. If the channel is of small capacity as compared with the information source to which it is connected, the flow through the channel must be carefully metered. We can still pass large amounts of information, but we must do so in small quantities over extended periods of time. Thus, we use the coding system to meter the information content of the message at any given instant. In this sense we reduce the message content per unit of time. We might think of such a use of

---

[2] For an extensive discussion of the mathematical relationships involved, the reader is referred to the work of Shannon and Weaver (1949).

coding as being a form of message reduction. The case of network television provides an example.

Message Reduction and Metering. Program material from the point of origin (often New York or Los Angeles) is distributed along a complex network of channels to numerous local stations for rebroadcast to home receivers such as your own. Often the television distribution channels are leased from carriers such as the Bell System. You may have noticed reference to such carriers when there is "trouble on the network." You may have assumed that these channels were very much like the ones used for telephone service, but the assumption is correct only up to a point. There is a considerable difference in capacity. As you can imagine, the image produced by the television camera is an immensely complex signal compared to that of the human voice. Indeed, the typical channel required for television transmission is of sufficient capacity to handle approximately 1,500 ordinary messages. We are assuming, of course, that at any given instant we wish the channel to convey all the information selected by the transmitter from the source. To do so is analogous to the transfer of all the liquid through the funnel in a very short period of time. To accomplish such a rapid transfer, we obviously will need a funnel with a capacity at least equal to the capacity of the transmitting container. In the case of the television networks, the decision was made to provide the large-capacity channels. However, there is another alternative. We can deal with the problem of high-capacity information sources by adjusting the coding system. Another type of television system provides us with an example.

You may recall that some of our early unmanned space vehicles which explored the moon sent back television pictures which were not broadcast in their entirety as they were received. The reason for this was quite simple: the pictures were not received in their entirety for instantaneous rebroadcast. Rather in the interest of conserving energy and channel capacity, the coding system was such that each picture was transmitted one horizontal scan line at a time over an extended period of time. In contrast, the image you see on your home receiver at any given instant results from 525 scan lines for each complete scanning of the scene. The scene is scanned 30 times per second; thus the image you see during this interval is composed of 15,750 horizontal scan lines. The obvious implication is that we may use the coding system to make trade-offs between channel capacity, capacity of the source, and the overall situational circumstances of a given communication system.

Interrelatedness of Communication-Process Elements. The ramifications of all this should be obvious. We must evaluate the capacity of a particular channel in terms of the information content of the sources to which it is *likely* to be connected and the messages it is likely to carry. If the former is equal to or exceeds the latter, we can adjust transmitter coding to achieve the desired accuracy in received signals.

However, the more sophisticated coding process does have a cost which can be measured in time or money. If channel capacity is less than the information content of the most probable messages, then considerable error in transmission will occur which cannot be offset by even the most sophisticated coding. Even in the best of circumstances where the capacity of the channel is adequate, the presence of noise will cause some doubt as to what the message is. This is why we previously noted the advantage of some redundancy in the coding system.

We can design a coding system which is capable of dealing with a particular source-channel-capacity relationship within limits, but there will be costs involved in doing so. Indeed, we find that many human communication systems are capable of just such adjustments of coding. This is why such systems as special jargon emerge. The beauty of human communication is that it provides a great deal of flexibility and such adaptations are common.

Further, in those communication circumstances where the most probable messages are to be high in information content, we *must* provide high-capacity channels or run the risk of error. This may seem a simplistic observation, but the reader is cautioned to think about personal organizational experiences. Many human-communication situations, particularly those which occur in organizations under the stress of some problem or crisis, will involve high-information-content messages (rich in content). Yet, we find managers in these same organizations limiting the capacity of available channels of communication. For example, they seek to restrict the use of the telephone or other forms of interpersonal communication. We shall come back to this matter in subsequent sections of this book.

SUMMARY

In this chapter we have discussed the nature of the general-communication process. The source-encoder, message, channel, and receiver-decoder were identified as the major component elements of the communication process. The nature of each was described and important interrelationships and constraints were identified.

It was noted in particular that systemic relationships operate. The effective functioning of one component is closely interrelated with that of the others. The basic nature of the information source was observed to involve alternative choices of message or meaning. It was seen that this results in a selection activity by the source person and uncertainty regarding which message will ultimately be transmitted. Channel noise and human perceptual differences were seen as important determinants of successful communication.

The panorama of all possible communication problems can be arranged into three categories: (A) the technical problem of conveying signals accurately; (B) the semantic problem of conveying meaning; and (C) the effectiveness problem of achieving the desired effect on behavior. It was noted that the levels B and C are clearly affected by events at level A. An analysis and understanding of level A is instrumental in effectively dealing with problems at levels B and C.

The notion of channel capacity was also discussed, and significant relationships were drawn between the capacity of the source, the capacity of channel, and the type of coding. Channel capacity was seen as a limiting factor in dealing with the information potential of a source, and the coding system was suggested as a feasible mediating variable. Source-encoders, channels, decoder-receivers, and situation must be compatible if the communication process is to be effectively implemented.

IMPORTANT TERMS AND CONCEPTS

source-encoder, receiver-decoder, message, channel, technical problem, semantic problem, effectiveness problem, channel noise

REVIEW QUESTIONS

1. Think of a specific personal communication experience and attempt to identify the major component elements as they were described in the process model.

2. Why is it useful to describe an information source in terms of alternative meanings and what are the implications for the communication system?

3. What is noise and how can we deal with it?

4. Discuss the interrelationship of source capacity, channel capacity, and coding. What are the implications of this interrelationship for the manager?

5. Discuss the general types of communication problems and give examples of each.

6. See if you can identify each subelement of the communication process as it occurs in a number of different communication situations.

INCIDENT: THE GREEN HOUSE

Janice and Martha worked several years together as salespersons for a real estate agency in a large Midwestern city. The two became close friends over the years of their association. Each was bright and ambitious and had planned eventually to start her own real estate venture after learning the ropes working for the large broker.

However, because they were such fast friends, they decided to become partners in a joint venture. Each woman invested her own funds and some additional financial backing was obtained from other sources. The two decided to start their venture by buying and selling properties in some of the more rapidly growing sectors of the United States. Houston and Dallas were selected as the target areas of their first efforts. Janice was to work out of Houston and Martha was to take the Dallas area.

Neither woman placed too much faith in formal organizations, procedures, and documentation. They preferred to operate informally. Each felt strongly about the importance of communication, however, and this led to one basic agreement governing the operations of their partnership. It was agreed that each partner would always notify the other in writing concerning the details of any transaction she made for the partnership. Shortly after they began operations, Martha received a telegram from Janice in Houston which read as follows:

> PURCHASED GREEN HOUSE FOR $20,000.00.
>
> Signed,
> Janice

1. How much has Janice really communicated to Martha?

2. List as many of the possible messages as you can.

3. Analyze this incident in terms of the basic elements and considerations of the communication process.

BIBLIOGRAPHY

Berlo, David K.: "Meanings Are in People," a film from the *Effective Communication Series* (Rockville, Md.: BNA Communications, Inc., 1965).

———: *The Process of Communication* (New York: Holt, Rinehart and Winston, Inc., 1960).

Dearborn, DeWitt C., and Herbert A. Simon: "Selective Perception: A Note on the Departmental Identification of Executives," *Sociometry,* vol. 21, 1958. Abridgement published in David Hampton et al. (eds.), *Organizational Behavior and the Practice of Management* (Glenview, Ill.: Scott, Foresman and Company, 1968).

Leavitt, Harold: "Perception: From the Inside Looking Out," *Managerial Psychology* (Chicago: The University of Chicago Press, 1964). Reprinted in David Hampton et al. (eds.), *Organizational Behavior and the Practice of Management* (Glenview, Ill.: Scott, Foresman and Company, 1968).

Shannon, Claude E., and Warren Weaver: *The Mathematical Theory of Communication* (Urbana: The University of Illinois Press, 1949).

Thayer, Lee: *Communication and Communication Systems* (Homewood, Ill.: Richard D. Irwin, Inc., 1968).

3

EXPLORING THE NATURE OF THE HUMAN COMMUNICATION PROCESS

In this chapter we shall briefly adapt the general-process model to the human-communication scenario. Some of the special relationships involved and the concept of effectiveness will be discussed.

In all its major attributes the human communication process parallels the general model we described in the preceding chapter, and it is subject to the same general principles. The remarks which follow are aimed at highlighting some factors and concepts which are considered particularly relevant to the study of human communication. We make no claim that such concepts either "are" or "are not" operative in the case of the more general model.

DATA AND INFORMATION DISTINGUISHED

Human communication has previously been defined as the establishment of a relationship such that the actions, thoughts, feelings, and intentions of one person evoke a response in another. It has been noted that in organizations we often seek a specific response. We wish to influence the behavior of others. Indeed, Thayer (1968) notes that communication occurs only when somebody "takes-something-into-account."

Yet, as was noted in the previous chapter, individuals react differently to the multiple potential meanings of a given information source. We cannot always be sure what a given source-encoder will elect to encode. We are equally unsure as to what the receiver-decoder will choose as "the message." Indeed, it is possible that the receiver-decoder will sense no message at all. The latter may simply choose not to take "that message" from "that source-encoder" into account at all. As far as the receiver-decoder is concerned, there is no input from that particular source.

Such complications necessitate that we differentiate data from information. For the special case of human communication, it is best to define *information* as data which has meaning to the receiver. Data which does not convey meaning to the receiver is the equivalent of nonsense. The purpose of human communication is to affect the behavior of the receiving person. Generally, the source-encoder wishes to influence the receiver-decoder by having the target person to take the message into account. For the moment, we will disregard the important special case in which the source-encoder inadvertently sends an unintended message.

Many managers (and others) take the attitude that communication has been accomplished once the *data* have been transmitted, but this is not the case. Managers who make such assumptions are subscribing to the conveyor theory of communication. Such a manager responds to a communication failure by stating, "but I sent you a memo." In the absence of an interpretive behavior, we have only raw data or perhaps noise or nonsense, and there is no behavioral response.

As an example, a message sent via telegraph using code is information to the receiving telegrapher who can read the code; it has meaning. To others it is data, a series of dots and dashes, or noise, but it has no meaning. The circuit diagram of a color television receiver is information to TV technicians; it has meaning and affects their behavior in that the information contained in the diagram influences their actions. To others who are unable to read circuit diagrams, it is a meaningless maze of funny-looking lines. The examples are endless; perhaps you should think of a few for yourself to be sure you have the distinction clearly in mind.

THE HUMAN COMMUNICATION PROCESS

The requirement that data must convey meaning in order for human communication to occur results in a special constraint for the source-encoder. The transmitting individual is not the sole determiner of whether there is meaning, or what the meaning will be. The transmitting person, of course, is aware of the meaning he or she wishes to convey, but this person has only limited control over what the receiving person will perceive, or which meaning will be selected or interpreted from the array of possible meanings received.

Recall Kissinger's experience in international negotiations. Each party was in agreement that an international control commission for ensuring the peace in Southeast Asia would be an important part of the treaty. In this sense each party selected a common meaning. However, later experiences revealed drastic differences as to what the actual makeup of the control commission was to be. The computer specialist feels that computer printouts are information; the accountant feels that the income statement is information. However, to individuals at the receiving end of such communications who do not happen to be computer specialists or accountants, the computer printout and the income statement can be meaningless data.

In the case of human communication systems, there is a need to convey meaning, but there is difficulty in doing so. The difficulty arises from the fact that the receiving person as well as the transmitting person can affect the meaning ultimately communicated. The person at the receiving terminal, by reason of personal psychological nature and background, may see no meaning at all in a given piece of data. Perhaps even worse, this person may select an incorrect or unintended meaning. We must adapt our newly discovered communication-process model to account for such difficulties. We can do so by recognizing the problem of motivational, perceptual, and semantic differences between transmitter and receiver.

The human communication process is presented in block form in Figure 3-1. The essential process elements still include source-encoder, message, channel, and receiver-decoder. However, we have elaborated beyond the basic process elements in order to draw attention to the problem of conveying meaning.

Four basic considerations have been incorporated to provide the model shown in this figure: (1) the addition of a semantic noise box at the source-encoder; (2) the differentiation of channel noise from semantic noise; (3) the addition of a semantic

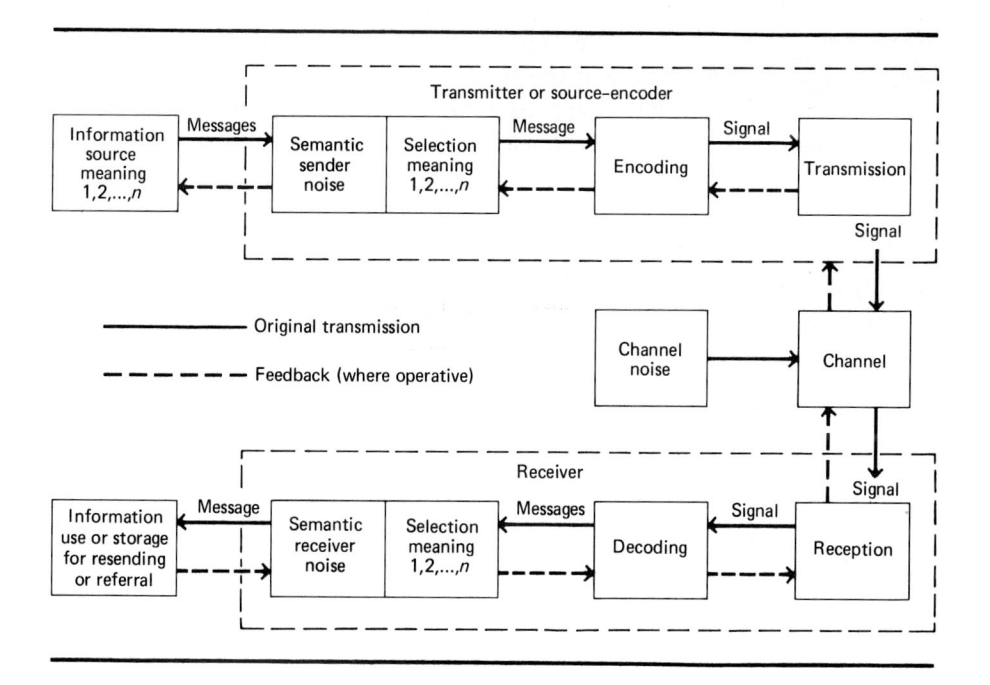

FIGURE 3-1 The human communication process.

receiver at the receiver-decoder; and (4) the possibility of a feedback path. The first three considerations arise from the levels B and C problems which tend to occur in human communication situations. A number of authors, including Shannon and Weaver (1949), have suggested that semantic considerations must be treated for the human model. The fourth consideration, providing and utilizing feedback paths, will be shown in subsequent paragraphs to be a most effective means for combating semantic problems.

Semantic Noise and Semantic Receivers

The choice of the word "semantic" to describe the noise inserted at the transmitter by the human operative seems most appropriate. Semantics can be described as a science which deals with meaning, whereas phonetics deals with sounds. As has been suggested previously, sounds or phonetics is the basis for some of our coding systems. We use sound symbols to construct signals which represent certain messages and which are capable of transmittal through the channel.

However, as was suggested in the opening paragraphs of this chapter, a problem arises when the meaning which emerges at the receiving terminal is different from the one intended at the transmitting terminal. Such a difference is a *semantic distortion* which occurs because our code fails us. The meaning of a particular sound is at variance between transmitter and receiver. The failure can result from numerous causes, including poor choice of symbols, emotional state, and perceptual set. Such matters will be discussed in detail in the remainder of the book. For now, we wish to give a brief example of the human communication dilemma, showing why the boxes are placed as they are and how feedback can deal with some of the problems which arise.

A Problem with Semantics. Consider, for example, an incident described by Reid (1963) in his discussion of the problem of "malicious obedience." The situation includes all elements of the communication process as we have discussed them.

Source-encoder	Farrow, the supervisor[1]
Receiver-decoder	Bentwick, model maker[1]
Messages	Several; see if you can identify them
Channel	Several; see if you can identify them

[1]The point should be made that the transmitting and receiving roles between Farrow and Bentwick are reversible under the proper conditions.

Be sure to follow these blueprints just the way John has drawn them. We don't want any slip-ups—if this model isn't ready by Thursday, we'll lose an important contract.

With this admonition, Matt Farrow, supervisor of the development department of a large electrical company, placed a set of blueprints for a new control device on model-maker Dave Bentwick's workbench. Dave nodded, but inside he was smoldering with repressed anger. Once more, he felt, Farrow had shown his favoritism toward John Bergen, the blueprint maker. It was John who got the lion's share of credit for a job well done. John was the one Farrow always consulted when he had a problem, while Dave's ideas usually got a quick brush-off.

When Farrow left the lab, Dave examined the blueprints—and his eyes widened with sudden interest. So Farrow wanted him to follow John's blueprints exactly, did he? That's just what he would do . . .

Dave finished the complicated model on Thursday, right on schedule. As Farrow hurried off with it, Dave gave his retreating figure a mock salute. An hour later, the supervisor was back with the model, his face a study in purple.

"The model doesn't work," he snapped. "We don't have a chance of getting that contract now, and my boss is screaming. What the devil happened, Dave?"

Dave scratched his head and looked baffled. "I can't understand it," he said. "I followed John's blueprints exactly, just as you told me to. Maybe he made a mistake."

Multiple Messages and Meanings. Several messages can be detected in this particular incident. Most of the messages sent by Farrow utilize the English language for encoding and decoding and the atmosphere as the channel. But as we examine the situation, we can see that Farrow is increasing the potential for *semantic sender noise,* if he is not outright inserting such noise. Semantic noise is any behavior by the source-encoder which interferes with the transmission of the intended meaning. Such behavior affects the state of interpersonal relations which exists between transmitter and receiver and disrupts communication.

Farrow's abrasive style, his lack of regard for the abilities of Bentwick, and the probable bad relations between the two in the past are all examples of semantic noise. As Reid (1963) observed, most such messages involve emotional content in addition to technical content; Farrow is woefully unaware of the existence of the former.

Clearly, Farrow intends to convey to Bentwick the importance of constructing an exact model prior to the Thursday deadline. After the model failed, Farrow clearly intended to convey his displeasure with Bentwick. But Farrow failed to recognize that in the first case, the message received by Bentwick had nothing to do with modelmaking and deadlines. Rather, Bentwick "took into account" that Farrow lacked confidence in anyone but Bergen, the blueprint maker. When Farrow attempted to register his displeasure, the message actually received by Bentwick was that Bergen was indeed capable of mistakes. It was something after the fashion of a "self-fulfilling prophecy."

Bentwick's emotional state which is brought on by the negative relationship between himself and Farrow clearly affects his reception of the message. Thus, we can say a semantic receiver has been inserted. By *semantic receiver noise* we mean the tendency of the receiver to distort incoming meaning to suit his or her psychosocial state. The receiver will place his or her own interpretations on the symbols received, and such interpretations are likely to be at variance with the intention of the source-encoder. Such effects seems to support the contention of Reid and others that some degree of emotional content is present in many human communication situations.

Intrinsic and Symbolic Meaning. Maslow (1941) has observed that for many human situations a given cue can be associated with two sets of meaning, the *intrinsic* and the *symbolic*. In the case of the intrinsic set, the information content is associated with the objective properties of the cue itself. For the symbolic set, the information content is associated with the emotional state of the perceiver (the receiver in the communication situation). As an example, Maslow suggests that when a mother deprives her child of ice cream, two general categories of interpretations are possible: (1) mother has refused to give me food which tastes good and may spoil my appetite for dinner; (2) mother doesn't love me. The first is the intrinsic set and is objective in nature though it may have only limited information value. The second array, though it is a distortion of reality, contains much more information.

Some individuals, because of their emotional state, tend to require much more information about a given situation and their relationship with others. As a result of their stronger need to know, such individuals turn to the symbolic set for an interpretation even though the particular meaning involved is a distortion of reality. The conclusion that "mother doesn't love me" can be highly realistic to the affected individual though it is illogical to others. Thus, in the case of the symbolic set of meaning, the information content can be as rich and as varied as are the emotional states of individuals. Such factors are clearly important influences on the semantic dilemma of human communication, and these as well as other similar factors will be discussed at length in subsequent sections of this book.

Feedback

Unacceptable levels of noise (channel or semantic) tend to decrease the probability of conveying the intended meaning. It has been noted in our discussion of the general-process model that we can counter the effects of noise through the redundancy of our coding systems or channels, but that certain costs were involved in doing so. We suggested at the time that an alternative was available for dealing with the effects of noise. Such an alternative exists to the extent we can avail ourselves of the opportunity to provide feedback.

Feedback Concerning the Effects of Communication. Feedback, in its simplest form, can be described as the provision for two-way communication.[2] If for a given communication situation, we consider the primary thrust of the communication as being from A to B, then we would consider the feedback path (if it exists) as being from B to A. It is A who wishes to affect the behavior of B by communicating something to the latter. In such a case, the feedback path can play a vital role by providing information concerning B's behavior, particularly whether or not the correct meaning was received or acted on. We have shown such a feedback path as a dotted line in Figure 3-1.

The preceding illustration, however, fails to convey the involved nature of the feedback concept as it occurs in the human-communication situation. Effective feedback is not simply a matter of providing the physical channel. Just as is the case for the primary channel, consideration must be given to such matters as motivational-emotional states and the specific interpersonal relationship which exists between those who are attempting to communicate. In the feedback case too, we find the presence of such phenomena as semantic noise, intrinsic information, symbolic information, and so on.

Opening the Feedback Channel. We can emphasize the role of feedback and some of the important influences on the process through a reexamination of the Farrow and Bentwick incident. Notice that Farrow from the outset seemed determined to minimize the occurrence of feedback. He gave explicit instructions to Bentwick

---

[2] As will be discussed in Chapter 14, the basic purpose of providing feedback is to permit the transmitter to evaluate the effectiveness of his or her communication. To do so, of course, will require two-way communication in some form.

which were primarily of a controlling nature. It seems clear that Farrow's basic assumption was that if Bentwick followed his (Farrow's) instructions and Bergen's plans, the project would be successful. Project failure was only a possibility if Bentwick "goofed." Accordingly, Farrow solicited no comments from Bentwick, and we might guess that he would not have been receptive had they been offered. Such a circumstance is interesting, and unfortunately is all too common in supervisor-subordinate relations. One would think that for such an important project, Farrow might have inquired as to the clarity of the blueprints, thus opening the door to comments as to the accuracy of the drawings.

Some such question, properly asked, might have opened the door to some very useful and productive feedback. But it would be misleading to suggest that one can get feedback only by asking questions. This is not the case. The face-to-face human communication situation provides feedback opportunities which are intrinsic to the situation itself. In the Farrow and Bentwick situation, we assume that a negative relationship had been building over some period of time. Clearly in this particular incident, Bentwick's emotional state is one of anger. It should not have been too difficult for Farrow to detect the symptoms of such an emotional state.

Sensitivity to the Presence of Feedback. Farrow's effectiveness as a supervisor is, in part, dependent on his ability to sense what his people are "feeling" and to control his own behavior in an appropriate fashion. This should not be construed as meaning supervisors "give in" to their subordinates. But it is suggested that supervisors can enrich the feedback they receive if they are sensitive to the various cues we all give off as we engage in interpersonal relationships. We all possess such sensitivity to some degree. An actor, a speaker, a comedian, or a politician continuously sizes up the receptiveness of the audience to the message, and adjusts his or her own behavior accordingly.

Think of some recent interpersonal, face-to-face experiences of your own. Did you detect anger, joy, resistance, apathy, or some other emotional state in your audience? What sorts of cues tipped you as to the mood of the other person? A cue may have been verbal, but the signal might just as well have been visual. The face-to-face setting provides a rich opportunity for nonverbal feedback such as the following: facial expressions, particularly about the eyes and mouth; skin tone and color; gestures with the arms and legs and other parts of the body; tone, pitch, and inflection of the voice.

Variations of such nonverbal channels can provide for almost unlimited kinds of messages which have a very high information content. It is foolish for the manager not to make use of such a potential. Our friend Farrow for some reason has not utilized these valuable channels. It should be noted in passing that Farrow received one final feedback message, the mocking salute. This one was, of course, too late, but its presence suggests that there were many others which also failed.

ACHIEVING EFFECTIVENESS IN HUMAN COMMUNICATION

In this section we wish to briefly examine the concept of effectiveness in human communication. What factors and considerations are involved if the manager and subordinates are to successfully implement the communication process in the human dimension? Clearly, to achieve effective human communication in the organization, the manager must deal with the problem of semantics as was seen in the preceding section. The focus here is on the nature and value of face-to-face communication channels. We will see that they offer advantages in terms of multiplicity of channels, richness, and timing.

Face-to-Face Channels

The discussion of the preceding section suggests an extremely important point concerning human communication (including feedback) which occurs in the face-to-face setting and which should be emphasized. When two or more individuals engage in face-to-face communication, the opportunity exists to utilize multiple information channels which have a very high information potential. It should be noted that the participants are not restricted to verbal channels or to a single signal direction except by individual or organizational choice. In a sense, the multiple nature of face-to-face channels is a form of automatic redundancy which has low cost.

Some individuals and some organizations intentionally choose to restrict channel choice, message content, and signal direction. Where such a choice has proved effective and there is full awareness of its consequences, we have no quarrel. Where the choice has proved ineffective and is done out of ignorance, we think it is unfortunate. Such a line of discussion implies the need to develop an organizational climate which can enhance the effective use of interpersonal channels, including feedback. Subsequent sections of this book will be aimed at this problem as well as the general problem of feedback.

The Concept of Richness

It has been suggested by some that any evaluation of the quality of a particular channel of interpersonal communication must account for two essential factors: (1) technical capacity; and (2) the ability to convey meaning. Of the two, technical capacity is a factor universally recognized and one which receives a fair amount of attention in the design of any communication system.

To call attention to the importance of each factor (technical capacity and the ability to convey meaning) in assessing quality, the notion of *richness* has been suggested (Bodensteiner, 1970, p. 40). To score high on a scale of richness, a communication system must have both *technical capacity* and the ability to *convey meaning*. A communication system which is lacking in either dimension will not be an efficient system except for the most trivial messages. We turn now to a further discussion of the two dimensions of richness.

Technical Capacity. Technical capacity seems closely related to the level A problem suggested by Shannon and Weaver: conveying the signal accurately. Suppose that we have two channels, say A and B, and that each can carry a given set of symbols (the message) with comparable accuracy between two assigned points. Where one channel, say A, can carry the message in a shorter period of time or perhaps carry other additional messages, we would say that it has greater technical capacity. As an example, if you wished to give instructions to your broker to buy or sell certain shares, you might do so via the postal service. However, that might be risky since several days would be required to do so whereas the same message could be given over the telephone in a very few minutes. In this situation, the telephone channel has a greater technical capacity.

It is difficult to discuss the concept of capacity without getting into matters of timing. As was indicated in the discussion of television transmission (Chapter 2), we can counteract the effects of limited channel capacity by making trade-offs between length of time consumed (in encoding-decoding or transmission) and the quantity of signals transmitted. If we are willing to allocate the time to encoding, decoding, and transmission, very complex signals can be sent over relatively low capacity channels. Or to turn it around, many very simple signals can be sent rapidly over the relatively high capacity channels. The nature of timing considerations will be examined more closely later, but for now, we turn our attention to the second dimension of richness.

Conveying Meaning. As had already been noted, signal transmission in and of itself is no assurance that the desired meaning has been conveyed. In the case of human communication, we want the receiver-decoder to "take into account" the message. Accordingly, a second factor which must be considered in assessing the quality of a human communication system is the ability to elicit the intended meaning in the receiver. In the absence of the ability to *convey meaning*, mere technical capacity has limited usefulness.

It may be possible to design communication networks which move huge quantities of signals, but unless the desired meanings are evoked, the intended behavior is unlikely to occur. The industrial world is replete with examples of such difficulties: the management information system (MIS) which nobody uses; the

PERT milestone which is ignored by all but the person preparing the PERT chart; the budget which everyone knows to be falsified; the interoffice memo which winds up in the waste can, etc.[3]

For a specific example of the nature of quality inadequacies in human communication, consider our friends Farrow and Bentwick. It seems perfectly clear that nothing was wrong with the technical capacity of the channel used by Farrow. Technically, he clearly should have been able to transmit the message. The evidence would suggest that the signals were received in fine fashion; perhaps the intended meaning was also evoked. Unfortunately, some other important meanings were also evoked in the mind of Bentwick. Particularly, Bentwick perceived that Farrow had a low regard for his (Bentwick's) ability, and it was this meaning which determined Bentwick's subsequent behavior. A further unfortunate circumstance was Farrow's inability to receive any of the meaning in the feedback path. Clearly, extant technical capacity in the absence of an ability to convey meaning is not enough for successful human communication.

Finally, it should be noted that though the basic notion of richness can be applied to the channel alone, this is a short-sighted perspective. The more complex case occurs with the communication system which includes semantic noise and the semantic receiver as is shown in Figure 3-1. As we have seen, it is the semantic factors (introduced by the human operatives) which tend to cause distortion and result in uncertainty as to the true message. Semantic noise and channel noise are important determinants of the richness of a given system. Therefore, we feel the concept of richness is best applied in the analysis of the total human communication system because it draws our attention away from a concern with mere capacity to the vital factor of conveying meaning.

The Importance of Timing

We have noted that *face-to-face* and *feedback* channels are important elements of the human communication system and have emphasized the importance of achieving *richness*. We have also observed that the semantic noise of interpersonal relations together with the channel noise of the technical system are important determinants of the richness of the system. We now wish to examine the importance of timing in achieving a richer human communication system.

The point is that if our messages (whether primary or feedback in nature) are not

---

[3] We do not mean to imply that all such efforts are failures, but rather that some difficulties do occur which could be avoided if people had a better awareness of the conditions under which such formal information systems are most effective. In Part Four, we shall discuss this problem further and suggest a solution.

timed properly, they are of little value in affecting behavior. At least two aspects of timing seem crucial, *duration* and *sequencing*. With reference to *duration*, one can think in terms of a continuum of possibilities. Some communication systems can convey a message in time intervals which are very small and approach being instantaneous, while for others the time consumed in transmission is of long duration. Clearly, duration is an important consideration for both primary and feedback communication. The duration requirements for a given system will be affected by the nature of the message involved, type of encoding-decoding, selection processes, and the type of channel.

Sequencing refers to the timing relationships which exist between the reception of a message and other important events in the communication situation. Sequencing is obviously influenced by duration and the factors described above as having an influence on duration. However, sequencing is also affected by important situational circumstances. A message which arrives *after* the occurrence of some important event is of little value, even if it conveys the proper meaning. A bank statement indicating your account has no remaining balance is of limited use if you have already written several checks.

The point regarding duration and sequencing can be made by examining the communication situation which existed between Farrow (the supervisor) and Bentwick. It is quite clear that the mock salute given by Bentwick was potentially a very rich signal. Disregarding (for purposes of this discussion) the fact that the signal was not received by Farrow, it still provided the opportunity to convey a very rich message in a very short period of time or *duration*. Had Farrow been receptive to this particular message, it would have taken only an instant for him to become aware of the sad state of affairs which existed between himself and his subordinates. *Sequencing* is illustrated by the fact that the mock salute was not received until after the problem with the drawing, and thus could not be of any use in dealing with that particular problem.

Channel Differences

This incident should clarify what we mean by duration and sequencing. For other channels and coding systems, the duration and sequencing relationships would be quite different. How much time would have been required to send the same message via telegram? Via telephone? Each of these two types of channels can be distinguished from the face-to-face channel with respect to the effects of duration and sequencing on the feedback channel. Certain advantages in terms of richness accrue to the face-to-face channel because of the unique potential of its feedback channel. Any of the three systems can provide feedback, but the methods for providing feedback and the nature and timing of feedback are quite different.

Telegram. In the case of the telegram, feedback (if it occurs) will be via a return telegram as initiated by the receiver. It is important to note that the feedback option rests primarily with the receiver; it occurs only if the recipient of the telegram chooses to reply. Further, with respect to timing, the duration will be determined by the time required for a telegram to be received and a response to be sent. Surely, the interval involved, even under the best of circumstances, would approach perhaps an hour as a minimum. No doubt the duration could be much longer under some circumstances. Clearly, communication situations occur in which an hour's duration will not be tolerable.

It should be similarly clear that duration will affect sequencing. However, it is possible to allow for such effects provided we know *when* the message must be received (in order to achieve its purpose) and *what* the duration of the message will be. Relative to a written letter which is sent through the U.S. Postal System, the telegram offers certain timing advantages. The telegram is unlikely to require as great a duration, and the system permits the telegram to be processed with much less delay. In many cases a telegram can be sent at any time of the day or night. The letter may be retained in a mailbox or a post office for extended periods of time, not to mention the probable requirement for greater transmission durations for the letter system.[4]

Telephone. In contrast to the telegram (or the letter for that matter), both the telephone and the face-to-face communication systems provide very definite feedback advantages. Relative to the telegram, either the telephone or the face-to-face communication system provides for greater transmitter control of the feedback choice and also more closely approaches an instantaneous timing capability.

Such a capability was the primary reason for the installation of the so-called "hot line" between Moscow and Washington during the 1960s. It was recognized by both parties that during stressful international crises, a two-way telephone communication between the two nations would permit a very rich exchange of information. Differences and misunderstandings are more susceptible to detection where the communication system permits the sender to directly ascertain the effect of his or her message on the receiver and vice versa. The "hot line" would appear to provide clear advantages in timing over the normal diplomatic channels. One would hate to rely on a telegram to advise the fire department that one's house was

---

[4]This example is mentioned only to make the point regarding timing (duration and sequencing). It is not intended to infer that telegrams are more desirable than letters; indeed, the latter system may provide the richer form of communication depending on the timing aspects of the specific situation. Further, as normally used, the letter may be richer than the telegram because of the advantages provided by a more flexible coding system. The typical letter has more of the qualities of a personal conversation than does the typical telegram.

burning or the local newspapers to warn of an impending tornado. Indeed, there is research which suggests that in the face of stressful situations, we tend to rely on the richest communication channels available (Bodensteiner, p. 27).

Face to Face. It is with respect to the quality of richness that we find the face-to-face communication system to be quite different from either the telegram or the telephone. The face-to-face interpersonal channel has the greatest capability to convey meaning and is, therefore, the richest type of interpersonal channel. The reasons for the richness of the face-to-face channel would include:

1. Feedback is to some degree automatic and is not dependent on the direct action of the receiver. It is easily available to the source-encoder at his or her option.
2. The face-to-face channel actually involves multiple channels (both primary and feedback).
3. The face-to-face channel permits greater freedom of choice in matching duration and timing to the communication situation.

Taking the matter of feedback initiation first, it should be clear that feedback is automatically present in the typical face-to-face situation. Though some communicators are not sensitive to feedback and fail to utilize it, it is nevertheless present. Bentwick was clearly giving off signals concerning his relationship with Farrow which could have been constructively used. The quarterback of a professional football team may change the play previously called in the huddle on the basis of feedback received from the opposing team. In doing so, he is using the reactions of the opponent (to his own team's offensive formation) as feedback information. This is really no different for any human situation. We can make rather good judgments concerning the impact of our messages on others by observing their responses: a smile, a frown, a red flush, etc.

This observation brings us directly to the second point about *face-to-face* communication, the existence of multiple channels. In the face-to-face situation, we are not constrained to the normal voice channel alone; all the human senses may be utilized. In addition to the various facial expressions suggested above, there is the opportunity to utilize gestures, body language, touch, smell, and the various nuances of language that might not be detectable over the telephone or in a report, memo, telegram, or letter. Such a multiplicity of channels greatly enriches the capability of the face-to-face channel.

The reader is well advised to think about this for a moment. Have there been some personal experiences which have highlighted the richness of face-to-face channels for you? Thinking through these specific circumstances will be beneficial to your understanding the basic importance of the face-to-face channel and our dependence on it.

The third point we wish to make which impinges on the richness of the face-to-face channel concerns its ease of use and flexibility. Assuming the face-to-face channel to be physically possible (which we admit is not always the case), the individual is free to use the channel as the situation demands. There are occasions when some human contrivance such as management rules tends to interfere with the free use of the face-to-face channel. The physical limitations are obvious and will not be discussed at all in this book. However, the actions of management or other forms of human interference in the face-to-face communication process will be dealt with in subsequent sections of this book.

The point to be made here is simply that excluding the foregoing constraints, the individual user of face-to-face communication has a free hand in structuring his or her communication system to meet the needs of the situation. One can select the desired receiver, send any message, solicit feedback, determine duration and sequencing, and tailor the system in an almost infinite variety of ways depending on one's interpretation of the circumstances. We know of no other system which permits such flexibility and selectivity. Table 3-1 is a comparison of the three channel types with respect to feedback, timing, and richness qualities.

In summary, the unique attributes of the face-to-face channel with respect to feedback and timing contribute to the richness of this type of channel. It is the richness of the face-to-face channel which makes it so desirable in resolving organizational problems under conditions of stress. It is the face-to-face channel which is the vital link in human communication. Thus, when we say this book is aimed at enhancing human communication, we are primarily saying it is aimed at improving our ability to use the face-to-face channel.

TABLE 3-1 Feedback, Timing, and Richness for Three Types of Interpersonal Channels

Channel type	Feedback: Receiver-initiated	Feedback: At option of transmitter	Feedback: Single or multiple channel	Timing[1]: Duration	Timing[1]: Sequencing	Channel richness[1]
Face to face		x	Mult.	Short to long	Variable	Very High[3]
Telephone		x	Sgl.	Short to long[2]	Variable[2]	High[3]
Telegram	x		Sgl.	Short[2]	Variable[2]	Low[3]

[1]The timing and richness qualities are equally applicable to either primary or feedback channels.

[2]In actual practice, it is felt that timing qualities are much in favor of the face-to-face channel in terms of flexibility and ease of use and become progressively more rigid as one moves to telephone and then telegram.

[3]High levels of semantic noise can reduce the level of richness.

SUMMARY

In this chapter, the process model of communication has been specifically focused on the human situation. We saw that the semantic aspects of the human situation necessitate special precautions if we are to successfully elicit the intended meaning at the receiver-decoder. Information was distinguished from other data and the nature of feedback was discussed. Channel richness was described as involving both technical capacity and the capability for conveying meaning.

Concepts of message timing such as duration and sequencing were seen as important considerations in the success of human communication. It was suggested that the richest form of human communication is the face-to-face system. The advantages of face-to-face communication were attributed to: the opportunity to utilize multiple channels; transmitter-controlled option for feedback; and flexibility in matching timing (duration and sequencing) to situational needs.

IMPORTANT TERMS AND CONCEPTS

information and data, semantic sender noise, semantic receiver noise, feedback, face-to-face channels, richness, timing—duration, timing—sequencing

REVIEW QUESTIONS

1. In what fashion is the human communication process differentiated from the more general communication process? Why?

2. What do we mean by semantic noise and how is it different from channel noise? What remedies are available for dealing with either type of problem?

3. Why is it important that data be differentiated from information?

4. Do you see any connection between our remarks (in Chapter 2) concerning the impact of uncertainty concerning which message is to be sent upon channel choice and our current remarks as to the value of face-to-face channels? Discuss.

5. What do we mean by feedback, richness, and timing, and how are these concepts interrelated?

6. Would you classify the problem in "communication" between Bentwick and Farrow as resulting from semantic noise, or channel noise, or neither? Why?

INCIDENT: THE CIRCUIT WAS OPEN, BUT WHERE?

A trouble report was received at the Webb City toll test room by Ralph Jaxson concerning some transmission difficulty with one of the long-distance circuits to Cruxton. In investigating such difficulties, a test person at the responsible test room will normally contact his or her counterpart at the distant point using some alternate circuit. The two test persons can then hold the alternate circuit open while attemtping to "talk out" the defective one. Should this procedure not be successful in isolating the source of the difficulty, further tests may involve the sending of test tones in the appropriate direction and testing for continuity at various intermediate points and equipment. Once the difficulty has been isolated it can be repaired or bypassed.

In the case of the particular incident at hand, Ralph contacted his friend in the test room at Cruxton, Sy Walton. The following conversation took place.

Sy: (Answering an incoming call at his testboard) Cruxton Testboard.
Ralph: Hello, Sy, how's the weather out there today?
Sy: Okay for fishing, not so good for working. Have you got a problem?
Ralph: Yes, the 102 Cruxton (Webb City–Cruxton) has been reported open. You want to hold this line open and try to meet me on the 102?
Sy: Sure, and if we can't talk to each other, I'll meet you back here.

At this time, each man moves his talking equipment to the 102 Webb City–Cruxton.

Ralph: Hello, Cruxton?
Sy: Hello, Webb City?
Ralph: Hello, Cruxton, Hello, Sy, Hello?
Sy: Hello, Webb City, Hello, Ralph, Hello?

At this point Ralph concludes that Sy is unable to hear his (Ralph's) voice and Sy concludes that Ralph is unable to hear his (Sy's) voice. They return to the alternate circuit.

Ralph: Hello, Sy?
Sy: Hello, Ralph; yeah, it looks as if we have a problem. But I could hear you okay.
Ralph: You could? Well I could hear you okay, too!
Sy: You mean we could hear each other but we were unable to communicate?

1. The above incident actually happened. As you think about this incident, try to associate it with the notions in Chapters 2 and 3, such as noise, signal, encoding, decoding, message, semantics, channel redundancy, symbols, language redundancy, selection.

2. The channel (102 Webb City–Cruxton) is not really in trouble. Why are Ralph and Sy unable to communicate?

BIBLIOGRAPHY

Bodensteiner, Wayne Dean: "Information Channel Utilization under Varying Research and Development Project Conditions: An Aspect of Inter-Organizational Communication Channel Usage," doctoral dissertation, University of Texas at Austin, January 1970.

Maslow, A.: "Deprivation, Threat and Frustration," *Psychology Review,* vol. 48, pp. 364–366, 1941.

Reid, Peter C.: "A Case of Malicious Obedience," *Supervisory Management,* July 1963.

Shannon, Claude E., and Warren Weaver: *The Mathematical Theory of Communication* (Urbana: The University of Illinois Press, 1949).

Thayer, Lee. *Communication and Communication Systems* (Homewood, Ill.: Richard D. Irwin, Inc., 1968).

4

THE COMMUNICATION PROCESS AND ORGANIZATIONS:
A Framework for Managerial Analysis

In this chapter the organization will be discussed as a goal-oriented association of individuals. It will be shown that the organization consists of a hierarchy of interdependent subgoals linked together by managers and other key individuals. The linking of subgoals and subunits into the overall organization structure is seen as a largely communicative function. Certain communication problems and factors which influence the process are described. An analytical approach to the study of organizations and communication is developed.

All kinds of organizations (whether business, social, or governmental) may be thought of as goal-oriented associations. People associate with one another for many reasons, but the essential motivation is simply that something (organizational and personal goals) can be accomplished by the collective which is not readily attainable by the separate action of the various individuals.

The relationship between organizational and personal goals is not always a clearly distinguishable one. It is not an absolute requirement that personal goals always be identical to or congruent with organizational goals. It may be sufficient that the individual perceives organizational-goal accomplishment to be a means for achieving personal goals. For a book dealing with communication, we need not be concerned with the precise nature of the relationship between organizational and personal goals.[1] It is, however, important to note that the potential dichotomy of

---

[1] These very brief remarks regarding goals are adequate for the purposes of a text in organizational communication. However, for an in-depth discussion of the subject, the reader is referred to a suitable text in organization and management.

goals as well as the general goal-oriented nature of organizations has important implications for management and communication.

ORGANIZATION GOALS: INTERDEPENDENCY AND STRUCTURE

An important aspect of the goal-oriented nature of organizations is the need for an effective division of organizational work among the various participants. In some fashion, the manager and others who plan the organization must divide the total work of the organization into an appropriate number of tasks and activities which are to be carried out by each participant. Overall organizational goals will be achieved as individuals accomplish their assigned tasks and activities. The process of goal subdivision creates an interdependency between goals and subgoals.

Means-Ends Chains

The nature of overall goals and subunit goals, as well as their interdependency, will influence the structural form of a given organization. The structural form of the organization, in turn, has implications for management and communication. In planning an organization, it is helpful to think first in terms of the broad overall goals which we wish it to accomplish. Once the broader goals have been established, we can begin to focus on the more narrow operational goals and activities which are specifically needed. Ultimately, the organization can be structured by grouping subgoals and activities consistent with the overall goals. Clearly, the nature and scope of a given goal-subgoal sequence will be influenced by the managerial and communication processes involved in its development. Conversely, a given goal-subgoal sequence will influence the managerial and communication processes involved in its implementation.

It is helpful to think of the organization as being composed of a hierarchy of interdependent goals and subgoals such as that shown in Figure 4-1. At the very highest level are the overall objectives or goals of the firm, which are represented at the first level (G1) of the figure. Such objectives are broad in scope and provide the organization with a long-term sense of direction. The objectives or *ends* at the second-highest level (SG2) are actually the *means* to the *ends* or objectives at the highest level (G1). Thus, the second-level objectives are more specific and operational than those at the first level. The analytical process is repeated throughout the hierarchy with lower levels providing a specific means for the accomplishment of the objective or subobjective for the succeeding higher level.

The resulting hierarchy of goals is sometimes called a *means-ends chain*. The

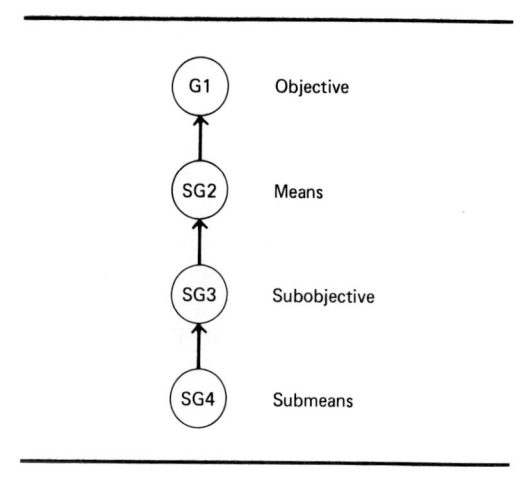

```
       G1   Objective
       ↑
       SG2  Means
       ↑
       SG3  Subobjective
       ↑
       SG4  Submeans
```

FIGURE 4-1 Hierarchy of goals.

means-ends chain represents the mainstream of the organization's work from the highest and most abstract level down to the very specific and detailed operational level (depending, of course, how far one carries the analysis). Perhaps a very brief example will clarify the nature of such interdependent means-ends chains.

An Example of Means-Ends Interdependency. Suppose that a state legislature has stated (in its legislation) that public higher education in the state is intended to provide the opportunity for quality education to all citizens of the state without regard to income or geographic location. Such a charge then becomes a major overall goal (level 1 of Figure 4-1) for the directors, administrators, and faculties of the state's higher educational system. The board of directors of a particular system might then determine that a number of separate component universities must be established at convenient locations throughout the state. The development of component universities at strategic locations then becomes a *means* (level 2 of Figure 4-1) to the accomplishment of the overall goal.

It should be noted that the development of component universities at various locations is simultaneously a *means* to the accomplishemnt of the system objective and an *end* or objective for the presidents of the individual universities. As these presidents work to develop their own universities, they are helping the system to accomplish the legislative mandate. The overall objective and the means to its accomplishment are highly interdependent.

Specificity of Means-Ends. The relationship is repeated at each level. However, as we move downward in the hierarchy, the objectives and means become more narrow in scope and more specific in form. The president of a given university seeks to meet the higher education needs of the public in his or her area, but does not teach classes. The *means* to the accomplishment of the president's objectives are provided by the deans of the various colleges which are established within each university. The objectives of each dean are, in turn, accomplished through the *means* of departmental chairpersons, staff, and faculty who actually plan, organize, and implement academic programs. Ultimately, each faculty member is teaching specific courses as the necessary *means* to the ends of his or her department. It should be clear that the broad-gauge, overall objectives of the state's higher educational system cannot be successfully accomplished if we are unable to effectively link the numerous means and ends. Significant inconsistencies at any level of the chain can be very disruptive. Communication will be essential in developing the overall plan of the system, in communicating it to individuals at each level, and in the day-to-day operation of the system.

Structuring Goals and Subgoals for Coordination and Communication

To ensure that the flow of organizational work represented by the means-ends chain is a smooth one, managers are usually assigned the responsibility for specific groupings and subsets of organizational activities. In effect, we divide up the work represented by the means-ends chain and assign responsibility for its accomplishment. Such a subdivision of responsibility causes the organization to take on a specific structural form and has implications for coordination and communication. The structural relationship between positions determines who communicates to whom and about what.

We can better understand the nature and impact of such structural relationships by mapping them in the fashion shown in Figure 4-2. Such maps of organizational task-responsibility relationships are called *organization charts* and are constructed for most "real world" organizations. In essence, the overall goals (G) of the organization shown in Figure 4-2 have been broken into subgoals and related activities which are assigned to the individuals who occupy the numbered positions. Obviously, if the overall goals (G) are to be reasonably achieved, the efforts of the various individuals must be coordinated. Typically, authority-responsibility relationships are established by assigning managers at key positions who ensure that the needed coordination takes place.

As an example, the individual at position 2 is responsible for subgoal $SG2_a$. This person must see to it that the efforts of numbers 5 and 6 are effectively blended to achieve $SG3_a$, which in turn assures that $SG2_a$ is accomplished. The relationships so created and represented on the organization chart can be very complex ones. The point for now is that we create a hierarchy of goal-subgoal relationships when

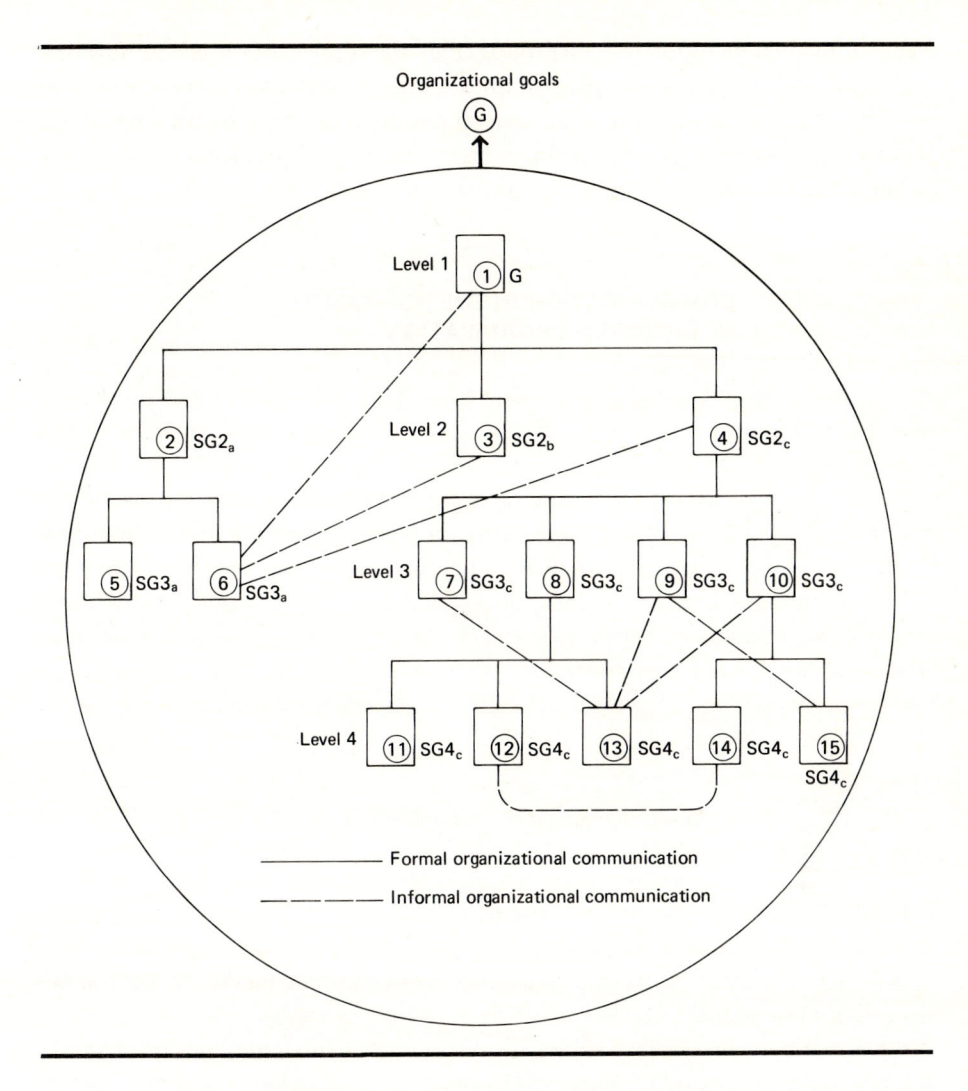

FIGURE 4-2 Structural effects of dividing work.

we divide the work of the organization. The structural effect is that a number of interdependent subunits are created which must be linked together. The linking-coordinating activity is largely a managerial function and is highly dependent on communication.

Each manager is a linking pin in the sense that each connects his or her group to the next-higher level of the hierarchy. Likert (1961) argues that successful managers are able to effectively link numerous task groups into an efficient overall organization. Such managers effectively represent their groups to higher management. Individual members of such groups enjoy the support of the group. Productivity and communication within groups are effective. It can be seen from this example that communication is of vital importance to the formally structured organization. We turn our attention now to the nature and problems of communication in the formally structured organization.

COMMUNICATION IN THE FORMALLY STRUCTURED ORGANIZATION

Any organization, including the one shown in Figure 4-2, involves a large number of actual and potential communication relationships. The linking function of the manager is one such relationship. For example, in Figure 4-2, the manager at position 2 must be in communication with the higher-level manager at position 1 and also with each of his or her subordinates at positions 5 and 6. It is obvious that in an ongoing operation, there will be numerous opportunities for interpersonal communication between the manager at position 2 and any one of his or her three potential communication partners. For each such occurrence, the communication process as described in the previous chapter will be operative. The communication process occurs via one of two broad categories of communication channels.

Formally Required Communication

One category of communication channels includes those which are formally prescribed and implemented by managers and others who are in authority. Usually, such channels are designed to provide downward, horizontal, and upward flows of information. Such channels are needed to connect and coordinate the activities of people at different locations in the structure.

Organizations have been traditionally viewed as involving a "scalar chain" of authority and responsibility relationships from the very highest to the very lowest level of the organization. Such a chain of relationships must have a corresponding communication overlay. The individual at the top level can, in theory at least, communicate "vertically" through this chain to the lower levels. Such a chain can be characterized as a series of two-person or "person-on-person" communication dyads which overlays the hierarchical structure of the organization. It is via such vertical channels that much of the manager's directive communication is accomplished. An example of this type of channel would connect positions 1 and 2 of Figure 4-2.

A second perspective of communication within the formal structure of the organization is the flow of upward communication. For successful operation, any organization must provide an upward flow of information which permits the responsible manager to know "what is going on." Such information is needed if the manager is to adequately carry out his or her control function. As an example, such a channel can be used to transmit performance-type information from position 15 to position 10 in Figure 4-2.

Finally, in most formally structured organizations we can detect a horizontal flow of communication which is of a coordinative nature. As an example, we might imagine that the Level 4 subtasks for positions 11 through 15 in Figure 4-2 are all associated in a sequential fashion to produce a common product. It is obviously necessary that the interrelated subtasks be coordinated such that the operations and outputs of one position flow smoothly to the next. Such coordination is sometimes provided via direct communication channels between the involved individuals. An alternate form of coordinative communication is, of course, the hierarchical chain mentioned above.

Informally Emergent Communication

Our remarks in the preceding section were aimed at those communication channels which are formally prescribed by the organization. It is probably obvious that many people in organizations do not restrict their communication to only the formally prescribed channels. Most of us have a natural tendency to communicate with our associates more frequently than the formally prescribed channels normally permit. Such tendencies lead to the emergence of a variety of other channels which are often referred to as *informal communication channels*. The broken lines of Figure 4-2 are used to represent such informal communication channels.

People in organizations use the informal communication channels to accomplish an almost infinite variety of purposes. For example, some may choose to use the informal channels as a means for gratifying individual personal needs such as the need for affiliation with others. Others may use informal channels to counter the effects of job boredom and monotony. We may also elect to use the informal channels to influence the behavior of others with whom we are associated. Finally, though it is often overlooked, the informal channels can also be used as a medium for obtaining job-related information. The well-known "grapevine" is one example of such an informal communication channel. In the absence of information in the formal channels, individuals may utilize informal channels as a source of information about their jobs.

One should not assume that informal channels are always undesirable sources of information. Rare is the organization that is able to move all the information needed by employees via the more formal communication channels. If you will recall your own experiences, you can probably think of numerous instances in which important job-related information was obtained from informal channels. Indeed, as we shall see later, it really is not feasible to provide a formal communication system which perfectly satisfies every information need.

Finally, as is suggested by the broken lines of Figure 4-2, informal channels are not restricted to any particular direction of flow. Informal communication channels connect *people*, not positions. Informal channels are ad hoc, not planned. Such channels interconnect people who find it convenient to communicate with each other for a variety of reasons. Under the proper conditions, informal channels are multidirectional and are not restricted to just the vertical or horizontal dimensions. We shall have more to say about informal channels in later chapters.

Communication Problems in Organizations

The division of organizational work into well-structured subunits has a very pronounced effect with respect to communication and management. It can be seen from our discussion of formally structured vertical channels that each manager is confronted by a number of person-on-person communication situations. A given manager is linked to his or her superior but is also linked to each subordinate. Each individual operates within the rather well-defined boundaries of his or her particular position. Communication between such paired sets of individuals will be influenced by both the formally structured roles of the participants and their personality peculiarities. The uniqueness of each situation with respect to types of roles and individual makeup makes it very difficult to anticipate the outcome of a given communication. However, we make our point by generalizing briefly concerning distortion and filtering as common kinds of communication problems which occur in organizations.

Distortion and Filtering. Likert (1961) and others have noted that communication upward tends to be filtered and distorted. Many of us tend to tell the boss what we think she/he wants to hear. We are reluctant to communicate information which is damaging to us as individuals. There is no reason to believe that communication downward through the hierarchy is any less subject to such distortion and filtering. It is also possible that the organization's horizontal communication channels can be similarly impaired. It should be clear that where the problem of distortion and filtering is severe enough, it will be very difficult for the manager to effectively coordinate and integrate the efforts of subordinates toward overall organization goals.

As an example, Likert (1961) observed that even where managers held group meetings to provide coordination and share information, there were still difficulties. Individuals tended to share only trivial information. The more important information was withheld until the person who possessed it could get "one-on-one" with the boss. Such information could then be used to the advantage of the individual or his or her associates. In general, distortion and filtering, as well as other communication problems in organizations, can be attributed to the manner in which four categories of factors interface for a given job situation.

Four Levels of Factors. Thayer (1968) observed that a given communication event is influenced by intrapersonal, interpersonal, organizational, and technological factors. Intrapersonal factors are the human attributes such as motivation and emotion which influence all of us. Interpersonal factors are those which arise from the interaction of two individuals. A negative interpersonal relationship such as the one between Bentwick and Farrow concerning the erroneous drawing is an example of such interpersonal factors. Examples of organizational factors include the structure which links organization participants into networks, prescribes behavior, and even links the organization to its environment. Technological factors would include channels, coding systems, language, and other similar operational aspects of moving data through the organization and storing data.

It should be emphasized that the four levels of factors interact, overlap, and affect one another as well as influence the communication process. An intrapersonal factor such as one's state of motivation or emotion at any given instant can and does influence the nature of one's interpersonal and organizational contacts. Clearly, the intrapersonal and interpersonal factors are of behavioral origin, but they can and do impair our ability to utilize the technological system. Thayer (1968) used a paradigm similar to the one shown in Figure 4-3 to demonstrate the interrelationship of the four levels of factors.

It can be seen in the figure that each level of factors intersects and overlays the other levels. Of particular importance for our purposes is the boldfaced area at

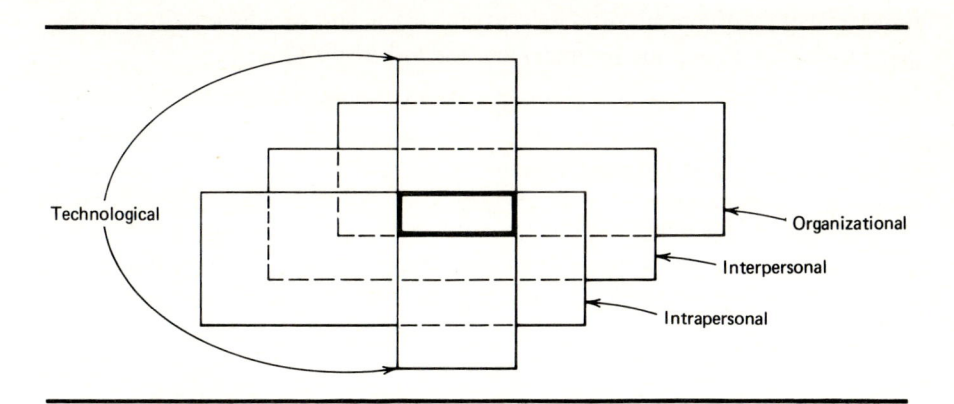

FIGURE 4-3 Four levels of factors which influence communications.

the center of the figure. It is here that all levels of factors interface. One might think of organization structure as being the matrix which brings the various factors together where they have a very complex effect on communication as well as other aspects of human behavior. Each position in the organization structure may be viewed as a focal point for a complex set of forces which act on the behavior of the individual occupant of the position. Indeed, it is our view that such a perspective of communication in organizations will be most useful. We intend to expand the viewpoint in the following paragraphs to enhance our understanding of human communication in organizations and to help us analyze communication problems.

AN ANALYTICAL APPROACH TO COMMUNICATION BEHAVIOR IN ORGANIZATIONS

We have seen that each position of the organization structure is the focal point of a complex array of forces. Some are physiological or technological in nature while others are psychological or sociological in nature. The effect of such forces influences the behavior, including communication, of the position occupant. Such effects are sometimes in an unpredictable and negative fashion. Yet, the organizational structure and plan are contrived and managed to achieve certain goals. What goes wrong?

The problem can be better understood if we realize that individual behavior in any organization is constrained by two systems which incorporate the forces we have been describing. We may refer to these as the *external system* and the *internal system* components of the organization. The external system is the contrived, rational plan which is designed and developed by managers to achieve organizational goals. The internal system is a set of behaviors which are not planned but rather emerge as the result of unique psychological and sociological forces within people who are attempting to implement the formal plan.[2]

The External System

As we saw in the opening paragraphs of this chapter, all human organizations exist for a purpose; they are goal-oriented associations. Organizational purposes are as varied as the needs of people and can include religious, social, economic, and/or

---

[2]The analytical approach suggested in this section and utilized throughout the remainder of this book is based on the work of George C. Homans, which we will credit here. Citations of this respected work will be given elsewhere only as warranted by the circumstances. Such action is taken only to preserve continuity and avoid excessive redundant citations. George C. Homans, *The Human Group* (New York: Harcourt Brace Jovanovich, Inc., 1950).

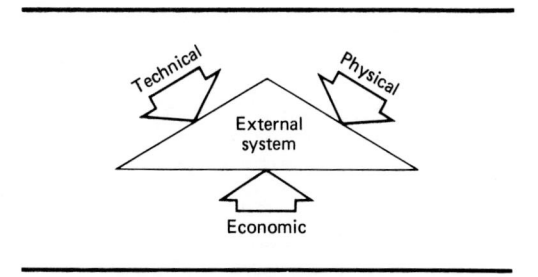

FIGURE 4-4 Origin of the external system.

survival considerations. Each human organization seeks to accomplish its purpose(s) and survive.

Homans suggests that major environmental circumstances create a pressure for the formation of human organizations. Such pressures are typically technical, physical, or economic in nature. Homans defines the *external system* as the essential state of human associations which are required to survive in a given environmental circumstance. The external system includes only such behaviors as are required to accomplish purpose and survival, nothing more and nothing less. This particular set of human relations is called an external system because its nature is determined by the technical, physical, and economic nature of the environment and not by the internal aspects of its constituents. It is external to the human participants and specifies the behavior expected of them. The organization chart shown in Figure 4-2 together with the associated job descriptions and procedures is an external system. It is the external system which configures the so-called "formal organization" as we know it. As such, the external system also characterizes formal organization communication. The origin of the external system can be shown as in Figure 4-4.

The Internal System

The external system is only one part of the total organization or social system. Consider the following from Homans.

> Social life is never wholly utilitarian: it elaborates itself, complicates itself, beyond the demands of the original situation. The elaboration brings changes in the motives of individuals. (Homans, 1950, p. 109)[3]

---

[3] Social life as used in this quotation refers to social associations in the "external" sense; that is, individuals are associated with one another to accomplish a purpose and survive as an entity.

```
┌─────────────────────────────────────────┐
│    Technical — Physical — Economic      │
│   ┌─────────────────────────────────┐   │
│   │      Psychological effects      │   │
│   │              ⇩                  │   │
│   │        ┌──────────┐             │   │
│   │        │ Internal │             │   │
│   │        │  system  │             │   │
│   │        └──────────┘             │   │
│   │              ⇧                  │   │
│   │      Sociological effects       │   │
│   │         External system         │   │
│   └─────────────────────────────────┘   │
│              Environment                │
└─────────────────────────────────────────┘
```

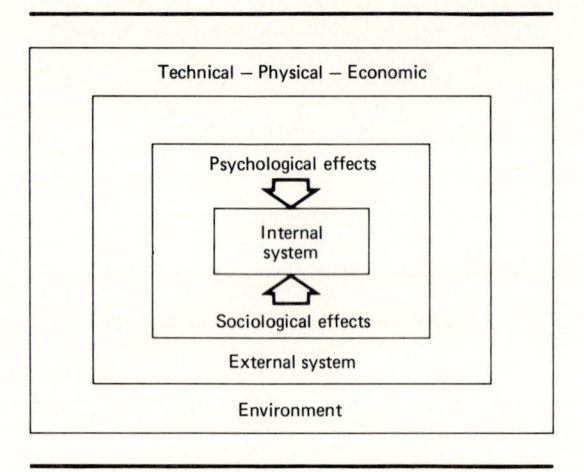

FIGURE 4-5 The social system.

We find that as individuals begin to function in the external system, certain behavioral patterns emerge which really have nothing to do with the requirements of the external system itself.

These emergent behavioral patterns are not determined directly by the environment. Rather, they are the result of sociological and psychological attributes of individuals who are associated with one another in a particular external system. Therefore, Homans has named this system the *internal system*. It encompasses those behavioral patterns which emerge from the "shell" of the external system in a somewhat spontaneous fashion.

It is the internal system which configures the so-called "informal organization" and informal communication. It is in the internal system that the intrapersonal and interpersonal factors, shown in Figure 4-3, operate to influence communication. The external system brings people together and requires certain behavior of them, but internal-system behaviors result from human qualities and human interaction. Figure 4-5 is a further elaboration of the relationships expressed in Figure 4-4 and accounts for the emergence of the internal system. The two subsystems (internal and external) in combination form the overall organization or social system.

Elemental Behavior in External and Internal Systems

Our analytical model of the organization or social system is taking shape but is not yet complete. Other than describing the required-emergent dichotomy, we have not accounted for the precise nature of either the internal or external systems.

Homans suggests that social behavior is comprised of three basic elements: activities, interactions, and sentiments. *Activities* (A) are the things which people do. Smoking, drinking, drilling, and soldering are examples. Activities are jobs and tasks or elements of jobs and tasks. *Interactions* (I) are events of contact or association between two individuals. George called Harry. Jim passed the note to Joan. Teachers met students. It should be specifically noted that communication is one form of interaction, but interaction is a more general word and is more desirable for the purposes at hand. *Sentiments* (S) refer to the internal states of individuals and include such things as drives, emotions, and feelings. In a word, sentiments refer to our attitudes—that is, how we feel about something or somebody.

All behavior in organizations (both the external and internal systems) may be described in terms of activities, interactions, and sentiments. It should be noted that each element interacts with the other two to affect the overall behavioral aspects of the given system, be it internal or external. Sentiments affect activities and activities affect sentiments (S $\rightleftarrows$ A). Activities affect interactions and interactions affect activities (A $\rightleftarrows$ I). Interactions affect sentiments and sentiments affect interactions (I $\rightleftarrows$ S).

External-Internal System Linkages. It is also important to note that interrelationships exist between the external and internal systems. We have already observed that the internal system emerges from the external system. We can now examine the relationship more closely by viewing it in terms of activities, interactions, and sentiments. One possible linkage between the two systems is expressed in Figure 4-6. The solid interconnecting arrows of this diagram reflect all the possible relationships between activities, interactions, and sentiments within either the external or the internal system. For the external system, the activities, interactions, and sentiments are those elementary behaviors required to accomplish the mission or purpose of the organization or group. Each behavior element of the external system is prescribed as part of the formal organization. Assuming the organization plan to be a good one, one element of the external system should affect the others in a supportive fashion. All three elements should be integrated in some logical pattern to achieve the desired outcome. The internal-system elements are similarly interrelated to one another. But activities, interactions, and sentiments in the internal system are not formally prescribed and planned. This system is strictly an ad hoc operation.

As has been previously noted, the internal system emerges from the external system. One obvious linkage between the two is that shown by the broken line in Figure 4-6. Homans commented that whatever sentiments we bring with us to the job are developed further through our associations on the job. We all bring sentiments to the job with us. However, as time goes by and we work with others,

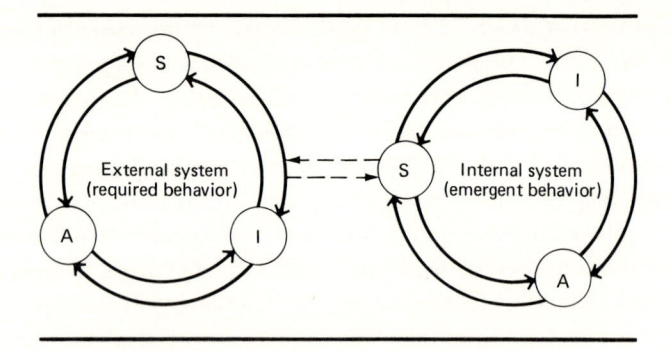

FIGURE 4-6 External- and internal-system linkage.

such sentiments are elaborated and modified. Perhaps we liked the job at first, but in time, exposure to the boss or others caused a change in attitude. The change might be positive, negative, or neutral in terms of its relationship to the organization's mission. The only point implied here is that elaboration and change occur in all three basic elements of social behavior. To quote Homans:

> If the interactions between members of a group are frequent in the external system, sentiments of liking will grow up between them, and these sentiments will lead in turn to further interactions, over and above the interactions of the external system. (Homans, 1950, p. 112)

Thus, in Figure 4-6 we have shown the primary linkage between the external and internal system as a broken line from the sentiment-interaction interface of the external system to the sentiment element of the internal system. It can also be argued that two-way relationships exist between paired sets of elements from each of the two systems—for example, from the activity element of the external system to the activity element of the internal system. We feel that such relationships are less direct than the primary sentiment connection, and they do complicate the model which we are trying to keep simple during this introductory discussion.

External Systems and Organizations All organizations with which we come in contact have external-system aspects. The local supermarket, the bank, Ford Motor Company, and the corner drugstore, all require certain activities, interactions, and sentiments of their employees. Often such required behavior is spelled out by organization charts and administrative manuals. Whether prescribed in writing or not, we are usually aware that such requirements exist and attempt to conform to them. Further, we can be equally sure that activities, interactions, and sentiments of the internal system will emerge from the external system. Our understanding of organizations and organizational communication will be greatly improved if we understand these basic components of the organization.

Perhaps an example will make the external-internal system interrelationship more explicit. Suppose you have a small company which is engaged in the sales and distribution of rubber baby buggy bumpers. This particular line of business has probably been selected because of prevailing economic and technological conditions. Let us further assume that the rubber baby buggy bumpers are purchased in bulk quantities and then packaged in matched sets for shipment to the customer. This is a very small company and four employees are sufficient to handle the volume of business involved. Two female employees handle sales and purchasing while two males perform the shipping and receiving tasks. Basic activities, interactions, and sentiments can be identified which form the *external* system. The formalized external system prescribes at least the minimum behavior that is essential for the firm to survive.

The following basic behavioral elements might comprise the external system. Required *activities* would include taking orders from customers, placing orders with suppliers, packaging the merchandise, and shipping the merchandise. Required *interactions* would include providing information concerning sales to purchasing, packaging, and shipping, and providing information concerning purchases to packaging and receiving. Required *sentiments* are not so easily detected but would include a necessity for reasonably favorable attitudes toward the job, the company, and one's associates on the job. Such favorable attitudes would be a minimum requirement. The individual cannot function effectively if his or her attitude toward the job, the company, or associates is too negative. At best, one's sentiment can be so favorable that it is a motivator of job performance.

Internal Systems as Functions of Ongoing Operations. In the preceding paragraph, we have described the external system of our hypothetical company. If we were to observe the behavior of people in the company immediately after the start-up of operations, we would probably see the specific activities and interactions described above. Similarly, if we were to conduct an attitude survey, we would likely find the participants feel reasonably positive toward their jobs, the company, and each other. In short, our first observations after start-up would probably reveal just what we expect to see. We would see people behaving as required by the external system.

However, as people interact within the framework of the external system, we would expect to see change and elaboration over time. Indeed, we might come back some day to find that new behavioral patterns have emerged. In addition to the ones described above, we now find people drinking coffee, engaging in horseplay, female talking to male, etc. A complete new set of behaviors has emerged though there was no formal requirement that this be the case.

Our examples (drinking coffee and horseplay) may seem to imply that the emergent internal system has undesirable effects. We do not mean to imply this at all. Such examples just happen to make better illustrations of the point because we have all experienced these forms of social behavior. Indeed, in subsequent sections of this book, we shall show that the emergent internal behavior can be very beneficial to organization purpose.

However, the point for now is simply that over time there will emerge from the external system an elaborate new set of activities, interactions, and sentiments. The emergent system has no legitimacy in the formal sense, and it does not result from managerial plan. But the internal system, like its external shell, does affect the behavior of organizational participants. Think of your own experiences with various kinds of organizations. How much of the behavior involved was of a required nature and spelled out by the external system? How much was emergent in nature and part of the internal system?

Communication and External-Internal Systems. It can be shown that communication systems parallel the external-internal system relationship just as do other kinds of organizational phenomena. Certain interactions are required in the external system and the other interactions are emergent in the internal system. As has already been noted, communication is a special form of interaction. The formal plan of the organization provides for and is dependent on communication. As was noted earlier, a variety of specific communication channels are formally required by the organization. Such prescribed channels are part of the external system. But as individuals communicate in the external system, we should anticipate relevant emergent behaviors in the internal system. These emergent behaviors may include communication channels which elaborate and reinforce the formal channels. Informal channels such as the "grapevine" are examples of the informally emergent channels which are components of the internal system. As might be expected, we may sometimes find that the emergent behaviors tend to work against the effectiveness of the formal communication channel. We may even find that informal communication channels compete with and disrupt the formal channels. Managers cannot effectively deal with such matters if they are unaware of the external-internal nature of the organization and its communication.

Some people (including some managers) tend to take a very restrictive view of the organization. Only the formal aspects of the organization are of importance to such individuals. Behaviors other than those called for by the external system are considered as irrelevant and perhaps even illegitimate. This is a very short-sighted perspective and assumes things about the organization which are simply inaccurate. The problem which results is much like having a road map that shows Houston at highway coordinates which, in reality, locate Kansas City. If we use such a map as a guide for our drive to Houston, we will have to spend our vacation in Kansas City.

Some managers have the same problem with organizations. Their assumptive map of the organization is based only on the external system and makes no allowances for the organization's internal system. Such a restrictive perspective can result only in problems. The manager is attempting to coordinate diverse behavior and effort toward overall goals, but he or she is, in effect, blind with respect to one-half of the efforts involved.

In this book we are concerned with enhancing the ability of the manager to achieve effective human communication for the organization. A prerequisite to the accomplishment of the purpose is that the manager possess an awareness of the nature of her/his organization. We hope to help provide this awareness by analyzing organizational communication according to the external-internal dichotomy. Part Two is aimed at the intrapersonal and interpersonal communication aspects of the internal system. Part Three treats the interrelationship of external and internal systems as they affect group communication. Part Four will integrate the internal and external system considerations into the organizational communication system. Readers are encouraged to be sure they understand these relationships now as they provide the key to an understanding of much of the material which follows. More importantly, we feel that the external-internal dichotomy is one of the most useful approaches for analyzing and understanding organizational phenomena. We encourage readers to develop their abilities to use the concept by applying it to their own organizational experiences as well as the cases and incidents encountered in this book. This can be a rewarding learning experience.

SUMMARY

In this chapter, we have characterized the organization as a goal-oriented association of individuals. The division of organization work among its participants creates a means-ends interdependency. The accomplishment of organizational objectives at any level is dependent on task performance at lower levels. To ensure that important tasks are performed and subgoals accomplished, responsibilities for subunit performance are assigned to managers.

It was noted that each manager must coordinate the activities of his or her group and effectively link them to the rest of the organization. Communication was seen to play a key role in achieving overall coordination. Both formal and informal communication were discussed and certain communication problems were examined. It was noted that communication is subject to the effects of four types of forces—intrapersonal, interpersonal, organizational, and technological. All the forces were seen to be focused by the organization structure on the occupant of a given position.

Finally, the external-internal system aspects of organizations were discussed. It was suggested that the phenomena of all forms of human association can be better analyzed using this approach. The two basic subsystems of any organization or social system were identified as the external and internal systems. The external or required behavior system was seen as having been contrived for, and necessary to, survival in a given set of environmental circumstances. The internal or emergent behavior system was seen as an elaboration growing out of the external system as a result of the sociological and psychological attributes of the people involved. The basic elements of human behavior in either system were identified as activities, interactions, and sentiments. Formal communication channels were seen as one aspect of formally prescribed interactions in the external system. Informal communication channels were seen to be part of the informally emergent internal system. It was emphasized that the effective manager is one who is aware of both the external and internal aspects of the organization. With an understanding of both systems, the manager is in a position to derive maximum benefit from both the formal and informal communication systems. The manager's potential as an efficient linking pin will be greatly improved.

IMPORTANT TERMS AND CONCEPTS

means-ends chain, hierarchy of goals, formal communication, informal communication, scalar chain, upward communication, horizontal communication, intrapersonal factors, interpersonal factors, organizational factors, technological factors, external system, internal system, activities, interactions, sentiments

REVIEW QUESTIONS

1. For an organization with which you are familiar, sketch the means-ends chain in as much detail as possible. Discuss the role of communication in the implementation of the organizational work represented by the means-ends chain.

2. Sketch the organization chart for several levels of an organization with which you are familiar. See if you can identify key managers who serve as linking pins for their groups. How is communication involved with the linking-pin concept?

3. Describe what we mean by formal and informal communication channels. Give some examples of each. How is communication involved with the managerial function of coordination?

4. Describe the major factors which influence communication in organizations.

5. Discuss the behavioral elements and systems which compose the organization or social system.

6. Think of a specific organization with which you are familiar and identify the behavioral elements which can be classified as components of the external and internal system.

7. Thinking further of the organization identified in question 6, which system seems to dominate? (That is, based on your day-to-day observations, do most of the elements seem to clearly fall within one system or the other?)

8. In an organization with which you are familiar, see if you can catalog specific communication events as to their occurrence in either the external or internal system.

INCIDENT: HEMO[4]

To others at Central Hospital it is known as "Hemo." Hemo is the department of the hospital which houses and operates the hemodialysis machines. These vital machines sustain life by performing the functions of an ailing kidney. The machines literally filter toxins from the bloodstream. A team of highly skilled specialists is required to efficiently operate the hemodialysis unit at Central Hospital.

Overall responsibility for the operations of Hemo rest with Dr. Benson, who is a member of the faculty of Central State Medical School. The medical school works closely with county authorities to operate Central Hospital. Dr. Benson's visits to Hemo are infrequent; however, he does assign a training specialist or fellow to oversee the treatment of patients at Hemo. Physicians rotate through Hemo on a monthly basis for training and the current fellow is Dr. Martha Winslow. All the fellows are highly skilled. They represent the "cream of the crop" at Central State Medical School.

The mission of Hemo and its attending fellows is essentially one of patient service and care. All efforts are directed at sustaining the patient's life and assisting the patient back to good health. Five skilled people are assigned as the permanent staff in Hemo and support the fellow in accomplishing the unit's mission.

A head nurse, three other registered nurses, and one technician are assigned to Hemo. In a sense, all five Hemo specialists are responsible to four different authority sources: the fellow, the hospital division manager, the nursing supervisor, and finally to the patient. Obviously, the role behavior required of each of the specialists is influenced by all four sources.

Each of the nurses is registered with the state and is approved to care for one or two patients on an individual basis. Working as a team they may serve the needs of several patients simultaneously. The technician cannot operate independently; his or her activities must be supervised by either a nurse or the fellow. The specialized tasks performed

[4]Based on material supplied by a former student.

by nurses and technician are critically linked to patient care and survival. Nurse, technician, and physician must work closely together. Communication is a vital link between them.

The nursing supervisor and physician provide instructions and medical information concerning patient care to the staff of Hemo. Administrative information comes from the division manager of the hospital. Much information at Hemo is passed via the communication book. Each member of the staff is expected to read and initial each entry in the book. Rich Manders, the technician for Hemo, indicates that there rarely are four sets of initials by a given log entry.

Manders feels that the communication book is an inadequate channel and offers the following observation: "Honestly, there are times when we find ourselves doing things (we think we're right) contrary to the instructions of the doctor, supervising nurse, or division manager. Too many times one nurse in particular comes to me, frowning in disgust, and complains, 'I don't know why so-and-so doesn't tell us these things.'"

According to Manders the staff of the Hemo unit normally will bring its patients from the other wards of Central Hospital and then return them after treatment. Patients have been "lost" in the sense that they were returned to the wrong ward after treatment. Patients are "hooked up" to the hemodialysis machines via tubes which connect to the veins. Treatment periods are determined by the physician and tailored to patient needs. The nurses help provide the treatment and carry out the physician's instructions in caring for the patient. The technician tends the patient-machine functioning under the guidance of the nurse or physician.

While on the machine, patients may pass the time reading or even eating a meal. The staff of Hemo may arrange for the dietary unit to send a tray of food and may even feed the patient. Patient blood pressure is monitored every half hour during treatment and weight gains and losses are checked during extended treatment intervals as a control measure. It is very important to monitor blood-flow rates so that the staff knows how much blood is being cleansed per minute. The dialysate fluid must be maintained at a proper level and in proper condition. There are many things the team must do while the patient is in Hemo, and mistakes do occur.

Manders noted that on occasion it is necessary to change or modify procedures, but such changes may not be fully communicated to the staff. As a result, obsolete procedures may be used for patient treatment. No serious threats to patient health have been involved, but the extra work necessary to compensate for incorrect procedures has been a source of frustration for all. Some of the physicians, including Dr. Winslow, have been quite angry with the technician or nurse on duty.

Those who work in Hemo must be willing to work with all kinds of patients. As a county hospital, Central receives patients from all walks of life. Many VIPs are treated at Central, but many more are treated who are poor, aged, and/or otherwise represent the underprivileged of our society. Included as patients at Central would be the dope pusher, the dope addict, and the alcoholic. Manders noted that it is easy for a staff member to give good patient care to those having a lifestyle and value system similar to one's own. One staff member at Hemo was known to cry when a patient who was particularly close was lost. At Hemo the staff is required to provide the very best care to *all* patients. This requirement includes caring for the unclean, the uncooperative, and others who may be considered undesirable. This is not an easy thing to do.

At Hemo the level of morale is only fair, but the care given to patients is good. Still, there is some room for improvement in both patient care and staff morale. The staff works fairly well as a team, but as mentioned above, there are occasional communication failures which affect operations at Hemo.

Another kind of communication failure concerns individual performance. As Manders indicated, "We never know whether we have performed an excellent job, an acceptable job, or a lousy job. Unless we do something drastically wrong, we have only our semiannual review, and it doesn't help for specific situations."

If absenteeism is an indicator, there may be some lack of dedication and loyalty. The staff of Hemo tends to fully utilize sick leave, emergency leave, jury duty, and other provisions which will permit them to stay away from their jobs. Some of the women have children and other family-related problems. They may not be able to leave their domestic woes at home and as a result aimlessly drag through the same recurring errors on the job at Hemo.

1. Map the activities, interactions, and sentiments of the external system for the Hemo unit at Central Hospital.

2. Map the activities, interactions, and sentiments of the internal system for the Hemo unit at Central Hospital.

3. Does the internal system at Hemo seem generally supportive of the external system?

4. What kinds of communication problems seem to be occurring?

BIBLIOGRAPHY

Homans, George C.: *The Human Group* (New York: Harcourt Brace Jovanovich, Inc., 1950).

Likert, Rensis: *New Patterns of Management* (New York: McGraw-Hill Book Company, 1961).

Thayer, Lee: *Communication and Communication Systems* (Homewood, Ill.: Richard D. Irwin, Inc., 1968).

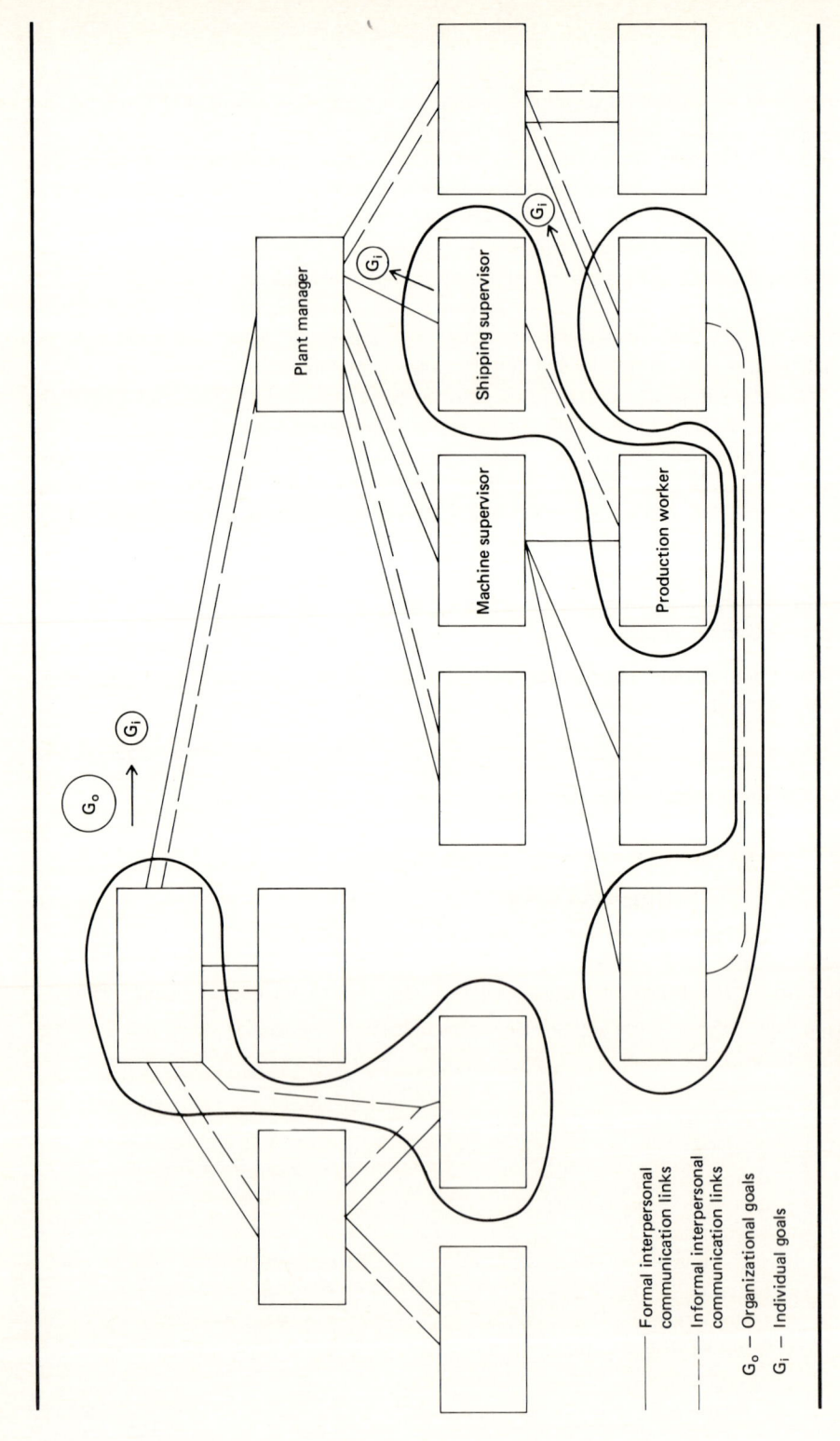

FIGURE 2 Organizational communication at the interpersonal level.

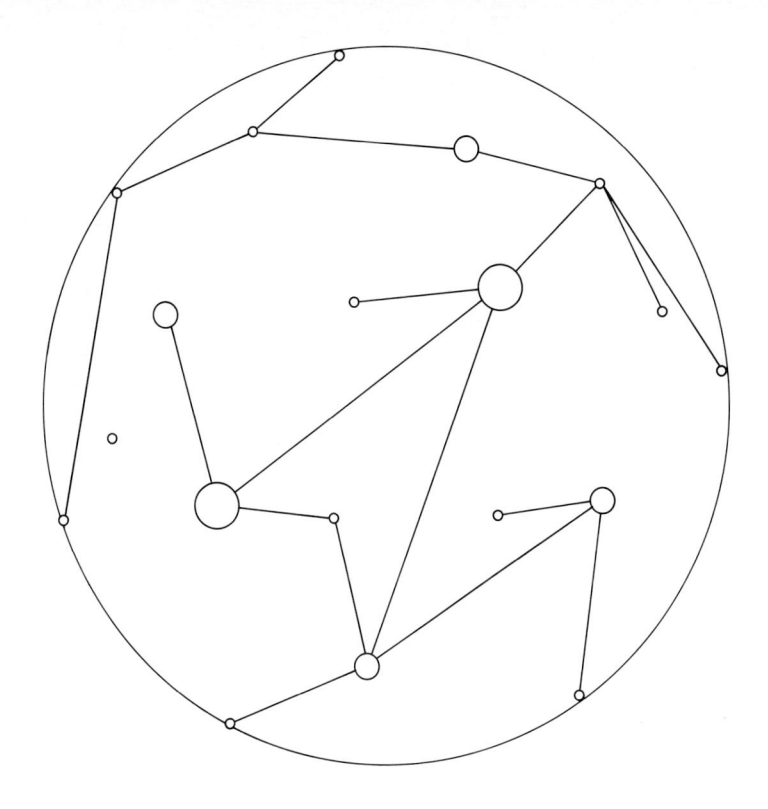

PART TWO

**MANAGING ORGANIZATIONAL COMMUNICATION:
Intra- and Interpersonal Communication**

In this section we will focus on the manager's role in interpersonal communication. Particular emphasis will be placed on those variables which influence the communication process as it occurs in interpersonal communication (the two-person relationship). As was suggested in the preceding section, managers must deal with numerous dyads as they carry out the managerial function. They are forming such dyads each time they relate to their superiors, subordinates, and peers. (See Figure 2, heavy-lined enclosure.) If managers are to effectively function in the two-person communication relationship, they must understand the underlying behavioral factors involved. They must effectively deal with both the external and internal systems aspects which affect the two-person relationship.

Chapter 5 introduces the concepts of interpersonal communication and looks at some major requirements for effective communication. Chapters 6 and 7 examine the effects of the intrapersonal factors of interpersonal motivation, interpersonal perception, emotion, and self-confidence as they affect communication. Chapter 8 presents the Exchange Theory, Johari window, and Transactional Analysis as models for understanding interpersonal relations. Chapter 9 examines the nature and the effects of six styles of communication which are used by the sender. Chapters 10 and 11 deal with the barriers and the gateways to effective interpersonal communication. Finally, Chapters 12 and 13 consider two of the interpersonal factors which are the results of communication: influence and conflict resolution.

5

MANAGEMENT OF INTERPERSONAL COMMUNICATION:
An Introduction and Overview

It is the purpose of this chapter to show the centrality of interpersonal (two-person) communication to the management process. The chapter emphasizes the often-neglected but critically important role of open and expressive interpersonal communication for effective organizational management.

THE EXTERNAL-INTERNAL SYSTEM AT THE INTERPERSONAL LEVEL OF COMMUNICATION

The Traditional Conception of the Manager's Role

The role of the manager has traditionally been defined in terms of the external system (those behaviors required to accomplish the purpose and survival of the organization). The conception of the manager's role has been concerned with the planning, organizing, directing, and controlling of the *activities* of people (in combination with money and machines). Relatively little emphasis has been placed on the manager's *interactions*, although we have shown in Chapter 1 that the major functions of managers are dependent on the communication process. Traditionally, managers have not concerned themselves with *sentiments*. Although one aspect of sentiments is motivation and managers obviously are interested in motivation, the subject of sentiments itself is avoided like the plague in most organizations. As Argyris (1970) states, managers feel that "cognitive rationality is to be emphasized; feelings and emotions are to be played down."

This lack of attention to interactions and sentiments carries over to the internal system. Managers almost universally agree that the significant human relations are the ones which have to do with achieving the organization's objective. In studies involving thousands of units of behavior, almost none show that managers spend some time in analyzing and maintaining effective relationships. This is true even though in many meetings, the group's effectiveness was bogged down and the objectives were not being reached because of interpersonal factors (Argyris, 1970).

The External System Requires Interpersonal Communication

The exact specification of the activities of the external system is impossible. The problematical situations that an organization may face cannot be completely anticipated. Consequently, policies, plans, and procedures cannot be established to cover all situations. In problematical situations, someone (or group of people) must decide what to do (plan), decide how to do it (organize and direct), and monitor the quality of the effort (control). All these processes involve communication and often involve two-person (interpersonal) communication. The following situations are illustrative of interpersonal communication made necessary by the incomplete structure of the external system:

1. Production costs have risen. The manager talks to the supervisor and/or production superintendent about possible ways of cutting costs.

2. Maintenance on a particularly critical machine has been performed repeatedly with no apparent results. The production supervisor talks to the maintenance supervisor about what to do.

3. A new office employee has frequently been late to work. Other workers notice this. The office manager talks to the employee.

4. The government has funded a new research project. Someone with administrative skills is needed to oversee the project. The manager interviews applicants.

5. An engineer has studied the production process and has stopped a five-year plan for technological change. The manager talks with the engineer about details.

6. The yearly budget figures have just been published and the process department budget is one-third as large as planned. The process supervisor talks with the superintendent.

In addition to the interpersonal communication situations which arise because of the incomplete specification of organizational structure, the interdependence of activities of individuals in the organization make it necessary for people to communicate interpersonally. The following situations are illustrative of the frequent need for coordinating activities between two or more individuals.

1. The doctor has determined that Mr. Jones needs a shot of a particular drug to combat his illness. The doctor instructs the nurse to administer a specified dosage of the drug.
2. The manager reports upward her analysis of the reasons that costs have increased.
3. The road construction engineer informs the logging supervisor (yarding and loading department) that the road into a particular sector will be finished at a particular time.
4. The office manager informs the production superintendent that overtime costs are up 20 percent over last month.
5. The supervisor tells the employee that his work is below standard.

As can be seen, a manager may be involved in many types of interpersonal communication situations which are related to the external system: downward communication (situations involving subordinates), upward communication (situations involving superiors), and lateral communication (situations involving peers). In addition, communication situations may be classified as formal (part of the organization's chain of command) or informal (arising to meet a need, either external or internal). Figure 5-1 (one segment of Figure 2) emphasizes by use of a heavy line the upward and downward interpersonal communication in the external system. Though the basic communication process describes the manager's communications with others at a general level, an in-depth understanding of the effect of important behavioral factors is needed to improve the manager's interpersonal effectiveness.

The Internal System and Interpersonal Communication

Let us return now to the example cited in Chapter 3 involving Farrow (supervisor of the development department) and Bentwick (model maker). Farrow takes the orientation of the traditional manager and is focused exclusively on the require-

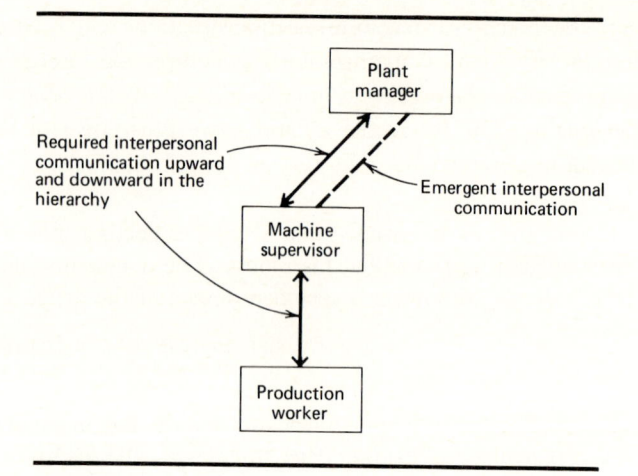

FIGURE 5-1 Interpersonal communication in the external system.

ments of the external system, i.e., the achievement of the company objectives. He directs Bentwick to follow the blueprints exactly. This appears to be a straightforward interpersonal communication. The effect of Farrow's directive is *not* toward achieving company objectives; instead Farrow's directive leads to the loss of the contract.

Where did Farrow go wrong? First of all he did not pay attention to the *interaction*. He was apparently so intent on telling Bentwick what to do that he completely excluded the possibility of feedback. Second, he did not pay attention to *sentiments*. His impersonal approach and probable impatience and Bentwick's hostility were not acknowledged. Finally, and most importantly, he entirely neglected any attention to the *internal system*. The implication of his directions to Bentwick and Bentwick's response is that the nature of their relationship had never been discussed. That is, Farrow had apparently given no attention to any factors except the defined roles of supervisor and subordinate. It is not surprising that Bentwick reacted with malicious obedience. If he agrees with Farrow's approach, he must also accept the sentiment that he is of little value since his opinions are apparently of no consequence.

As defined in Chapter 4, the internal system is the behavior patterns which emerge from the external system. Figure 5-2 (development of Figure 5-1) emphasizes by a heavy dotted line interpersonal communication at the internal-system level. More specifically, the interactions required by the external system (in this case, Farrow's directions) elicit sentiments (Bentwick's hostility) which form the context for future interactions. The concept of interpersonal relations is shorthand for this social-behavioral context. Thus, the interpersonal communication required by the external system leads to an interpersonal relationship. Further, interpersonal communication occurs within the context of the interpersonal relationship. As we can now see, the traditional management orientation which gives almost exclusive attention to the requirements of the external system paradoxically leads to the inability of the external system to function.

Internal-System Issues Are Necessarily a Manager's Responsibility

The traditional manager is unlikely to see his or her part in the communication breakdown leading to the failure in the external system. Farrow is unlikely to see that his failure to pay attention to the nature of the relationship between himself and Bentwick is at least partially responsible for the failure to gain the contract. Farrow is more likely to "blame" John, the blueprint maker, and/or Bentwick. He might make such comments as, "People just don't take pride in their work any more," or "They probably think the world owes them a living." If Farrow accepts any responsibility for the failure to gain the contract, it will probably be in terms of the external system. Thus, Farrow might acknowledge that he "should" have checked or had someone else check the blueprints.

One of the reasons that Farrow is unlikely to see his part in the external-system failure is because his view of his responsibilities probably does not include interpersonal relations. It is important, therefore, to emphasize that the manager's role is concerned with planning, directing, organizing, and controlling activities in order to accomplish the company's objectives *and* with integrating the external and

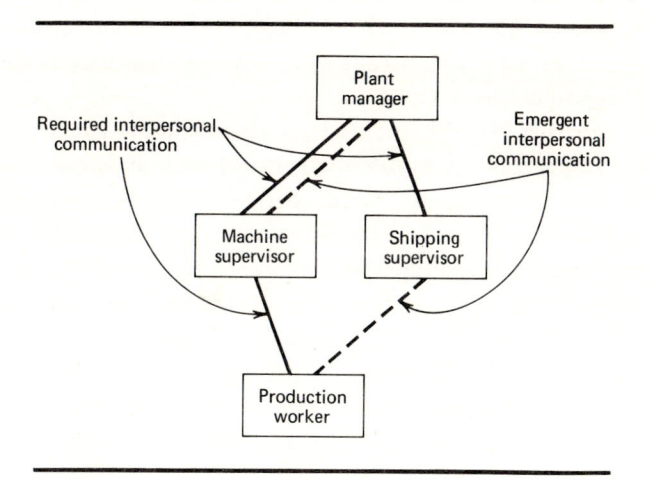

FIGURE 5-2 Interpersonal communication in the internal system.

internal systems. The manager whose planning, organizing, controlling, and directing appear to be adequate is still likely to fail unless he or she is also competent in interpersonal communication within the emergent internal system.

Given that attention needs to be devoted to interpersonal relations if organizational objectives are to be achieved, to what aspects of interpersonal relations does the manager need to pay attention? Another way of putting this question is to ask what causes "breakdowns" in communication and how are they avoided or alleviated. The remainder of this chapter examines the primary factors which cause communication breakdowns such as that of Farrow and Bentwick.

THE PRIMARY PROBLEM AREAS IN INTERPERSONAL COMMUNICATION

In order to understand how to improve interpersonal communication, we must first know *what* is to be improved. Thus, we shall look first at where problems or breakdowns in interpersonal communication occur. Often breakdowns in communication are referred to as "personality conflicts"—or they are "explained away" by statements such as, "He doesn't like me," or "She just doesn't understand me." Such statements simply suggest that communication breakdowns are inevitable. This viewpoint is largely a result of not paying attention to the process of interpersonal communication.

In order to see how communication breakdowns occur, it is important to again examine a model of communication. Figure 5-3 represents such a model and is a minor modification and simplification of the model presented in Chapter 3. We assume that any interpersonal communication contains an interpersonal motive which is usually not made explicit. For example, Farrow's interpersonal motive in his conversation with Bentwick may have been to get Bentwick to comply with directions without question.

We also assume that people consciously or unconsciously guess what interpersonal motive(s) is(are) contained in an interpersonal communication. Such guesses are called *interpersonal perception*. In the Farrow-Bentwick example, Bentwick perceives that Farrow does not like him and therefore does not appreciate his ideas.

Third, we assume that such interpersonal perceptions result in sentiments. In the Farrow-Bentwick example, the perception that Farrow does not like him or his ideas leads Bentwick to feel hurt and angry.

Finally, the model suggests that these sentiments or reactions affect our interpersonal motives. Bentwick translates his anger into malicious obedience.

We shall see through the remainder of Part Two that an essential requirement for effective managerial communication is an awareness of and attention to intrapersonal factors (within a person) and interpersonal factors (between two persons).

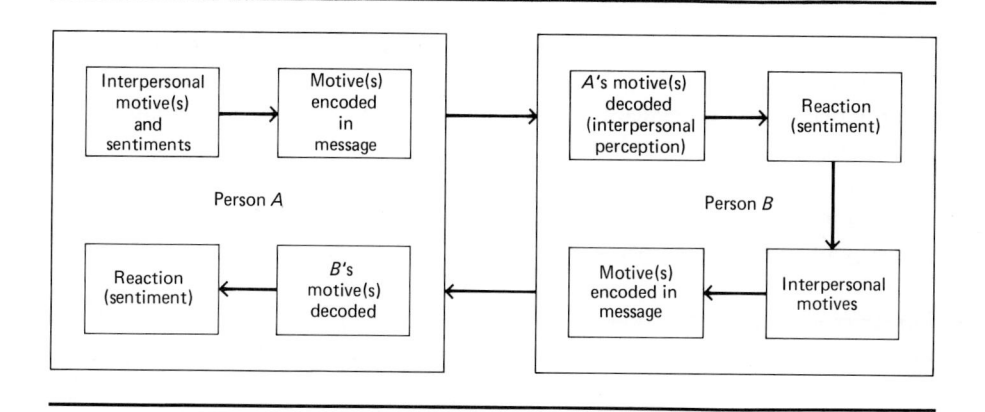

FIGURE 5-3 A model of interpersonal communication.

Examining the model of Figure 5-3, we can point to some specific areas where breakdowns occur at both the intrapersonal and interpersonal levels. *First, a person may be unaware of his or her motives.* Farrow probably feels that he is simply responding to the external system—the need to have the model finished according to plan by a certain time. He is probably looking forward to the successful procurement of the contract as a feather in *his* cap which will gain *him* recognition. He is only dimly aware that Bentwick's ideas, questions, and feelings represent an obstacle to his own personal goal.

The second area in which communication breakdown originates is in the encoding of motives. This encoding also occurs at the intrapersonal level. Fear of retaliation and lack of self-confidence are among the intrapersonal factors which restrain the expression of our true wants and needs.

The third area of breakdown results from interpersonal perception. Problems of interpersonal perception have their greatest impact at the decoding stage. We tend to see the actions of another person in the context of a general impression that we have formed. Thus, Farrow will see Bentwick's "playing stupid" in the context of his perception of Bentwick. We infer from the example that Farrow's impression is that Bentwick is not very intelligent.

Finally, communication breakdowns often occur as a result of failure to recognize and deal with the intrapersonal factor of emotion. When people are unaware of their own feelings, their interpersonal perceptions and their interpersonal communications will be influenced by their feelings indirectly. Thus, the manager who has been "disciplined" by her boss may react angrily without realizing it. Thus, she may express her anger indirectly by being unnecessarily harsh with her subordinates. In addition, she may unjustly "see" the boss as an "ogre" who does not like her. If this manager becomes aware of her feelings and expresses them appropriately, her interpersonal perception and communication are likely to be less irrational. That is, by becoming aware of and by expressing feelings, the individual is more apt to act rationally.

Now that we have a general understanding of how breakdowns in communication occur, we are in a position to state some general guidelines to avoid such breakdowns and to increase the effectiveness of interpersonal communication. These guidelines are aimed at increasing self-awareness, self-disclosure, and the accuracy of interpersonal perception.

Increasing Self-Awareness. The major block to increasing self-awareness is that it is psychologically painful and we are afraid of pain. The reason that it is painful lies basically with our need to hold a positive self-image. The protection of self-image keeps us from recognizing the "true" self.

Awareness of Feeling. The most obvious way to develop awareness of one's feelings is to pay attention to them. A helpful notion to be aware of in this regard is that physical feeling is closely related to emotional feeling. For many people, increasing the awareness of body sensations is the place to begin. Thus, we talk about a person giving us "a pain in the neck" or about getting "cold feet." (See, for example, Schutz, 1967, and Lowen, 1958.)

Awareness of body sensation may take the form of noticing when certain muscles become tense and then seeing if a feeling is being kept from conscious awareness. The term "being uptight," muscle tension, and repressed feelings are virtually the same thing.

Self-Disclosure of Feelings. The expression of feelings, attitudes, and motives is termed *self-disclosure*. Basically, self-disclosure increases interpersonal competence by increasing self-awareness and by increasing the likelihood of being perceived accurately by others. As was suggested, the major block to self-disclosure is fear.

When one becomes aware of feelings, it is important to express them. In order to strengthen the awareness of feelings, it is important to exaggerate the expression of feeling. Here, the person is likely to encounter fear. This happens for two reasons. First, the person is on unfamiliar ground and is therefore afraid that he or she might look silly or phony. Second, the expression of feeling carries with it the fear of self-discovery. That is, awareness of one's feelings, especially one's repressed feelings, is likely to lead one to confront one's self-image.

Self-Disclosure of Interpersonal Motives. Self-awareness and interpersonal perception may be increased through disclosing one's interpersonal motives. You must begin by paying attention to your own motives. What is it that you want? Verbalize it.

Tell others what you want from them. This eliminates the guessing game and establishes a basis for understanding.

In our example, Farrow is probably picking up the resentment which Bentwick feels and is indirectly expressing. Thus, it may very well be that Bentwick's expression of ideas is irritating to Farrow because of the hidden resentment. In such a case, Farrow might very well avoid contact with Bentwick as much as possible. This might then appear to Bentwick that he is getting brushed off and that Farrow is "playing favorites."

Clarifying Interpersonal Motives. We may be unclear of what our own motives are. Lack of awareness concerning our own motivations tends to be a safe retreat for us. For example, suppose that Bentwick "really" wants Farrow to help him. For Bentwick to disclose this motive, he may have to acknowledge that he is not as smart and self-reliant as he pretends. This acknowledgement and consequent destruction of self-image may be psychologically painful; thus, it is "safer" for Bentwick to not pay attention to what he wants.

A simplified model for increasing interpersonal competence by increasing self-awareness can now be stated in "how to" form. As you become aware of feelings, express them. Pay attention to the thoughts, perceptions, and feelings which arise following the expression of emotion. As you continue to express emotion, pay attention to and verbalize what you want. In addition, ask for and listen to feedback given to you by others.

Interactions with others is implicit in the model, i.e., self-disclosure implies disclosure to others. Generally, such an interaction can work only if others are also disclosing themselves. The "task" of increasing interpersonal competence through increasing self-awareness is a joint adventure.

Increasing the Accuracy of Interpersonal Perception. We have suggested that one way of increasing the accuracy of interpersonal perception is by self-disclosure of feelings and interpersonal motives. If you know what a person feels and wants, you are less likely to misinterpret that person's actions. Another way to increase the accuracy of interpersonal perception is to pay attention to the process, i.e., observe yourself interpreting the actions of others. Finally, the most straightforward way of increasing the accuracy of interpersonal perception is by noting what observations lead one to a particular conclusion and then checking whether or not the conclusion is accurate.

Checking to determine whether particular observations justify particular conclusions or interpersonal perceptions is the guts of improving interpersonal relations. Breakdowns in communication are usually a result of faulty assumptions. When assumptions are checked out and feelings and interpersonal motives are disclosed, communication breakdowns are unlikely. Unfortunately, *an individ-*

ual manager who sincerely wants to increase his or her interpersonal competence and embarks on such a program as outlined above is likely to meet considerable if not overwhelming opposition.

Forces against Increasing Interpersonal Competence

It is probably obvious that what is being suggested in this chapter is considerably at variance with the typical behavior of the manager. For example, we are suggesting that in order to avoid breakdowns in communication, and thus to increase the effectiveness of the external system, individuals need to increase their self-awareness. Such a statement implies that no management techniques—no system of accountability, rewards and punishments, policies and procedures—can avoid breakdowns unless the individuals in the system are aware.

Norms against Discussing Interpersonal Issues. Any actions leading toward awareness are feared and therefore resisted. One of the problems which an individual manager attempting to improve his or her interpersonal competence inevitably encounters can be labeled "social norms." Norms are unwritten rules about acceptable behavior. New members of an organization are taught these behaviors by social conditioning. If someone persists in deviating from social norms, sanctions will be placed against that person. People might make snide remarks; the person might be ignored or gossiped about; in short, that person would likely become a social isolate.

There exists in most organizations a social norm against the discussion of intrapersonal or interpersonal issues. The manager who deviates from this norm is likely to receive sanctions from others in the organization. Thus, managers attempting to improve their interpersonal competence in these organizations are likely to experience strong social sanctions against discussing what are considered inappropriate issues. Such sanctions would likely be brought to bear on the deviant by managers with equal or greater organizational power. Imagine a manager with the audacity to express his own feelings and motives to his superiors! Try to imagine a manager with the audacity to check out her assumptions about her superiors' motives and feelings by asking them how they feel about her or what she has done!

Lack of Self-Confidence

If managers are to "brave" the possibility of strong social sanctions being placed against them, they must be self-confident. It takes a self-confidence to encounter others openly. This assertion leads to an obvious dilemma. In order to be confident in interpersonal situations, one needs to have positive feelings regarding one's own interpersonal competence. In order to acquire interpersonal competence, a manager needs to "practice" the skills associated with interpersonal competence. In order to practice these skills, one must be self-confident.

Most managers are aware that effective interpersonal communication is essential to the success of an organization. However, most managers do not realize that effective interpersonal communication requires an awareness of and a disclosure of feelings. They do not check out their interpersonal perceptions or discuss their emotions or motives. Our aim in the remaining chapters of Part Two is to explore in greater detail the intrapersonal and interpersonal factors in effective organizational communication and to demonstrate how interpersonal communication and interpersonal relationships can be improved.

SUMMARY

In this chapter we have examined communication between two persons as it relates to the external and internal systems. We have seen that the manager is constantly involved in interpersonal communication at both the external and the internal levels.

The necessity for the effective manager to develop skill in interpersonal communication was clearly demonstrated. Some of the primary areas in which breakdowns in interpersonal communication can occur were explored. Approaches to avoiding these breakdowns were also examined.

The manager who wishes to become effective at interpersonal communication must be willing to develop an awareness of his or her own feelings and thoughts and must be able to openly reveal these to others. The manager must be receptive to feedback from others.

IMPORTANT TERMS AND CONCEPTS

interpersonal communication, intrapersonal communication, internal system, external system, communication breakdowns and problems, interpersonal motive, interpersonal perception, emotion, self-awareness, awareness of feelings, self-disclosure, sanctions, self-confidence.

REVIEW QUESTIONS

1. Explain why Farrow (in the example cited in Chapter 3) is responsible for losing the contract. What did he do or not do that "caused" the company to lose the contract?

2. Describe how a "traditional" manager would react to your answer to question 1.
3. It is suggested that managers avoid the expression of feelings. Why do you think this is so?
4. How is the avoidance of the expression of feelings dysfunctional to the organization? (Or more generally, how is the avoidance of discussing interpersonal factors harmful to the organization?)
5. Specify where communication breakdowns are likely to occur.
6. Give three examples of interpersonal motives you have attributed to others.
7. a. What is your self-image? (Give at least five adjectives, such as intelligent, attractive, shy, cheerful, uptight.)
   b. What observations support these conclusions?
   c. What other conclusions are consistent with the same observations?
8. How would you go about increasing the accuracy of your interpersonal perception?
9. How can you become more aware of your own motives?
10. How can lack of awareness of your own interpersonal motives lead to breakdowns in communication?
11. How can lack of awareness of your own interpersonal motives (and feelings) lead to depression or violence?

EXERCISE 1

1. Print at the top of a sheet of paper the words, "Who Am I?"
2. List eight adjectives which best describe you.
3. Pin the list to the front of you.
4. Circulate through the class. Read as many lists as possible in the time allowed.
5. Find two other persons about whom you would like to know more.
6. Explain your adjectives (each member of each triad). Discuss any thoughts or feelings.
7. Discuss how you felt about the exercise (the class as a whole). How did you feel while writing your list? While looking at others' lists? While discussing the lists?

BIBLIOGRAPHY

Argyris, Chris: *Intervention Theory and Method: A Behavioral Science View* (Reading, Mass.: Addison-Wesley Publishing Company, Inc., 1970), p. 64.

Lowen, Alexander, M.D.: *Physical Dynamics of Character Structure* (New York: Grune & Stratton, Inc., 1958).

Schutz, William: *Joy: Expanding Human Awareness* (New York: Grove Press, 1967).

6

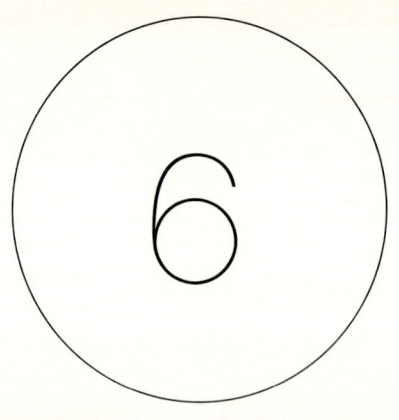

INTRAPERSONAL FOUNDATIONS FOR INTERPERSONAL COMMUNICATION

In this chapter we are concerned with examining in more detail the concepts of interpersonal motivation, interpersonal perception, and emotion introduced in the last chapter.

Motivation, perception, and emotion are three intrapersonal variables which operate within the individual and strongly influence interpersonal communication. As was pointed out in the previous chapter, the lack of awareness of how motivation, perception, and emotion operate in ourselves and others accounts for a large percentage of breakdowns in communication. For a manager concerned with increasing his or her interpersonal competence, an understanding of these important determinants of interpersonal communication is obviously necessary.

MANAGING MOTIVATION TO INFLUENCE INTERPERSONAL COMMUNICATION

As we have seen, many managers are so strongly focused on the task and the achievement of company objectives as prescribed by the external system that they are largely unaware of these intrapersonal variables. The unaware managers are likely to view ideas concerning motivation as pointing to ways to get the subordinates to perform at a higher level. The implication for these managers is that there is something the manager can do which will "magically" get the subordinates to produce like crazy because the subordinates now want to achieve the company objectives. That is, when many managers speak of motivating subordinates, they really mean changing the subordinates' motives. While changing the motivation of others is possible (McClelland and Winter, 1969), it is difficult to conceive of such a change as these managers have in mind unless they have much greater control over the environment of the subordinates.

It is much more feasible for managers to understand the subordinates' present motives rather than to change their motives. If managers understand subordinates' motives and accept them as unchangeable, they may be able to influence the behavior of the subordinates. Thus, if the manager knows what motivates Fred, and he wants Fred to expend more effort toward satisfying company objectives, all he need do is make it to Fred's advantage to work harder for the company—i.e., he needs to make the satisfaction of Fred's motives integral with Fred's achievement of company goals. This integration of individual and organizational objectives is one of the primary issues facing managers in today's world.

THE EFFECTS OF INTERPERSONAL MOTIVATION UPON INTERPERSONAL COMMUNICATION

In Chapter 5 we suggested that lack of awareness of one's own interpersonal motives leads to a confused way of expressing them and thus to communication breakdowns. We will proceed to describe that confusion and how it arises. As will become evident from our discussion, people who are either unaware of or refuse to acknowledge their interpersonal motives are acting defensively by protecting their self-image. The evidence very strongly indicates that everyone has interpersonal motives and that all communication acts are attempts to satisfy these motives (Berne, 1964).

Schutz (1967) has suggested that there are three basic interpersonal needs which underlie all interpersonal behavior. These three basic needs are for inclusion, control, and affection. He suggests that our methods of dealing with these needs are shaped by childhood experiences and that some methods lead to more "healthy" individuals than others. Examples of each are given in Figure 6-1.

The Need for Inclusion

The need for inclusion is concerned with having people to interact with who pay attention to you and what you have to say. This need is manifested each time you enter a new group of people.

People learn to deal with their need for inclusion in one of *three basic ways*. They may deny their need for inclusion by remaining aloof from others. These are the

Inclusion expressed:	Asking others to join in activities
	Joining others in activities
Inclusion wanted:	Others to ask you to join them
Control expressed:	Influencing others
	Deciding for others
Control wanted:	Allow others to influence you
	Want others to take charge of the situation
Affection expressed:	Being close and personal to others
Affection wanted:	Wanting others to be close and personal toward you

FIGURE 6-1 The three categories of interpersonal needs and their expressed and wanted dimensions.

undersocial type. They maintain *distance* between themselves and others and tend to be social isolates rarely initiating or even accepting interpersonal interactions with others in the organization. People of the undersocial type create a world of their own in which they feel secure because they unconsciously "feel" that other people in the organization are not interested in them. In this way they need not risk the pain of rejection, but instead endure the pain of being lonely.

This is an extreme example of people who express their need for inclusion in a very confused way. They are denying their need for inclusion altogether! They have such a strong motive to avoid rejection that they avoid inclusion in order to avoid the possibility of rejection.

A manager who maintains such aloofness is likely to experience poor interpersonal communication even when he or she does interact with others. Other people are likely to interpret the manager's aloofness to be snobbishness or arrogance so that any effort the manager does make at interaction may not be received very well. The manager is then likely to view this poor reception as confirming his or her original "feeling" that others in the organization are not interested in him or her (a self-fulfilling prophecy).

The *oversocial type* of person learns to deal with inclusion needs by constantly interacting with others. Such persons attempt to focus attention on themselves by exhibitionist-type behavior or by acquiring some special status. Oversocial managers are likely to spend so much time demanding attention that they neglect other things. They are likely to tell amusing "stories," but others are likely to interpret their sociability as suggestive of low interest in the task. Subordinates may attempt to gain favor with such managers through paying attention to them rather than through accomplishing tasks. Thus, the need for inclusion is expressed unclearly, resulting in low task orientation.

The third type of manager is the *adaptable-social type*. This type can be a high participator or a low participator in a group depending on the situation. Such managers are comfortable being with people and are also comfortable being alone. They have resolved the need for inclusion in a constructive way so that they can maintain identity and individuality. They are not afraid of interaction and showing their identity, as are the undersocial managers; nor are they compelled to submerge their identity by constantly pleasing others as are the oversocial managers.

In general, in work organizations, one is formally included in the organization and the work group by an organization chart. However, the attainment of the status of membership in the informal social groups that form "spontaneously" is not guaranteed by a chart. One might be isolated from the group because one differs in attitudes, age, education, etc., or because one chooses to be isolated. The need for inclusion is a strong motivational force in organizations. For example, the desire not to be excluded from the group because of being judged to be a rate-buster may cause some people to produce less than they are capable of even when this results in lower pay (Roethlisberger and Dickson, 1938).

The Need to Control

The interpersonal need for control can also be discussed in terms of three types of people. There are those people who have learned to avoid interpersonal situations in which they have *control of others*. This type of manager is one who does not like to make decisions which affect other people and generally makes a poor leader. Such managers are happiest when others control them by making decisions for them. "Unconsciously" they feel incompetent and seek to avoid situations in which they will have to face these feelings of incompetence. Second, there are those people who are comfortable *only* when they are controlling others. Managers of this type seek to dominate other people as a way, perhaps, of proving to themselves that they are competent. People of the third type feel comfortable both in situations where they control others and in situations where others have control over them. Managers with this orientation do not feel it necessary to constantly assert their competence; nor do they refrain from leadership positions when such positions are appropriate.

The "control" area of interpersonal relations is often where people in business organizations get "hung up." A subordinate who dislikes being controlled even when control is appropriate may resist the boss in many ways. Such a person may consciously or unconsciously "misunderstand" directions—doing what the boss said but not what the boss meant.

People who resent control may also cause problems with equals in the organizations. They may be so concerned with getting their way that they fail to get anything constructive done. Sometimes business meetings result in an endless parade of people to the blackboard because people feel that the person with the chalk in hand has control of the group. It is unlikely in this situation that much will be accomplished until the control issue is resolved.

The need for control can also affect intergroup relations. Often in organizations which have a research and development group and a production group, the control issue interferes with organizational effectiveness. Research may assume that production should produce the product that research has designed and specified, whereas, production may rebel at this assumption, feeling that research has not taken into account the special problems of production. If the research group fails to work with production people in the developmental stages, it is likely that there will be a delay in the start-up of production. In some industries this delay may reduce the competitive advantage of the company and result in a reduction of profit.

The Need for Affection

The third interpersonal need, that of affection, also involves three types of people. First are the people who deny their need for affection. Managers of this type may be openly antagonistic or may remain emotionally distant from others by treating everyone the same, not singling anyone out with whom they become especially close. They feel unconsciously that they are not worthy of being loved and thus are determined to avoid situations where people may express their feelings toward them. People of the second type also fear that they are not worthy of being loved. They react to this by trying to please everyone. Unfortunately, the more they seek the approval and love of others, the less likely they are to receive it (Crowne and Marlowe, 1964). They are likely to be overly permissive, failing to balance their attention to others with their attention to task. Managers of the third type in the affectional area, the ideal type, are those who feel comfortable being close to other people but who also are able to understand that they are worthy persons even if some people do not want to be close to them.

It is easy to see the problems caused in a business organization by the first two types. The person who withholds expression of feeling may frustrate others who need to feel close. A boss who does not express positive feeling toward a subordinate makes the subordinate feel uncertain about where he or she "stands" with the boss. This, in turn, makes it unlikely that the subordinate will tell the boss about the problems encountered on the job, which in turn makes it difficult for the boss to give adequate supervision. This is evident in the case of the development department of the electrical company cited in the previous chapter. On the other hand, a manager who is overly concerned with people liking him or her is not likely

			I initiate interaction with others	
			Low	High
Inclusion	I want to be included	High	Dependent on others for inclusion	Avoids being alone
		Low	Isolate	Controls relations by initiating inclusion but not responding to others' initiatives

			I try to control others	
			Low	High
Control	I want to be controlled	High	Avoids responsibility	No middle ground—either dominates or submits
		Low	Avoids confrontations; rebellious	Satisfied only in relationships where he/she is dominant

			I am close and personal with others	
			Low	High
Affection	I want others to be close and personal with me	High	Dependent on others for intimacy	Tries very hard to be liked
		Low	Aloof; distant	May use this style to "possess" and control friends

FIGURE 6-2 Personality types according to interpersonal needs. [*After* W. Schutz, The Interpersonal Underworld *(Palo Alto, Calif.: Science and Behavior Books, 1966), p. 60.*]

to be demanding and confronting even when it is necessary. This is the type of manager who "misuses" the human-relations approach and then perhaps decides: "Alright, if they don't respond positively when I treat them nicely, I'll just be an S.O.B." Figure 6-2 outlines "personality types" according to interpersonal needs as discussed above. The ideal is to be moderate on all dimensions.

APPLICATION OF INTERPERSONAL-NEEDS CONCEPT TO ORGANIZATIONAL RELATIONSHIPS

The above analysis of interpersonal needs points out some of the difficulties which arise in relationships because people have learned ways of dealing with interpersonal needs which are inadequate. How does a manager use the understanding of interpersonal needs to "motivate" his or her people in a positive direction? The manager needs to recognize these interpersonal needs and try to create conditions where these needs can be satisfied in the context of achieving organizational objectives. The Hawthorne studies (Roethlisberger and Dickson, 1938) provide an excellent example.

Six women who assembled electronic gadgets were isolated from the rest of the factory so they could be studied. They were informed that the experiment was very important but that they were not to work any harder than usual. There were a number of experimental periods where the rest pauses, pay incentives, and amount of illumination were changed. The interesting finding was that no matter what the experimental condition, whether for better or for worse, production increased.

Despite the increase in production, the women maintained they were not working harder and, in fact, that they found it easier to work under the experimental condition. The experimenter concluded that no experimental variable could account for this increase in production. Then, observations and interviews led the experimenters to conclude that the increase in production came about because: (1) the women felt that they were important since they were involved in an important experiment, (2) there was less supervision (there was no supervisor—only an experimental advisor was present), and (3) these conditions led to a close-knit group where the women exchanged birthday presents, etc.

In Schutz's terms the inclusion area was satisfied since attention and interest were directed toward the women, the control issue was more adequately dealt with since the women no longer felt that they were under close company surveillance, and the affection needs were satisfied by the close relationships developed within the group. Since all the interpersonal needs were effectively satisfied, work was less of a chore and production increased!

INTERPERSONAL PERCEPTION UPON COMMUNICATION

As can be seen from the discussion of interpersonal motives, when people are unaware, they interact with others in ways which often lead to communication breakdowns. People guess from inferences about others' motives. If these motives are expressed in a confused way, they are likely to be misinterpreted. This misinterpretation or inaccurate perception can happen for a number of reasons.

First, the same interpersonal act may be motivated by one of several different motives. The impact of the interpersonal act depends somewhat on how one perceives the motivation underlying the act. For example, if Joe invited Fred, his boss, to dinner, this might be interpreted by Fred as an act of friendship, or as paying or repaying a social obligation; or it might be interpreted by Fred as an attempt to influence him.

A second reason for inaccurate interpersonal perception is that the way the interpersonal act is perceived depends on the perceiver as well as the act. If Fred feels uncomfortable being close to other people, he is more likely to treat the invitation to dinner as an attempt to influence him, rather than as an expression of positive feeling by Joe. We tend to interpret other people's actions in terms of our own motives. For example, if Fred is the type of guy who is concerned about influencing and manipulating others, he is more likely to see others as trying to manipulate him.

Finally, a third reason for inaccurate interpersonal perception is that we tend to interpret interpersonal actions in terms of our image or stereotype of the person with whom we are interacting. Thus, if the person is a Negro, or a business person, or a union member, or a "hippie," or an older person, etc., we use the information or misinformation we have accumulated about the group to which that person belongs as a means of interpreting his or her motives. If we have a *stereotype* of union members which says that all they want to do is to avoid work—that they want to make a lot of money without really contributing to the company—then we will tend to interpret their actions in terms of this image. In fact, the image may be so strong that we will have to distort or ignore information we have about the particular union member with whom we are interacting, in order to continue to perceive that person as our stereotype describes him or her. Eventually, as we continue to interact with the person, we may accumulate enough information about him or her to force us to reject the stereotype. Usually we simply admit that we were wrong in assuming that the particular person involved fits the stereotype. Rarely do we examine the validity of the stereotype.

Perceptual errors have strong effects on the nature of subsequent interactions. Often these errors operate as self-fulfilling prophecies—i.e., by our own actions we tend to make our "inaccurate" first impressions come true. In the example of Figure 6-3, if Alice judges that Bill doesn't like her—whereas in reality Bill is simply a "shy" person—then Alice may act in such a way as to "cause" Bill not to like her. Alice may say to herself, "I'm not going to be nice to Bill because he doesn't like me." Bill, seeing that Alice is ignoring him, may reciprocate. Then Alice can conclude that Bill doesn't like her.

Often people are unaware that they are forming impressions of others; they are very often unaware of *how* they form these impressions. Alice may be unaware of what observations lead her to the conclusion that Bill doesn't like her. That is, Alice may not be aware that her interpretation of Bill's feelings is based on the observation that Bill does not smile at her and does not talk to her. If she is not aware of the observations she used to reach her conclusion (perception of Bill), she is unlikely to be able to change the conclusion. This is because we tend to "see" what

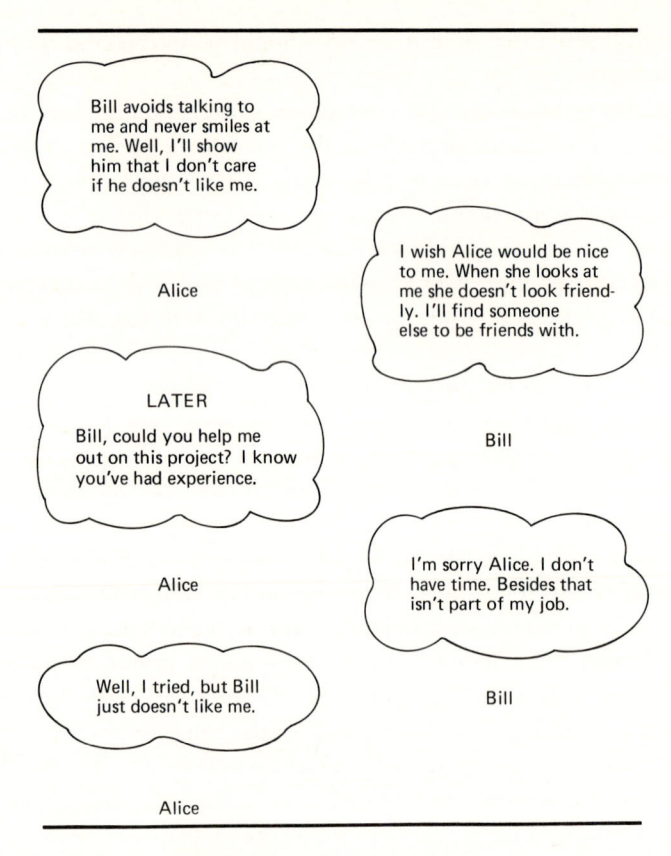

Alice: Bill avoids talking to me and never smiles at me. Well, I'll show him that I don't care if he doesn't like me.

Bill: I wish Alice would be nice to me. When she looks at me she doesn't look friendly. I'll find someone else to be friends with.

LATER

Alice: Bill, could you help me out on this project? I know you've had experience.

Bill: I'm sorry Alice. I don't have time. Besides that isn't part of my job.

Alice: Well, I tried, but Bill just doesn't like me.

FIGURE 6-3 Self-fulfilling prophecy.

we are prepared (or want) to see (Hastorf et al., 1970), so that in future encounters Alice will tend to "see" those actions of Bill which support her conclusion.

If Alice is aware of what observations she is using to support her conclusion, she may still misinterpret the observations. As was suggested in the example, Alice interprets Bill's behavior as indicative of Bill's dislike for her. In actuality, Bill is apparently attracted to Alice, but is shy. Thus, Alice's perception of Bill is inaccurate because she has misinterpreted the facts.

The most straightforward way of increasing the accuracy of interpersonal perception is by noting what observations lead one to a particular conclusion and then checking the conclusion for accuracy. Thus, in the example, Alice might say to Bill: "I've noticed that you don't smile at me and that you seem to avoid talking to me. Does this mean that you don't like me?" Bill, if he is a sincere individual, may then confirm or disconfirm the accuracy of the perception. This is also good feedback for Bill—he may now see that his shyness is interpreted by others as unfriendliness.

The checking out of assumptions to see whether particular observations justify particular conclusions or interpersonal perceptions is the guts of improving interpersonal relations. Breakdowns in communication are usually a result of faulty assumptions. When assumptions are checked out and feelings and interpersonal motives are disclosed, communication breakdowns are unlikely. Unfortunately, an *individual* manager who sincerely wants to increase interpersonal competence and embarks on such a program as outlined above is likely to meet considerable if not overwhelming opposition.

INTERPERSONAL PERCEPTION AND SUPERIOR-SUBORDINATE RELATIONS

Unless interpersonal perception is reasonably accurate, communication breakdowns are likely to occur. Superior-subordinate relations are often characterized by faulty perceptions. This is the case because both social norms (discussed in the previous chapter) *and* the power of the superior act to inhibit the subordinate's openness to the superior. Suppose, for example, a manager initiates the following conversation with a subordinate.

Manager (Susan): "Bill, I would like to talk to you about your personal objectives and what role they have in achieving company objectives." (Susan is thinking about promoting Bill and would like to hear what Bill's interests are and what future he sees with the company.)

Bill (Subordinate): "Sure, shall we meet in your office?" (Bill is distrustful of Susan because she is stereotyped as an authority figure and he distrusts people who have authority.)

Susan: "I'm wondering what you see as your future with the company."

Bill: "Well, I'm just doing as good a job as I can. Hopefully, I'll be able to get a more interesting job when people see that I'm capable of handling it." (Bill is playing it pretty tight. Since he distrusts Susan, he suspects that she might be talking to him for some other reason than she's willing to admit.)

Susan: "Well, I've noticed that you are a capable young man who may be deserving of a promotion sometime soon. We ought to talk about what things you need to learn before you can qualify for a promotion."

Bill: "OK, whatever you say." (Bill suspects that the suggestion of a promotion may be a manipulative attempt to get him to work harder and is not going to commit himself until he learns more.)

Susan: "Well, I would like you to learn Larry's job. It will mean staying late for a few weeks but I think you can handle it."

Bill: "Well, I don't know. I don't think I'll have the time to stay late."
Susan: "OK, we'll see if we can work something out." (Susan is encountering some resistance. She "realizes" that young people often don't want the responsibility that goes with a promotion. Bill's reluctance to put in a little overtime suggests to her that he would be a poor chance for a promotion.)
(Bill's suspicions are mounting.)

The above conversation, although a caricature of real situations, points toward a common issue between superior and subordinate which is due to (or at least compounded by) inaccurate interpersonal perception. The subordinate is likely to perceive that the manager is trying to manipulate him or her. In this case, Bill's stereotype of people in authority may account for some feeling of manipulation. This feeling of manipulation and distrust may be enhanced by Bill's protection of his self-image. To see Susan as trying to help him may lead Bill to recognize a need for help that is inconsistent with his self-image. Thus, Bill may have a "predisposition" to see Susan's actions as manipulative.

On the other hand, the manager often is distrustful of subordinates, viewing them as unwilling to accept responsibility. Such a manager is likely to be cautious in delegating responsibility and is likely to look for "clues" revealing whether the subordinate would act responsibly if given more authority. In this case, Susan is unsure how responsibly Bill will act and is testing him. Her caution (distrust) concerning Bill "plays" into Bill's distrust of her. Thus, when Bill is reluctant to work overtime, she perceives Bill as not having sufficient *motivation to act responsibly*. She may very well decide not to promote Bill for this reason.

It is possible to see by examining this particular superior-subordinate issue (responsibility vs. manipulation) that inaccurate perception may lead both parties in an interpersonal relation to act in such a way as to perpetuate the misperceptions. Bill, by assuming Susan is manipulative, acts in a way which allows Susan to see him as irresponsible. Susan, by assuming that Bill is possibly irresponsible, acts in a way which allows Bill to see her as manipulative. Eventually, there is likely to be a communication breakdown (see Figure 6-4).

It is very difficult to avoid this type of inaccurate perception. Bill "should" check out his assumptions. This might go: "Susan, I've noticed you watching me in various situations. I am also aware of specific promises that you have made to other individuals which you have not carried out. For these reasons, I do not trust you. I think you are trying to get me to work harder to make you look good. I don't think you are interested in developing my talents and I am uncertain whether you would promote me." This seems ridiculous! How is Bill going to let loose such a bombshell when he doesn't trust Susan in the first place?

On the other hand, Susan might be more specific about her intentions and less

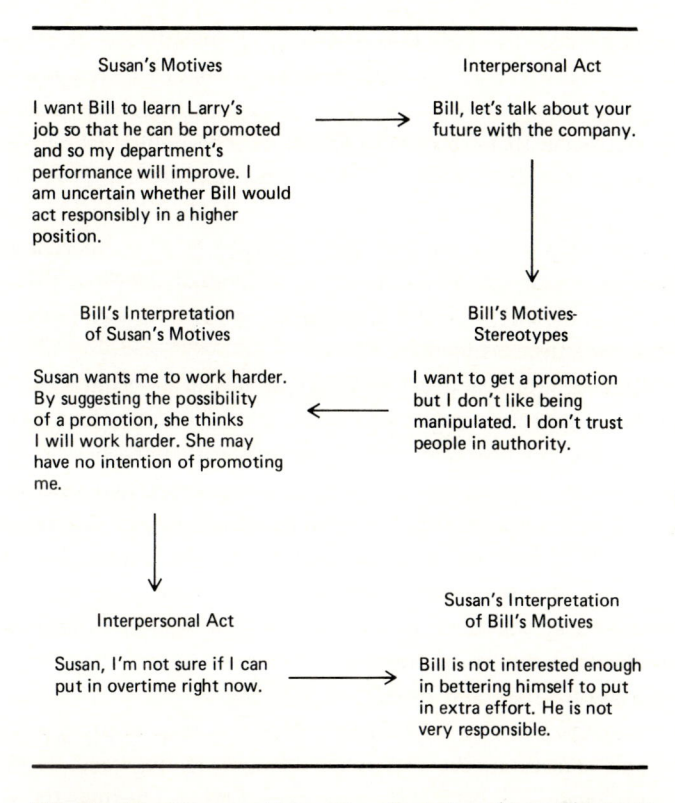

```
          Susan's Motives                        Interpersonal Act

I want Bill to learn Larry's          →    Bill, let's talk about your
job so that he can be promoted             future with the company.
and so my department's
performance will improve. I                              │
am uncertain whether Bill would                          │
act responsibly in a higher                              ↓
position.

       Bill's Interpretation                    Bill's Motives-
        of Susan's Motives                       Stereotypes

Susan wants me to work harder.             I want to get a promotion
By suggesting the possibility         ←    but I don't like being
of a promotion, she thinks                 manipulated. I don't trust
I will work harder. She may                people in authority.
have no intention of promoting
me.

            │
            ↓

          Interpersonal Act                 Susan's Interpretation
                                               of Bill's Motives

Susan, I'm not sure if I can          →    Bill is not interested enough
put in overtime right now.                 in bettering himself to put
                                           in extra effort. He is not
                                           very responsible.
```

FIGURE 6-4 Diagram of interaction: illustrative of how misperceptions are perpetuated.

cautious about delegating responsibility. Certainly when Bill backs off, she "should" not be so quick to leap to the conclusion that Bill is not responsible. If she pursues Bill to find out what his reluctance is concerned with, he may "open up."

The likelihood of two people "opening up" to each other (disclosing their feelings and perception about each other) when they distrust each other is very slight. We now see that the establishment of *interpersonal trust* is a necessary precursor to avoiding breakdowns in communications. We shall elaborate upon the importance of interpersonal trust in Chapter 11.

THE ROLE OF EMOTIONS IN INTERPERSONAL COMMUNICATION

As pointed out in the previous chapter, lack of awareness of emotion can lead to breakdowns in communication. This is because feelings influence interpersonal perception and interpersonal motives. In fact, the expression of any interpersonal communication reflects the individual's feeling. If people are unaware of their feelings, they are unaware of a significant aspect of what they are communicating.

Many people *are* aware of only their very strong feelings. This unawareness of feelings does not mean that feelings do not exist. The individual has "repressed" his or her feelings from consciousness. The repression of feelings is the result of extremely strong social conditioning. "If you can't say anything nice, don't say anything" is one example of the way parents teach children to repress feelings (especially negative feelings). Eventually, the individual may fear the expression and even the awareness of "forbidden feeling." This is how social norms work in the organization to suppress feelings.

When emotion is suppressed or repressed, it acts in an accumulative fashion. Thus, when one suppresses emotion, it generally acts to produce more intense feeling. Finally, the emotion may become so strong that the person "explodes." Managers who allow "minor" irritations to go unexpressed may one day unleash their anger at an individual who has deserved perhaps only a "slap on the wrist." The "victim" is left dumbfounded, unable to see what could have possibly angered the boss so much. This phenomenon is so frequent there is an expression for it: "The straw that broke the camel's back." Thus, repressed or suppressed feelings may eventually have the effect opposite to that intended; they may intensify emotional "displays."

In addition to the fact that expressing feelings as they occur tends to reduce irrationality and confusion, the expression of one's feelings acts to bring other feelings to consciousness. That is, when we have repressed feelings for most of our lives, there are a *lot* of feelings which we have not expressed. When we express one, this expression tends to bring others to awareness. As was pointed out in the previous chapter, when (and if) Bentwick expresses his resentment, he is likely to make contact with other feelings—in this case, probably fear and competition. As we become aware of our feelings we can choose how to express them. If we are unaware of our feelings, we have no choice. Thus, the expression of feeling leads to greater self-awareness and the possibility of more straightforward interpersonal communication.

In order to illustrate the above statements, let us address our attention to specific emotions. The identification and constructive use of negative emotions pose special problems. The two negative emotions which seem to cause the most problems interpersonally are fear and anger.

Fear in Interpersonal Communication

Fear is the anticipation of physical or psychological pain. If one is paying attention to what might happen rather than to what is presently happening, one's ability to respond to the situation is impaired.

In order to understand how fear inhibits performance and development, let us examine a common fear-provoking situation. A manager may be afraid of making presentations to committees or other groups. If the fear is great, the manager is likely to perform poorly. This person may then conclude that he or she is a poor speaker and thus avoid speaking in front of groups. The avoidance of a fear-producing situation relieves the fear and thus is rewarding. The individual forms a habit of avoiding such situations, and this habit becomes stronger each time this manager avoids public speaking. The only way of reducing the fear is by speaking to a group and performing well. In that event, the manager will be reinforced for this action and will be less likely to avoid the situation. By speaking on numerous occasions, the manager's ability as a speaker should improve, yielding additional reinforcement and thus strengthening his or her positive feelings about speaking to a group and decreasing fear.

The role of fear in interpersonal relations may be made more explicit by considering another specific situation. Suppose your supervisor explains a difficult task and you are not sure you understand it. You realize that you will be expected to perform it later, but rather than ask the supervisor for clarification, you decide that you will be able to do well on the task if you try it on your own later. Later you attempt the task and break the equipment. What happened? You may have felt that you "should" understand the task after the supervisor explained it, and that to question the supervisor would show your coworkers, and the supervisor, that you were stupid. Rather than recognizing that the failure in communication may have risen for other reasons, you have supposed that it is your inability to understand. Your lack of self-confidence and your fear of appearing stupid have led you to fail, and failure is not likely to improve your self-confidence. Furthermore, your avoidance of asking a question makes it more difficult for you to ask questions in the future and thus you will probably again think that such problems in communication are due to your own stupidity.

Confronting Fear

As can be seen from the two examples, fear does inhibit performance and development and also tends to lead to communication breakdowns. How can people conquer fear? The first step is to recognize that fear is involved! As long as individuals see themselves as "too stupid" or as "a poor speaker," they are not going to conquer their fears. They need to see themselves as afraid.

When people have identified what they are afraid of, they need to systematically go about preparing themselves for the fear-producing situations. If they are afraid of speaking to groups, they can take courses in public speaking. If they are afraid to take the courses, they can construct less fearful situations—e.g., making presentations to friends. Essentially, what people need to do is to take on similar but less fearful situations and master them. This builds self-confidence and competence so that these people are eventually able to "deal" successfully with the fear-producing situations—e.g., speaking to committees. When they prove to themselves that they can do this, they will reduce the fear and increase their self-confidence.

It should be obvious that people with low self-confidence will have difficulty in interpersonal relations. People with low self-confidence tend to avoid problems, feedback, and stress, and therefore restrict self-awareness. Individuals who have restricted their expression of ideas, opinions, and feelings to those which are unlikely to be challenged have little to say that is worth saying. Conversely, development of self-confidence is likely to increase interpersonal competence even if the fear that the individual confronted was unrelated to interpersonal relations.

Anger in Interpersonal Communication

Another emotion which often results in communication problems is *anger*. The norm in our culture—and certainly in the culture of business—is to avoid the expression of anger or control one's anger. This may be detrimental in many ways even in business. If the person cannot directly express anger, it is likely to be expressed indirectly. The manager who is angry at the boss but afraid to express this anger may take it out on a subordinate or spouse. This is called *displaced aggression*. Some may take it out on themselves. This is especially true of people with low self-confidence who tend to attribute relationship problems to their own inadequacies. Being angry at oneself, of course, only contributes to lower self-confidence. Finally, the individual may simply internalize anger (not express it at all). The failure to express anger, however, may increase tension to a point where it affects task performance adversely.

An additional problem with not expressing anger directly is that the situation which produced the anger is unlikely to change. A good deal of evidence supports the contention that the impact of a communication (i.e., the tendency of the message to produce action on the listener) is associated more strongly with the emotional force of the speaker than with the content of the message. This is generally accepted by people who talk about the enthusiasm or dynamism of a speaker, but it is also true with anger. The danger with the expression of anger is not that it will fail to have an impact on the listener, but that the listener may act in a destructive or negative manner rather than attempt to constructively change the anger-producing situation.

Bach and Wyden (1969), in their book *The Intimate Enemy*, suggest ways of learning to "fight" which are constructive—i.e., ways in which the expression of anger can improve the relationship. Basically, the techniques center around creating a positive relationship strong enough to survive the expression of negative emotion and establishing a norm where both parties encourage the other to express their anger. The angry individual should focus on those behaviors of the other person which are particularly irritating and which the other is capable of changing. If the person feels positively toward the angry person and perceives that the anger is directed toward behavior which is in his or her power to change, then it is likely that the expression of anger will be constructive—will produce better relations. If the angry party controls anger, he or she is likely to remain consciously or unconsciously angry at the other and the relationship will deteriorate. Thus, Bach and Wyden conclude, the inability to express anger erodes a positive relationship and the constructive expression of anger improves it.

An example of an interpersonal situation in which anger is not directly expressed may clarify the above discussion. This example is concerned with marketing in an expanding small company. Al is president of the company; Sally is a young college graduate recently hired; and Charlie has been handling the marketing for the company since its inception ten years ago. Al hired Sally to assist Charlie in marketing the company's line of products. Sally was hired at a salary almost equivalent to Charlie's, who has had ten years' experience but has completed only high school. Sally asked Charlie to fill her in on the present procedures and then suggested to Charlie that she could conduct a customer survey using techniques that she had learned in college. Charlie told Sally that this was not necessary, but she insisted on explaining how such a survey would improve the marketing strategy. Later, Charlie met with Al and told him that if Sally was going to stay with the company, then he was leaving. She is too pushy and impractical.

An analysis of this simple situation allows us to see the complexities of interpersonal communication and specifically the role that anger plays in communication problems. Charlie's perception of Sally is the consequence of an emotional reaction to the whole pattern of events. Charlie may feel threatened by Sally because she has more education and also because the boss apparently values this education almost as much as Charlie's ten years of experience. In addition, since Al did not consult with Charlie before hiring Sally, it is easy enough for Charlie to conclude that Al was not entirely happy with his performance. Within this context, it is unlikely that anything that Sally does will be seen positively by Charlie. So the fact that Charlie sees Sally as pushy and impractical is not surprising.

The emotional reaction of Charlie to the new situation is probably complex. Let us speculate about it. As was suggested above, the major reaction may be fear (threat). Charlie is also likely to feel hurt. Al's hiring of a new person with superior education without consulting him may be interpreted by Charlie as rejection. Finally, Charlie is likely to be angry at Al for rejecting him. That is, the emotional reaction of hurt and anger is probably aimed at Al. Certainly Charlie's ultimatum to Al suggests that there are strong feelings present. Unless Al is perceptive and interpersonally competent, he is likely to have to choose between Sally and

Charlie. If Al listens carefully, he may hear that Charlie is hurt and angry and needs reassurance from Al concerning his status and competence. Assuming that Al can honestly give such reassurance, the conflict might be diminished. If Al does not hear that Charlie is hurt and angry at him, then Charlie is likely to express his anger indirectly and destructively by carrying out his ultimatum, sabotaging Sally's efforts, withholding information from Al, or some other act of revenge.

From Charlie's side, a direct expression of anger is more likely to bring positive consequences. He might confront Al and tell him that he is angry that a new person was hired without consulting him and at nearly the salary he is getting after ten years. This confrontation would probably force Al to level with him. If Al tells Charlie that he thinks he is competent and is doing a good job but just needs assistance, then Charlie could demand a raise and a confirmation of his status in the company. If Al feels that Charlie is not doing as well as he would like, at least Charlie will find out where Al feels he is deficient and know where he stands with Al. In the latter situation, although the truth may hurt Charlie, at least he is in a situation to do something about it. From the analysis of this hypothetical situation, we arrive at the conclusion of Bach and Wyden: The inability to express anger erodes a positive relationship and the constructive expression of anger improves it.

SUMMARY

The present chapter discussed in detail the role of motivation, perception, and emotion in interpersonal communication. Interpersonal motivation was discussed in terms of three basic interpersonal needs: inclusion, control, and affection. The need to be included (paid attention to and accepted) by others is denied by the undersocial manager and overemphasized by the oversocial manager. Both extremes are primarily the result of low self-confidence. The need to control (influence) others may also bring about inappropriate responses: the manager who insists on having his or her way at all times (overcontrolling) and the manager who abdicates any leadership responsibility. Again, extreme behavior on this dimension is a result of low self-confidence. Finally, the need for affection may be met by being overly affectionate or by denying it. The "ideal" lies somewhere between the extremes in all cases.

Interpersonal perception (guesses about the other person's motives, feelings, etc.) is often inaccurate because a given interpersonal act may be motivated by one of several different motives. In addition to the ambiguity of the interpersonal act, there are numerous aspects of the perceiver which tend to influence how the interpersonal act is perceived. One's own interpersonal motives toward the other person may influence one's perception. What the interpersonal act would "mean" if one had made it (i.e., one's way of expressing one's interpersonal motives) influences one's perception. Finally, the individual's stereotype of the group or class of people represented by the person with whom he or she is interacting is also likely to influence his or her perception. For example, if the other person is a union member, the manager's stereotype or image of union members is likely to influence that manager's perception.

The role of emotion in interpersonal relations was also examined. It was shown (by examples) that the repression of feelings tends to lead to the indirect expression of feelings and to communication breakdowns. When people express their feelings openly *and* the listener is able to listen without defensiveness, relationships become stronger (even if the expressed feelings are negative).

IMPORTANT TERMS AND CONCEPTS

inclusion, control, affection, stereotype, interpersonal trust, repression of feelings, displaced agression

REVIEW QUESTIONS

1. What basic strategy can a manager use to get a subordinate to work harder?
2. What type of communication problems might arise for an "overly social" manager? Why?
3. Suppose you are a manager with an "undersocial" subordinate. What can you do to make that subordinate more a part of the work team?
4. Suppose you are a manager with a subordinate who resents being controlled. What can you do to utilize his or her talents?
5. Compare your answer to question 4 with the conversation diagrammed in Figure 6-3. How are you approaching the subordinate differently than Susan?
6. Suppose your superior is an "abdicrat" (exercises little control). How might this lead to a communication breakdown? What could you do to avoid such a breakdown?
7. Why is interpersonal trust necessary if most superior-subordinate relationships are to be improved? (Use any example cited in the book.)
8. Why do you think managers allow "minor" irritations to go unexpressed?
9. What steps can a person take to improve self-confidence?

EXERCISE 1

Photograph courtesy of J. Paul Kirouac, A Good Thing, Inc.

Using the following list of adjectives, describe the person in the picture. Place a circle around the number which indicates the degree to which the adjective applies to the person.

Dominant	1	2	3	4	5	6	7	Submissive
Happy	1	2	3	4	5	6	7	Sad
Responsible	1	2	3	4	5	6	7	Irresponsible
Sophisticated	1	2	3	4	5	6	7	Unsophisticated
Intelligent	1	2	3	4	5	6	7	Unintelligent
Tolerant	1	2	3	4	5	6	7	Intolerant
Self-confident	1	2	3	4	5	6	6	Insecure
High achiever	1	2	3	4	5	6	7	Low achiever
Rigid	1	2	3	4	5	6	7	Flexible
Firm	1	2	3	4	5	6	7	Soft
Anxious	1	2	3	4	5	6	7	Relaxed

Sociable	1	2	3	4	5	6	7	Unsociable
Stable	1	2	3	4	5	6	7	Unstable
Introverted	1	2	3	4	5	6	7	Extroverted
Capable	1	2	3	4	5	6	7	Incapable
Industrious	1	2	3	4	5	6	7	Lazy

EXERCISE 2: LOG OF FEELINGS

1. For a two-day period maintain a log of your feelings. Identify each feeling: when it occurred, what the emotion was, how it showed up in your body, what the circumstances were, and how you showed or concealed the feeling from others.

2. Pair up with two other class members. Discuss your logs. Did you experience the following emotions?
    a. Happiness
    b. Sadness
    c. Jealousy
    d. Anger
    e. Liking
    f. Loving
    g. Hurt
    h. Fear
    i. Anxiety
    j. Other feelings

    Are you normally aware of your feelings?

EXERCISE 3

The following role-play exercises are designed to give the student practice in dealing with situations where interpersonal issues are largely concerned with control. In order to experience the different possibilities of dealing with a situation, it is important to play both supervisor and subordinate (at different times) and to play each role in different ways. Thus any one role play may be played several times. Following the role play students should discuss their reactions to different styles of interacting. Some useful questions are listed below each role play. In order to get maximum use of these exercises, it is important to be as imaginative as possible in "getting in" the role.

A. Poor attendance in a manufacturing plant: Find a partner and decide who is to be Ted and who is Sam. Afterwards, switch roles and partners, etc. (This exercise is best done in class.)

First-line supervisor (Ted): Employee has poor attendance record. He misses usually every other Friday or Monday. When he does come to work he complains that he didn't get any sleep. He complains about his work and his fellow workers. He goes over to first aid for some little thing on a regular basis.

Employee has been working for six months. He has been in this department for almost all of this time. His work performance—when he works—is adequate. I have not spoken to the employee about absenteeism—except to inquire why he was absent. I have not spoken to employee about his frequent trips to first aid. There is nothing in the employee's file.

Employee (Sam): This job is no fun. This whole mill is a drag. I get a headache just coming into this place. I used to play hookey from school because it was so boring, but this place makes school look like the Garden of Eden in comparison. I am making a reasonable amount of money and want to continue working here for that reason. My supervisor seems to be a bit unfriendly toward me, but I do my work so he has never said much to me.

Discussion Questions:

1. How does Sam feel about the way the supervisor acted in the situation?
2. Does Sam think that he will reduce his absenteeism? Why or why not?
3. What did Sam do or say that was difficult for the supervisor to handle? How would others handle this particular situation?
4. What long-term plan might work to "motivate" Sam?

B. Safety problem in a manufacturing plant:

First-line supervisor (Don): The fork-truck driver likes to "cowboy" his vehicle around the plant. Sometimes he does not slow down for corners and has narrowly missed hitting the chief engineer. Otherwise, he is a good worker.

Fork-truck driver (Bob): I like to work fast and see how much I can get done. Sometimes pedestrians do not watch where they are going. The company should do something about them.

Discussion Questions:

1. How did Don approach the situation? What was the first thing he said?
2. How does Bob feel about the different approach?

BIBLIOGRAPHY

Bach, G., and P. Wyden: *The Intimate Enemy* (New York: William Morrow & Company, Inc., 1969).

Berne, Eric: *Games People Play* (New York: Grove Press, Inc., 1964).

Crowne, D., and D. Marlowe: *The Approval Motive* (New York: John Wiley & Sons, Inc., 1964).

Hastorf, Albert, David Schneider, and Judith Polefka: *Person Perception* (Reading, Mass.: Addison-Wesley Publishing Company, Inc., 1970).

McClelland, D. C., and D. Winter: *Motivating Economic Achievement* (New York: The Free Press, 1969).

Roethlisberger, F., and W. Dickson: *Management and the Worker* (Cambridge, Mass.: Harvard University Press, 1938).

Schutz, William: *Joy: Expanding Human Awareness* (New York: Grove Press, 1967).

7

SELF-CONFIDENCE AS AN ESSENTIAL INTRAPERSONAL VARIABLE FOR EFFECTIVE COMMUNICATION

Lack of self-confidence can be a critical barrier to interpersonal communication. This chapter examines the importance of self-confidence and considers how self-confidence can be developed. The manager's role in facilitating the development of self-confidence in subordinates is examined.

Openness in interpersonal communication requires self-confidence. The more confident one is intrapersonally, the easier it is to express one's feelings and opinions, and the more receptive one becomes to feedback from others. As people increase their self-confidence, they are more likely to take the risks associated with exposure of themselves and other's opinions about them.

INTERPERSONAL COMPETENCE REQUIRES SELF-CONFIDENCE

Why is it so difficult to openly expose true feelings and ideas and to accept openness from others? A pattern of openness and receptivity to feedback has certain payoffs and costs. To give up these payoffs and seek new ones requires effort and immediate loss for a possible long-term gain.

Take, for example, the "typical" superior-subordinate relationship. If subordinates reveal their true feelings, they may be asked to act on them by taking more responsibility. They may be afraid that they will be unable to handle this increased responsibility which could result in personal failure for them. On the other hand, if subordinates do increase their initiative and responsibility, the superior needs to change his or her behavior in order to support the change in the subordinates. As the supervisor becomes more of an equal by delegating responsibility, he or she is likely to get less status recognition and compliance from subordinates. The supervisor may lose self-confidence because of the loss of ego-bolstering comments from subordinates. Thus, with both superior and subordinate feeling "shaky" in their newly defined relationship, both are likely to revert back to their old ways under stress. From this description, it is apparent that the development of interpersonal competence necessitates the development of self-confidence. A person must have the self-confidence to accept the risk involved in an open relationship.

DEVELOPMENT OF SELF-CONFIDENCE

Recognition of Anxiety

The first step in increasing self-confidence is the recognition of situations which are associated with feelings of low self-confidence. Since feelings of anxiety are often associated with low self-confidence, we begin our discussion by describing the state of anxiety and how persons with low self-confidence react ineffectively to feelings of anxiety.

When a person is uncertain concerning his or her ability to avoid physical and/or psychological injury, he or she is likely to experience a negative emotion which psychologists have labeled "anxiety." Anxiety is characterized by frequent worrying, being easily upset, having frequent headaches, lacking energy when faced with difficulties, and responding with reduced effectiveness when under pressure. Feelings of inadequacy are often associated with anxiety because the individual perceives himself or herself to be unable to cope with many situations. Thus, anxiety may be interpreted as an indication that the individual feels inadequate with respect to whatever situation he or she currently faces.

Defense Mechanisms

Ingenuous characters that we are, we humans have figured out ways to avoid or reduce anxiety without coping with the situation. In this way we need not test our adequacy and risk physical and psychological injury. The methods of reducing anxiety which most people discover are called *defense mechanisms*. These behaviors may successfully defend a person, but they do not build feelings of adequacy. For example, the fear or anxiety produced by public speaking may be reduced by avoiding such situations rather than mastering them. Since defensive behavior reduces anxiety and is reinforced by the reduction of this negative state, defense mechanisms become strong habits which are highly resistant to change and which need to be unlearned in order to develop self-esteem.

Since defensive behavior is often a habitual reaction to anxiety and since such behavior is counterproductive, it is useful to recognize one's own and others' defenses. An awareness of defenses is useful in the pursuit of both self-esteem and interpersonal competence. Awareness of one's own defenses allows one to pinpoint behavior of others and provides an insight into the communication process, since the sender may be the stimulus which provokes defensiveness in the receiver. A brief description of commonly used defenses should provide the reader with a clear idea of defense mechanisms. Some of the most frequently used defense mechanisms are avoidance, repression, projection, regression, and rationalization.

The defense mechanism of *avoidance* is well illustrated by the example of avoiding expressing one's ideas in committees. In organizations, avoidance might be used in several ways. A recently promoted manager may spend a disproportionate amount of time working on situations relevant to his or her old job rather than tackling more difficult and less familiar problems of the new job. Similarly, groups often choose to deal with problems which they are confident they can solve, rather than attacking issues critical to organizational success.

Repression is a defense which is generally used to protect the person from being aware of motives or feelings which he or she believes to be undesirable. For example, if the feeling of hostility is believed to be undesirable, then the person may repress it by not allowing it to become conscious. A manager may repress anger toward a colleague since expression of anger is generally socially unacceptable in business organizations. As was pointed out in Chapter 5, anger which is not expressed directly is likely to be expressed unconsciously toward oneself, an innocent bystander, or indirectly toward the person who has aroused the anger. Thus, the manager may become depressed, may be unnecessarily harsh with a subordinate, or may neglect to relay information to a colleague. None of these alternatives are constructive either in terms of the development of self-esteem or in terms of organizational success.

Projection can be seen as functioning with repression. Here the individual may project his or her feelings outwardly. Thus, the perceived source of anxiety is transferred from the individual to the environment. This protects the individual from feeling inadequate, since the individual says, in effect, "I do not have this undesirable feeling. I am just a victim of circumstances." Thus, a manager might feel that colleagues, boss, or subordinates are angry at him or her rather than accept his or her own anger. If they are hostile toward the manager, then, of course, his or her own aggressiveness is justified as self-defense.

Regression is a defense mechanism which is frequently used to reduce anxiety. When an individual is faced with a situation provoking anxiety, he or she may revert to behavior more appropriate to satisfying lower-level needs. A manager may use regression to reduce anxiety by showing excessive concern about the size of his or her desk or the thickness of the office carpet. Such behavior is generally coupled with avoidance of situations which might provoke anxiety.

Rationalization is perhaps the most frequently used defense mechanism. People often invent excuses or explain away frustrations. For example, a manager who does not get a promotion may rationalize that this had nothing to do with his or her managerial skill but was in reality a result of not playing golf with the boss.

The Change Process

After a person recognizes those situations which "trigger" anxiety and feelings of inadequacy, and those behaviors which reduce anxiety but do not promote self-confidence, the next step is to try to limit the use of such behaviors. When one begins to stop using these defenses, one encounters an increase in anxiety! Having divested oneself of one way to reduce anxiety, now one needs to adopt another way to decrease anxiety which will also increase self-confidence.

People can adopt many behaviors in order to obtain temporary relief from tension. The ultimate relief of negative tension or anxiety will be gained upon achieving self-confidence. These temporary tension-relieving behaviors are called *coping mechanisms* (Mennenger et al., 1963).

The coping mechanism is used until tension has declined, and discontinued until the need arises again. When not used temporarily, as in the case of alcoholism or drug addiction, they are not coping mechanisms.

There are numerous coping mechanisms. Some of the most frequently used are:

1. Eating and other oral behaviors like smoking and chewing gum

2. Ingestion of alcoholic beverages and drugs

3. Sleeping

4. Talking out; discussing one's problems with a sympathetic listener

5. Working off, as in direct physical exercise

6. Pointless overactivity, such as walking up and down, finger tapping, etc.

7. Retreating into fantasy and daydreaming

Only the coping mechanisms of talking out and working off seem related to increasing self-esteem. Talking out may improve self-esteem because it may lead the individual to see alternative behaviors which increase feelings of adequacy, and working off may help because it may produce a better feeling about one's body, which is in turn closely related to one's self-concept.

In confronting the anxiety which initially accompanies decreasing defensiveness, a person's first task is to believe that he or she can be adequate. One needs to reprogram oneself, replacing fears about inadequacy with workable plans. One also needs to rehearse what one is going to do when the particular anxiety-provoking situation arises. Furthermore, one needs to see oneself in the process of change and put one's concentration on the change without evaluating progress. The more effort and attention that is directed toward change and the less attention directed toward the evaluation of the results of that effort, the more likely that the change will be positive. Instead of wondering whether people will respond favorably to one's actions, one needs to find enjoyment in the actions. As one begins to enjoy the process, one will be less concerned with the effect. As one learns to project oneself into one's actions rather than being a spectator wondering about their effects, one will understand better what one is doing and consequently do it better. This change process is summarized in Figure 7-1.

DEVELOPING SELF-CONFIDENCE IN SUBORDINATES

Many of the influence methods open to the manager can also build the subordinate's self-confidence. For example, attention and positive recognition of effort and accomplishment are certainly builders of self-confidence. The following discussion is extrapolated from Stanley Coopersmith's study, *The Antecedents of Self Esteem* (1967), and will deal with basic approaches to building self-confidence in others rather than with particular techniques.

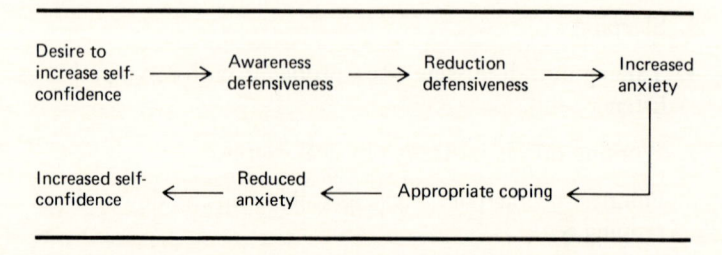

FIGURE 7-1 Cycle for increasing self-confidence.

Total Acceptance of Subordinates

Coopersmith's study suggests that high self-confidence is related to three conditions: total acceptance of the subordinates by the manager, clearly defined and enforced limits, and managerial respect for individual action within the defined limits. Total acceptance is communicated by showing concern and being attentive to the needs of subordinates.

Initiation of Structure

As suggested above, managers who want to develop the self-confidence of subordinates need to provide structure in the form of clearly defined and enforced limits for their subordinates. That is, the manager needs to tell the subordinates what is expected of them, what his or her own attitudes are toward work, how he or she feels about the subordinates' progress, etc.

In order for the manager's structuring to have positive effects, the manager needs to have a personal commitment to the validity of this structure. If the manager disagrees with decisions and policies passed down from above, his or her structuring of the subordinate's situation is likely to be unclear or insincere and consequently is likely to have less impact.

Respect for Individual Action

The third condition important to the development of self-confidence in subordinates is the permission and encouragement by the manager to act freely and responsibly within the structure established by the manager. This is an important and difficult middle ground between allowing the subordinate to act as he or she pleases (permissiveness) and telling the subordinate exactly what to do and how to do it (authoritarianism). It is often difficult for the manager to allow the subordinate to make some mistakes; however, only by encountering and overcoming difficulty is the subordinate going to increase his or her self-confidence.

The respect for individual expression requires that the superior spend less time in directing and controlling the subordinate; however, this does not imply an abdication of the supervisor's responsibility but rather implies a redirection of the supervisor's energies toward structuring the environment, i.e., specifying limits rather than directly controlling the subordinate's behavior. The manager attempts to guide subordinates and channel their individual efforts toward achieving group goals rather than telling them what to do. To the extent, then, that the subordinates succeed in their individual efforts, they can experience success and bolster their self-esteem. On the other hand, when the manager does not allow expression of individual initiative, the subordinates cannot attribute the group's success to their own efforts and therefore cannot experience successes necessary for the enhancement of self-esteem.

The manager who allows and encourages individual initiative but does not adequately specify limits is not likely to be successful. This abdication of responsibility is likely to leave subordinates unclear about what constitutes success. In this case, subordinates are not likely to experience the successes necessary to produce high self-esteem. *Only* if subordinates already clearly understand the problem they are faced with and already possess the self-esteem, responsibility, and expertise necessary to successfully attack and solve the problem will such a manager be successful.

An Example of Building Self-confidence in Subordinates

Returning to the example of Al, Sally, and Charlie in Chapter 6, we can illustrate the managerial approach for building self-confidence in subordinates. In this example, Al's apparent lack of communication with his subordinate, Charlie, has the consequence of undermining Charlie's self-confidence. Al apparently considered Charlie's academic knowledge of marketing to be inadequate and therefore hired someone with this background for the expanding operation. If Al were concerned with the development of Charlie's self-esteem, he might have talked with Charlie rather than taking unilateral action. In this conversation, Al might have pointed out that, although Charlie was working hard and doing a good job (if this was in fact the case), his lack of knowledge about certain marketing techniques restricted his effectiveness. In addition, he might have pointed out whatever considerations led him to believe that an additional person was needed.

After the problem was presented to Charlie, the two of them could have discussed possible solutions to the problem. The eventual decision to hire a person like Sally with academic training might have been the same, but the effect on Charlie would likely have been far different. The fact that Charlie was consulted and participated in the decision is likely to make Charlie see Sally in a far different light. Charlie is much more likely to use Sally's knowledge because of the way the decision was made, and thus, Charlie is much more likely to gain competence. His self-confidence is likely to improve with his gain in competence. Communication between Charlie and Al and between Charlie and Sally is likely to be significantly better. Finally, Charlie is likely to make the decision work since he had a part in it. This is an example of participative decision making.

Al's failure to show concern about Charlie's development may have arisen because of his past relationship with Charlie. That is, he very likely has a friendly relationship with Charlie since the two have worked together for ten years, and thus he finds it hard to confront Charlie with his shortcomings. This is analogous to the reaction of the permissive parent who too often fails to confront the child. The initial reaction of the child and the subordinate to such a confrontation may be anger or feelings of rejection. A manager or parent may prefer to avoid such a reaction. However, in the long run such avoidance is destructive. Managers who avoid such confrontations may do so because they want the subordinates to like them. This need for affection or approval from subordinates may indicate that such a manager is trying to bolster his or her own self-confidence. Thus, a manager with low self-confidence is likely to avoid the confrontations with subordinates which are essential to the development of the subordinates' self-confidence. For a summary of this process by which the manager assists the subordinate in gaining self-confidence, see Figure 7-2.

CONSEQUENCES OF BUILDING SELF-CONFIDENCE

People with high self-confidence are interpersonally competent individuals. They tend to be socially skilled, have good social relationships, and are direct and incisive in dealing with the real world. They expect success and are assertive and curious. They will probably insist on their rights and resist any authority that suggests that they are not equals. Conversely, persons of low self-confidence feel incapable of expressing and defending themselves and feel that they are too weak to

---

High managerial self-confidence

Acceptance of subordinate (sees subordinate as potentially responsible)— Theory Y manager → Guides, encourages, and reinforces responsible behavior → Subordinate identifies with manager → Copes successfully → Subordinate self-confidence

Clear enforced limits

Freedom of individual expression —participative decision making → Gives tasks which require responsibility, sees guidelines, and encourages participation → Commitment to task → Copes successfully → Subordinate self-confidence

---

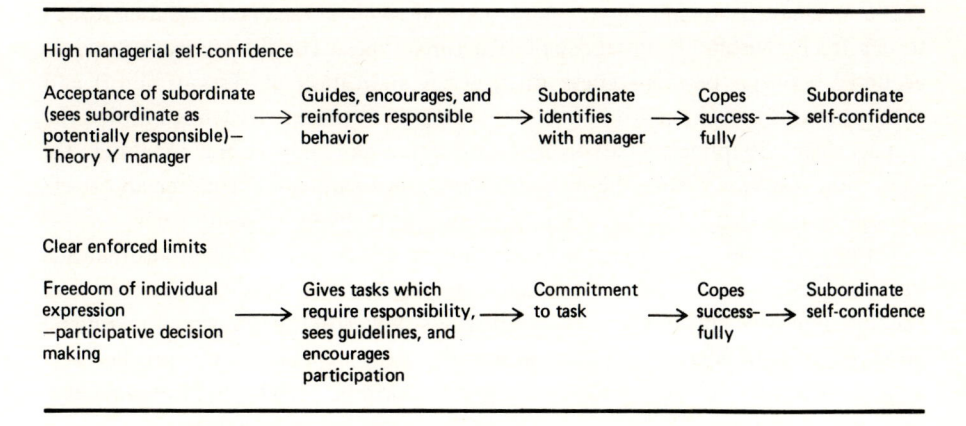

FIGURE 7-2 Two ways of building self-confidence in subordinates.

overcome their deficiencies. They tend to withdraw and be apathetic. They expect failure and are likely to have little motivation or energy to deal with problems.

It is easy to see that organizational members who possess high self-confidence are threatening to less confident but more organizationally powerful individuals. The high-self-esteem subordinate who demands equal rights is denying the superior's "right" to control. The superior has probably been defending a public image and denying his or her feelings of insecurity by insisting on control. If the superior allows the subordinate to have some control (influence), then the superior's feelings of inadequacy may be exposed. Of course, the superior's insistence on controlling the subordinate tends to restrict the development of self-confidence in the subordinate.

Finally, it should be clear that where organization members have high self-confidence, interpersonal communication will be significantly more open. Confident individuals are more likely to communicate with others in accordance with situational needs. Effective managers will strive to achieve such openness.

SUMMARY

The present chapter has detailed a basic approach for developing self-confidence. Anxiety, defense mechanisms, and coping mechanisms were detailed in order to give the manager an understanding of the process of developing self-confidence.

The manager's role in facilitating the development of self-confidence in subordinates is concerned with three basic conditions: (1) the total acceptance of the subordinate as a person by the manager; (2) clearly defined and enforced limits for the subordinate by the manager; and (3) managerial encouragement to subordinates to act freely within the established structure. These conditions are a "middle ground" between permissiveness (managerial abdication of responsibility) and authoritarianism (rigid control of the subordinate). With clearly defined limits, the manager can discipline the subordinate in a consistent, nonarbitrary manner. By exercising freedom within these limits, the subordinate can encounter and overcome difficulties and thus has the opportunity to develop self-confidence.

An organizational consequence of developing self-confidence in subordinates is that they may pose a threat to insecure managers. The insecure manager may become defensive and insist on controlling less powerful organizational members; however, self-confident employees do not like being unreasonably controlled and may challenge the manager. If the manager is unwilling to delegate responsibility, then the employee is likely to suffer some unhappy consequences.

IMPORTANT TERMS AND CONCEPTS

self-confidence, anxiety, defense mechanisms, avoidance, repression, projection, regression, rationalization, self-esteem, coping mechanism

REVIEW QUESTIONS

1. How is self-acceptance (of one's weaknesses and insecurities as well as one's good points) related to the development of self-confidence?
2. How is self-disclosure and feedback related to self-acceptance (and self-awareness)?
3. In light of questions 1 and 2, how is interpersonal competence related to self-confidence?
4. How do we limit our self-awareness (defend our self-image)?
5. Give an example of how you use the defense mechanisms of avoidance, projection, and rationalization.
6. What can a manager do, in general, to help subordinates develop self-confidence?
7. Why are the establishment and enforcement of limits desirable?
8. How do self-confident subordinates threaten insecure managers?
9. Describe the process of developing self-confidence.
10. Can a manager who is insecure but willing develop self-confidence in subordinates? Why or why not?

INCIDENT: BELLA DONNA CHEMICAL CO.

The following case may provide a focus for talking about the development of self-confidence.

Sam Davidson is a manager of the accounting function for a large chemical company (Bella Donna Chemical Co.). Although he is forty-five, he has recently married for the first time. He is very hardworking, spending many unpaid overtime hours in order to ensure that all work is accurate and up to date. One of his subordinates, Bill Pender, is very difficult for Sam to supervise. Bill is very bright and routinely does all his work. Bill is also very innovative and has made a number of suggestions which have proved to be extremely beneficial to the company.

The problem that Sam has with Bill centers around what Sam calls Bill's "eccentric ways." Bill makes sarcastic remarks about Sam and others in front of clients and outsiders. He refuses to wear a tie even though Sam has suggested that this would ease things with upper management. Sam has encouraged Bill to apply for higher-paying jobs in accounting both within and outside the company. Bill says he likes his present job and does not want to move.

Discussion Questions:

1. What can Sam do to help Bill? Role-play a discussion between Bill and Sam.
2. What can Sam's boss do to help Sam? Role-play a discussion between these two.
3. How can this situation be approached if Bill and/or Sam do not want to discuss anything?

EXERCISE

From the list of slogans below, identify a statement that is most descriptive of each of your classmates.

____ I'd rather fight than switch. (Tareyton)

____ . . . has a better idea. (Ford)

____ Quality. The endangered species. (Whirlpool)

____ When you care to send the very best. (Hallmark)

____ . . . helps make it happen. (Westinghouse)

____ The seven-day wonder. (Kraft dressing)

____ Things go better with . . . (Coca Cola)

____ Put a tiger in your tank. (Esso)

____ It lets me be me! (Nice 'n Easy)

____ Come to where the flavor is. (Marlboro)

____ The way you look says a lot about you. (Vitalis)

____ You've come a long way, baby. (Virginia Slims)

____ Pleasing you more. (Ozark Air Lines)

____ Once you try it, you'll love the difference. (Dr. Pepper)

____ To know you're the best you can be! (Miss Clairol)

____ We try harder. (Avis)

____ It's the real thing. (Coca Cola)

____ We're trying to make things better. (Shell Oil)

____ Since we're neighbors, let's be friends. (Safeway)

____ We're specialists. We have to do a better job. (Midas)

____ I'd walk a mile for . . . (Camel)

____ The quality goes in before the name goes on. (Zenith)

____ You're in good hands with . . . (Allstate)

____ Put the snap, crackle, pop into your life. (Kelloggs)

____ You only go around once in life, so reach for the best. (Schlitz)

____ Life is too short not to go first class when you can. (Mercedes)

____ As you travel, ask us. (Standard Oil)

____ Think small. (Volkswagen)

____ The slowest ketchup in the West. (Heinz)

____ I can't believe I ate the whole thing. (Alka Seltzer)

____ Getting people together. (Boeing)

BIBLIOGRAPHY

Coopersmith, Stanley: *The Antecedents of Self Esteem* (San Francisco: W. H. Freeman and Company, 1967).

Mennenger, K., M. Mayman, and P. Pruysner: *The Vital Balance: The Life Process in Mental Health and Illness* (New York: The Viking Press, Inc., 1963).

8

MODELS FOR UNDERSTANDING INTERPERSONAL RELATIONSHIPS

Now that we have examined the intrapersonal variables which affect interpersonal communication and interpersonal relations, we are in a position to examine the interpersonal relationship itself. In this chapter we shall examine three models for understanding interpersonal relationships and interpersonal communication—exchange theory, Johari window, and Transactional Analysis. Each of these models aids in our understanding the underlying relationship upon which interpersonal communication is based.

Interpersonal relationships serve as the framework within which interpersonal communication occurs. If we are to fully understand a communication event between two people, we must know the relationship of these people. Jane says to Harry, "I really care about you." If we know that Jane and Harry are a happily married couple, this statement has a certain meaning; if we know that Jane is a therapist and Harry is a patient, we have a different interpretation; and if we know that Jane is the supervisor of Harry and that Harry has just been given disciplinary action, we have a third interpretation.

Compatibility of such intrapersonal variables as motives, values, attitudes, and interests is an important foundation for a positive interpersonal relationship. Within an organization, we are often required by the external system to enter an interpersonal relationship in which we do not find compatibility. To accomplish a required organizational objective, we may be forced to interact with a person with whom we have little or no compatibility. As a consequence, the interpersonal communication is severely hampered.

We can find good reason to suspect that the constraints of business organizations often hinder effective interpersonal relations. A power hierarchy within the traditional organization exists to ensure commitment to company objectives. This force is seen as necessary since cooperation is unlikely between people who are not particularly compatible and whose personal objectives may be largely unrelated to company objectives. We have also suggested that this force may frustrate the satisfaction of interpersonal and/or achievement needs. Finally, we can now conclude that this frustration may eventually lead to retaliation as a negative exchange. Perhaps, then, the Farrow-Bentwick example which so clearly illustrates this argument is typical of interpersonal relations in organizations. We shall examine more thoroughly the nature of these interpersonal relationships using three models: the exchange theory, the Johari window, and Transactional Analysis. The exchange theory considers the nature of a relationship in terms of compatibility of values exchanged. The Johari window considers the compatibility of persons in the level of self-disclosure and feedback. Transactional Analysis examines the compatibility of the roles taken in a relationship.

EXCHANGE THEORY AS A MODEL FOR INTERPERSONAL COMMUNICATION

Exchange theory provides a conceptual framework by considering what is being exchanged in interpersonal relations. This concept holds that interpersonal motives depend on the *reward value gained from the relationship* and that individuals involved in a relationship need to feel that each is contributing equally, i.e., the rewards are equal to what is given. If over a period of time one person feels he or she is contributing too much or too little to a relationship, that person is likely to discontinue that relationship. In this theory, one can view interpersonal acts as commodities to be exchanged. Such commodities would include information, expertise, status, and love, as well as money. Thus, if I invite you to dinner, you may attempt to repay my effort and expense by conferring status on me. This might take the form of thanking me and remarking about the excellent food—perhaps asking for the recipe in order to show how pleased you were with the dinner. Eventually, however, you may need to reciprocate in some manner—perhaps by asking me to dinner.

In a business organization, the existence of unbalanced exchange may cause a strain in interpersonal relations. For example, Fred, a new man, may need to ask Joe for some help in solving a particular problem. In this situation, Fred is conferring status on Joe by acknowledging his expertise, and in return is receiving help. However, if Fred continues to go to Joe for help, the value of the status conferred may become less than the time and effort necessary to give help justifies. In this case, the relationship is unbalanced and either Fred will become reluctant to seek help from Joe or Joe will be less willing to give of his expertise. This problem may be solved by changing the nature of the exchange. If Joe is made responsible for "breaking" Fred in, then he has the opportunity to gain recognition from his superiors for helping Fred. In this case, Joe need not feel that he is doing something and receiving nothing in return.

Another example of unbalanced exchange is the manager who allows his or her subordinates to break some company rules of little consequence—e.g., taking unauthorized breaks if they have completed a job. When a rush job comes up where a little extra effort is needed from the workers, the manager is in a position to ask them for extra effort since they have received something from the manager in exchange.

A typology of relationships based on the units of exchange in interpersonal relationships is outlined in Table 8-1. This classification is not exhaustive—it is merely illustrative. We believe it provides an interesting way of viewing interpersonal relations. For example, what is the character of interpersonal relations for a manager who complains that his or her workers are no longer loyal? The table suggests that this manager views his or her relationship to the workers as one where money (salary) buys love (loyalty). As long as the manager can recruit "prostitutes," he or she can enjoy this type of relationship. It appears, however, that workers are no longer willing to give loyalty (love) for money.

In addition to positive exchanges (transactions), exchange theory also suggests that negative exchange may occur. As Whyte (1969) indicates, the existence of negative exchange is supported by comments that people make about "paying back" or "getting even." This idea of negative exchange goes back at least as far as Hammurabi (2000 B.C.): "an eye for an eye." For example, individuals who resent being controlled may find a way to get even. The Farrow-Bentwick example cited in Chapter 3 illustrates such a situation.

JOHARI WINDOW AS A MODEL FOR INTERPERSONAL COMMUNICATION

The Johari window is a theoretical conceptualization developed by Joe Luft (1961). We use it here as a focus for our discussion on the information flow between two persons. Imagine a window frame (Figure 8-1). Inside the frame is everything there is to know about you: your opinions, feelings, likes and dislikes, goals, needs, etc.

You are not aware of everything about yourself. You learn more about yourself all the time. Others with whom you have relationships do not have full knowledge of you either. The Johari window is a model for examining those areas of a person which are known, and those areas which are not known to the person and others.

The Johari window divides knowledge about an individual into four areas

TABLE 8-1 Examples of Interpersonal Relationships Based upon Various Exchanges

	Status	Information	Love	Expertise	Money
Status	Very formal relationships—as characterized by heads of state where protocol is important.				
Information	e.g., Superior may give subordinate inside information—in return subordinate shows respect for superior (agrees with superior).	Business-type relationships—"I just want the facts."			
Love	The traditional paternalistic view of human relations—subordinate gives status to boss. Boss in return shows concern for subordinate.	Concern shown for subordinate—in return subordinate feels free to give information about how things are going at lower levels.	Close personal relationships.		
Expertise	Traditional staff role of giving expertise and in exchange hoping that one will be accorded organizational status.	A highly competent person may give technical know-how to another person and in exchange receives information about organizational politics.	Often a helping relationship where the helper uses expertise and generates goodwill in return.	Mutuality in problem solving where each person equally contributes.	
Money	Buying influence.	Buying information.	Prostitution of some sort—"If I pay you enough money, I expect you to show concern about me." Production-oriented individual expects loyalty from worker in exchange for money.	Consultant relationships in traditional view—boss pays consultant for advice. Personal orientation.	Pure economic exchange.

```
┌─────────────────┐
│   Everything    │
│     about       │
│      you        │
└─────────────────┘
```

FIGURE 8-1 Window frame enclosing everything about a person.

according to the degree of self-knowledge and the knowledge others have of the individual (Figure 8-2). The *arena* (I) is those aspects of a person of which both the individual and others are aware. This might be termed the "open area." It represents the image one presents to others. One's arena is often largely defined by the role and activities one pursues, such as student, housewife, businessperson, amateur photographer, father, etc. The second area, the *blindspot area* (II), might better be called the "bad-breath area." This is the area where one is unaware of oneself although others are aware. The third area is the *facade* (III). This area has to do with a person's fears, troubles, negative feelings about self, etc., which the person is afraid to show others for fear they might reject him or her. Finally, the fourth part of an individual is that which is completely unknown—the *unknown* (IV). This part of the person has not been revealed because the person has not put himself or herself in situations which reveal it. For example, if one has never been under extreme stress, how one would react under extreme stress is unknown both to oneself and to others.

These four areas are interrelated and may change in size in the process of interpersonal relations and personal growth. As one gains confidence in oneself and the strength of one's relationship with another, one may reveal some hidden area to the other person. This is an act of trust in that the individual figures that aspects of himself or herself in the facade area are potentially damaging and thus he or she is freely providing "ammunition" to the other. This "letting down one's hair" usually is reacted to as an attempt to increase the intimacy of the relationship and is usually

	Known to self	Unknown to self
Known to others	I Arena	II Blindspot
Unknown to others	III Facade	IV Unknown

FIGURE 8-2 Areas of the Johari window. [*After Luft, 1961.*]

perceived to mean that the individual feels positively about the other person and may lead him or her to reciprocate. In any event, making more of oneself open tends to also increase the size of the blindspot area. The better a person knows you, the more likely that the person knows things about you of which you are unaware.

In an interpersonal relationship, two persons may be viewed as engaging in a process of exposure and feedback. One exposes one's thoughts and feelings to another and receives feedback about oneself and one's messages from the other.

In Figure 8-3 a Johari window has been drawn for each of two persons who are attempting to communicate. Person A's window is reversed to show that it is the arena that provides the open area for communication. The communication is limited to the level of the arena for either person. As seen in Figure 8-3, the restricted arena for person B limits the flow of information from person A (his or her exposure) and the flow of feedback from B to A. Effective interpersonal communication requires a large arena area on the part of both persons.

TRANSACTIONAL ANALYSIS AS A MODEL FOR INTERPERSONAL COMMUNICATION

Transactional Analysis (T.A.) provides a useful framework for focusing attention on how exchanges take place. Transactional Analyst Berne (1964) suggests that there are three basic ways that individuals use to relate to others. These modes of behavior are called the Parent, the Adult, and the Child, since they are roughly analogous to these "roles." (See Figure 8-4.)

Parent-Adult-Child

The Parent mode of communication (ego state) is learned from one's parents. People record the attitudes, values, and morals of their parents during their

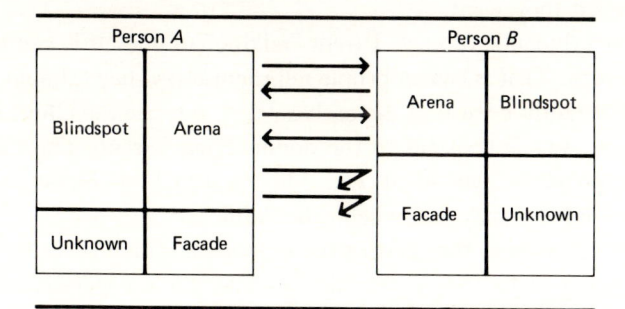

FIGURE 8-3 Johari windows of two communicating persons.

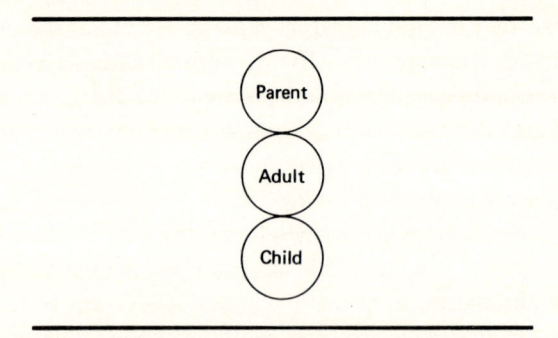

FIGURE 8-4 Parent, Adult, and Child ego state.

childhood at a time when they are in no position to question or evaluate their parents' ideas. Young children observe their parents' behavior, how the parents relate to them, etc. When situations arise which touch on one's Parent (i.e., situations where others are dependent on one, or where values or morals are involved), the Parent ego state is likely to be activated.

Many managers seem to operate almost entirely from the Parent when talking with subordinates. If their Parent is critical and evaluative, they tend to criticize and interrogate their subordinates. If their Parent is warm and supportive, they tend to "mother" their subordinates. If the manager is operating from the Parent, the subordinate is receiving a lot of pressure to act the Child: compliant, dependent, seeking approval, or rebellious, counterdependent, seeking independence.

It is generally easy to recognize Parent communication. If the tone of voice is moralistic, if the person shakes a finger at the listener, if authority is used instead of reasoning, and if the speech is sprinkled with "shoulds," it is very likely the Parent that is speaking.

People who come on Parent to others probably come on Parent to themselves. They are likely to be perfectionists who never do as well as they "should." They may spend little time doing what they want; in fact, they may be completely out of touch with what they want.

The internal dynamic of one's Parent "talking" to oneself is similar to transactions with others. That is, when people tell themselves they "should" do thus and so and are constantly critical of themselves, they activate the Child in themselves which in some way is resistant to the domineering Parent. The Child wants to play, be irresponsible, dependent, etc. The Parent-Child conflict in people is an energy drain and also may overwhelm the Adult.

The *Adult* ego state is that part of the individual which is reality-oriented and problem-centered. The Adult attempts to take life's experiences as data and rationally deal with them. The objective of the maturing individual in T.A. terms is to emancipate the Adult—i.e., to free oneself both from the Child's feelings of helplessness and dependency ("I'm not OK") and the Parent's edicts which cover everything from sex to work.

Perhaps the best indicator of the Adult state is the ability to cope responsibly with stress. As we shall see later, most people's Adults are contaminated with Child and/or Parent ego states so that often what seems to be an Adult communication (reasonable, responsible, etc.) may, in fact, also contain Child or Parent messages.

The *Child* ego state contains all the impulses that come "naturally" to a young child. It also contains the memories of childhood experiences and how one responded to them. The Child has experienced situations where the individual was helpless and dependent, which may have led the Child to conclude that he or she is "not OK." The Child has also experienced being held, loved, consoled, and being taken care of. Thus, positive feelings of dependency also reside in the Child. The Child also contains the playfulness and curiosity that are so obviously a part of the young child's life. Characteristics of the Child which are easily recognized are rebelliousness, submissiveness, whining, wanting its way, impulsiveness, curiosity, playfulness, etc.

The Adult is the only ego state which is interested in and receptive to information. The Child is primarily interested in fulfilling its wants. It sends messages in an attempt to convey its needs. The Parent assumes the role of the sender in presenting its controlling messages. It is the Adult which receives, processes, and feeds back information in an attempt to understand the other person.

Games in Superior-Subordinate Relations

We shall describe in detail a "typical" transaction that takes place when the subordinate resists (or rejects) influence attempts by the superior. This description illustrates a difficulty that a manager is likely to encounter. We shall analyze this transaction and then suggest a way of overcoming the subordinate's resistance which can lay the groundwork for establishing interpersonal trust.

Consider the situation of Cecil, a very capable machine operator. Some days Cecil's output is very high; some days his output is very low. Bill, the new supervisor, has spoken to him on several occasions about this. The very next day after one of these talks, he sees Cecil standing around with the machine idle for no apparent reason. Cecil sees Bill looking at him but pays no attention. Bill goes up to him and asks him what is wrong, and Cecil replies, "Nothing." What can Bill do? Obviously, talking to him has done little good. Firing him or otherwise disciplining him is difficult because there are other operators who, on the average, are less productive than Cecil.

Figure 8-5 suggests what is happening in T.A. terms. Although on the surface the conversation is Adult to Adult, the hidden messages are Parent to Child: "Get

140 INTRA- AND INTERPERSONAL COMMUNICATION

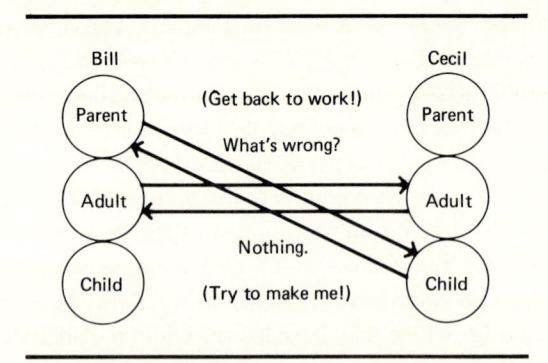

FIGURE 8-5 Bill and Cecil's interaction in T.A. terms.

back to work!" and Child to Parent: "Try to make me!" Bill sees that telling Cecil to work more consistently does not have any effect and he is stymied because Cecil has called his bluff. If Bill continues to pressure Cecil, he will likely get continued resistance (from the Child). Bill seems to be in the position of either being a persecutor (being tough on Cecil while other workers are really no better) or being a patsy (accepting the situation as it is). Essentially, this is the control issue, and as long as Bill responds on this dimension, he is not likely to have much luck.

The consequences of such a relationship are highlighted in the study of supervisors in a manufacturing plant (Cummins, 1972). The study concludes that leaders who have high needs for structure are relatively unsuccessful in groups which are uncooperative. This is interpreted in terms of Parent-Child transactions where the supervisors operate primarily in the Parent mode—"Do as I tell you"—and the workers operate primarily in the mode of the rebellious child—"Try and make me!" As the workers resist the Parental authority, the supervisor becomes frustrated and increases efforts to get compliance. The workers in turn increase their resistance (low-quality work, sabotage, etc.), and since the supervisor often does not have the power to break the workers' resistance because of union protection and peer-group protection, the relationship may deteriorate to the point that the supervisor gives up.

The Parent-Child transactions of superior-subordinate relations are not always initiated by the superior. The subordinate may prefer to play the Child since this role entails few risks. He or she, by playing the Child, puts pressure on the superior to play the Parent. This type of relationship allows the subordinate to blame the superior for whatever dissatisfactions arise in the job situation. A person playing the Child is likely to have both positive and negative feelings toward his or her protector. Thus, even though the subordinate may prefer to be told what to do, he or she is still likely to feel hostile toward the superior.

We shall describe two defensive reactions (games) which are often used by managers, in order to illustrate how the lack of self-confidence (defensiveness) of the manager severely restricts the process of gaining the commitment necessary to organizational success. These two games are typical of the two basic interpersonal orientations indicative of low self-confidence mentioned above.

The position "I'm OK, you're not OK" is perhaps best illustrated by the game Berne (1964) calls "Now I've Got You, You S.O.B." In this case, the manager whose influence attempts have been unsuccessful "lies in wait" for the offender. When that individual does something which is in violation of company policy, procedures, etc., the manager can then unleash the full fury of his or her Parent and feel "justified." The manager has "successfully" defended himself or herself but in the process has eliminated any chance of establishing interpersonal trust.

The position of "I'm not OK, you're OK" is perhaps best illustrated by the game Berne calls "Why Does This Always Happen to Me?" Here, the insecure manager tries to be nice to the subordinate by "overlooking" certain inadequacies. The subordinate interprets this behavior as indicative of the manager's lack of "backbone." When the subordinate later challenges the manager, the manager backs down wondering, "Why does this always happen to me?" This type of game is equally unlikely to establish interpersonal trust.

The payoff to the manager who is playing "Why Does This Always Happen to Me?" is not obvious. Essentially, this game allows the manager to avoid his or her feelings of inadequacy which are aroused by interpersonal conflict. By not owning responsibility for what happens ("it always happens *to* me"), the manager can see himself or herself as unlucky rather than inadequate. More subtly, the "put down" which he or she has invited confirms the inner feeling that he or she is "not OK" and this confirmation has payoff.

Breaking the Game

The best strategy that the manager can adopt when interacting with others who are playing games is to refuse to play the game. The manager needs to do this in a way which reduces the defensiveness of the other person if he or she wants to establish interpersonal trust. This essentially means avoiding the use of Parent communications. The object of the manager is to convert the transaction to Adult-Adult rather than playing Parent to the subordinate's Child. This can be done by simply picking up on the Adult messages that the Child is pretending to give. Alternatively, the manager can escape the game by first changing the transaction to Child-Child and then later moving it to Adult-Adult. In order to illustrate this latter strategy, we will show how it might be used in the game situation discussed above.

The following hypothetical conversation shows how Bill—by skillfully blending Adult-Adult and Child-Child transactions—redefines the relationship in such a way that Cecil is unable to play the game.

Suppose the following conversation takes place:

Cecil: (Resting, baiting Bill)

Bill: "Hey man, you tired already? It's only 9 o'clock."

Cecil: "Yeah, I'm tired."

Bill: "Maybe we can get you some Geritol."

Cecil: "Well, I was up late last night."

Bill: "Ah, does your wife know about that?"

Cecil: "Well, she was with me."

Bill: "Did you have a good time?"

Cecil: "Yeah."

Bill: "Great! See if you can get it going. I'll see you later. I've got to see the ol' man."
. . . (As a parting shot) "Maybe I can sneak you some raisins for that tired blood."

In this short conversation, Bill has done a lot to break up Cecil's game. Instead of moving on the control issue, Bill immediately redefined the issue: Cecil is tired. What can Cecil say? If he says, "No, I'm just standing here and you can't make me work," then he has put himself in a position where Bill is justified in taking disciplinary action. Besides, this would eliminate the fun of the game.

Bill quickly follows this advantage by suggesting that Cecil's tiredness is a weakness. (The image of Geritol is associated with older women who have lost their vitality.) This is done within the context of the game by keeping the conversation "light." Cecil is on the defensive and says he was out late. Bill, still joking with Cecil's Child, suggests that he was being a "naughty" boy—out carousing with another woman.

Cecil comes on straight again when he acknowledges that his wife was with him. Bill, seeing that Cecil is answering in the Adult mode, returns the favor: "Did you have a good time? Great!" He has now converted an apparent Parent-Child conflict into an Adult-Adult transaction.

Bill's comment, "See if you can get it going. I'll see you later," is now in the context of Adult-Adult. Even after this brief conversation, it will be hard for Cecil to hold the attitude "Try to make me work."

Bill again initiates the Child-Child transaction: "I've got to see the ol' man. Maybe I can sneak you some raisins for that tired blood." "Ol' man" and "sneak" are both phrases likely to trigger the Child. By speaking directly to Cecil's Child from his own Child, Bill short-circuits the Child-Parent response. Finally, Bill reemphasizes the definition of the situation—Cecil is tired. By avoiding any Parental messages, Bill has deemphasized the control issue without being either the patsy or the persecutor.

When Bill returns later, he can reemphasize the definition of the relationship. If he finds Cecil working, he can communicate in the Adult mode: "Glad to see you got it going. Here are some raisins for that tired blood." (Throws the box to Cecil playfully.) The playful touch underscores the Child-Child transaction earlier. If he finds that Cecil is still not working, he can still stay in the Adult: "Look, Cecil, if you are that tired, maybe you should go home and sleep it off" (with concern). The concern is basically Adult-Adult, with some underlying Adult-Child qualities. Now, Cecil is in a bind. If he goes home, he is essentially responding to the Adult concern shown by Bill; if he begins work, he is also responding to the Adult message of working consistently at his job.

Suppose that Cecil elects to go home. Bill can still toss him the box of raisins as a parting present. In this circumstance, it is very difficult for Cecil to continue playing the upset Child. Bill has refused to play Cecil's game, so there is no game.

What happens if Bill immediately reacts to Cecil's Child by coming on Parent: "Get back to work or we'll find someone else to do your job"? Cecil might respond by being the compliant Child and returning to work. It is not likely, however, that Cecil will feel very good about it. The control issue will become dominant in the relationship and Bill will probably have to assert his authority. At best, Cecil will operate as the compliant Child, simply doing what he is told but in no particular hurry. At worst, the Parental message will "hook" Cecil's rebellious Child and he will seek ways to undermine Bill's authority: sabotaging the machines, promoting dissatisfaction among other workers, etc.

In the above example, Bill's Child-Child communication was an attempt to "hook" Cecil's playful Child. If this is successful, playful Child responses are much easier to tolerate and are probably a lot less counterproductive than the rebellious Child. A study by the author suggests that in situations where the work is of a repetitive nature, "horseplay" (the playful Child) breaks the monotony and is often associated with high productivity (Cummins and King, 1973).

The ability of the manager to refuse to play the game is directly related to the manager's self-awareness and self-confidence. If the manager opts to use his or her position power to attempt to coerce or manipulate the other person, this is equivalent to the interpersonal orientation "I'm OK, you're not OK" (Harris, 1967). This orientation suggests a basic insecurity which is defended by aggressive behavior. With this orientation, the manager can bolster his or her own ego only by "putting the other person down."

On the other hand, if the manager allows the other person to reject his or her attempts to gain commitment, this may be equivalent to the interpersonal orientation "I'm not OK, you're OK." This orientation suggests a basic insecurity which is defended by withdrawing from conflict and abdicating responsibility, i.e., playing patsy.

The manager is able to respond to the subordinate's game in a nondefensive manner only when he or she values the self-worth of both himself or herself and the subordinate. That is, the manager can avoid the game only when his or her interpersonal orientation is "I'm OK, you're OK." If the manager refuses to play the subordinate's game so that the manager can play his or her own game, then the manager is simply outmanipulating the subordinate. Manipulation also comes from the interpersonal orientation "I'm OK, you're not OK" and is potentially destructive of interpersonal trust.

SUMMARY

Interpersonal relations occur within the context of the business organization. Since the primary motive for joining the organization is often financial, incompatibility between individuals is likely. If individual motives are financial, commitment to organizational objectives is likely to be indirect. The structure of the traditional organization has been devised to gain commitment through a power hierarchy. Unfortunately, such a structure also often leads to breakdowns in communication.

Interpersonal relations can be viewed as exchanges of such commodities as information, expertise, status, money, love, etc. When the exchange between two individuals is "balanced," the relationship is stable. When the exchange is not balanced, one person or the other will act to establish this balance in the exchange. This may be either in a positive or in a negative way.

The Johari window was discussed as a theoretical concept which assists in viewing information flows between two individuals. By using this concept it can be seen that each individual must strive for large active arenas via the use of exposure and feedback. If this goal can be accomplished, communication will be effective.

Transactional Analysis suggests how people interact in exchanges. They may use the Parent ego state in communication, unconsciously indicating a parental attitude toward the person with whom they are interacting. They may adopt a Child ego state in interacting, indicating a childlike attitude (rebellious, conforming, dependent, or insecure). Finally, they may communicate in the Adult ego state, suggesting a problem-solving approach to reality and the persons with whom they are interacting. Transactional Analysis can be appropriately applied to the organizational situation since many managers tend to take a "parental" approach in their relationship with subordinates.

Managerial games are played as a means of defending one's position, or resisting influence attempts of a superior while pretending to be in an objective Adult ego state. The manager can refuse to play the game and move to an Adult-Adult relationship. To break the game requires self-confidence and interpersonal competence.

IMPORTANT TERMS AND CONCEPTS

Johari window, exchange theory, Transactional Analysis, Parent, Adult, Child, games

REVIEW QUESTIONS

1. How do the characteristics of the business organization make it likely that interpersonal conflict will occur?
2. In what manner does the traditional business organization handle the problem of gaining commitment to company objectives?
3. What difficulties in interpersonal relations are precipitated by the above method (question 2) of gaining commitment?
4. What is exchanged in relationships?
5. What happens if the exchange is perceived to be unbalanced?
6. Describe the three ego states (modes of interacting) used in Transactional Analysis.
7. How is a supervisor likely to relate to a subordinate? What are the consequences of this way of relating?
8. How is Cecil's unspoken challenge to Bill a game?
9. Describe a basic approach to breaking games. How does this differ from manipulation?
10. What strategy can you think of to break the power game of a superior?
11. How is interpersonal orientation related to playing games?
12. How is "Now I've Got You" a game?
13. Give an example of a contradictory message.

EXERCISE 1

Draw a Johari window that you believe represents you in relationship to other members of your class. Now draw a Johari window that represents you in relationship to a person who is close to you: a boyfriend, girlfriend, buddy, spouse, or parent.

From these windows answer the following questions:

1. Are you an open person?
2. Are you a listening person?
3. Can others feel confident that they *really* know you?
4. Do you place great emphasis upon knowing the feelings and thoughts of others?

EXERCISE 2: BREAKING GAMES

1. Divide class into pairs.
2. The pairs are to develop a skit in which a T.A. game is played. In the skit one person will play the Child while the other person plays the Parent (either the harsh, judgmental persecutor or the kind, supportive rescuer). After the game is in full motion, the pair shifts and attempts to "break the game." (Avoid the temptation to shift from persecutor to rescuer.) These are the games that may be played:
   "Now I've Got You, You S.O.B."
   "Why Does This Always Happen to Me?"
3. The pairs play their skits before the class. The class attempts to guess what the game is and then discusses it. Special attention should be given to how the game was broken.

BIBLIOGRAPHY

Berne, E.: *Games People Play* (New York: Grove Press, Inc., 1964).

Cummins, R.: "Leader-Member Relations as a Moderator of the Effects of Leader Behavior and Attitudes," *Personnel Psychology,* vol. 25, pp. 655–660, 1972.

Cummins, R., and D. King: "The Interaction of Group Size and Task Structure in an Industrial Organization," *Personnel Psychology,* vol. 26, pp. 87–94, 1973.

Harris, T.: *I'm OK, You're OK: A Practical Guide to Transactional Analysis* (New York: Harper & Row, Publishers, Incorporated, 1967).

Luft, J.: "The Johari Window," *Human Relations Training News,* vol. 5, pp. 6–7, 1961.

Whyte, W. F.: *Organizational Behavior* (Homewood, Ill.: The Dorsey Press and Richard D. Irwin, Inc., 1969).

9

STYLES OF HUMAN COMMUNICATION

The purpose of this discussion of communication styles is to lay a foundation for categorizing and evaluating events of communication behavior and to understand the effects of particular styles upon organizational climate and performance. We shall describe and illustrate six broad styles of communication behavior. The effectiveness of each style will be analyzed within the context of influencing environmental situations of the organization.

You are the manager of a civic theater. A stagehand comes rushing up to you shouting, "A fire has started backstage; we can't get it under control!"

Choose your response.

____ "You call the fire department while I clear the audience from the building."

____ "Calm down, Joe, let's see if we can come up with some ideas on what would be the best thing to do."

____ "The rules on what to do in case of fire are posted on the bulletin board. Let's go back and see what the rules are."

____ "Don't waste time; you call the fire department, and I'll run out on the stage and tell the audience to leave!"

____ "You know what the situation is; what should we do?"

____ "Don't tell me about it; you handle it."

The particular style of communication used by a person in any situation will reflect both the external- and the internal-system factors. External factors specific to the particular organizational situation in which the communication occurs clearly affect the resulting communication style. The burning-theater situation makes this point rather strikingly. The internal factors emerging out of the personal makeup of the individual communicator are of equal importance.

A communication style might best be defined as a specialized set of interpersonal behaviors which are used in a given situation. The communication process describes in elemental terms "what" takes place when people communicate. Communication style characterizes the set of behaviors involved in the elemental process.

A communication style differs from a specific communication action in two distinct ways: (1) each communication style represents a category of communication behaviors which have related purposes and similar approaches and (2) a particular style will be used with consistency by a person for similar situations. As a general rule we are able to distinguish one style from another. If you will look back at the opening example, you can see that the six styles are different. Which style is appropriate depends on both external- and internal-system variables. The fire faced by the manager probably demands the distinct, efficient commands expressed in the first alternative. Many other kinds of crises might demand the same style (controlling style). However, to determine which style is most appropriate for a situation, one must also take into account the internal-system effects. For example, the manager of an accounting department will assign the task of preparing a report to his or her staff using the same communication style that he or she has used previously for this and other similar assignments. The manager may find this necessary because of the particular personal relationship and sentiments which have developed. We shall examine the nature of the six basic communication styles and then look at their effects for people in an organization.

DESCRIPTION OF THE COMMUNICATION STYLES

Since communication is at the heart of each person's organizational functioning, we need to be able to identify and to analyze the styles of communication which we use. To improve our communication behaviors, we must be able to understand them and to compare their effects for the situations in which we operate.

Six basic communication styles appear in the organizational situation—the controlling style, the equalitarian style, the structuring style, the dynamic style, the relinquish style, and the withdrawal style. Each of these styles is represented (in the order listed) by the response choices available to the theater manager of our chapter-opening incident. Let us consider the nature of each communication style.

The Controlling Style

The controlling style is one in which the communicator constrains and directs the actions or thoughts of others. The controlling style is essentially one way, with any feedback being basically for the purpose of clarification. Communicators using this style tend to formulate their ideas prior to discussion and then gain the compliance of others. They do not like to consider alternatives which others may propose. They persuade others by showing the incentives (both positive and negative) which may accrue from a given course of action. They often engage in the process of selling themselves and their status to others. In addition to the persuasive and selling aspects of the controlling approach, the element of constraining others is also present. Communicators indicate that they will use their authority or power to assure compliance to their wishes. The approach of selling is replaced by one of telling. By virtue of their power, the communicators tell others what the others will or will not do. If direct threats or promises do not apply or are not effective, such a communicator may manipulate the receiver into the desired action. Since the disappointment that follows for the receiver usually damages future communication, manipulation is usually reserved for short-term relationships. The ramifications of using manipulation as an approach to influencing others have been explored in more detail earlier in the book.

Roethlisberger (1953) presents a case in which a supervisor uses the controlling style in a manner that leads to conflict. Let us reconstruct the conversation underlying the case in the following interchange between Hart and Bing.

Hart: "Bing, I want you to know that your taking double and triple setup time in inspection panels is cheating. I'll not tolerate the practice any longer."

Bing: "We've always done it this way. You did it this way yourself before you were promoted."

Hart: "Look, I'm not arguing with you; I'm telling you. I'm going to take official action with my boss to have you fired if this continues. And another thing, you've been going to lunch early for a week; this is upsetting the department."

Bing: "I have not been taking off for lunch early for a week."

Hart: "You won't listen, will you. Let's get some things straight. Starting now, you go to lunch at 12:00 sharp. And stop that noisy singing during work hours."

Bing: "I want a transfer."

Hart: "We'll see about that. But first, I want to get some cooperation."

Not all controlling communication is as harsh and threatening as that of Hart. It can as easily be benevolent and gentle. Unfortunately, controlling communication is often given and received with expressions of negative emotions. Bing, like most other people, does not respond well to the hostile approach to control. It simply evokes a defensive reaction from him. As we pointed out earlier, problems of resistance and malicious obedience are often the response of the person being controlled. When we use the controlling style, we are taking the Parent role of Transactional Analysis and inviting a Child response on the part of the person with whom we are communicating. It should be clear that the directive aspect of the management process often calls for the use of the controlling style. It is important that we understand its nature so that the potential for negative consequences is reduced.

The Equalitarian Style

The equalitarian style is characterized by a two-way flow of exchange in which the influence flows back and forth between people. The communicator stimulates others to personal initiative in planning, setting goals, taking action, or thinking. The discussion is open, with each person freely expressing ideas in an atmosphere of acceptance and mutual understanding. With the equalitarian style, the communicator does not assume personal superiority or expertise, but receives information as well as giving it. The communicator shows genuine interest in the ideas of others. Decisions are often based upon a consensus rather than being unilateral in nature. The atmosphere established by the equalitarian style is relaxed and often informal. The communicator may spend time chatting casually about personal or trivial things. His or her relationships are often on a close and friendly basis.

In a description of Philip Morris, Inc., and its board chairman, Joseph F. Cullman, III, *Business Week* quotes one of the members of the corporate products committee as saying, "While Joe is far more equal than anyone else on the committee, these meetings are fairly democratic and often fairly heated. In the end, of course, Joe has the final word." From this description, it is apparent that Cullman uses a combination of controlling and equalitarian styles in the stimulation of a "fairly democratic" interchange.

The Structuring Style

The structuring style is used by the communicator who is oriented toward establishing order, organization, scheduling, and structure through the communication process. This communicator influences others by discussing with them the goals, standards, schedules, rules, or procedures that seem to apply to the situation. The communication is directed toward either establishing and clarifying these systems of structure or applying them to activities. Structuring communications rarely involve the expression of strong emotion. The communications usually are objective in nature.

One may feel at the outset that this would be a rather narrow range of communication and rarely a basis for discussion, but in fact, if we consider the many social mores, religious customs and principles, local regulations, business procedures, governmental requirements, and so on, we discover that we use the structuring style rather frequently. Clearly, the organizing, directing, and controlling elements of the management process must involve the structuring communication style. We have already seen that a reasonable balance of structure and freedom within that structure are important ingredients in building self-esteem.

In a written communication of a university president to the faculty, we find an example of the structuring style of communication which reads:

> Nonrenewal of a faculty appointment as provided for in the University Regents' Rules and the guidelines of AAUP is primarily the responsibility of the department involved with review by the Dean, Vice President for Academic Affairs, the President.... This procedure for review of nonrenewal of probationary faculty appointments will remain in effect until superseded by provisions in the Institutional Handbook of Operating Procedures or until modified or rescinded by the President.

The president is communicating structure in the form of policies, procedures, and lines of authority. A hint of controlling is also implied in this statement in that the president is indicating that the rules as communicated will be applied as constraints to future decisions dealing with nonrenewal of faculty appointments.

The Dynamic Style

The dynamic style is employed by a communicator who is highly active and aggressive. The communication tends to be brief and to the point. It is frank and open, with an absence of evasion. The communications of the dynamic style are not deep and philosophical but are oriented to the pragmatic, immediate problems confronted. They rarely deal with plans or strategies of the distant future. This approach to communication is more at home in the fast-moving business than in the halls of the ivy-covered university.

The dynamic entrepreneur Ross Perot says to his employees, "We have the guts to give you responsibility to make mistakes, if you have guts enough to make mistakes. Don't make the same mistake twice and make all mistakes at full speed." This is a frank and direct statement of management's position, which has the action-oriented tones typical of the dynamic style.

Robert Townsend (1970), in *Up the Organization*, provides a clear example of the dynamic style in his statement of what one might say to a supplier executive in telling him that you are delegating authority to "John" for handling a contract: "With John on an extension, you phone the top man involved at each supplier, and after the amenities, you say, 'This is John. I've asked him to negotiate this contract. Whatever he recommends, we'll do. I want a signed contract within thirty days.'" This is a succinct and straightforward statement of an active and pragmatic person. Unlike a strictly structuring style of communication, this statement avoids the description of specific policies, procedures, or regulations for the contract. The one statement restricting the negotiations to thirty days is controlling, but the tone and content of the communication is thoroughly the dynamic style. The delegation of authority which Townsend is advocating provides a clear indication of confidence in John and is an effective mechanism for building John's self-esteem. Such a style is perhaps most likely to come into use as the organizing and directing elements of the management process are performed.

The Relinquish Style

The relinquish style involves a subordination of one's position to that of another person. The communicator defers to the desires of the other person. A communicator takes a receptive rather than a directive position and shows interest in the contributions of others. The communicator shows preference for a supporting role rather than for a directing one.

Townsend also provides an illustration of the relinquish style when he says to his general counsel: "I don't want to read any legal document covering transactions I've approved. If I have to sign them, then you initial them for legal aspects, and get the affected division or department head to initial for operating aspects. But remember, if you send it in with two sets of initials, I'll sign it without reading it." Townsend advocates the total relinquishing of authority as a method of getting others to assume responsibility. In this example, we see the interchange of two styles of communication. Townsend relinquishes by "structuring" his relationship to the general counsel. Many managers will find this style an appropriate one for delegating to subordinates.

The Withdrawal Style

The withdrawal style involves an avoidance of interaction. It is almost a misrepresentation to refer to the person using this pattern as a communicator. In fact, the users do not wish to communicate but prefer to withdraw from others. They do not wish to influence others and prefer not to be influenced. In a discussion, withdrawal may take the form of diversionary tactics to get away from the topic. The diversionary approaches may include joking about the problem. The person assumes an independent stance either to perform a task alone or to allow others to do so.

Withdrawal statements are typified by the following: "I don't want to get involved in that issue." "Sorry, but I have no opinion on that." "Don't bother me with your problems." "Obviously there is no point talking with you about this, you just don't understand." "What do you mean, we should let them have the sales, that's the kind of stupid idea typical of you." These statements do not simply relinquish by giving others responsibility, but they indicate a desire to avoid the entire process of communication.

Each of the roles conceptualized in Transactional Analysis (Parent, Adult, and Child) involves the use of two styles of communication. The Parent uses the controlling and the structuring styles in directing and establishing rules and restrictions for others; the Adult objectively handles problems by the use of the equalitarian or the dynamic styles; while the Child responds to interpersonal situations by employing the relinquish or the withdrawal style. Persons who are strongly oriented toward a particular role tend to rely heavily upon the use of the communication styles which relate to that role, i.e., the person playing the Parent role has a high frequency of controlling and structuring. A typical conversation will include more than one style. A lengthy conversation may involve all six styles.

Figure 9-1 depicts the direction and flow of communication. The equalitarian and dynamic styles involve two-way communication, while the other styles are basically one directional. In the case of the controlling and structuring styles, the sender takes the initiative and assumes a more active role; whereas, in the withdrawal and relinquish styles, the sender tends to be passive in the interchange.

In terms of the concept of communication richness which we discussed in Chapter 3, it is clear that the equalitarian style will typically be the richest. The equalitarian style provides the fullest degree of feedback and has the most flexible duration. Withdrawal has the least richness in that it allows little feedback and tends to be short in duration. The sequencing is also difficult to arrange with a person who uses the withdrawal style.

The six styles have direct influence upon the development of the Johari window of interpersonal perception. The withdrawal and relinquishing styles tend to

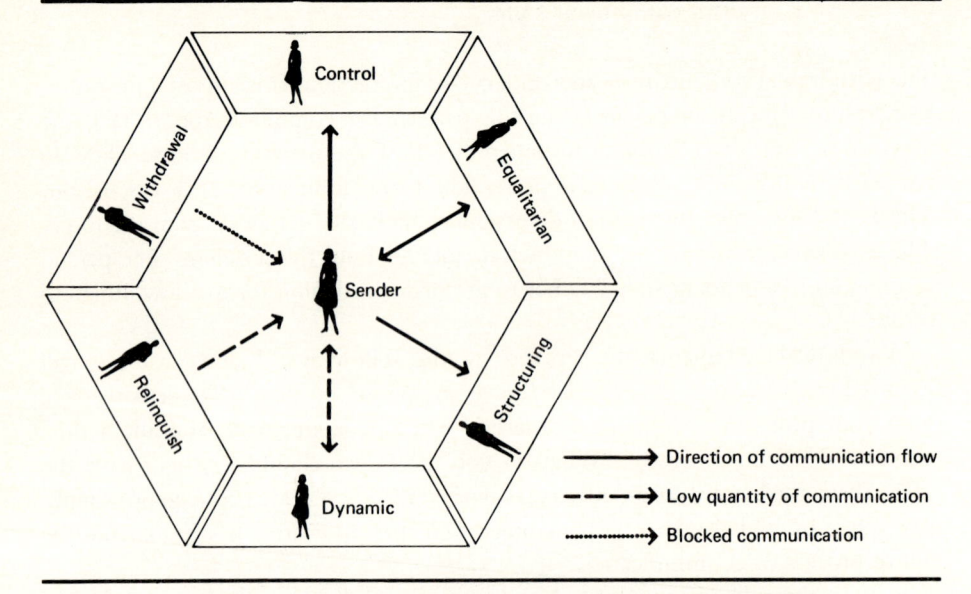

FIGURE 9-1 Direction and flow of the six styles of communication.

increase the blindspot and unknown-self areas by limiting both feedback and self-disclosure. The arena is reduced. Relinquishing in allowing feedback but limiting exposure builds the facade area. Controlling operates in the opposite fashion and gives maximum exposure with little feedback. It builds the blindspot area. Structuring and dynamic styles add little to self-knowledge or the awareness of others. Structuring is a more objective and less personally revealing communication that is basically one way, while dynamic is rapid, brief, and problem-oriented. Use of these styles builds blindspot and unknown areas. The style which contributes most to the arena is equalitarian. This style provides exposure of oneself to others and feedback from others.

Summary of Typical Behaviors of the Styles

The patterns of communication may be characterized by the following typical behaviors:

The Controlling Style

- The communication is usually one way.
- The communicators are directive, demanding, and controlling.

- The communicators insist that their ideas be tried first.
- The communicators persuade others to follow their course of action.
- The communicators use power and authority in gaining compliance.
- The communicators may use manipulation.

The Equalitarian Style

- The communication is two way.
- The communicators stimulate and draw out the thoughts and intents of others.
- The communication is free and fluid.
- The atmosphere is one of mutual understanding and personal interest.
- The communication is friendly and warm.

The Structuring Style

- The communication is oriented toward systematizing the environment.
- The communicators influence others by citing the standards, procedures, or rules which apply to a situation.
- Communication is directed toward clarification of the structure or establishing structure for a problem.

The Dynamic Style

- The communicators are brief and to the point.
- The communicators are frank and direct.
- The communication content is pragmatic and action-oriented.

The Relinquish Style

- The communicators submit to the desires of others.
- The communicators comply with the other person's point of view.
- The communicators are receptive to other people's ideas and contributions.

- The communicators shift responsibility to the other person.
- The communicators assume a supporting role.

The Withdrawal Style

- Communication process is avoided.
- No influence is sought or desired.
- An independent rather than an interactive approach to decision making is used.
- The communicators avoid the subject under discussion by talking about something else or by shifting to a verbal attack of the other person rather than responding. (Shaw, 1968)

The six styles of communication relate in varying degrees to the external or the internal systems of organizational communication. The structuring style is used almost exclusively in establishing and implementing the formal, external system. Controlling is used as an interaction in both systems but perhaps more frequently in the external system than in the internal system. The relative balance of each style in external systems as compared to internal systems is shown in Figure 9-2. Both systems employ each style; however, the structuring and controlling styles are more often used in external systems and the withdrawal and equalitarian are more often used in internal systems. The extent of the use of the equalitarian style in the external system has increased in recent years with the growth of MBO (management by objective) and participative decision making in organizations.

THE EFFECTS OF COMMUNICATION STYLES

The effectiveness of communication patterns may be evaluated in terms of their influence upon task performance and individual morale. The assumption growing

Styles	Structuring	Controlling	Dynamic	Relinquish	Withdrawal	Equalitarian
Systems	External system					Internal system

FIGURE 9-2 Relationship of organizational communication system to styles.

out of the human-relations movement was that the equalitarian style would be effective both in attaining task performance and in lifting morale, while the controlling style would have a negative impact on both factors. Recent research has shown this conclusion to be erroneous. Each situation in which a person lives, works, or plays facilitates the effectiveness of certain communication styles and retards others. Our problem becomes one of identifying the situations in which a given style is most effective. For the manager, this problem is particularly significant because use of effective communication styles is essential to effective performance as a manager.

The Effects of the Controlling Style

The controlling style serves effectively in several situations. One such situation is that in which the communicator has superior knowledge and expertise in the field of discussion. Morale and performance motivation are threatened by the communicator who presumes to take control and to issue directives in an area in which he or she has a lack of competency. Others are often willing to submit to the person whom they perceive to have more facts, experience, knowledge, or competency; they are rarely willing to do so for the person who is of equal or lower capability. When persons are promoted to supervision of a wider scope of activities for which they lack experience and knowledge, they will usually falter. For the same reasons the supervisor may effectively use the controlling style with a new and inexperienced subordinate. Since the situation is unfamiliar for the new person, direction and instruction are readily accepted. Lacking information, the person prefers to relinquish to the leader. The orientation and training period for a new person calls for the controlling style. The wise leaders are able to perceive the changing competency of their employees and to adjust their communication styles to adapt to the current level of knowledge of the employees.

The controlling style may also be effective for leaders of persons who are either dependent or lacking in motivation. These persons prefer to take a receptive role in communication. They need the dominant and informed leader to provide the security and stimulation that they do not find within themselves (Vroom and Mann, 1960).

The controlling style is often intended to persuade or stimulate employees to perform effectively, and in such situations criticism is frequently used as an ingredient of the attempts to improve performance. General Electric has conducted research to analyze the effects of the use of criticism by managers in their attempt to influence the subsequent performance of employees. The number of criticisms used by the managers in their discussions with the employees was recorded. During the next twelve weeks the percentage of the employees' goals that were achieved was assessed. The GE researchers concluded that criticism has a deleterious effect upon the employee's performance. This effect was most pronounced among employees who held a low self-esteem. For these employees the threat of the criticisms seemed to hinder future performance. These results suggest that a positive approach in discussing performance is more effective than a critical one. Criticism should be expressed tactfully and in specific terms. The communicator should avoid unnecessary threats to the self-esteem of the other person by taking a nonevaluative problem-oriented approach (Kay et al., 1962).

The controlling style seems to be quite appropriate in a crisis situation such as that of the burning theater, the combat squad under fire, or the street riot. Crises of this type usually do not allow an opportunity for an equalitarian discussion or a structuring of the procedures. Crises require a firm decisive action preferably by a confident individual (Hamblin, 1958). Similarly, a situation which allows only brief interaction between people often requires a controlling style. Since the control is very temporary, the resentment that prolonged dominance usually provokes is not elicited (Vroom and Mann, 1960). Groups of larger than about twenty persons require a predominance of the controlling communications. When large groups meet, the purpose is usually one of presenting information or persuading rather than the mutual sharing of thoughts (Hemphill, 1950).

The controlling style often elicits dysfunctional consequences. A supervisor may be complacently content with employees who follow directives to the letter and who complete the necessary written reports to show their compliance, while others with the organization know that it is all a "paper whitewash." Instead of carrying out the intent and objective of the supervisor, the employees expend their energies in preparing the forms, writing the justifications, or juggling the data to give the false appearance of success. The control has detracted from rather than facilitated goal attainment.

A similar effect may occur from the use of goal setting as a controlling device. General Motors is among the companies which have found that when goals for the quantity of productivity are emphasized, quality is reduced; when goals for quality and quantity are both emphasized, maintenance is neglected. Well-intentioned goals may draw attention away from areas not included in the goals; this results in an imbalance.

The controlling style may also bring about resistance on the part of its recipients. Supervisory directives are often met with passive resistance or open rebellion. The resistance by the employee yields lower performance, which evokes stronger measures of control and pressure from the supervisor. These in turn bring about a greater resistance and still lower performance. The downward spiral becomes a whirlpool that is difficult to reverse and may destroy the communication relationship (see Figure 9-3).

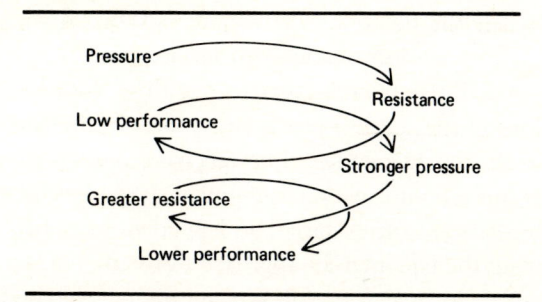

FIGURE 9-3 Spiraling effects of controlling pressures.

The Effects of the Equalitarian Style

In his book *The Human Organization*, Rensis Likert (1967) reports on the results of a survey of the opinions of top managers of several of the major companies of the United States. He notes that these managers preferred the use of participative management. However, they evaluated their own behavior and that of their subordinates as more toward the controlling end of the continuum than the fully participative approach which they viewed as ideal. Since the equalitarian style is basic to participative management, to close the gap between the desired and the actual managerial approach will involve an increase in equalitarian behaviors and a decrease in controlling ones. Managers must be able to identify their current communication style and understand the characteristics of the style which is more effective for their situation.

The situations in which the equalitarian style serves most effectively are almost the direct opposite of those for the controlling style. The equalitarian style is an effective approach for the leaders who wish to build teamwork and to strengthen the closeness and understanding between themselves and those with whom they work. The equalitarian style often serves to facilitate communication. It is used to "draw out" the other person in order to improve understanding. This approach is effective for a wide range of situations (Wofford, 1971).

In contrast to the controlling style, the equalitarian style is not effective for the leader when communicating with people who lack experience, knowledge, or competence. The equalitarian style is not effective in communicating with people who are highly dependent in personality. The style is also ineffective for crisis or emergency situations, or for communication to a large group. Instead, the equalitarian style is effective when used with small groups, particularly when time for thorough discussion and decision making is possible (Parker, 1963). This approach helps to stimulate motivation and to build commitment on the part of those involved in the decisions. People who participate in a decision are more ego-involved in its outcome. Improved decisions can also be developed by the equalitarian approach when the decisions are complex. When others are involved in decision making, additional information can be brought to bear which no single person would possess, thus giving a greater breadth of available information.

The qualifications of the receivers have an important influence upon the use of the equalitarian style by the sender. The receivers need to have a worthwhile contribution in terms of information, judgment, experience, and independent thought. If the receivers are authoritarian or dependent, it is difficult to communicate with them using the equalitarian approach (Vroom and Mann, 1960).

The equalitarian style is also useful as a means of overcoming resistance to change. Coch and French (1948) reported results of a classic study which yielded the conclusion that the participation involved in equalitarian communication leads to a high acceptance of change. They found that the controlling approach to communication, whether used by industrial engineers or supervisors, brings resistance to change. Employees who were told that their jobs would change to a more efficient procedure became distrustful and hostile toward management and restricted output after the change. Those who were permitted to discuss freely the changes needed and to help determine the nature of the changes showed a marked improvement in output following the change. Participation led to a better attitude toward the work as well as a more cooperative atmosphere.

The Effects of the Structuring Style

The structuring style is particularly important in a complex environment. If the tasks are highly flexible, then the complexity may create severe difficulties in grasping and handling the problems involved. The structuring style aids in bringing system and order into this complex situation. Even after the procedures policies, plans, goals, etc. have been established which build the needed structure, the structuring style is still required as a means of clarifying, interpreting, and transmitting the structure to others. The Ohio State Leadership Studies identified the dimension of "initiating structure" as one of the two basic factors of leadership behavior. Leaders were found to use structuring communications to perform such activities as establishing goals, making work assignments, encouraging overtime, emphasizing meeting deadlines, and spelling out what should be accomplished.

Often a great deal of time and energy is spent in the process of developing structure which will never be used. Many hours are spent in developing job descriptions, writing operations manuals, or preparing policy statements, which are never referred to after they are approved. Frequently, such paper manipulations simply do not face the realities of the situation and are used to soothe feelings or to make a show of effort while a crisis point passes.

When tasks are relatively simple and the environment stable, little of the communication should involve the structuring approach. The person who is so strongly oriented toward orderliness that he or she focuses attention on structure when little is required will waste time and energy needlessly and will tend to limit his or her own creativity as well as that of others.

Another common misuse of the structuring style is that of hiding behind rules and regulations rather than facing issues squarely. Persons who are unsure of the reaction of others to their opinions may find a rule or policy which they can interpret to their advantage. This shifts the attention away from the actual problem and its solution toward a question of legality and correct methodology. It may serve the persons involved by forcing their position upon others without directly exposing their desires, but it usually produces frustration and discontent among those with whom they are communicating. Others see their own opinions being ignored and their positions lost without a fair hearing.

The Effects of the Dynamic Style

The dynamic style is most appropriate for persons in a fast-moving and rapidly changing environment. The communicators speak briefly and serve as stimulants for others rather than working directly with them. The approach is effective in dealing with environments which have frequent crises and in which others are competent to handle the problems. The communicators give a brief statement of their positions but delegate to the other persons authority to make decisions and to take action.

The dynamic style, like the controlling style, is appropriate when the communicators have only a brief contact with the other persons. Whereas brevity for the controlling style avoids eliciting the resentment that often emerges under prolonged domination, brevity for the dynamic style provides the most compatible context for the communication approach. The communicator states his or her position succinctly and with enthusiasm. If the style is used effectively the receivers of the communication are challenged and stimulated to action.

Since the primary purpose of the dynamic style is to stimulate others, the motivation and competence of the other person is important. When the receiver of the communication feels inadequate to perform in the way the communicator is urging, he or she may find the experience frustrating (Wofford, 1971). Managers who use the dynamic style should surround themselves with highly competent people.

The Effects of the Relinquish Style

The relinquish style is often used in counseling others or in communicating confidence in others. This confidence may be shown by yielding a decision to the other person's judgment. The style may be used to prevent others from unduly shifting responsibility which they should retain. Counselors often wish to show that they understand and support their counselees, but they do not want the counselees to become more dependent on them. Similarly, managers may wish to build confidence and competence in their subordinates. A person whose personality structure is basically dependent will respond to the relinquishing style with frustration, resentment, and resistance. Dependent persons will often describe a relinquishing supervisor as weak and indecisive. The subordinates are fearful of being given authority and resist efforts on the part of the supervisor to give control to them.

A communicator may also appropriately use the relinquish style when another person clearly has superior information, experience, and understanding. For example, the patient will yield to the superior knowledge and information of the doctor in selecting treatment of an ailment. Most people relinquish influence to the lawyer or tax accountant in areas of their expertise. The relinquish style can be used only when the other person is willing to assume responsibility. It is inappropriate to use the relinquish approach as a way of avoiding responsibility or of avoiding an unpleasant situation. A person who uses the relinquish style for this purpose will experience a rapid deterioration in the confidence that others have in him or her.

The Effects of the Withdrawal Style

There is a limited number of situations in which the withdrawal style is effective. When discussing a subject which involves information that has been received in confidence, it is often expedient for the communicator to withdraw from the discussion which might cause him or her to reveal more than should be revealed. This would also apply to discussions requiring comments which would tarnish the company's image.

In a few situations the expression of anger may serve to demonstrate disapproval more effectively than logical argument. Suppose, for example, that an employee recommends that the organization engage in an unethical or immoral practice. An emotional, attacking, withdrawal response may help to communicate emphatically that this is not an alternative open for discussion.

With few exceptions, the withdrawal style cannot be recommended as a communication approach. Rarely will withdrawal from a problem produce a solution or improve a condition. The more frequent effect is to bring about a deterioration in relationships and delay problem solving. Highly aggressive withdrawal places a thick barrier to further communication. Hostile aggressive actions rapidly cut one off from the opinion of others.

From the foregoing discussion, it should be obvious that no single style is preferred for every situation. We must employ the communication style that is appropriate within the context of a particular situation or environment. Warren Bennis (1966) argues persuasively that our social and business culture is changing from one that is predominantly authoritarian to a more democratic orientation. Bennis points out that organizational life is becoming more technologically oriented and complex; the work force is becoming more educated and mobile and has higher expectations; jobs are requiring more involvement, participation, and autonomy. As organizations become more democratic in philosophy, the equalitarian style will be used more frequently, while the use of the controlling style will diminish. A complex, rapidly changing company will require the dynamic approach more often than the older, more stable organization. Thus, we can see broad environmental conditions that set the stage for the use of certain styles, but it is the day-to-day situation that is most significant in determining which style will be most effective.

Styles of communication are an integral part of both the internal and external systems. Communication style is an important determinant of the internal and external relationships which exist. Communication styles are applied to both the interpersonal and the small-group context. Each of the styles which we have discussed apply equally well to interpersonal and to small-group communication. As concepts of leadership and communication nets in small groups are discussed, the close alignment of these topics with communication styles will become apparent.

SUMMARY

In this chapter we have discussed the nature and effects of six styles of communication behavior, i.e., controlling, equalitarian, structuring, dynamic, relinquish, and withdrawal. The styles have been described within the context of public and private organizational settings. The major behavioral items making up each style have been outlined.

We observed that these styles are related to the organizational system. The structuring and controlling styles are more formal and external-system-oriented, while the equalitarian and withdrawal styles are normally the basis for the more informal relationships of the internal system.

The effectiveness of each style must be discussed in terms of the environmental situation. Each style has situations in which it serves effectively to accomplish the desired results. The controlling style serves best for a person who is respected, who is communicating to inexperienced, dependent, or unmotivated persons. The controlling style is particularly appropriate within a crisis situation and in communication within a large group. The equalitarian style is effective in stimulating communication within an organization. This style is effective in dealing with complex problems, in interacting with mature, well-motivated, experienced, and independent persons. The structuring style is effective in a complex and highly organized organization in which uniform policies and procedures are required for efficiency and consistency. The dynamic style is most appropriate in a rapidly changing environment in which people are capable of carrying out activities with minimal interaction. The relinquish style serves as a means of delegation to persons who have capabilities or expertise for assuming responsibility. The withdrawal style is rarely effective in communication because it blocks interaction. In the circumstance in which an issue is so dangerous as to require an angry outburst to demonstrate the intensity of one's reaction to the question and to avoid the hazards of pursuing the discussion, the withdrawal style is appropriate.

IMPORTANT TERMS AND CONCEPTS

communication styles, controlling, equalitarian, structuring, dynamic, relinquish, withdrawal

REVIEW QUESTIONS

1. Which styles of communication would you expect each of the following persons to use most frequently in the routine of a day's work? Vince Lombardi, Winston Churchill, John F. Kennedy, Gerald Ford, Adolph Hitler, William Buckley, and Johnny Carson.
2. Do you believe that the styles of communication used in an Exxon corporate board room would be essentially the same as or different from the end-of-month discussion between three partners in a corner shoe store? Explain.
3. Suppose you find that one of your subordinates is angry with you about an office procedure change. You know that the change must be put into effect, but you do not wish to alienate the subordinate. What style would you use in communicating to the subordinate?
4. In general, do you think that reliance on a single communication style, using all styles equally often, or using some mix of styles is more effective?
5. In what situations would you use each style of communication?
    a. Controlling style
    b. Equalitarian style
    c. Structuring style
    d. Dynamic style

e. Relinquish style
f. Withdrawal style

Attempt to be specific by describing an interpersonal or group situation in terms of the characteristics of the receiver, tasks, timing, etc.

EXERCISE 1

For the conversation below, evaluate each statement by a C, E, S, D, R, W, indicating whether it is a *control, equalitarian, structuring, dynamic, relinquish,* or *withdrawal* statement.

A marketing manager (John) and his salesperson (Joe) are discussing the sales prospects for the next quarter and are evaluating recent historical events.

____ John: "Joe, the first duty listed in your job description indicates that you are to investigate customer complaints."

____ Joe: "Yes, I think I should place more emphasis in that area in March. Our number of complaints seems to be growing for Grade C, and I need to get to the bottom of it. What do you think?"

____ John: "I'll leave that entirely up to you, Joe. You know that I don't want to tell you how to do your job."

____ Joe: "John, I've gotten a very good reception from fiber grade products in my area and the profit margin on them is good; we should put them at the top of our priority list."

____ John: "I know you've been sold on fiber grades from the beginning, Joe, but you're dead wrong. You've poured time into them and yet your sales for them is only a trickle. I want to make it clear that not only am I not encouraging the other men to push these grades, but I'm telling you to stop wasting your time with them."

____ Joe: "If that's what you want, all right. I'll go along with you on it."

____ John: "Joe, you have a tendency to run after fads. What's the matter with you, anyway?"

____ Joe: "Look, I thought the fiber grades would go, but since you feel so strongly about them, let's drop it. Maybe I should come back when you're in a better mood."

____ John: "Hold it! Let's not waste time and energy on losers."

____ Joe: "I like to ride a winner too!"

____ John: "What do you think of the asbestos grades?"

____ Joe: "The asbestos products were introduced in the wrong manner. We should make it standard procedure to let the salespeople check these products out with the potential customers and take our recommendation on specifications to R&D rather than allowing R&D to come up with these brainstorms that nobody will buy."

____ John: "You're right, Joe. I've been trying to make that point with J.B. for years, but he won't listen."

____ Joe: "It sure would make things better for us in the field. Keep trying to get him to buy the idea."

EXERCISE 2: STYLES OF COMMUNICATION

Harry was critical of his work group almost from his first day on the job. He considered them lazy and inefficient. A hard worker himself, Harry found their frequent breaks in production and the lack of concern for quality to be annoying. On the third day of Harry's employment, Bart came to him and in a friendly manner said, "Look fellow, you keep working your head off and it will make it tough for everyone. Slow it down. It'll be here tomorrow." That began a feud that lasted for months. Bart became the object of Harry's anger and Bart responded in kind. In time, Harry's performance began to slip; his absence record became highly unfavorable. The disharmony was having a negative impact on the entire operation.

1. The class is divided into groups of six to eight members each.

2. Each group discusses the topic "How would you as a manager resolve the conflict between Harry and Bart?" for ten to fifteen minutes.

3. The discussions are tape-recorded or video-taped. Following the discussion the tape is replayed. Then, using the table shown on page 167, each group member identifies the style of communication being used by each participant and notes the reaction that the group had for the communication item. The tape should be stopped at regular intervals to discuss the communication items.

4. The group should categorize, evaluate, and discuss each item and its effects.

BIBLIOGRAPHY

Bennis, Warren G.: *Changing Organization* (New York: McGraw-Hill Book Company, 1966).

Coch, L., and J. R. P. French, Jr.: "Overcoming Resistance to Change," *Human Relations,* vol. I, pp. 512–532, 1948.

Hamblin, R. L.: "Leadership and Crises," *Sociometry,* vol. 21, pp. 322–335, 1958.

Communication item	Style used	Response and effect			
		Positive response	Negative response	Facilitated discussion	Hindered discussion
1.					
2.					
3.					
4.					
5.					
6.					
7.					
8.					
9.					
10.					
11.					
12.					
13.					
14.					
15.					
16.					
17.					
18.					
19.					
20.					
21.					
22.					
23.					
24.					
25.					
26.					
27.					
28.					
29.					
30.					

Hemphill, J. D.: "Relations between the Size of the Group and the Behavior of Superior Leaders," *Journal of Social Psychology,* vol. 32, pp. 11–22, 1950.

Kay, E., J. R. P. French, and H. H. Meyer: *A Study of the Performance Appraisal Interview* (New York: Behavioral Research Service, General Electric Co., 1962).

Likert, Rensis: *The Human Organization* (New York: McGraw-Hill Book Company, 1967).

Parker, T. C.: "Relationships among Measures of Supervisory Behavior, Group Behavioral and Situational Characteristics," *Personnel Psychology,* vol. 16, pp. 319–334, 1963.

Roethlisberger, F. J.: "The Administrator's Skill: Communication," *Harvard Business Review,* vol. 31, no. 6, pp. 55–62, November–December 1953.

Shaw, Malcolm E.: *Developing Communication Skills* (Westport, Conn.: Educational Systems and Designs, Inc., 1968).

Townsend, Robert: *Up the Organization* (New York: Alfred A. Knopf, Inc., 1970).

Vroom, V. H., and F. C. Mann: "Leader Authoritarianism and Employee Attitudes," *Personnel Psychology,* vol. 13, pp. 125–140, 1960.

Wofford, J. C.: "Managerial Behavior, Situational Factors, and Productivity and Morale," *Administrative Science Quarterly,* vol. 16, no. 1, pp. 10–17, 1971.

10

BARRIERS TO COMMUNICATION

This chapter describes barriers to communication with which the manager must contend. It discusses in some detail how differences in power attributable to role can become a barrier to communication. It also addresses barriers to communication which may arise from language differences (jargon) between organizational subsystems. Third, and perhaps most important, it discusses types of communication which may provoke defensiveness and therefore act as a barrier to communication.

In previous chapters we have examined a number of ingredients which are basic to effective communication. We have explored the importance of self-awareness, self-disclosure, self-confidence, and attention to intrapersonal factors for effective communication. In this chapter we shall examine some of the variables which interfere with these important ingredients. We shall see how the ineffective use of power may be a barrier to self-disclosure and self-confidence. We shall examine language as a problem for self-disclosure. It is difficult to disclose to others who are unfamiliar with our "special" language. We shall see how certain types of communication (such as evaluative, dogmatic, and manipulative) create problems of defensiveness and lack of self-confidence.

POWER DIFFERENCES AS A BARRIER TO COMMUNICATION

Essentially, power (influence, control) is exercised in the decision-making processes. Decision making is part of the organizational process and affects who does what, when, where, and how. Decisions must be made; in fact, the avoidance or delay of decision making is itself a decision. From this viewpoint, power itself is neither good nor bad; it simply is.

The way that organizational decisions are made and power is exercised affects interpersonal relations. For example, if lower management has little upward influence, then managers on this level are not in a position to attend to the needs of their subordinates, since decision making is out of their hands. Such lack of attention to subordinates' needs is detrimental to the relationship. Thus, if managers have little power, their ability to function interpersonally within the organization is restricted (Pelz, 1952).

Power Tactics of the Relatively Powerful

It is apparent that the most powerful managers decide how decisions are to be made. That is, they can use their power to encourage or restrict the participation of the less powerful in the decision-making process. Since the decision about how decisions are made is such an all-encompassing one, a brief "look" at the probable "psychology" of these powerful managers is in order.

In North America, the powerful managers are likely to be men in their early fifties who grew up in the Depression. They were successful at acquiring power when the "rules of the game" were more authoritarian than now. Thus, they probably have a healthy respect for the "work ethic" and are not likely to challenge authority, or tolerate their authority being challenged. Also, they are probably very conscious of how things are organized and are well-disciplined and orderly, since this trait might have gained them favor in their rise to power.

Having devoted a large part of their adult life to the attainment of power, they are likely to be familiar with various power tactics. These power tactics essentially revolve around controlling the communication process in order to maintain or augment their personal power. Such tactics are barriers to communication, although they may be used "successfully" to maintain power. Martin and Sims (1956) suggest a few power tactics often used by people whose primary motive is to maintain power:

Taking Counsel. Executives should seek advice only when they think it is necessary. If they allow subordinates to give advice when it is not necessary, they are likely to find themselves under pressure to act in accordance with the advice, even when they see that such action may be disastrous.

Maneuverability. Wise executives should never fully commit themselves to any position or program. Otherwise they may find themselves committed to positions which are untenable. They must be careful to leave themselves a number of options so that they do not have to retract previously made commitments since such retractions are harmful to their credibility and diminish their power.

Complete Communication. It is not a good strategy to communicate everything one knows. Completely open communication deprives the executive of determining who gets to know what, when. Future plans may not materialize, but if they have been openly communicated it may be difficult to extricate oneself from the commitment to action. Also, if other power figures in the organization are aware of one's plans, they may move against them.

Compromise. Executives who wish to maintain their power may openly compromise but should continue to work toward their own goals. That is, any concession made should be seen as a way of delaying the opposition rather than as an act of cooperation.

Negative Timing. Sometimes pressure from subordinates, powerful colleagues, etc. may "force" executives to move in directions in which they do not agree. The appropriate tactic here is to take action but proceed so slowly that little harm is done. Thus, the inadvisable program dies "in committee" or "under consideration." In this way executives cannot be openly challenged. They are taking action, but by using negative timing, they make sure that nothing comes of the proposals.

We can see from the above discussion that from the power-seeking executive's viewpoint, the exercise of power is a foremost concern. Power tactics that executives often use are antithetical to cooperation and open communication. Such executives tend to view the concentration of power as necessary to organizational as well as individual success. The difficulty with such a position is that individual success can often become the driving concern. Further, power concentration tends to alienate the powerless. On the other hand, the equalization of power may bring an anarchical conflict of interest if there is not equalization of responsibility and expertise. Powerful executives thus justify their roles as necessary to the good of all, since organizational anarchy is likely to be disastrous where organizations are competing on the market.

The counterargument that we have suggested is that such power tactics tend to lead to inefficient communication, destructive conflict, dissatisfaction in the organization, etc. Hidden in the power-seeking executive's value system is the assumption that less powerful organizational members are less capable and less responsible. Of course, the exercise of power tactics tends to limit less powerful organizational members from becoming responsible. We have suggested that the more powerful person can adopt the viewpoint of developing the less powerful organizational member. This viewpoint leads to an increasing delegation of power as the subordinate develops responsibility and expertise.

Conformity

The relatively less powerful organizational members have little direct influence on decisions. They are at the mercy of the more powerful; they "must" conform to the decisions made by the more powerful. Within this context, one way of gaining influence is through gaining the favor of a relatively powerful manager who himself or herself can influence decision making.

One way the lower-level manager can gain influence is by using the Machiavellian strategy of agreeing in appearance with the ideas and attitudes of the more powerful manager. Support of the more powerful manager "causes" one to be liked by this powerful manager and lays the groundwork for later influence attempts. As was discussed in Chapter 8, this is a Machiavellian strategy to gain interpersonal influence.

This type of conformity, which has an ulterior motive, is described by Jones (1964) in a book entitled *Ingratiation*. He suggests that the effectiveness of ingratiation through conformity depends on clever concealment of ulterior motives. Thus, the lower-status person disagrees with the higher-status person on unimportant issues in order to appear to be a nonconformist. Conversely, a high-status person who is attempting to ingratiate himself or herself with lower-status people will agree on unimportant issues, but not on important ones. Thus, in organizations where ingratiation is a way of life, public agreement on issues appears to be at a high level. Indeed, for the ingratiation situation, the lack of disagreement is an indicator of poor communication!

Another way of handling the power issue is also often used by the less powerful. This is what Kelman (1958) terms *compliance*. This amounts to reluctant obedience; obeying the letter of the law but not the spirit of the law. The individual does what he or she is told but with little enthusiasm. This type of conformity may erupt into malicious obedience if the opportunity to express resentment without fear of reprisal is presented.

Consequences of Conformity. Conformity through either compliance or ingratiation restricts personal development since the individual does not express his or her own ideas and feelings. The long-range effect of conformity is to produce an organization of "yes men" with no initiative. Such an organization is likely to have difficulty changing to meet unforeseen circumstances.

If new ideas are eliminated through conformity, the organization becomes inflexible and unable to adjust to changes. A managerial strategy aimed solely at gaining cooperation through conformity is therefore unlikely to be successful even if all the conformists are contented ones. The organization is faced with the need for both cooperation (stability, law, and order) and innovation. The important thing from the organizational viewpoint is to meet both needs. We shall have more to say about achieving a balance between innovation and conformity in Part Four of the book.

Conformity and power tactics in combination tend to lead to a situation where task accomplishment is less important than the maintenance of the "power structure." Both sides pretend, however, that company objectives are of primary importance. In this context, open communication is not only unimportant, it is intentionally avoided.

The consequences of conformity are to deaden interpersonal relationships. Bach and Wyden (1969) suggest that the absence of conflict is an indicator of an unexciting and unproductive relationship. Conformity is a means of avoiding conflict essentially through the sacrifice of one's individuality. Such a sacrifice will eventually deaden the relationship, since a relationship by definition consists of two *individuals* relating to each other. Such a sacrifice may produce feelings of resentment, alienation, etc. In any event open communication is unlikely in such circumstances.

Facing Conflict. The manager who wishes to improve interpersonal relations in the organization needs to resolve the power issue more constructively. This essentially means that conflict must be faced rather than avoided. It is faced best through self-disclosure and feedback sequenced in a way which builds interpersonal trust.

LANGUAGE AS A BARRIER TO COMMUNICATION

The manager who wants to improve interpersonal relations needs to be aware of another barrier to communication often found in organizations. This barrier arises from differences in the use of language associated with the segregation of people into various groups within the organization.

Language Differences within Organizations

Some obvious characteristics of present-day organizations are that they are large, complex, and hierarchical. These characteristics of organizations tend to produce numerous groups of people which are separate from each other on the basis of specialty, status, and physical location within the organization. This separation of groups tends to be accentuated by differences in the use of language between groups. These differences in the use of language act as barriers to communication.

Virtually each specialized function in organizations has evolved a precise language to describe its experience. So accountants, engineers, scientists, psychologists, etc., all have terminology which they use to precisely communicate to others who share the same background. The specialization of language is directly related to the way one looks at the organization.

For example, consider various viewpoints concerning a library. An accountant would probably view the library in terms of cost-benefit ratios. Thus, circulation of books might be compared to cost of books so that particular categories which have a large circulation might justify additional purchases. An architect, on the other hand, would be prone to look at the use of space and materials. Is it constructed in such a way as to produce an environment suitable to its intended use? Students, depending on motivation, might see the library as a place for socializing, a place to find a date for Saturday night, a place to study, a place to get help in assembling information, etc. The librarian might look at the library in terms of the ease of locating books. These various viewpoints are related to one's motives and conceptual tools (language). That is, one's awareness of the various aspects of the library is directly related to motives and to the possession of vocabulary which is capable of describing perceptions.

Specialized Language for Specialized Functions

A specialized language develops when individuals in organizations perform different specialized functions as a result of the division of work which occurs in organizations. Accordingly, specialized language is inappropriate for communication between people performing different organizational functions. Since the accountants generally do not have engineering experience or an engineer's specialized vocabulary, the engineer's specialized vocabulary is jargon to the typical accountant. Communication problems frequently arise because engineers, for example, are sometimes unaware that their terminology is outside the experience of an accountant. In such a case, the information that is actually transmitted may be minimal. In a sense there are communication barriers or boundaries between such specialists. Methods for spanning such boundaries will be discussed in the last part of this book.

Specialized Language for Top-Management Policies

Similar difficulties are likely to occur when top management formulates policy. If policy decisions are made using information which is inaccessible to lower levels of management, then it is likely that managers at lower levels will not be able to interpret the policies once they are established. This is especially true if top management is unaware of the problems and routines of lower management. The language used to formulate policy is likely to be ambiguous (imprecise), since the information and experience on which policy is based are not shared.

For example, consider the decision to institute a companywide management-by-objective (MBO) program. Often an outside consulting firm has sold the program to top management on the basis of data reflecting the effectiveness and profitability of the MBO program in other companies. Top management then decides to institute MBO and sends operating details to lower management via office memo. Lower management, without benefit of the presentation by the consulting firm, may not understand the purpose of the program and specifically how it applies to their situation. Under such conditions, managers at the lower levels will not be familiar with the jargon of MBO and will not be able to communicate effectively about the new program.

Though similar, the MBO example is a more subtle variation of the limitations of language than are the communication difficulties arising between the engineer and accountant. In the latter case, the accountant is aware that he or she does not understand the jargon of the engineer, whereas lower managers may not be aware that they do not understand the implications of policy decisions made by top management. The language of the policy decision may seem to be perfectly clear, yet communication may be poor. The two illustrations are similar in that the communicator has firsthand knowledge based on experience, whereas the receiver has limited experience with the subject of communication. However, in the MBO example it seems likely that neither top nor lower managers have firsthand experience with the subject of the communication. In any event, that which may seem perfectly clear to the communicator may be uninterpretable to the receiver.

Language is such an all-pervasive part of our experience that it is difficult to recognize its limitations. A good place to start is the recognition that language is an abstraction, a labeling of experience which is at best an approximation. Try a little experiment: Look around you and describe your visual experience fairly accurately. Yet, to say that a rug is brown or green is to make a gross approximation. What is the texture of the rug? What do you mean by brown? If it were really important to describe your experience more accurately, you would have to come up with a more precise language. For an interior decorator, brown is not good enough—there are literally dozens of labels for different colors which the lay person would simply call brown. It is very important that we understand this interaction between language and experience. Each of us through our individual experience has acquired a vocabulary which is particular to those experiences which we are most interested in communicating.

COMMUNICATION WHICH PROVOKES DEFENSIVENESS

Perhaps the greatest barrier to communication, however, goes beyond the difficulties associated with terminology and jargon. The style of communication used by the manager may itself act as a barrier to communication. That is, when a manager sends a message in a way that provokes defensiveness, he or she contributes to the "poor" interpersonal relationship. When relationships are strained, the chances of experiencing communication breakdowns are greatly increased.

Four types of communication which often provoke defensiveness are: evaluative, manipulative, dogmatic, and communication which implies superiority.

Evaluative Communication

By "evaluation" we mean the use of labeling, particularly as it implies to negative comparison—for example, "pushy," "lazy," or "incompetent." Labeling or attributing characteristics to people even when the attributes are positive is essentially a stereotyping procedure. Once the person is labeled, it is difficult to see the whole person. Instead, one tends to see the label.

An example of evaluative communication and its provocation of defensiveness which the author observed recently was a transaction between a manager and his personnel supervisor. The manager sat in on a meeting with union representatives conducted by the personnel supervisor. The meeting was concerned with ways to improve training. After the meeting the conversation went something like this:

Manager: "That meeting was a complete waste of time. You are a poor discussion leader."

Personnel supervisor: "You just don't understand the difficulties in dealing with this union. I thought the meeting was reasonably productive."

Manager: "Well, maybe it wasn't a *complete* waste of time, but the major issues were not really resolved."

Personnel supervisor: "Well, with these guys you have to be careful how you proceed."

Manager: "Look, I don't want to fight with you, but I just don't see what was accomplished."

Personnel supervisor: "OK. Then don't fight with me. Look, if we did things your way, we would be in a real conflict situation with the union, but if that's what you want me to do. . . ."

Manager: "What is my way?"

Personnel supervisor: "Oh, I don't know."

Whether or not the meeting was unproductive, the above conversation between the personnel supervisor and the manager was certainly unproductive. The evaluative statement, "The meeting was a complete waste of time," provoked a defensive response and the rest of the conversation was concerned with the control issue (whose *way*) rather than the real issue (how to proceed with the union).

A replay of the same conversation with descriptive rather than evaluative communication might be as follows:

Manager: "I sure felt frustrated in there." (Describing feelings)

Personnel supervisor: "Yeah." (Sigh) "It is hard working with those union guys."

Manager: "I wonder how we could get them to talk about problems more directly?"

Personnel supervisor: "I don't know; they are pretty tricky characters."

Manager: "You think that they really don't want to resolve the issues?"

Personnel supervisor: "Yeah, they want to resolve them, *their* way."

Manager: "And we want to resolve them *our* way?"

Personnel supervisor: "Yeah."

Manager: "So, how do we break this deadlock?"

Personnel supervisor: "I don't know."

Manager: "Well, maybe we could give them a better understanding of our problems."

Personnel supervisor: "You think that might work?"

Manager: "It would be a start."

The above conversation is very slow and tedious because the personnel supervisor is very protective of his viewpoint that the union members are trying to trick him. That is, he has labeled the union members and is now trapped by this label into making a possible problem-solving discussion into the Paris peace talks. The manager carefully avoids any attacks on the personnel supervisor and has some success in moving him toward relaxing his stereotypes.

Dogmatic Communication

The personnel supervisor's resistance to feedback and his tendency to see the situation in black-and-white terms are aspects of a form of communication which we have labeled "dogmatic." Of all the barriers to communication which have been described and investigated, dogmatism is perhaps the most difficult to overcome. The research initiated by Rokeach (1960) suggests that dogmatism is a personality trait that is difficult to change. Dogmatic or closed-minded individuals are resistant to new ideas and are unable to see other people's points of view. They usually turn a discussion of alternatives into a debate. Their approach to communication seems to start from the premise that they are correct and other people are incorrect. This tends to severely limit communication since the possibility of mutual influence and the exchange of exclusive information are eliminated. When one person insists he or she is right and refuses to accept any other possibilities, the interpersonal situation tends to become polarized. The other person in the relationship is likely to become more defensive of his or her own viewpoint.

Dogmatic people very rarely listen to what other people say as they are already busy preparing their own arguments. They are highly resistant to feedback and generally react to any negative feedback by counterattack rather than trying to understand it. Because of their rigid belief system, dogmatic people tend to have little creativity and little flexibility in any endeavors.

Communication Which Implies Superiority

People who believe that their possession of superior knowledge, expertise, experience, etc. necessarily makes their contributions more important often excite the same defensiveness as dogmatic people. If a manager is constantly implying his or her superiority, this in turn implies that the other person(s) is(are) inferior. Such implications are likely to lead to defensiveness.

It might be noted that if the manager is clearly superior, the superiority of his or her viewpoints will probably be recognized and appreciated by others. In any event, the insistence on superiority is generally not a successful communication strategy. Given that an organization is relatively stable in terms of personnel, most members of the organization will know a person's position, expertise, and reputation. A manager who has a superior reputation will probably be listened to, and indeed, his or her advice will be actually sought. (We will discuss this concept further in Part Four as the special communicator.) In this case, the manager has the opportunity of establishing rapport simply by listening to other viewpoints. People are usually flattered that a "great" person listens to what they have to say.

Manipulative Communication

As has been suggested repeatedly, when people perceive that someone with some ulterior motive is trying to influence them, they tend to react negatively. Rather than seeing the communication as neutral, they tend to oppose the communication even if the opposition is not in their best interests. That is, manipulative communication excites the control issue and the reaction to the communication is based on not wanting to be controlled rather than on the content of the communication.

Managers who are aware that coercion meets resistance often try to manipulate subordinates to accept a decision that has already been made. They may ask for advice and cast the choices in such a way as to "stack the cards" in favor of the choice they prefer. Once subordinates see this consultation as a manipulative strategy, their acceptance of decisions is likely to deteriorate. They are likely to become defensive, become increasingly critical of management, etc. What is communicated when manipulation is used is that subordinates are easily influenced and are incapable of participating in decision making. In order to show that this is not the case, subordinates resist.

In many organizations, manipulation appears necessary for survival. The end result of manipulation, however, may be disastrous. The only way out of this dilemma appears to be to change the nature of the organization. If short-term payoffs for manipulation are minimized, then more honest communication is likely to take place.

Defensiveness

We have talked about four types of communication which provoke defensiveness. It should be clear that these types of communication are themselves defensive in nature. When a person evaluates another person, it is often in self-defense. The example of the new marketing manager given in Chapter 4 clearly illustrates this point. Al saw Sally, the new person, as "pushy" at least partly because he was insecure himself.

Manipulation is generally used because the person thinks that his or her true feelings or motives may be misunderstood or unaccepted. Such a perception may be an accurate one, and if so, it has been suggested that manipulation is perhaps justified. It would be better, however, if the organizational climate was such that the individual did not feel that expression of his or her real feelings was detrimental to personal success.

Clearly, dogmatic, closed-minded individuals are so busy defending their ideas and beliefs that they are not receptive to new ideas. This defensive posture may well be associated with hidden feelings of insecurity or inadequacy which they cannot accept. People who imply superiority are more directly defending their self-concept; it is important that others believe that they are superior so that they can continue to believe in their own superiority. Again, we see that the best way to increase effective communication is to increase one's self-confidence and to decrease one's defensiveness.

The manager who is trying to improve the climate of interpersonal relations needs to be able to distinguish between confronting others constructively and provoking defensiveness. Confrontation of conflict through self-disclosure and feedback involves the description of one's own ideas, attitudes, feelings, opinions, etc. The way to avoid provoking defensiveness in confronting conflict is to describe one's own position while encouraging the other person to describe his or her position. When a manager communicates the "message" that he or she values the ideas of others, then defensive reactions are considerably lessened.

SUMMARY

Managers who attempt to improve interpersonal relations in organizations are likely to run into several barriers. First, they may find that open communication is at cross-purposes with the way the power issue has been resolved. The relatively powerful manager may intentionally use tactics aimed at reducing communication as a means of maintaining power. Less powerful organizational members may appear to conform but are restricting communication themselves. They may distort communication or withhold it while ostensibly doing what the more powerful person wants. Conformity and power tactics in combination tend to produce an organization of people unable to adjust to change.

Another barrier to communication the manager is likely to encounter is associated with differences in languages (jargon). This difference in language arises from differences in task specialty and organizational status and may lead to communication breakdown.

Finally, the manager's own style of communication may be a barrier to communication. The manager may unintentionally provoke defensiveness and create barriers to communication by use of evaluative, dogmatic, manipulative, and "superiority" forms of communication. The best way to reduce this barrier to communication is for the manager to decrease his or her own defensiveness.

IMPORTANT TERMS AND CONCEPTS

taking counsel, negative timing, conformity, ingratiation, evaluative communication, dogmatic communication, manipulative communication, compliance

REVIEW QUESTIONS

1. How does the way that decisions are made affect interpersonal relations in organizations?

2. Describe the power tactic of "negative timing." How does it limit the "openness" of interpersonal communication?
3. Describe "ingratiation." What effects might ingratiation have on organizational effectiveness?
4. How can a manager resolve the power issue in a way which eliminates ingratiation?
5. How does evaluative communication provoke defensiveness in others?
6. How does compliance differ from ingratiation?
7. Comment pro and con on the following statement: "A capable manager will consult others so as to get their input, but once the manager has made a decision he or she should not tolerate dissent. If the manager allows such dissension, the organization is likely to fail."
8. Suppose an organization had a few powerful managers who used power tactics similar to those described. Suppose that most of the rest of the managers were using ingratiation tactics. How would a new person entering the organization find this out? That is, what observations would support the above conclusions?

INCIDENT 1: COMMUNICATION ABOUT PERFORMANCE

"Martha, I asked you to come by the office today because I'm evaluating the performance of everyone in my department. You've done a lot of good work this year, and I want you to know that I appreciate it. I do notice what is going on in your department. You are to be commended.

"Of course, there are a few areas in which you could improve, but let's start the evaluation with the good side. You've done a fine job in getting your people involved in team decision making. Your department has an effective system of planning and scheduling of activities which increases your output. I'm also glad you're taking an active role in my staff meetings. . . .

"Now, Martha, let me tell you where I think you need some improvement. I hope these remarks may help you to do an even better job next year. Your attitude toward your work and the division is bad and I believe that it is rubbing off on your people. You also need to set an example in the area of promptness for your people. You often are late to meetings, arriving at work or returning from lunch. Be more conscientious about promptness. I think you need to be more imaginative and creative in your approach to your job. You do the things that are required, but that's it, nothing extra or innovative.

"Do you have any thoughts or questions on this?"

1. What response do you anticipate from Martha?
2. What are the barriers to communication in this incident?
3. How might the discussion be handled more effectively?

INCIDENT 2

At the United Paper Mills, the maintenance department had had difficulties for a number of years. Recently, things had gotten worse. Several employees, for example, were "known" to have spent company time working on projects for their own boats and cars and in addition were "known" to have used company materials. Many supervisors had apparently "given up" trying to discipline workers because they felt that the company would not back them up.

Jerry, a newly promoted maintenance supervisor, had a crew that was working pretty well. One of the difficulties was that workers under him often changed to other crews and supervisors because of absenteeism and emergency rush jobs. Wednesday, he caught one of his workers, Hal, quitting early. He told him that quitting time was not for another hour and he expected him to work that amount of time. Hal proceeded to do so but seemed to be disgruntled.

The next day Hal was assigned to another supervisor and, sure enough, Jerry saw him quitting early again. Hal saw Jerry see him but paid no attention to him. Jerry knew that some of the other supervisors "looked the other way" when workers quit early and suspected that Hal's supervisor for that day probably did not want to know about Hal quitting early.

Discussion Questions:

1. What can Jerry do?

2. Role-play a discussion between Jerry and Hal.

3. Role-play a discussion between Jerry and Hal's supervisor for that day.

4. What issues are at stake here? What are the barriers to communication?

BIBLIOGRAPHY

Bach, G., and P. Wyden: *The Intimate Enemy* (New York: William Morrow & Company, Inc., 1969).

Jones, E. E.: *Ingratiation: A Social Psychological Analysis* (New York: Appleton-Century-Crofts, Inc., 1964).

Kelman, H.: "Compliance, Identification, and Internalization: Three Processes of Attitude Change," *Journal of Conflict Resolution,* vol. 2, pp. 151–160, March 1958.

Martin, N. H., and J. H. Sims: "Power Tactics," *Harvard Business Review,* pp. 25–29, November–December 1956.

Pelz, D. C.: "Influence: Key to Effective Leadership in the First Line Supervisor," *Personnel,* vol. 29, pp. 209–217, 1952.

Rokeach, Milton: *The Open and Closed Mind* (New York: Basic Books, Inc., Publishers, 1960).

11

GATEWAYS TO EFFECTIVE INTERPERSONAL COMMUNICATION

Effective interpersonal communication involves a number of essential skills. In this chapter we examine several of the most significant interpersonal skills which are at the heart of effective communication.

Effective communication requires the manager to open several essential gateways. These gateways provide a basis for increased self-awareness, self-disclosure, self-confidence, and reception of feedback. Interpersonal trust, listening, feedback, nonverbal communication, and nondirective counseling are the gateways which we shall explore in this chapter.

INTERPERSONAL TRUST AS A GATEWAY TO COMMUNICATION

A key to effective interpersonal communication is trust. Employees will not send accurate and open messages to their supervisor unless they trust the supervisor. They must have confidence that the supervisor will not use the information the subordinates send to their detriment. They must believe that the information will not be inappropriately or inaccurately transferred to others. They must believe that promises will be kept. They must believe that their expressions of feelings will be accepted without defensiveness or retaliation from the supervisor. In effect, the subordinates must believe that their supervisor is "on their side" and can be depended upon.

Developing Interpersonal Trust

How is interpersonal trust developed? The level of interpersonal trust is established by intrapersonal factors, interpersonal factors, and organizational factors. Each of us brings to a relationship a level of expectation about the degree of trust we can have in other people. This level of intrapersonal trust is developed early in life from relationships of childhood and adolescence. If our early associates are consistent, fair, and trustworthy, we hold a favorable expectancy about new associates. Early negative experiences predispose us toward distrust. Similarly, expectancies concerning trust within organizations are built through our experiences with people in organizations.

The interpersonal factors also contribute to the level of trust for a person. Past experiences with a person influence our present feeling of trust for that person. If a supervisor has been trustworthy in past associations, we expect him or her to continue to be trustworthy.

The total climate of an organization may be favorable or unfavorable for interpersonal trust. This climate is usually established by top-level managers. If managers at the top of an organization trust one another, and are fair, open, and receptive, this atmosphere will permeate the entire organization. If top managers are cautious, defensive, and deceptive, the total organization will show a lack of trust.

Establishing Interpersonal Factors for Trust

What can the individual manager do to establish interpersonal trust? The manager at the middle or lower levels of an organization cannot change the climate of the total organization. He or she cannot quickly change the intrapersonal trust of another person. But the manager can change the interpersonal factors which influence his or her own trust relationships. This is accomplished by communicating standards of fairness and integrity and in living by those standards. Trust is enhanced when others observe a consistent devotion to commitments, consideration of others, and fairness on the part of a person. The trust level is further developed when the person is tempted to violate the trust for personal gain but does not: for example, a supervisor who could blame subordinates for faulty work but accepts the failure as his or her own, or a subordinate who could have withheld important information but does not do so.

The Constructive-Destructive Trust Cycles

A manager is in one of two cycles with each of his or her associates (see Figure 11-1). The constructive trust cycle is one in which there is a relationship of trust.

	Constructive trust cycle	Destructive trust cycle
Person A	→ High trust →	→ Low trust →
Person B	← Effective communication ←	← Ineffective communication ←

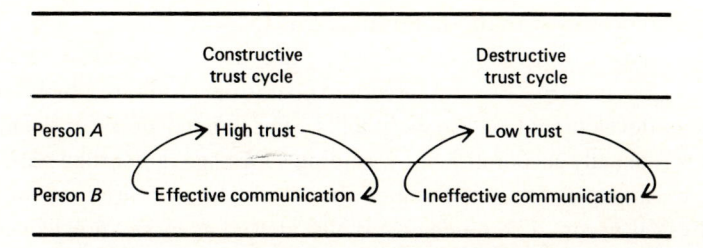

FIGURE 11-1 Trust-communication cycles. [*After Haney, 1973.*]

Trust on the part of person A for B results in more accurate and more open communication on the part of B. This open communication can then provide A with an added opportunity to be trusting of B. If A responds with integrity, B will feel more confident to increase his or her self-disclosure. And so the constructive cycle builds in a positive direction.

The second cycle is not so favorable. It can begin with a lack of trust by person A for person B. Since A does not trust B, the communication of B to A tends to be guarded and/or deceptive. A probably responds by being less personal, more negative in his or her feelings for B, and less supportive of B. B responds by having less trust for A and by being less open, more cautious, and more deceptive. This results in a continuing response of less support and less effective communication.

Either person A or person B can break the destructive cycle. A can do so by being consistently honest, fair, supportive, and nonpunitive even though he or she knows that at the present B is being deceptive. B, in seeing this response of A, will then begin to become more open and accurate in his or her messages. B can break the cycle by taking the risk of being open and disclosing thoughts and feelings even when he or she believes that A may use this against him or her. In seeing this openness, A will become more supportive, thus shifting to the constructive trust cycle.

Trust is a key ingredient of communication effectiveness and ultimately of organizational effectiveness. The manager should make a concerted effort to build the trust relationship with associates.

LISTENING AS A GATEWAY TO COMMUNICATION

One of the most talked about and least practiced communication skills is listening. Listening is the concern of almost 50 percent of this book. All the elements involved in the reception and processing of the message are aspects of listening. Obviously, then, effective communication requires effective listening.

Wide differences exist in the ability to listen. Like other human skills, listening must be developed by careful, attentive practice. One is not likely to become a good listener by accident. Several forces are operating within us which hinder the spontaneous development of listening skills. The immediate satisfaction of personal needs is usually accomplished by sending a message rather than receiving. As children, we must ask for something or show concern or desire for something to satisfy physical needs. The sender is usually viewed as more knowledgeable and more interested in a topic than the listener. The sender has a more direct influence upon the activities of others than does the listener. We build our ego by sending a message that sounds astute. These forces prevent most of us from developing effective listening skills.

Listening is an essential skill for the manager. Nichols (1957) estimates that at least 40 percent of the white-collar worker's day is devoted to listening. Effective decision making requires the ability to obtain information in auditory as well as visual form. In addition, the ability to listen is a primary skill for the manager in improving relationships with subordinates.

Nichols (1957) compared the listening behaviors of 100 persons considered to be the best listeners of a university freshman class with those of the 100 worst listeners of this class. He identified the following ten components of effective listening: (1) The listener must find an area of interest in what is being said. (2) The listener must judge the content of the message rather than the weakness of the speaker. (3) The listener does not evaluate the message until he or she thoroughly comprehends it. (4) He or she listens for the central idea. (5) The listener should be flexible and not expect the message to follow a fixed pattern. (6) Since listening is difficult, the listener must work hard at it and pursue it actively. (7) The listener must fight distractions and concentrate on the message. (8) The listener must be mentally alert to grasp the meaning of the message. (9) The listener must be open-minded. (10) The listener has an advantage in that "thought" processes are more rapid than "talk" processes. He or she must capitalize on this advantage by focusing intensive thought on the speaker's hidden meanings and central ideas.

Listening is an essential skill for feedback and nondirective counseling. As we shall see on the following pages, these are important communication skills for the manager.

FEEDBACK AS A GATEWAY TO COMMUNICATION

Feedback may be defined in a general way as any information which allows the sender to evaluate the effects of his or her own communication on the receiver.

Thus, former President Nixon might have seen the march on Washington as feedback concerning his Vietnam policies, an individual might see the receiver's emotional reaction as feedback concerning the effects of a message sent, the absentee record of a company might be seen by the personnel manager as feedback concerning job satisfaction of employees, etc. Since every system (for example, an individual, a group, an organization, a society) is faced with the problem of adapting to a changing environment, feedback on the appropriateness of its responses is essential to effective functioning. Without feedback the system cannot effectively adjust to the environment within which it operates.

The importance of feedback to organizational success is highlighted by the experience of Edward J. Feeney, vice president of System Performance, Emery Freight Corporation, Wilton, Connecticut. Tangible savings of $600,000 for Emery were achieved one day after the installation of an effective feedback system (Laird, 1971). (We will elaborate on this example later in the chapter.) The present chapter will look at the feedback process at two different levels: intrapersonal (within the individual) and interpersonal (between individuals). The focus will be on the use of feedback as a means of increasing effective functioning.

Intrapersonal Feedback

Let us look at the feedback that is available to us intrapersonally. For illustrative purposes, consider the feedback which we have concerning diet. Most of us have evolved habits of eating which are grossly unhealthy: beer, soft drinks, french fries, fried foods, etc. form the basis of our diet. We give little thought to our food intake until some gross indicator suggests maybe we should alter the program, e.g., we find that we no longer fit our clothes. There is well-documented evidence that the type of food that we eat as well as the quantity has effects on our emotional and physical well-being. Most of us are so insensitive to feedback about food that we do not realize we are eating an unbalanced diet until we have a heart attack! How does one become sensitive to the physical and emotional feedback which research tells us is the result of dietary habits?

There is no simple answer. One could adopt a balanced diet and see if one feels the difference. Unfortunately, the experiences of the author and acquaintances suggest that this difference is generally not felt, although gross indicators like weight change are often noticed. The problem probably lies in our general insensitivity to our bodies. Thus to be sensitive to feedback about diet, perhaps we need to first increase body awareness in general. (There are many ways of doing this, such as yoga and body-awareness exercises such as advocated by Moshe Feldenkries, 1972.) Another problem related to sensitivity to feedback concerning eating habits is that feedback is often delayed. For example, when one eats sweets, one experiences a pickup. Physiologically, sugar is quick energy. The tendency of the body is to accept this pickup as feedback and continue to eat sweets. The consequence of eating sugar over time, however, is to first experience the quick high and later experience fatigue. It is much more difficult to associate this delayed consequence with the eating of sugar.

Perhaps the most difficult problem is that the effects of eating on emotional and physical well-being is compounded by many other influences. So, maybe I feel bad because I didn't get enough sleep or because my income tax is due, or because I had an argument with my wife.

This dissertation on the difficulty of becoming sensitive to feedback concerning dietary habits is presented to show that the feedback process, while simple in theory, is difficult in practice. To really function optimally, individuals, groups, and organizations need to be much more sensitive to feedback. Thus, we are faced with a very difficult task of increasing awareness.

Types of Intrapersonal Feedback

We will briefly describe other indicators of physical-emotional well-being which can act as intrapersonal feedback.

1. *Posture*. The way we sit, stand, and walk communicates a lot to others and to ourselves about the way we feel about ourselves. A person who sits relaxed, back straight, usually feels self-confident. A person who slouches or is bent over usually does not feel self-confident. The way one stands can indicate how solid one feels (feet on the ground). Walking often shows aggressiveness (chest stuck out), sexuality (movement in the pelvic area), importance of intellect (head stuck out, literally head before body), looseness (openness), or tightness, (defensiveness).

2. *Muscle Tension*. Often emotional tensions express themselves in the body by creating muscular tension. The phrase "you give me a pain in the neck," literally translated, means I am so angry at you that my neck muscles are painfully tense.

3. *Sleep*. Irregularities in sleeping or the inability to sleep is a rather gross indicator of emotional upset.

4. *Use of Tranquilizers.* Drugs, food, alcohol, tobacco, television, even sex can function basically as tranquilizers. When you find yourself overindulging in tranquilizing yourself, this is good feedback. What impulses to action (what energy expenditures) would be used if you were not tranquilizing yourself? More specifically, what are you afraid of?

5. *Emotion.* Emotion provides a much more direct and immediate feedback process than body awareness (muscle tension, posture, etc.). However, we often are not sensitive to our emotions. In fact, the awareness of emotion and the ability and openness to express emotion is perhaps the single most important characteristic which differentiates the psychologically healthy and interpersonally competent from the neurotic.

Fear as Intrapersonal Feedback

Let us look at how emotions function as intrapersonal feedback. Specifically, we will describe the feedback process arising from the emotion of fear. Our discussion of anxiety and ways of coping with anxiety in a previous chapter provides us with a good background. As was suggested then, anxiety-fear allows us to pinpoint the situations which are blocking our psychological-interpersonal growth.

Fear might be defined as the anticipation of psychological and/or physical injury (i.e., pain). The trouble with fear is that it tends to generalize situations and thus restrict our behavior. For example, if I am in a car accident and break my leg, I may become afraid of riding in cars, anticipating that it might again prove painful. Thus, the tendency is to stop riding in cars, i.e., to restrict my behavioral sphere. If my wife leaves me for another man, I may become afraid of emotional involvement with other women, for fear that I again may be rejected and feel emotional pain. Again, the tendency is to restrict my behavioral sphere. Thus, the more fear I have, the more narrow my life becomes.

Fear can be used as feedback in a way that promotes rather than restricts personal growth. The trick is to be aware of fear and be interested in the way it works. I can observe physical characteristics, the tightening of the viscera, the quickening of the heartbeat, etc. If I watch closely I can observe many ways in which fear affects my behavior. For example, when I want something from you, I can observe how fear changes my voice, how I try not to alienate you, etc. When I see clearly how fear affects my behavior, then it no longer has the same hold on me. I begin to see other ways of responding to the same situation.

Interpersonal Feedback

Now that we have some idea about the difficulties of becoming sensitive to feedback and the diversity of indicators which can be used as intrapersonal feedback, let us look at the feedback process in interpersonal communication.

First of all, there are some general guidelines for effective feedback, i.e., feedback which the receiver will act on. These follow recommendations of the National Training Laboratories.

1. *To be useful, feedback should be descriptive rather than evaluative.* In general, the person giving feedback describes his or her emotional reaction to the other person's behavior. For example, "I am disappointed that we are not achieving our objectives." This description of feelings avoids evaluation. When the manager makes an evaluative statement such as, "You guys are not working hard enough," or "You're lazy," in reaction to the same situation, the feedback is likely to be less effective. In the latter instance, the manager is provoking a defensive response. The workers are left with little alternative but to dispute the charges or to rationalize their behavior by pointing to problems in work assignments, etc. When the manager describes his or her feelings, it is more likely that the workers will respond in a nondefensive manner since they are not placed in the position of justifying their behavior.

2. *Feedback should be specific rather than general.* For example, the marketing manager might tell the production manager, "You don't cooperate enough with us." This rather general feedback is not nearly as helpful as, "I wish you guys in production would consult us as to the delivery needs of our customers before you make your weekly production schedules out."

3. *Feedback is useful only when directed toward behavior which the receiver can do something about.* For the production manager to complain to the quality-control manager about the number of rejections for poor quality misses the point. The manager needs to direct the complaint to the workers or get engineering to change the standards.

4. *Feedback is most useful when it is solicited rather than imposed.* If the manager can create the climate such that employees approach him or her about problems that they are experiencing, feedback is much more likely to be effective. Work-

ers are likely to know specifically what kind of feedback the manager needs.

5. *Feedback should be given at the earliest opportunity (depending, of course, on the person's readiness to hear it, support available from others, etc.).* This concern should be obvious: When feedback is delayed, memory distortion, irrelevance, and defensiveness are likely to increase. Thus, the manager who says, "You didn't listen to me three weeks ago; I was trying to suggest a way of solving that problem but you didn't give me enough time to explain the solution," is likely to get the response, "Heck, all you had to do was continue talking; I was listening. Besides, it's too late to use your solution now."

6. *Feedback is most effective when it is checked to ensure clear communication.* One way of doing this is to have the receiver rephrase the feedback received to see if it corresponds to what the sender had in mind. It is surprising how often feedback is not received because the person giving feedback does not get feedback on the clarity of the initial feedback.

Initiating the Feedback Process

The guidelines to effective feedback given above assume that the feedback process is functioning but may need to be improved. In many hierarchical organizations, the feedback process is almost nonexistent. In the previous chapter, we pointed out why this is the case: There are usually strong organizational norms against the expression of emotion and against the discussion of interpersonal behavior. As was argued in the previous chapter, these norms generally lead to a situation where organizational members are unsure of their standing and thus are reluctant to express any ideas which might lead to the exposure of suppressed feelings. Thus, when feedback about interpersonal behavior and the expression of emotion are contradictory of organizational norms, feedback on substantive matters also tends to be suppressed. The manager, therefore, is often in the position of trying to initiate the feedback process. How does the manager go about encouraging feedback? Borman, Howell, Nichols, and Shapiro (1969) suggest eight steps for encouraging feedback.

1. *Tell people you want feedback.* Although subordinates may be cautious about taking you up on your invitation, this initial overture may "unfreeze" some of the less defensive subordi-

nates. The others will be watching to see if you really mean what you say. That is, are you willing to deal with negative as well as positive comments?

2. *Identify some areas in which you want feedback.* A general invitation to give feedback is usually nonproductive since subordinates are unsure about your intentions. When you specify particular areas in which you want feedback, this reduces their uncertainty. It is perhaps wise to originally specify a limited number of areas which you anticipate will be productive, i.e., where risk is low and interest relatively high.

3. *Set aside time for regularly scheduled feedback sessions.* Again you are reducing the risk for your subordinates to give you feedback by taking the initiative yourself. You are also communicating in a very concrete way your desire for feedback.

4. *Use silence to encourage feedback.* At a regularly scheduled meeting with your subordinates where you have asked for feedback on specific topics, it is not necessary for you to do much talking. This entails a role reversal since people of lower status are used to listening. If you make it easy for them to listen, they will fall into their established role. Thus, it is important to demonstrate your desire to listen by remaining silent. Since it is also usual that when people meet someone does the talking, if you refrain from talking, it is likely that your subordinates will talk.

5. *Watch for nonverbal responses.* If your subordinates are still reluctant to give feedback, you may be able to ascertain who is most likely to give feedback by their nonverbal responses. If they look displeased, then you might ask them why they appear that way. It is generally easy to spot people who have something on their minds by their posture, expression, etc. This is true for any communication, whether or not it is at a feedback session.

6. *Ask questions.* Often a specific question to a specific person will elicit a response which might otherwise not be made. People who are uncertain about the situation are more likely to respond if you clearly indicate that you expect it. When you do receive feedback, it is important to ask questions so that they will see your interest and feel free to clarify their initial remarks.

7. *Use statements that encourage feedback and clarifications.* When a person states a problem, an opinion, or idea rather than immediately reacting to the statement, encourage elaboration by such statements as "I see" or "That's interesting." Rephrasing the statement to see if you really understand what was said also encourages clarification.

8. *Reward feedback.* A manager who has asked for and received feedback is obligated to respond to feedback. That is, if the manager appreciates the feedback, he or she needs to treat it as important and act on it, if possible. If managers want feedback, they need to demonstrate that their openness goes farther than just being good listeners.

Encourage the Expression of Emotion. In addition to these eight points, it is important to allow and encourage the expression of emotion. As was emphasized above, feedback is not likely to exist in a situation where norms are against the expression of emotion and/or the discussion of interpersonal behavior. The manager must be prepared to accept the anger and dissatisfaction of subordinates. That is, the manager must allow the expression toward specific behaviors or issues. Thus, if subordinates express dissatisfaction with company policies, ask for their recommendation. If, as a manager, you have upward influence, use it judiciously to forward subordinates' ideas. When subordinates see that legitimate grievances are resolved, the feedback process is likely to improve. They are likely to be more receptive to feedback and also more likely to give feedback.

Address the Interpersonal Issues. Eventually, interpersonal behavior will probably need to be discussed. Managers must be willing to take time out from task considerations to address interpersonal issues. They may need to act as a third party to resolve interpersonal conflict. They may need to encourage more initiative or more cooperation by drawing attention to specific behaviors of specific persons which inhibit positive group action. They definitely need to share their feelings, what they like and dislike about specific behaviors of specific persons. They need to make clear their attitudes and ideas about work methods, organizational policies, etc. They need to show by example and by making statements that expression of emotion and feedback concerning interpersonal behavior are acceptable and important. Here, they need to make sure that their feedback and the feedback of their subordinates meet the guidelines for useful feedback outlined earlier.

The process of introducing feedback on interpersonal behavior is a radical change from traditional organizational practices. It is difficult and entails personal risk. The manager might seek training, perhaps outside the organization, to increase his or her skills at giving and receiving feedback. The manager needs to seek organizational support for his or her efforts. It is important to bear in mind the analogy to the feedback process concerning diet made earlier. Generally, we are sensitive only to very gross indicators such as hostile reactions of subordinates. The manager needs to become increasingly sensitive to feedback so that he or she can sort out what is meaningful. It is easy enough to mistake the pickup that sugar gives for the well-being that real food brings. It is just as easy to mistake a good feedback session for the establishment of good communication.

The point should be made that the feedback process is not a cure-all. Most managers are unaware of their own feelings, and even when they are aware, find it very difficult to specify what behavior on the part of another person gave rise to a particular feeling. Even when managers can specify a particular behavior as causing a particular feeling, there may be other factors influencing that feeling of which they are unaware. Thus, feedback may often be misleading rather than helpful. The fact that individuals are giving feedback to each other does not guarantee that interpersonal problems will be resolved; however, the absence of feedback makes resolution of interpersonal problems extremely unlikely.

Positive Reinforcement at Emery Air Freight

The particulars of the dramatic benefits of feedback to Emery mentioned earlier in the chapter serve as an apt conclusion to the discussion on feedback. The basic approach is to establish performance goals and to use positive reinforcement and feedback to shape behavior toward meeting these goals. The first step, then, is to perform a performance audit. The aims of this audit are twofold: (1) it indicates the areas in which the biggest potential payoffs exist, and (2) it convinces previously skeptical managers on quantitative grounds that there is need for substantial improvement.

As Feeney notes, "Most managers genuinely think that operations in their bailiwick are doing well; a performance audit that proves they're not comes as a real and unpleasant surprise." The performance audit is structured to ensure cooperation; managers are heroes for making the audit and are reassured that regardless of the current level of performance, they will look good if they can improve.

The managers are then given elaborate programmed instruction on recognition, rewards, and feedback. In the beginning, positive reinforcement (praise and recognition) is given frequently and as soon after the behavior to be reinforced as possible. Censure and criticism are completely avoided. Such statements as, "Joe, I liked the ingenuity you showed just now getting the crates into that container. You're running pretty consistently at 98 percent of standards and I can see why," are expected of managers.

Even with the below-par employee, the manager is positive—waiting for a period of even slight improvement and then giving recognition. What about the problem employee who does not respond to recognition and feedback? Feeney suggests that low performance in these cases is often due to conditions beyond the employee's control. In those few cases where it is not, a custom-tailored, positive-reinforcement program is often the answer.

As the desired behavior is reached, the manager increasingly relies on feedback procedures inherent to the job. Daily feedback reports on particular aspects of the job (often kept by the employees themselves) serve to reinforce. The manager continues to reinforce with praise and recognition—but infrequently and irregularly. In Feeney's experiences when daily feedback was discontinued for various reasons, performance in the periods without feedback dropped to the previous level. Thus, the internal reinforcer, the satisfaction of doing a good job, is confirmed and reinforced by the daily feedback reports and the more "artificial" reinforcement of the manager is no longer necessary.

This above example illustrates a number of principles of effective communication. It was noted that the manager needed objective feedback via the performance audit in order to see a need to change. This is the idea of "unfreezing." In conjunction with the performance audit, the importance of reassuring was noted. This is consistent with the approach to building self-esteem where the manager has clearly enforced guidelines but gives "total acceptance" to the individual within these guidelines. The negative consequences of evaluative interpersonal feedback are escaped by avoiding criticism and using objective feedback reports on performance. The control issue is deemphasized as the employees ultimately "control" themselves by generating their own feedback. Finally, the effects of specific, immediate feedback are shown as effective.

NONVERBAL COMMUNICATION AS A GATEWAY FOR THE MANAGER

The manager who is effective in interpersonal communication must be aware of the many hidden messages contained in apparently straightforward communication and must respond appropriately to these messages. These "messages" are conveyed by means other than the dictionary meanings of the words employed. That is, these "messages" are nonverbal, since they are not concerned with the meaning of the words but rather with such things as facial expressions, gestures, tone of voice, etc.

Looking back at the example of Bill and Cecil, we can appreciate the importance of nonverbal communication. Bill picked up cues from Cecil that Cecil was challenging his authority. These cues or nonverbal messages had to do with the way Cecil was standing, the tone of his voice, his continued erratic performance, etc. At no point did Cecil actually say he was challenging Bill's authority, since this was part of the game.

Being sensitive to the nonverbal message, Bill avoided the challenge nonverbally. Bill did this by joking with Cecil, by communicating Adult concern, by communicating support (the box of raisins), etc. If Bill replies to Cecil's challenge, he is playing Cecil's game and Cecil's game is destructive. If Bill exposes Cecil's game (points out to Cecil that he feels challenged, etc.), Cecil may become more defensive. Cecil's game is itself defensive and to expose it is likely to threaten Cecil.

Importance of Nonverbal Communication

The importance of nonverbal communication cannot be overemphasized. A study by Albert Mehrabian (1970) concerned with the influence of attitudes brings this point home dramatically. He found that only 7 percent of attitude change was accounted for by the verbal content of the message, whereas 38 percent was accounted for by vocal characteristics (rate of speech, inflection, quality, etc.) and 55 percent was accounted for by facial expression. This makes sense when one considers that the nonverbal aspects of the communication reveal the enthusiasm, sincerity, and trustworthiness of the sender as well as how the sender feels about the receiver.

Usually nonverbal aspects of communication (such as body posture, eye contact, distance from the receiver, voice inflection, rate of speech, gesture, emphasis of particular words, silence, etc.) are not calculated. Because they are not calculated, they tend to be a better indicator of what a person truly thinks than the words the person uses. An example cited by Edward Hall (1959) illustrates how the nonverbal use of space and time often communicate more than the words employed in conversation.

Hall was assigned the job of finding out what the chances were of nondiscriminatory practices being adopted by different city departments. He set up interviews with each department head. Every department head expressed willingness to adopt nondiscriminatory labor practices; however, Hall concluded that in only one case was there a chance for change. How did he come to this conclusion? By observing how they used the silent language of space and time. Department heads were informed in advance of the meeting time and that the meeting would take at least an hour; nevertheless, appointments were forgotten, long waits in outer offices were common, and the length of the interview was cut down in most cases to ten or fifteen minutes. Further, Hall was kept at an impersonal distance during the interview and in only one case did the department head come from behind the desk. It was this person who, in fact, was open to change. The implication of this example is that one can more often trust what people do (communicate nonverbally) than what they say.

Nonverbal Communication of Status

The manager who wants to influence compliant behavior from others may seek to use nonverbal communication to underscore his or her status. Often people will "unconsciously" respond to nonverbal displays of status, although they may resist more obvious control. On the other hand, the manager who wants to facilitate open communication should eliminate displays of status.

Given the importance of nonverbal communication, let us describe some aspects of nonverbal communication important to managers. Status or power is often communicated nonverbally. The size of the office, whether one has a personal secretary, where one sits when a group is meeting (the high-status person generally sits at the end of the table), whether the manager requires subordinates to come to his or her office for discussions, interrupting another person's activities or speech, having the last word in a conversation, talking a higher percentage of the time than others in a conversation, etc.—all are nonverbal indicators of status or power. When a manager uses these nonverbal communications, he or she is saying—intentionally or unintentionally—"acknowledge that I am more important or more powerful than you and pay me the proper respect." That is, the manager is communicating nonverbally that he or she expects to control the relationship.

Contradictory Messages

This brings us to another important aspect of nonverbal communication: the case where the nonverbal message contradicts the verbal message. The manager who says, "I want you to express your ideas openly with me," but also communicates nonverbally that he or she expects agreement is sending contradictory messages. As mentioned above, if the messages are contradictory, the nonverbal message probably is closer to the sender's "real" feelings since it is much more difficult to control. Indeed, the sender often is unaware that he or she is sending contradictory messages.

The contradiction of nonverbal and verbal messages constitutes what we have called "games." In the above case, the subordinate who openly discusses only those issues on which he or she agrees with the manager is playing the manager's game. The subordinate who openly refuses to play the manager's game by actually voicing disagreement with the manager threatens the manager. When managers are threatened, they are likely to defend themselves by attacking the less powerful subordinates.

This "power or status" game (which we have called "ingratiation" and "conformity" on the subordinate's part) seems to be the most prevalent organizational game. The manager who refuses to play the power game can establish interpersonal trust with subordinates but may prove threatening to superiors.

Nonverbal Communication between Subordinates

The awareness of nonverbal communication can also help the manager detect interpersonal conflicts between subordinates. A manager can easily observe such clues as: (1) who talks to whom; (2) who interrupts whom; (3) who listens to whom; and (4) what is the frequency of eye contact. These uncomplicated nonverbal messages are likely to reveal the type of interpersonal relations existing between the various subordinates. Such an awareness may prove invaluable in facilitating cooperation among them.

NONDIRECTIVE COUNSELING AS A GATEWAY FOR THE MANAGER

In the process of giving and receiving feedback, the manager is likely to uncover "problem" areas of subordinates, peers, or superiors. The manager who is able to help the other person solve his or her own "problem" is contributing to the quality of interpersonal relations as well as organizational effectiveness.

The Nature of Nondirective Counseling

Nondirective counseling is an approach to providing help which can prove particularly useful to the manager. With this approach, the manager is concerned with helping the person examine his or her own ideas, feelings, and attitudes regarding the "problem." This is done by listening attentively, asking appropriate questions, and in general providing support for the person. The manager essentially is providing a "sounding board" for the person, enabling the person to think through the problem.

The manager needs to be nonevaluative, nonmanipulative, and nondogmatic. He or she needs to accept the person without criticizing or even implying criticism.

This is because the person with the problem is probably feeling tense and irritable anyway. More specifically, the manager guides the conversation by questions, restatements, silences, and indications that he or she is following and is interested.

Responses such as "I see" or "um hmm" tend to indicate attentiveness. This can be emphasized by posture (e.g., leaning forward) and facial expression. Silence, in combination with nonverbal expressions such as eye contact, indicates willingness to listen. Restatements indicate that the manager has correctly heard the other person and also gives the other person a chance to clarify what was meant. Questions can lead the other person to explore other areas related to the problem.

An Example of Nondirective Counseling

Let us take as an example Joe's exploration of his feelings about his boss. Joe comes to Fred and expresses dissatisfaction about their mutual boss, George:

Joe: "You know, I really get frustrated working for George sometimes."

Fred: "What do you mean, frustrated?"

Joe: "Well, I don't feel that George values my opinions."

Fred: "What makes you say that?"

Joe: "I don't know. I just don't feel that he listens to me."

Fred: "You don't feel that he listens to you?"

Joe: "Well, it seems like everytime I have something to discuss with him, he has some meeting to go to or prepare for."

Fred: "That frustrates you?"

Joe: "Yeah."

Fred: "Well, that is a frustrating experience, having something to discuss with him and then not being able to communicate it."

Joe: "I guess it isn't really that. I mean sometimes he does listen."

Fred: "But?"

Joe: "But, somehow I just don't get through to him."

Fred: "Um hmm."

Joe: "I mean he understands what I say, but somehow I go away feeling it wasn't very important."

Fred: "You think that George feels your ideas are not important?"

Joe: "Yeah, and when I walk away from the discussion I wonder what I had to say that was so important."

Fred: "You wonder whether your ideas are important?"

Joe: "Kind of. It's like when I talk to George I don't really make him see how strongly I feel."

Fred: _____ (Listens silently)

Joe: "I get self-conscious and I don't say things the way I want to."

Fred: "Why do you suppose that happens?"

Joe: "I don't know."

Fred: "What would be your guess?"

Joe: "George is just the type of person who I have trouble talking to."

Fred: "Does anybody else affect you that way?"

Joe: "No. . . ."

Fred: "Nobody else makes you feel self-conscious?"

Joe: "The only other person that I can think of is my father-in-law."

Fred: "Somehow George and your father-in-law affect you the same way."

Joe: "My father-in-law, Man, he is a difficult person. . . ." (Laughs nervously)

Fred: "In what way?"

Joe: "He's a doctor, and I always get the feeling that he wanted his son-in-law to be a doctor or something."

Fred: "You feel that your father-in-law is dissatisfied with you because you aren't a doctor?"

Joe: "Or at least some kind of professional."

Fred: "Does that make any sense in terms of George?"

Joe: "Maybe . . . George wants me to be something that I'm not."

Fred: "You think that George wants you to be something that you are not?"

Joe: "Well . . . I never finished college and I think George sees that as negative."

Fred: "You do?"

Joe: "I don't know. . . . But he's so demanding. Everything has to be just so. Just like my father-in-law."

Fred: "And that makes you feel self-conscious?"

Joe: "I just don't know whether I can live up to those demands. I get so uptight. I guess I just get tongue-tied."

Fred: "Um hmm."

Joe: "I guess that's it. What should I do, Fred?"

Fred: "What do you think you should do, Joe?"

Joe: "I don't know. Somehow I've got to learn to be less 'uptight' with George."

Fred: "What would help?"

Joe: "If you could just talk about things . . . other than business. Like, I don't know, football or movies or something."

Fred: "Um hmm."

Joe: "Yeah, I guess I'll try that."

Let us look closely at this example in order to see that even though the nondirective approach appears simple, there are many pitfalls to avoid. Fred works with Joe and probably has a pretty good idea that Joe's frustration stems from his being "uptight" when he talks with George. What if Fred simply advises Joe that he needs to relax and say what he has to say; that is, form a relationship with George rather than waiting until something is really pressing before he talks with him? Since this is Fred's analysis (not Joe's), Joe is less likely to accept the analysis. He may become defensive since Fred is setting himself up as being superior to Joe; he knows Joe's problem better than Joe. Even when Joe directly asks Fred what he should do, Fred carefully avoids giving advice. Such advice giving generally leads to a game which Eric Berne (1964) calls "Yes, But," and Joe is likely to search for counterarguments to Fred's advice. So Joe may reply to such advice, "Yes, but George isn't willing to talk about anything except strictly business."

Fred also was careful not to ally himself with Joe by agreeing that George is hard to approach. Such an agreement would provide a convenient "out" for Joe. He could conclude that the problem lay with George and remain dissatisfied. Even Fred's agreement that not being listened to was frustrating provides a possible "out" for Joe. By expressing his frustration to Fred, Joe can reduce his dissatisfaction temporarily without ever getting to the heart of the problem. Apparently, Joe recognizes that the problem is not completely external and thus is not content to stop at that point.

Fred's probe, "Does anybody else affect you that way?" is an attempt to move from an apparent dead end. Joe is unable to get a handle on why he finds George difficult to talk to, so Fred looks for another way for Joe to investigate the problem. Apparently, it is easier for Joe to examine his relationship with his father-in-law.

This is indicated by Joe's apparent lack of insight into the question, "Why do you suppose this happens?" and the follow-up question "What would be your guess?"

Upon returning to Joe's relationship to George, Joe is somewhat tentative. He initially responds to Fred's questions with questions himself: "Maybe . . ." and "I think George sees that as negative." Fred carefully refrains from giving his opinions, simply reflecting Joe's tentativeness by questioning whether Joe really believes his own statements. Finally, Joe makes the insightful statement: "He's so demanding." This is the key statement of the discussion and sensing this Fred makes an interpretation: "And that makes you feel self-conscious?"—a leading question. It may have been more appropriate for Fred to have simply allowed Joe to speak for his own feelings. In this situation, Fred correctly sensed that Joe was now ready to see his own side of the problem.

The danger of such an interpretation is that Joe may retreat from examining his part of the problem, i.e., become defensive by disputing the interpretation or by playing "Yes, But." For example, Joe might reply, "Yes, but who wouldn't feel self-conscious when faced with such a demanding person?" Also, Joe may agree with the interpretation when it is inaccurate. Perhaps Joe becomes angry at George, represses his anger, and withdraws without realizing that the withdrawal is an unconscious expression of his repressed anger. Thus, any leading or interpretive question may have bad results and the helper is wise to refrain from interpretation.

SUMMARY

Interpersonal trust, nonverbal communication, listening, feedback, and nondirective counseling serve as gateways to effective communication.

Interpersonal trust is a prerequisite to open and accurate interpersonal communication. The manager should build associates' trust for his or her fairness and integrity. By so doing, the manager can establish the constructive cycle which brings effective communication.

Listening requires an active thinking receiver. To develop the skill of listening requires hard work and careful thought.

The manager can use intrapersonal feedback such as emotion, sleep habits, muscle tension, and posture to increase self-awareness.

Effective feedback is descriptive, specific, and directed toward behavior which the receiver can do something about. Timing, clarity, and openness to feedback also determine how effective it will be.

The initiation of the feedback process in the first place is sometimes difficult. Asking for feedback on particular points at particular times certainly encourages others to give feedback. Asking questions, using nonverbal clues, and remaining silent at appropriate times are also methods of encouraging feedback. Perhaps the most important method of gaining feedback is the demonstration of willingness and ability to respond positively to it.

Nonverbal communication is much more impactful in terms of influence and more accurately reflects the true feelings of the sender than what the sender says (verbal communication). By observing such things as tone of voice, eye contact, who talks to whom, etc., the manager may be able to effectively "manage" interpersonal relations.

Nondirective counseling has many similarities to the feedback process. Here, the manager is concerned with helping the person solve a problem. Thus, rather than giving or receiving feedback, the manager gives support and encourages self-exploration. The manager encourages self-exploration by using silence, restatements, questions, and indications of attentiveness. Both the feedback process and nondirective counseling require nonmanipulative, nondogmatic, nonevaluative communication in order to be effective.

IMPORTANT TERMS AND CONCEPTS

interpersonal trust, constructive trust cycle, destructive trust cycle, listening, intrapersonal feedback, interpersonal feedback, performance audit, nonverbal communication, contradictory messages, nondirective communication

REVIEW QUESTIONS

1. How can a manager build an atmosphere of trust in his or her organization?
2. How would the ten keys to listening apply to the manager in working with employees?
3. Give an example of descriptive rather than evaluative feedback.
4. How does effective feedback improve interpersonal relations?
5. When somebody comes to you with a problem, why is it important not to solve the problem for the person (i.e., tell the person what to do)?
6. When would it be appropriate to solve the person's problem by telling him or her what to do?
7. Take the Bentwick-Farrow situation originally discussed in Chapter 3. What can Farrow do to establish feedback effectively? How might this improve the organization's effectiveness?

8. If the feedback process is as effective as the Emery Freight Corporation's experience suggests, why don't more companies use it?
9. What are the most obvious nonverbal clues which you have observed in your contacts during the past day?
10. Under what conditions would nondirective counseling be least effective? Most effective?

INCIDENT: OPENING COMMUNICATION GATES

Fran: "Mr. Colbert, I have a problem with one of my crew members I'd like to discuss with you. I just can't seem to be able to get Bart to cooperate. He seems to dislike me."

Mr. Colbert: "Fran, you seem to be rather upset about it."

Fran: "Yes, it has been on my mind day and night for weeks. He is always doing something to irritate me."

Mr. Colbert: "You think that he is intentionally trying to irritate you?"

Fran: "Well, yes I do. He knows that I expect the work area to be kept clean. Yet his area is always dirty. He will get 95 percent of a job done before the deadline and then set the job aside until the deadline is passed. When I try to talk to him he only grins that impish little grin and makes his hollow promises to do better."

Mr. Colbert: "You feel angry at him because he seems to be uncooperative."

Fran: "I try to keep from showing my anger, but yes, I get hopping mad. I think he has some hidden resentment for me. Maybe it's a personality clash. I just don't know."

Mr. Colbert: "I see."

Fran: "What do you think the problem could be?"

Mr. Colbert: "It could be any number of things. Perhaps you should have a discussion with Bart."

Fran: "I try to talk with him, but he just won't listen. When I talk with him he just gives some phoney excuse."

Mr. Colbert: "He always tries to defend himself."

Fran: "Yes. Of course, I have to admit that I really talked to him only about something he's done wrong for a long time. I guess I'm letting this thing interfere with the usual discussion that I like to have with each of my people.

Mr. Colbert: "I see."

Fran: "Perhaps I should try to start off on a new foot with Bart. How do you think he would react if I went over to his station and just had a chat with him about the work in general?"

Mr. Colbert: "Sounds like a good idea. But, you know it may take several tries before he responds. It's not as though you were starting from scratch you know."

Fran: "Yes, we have built up some resentment over these past months. But someone has to break this cycle and I think it should be me."

1. What gateways to communication do you find in this incident?
2. Evaluate Mr. Colbert as a communicator.
3. What other approach(s) might he have taken?

EXERCISE 1

Your instructor will appoint a class member to describe two pictures.

1. During the description of the first picture you may not ask any questions. The sender of the descriptive message will turn away from the class so that the visual cues will be minimized. You are to make no sounds during the time of this description.
2. During the description of the second picture the sender will receive any feedback you desire. You may make any sound or statement or ask any question you wish.

EXERCISE 2: COUNSELING

Form groups of three. Each person then should think of some problem which he or she would like help on. Person A then begins by presenting a problem. Person B helps A using a nondirective approach. Person C is an observer. Allow about ten minutes for the consultation. Then the observer should make comments on what happened (e.g., how effective the helper was). The observer should attempt to make comments which constitute effective feedback. A discussion could follow. If time allows, everyone should take each role once.

EXERCISE 3: FEEDBACK

Form groups of five or six. One person then gets in the center of the circle. The other members give positive feedback to that person. Each person, in turn, goes into the center.

Following this, a second round can be done involving "negative" feedback. After this round, a discussion concerning reactions, feelings, etc. about the process is appropriate.

BIBLIOGRAPHY

Berne, E.: *Games People Play* (New York: Grove Press, Inc., 1964).

Borman, E., W. Howell, R. Nichols, and G. Shapiro: *Interpersonal Communication in the Modern Organization* (Englewood Cliffs, N.J.: Prentice-Hall, Inc., 1969).

Feldenkries, Moshe: *Awareness through Movement: Health Exercises for Personal Growth* (New York: Harper & Row, Publishers, Incorporated, 1972).

Hall, Edward: *The Silent Language* (Garden City, N.Y.: Doubleday & Company, Inc., 1959).

Haney, W. V.: *Communication and Organizational Behavior: Text and Cases* (Homewood, Ill.: Richard D. Irwin, Inc., 1973).

Laird, Dugan: "Why Everything Is All Loused Up, Really (And What to Do about It)," *Training in Business and Industry,* March 1971.

Mehrabian, Albert: *Tactics of Social Influence* (Englewood Cliffs, N.J.: Prentice-Hall, Inc., 1970).

Nichols, R. G.: Listening Is a 10-Part Skill, *Nation's Business,* vol. 45, pp. 56–60, 1957.

12

COMMUNICATION FOR INTERPERSONAL INFLUENCE

A primary purpose of communication by a manager is that of influencing others. This chapter discusses how the manager can attain and develop interpersonal influence and influence others to develop and utilize their talents.

THE INFLUENCE PROCESS

As was suggested in the previous chapter, the traditional business organization gains the commitment of the individual to company objectives via hierarchical power. The relationship is such that it implies the threat of force if the individual's behavior is not consistent with company objectives. However, a manager who is interested can gain commitment to company objectives in other ways. These options come under the broad heading of interpersonal influence.

Influence of Behavior through Shaping

Because of the power of the position, the top manager potentially has more influence than any other single member of the organization. He or she can "shape" behavior by rewarding appropriate behavior and not rewarding (or penalizing) inappropriate behavior; encourage people to model his or her behavior; counsel and/or coach people; restructure the organization, redesign jobs, introduce new policies and change old ones; and involve people in the decision-making process. Depending on the target person and the skills and awareness of the manager, any one method or combination of methods may be successful.

Shaping of behavior is probably the single most powerful method of influencing behavior available to the manager. "Shaping" is a technical, psychological term derived from learning theory. It involves the reinforcement (or reward) of those behaviors which are consistent with the desired behaviors and then shaping the behavior by gradually deferring reinforcement until the behavior by successive approximations gradually approaches the desired behavior. For example, Skinner taught pigeons to play Ping-Pong by shaping their behavior. First, they received reinforcement, some grain every time they approached the table; then later they were reinforced only when they actually were on the table; then only when they approached the paddle; then only when they picked it up; then only when they hit the ball; and finally only when they won the point.

Suppose the manager is trying to shape subordinates to adopt a new style of management. The manager needs to be clear about what steps the subordinates should pass through and what specific behaviors constitute reaching a particular step. Given this knowledge, the manager must reinforce the subordinate's behavior as it successfully approximates the new style of management. That is, after the attainment of a particular step, the manager withholds reinforcement until the subordinate approaches the next step. The assumption when only "shaping" is used is that the increments are small enough that the target person is able to move from one step to the next on his or her own. It may very well be that some or all of the other methods mentioned above (counseling, involvement in decision making, modeling, and restructuring) are necessary in order to facilitate the progression of the subordinate from one step to the next.

Influencing Behavior through Modeling

A second approach to influencing behavior is by *encouraging modeling*. The effectiveness of this approach lies in the strength of the identification (personal attraction) toward the manager. Modeling is an extremely powerful adjunct to shaping. The manager who is well-liked and/or respected, who can demonstrate success with a particular managerial style, and who also clearly understands and structures the acquisition of this style for subordinates is likely to successfully influence their behavior.

Influencing through Counseling and Coaching

Third, the manager can *counsel and/or coach* people. The basic dynamics of counseling is similar to shaping. The manager encourages discussion of critical problems.

He or she shapes this discussion gradually by guiding it toward an examination of the subordinate's managerial style—using the particular incidents discussed by the subordinate as examples. The counseling/coaching process is a complex skill—many components of which are important aspects of interpersonal skills in general. We will only briefly describe this process here.

One of the primary skills of the manager-counselor is to listen to the subordinate. This means maintaining eye contact, checking out to make sure that what the subordinate has said is understood, and noting nonverbal indicators—such as tone of voice, positioning of furniture, facial expressions, etc. In addition, the manager needs to be able to "sense" what the subordinate feels, sees, and thinks—i.e., to be able to empathize with the subordinate and be able to communicate this empathy. Third, the manager needs to continually push the subordinate-counselee to be specific in discussing the managerial problems that the subordinate encounters. Fourth, the manager needs to share his or her experience with the subordinate—by self-disclosure, by expressing feelings, by confronting the subordinate's ideas and attitudes, and by giving the subordinate alternative ways of looking at the same situation. Finally, the manager who has guided the subordinate through a maze of self-exploratory discussions can follow through by helping the subordinate plan an action program.

Personal Influencing

A fourth approach to interpersonal influence open to a manager is to use personal influence to persuade the subordinate to adopt new behaviors. As long as the subordinate does not fear managerial action if he or she does not comply, the subordinate may become committed to the behavior *after* he or she initiates it. That is, attitude change may be and often is preceded by behavioral change (Zimbardo and Ebbesen, 1970).

Influencing through Participation

Fifth, a manager can gain commitment from the subordinate by getting him or her to participate in decision making. There is considerable research which documents this assertion. This may be resisted by the subordinate, who may wish to continue in the role of the Child (in T.A. concepts). If the subordinate enters into the decision-making process in an Adult way, it becomes very difficult for him or her not to support the decision. The skills and difficulties of reaching truly participative decisions which are also of high quality are discussed in Part Three.

Influencing through Changing the Work Environment

Finally, the manager can influence the subordinate's behavior by *changing the work "environment."* The manager might change policies, procedures, the formal organizational chart of responsibility and authority, the geographical or physical location and/or layout of offices, etc., or he or she might introduce technological change. All these can be seen as influence attempts where the manager is trying to influence the behavior of the subordinates.

As detailed in previous chapters, when the manager unilaterally decides to change the work environment, he or she may create an adverse reaction in the subordinates. Participative decision making (PDM) is a powerful adjunct to changes in the work environment. Here, PDM and environmental changes may operate supportively to produce the desired behavioral changes.

Each type of influence described above is accomplished by interpersonal communication; each occurs within the context of an interpersonal relationship; and each has consequences which affect the relationship and subsequent communication. For example, shaping is done by giving positive comments, attention, or recognition immediately following a "hoped for" response by the subordinate. This shaping takes place within the context of the relationship. If the manager has generally been critical and/or aloof, then subordinates may distrust positive exchanges, suspecting that the boss is "buttering them up" for some reason. If the subordinates like and respect the manager, such encouragement (reinforcement) is likely to be a powerful influence on them. Finally, the shaping has consequences on the relationship and communication.

If a positive exchange is happening, then the manager and subordinate are likely to improve their relationship. Communication is likely to be more open. Important issues are likely to be discussed instead of avoided. If the relationship is poor, the subordinate is likely to feel manipulated. In this circumstance, unless interpersonal trust is established, the use of shaping by the manager may actually work in the direction opposite to the intention of the manager. This is because, in general, people tend to resist influence attempts which they view as manipulative (Brehm, 1966).

RESISTANCE TO CHANGE

We have repeatedly pointed out that when people feel coerced or manipulated, they are likely to react negatively. Practically every managerial decision requires that someone change his or her behavior. As we saw with shaping, when a manager attempts to influence others to change, those people may feel manipulated and therefore resist the change openly or secretly. Once resistance to change has become actualized, it is much more difficult to reverse than if the manager had recognized negative attitudes and attempted to change the attitudes before implementing the actual change. In other words, behavioral resistance tends to reinforce negative attitudes and makes these attitudes more resistant to change.

Becoming Aware of Resistance

Recognizing that any proposed change may encounter resistance, the manager needs to "sound out" the target person to find out if there is resistance. The "sounding out" of the target person to find his or her initial attitudes may seem straightforward, but there are some pitfalls to avoid. The manager should structure the canvassing of attitudes so that the expression of negative attitudes does not increase the strength of these attitudes. It should be borne in mind that the public expression of attitudes tends to produce commitment to these attitudes, and once people have committed themselves to a position in front of others who are significant to them, they tend to view a change in attitudes as a sign of weakness or lack of conviction. Thus, the discussion of change should take place in a problem-solving situation where individuals do not become identified with particular ideas, but instead see themselves as part of a group problem-solving effort. Alternatively, such discussion could be private, one to one. Additionally, the manager should be cautious not to sensitize or alert the target person that an influence attempt may be coming. In this case, the target is likely to feel manipulated and resist change because of these feelings, regardless of his or her actual attitudes toward the change.

In order to illustrate the importance of sensitivity to the target person, let us examine a specific situation. Suppose that you are going to introduce a computer into your business operation. You are sophisticated enough to realize that people often resist change and you also know that acceptance of the computer must be enthusiastic and without reservation if you are to get maximum benefits from its use. You have sounded out an employee (Joe) and found his attitude to be negative although he is unable or unwilling to say why. You are now in the position of having to develop some hypotheses as to why his attitudes are negative. These hypotheses should be based on your understanding of the individual and the situation. It may be that Joe's attitude is essentially *ego-defensive*. For example, he may believe that the introduction of the computer implies that his previous job performance is inadequate. Further, he may be concerned about his ability to handle his new job. Thus, his negative attitude toward the computer may be a nonthreatening way of dealing with basic feelings of insecurity and inadequacy. It is up to you to decide, based on your dealings with Joe, whether such concerns are at the root of his attitude. It is critical that you, as manager, recognize that if the negative attitude is held for ego-defensive reasons, Joe may be content to search for ways to justify failure rather than invest his energies into trying to make the new computer operation a success.

Approaches to Overcoming Resistance to Change

One approach for the manager in this situation is to clearly place responsibility for success or failure in the hands of this key employee. Have him participate in decisions, change things which he thinks unworkable, etc., so that the possibility of blaming you or the system is eliminated. The adoption of this strategy, of course, would depend on your judgment of Joe's chances of success in such a situation. As a manager you may be unwilling to risk the success of the operation on Joe's ability to cope with this kind of responsibility. In this case, it is best to find a less demanding situation for Joe. In any event, if Joe's negative attitude is based on feelings of insecurity, arguments concerning the value of the computer are unlikely to have any effects on his attitude.

Another possibility is that Joe may be uncertain about the eventual effects of installing the computer. His negative attitude may be a result of experience or observation of other computerized operations where there were personnel cutbacks or undesirable changes in jobs such as decreased status or increased work loads. If his negative attitude is held for these reasons, then persuasive argument, information, and assurance about his eventual job may allay these fears and change his attitude.

A third possibility is that Joe's fellow workers may have a negative attitude toward the computer, and thus may have influenced Joe to hold the same attitude. In this event, Joe's attitude has the utility of making him acceptable to his fellow workers. Your attempts at influencing Joe's attitude should then take the direction of either changing his evaluation of the importance of membership in this group or of changing his perception of the importance of holding this negative attitude as a means of maintaining membership in the work group.

A fourth possibility is that Joe is not particularly negative toward the introduction of the computer per se, but is using this issue to express hostile feelings. It may be, for example, that he has resentment toward you or the company for past wrongs. If this is the case, then it is up to you to find a more productive or at least less counterproductive means for him to express hostile feelings. This situation is similar to the discussion of the expression of anger in Chapter 6. As was suggested there, the most productive strategy is to uncover the cause of the negative feelings and get Joe to express them. In this way, it may be possible to discover ways of changing the situation which may eliminate whatever is irritating Joe. Otherwise, Joe may continue to find nonproductive ways of expressing his anger.

The key point in the discussion is the necessity of anticipating resistance to change. Awareness of resistance is a necessary but not sufficient condition for successfully influencing the target person's attitude and behavior. Many times organizational objectives are in conflict with individual needs. When influence attempts are aimed at getting the individual to accept changes which in no way can be construed to be in that person's best interests, then the best the manager can do is demonstrate the fairness of the decision-making process. The decision-making process which is most likely to be seen as fair is one in which all those affected are encouraged to participate in the decision. In this case, the individual may be able to put aside his or her individual desires to pursue the course of action deemed most appropriate by the group.

THE PROCESS OF CHANGING ATTITUDES AND BEHAVIORS

We have concluded that in order to adopt an appropriate influence strategy, a manager needs to be aware of the attitudes of those he or she intends to influence. It is also important that a manager have an understanding of the process of attitude and behavior change. The conceptualization of Lewin as elaborated by Schein (1969) of the process of change is particularly useful for our purpose. Lewin suggests three stages in the change process: (1) unfreezing, creating motivation to change; (2) changing, developing new responses; and (3) refreezing, stabilizing and integrating the change.

Unfreezing

As Schein notes, changes in behavior or attitude which are central to the individual are generally resisted. Change of this sort implies giving up attitudes and/or behavior to which the individual feels commitment. The process of unfreezing needs to take into account the threat involved in changing attitudes and behavior to which a person is committed. The threat involves admitting to oneself and to others the inadequacy of one's previous attitudes and actions.

Schein suggests two basic mechanisms appropriate to unfreezing: lack of confirmation (or disconfirmation) and reduction of threat. Lack of confirmation takes place when the individual finds no support for his or her attitude or behavior. For example, an employee who has a negative attitude toward work might be placed in a work group where everyone else is enthusiastic. When the employee finds no support for the negative attitude, his or her attitude is likely to decrease in intensity, or unfreeze. Disconfirmation takes place when the individual receives negative reactions to his or her attitude or behavior. Thus, in the above situation, the employee's negative attitude might be disconfirmed by the other workers' pointing out that the employee would be satisfied if he or she would act differently. The disconfirmation acts to unfreeze the negative attitude.

Another type of disconfirmation is the specification of inconsistencies in the target person's attitudes and/or behavior. The manager might say, for example, "Look, you have been asking for a more challenging job and now when you get the opportunity you don't want it." The specification of an inconsistency may lead the change target to question his or her attitudes and behavior. Disconfirmation acts to unfreeze previous attitudes and open the individual to learning new behavior and attitudes.

Unfreezing may also take place through the reduction of threat. In the superior-subordinate relationship, the manager can assure the subordinate of support in the change effort. Thus, in the case of the introduction of a computer, the manager could assure the subordinate that he or she will not be laid off, that performance expectations will not be rigid during the transitional period, etc. Such assurances tend to facilitate openness to change.

Changing

After unfreezing the individual is open to information which he or she would have rejected previously. The change process itself involves actually using this new information to arrive at new or changed attitudes and behavior. Schein suggests two forms for acquiring this information: identification and scanning.

Identification involves getting information from a single source or model. In order for the identification to be positive, the model must have personal attraction rather than merely position, power, or expertise. If the target person trusts and is attracted to the influencer (model), then the new behavior learned from the model will be a result of seeing the world through the model's eyes. In this case, the change may be dramatic. On the other hand, if the target feels helpless in the face of the model, he or she may decide to copy the attitudes and behavior of the model rather than submit to continual disconfirmation of his or her old attitudes and behavior. In this event, the new behavior is likely to be imitative and rigid because the target does not have any attachment to the behavior, merely adopting it to avoid disconfirmation. Effective influence is associated with the subtle use of power.

Information may also be gained from a number of sources where a strong emotional relationship does not exist. This *scanning of information* involves more time and energy, but ultimately the behavioral change is likely to be a better adjustment for the individual since it is internal rather than external.

Refreezing

After adopting new behaviors and attitudes to replace the old disconfirmed ones, there remains the question of whether the new ones have payoff. If not, these new attitudes are themselves likely to be disconfirmed. Thus, for attitude change to be successful, the new attitudes and behavior have to be assimilated or refrozen. The influencer must make sure that he or she reinforces the change in the target person.

As the change process is actually implemented (for example, the computer is introduced, accompanied by changes in job specifications and/or changes in the social structure), the employees as well as the manager are faced with learning new behavior and attitudes. It is often the case in introducing change that things get worse before they get better. People, under the stress of learning new behaviors, are likely to have second thoughts about the change. Questions are likely to arise: Will it really work? Am I capable of performing the new job or adjusting to my new role in the organization? Thus, the commitment to change is likely to be sorely tested in the change process itself.

Given that the employees are persuaded of the necessity and importance of the change, what can a manager do to promote the successful change of behavior? Let us take Fred, a typical worker, and look at his situation as he undergoes change. Fred experiences many frustrations. Since there is no established routine, he makes mistakes and often has to redo work he has already done. He is rapidly becoming discouraged since he is not getting the satisfaction of achieving results that he did prior to the change.

In this situation, the manager needs to distinguish between discouragement and resistance to the change effort. If Fred is simply discouraged, then the manager needs to find ways of giving psychological support. The manager should find ways to reinforce the subordinate's effort to change since the effort may not presently be reinforced by results. One thing the manager can do is redefine the situation to Fred by pointing out that acquiring new skills takes time. The manager can point out to Fred that learning means willingness to make mistakes, and that if he keeps at it he will eventually succeed. If Fred is showing progress, the manager can point this out also. Perhaps Fred needs more than psychological support. The manager might supply assistance in terms of on-the-job training or temporarily decreasing Fred's responsibilities until he is more able to cope with the new situation. The manager might also invite Fred to suggest ideas which would increase his effectiveness. As pointed out before, in addition to the possibility of finding better ways to accomplish the change, this managerial approach is likely to increase commitment to change, and thus Fred is likely to continue to expend effort even if he is having difficulty.

If Fred is beginning to resist the change, then the manager may need to resort to stronger measures. For example, the manager might communicate to Fred disappointment in Fred's lack of commitment to the change effort. Fred might be reminded that the entire department or company is depending on Fred to hold up his end, and that if Fred puts a little more effort into his work, everything will work out fine. That is, Fred might be reminded of his part in the decision and of his commitment to carry through with the decision. This type of pressure is not likely to produce commitment if Fred did not originally accept the change effort; however, individual and group pressure of this variety may reestablish Fred's resolve to succeed if he was part of the decision process in the first place.

There are numerous studies which show that verbal agreement with a change and actual behavioral change are often not related. The results of these studies may be best summarized by noting that when emotional forces are in conflict with the change, intellectual agreement may not be sufficient to produce behavioral change. That is, verbal agreement to the change effort may be in conflict with emotional feelings of inadequacy (low self-esteem). This observation underscores the importance of the manager's role in the change process by pointing out that verbal agreement associated with the initial attitude change is not enough. The manager should expect that resistance to change may arise at some point in the change process even if he or she has carefully gained acceptance prior to the actual implementation of change.

There are many experimental and actual organizational studies which have shown that often behavioral change precedes attitude change. In a study of the Weldon Company, very dramatic changes in job performance and production were made while employees still held negative attitudes toward the company (Marrow et al., 1967). Apparently, openness to attitude change (unfreezing) often allows behavioral change, which then eventually produces the attitude change necessary to sustain the behavioral change.

ORGANIZATIONAL LIMITATIONS TO INTERPERSONAL INFLUENCE

Resistance in the Organizational Environment

In addition to resistance to change, experience has shown that there are certain organizational limitations to the manager's use of interpersonal influence and communication. The limitations of interpersonal influence in an organization stem from the fact that decisions, policies, and actions of individuals outside the immediate work relationship may strongly affect both the influencer and the target person. Many of the individual's attitudes which managers wish to influence are rooted in orientations toward the company, supervisor, and work group and are unlikely to be influenced significantly unless there are organizationwide changes in attitudes and behavior. The results of a study by Flieshman (1953) in the early fifties may clarify this assertion.

In this study, the first-line supervisors at International Harvester attended leadership classes aimed at increasing their sensitivity and consideration for their subordinates. Immediately following the course, the attitudes of the supervisors were significantly more considerate toward subordinates. Six months after training, the attitudes of the supervisors had shifted in the reverse direction; they had become significantly less considerate of subordinates than before training. Further, supervisors favored significantly greater emphasis on enforcing particular rules and procedures regardless of the needs and talents of subordinates than they had immediately following the training period. Thus, the long-run result of the training program (a major influence attempt) was to change attitudes in a direction opposite to that intended!

Interviews and observations of supervisors suggest the following explanation of the results. Immediately after training, the supervisors' attitudes were much more considerate toward subordinates than before and they behaved accordingly. The subordinates apparently saw such consideration as permissiveness and attempted to take advantage of their supervisors. The supervisors, under pressure from their bosses and in competition for promotions and raises with other supervisors, felt it necessary to curb the irresponsible behavior of the subordinates. Relations between supervisors and subordinates deteriorated to the point that only a very controlling leadership style seemed viable. In this case, then, the attitude change in the supervisors was short-lived at least partially because the attitudes and behavior of subordinates and superiors did not change.

The results of the above study point to a very common difficulty of first-line supervisors. In Transactional Analysis terms, the supervisor wants to move the relationship from one characterized by Parent-Child transactions to one characterized by Adult-Adult transactions. This entails delegating increasing amounts of responsibility and allowing (encouraging) free choice by subordinates within this area of responsibility. One of the necessary conditions of this change in the supervisor-subordinate relationship is that the supervisor can support this increase in responsibility. If the subordinate suggests reasonable changes in policies, need for maintenance, or redesign of the job, etc., the supervisor needs to be able to follow through on such suggestions. Otherwise, the subordinate has no way of exercising his or her responsibility, and therefore the relationship will not change.

Lack of Influence by the Supervisor

In many organizations the supervisors themselves have little influence over the factors which affect their subordinates' jobs. Until supervisors achieve such influence—that is, until the nature of their relationships to their superiors is changed—they are in an obvious bind. The conditions necessary for improving their relationships with their subordinates are outside of their control. The bind of first-line supervisors points out the limitation of interpersonal influence imposed on individuals by the organization and implies that organizationwide change in the nature of relationships is often necessary before first-line supervisors can create more effective relations.

Restraints of Group Interdependence

In addition, the interdependence of groups and departments limits the amount of unilateral change possible in a given group or department. A couple of examples may be helpful as illustrations. One department in a rather traditional organization increased the responsibility of secretaries, giving them some coordinating and administrative functions. With this increase in responsibilities, the secretaries naturally pushed for a corresponding increase in pay through reclassification of their jobs. The reclassification was eventually vetoed because other departments were worried that their secretaries would become unhappy and push for similar changes in their responsibilities and pay. The veto came as a shock and a great disappointment. Two secretaries subsequently quit the company and the other applied for a transfer.

Another example of this is related to a maintenance department. Responding to the expressed desires of the other people in the maintenance department, the department head arranged for paychecks to be distributed on Thursday afternoon so that the employees or their spouses could deposit them in the bank the next day rather than waiting until the following Monday. The rest of the departments continued distributing checks on Friday because they were afraid that the absentee rate would be high on the Friday following payday if the checks were distributed on Thursday. This situation produced a considerable strain on the payroll department since workers aware of the favorite treatment given to the maintenance people focused their dissatisfaction on those they felt were responsible.

In both of these examples, managers were trying to increase their influence with the workers by responding to the needs of the workers. In both situations, the end results were far more negative than positive because the managers failed to consider how their actions would affect the rest of the organization. Again, we see that attitudes and behaviors throughout the organization affect and often limit the potential amount of interpersonal influence between any two members of the organization.

THE ATTAINMENT OF INTERPERSONAL INFLUENCE IN ORGANIZATIONS

We have suggested that the traditional business organization is a difficult context in which to exercise interpersonal competence. One way of circumventing these restrictions is through the attainment of interpersonal influence with organizational members who have power.

The attainment of interpersonal influence in an organizational setting is an art rather than a science. We shall briefly discuss the influence or political structure of organizations and follow this discussion with a brief description of a few techniques which might be useful in organizations.

Organizational Politics

Anyone who has observed the dynamics of organizations realizes that almost invariably factions form. People who have gathered together for some common purpose or goal also have individual goals. Factions are often formed by individuals who perceive that their individual goals are similar relative to the remaining members of the organization. The most clear-cut example of this is the factions which are formed along departmental lines. Clearly, the members of an engineering department, in addition to sharing common goals associated with the organization and the engineering function, have individual goals such as better pay, better working conditions, promotions, etc. These individual goals are likely to be served best by a politically strong engineering department. That is, the greater the influence of the engineering department relative to other departments in the organization, the more likely that budgetary requests of the department will be met. This will further the attainment of individual goals by making available more money for salaries and equipment.

In addition to the force of common political interests, the usual physical segregation in the company often results in departmental members associating almost exclusively with each other. Other forces which are usually operating to factionalize organizations along departmental lines include interactions involved in the daily work routine and similarity of personalities. Personalities of people in a particular department tend to be relatively similar because people tend to choose jobs which fit their personalities.

In addition to such departmental factions, less strongly defined factions are also likely to develop. These factions often develop along the dimensions of conservative-liberal, age, sex, race, religion, or attraction to a particular organizational leader.

Within these rather broad factions, subgroups usually form. For example, within the engineering department, there are likely to be several political subgroups or coalitions. Again, these are often formed on the basis of common political interests. Just as the engineering department competes for scarce resources with other departments in the organization, so coalitions within the department are also in competition. This intradepartmental competition may be over which projects should be funded, what operations should be expanded, etc. Again, coalitions might also form because certain members attend the same church, bowl in the same bowling league, have similar educational backgrounds, have common social interests, etc. It is important to note that although such factions and coalitions may initially be formed for nonpolitical reasons, almost invariably they become political in nature. These coalitions and factions generally come to have either formal or informal leaders or both. These leaders form the network which might be called the power structure of the organization. It is within this context that interpersonal influence takes place.

Emergent Leadership

Hollander (1961) has suggested a theoretical framework for describing the emergence of leadership in groups with no formally appointed leader which has implication for attaining influence in organizations. The main thrust of this theory deals with the accumulation of personal credits or what Hollander labels "idiosyncracy credits." Before there is an agreed-upon group leader, there is a power vacuum which draws the strong personalities of the group to compete for the leadership position. The winner of this competition is likely to be the person who has accumulated the most credits. A potential leader may antagonize the group by being more assertive than his or her credits justify. One builds credits by being a good listener, by making positive contributions to the group, by building on the ideas of others without being overly critical, by conforming to whatever practices or norms the group informally establishes, etc. Thus the emergent leader is not likely to be the one who has talked the most, or who has been the most innovative, or who dresses the most conservatively or nonconservatively, etc. Initially, such a person takes the role as a positive, active group member whose actions do not appear to be aimed at attaining the leadership position. When this person perceives that he or she may be accepted as the leader (i.e., has accumulated enough credits), then he or she takes on the more assertive, aggressive manner associated with leadership.

In an organizational setting, each member of a faction or coalition brings certain initial credits to the group. These include position power in the formal organization, reputation of competency and sincerity, known friends or alliances within the organization, etc. It is often these initial credits which determine the potential leaders. The initial role that a potential leader takes is thus determined by his or her initial credits in the group relative to other group members. One may increase these credits by forming alliances or coalitions with members of the group (faction or coalition) outside of the group context.

Since this person has a hidden agenda (leadership of the group), he or she probably has some advantage over those who are not aware of the leadership struggle at a conscious level. This person's basic strategy then becomes Machiavellian (see next section of chapter), and he or she attempts to determine attitudes and positions which will be acceptable to the largest number of group members. It should be obvious from this discussion that a new organizational member is relatively unlikely to attain a leadership role in a coalition or faction since he or she possesses few credits. One's first task, if one eventually desires a leadership position, is to seek out alliances with leaders in the political power structure, to make a reputation of competency and sincerity, etc.

This brief description of organizational politics and influence is not far different from a description of national politics. It is rather cynical since it suggests that alliances, friends, and manipulation are important to the attainment of power. To balance this description, it should be noted that there are other forces in the organization where competency, nonmanipulative communication, and relationships based on considerations other than power are important. Participative decision making, management by objectives, and organizational development are all efforts to limit the scope of power politics in the organization. Readers should realize, however, whether or not they personally are concerned with attaining influence, that no organization is totally devoid of influence seekers and that such influence or power can be used constructively.

Foot-in-the-Door Technique

A simple but amazingly effective influence tactic has been labeled the "foot-in-the-door technique." The wide use of this tactic by salespeople makes it an almost universally known technique. This approach basically entails asking the target person to perform an almost innocuous favor. Encyclopedia salespeople, for example, often gain admittance to the home under the guise of taking an opinion survey. If the prospective target agrees to answer a few brief questions, the salesperson has accomplished two things. First, he or she has gained admittance into the home and established some type of rapport. Second, he or she has enlisted the aid of the target and established the willingness of the target to help. Thus, a mental set in the target person has been established which makes that person more open to the real influence attempt. The salesperson then asks if he or she might have a few minutes to show the target person his or her wares. The agreement of the target person is much more likely now that the salesperson has gained a foot in the door than it would have been had this been the initial move of the salesperson.

Conditioning

The salesperson has already established a foot in the door, and more importantly, is also conditioning an acquiescent response. That is, each agreement or acquiescent response of the target is positively responded to with a smile and an affable manner so that agreement becomes a conditioned response. The salesperson can condition the agreement response in many ways. He or she might simply ask leading questions which are constructed so that the target is likely to agree. For example, "Don't you think that these illustrations are effective?" The salesperson might look for nonverbal cues showing interest in particular aspects of the product and then elaborate on these. He or she might try to determine those attitudes which are held by the target person which are consistent with the influence attempt and play on these attitudes. Thus, a standard probe for an encyclopedia salesperson is: "Don't you think that your children could profit from the use of these encyclopedias?" With such a question, the salesperson is attempting to hook the target person by playing on the target's desires for his or her children to gain a good education. When it comes time for the sales pitch, the target is much more likely to buy since he or she has been programmed to agree with the salesperson.

The foot-in-the-door technique and conditioning are easily adapted to the organizational scene. As was mentioned in the description of emergent leadership, the potential leader is interested in making alliances. The foot-in-the-door technique can be used to establish these relationships. For example, the potential leader might approach the target person and ask him or her about ideas he or she has concerning some rather trivial organizational matter. The target can hardly refuse without appearing impolite. As the relationship is established, the potential leader can then attempt to find issues of agreement. This tends to condition the target to agree with the potential leader.

Since there is a good deal of evidence which supports the conclusion that people who have similar attitudes are attracted to each other, such a tactic is likely to result in the attraction of the target person to the potential leader (Byrne, 1961). At this point, the potential leader is in a position to use this conditioned agreement and attraction to gain support for his or her own ideas. Eventually, such support can be used to gain acceptance for his or her leadership of the group.

In the organizational setting, the influencer needs to be very cautious about manipulation since the target person's discovery of the manipulation is likely to prove disastrous. The salesperson is usually content to be successful in his or her one influence attempt, whereas the organizational setting does not allow such a hit-and-run strategy. Thus, such manipulation needs to be over an extended period of time and interspersed with many nonmanipulative transactions.

The "influence game" is likely to be destructive to organizational functioning since the focus is placed on the accumulation of power rather than directly on organizational goals. People are valued on the basis of their power and their orientation to various power figures in the organization rather than on the basis of their own contributions to the organization. Information is likely to be withheld and distorted since communication tends to be a move in the influence game rather than an attempt to reach organizational goals. We will address this issue in the following section on Machiavellianism. It is the opinion of the authors that the destructiveness of the influence game may be the most critical issue that present-day managers face.

INTERPERSONAL INFLUENCE BY THE MACHIAVELLIAN APPROACH

In recent years, there has accumulated strong evidence that there are certain attitudes and characteristics which are generally descriptive of individuals who are capable of interpersonal influence. The most systematic approach to understanding the nature of these individuals who have demonstrated their abilities for interpersonal influence is the research which has centered on the development of a particular test of social "psychological" attitudes called the *Machiavellian scale*—so named because many of the items on this scale are statements directly attributable to Niccolo Machiavelli. Machiavelli was a fifteenth-century political theorist who authored—among other things—*The Prince*. This treatise was written essentially as a handbook of political action for those heads of state interested in accumulating and maintaining political power.

The conclusions from thirty-eight studies reviewed by Christie and Geis (1970) indicate that high Machs (high scorers on the Machiavellian scale) manipulate more, win more, are persuaded less, and persuade others more in situations in which subjects interact face to face with others. Christie and Geis suggest that the fundamental difference between high and low Machs is that high Machs have greater emotional detachment or what has been labeled the "cool syndrome." "One consequence of the high Mach's cool, cognitive, situation-specified strategy is that they never appear to be obviously manipulating, when being obvious would be a disadvantage. The high Mach is the one who gets others to help him win in such a way that, in the process, they thank him for the opportunity."

Low Machs have not suffered from a lack of enthusiasm or motivation in the situations studied. However, they become so engrossed with the particular person or content they are dealing with that they get carried away and neglect to manipulate, implicitly assuming that fair play will prevail. This appears to be a losing tactic. Another way of stating this observation is that high Machs will endorse whatever values and attitudes that have utility to them personally, whereas low Machs may be outsmarted because they stick to values of honesty, justice, etc.

Christie and Geis make some observations about Machiavellianism with respect to administrative success which are enlightening. They suggest that people who are extremely low Machs would make poor administrators. This is based on research evidence which indicates that such administrators would be unable to sufficiently detach themselves from subordinates to enable them to make decisions having negative consequences on individuals, such as firing an ineffective worker who is a nice guy.

The problem with high Machs is that their analysis of organizational needs together with disregard for individual needs could easily lead to morale problems. The high-Mach executive would be most successful in organizations where relationships to external organizations are critical. In this situation, high Machs would be effective in transactions with other organizations and these positive outcomes might negate whatever negative outcomes might arise from insensitivity to organizational members.

Attitudes in the United States population are moving toward greater support of those attitudes held by high Machs. This observation suggests that the problems of managers (whether high or low Machs) will be increasingly "political." It appears that managers will have to pay increasing attention to clarifying and structuring organizations so that the individual's organizational rewards are attributable to achievement of organizational goals rather than political finesse.

As may be inferred from the above discussion, the ability to influence attitudes and change behavior is important to managerial success. An awareness of tactics exercised by Machiavellians and the ability to adopt these tactics when appropriate also appear important to a manager's success, although such behavior may not promote organizational success. It appears essential both to managerial and organizational success that the manager develop "political finesse" so that he or she is not outmaneuvered by high Machs seeking personal gain at the organization's and/or the manager's expense.

SUMMARY

One of the most important skills of a manager is the ability to influence others. The manager can influence others by shaping behavior (strategic use of reinforcement), by encouraging modeling (identification), by counseling, by using participative decision making, and by restructuring the work environment. People are often resistant to change (influence). An understanding of the change process aids managers in coping with this resistance.

The change process involves: (1) unfreezing in preparation for change through disconfirmation and reduction of threat; (2) the change itself; and (3) refreezing the newly acquired behavior through reinforcement. The change process takes place within an organizational context where forces resistant to change may also be influencing the target person.

The manager concerned with attaining influence does so by demonstrating his or her security and competency and by cultivating influence with powerful allies. Two tactics useful in gaining allies are the foot-in-the-door technique and conditioning; these tactics are often used by "Machiavellians" intent on establishing a relationship which they can later use as leverage in influence attempts.

Machiavellians tend to be successful at influencing others because they adopt attitudes and behaviors aimed at influencing others, whereas other people may become concerned with such values as "honesty" and "fair play." Since Machiavellianism is becoming increasingly characteristic of people entering organizations, such behavior presents a substantial challenge to managers concerned with facilitating open communication.

IMPORTANT TERMS AND CONCEPTS

shaping, participative decision making, resistance to change, ego-defensive, unfreezing, lack of confirmation, reduction of threat, identification, scanning, refreezing, emergent leadership, foot-in-the-door technique, conditioning, Machiavellianism

REVIEW QUESTIONS

1. What ways of influencing subordinates are open to managers?

2. In the example of Farrow and Bentwick in Chapter 3, what method of influence might Farrow have used with Bentwick most appropriately? Why?

3. Why do people resist change?

4. Describe briefly the change process. Describe how a particular attitude or behavior of your own has changed. Did this change fit the description of the change process?

5. How does the organizational context of a relationship limit the degree that one person can influence another?

6. How does the organizational context of a relationship increase the degree that one person can influence another?
7. Give an example (not one given in the book) of the foot-in-the-door technique of gaining influence.
8. What are some other ways of gaining upward influence?
9. What are the characteristics of Machiavellians?
10. Would Machiavellians make good adminstrators? Why or why not?

INCIDENT 1: INFLUENCE WITHOUT AUTHORITY

Steve had looked forward to serving on the board of directors of AMI Corporation. He had been president of his own small company for four years, but this board membership was an opportunity to learn of the operations of a large corporation. After only a few meetings he could see that even though his own company was small, it was much better managed than AMI. It soon became apparent to Steve that AMI followed a number of policies and strategies that were antiquated.

He went to much effort beyond his responsibility as a board member to collect information and to develop proposals for corrective policies and approaches. With a true sense of pride he began to point out the problems and make his proposals. To his surprise and dismay, Steve found his words to fall as if in an empty room. The members agreed with the existence of the problems; these had been aired often. But when Steve made constructive proposals, the reaction was a strained silence.

Instead of giving thought or study to Steve's work, the board members followed their usual practice and turned to Bill for a response. Bill was one of the company's founders. He was outspoken and forceful. As was his usual practice, he reacted to Steve's proposals with little thought. Bill found a humorous or critical statement for each of Steve's ideas. Steve was amazed to discover that Bill's off-the-cuff ideas with their obvious flaws received attention and acceptance while his carefully structured proposals were hardly heard. The board members were surprised and disappointed when Steve quietly and tactfully resigned.

INCIDENT 2: UNITED PAPER MILLS

The following case study may provide a focus for talking about interpersonal influence in business situations. It could also be used as a role-play exercise.

Part A

United Paper Mills was a division of a large forest-product company. Fred Johnson, the new production superintendent, had recently moved to United Paper from a small independent mill where he had been the manager. The three key line managers reporting to Fred had all had fifteen or more years' experience with United Paper. They had seen it go from a highly productive mill to "one that was full of union strife and problem workers."

In talking with some of the supervisors, Fred learned that a good many of them were upset over the fact that they had to report any machine breakdown to the production manager or one of his assistants within fifteen minutes of its occurrence. They felt that this did not give them the responsibility of taking care of their own machines and weakened their position with their workers. The assistants, however, told Fred that the present supervisors did not have the experience and/or the ability to handle major "breakdowns."

Discussion Questions:

1. What should Fred do? Why?
2. What other problems (unidentified by Fred) might be present?
3. What additional steps might the supervisors take?

Part B

One of the major difficulties that Fred Johnson faced was that only about 40 percent of the jobs listed for scheduled maintenance shutdowns were performed (on the average). The personnel supervisor in an informal conversation had told Fred that it was estimated that maintenance was operating at 28 percent efficiency. The personnel supervisor also said that maintenance workers had recently spearheaded a "slowdown" in order to "force" the company to increase their wages, and although they had been successful they were still disgruntled. In addition, the personnel supervisor told Fred that several new maintenance supervisors had told him it had become "common practice" for maintenance workers to quit about an hour early in order to "wash up."

The maintenance superintendent was a man who had worked his way up through the ranks. His rationale for the "inefficiency" was that there were not many capable workers available so that the company had been forced to hire just about anybody.

Discussion Questions:

1. How might Fred approach the maintenance superintendent?
2. What questions might Fred ask the personnel supervisor?
3. Who else might Fred talk to? What would be the purpose of these conversations?

Part C

Many weeks after Fred Johnson joined United Paper the following conversation took place between Fred and the assistant personnel supervisor, Jonah Jamison.

Jonah: "Hey, Fred, can I talk with you for a minute?"

Fred: "Sure, what is it?"

Jonah: "Well, I was talking with one of your supervisors that I know pretty well. Kind of an off-the-record little chat."

Fred: "Yeah?"

Jonah: "And he told me this company's management style is the old mushroom style: keep 'em in the dark and feed 'em a lot of manure. He said for one thing that nobody knew that you had been hired for your job until you walked in the door and introduced yourself. This includes your assistants, Fred."

Fred: "Yeah, I guess so."

Jonah: "This supervisor says that he has been in his job for ten years and not once has anybody talked to him about how he might advance in the company, what his strong and weak points are, etc."

Fred: "Yeah, I guess that's probably true."

Jonah: "The clincher was his statement that Bill Jennings, the new head personnel supervisor for the mill, has not talked to or even been introduced to anybody in the paper-machine area and Bill has been on his job for four months now.

Fred: "Well, how widespread do you think this feeling is about mushroom management?"

Jonah: "I don't know, Fred, but I think you ought to find out."

Discussion Questions:

1. What steps can Fred take?

2. What does this conversation tell you about the role of personnel in the company? What about Jonah's role in the company?

3. What steps can Jonah take?

4. How does this situation relate to Part A and Part B?

5. What steps can the supervisor take?

BIBLIOGRAPHY

Brehm, J.: *A Theory of Psychological Reactance* (New York: Academic Press, Inc., 1966).

Byrne, D.: "Interpersonal Attraction and Attitude Similarity," *Journal of Abnormal and Social Psychology,* vol. 62, pp. 713–715, 1961.

Christie, R., and F. Geis: *Studies in Machiavellianism* (New York: Academic Press, Inc., 1970).

Flieshman, E.: "Leadership Climate, Human Relations Training, and Supervisory Behavior," *Personnel Psychology,* vol. 6, pp. 205–222, 1953.

Hollander, E. P.: "Emergent Leadership and Social Influence," in L. Petrullo and B. M. Bass (eds.), *Leadership and Interpersonal Behavior* (New York: Holt, Rinehart and Winston, Inc., 1961), pp. 30–41.

Marrow, Alfred, D. Bowers, and S. Seashore: *Management by Participation: Creating a Climate for Personal and Organizational Development* (New York: Harper & Row, Publishers, Incorporated, 1967).

Schein, Edgar: "The Mechanisms of Change," in W. G. Bennis, K. D. Benne, and R. Chin (eds.), *The Planning of Change* (New York: Holt, Rinehart and Winston, Inc., 1969), pp. 98–107.

Zimbardo, P., and E. Ebbesen: *Influencing Attitudes and Changing Behavior* (Reading, Mass.: Addison-Wesley, Publishing Company, Inc., 1970).

13

RESOLVING INTERPERSONAL CONFLICT

The manager, by virtue of his or her leadership position, can be instrumental in developing the interpersonal competence of subordinates. One of the avenues open to the manager in this task is the role of a third-party mediator in resolving interpersonal conflicts. The present chapter is concerned with describing a basic approach to managing interpersonal conflict.

THE IMPORTANCE OF CONFLICT RESOLUTION

The manager who influences subordinates in a noncoercive way (i.e., through shaping, modeling, counseling, persuading, or participative decision making) is "teaching" them self-respect and responsibility. With this increased sense of responsibility comes the need for the subordinates to work more closely together. That is, as subordinates take on more responsibility, they come to see their role more as members of a team and less as subordinates trying to satisfy the wishes of the manager. In Transactional Analysis terms, the subordinate's increase in responsibility tends to change the subordinate's mode of interacting from Child to Adult.

We return to the Farrow-Bentwick example first presented in Chapter 3 to illustrate this point. Suppose that Farrow, instead of rejecting Bentwick's ideas, had listened to them and through coaching, modeling, or participative decision making had helped Bentwick develop his ideas. As Bentwick increases his self-respect and becomes more responsible in the organization, he needs to gain the cooperation of others. For example, John, the blueprint maker, might be very helpful or even necessary if Bentwick's ideas are to become actuality. Bentwick will need to develop a better relationship with John than he probably now has if he is going to enlist John's full cooperation. If Farrow had a high degree of interpersonal competence, he could "facilitate" the development of this relationship and the development of his subordinates' interpersonal competence by acting as a third-party mediator.

Anyone who has worked in an organization has probably observed interpersonal conflicts. It seems that the very structure of the organization with its great number of interdependencies makes interpersonal conflict inevitable. If you have observed interpersonal conflicts in organizations, you probably also realize that such conflicts often prove destructive to organizational goals. Instead of cooperating to achieve organizational goals, the antagonists may expend energy and time in attempts to sabotage the efforts of the other. Thus, it is reasonable to conclude that skills at controlling and/or resolving interpersonal conflict can be critical to organizational success.

A cautionary note is necessary. This discussion on the management of interpersonal conflict is not intended to provide enough information to allow the reader to become an expert; it is simply an attempt to illustrate an arena of action in which communication skills are critical to managerial success. It should also be pointed out that conflict is not necessarily destructive—indeed it appears necessary to a dynamic organization. If people go along with the majority, if there is no dissent or struggle for leadership—there may be stagnation.

A good place to begin this discussion of interpersonal conflict is to reiterate the observation made in Chapter 6 that the expression of anger (and in fact, emotional expression in general) is contrary to the norms presently existing in most organizations. As was suggested in that earlier discussion, the failure to express anger directly often leads to an indirect expression. Since indirect expression of anger may leave the target person with no understanding concerning why he or she is being attacked, the target person is not in a position to change whatever it is that is angering the attacker. Further, if the target person follows the norms, his or her response is also indirect. Such interaction creates a situation where conflict is likely to escalate, since the possibility of addressing the issue which is at the base of the conflict is remote. In this situation, a manager acting as a third party may be instrumental in uncovering the underlying issue(s) and thus set the stage for conflict resolution.

The manager's basic approach is to help the "combatants" acquire the interpersonal skills of self-disclosure, feedback, and pacing necessary to the establishment of interpersonal trust. That is, the manager does not resolve the conflict, but instead facilitates the resolution *by* the two people in conflict.

THEORY OF INTERPERSONAL CONFLICT

Walton (1969) suggests that there are two basic types of interpersonal conflict—substantive conflict and emotional conflict. Substantive issues involve disagreement with policies or actions, differing concepts of areas of responsibility and roles, and direct competition for the same personal objective. To resolve substantive issues, the third party needs to set the stage and mediate a bargaining and/or problem-solving meeting. Emotional issues generally cannot be resolved through negotiation or problem solving. Generally the third party must facilitate a "working through" of the feelings and perceptions involved. That is, resolution of emotional issues involves dealing with emotions, whereas resolution of substantive issues can be more "intellectual" or cognitive. Unfortunately interpersonal conflicts tend not to fall totally into either category. It is often the case that a substantive issue will lead eventually to emotional issues (or vice versa). For example, two people competing against each other come into conflict and are likely to eventually "discover" things about each other which irritate them. Studies on prejudice suggest that, in fact, perceived substantive conflict may account for the development of prejudice (Sheriff, 1961).

The management of conflict generally involves both emotional and cognitive approaches. As Walton points out, the nature of interpersonal conflict is that it is cyclical. Only periodically do the opposing people actually engage in conflict. In between the battles, other things take precedence until something happens which again triggers the conflict. In order to understand and thus manage an interpersonal conflict the third party needs to discover what triggers the conflict and what forces operate to keep the conflict from being expressed. Examples of the latter are: (1) job requirements which limit amount of time for interaction, (2) feelings by the superior that open conflict will affect his or her ability to supervise, and (3) perception of vulnerability to the other's conflict tactics. Awareness of why conflict is not always being engaged in allows the manager some understanding of limiting conflict behavior. For example, the manager could attempt to limit conflict by limiting the amount of interaction time available to the two opposing persons.

THE CONFRONTATION MEETING AS AN APPROACH TO CONFLICT RESOLUTION

If the third party judges the two people in conflict to be strong enough to be capable of "weathering" a direct confrontation, he or she may choose to attempt to resolve the conflict by getting them together. In this event, the time, the place, and the decision process leading to the eventual meeting are critical to the success of the confrontation. Since a confrontation is an emotionally draining affair, the two opposing parties need advance notice of a proposed confrontation and the time should be set such that neither feels overburdened with other problems. Likewise, the place of the confrontation is important. If a confrontation is held between boss and subordinate in the boss's office, the subordinate is unlikely to be in a position to openly talk about issues which provoked the conflict. In order to equalize the power, the meeting might be held in a neutral place and perhaps the subordinate should have an ally present, in addition to the third party, so that the conflict can be more openly confronted. In addition, both parties need to feel some commitment to conflict resolution. This is likely only if both have entered into the decision concerning meeting to confront the conflict.

Before setting up the confrontation meeting, it is probably best that the third party talk with each person individually in order to diagnose the nature of the interpersonal conflict in an atmosphere less likely to provoke conflict behavior. These individual meetings have the added advantage of leading both parties to the conflict to think out and verbalize the factors contributing to the conflict without worrying that the other will try to take advantage of such an analysis.

The role of the third party in the confrontation meeting is difficult to blueprint since it is dependent on the nature of the conflict, the persons involved, etc. Instead we will discuss some overall strategies that the third party may adopt and some particular tactics that may be used. First, the third party needs to be aware of two stages in conflict resolution, those of differentiation and integration.

The Differentiation Stage of Conflict Resolution

It is necessary for the two opposing parties to fully describe their viewpoint of the conflict; this is the differentiation stage. In this stage the third party needs to caution each opposing party to refrain from looking for possible solutions. They should simply lay out the problem as they see it. Generally, the third party is acting as a referee, allowing or encouraging first one party and then the other to give honest opinions on specific issues.

An important strategy in the differentiation stage is to introduce a great deal of feedback into the discussion. A technique developed by Carl Rogers is useful in this regard. This technique involves having each party *restate* the other's position. Although this may sound surprising, it is often the case that the opposing parties are so wrapped up in their own viewpoint and what they are going to say that they really do not listen to the other. This technique tends to create a problem-solving orientation which reduces the amount of emotion in the discussion. The encouragement of the third party for the use of this rule (restatement of one's viewpoint to the satisfaction of the other) tends to decrease defensiveness behavior which has probably characterized the interactions between the two conflicting persons in the past.

Other activities of the third party which may help in the differentiation stage are: (1) initiating agenda items, (2) eliciting reactions, and (3) making observations concerning the interaction process of the confrontation. Especially in the initial part of the confrontation process the third party may find it necessary to focus attention on diagnosing the conflict by pointing out what he or she believes to be important issues. The third party might, for example, suggest that since both parties mentioned a particular issue as important in their private discussions with him or her, this might prove a useful place to start the discussion. If the third party does not make such a suggestion, the two conflicting persons may address trivial differences with a "wait and see" attitude. In this situation neither wants to make a move which might be seen as reconciliation by the other, for fear that the other might reject the overture or perhaps try to take advantage of him or her. Thus, the third party can remove this pressure of being first by taking the initiative.

Another concern that conflicting parties might have is that if one "opens up" the other may use this openness to find one's "weakness" without responding openly. Thus, the third party may need to pace the exchange of viewpoints in the differentiation stage by eliciting reactions first from one person, then from the other. If the two parties are still communicating in a "defensive manner," the third party may feel it necessary to intervene by making observations about how they are communicating in the present situation. It might even be necessary to question the commitment of one or both parties to a resolution of the conflict and have them look at their own openness to communicating to the other before a commitment to problem-solving communication can be produced.

The Integration Stage of Conflict Resolution

In the integration stage of confrontation the third party attempts to get the opposing parties to acknowledge those viewpoints which are similar and discuss resolutions to issues on which they continue to differ. If these issues turn out to be primarily substantive, then the third party should act essentially as an arbitrator in a negotiation session. The strategy is to ensure that it has a chance of working. The third party is also concerned about creating commitment on the part of the persons in conflict to honor the negotiated solution and also a commitment to renegotiate if the first solution proves unworkable.

If differences on issues are largely emotional, then the integration phase involves greater attention to emotion. Although it is important in any conflict resolution for the opposing parties to express positive feelings toward each other, it is particularly important when the issues are basically emotional.

Emotional Issues in Interpersonal Conflict

Emotional issues which often lead to interpersonal conflict can best be talked about by referring to the interpersonal needs discussed earlier. For example, frustration of the need for inclusion may lead to interpersonal conflict. Person A might initiate interactions but also desire to be a receiver of such initiation; whereas the other, person B, may enjoy receiving interaction but dislike initiating interaction. Eventually, person A is likely to become frustrated and discontinue initiating interaction since person B does not initiate any. Person A may feel that person B does not like him or her whereas person B may conclude that he or she has become "out of favor" with person A.

These feelings of frustration may be translated into retaliatory action. When person B needs person A to help in performing an organizational task, person A may be unavoidably "tied up." When person A needs support to influence the boss, person B may withhold support even though he or she agrees with person A's proposal. These incidents may then become the events which lead to an escalation of the conflict. If the underlying incompatibility can be clarified in the confrontation, then an agreement concerning behavior and/or attitude changes may be reached. In this example it should be apparent that person A needs person B's assurances that B likes A even though B failed to respond in the manner A wanted. This same reassurance needs to be made by person A. Thus, it is apparent that an emotional as well as cognitive exchange in dealing with "personality" conflicts is important.

A similar diagnosis can be made concerning incompatibility of persons on the need for control and how such incompatibility may lead to conflict. If both parties need to control, then a battle over who will be dominant in the relationship may overshadow the areas where cooperation would be mutually beneficial. Concentration on the control issue leads to a win-lose situation. The antagonists may seek to find ways of undermining each other and neglect the possibility of interacting cooperatively. In this situation, the third party might focus the discussion in the integration phase on how to accentuate the positive, i.e., how each could help the other. Later the third party might attempt to gain resolution through negotiation on those issues on which cooperative solutions are not apparent. Again the expression of positive emotion is important to an effective resolution. Without trading of positive feelings, the battle for control will likely escalate. It is not up to the third party to produce these feelings. Presumably they exist or there never would have been an agreement to meet to confront the conflict. The third party simply needs to create an atmosphere where this exchange of positive feelings can take place. As discussed earlier in reference to anger, this involves first communicating the negative feelings accumulated during the conflict. When these negative feelings have been expressed (in the differentiation phase), then positive feelings are much more likely to be expressed (if they exist).

Follow-up in the Conflict-Resolution Process

It is important during the integration phase to agree to meet at some specific time and place in the future, preferably less than a week hence. The importance of this agreement is that a verbal solution does not constitute an actual solution but rather points out behavior which needs to change in order to accomplish a resolution. Since behavioral change is a difficult proposition, it is likely that there will be a transition period where both parties try without complete success to implement the verbal agreement. In the transition period there is the possibility that conflict will again arise as one or both persons react to the stress involved in changing behavior by reverting back to more habitual responses. Thus frequent meetings aimed at defusing antagonisms and reemphasizing the desirability of changing behavior are necessary.

TYPES OF POSSIBLE SOLUTIONS IN CONFLICT RESOLUTION

We will briefly discuss some of the possible kinds of "solutions" to conflict in order to clarify the goals of the manager in conflict resolution. One important approach to managing conflict is aiding the parties in conflict to find behaviors which are mutually advantageous. This can be done by establishing a joint payoff situation where *only* through cooperative behavior can a payoff be reached. An example of this would be for Farrow to assign Bentwick and John a project to work on together where recognition and rewards would come equally to both for the success of the project.

Alternatively, the manager might encourage the conflicting individuals to form a trading relationship. Thus Bentwick might cooperate with John on one project if John in return would cooperate with Bentwick on another one.

A third way of constructing a situation is to change the reward structure so that it would be mutually advantageous to both parties in conflict to cooperate. An example from the automobile industry illustrates this point. A large assembly plant was experiencing "communication breakdowns" between supervisors responsible for the same machines on various shifts. A supervisor on the first shift would have a machine breakdown. This supervisor would not report this problem to the supervisor on the next shift and would only repair the machine well enough so that it would get through the rest of the shift without breaking down. Thus, the machine would again break down on the next shift.

The solution to this "communication breakdown" which was causing a lot of lost production was for the manager to change the reward structure. The manager had been evaluating supervisors on how much production they got relative to other shifts. Such evaluations and the rewards associated with them led the supervisors to be fiercely competitive across shifts and made it in the best interest of the individual supervisor to not communicate to counterparts on other shifts. The elimination of such evaluations and their concomitant rewards went a long way toward eliminating the destructive competition.

Another possible solution to interpersonal conflict is to change the nature of the work situation so as to minimize the potential for conflict. An example from the author's consulting experience illustrates this point. The chief administrator and the assistant administrator of a welfare agency were constantly "fighting" although they basically liked each other. An analysis of the situation suggested that the major instigator of conflict was when the chief administrator intervened in the affairs of the assistant. This happened rather frequently, since the chief's office was right across the hall from the assistant's. A lot of "work" at resolving the conflict had led to little resolution. Finally, the obvious solution of separating the location of their offices was tried. Almost instantly, things began running more smoothly.

Finally, the manager needs to recognize that one of the best solutions to conflict is to recognize its inevitability and set up procedures for identifying and confronting it. Regularly scheduled meetings aimed at surfacing any potential conflicts are important in this regard.

SUMMARY

The managing of interpersonal conflict is important to organizational success since conflict is potentially destructive. The managing of interpersonal conflict is also a means by which the manager can aid in the development of the interpersonal competence of employees.

The resolution of interpersonal conflict involves many of the communication behaviors necessary to interpersonal competence. Interpersonal conflict generally involves both substantive conflict over issues related to the job and emotional conflict over incompatibility of personal styles. The confrontation meeting facilitated by a third party is probably the most effective way of resolving such conflicts. Such confrontation meetings generally proceed through a differentiation stage in which negative feelings and the central substantive and emotional issues are identified to an integration stage in which cooperative strategies are planned and positive feelings are expressed.

Without intervention and mediation by a third party, interpersonal conflict and its destructive consequences are likely to escalate. The skills involved in acting as a third party include sensitivity, counseling, and the ability to manipulate the "environment" to reduce threat. These manipulations may include the location of the meeting, the pacing of the exchange, and the institution of communication rules aimed at increasing the chances of establishing interpersonal trust.

Solutions to interpersonal conflict involve the establishment of situations where cooperative behavior is mutually advantageous. This can be done through establishing joint payoffs, trading, changing the reward system, or changing the work environment.

IMPORTANT TERMS AND CONCEPTS

substantive conflict, emotional conflict, confrontation meeting, differentiation, integration

REVIEW QUESTIONS

1. Suppose you are Farrow's (Chapter 3) manager and have discovered the "causes" underlying Bentwick's malicious obedience. Outline a basic approach to resolving the conflict between Farrow and Bentwick.
2. When would a "confrontation" meeting be undesirable?
3. What can be done to lessen the destructive nature of a conflict when a confrontation meeting is undesirable?
4. What are the types of things which lead to interpersonal conflict?
5. What does the third party do to facilitate in the differentiation phase of conflict resolution?
6. How can the manager use interpersonal conflict to facilitate the development of interpersonal competence? What can the manager do in the integration phase of conflict resolution?
7. How does interpersonal conflict arise?

INCIDENT 1: A CASE OF INTERPERSONAL CONFLICT

Robert joined the management development staff of the Daem Corporation immediately upon receiving a Ph.D. degree in industrial psychology. His first assignment was to develop a performance-appraisal system. He soon became aware of a deep conflict between his supervisor, Harry, and the director of the industrial relations department, Dick.

Harry was convinced that only a broad-scoped program which wedded the performance-appraisal system to a total effort of management development could be effective.

However, to complete the total effort would require a staff of ten people where there were now three. Dick did not wish to expand the staff to this level, but wanted a strong effort toward implementing the appraisal system.

Dick urged Harry to move ahead with the appraisal program, but to no avail. Harry would not compromise his position. Unexpressed resentment between Harry and Dick became apparent to everyone. Finally, in an uncharacteristic display of emotion and authoritarian control, Dick called both Harry and Robert to his office and spelled out in detail exactly what was to be done. Upon return to Harry's office, Harry said to Robert, "Well, he was certainly angry, wasn't he. He wasn't too clear on what he wants done, so I plan to continue with our present course of activity."

INCIDENT 2: TRUMAN AND MACARTHUR[1]

The following incident is based on President Truman's recollection of a meeting between himself and General MacArthur concerning the war in Korea. There had been some controversy between the two concerning the manner in which the war was being conducted. MacArthur had made some public statements which angered President Truman. A meeting between the two men was arranged to settle their differences and Wake Island was selected as a neutral meeting site. It was Truman's impression that the general deliberately delayed his own appearance to keep the President waiting, thus upstaging the Commander in Chief.

"Finally, the son of a bitch walked out of one of the buildings near the runway there. He was wearing those damn sunglasses of his and a shirt that was unbuttoned and a cap that had a lot of hardware. I never did understand . . . an old man like that and a five-star general to boot, why he went around dressed up like a nineteen-year-old second lieutenant.

"I'll tell you this. If he'd been a lieutenant in my outfit going around dressed like that, I'd have busted him so fast he wouldn't have known what happened to him.

"But I . . . I decided to overlook his getup, and we shook hands and arranged . . . we had a meeting. I got there on time, but he was forty-five minutes late, and this meeting—it was just between the two of us, you understand, and was the only one like that.

"When he walked in, I took one look at him, and I said, 'Now you look here. I've come halfway across the world to meet you, but don't worry about that. I just want you to know I don't give a good goddamn what you do or think about Harry Truman, but don't you ever again keep your Commander in Chief waiting. Is that clear?'

"His face got as red as a beet, but he said . . . he indicated that he understood what I was talking about, and we went on from there.

"I didn't bring up what he'd written to the Veterans of Foreign Wars; I didn't have to. He did it. He said he didn't know what had got into him, and that it had been a mistake, and nothing like that would ever happen again.

---

[1]Reprinted by permission from *Plain Speaking: An Oral Biography of Harry S. Truman* by Merle Miller. New York: Berkley Medallion Books, pp. 316–318, 1974.

"I didn't mention 1948[2] either, but he did. He says, 'Mr. President, I was just taken in by the politicians, and I apologize for that, too. It won't happen again. I've learned my lesson.'"

He seems to have been very apologetic and contrite that morning.

"He was. He was. When you were alone with him, he was a very different kind of fella. Butter wouldn't melt in his mouth. But . . . I've known a few other fellas like that, and when they're out in public, it's an entirely different story. They're always playacting out in public.

"I asked MacArthur point blank if the Chinese would come in, and he said under no circumstances would they come in. He says, 'Mr. President, the war will be over by Thanksgiving and I'll have the American troops back in Tokyo by Christmas,' and he went on like that.

"We must've talked for an hour or so, just the two of us, and I believe I made it more than abundantly clear to him that I was his Commander in Chief and that he was to obey orders and keep . . . not issue any public statements of any kind that hadn't been approved by me personally.

"He was just like a little puppy at that meeting. I don't know which was worse, the way he acted in public or the way he kissed my ass at that meeting."

1. What barriers to communication can you identify in this incident?

2. Do you see any evidence that either Truman or MacArthur are trying to open communication gateways?

3. Has there been effective interpersonal communication between Truman and MacArthur?

INCIDENT 3: OMEGA DIVISION

The following case study may provide a focus for talking about interpersonal conflict in business situations. It could also be used as a role-play exercise.

---

[2]That year nobody knew much about MacArthur's views on anything, but the Chicago *Tribune* and the Hearst press thought they knew enough to be sure he wasn't one of your left-wingers and to start trying to drum up support for him.

In mid-March MacArthur, with his usual flair for understatement, allowed as how, "In this hour of momentous importance . . . I can say, and with due humility, that I would be recreant to all concepts of good citizenship were I to shirk any public duty to which I might be called by the American people."

Since he was on active duty in Japan, he couldn't do any active campaigning. His name, nevertheless, was entered in the Wisconsin Republican primary. He had, after all, once gone to school in Wisconsin and was appointed to West Point by a Congressman from that state, although he hadn't been in Wisconsin or anyplace else in the United States for eleven years. Some people even said he was the state's favorite son.

On primary day, however, the general got only eight of the twenty-seven delegates, and that more or less finished off talk about the duty the general wouldn't be able to shirk.

John Jackson had been transferred to Omega Logging Division to take the job of office manager. He had previously been an accountant at Delta Logging Division where the management style was pretty authoritarian. Omega Division was in the midst of an organizational development project aimed at improving morale and consequently production. Omega Division's manager encouraged more participation from his employees in hopes of gaining greater influence.

The office staff at Omega Division was composed of seven employees who were all nonunion. In addition to John, the office manager, there was Bill, the cost accountant, Barry, an assistant accountant, Art, the timekeeper, Susan, the receptionist, Jane, a stenographer, and Pam, who had production scheduling and clerical duties. As part of the organizational development project the office group had started making some decisions as a group. In addition, an effort to provide training in the different office functions had been initiated so that eventually everybody would know something about each job. The scheduling for this "training" had been arrived at through group discussion.

The company had for several years provided transportation from town to the marshaling yard (or office in this case) for all employees. The company furnished buses and paid workers for bus driving. This bus-driving job was considered a real plum. Hourly workers (unionized) received this job on the basis of seniority.

The office group was provided with a large van. Art, who happened to have the most seniority, had been driving the van. He seriously hurt his leg in a hunting accident, making it necessary for someone else to drive. John, the office manager, designated Bill as the driver because (as he later explained) Bill was the most irreplaceable member of the office staff and the driving job which essentially constituted a raise made it more difficult for competitors to bid Bill away to another company.

The three women were young and assertive and were very upset with this decision because Jane had more seniority than Bill. They felt that the decision was discriminatory against women and demanded that John change his decision. John, unused to seeing any managerial decision questioned, got angry and told them to get out of his office. The aftermath of this confrontation left the whole office morale in bad shape.

Discussion Questions:

1. If you were John's boss, would you talk to John about this matter? If so, how?

2. How might a "confrontation" meeting be structured by a third party? Should all three women be there? Where should it take place?

3. At this point, what action can John take?

BIBLIOGRAPHY

Sheriff, Muzafer: *Intergroup Conflict and Cooperation: The Robbers Cave Experiment* (Norman, Okla.: University of Oklahoma, Institute of Group Relations, 1961).

Walton, Richard: *Interpersonal Peace-Making* (Reading, Mass.: Addison-Wesley Publishing Company, Inc., 1969).

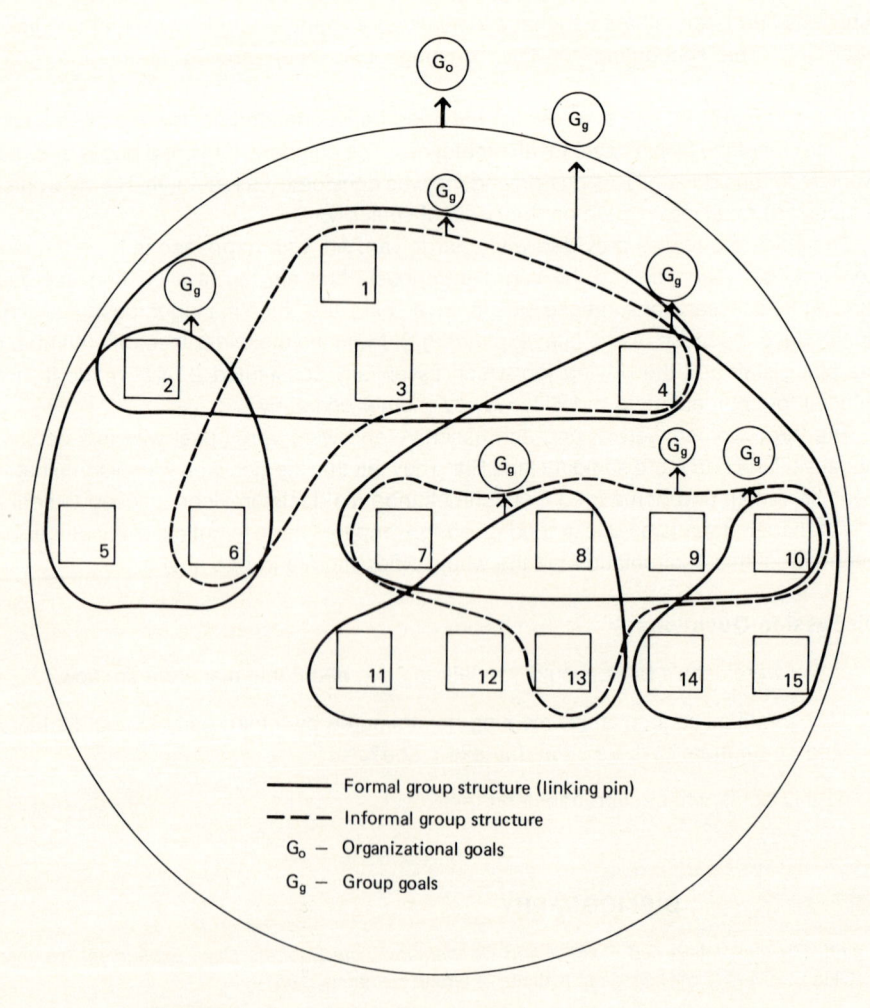

FIGURE 3 Organizational communication at the group level.

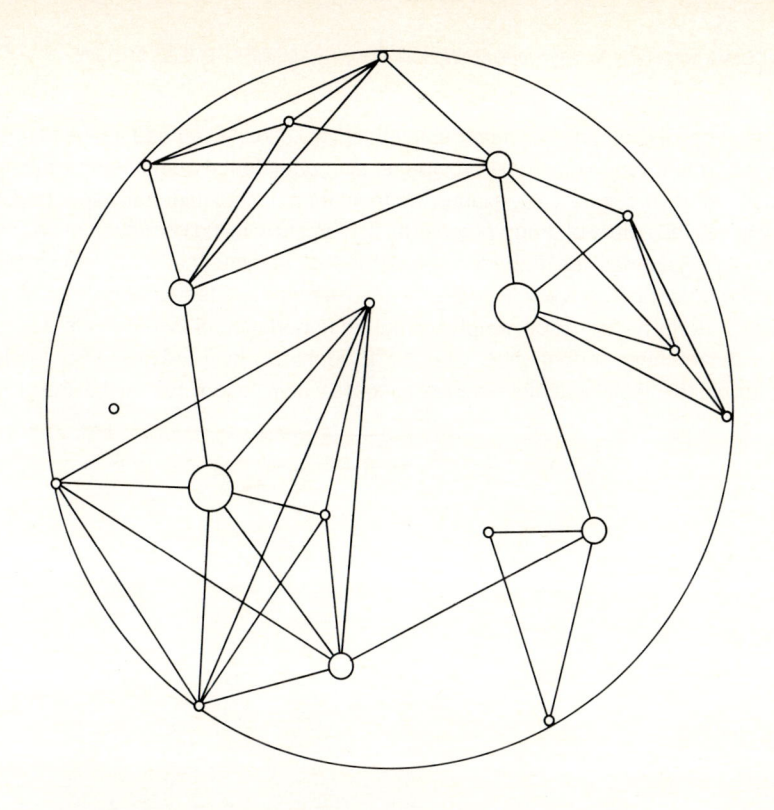

PART THREE

MANAGING ORGANIZATION COMMUNICATION:
Communication within Organization Subsystems and Small Groups

In Part Three we shift our focus beyond the two-person level of analysis to that of the small group. The small group is the basic building block of the organization and a major subsystem of any organization (see areas enclosed by heavy lines in Figure 3). The small groups and their functions are vital to the success of the organization and its management. The manager must be able to deal with the communication process within the small group. Communications are more complex at the group level than at the dyadic level because larger numbers of people are involved. However, many of the concepts critical to interpersonal communication also operate at the small-group level.

Our discussion of small-group communications will show that the manager must comprehend both the external and the internal systems of small-group activity in order to effectively use this important type of organizational subsystem. Chapter 14 will provide an external-internal orientation to small-group communication processes by examining their formal and informal aspects. Chapter 15 discusses the nature of group process as it interacts with the communication process. Chapter 16 examines the important properties of communication networks from an external-internal point of view. Chapter 17 focuses on the effect of communication with respect to group performance, emphasizing the importance of external-internal interactions in determining performance. Chapter 18 identifies key dimensions of leadership behavior which affect the achievement of success within the environment of the group.

14

AN EXTERNAL-INTERNAL SYSTEMS ORIENTATION TO THE MANAGEMENT OF COMMUNICATION WITHIN SMALL GROUPS

The objective of this chapter is to examine the small group and its communication process in terms of the external-internal systems. We shall consider the nature of the external and internal small-group systems and their relationship to group communications.

The small group is a building block of the total organization. The small group has the same formal, required, external-system aspects and informal, emergent, internal-system aspects as exist at the interpersonal and the total organizational levels. If you look at the chart presented in Figure 3, you will see that the total organization may be appropriately viewed as a set of overlapping small groups and dyads. These subsystems are linked together into a total organization by the managerial structure. The managers act as organizational "linking pins" through the communication process. Let us look at this process in action for an illustrative small group.

Suppose you have been appointed the case observer to evaluate the communication process for a newly formed group of market researchers. Previously your company had used its sales force to study the market needs for product Y. It is establishing this new group from a combination of experienced people and recent college graduates. The corporate communication section of the personnel division sees this as an excellent opportunity for the company to study the communication process in small groups and you have been appointed to conduct the study. Your assignment is to observe, record, and analyze the small-group system and the communication content and flow for the research group.

Five persons have been appointed to the group. Sam, an experienced market researcher from another part of the corporation, is the manager. Betty has a couple of years of market-research experience also. Keith is the third person in experience, but is being brought in from another company. Bryant and Dutch are recent BBA graduates of business schools and have had course work in market research. The new group begins its work on October 10 and you are there as they come to work. They have already been informed of your purpose and instructed to ignore your presence as much as possible. As they gather for the first time on Monday morning, you observe several phenomena which you record. They are uneasy about the situation. They are obviously emotionally mature people, but they appear tense, especially Bryant and Dutch. They begin their group relationship by making introductions. At Sam's suggestion, they tell a little about themselves. Each seems to focus upon work background and the aspects of educational background which relate to the tasks of this group.

Finally, Keith says to Sam, "Well, they have told me where to report and what my job title is, but I don't know what I'm supposed to do. This is a new territory and a new product for me." Sam responds, "Yes, we are supposed to develop our own team and assign responsibilities to each person. I feel the best way to do this is through discussion. I don't know you people and you don't know me. I would like for us to decide what we think should be our goals and how we should accomplish these goals—who will do what."

In the next few hours there is much talk about what market research is and should be as it relates to product Y. At the coffee break, Sam, Keith, and Betty remain in the coffee room, while Bryant and Dutch return to the conference room to have their break. At lunchtime they go to the cafeteria, and again divide into the two groups which emerged at the coffee break.

Later, after the goals are decided, attention turns to discussions of responsibilities and reporting relationships. After much discussion of tasks, it is decided that Betty and Keith will visit potential customers and collect data. Bryant will analyze the data, while Dutch organizes and develops reports for management. Sam will visit key customers, coordinate the efforts of the group, and handle relationships with other company departments.

Following this series of meetings, the group members begin work on their tasks with a sense of involvement and dedication. They are quick to give a word of encouragement or even criticism to a member of the group who falls behind schedule in the work. Even though they are performing their roles well, Sam becomes concerned about the lack of closeness of the group. Conflicts arise frequently between the field people and Bryant or Dutch. This is a surprise to Sam since he had made a special effort to instill a team spirit in the group. As the case observer, how would you evaluate this market-research group? Your analysis should include most of the elements of the group social system and the communication process.

ANALYSIS OF THE EXTERNAL SYSTEM OF THE GROUP

Even a superficial analysis of the market-research group identifies a basic external-system attribute. The group has been appointed by higher-level management to carry out an activity that is required by the total organization in order to adapt to environmental demands for new products. The group manager, Sam, is appointed by higher-level management. The group work location, membership, and general objectives are specified by higher management. These required elements make up the external system for the market-research group. They possess the basic characteristics of an external system in that they are formal, required, and specified factors. They are directly influenced by the technical, physical, and economic aspects of the environment which were discussed in Chapter 4.

As a member of the organization, the manager must deal with many of these types of small groups which are formally structured to perform certain activities. The environment and task structures often require that small groups be established. A work team may be required in order to apply a variety of skills to a single task. A committee may be required in order for the full group of people with responsibility for a decision to be involved in making that decision. The physical layout of an assembly operation may require the formation of a small group of people who work together in the production of each unit. A complete list of such required groups would be impossible because each organization has its own unique requirements. Some of the typical types of small groups which are required of organizations are conference groups, staff groups, committees, training groups, and boards.

THE GROUP AS AN ORGANIZATIONAL SUBSYSTEM

The group is a basic *subsystem* of the total organization. Subsystems include large units, small groups, and dyads which exist to carry out one or more functions that are required to meet organizational goals and environmental requirements. These subsystems do not operate in isolation. They must interact with other subsystems in order to coordinate their activities.

The manager is normally the most active coordinator. He or she is typically the member of at least two subsystems. Sam is a member of the market-research group and has free access to communicate with each member of the group. In addition, he is a member of the marketing-management group (see Figure 14-1). In meetings of the marketing-management group, he communicates the interests and needs of

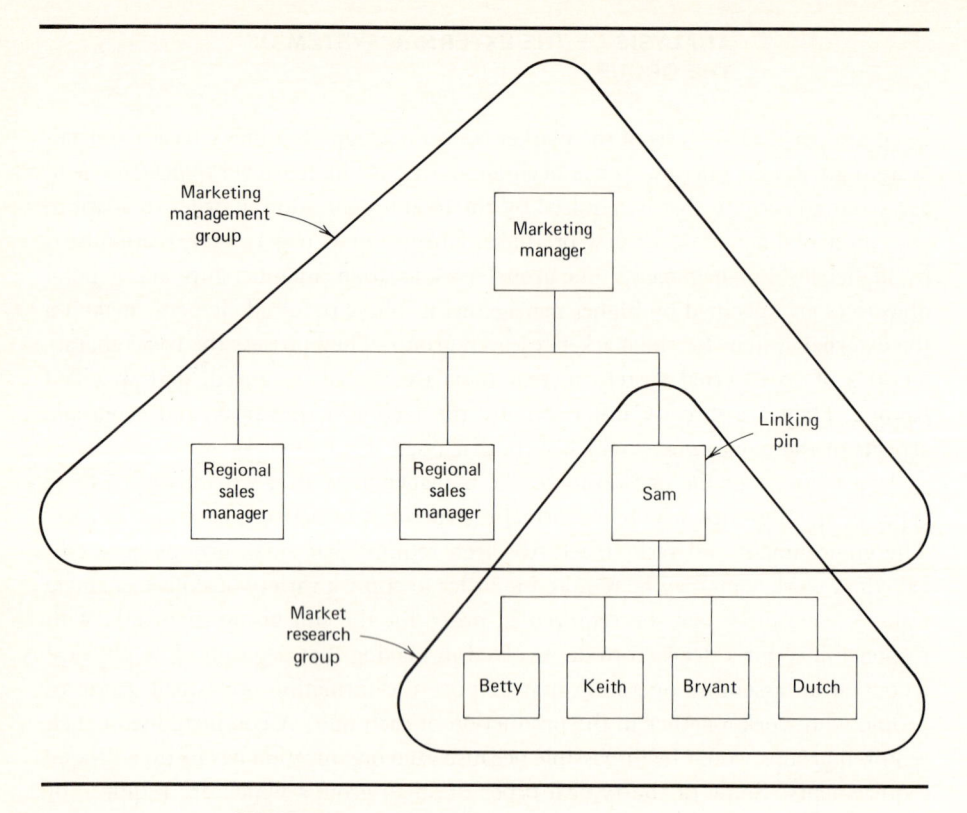

FIGURE 14-1 Linking-pin function of group manager.

the market-research group to his boss and peers. In the meetings of the market-research group, he communicates the goals and needs of the boss and other subunits represented in the marketing-management group to his group members. In this way he is performing the *linking-pin* function (Likert, 1961). He is forming a communication link between two groups of which he is a member. The array of linking-pin positions within the organization provides the adhesive that binds the organization together.

ANALYSIS OF THE INTERNAL SYSTEM OF THE GROUP

Within the required organizational framework, internal systems of small groups emerge. They arise as a result of informal, unspecified forces. Certain personal attributes attract people into small groups. Common values, beliefs, or needs weld individuals into a single group unit. Similar status levels, common expectations, or common goals may cause individuals to form a small group. Examples of these internal-system groups are found in coffee groups, lunch groups, grievance committees, social clubs, office parties, car pools, office sports groups, professional groups, and interest groups.

As the case observer, you will quickly see the emergence of the internal system for the market-research group. Bryant and Dutch form a subgroup or clique. Betty, Keith, and Sam become a second one. The subgroups emerge in response to common backgrounds of education and experience and certain personal attributes such as age and income. The nature of their individual tasks and work location facilitate the emergence of this informal, internal system.

The internal system has an important impact upon communication activities. Communication flows more smoothly with greater openness and trust within close-knit subgroups. Conversations over coffee or at lunch are relaxed and friendly. Conflicts within the subgroups are usually handled easily because of the closeness between the people.

In addition to the subgroups, you can identify other internal-system variables in operation. Differences in status levels exist. Involvement and dedication to responsibilities have emerged above the level actually required. These have largely been an outgrowth of Sam's participative style of management. Encouragement and constructive criticism are used freely by the group.

THE IMPACT OF THE EXTERNAL AND INTERNAL SYSTEMS UPON THE COMMUNICATION PROCESS

The manager must understand the importance of the relationship between the external and internal systems and their impact upon communication. The dynamics of the internal system influence the activities of the external system. Communication about product studies and market analyses flow smoothly between persons of equal status, between friends, and between persons who support and encourage one another. Conflicts growing out of the internal system of the group can hinder the communication regarding external activities. The manager must give attention to both the internal- and the external-group systems. He or she must properly balance these systems in order to attain the required objectives.

As the group manager, Sam must be aware of the impact of these social systems upon the communication process. He must recognize that the form and content of information from the *sender* will be influenced by the nature of the system in operation, as well as by the content of the message. To properly interpret a message in the role of *receiver*, the manager must be aware of the informal as well as the formal aspects of its content. The manager should consider both the formal and informal factors in determining the transmission and channel used in sending the message. Personal attitudes, animosities, or fears may have been the reason for a message being sent in written form rather than in oral form. On the other hand, the written form may have been best for the requirements of the group. Effective communication within a group requires the manager to apply an understanding of the group's social system.

As the case observer for the market-research group, your assigned task is only half complete. You have analyzed the external-internal systems of the group and their relationship to the group communication. You have not considered the nature of the group process and its relationship to the communication process. We shall examine these concepts in the next chapter.

SUMMARY

In this chapter we have introduced the external- and internal-system aspects of the small group using a business group as an illustration. The group as a subsystem of a total organization was discussed with a view of the manager as a communication link between two or more subsystems. Several emergent, internal-system factors of the group were discussed and illustrated. Finally, the impact of the mix of external- and internal-system factors upon the communication process was considered.

IMPORTANT TERMS AND CONCEPTS

small group, external-system groups, internal-system groups, subsystems, linking pin

REVIEW QUESTIONS

1. Identify several external-system-oriented groups common in business and explain why you consider them to be external-system-oriented.
2. Describe the linking-pin concept as a communication phenomenon.
3. What types of factors facilitate the emergence of internal systems in groups?
4. What aspects of the external-internal systems of the group are important to the manager?

BIBLIOGRAPHY

Likert, R.: *New Patterns of Management* (New York: McGraw-Hill Book Company, 1961).

15

ELEMENTS OF GROUP BEHAVIOR AND THE COMMUNICATION PROCESS

This chapter examines the processes by which small groups operate as a foundation for understanding small-group communication. The implications of each group-process variable for communication are discussed.

Much of our communication occurs in small groups. From the family of our birth to our funeral entourage, groups have a significant impact on our development and behavior. Communication is the basic tool for the operation of these groups. Whether it be the family members influencing one another in the daily conduct of life affairs, the work team on the engineering project, the board of directors, the chamber of commerce, the church school, or the social group, communication is the vital thread that holds the group together and provides the conduit for influence and action.

We are members of many more groups today than at any other time. These groups tend to be less permanent, stable, and enduring in nature. Consequently, communication skill becomes increasingly more important; one must be able to interact quickly and to relate effectively on a limited time basis. The successful manager today must become adept at establishing close, open relationships. One who remains guarded and defensive in the group context will be unable to succeed in a wide range of situations in the work environment. The typical manager spends much time in small groups. To perform effectively, the manager must be able to communicate effectively in the group for decision making, planning, and task execution. An understanding of certain group processes is an important determinant of the manager's ability to communicate effectively.

In the present chapter, we shall examine more closely the basic processes of group functioning and how they relate to the communication process. You are again asked to assume the role of the case observer for the market-research group and examine the group-process variables. The variables which concern us include group identity, social structure, goals, cohesiveness, and norms. These variables define the nature of the group and establish the group behavioral patterns.

Each of the group-process variables influences the flow, form, content, purpose, and quality of the communication process. Each is in turn influenced by the communication process (see Figure 15-1). You might begin your case observation with a look at the process of establishing group identity.

ESTABLISHING THE GROUP IDENTITY THROUGH THE COMMUNICATION PROCESS

The communication which establishes the identity will vary widely from one group to another. Groups which have vague purposes and structure spend a great deal of time and communication in developing their identity. If the association with the group is only to be of a temporary nature, less attention will be given to group identity. Groups which are established for a five- to ten-year duration give much more attention to identity. In addition, if the members are strongly ego-involved in the group, greater attention will be given to the discussion of identity.

The identity of our market-research group was defined in terms of *location* and *time*, which were already set when the group was first formed. Members learned that they were to appear at a particular address on a certain date. However, from the moment they first entered the building, the locational aspects of their future

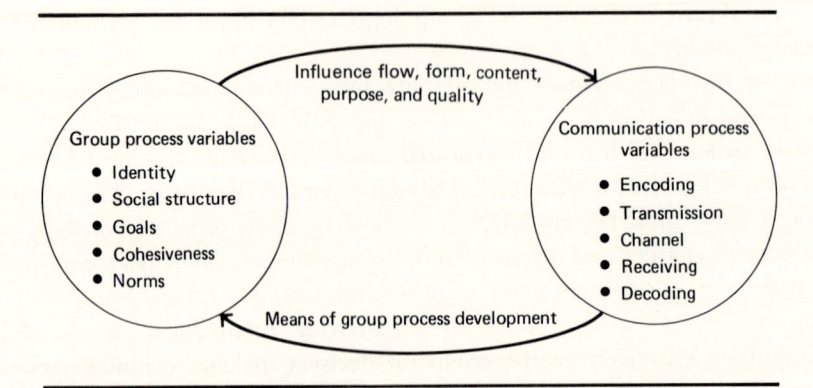

FIGURE 15-1 Interaction of group-process variables and communication-process variables.

group activities rapidly refined and expanded. A more explicit, fuller, and richer perception of the group's identity is formed over time.

For this market-research group, the *membership* is externally assigned and is easily identified. Since it is small, each member knows the other members. Large groups with fluctuating memberships such as university student bodies have a far less defined membership identity than is the case for the market-research group. The defined, stable membership of the group facilitates communication in that senders and receivers can build their understanding and their awareness of the language and semantics typically used by one another. Encoding, transmission, and other elements of the communication process will be enhanced through continuous practice and use. An enlightened manager can make good use of such effects in linking his or her group to other units of the organization.

The group has a defined *territorial space*. Certain offices, conference rooms, coffee lounges, and buildings "belong" to the group. The members refer to them as "our" or "ours." This territorial space may be expanded or contracted informally. Once established, the group tends to resist variations in the use of the space. Seating patterns become fixed. Particular locations become associated with specific activities. In groups such as an inner-city gang, the territorial space may be defended to the death against invasion. While not to this extreme, we all hold a degree of proprietary protectiveness for "our" territorial work space. Group communication may be directed toward defining or protecting the group's territorial space.

The *values* of the members also begin to be revealed early. As the members describe their backgrounds, they reflect their values. In our market-research group, the introductory discussion focused upon work and educational background. These were the valued aspects of their history as it applied to this group. In time, the values of the members will be reflected in many different ways and will become a point of identity for the group. These values become a basis for exercising control within the group.

With continued interaction, *expectations* about a number of factors become apparent. These expectations include those regarding various roles, interaction patterns, and member behavioral patterns. In our market-research group, the members developed the expectations that would assure Sam's leadership role. They also developed the expectation of a close interaction and participation in decisions. Job-performance expectations were discussed and agreed upon in open communication. By their behavior at coffee breaks and lunches, they developed clear expectations about who would interact with whom. These communication channels become the tasks for group activities.

The group establishes its identity when its members define the situations and characteristics which set them apart as an entity. The awareness of group identity may be either conscious or subconscious. The identity may be either external- or internal-systems-oriented. The primary external-system-oriented elements of identity include location, routine patterns, and membership. Values and expectations are elements of identity that relate closely to the internal system.

THE RELATIONSHIP OF SOCIAL STRUCTURE TO THE COMMUNICATION PROCESS

The second phase of development of the group process involves the social structure. The establishment of social structure and group identity are not totally independent processes. The structure of the group is one of the bases for group identity. Social structure includes *status systems, role relationships, subgroups, interaction relationships*, and *social-influence patterns*. The effectiveness of both the managerial and communication processes will be influenced by the social structure within which they occur. Accordingly, the manager and the communicator should be acquainted with the important variables which determine social structure.

The Relationship of the Status System within the Group to Communication

Achieved and Ascribed Status. Status is the social position a person holds as compared with that of other members of his or her group. Status identifies the evaluation of a position of an individual in the group. Status may be sought through striving and competitive mastery of the roles linked to status, or it may be ascribed to a person on the basis of characteristics such as sex, age, race, and kinship. The first type of status is referred to as *achieved status;* the second is *ascribed status*. Achieved status is attained through performing valued roles, activities, and efforts. On the other hand, the personal qualities of the individual are the basis for ascribed status and cannot be readily altered. In the film *The King and I*, the King of Siam is asked by his son how he will know when he possesses the omniscience associated with inheritance of the kingship. The King explains, "When you become King you will know." The King is suggesting that the ascribed status must precede the attainments associated with the status. This is not always the order of events.

In our market-research group, we can see evidence of both ascribed and achieved status. Sam comes to the group with the assigned, formal authority and position of group manager. This position within the external organizational system gives him a certain level of status. He has the authority to direct the work of others in the group, yet he elects to maintain a flexible group structure and to allow participation. As the group structure develops into an internal system, Keith and Betty appear to be striving to achieve a higher status rank than that aspired to by Dutch and Bryant. The status ascribed to them by virtue of their age and experience facilitate their ability to attain the desired status rank.

Deference. When group members act as if a group member holds status, these acts are referred to as *deference* behaviors. The group immediately shows deference for Sam. They accept his right to determine the group's method of organizing action. Deferential behavior takes the form of responding to the influence of the person with high status rank in satisfying that person's needs and aiding the achievement of his or her goals. The use of ingratiation as a deference behavior to gain conformity from a higher-status person was discussed in Chapter 10.

In an organization, the amount of status is usually tied closely to the organizational position, power hierarchy, and chain of command. Status symbols are acquired to communicate the existence of the status and to facilitate its recognition by others within the organization. Deferential behavior generally includes providing the most well-decorated and spacious rooms, most courteous treatment, gifts, attentiveness, praise, and imitation. Consequently, people with high status generally will carry with them symbols which help others recognize their status position.

Distributive Justice. Distributive justice refers to the perception of a person's status rank as proportional to the deferential behavior and the rewards associated with that rank. If people feel that their status rank is commensurate with their rewards and recognition, then distributive justice is maintained. If, however, this perception of their rank by virtue of achievement or ascribed status is below the level of the rewards and benefits afforded to them, then they feel a lack of distributive justice. Lack of distributive justice is usually attributed to favoritism and produces disharmony within the organization. Distributive justice is a significant consideration for the manager in determination of the relationship of wages and performance. Workers who perceive the status of their work to be low relative to the level of their pay will attempt to offset this imbalance by increasing their performance (Adams and Rosenbaum, 1962). If the manager arranges the work so that quantity cannot be increased, the quality of the work will be increased (Adams and Jacobsen, 1963).

The Impact of Status on Communication. Status has a significant impact upon the communication process in groups. Communication variables such as "how often," "who," "to whom," and "what" are influenced by status. High-status people generally communicate more frequently than do low-status people. They also have greater influence and more power than low-status people. Communication patterns tend to emerge along status lines. Persons of equal status tend to communicate with one another rather than with persons of different status. Consequently, status differentials facilitate communication at the same or similar status rank, but inhibit communication between people of differing ranks.

When people are introduced without the benefit of identifying status cues, there is a tendency to avoid communication. The ambiguity of the status positions results in discomfort in communication and is a threat to the status-related communication. To continue communication in the face of ambiguous status risks the loss of status position. The person may communicate in a manner that denotes lower status when his or her status is actually higher. Communication among persons of different status levels tends to be directed with more upward than downward reference. Persons of a given status position tend to direct their communication to higher-status persons rather than to persons of a lower-status level. Consequently, communication is greater among and toward high-status persons in a group.

The content of communication also varies among status levels. In group discussions, high-status people tend to give information and opinions, whereas low-status people assume a more passive role involving such responses as agreement, disagreement, and requests for information. Higher-status people also tend to sustain their positions by avoiding criticism of their role and tasks. Low-status people tend to be more critical of their own role.

The implications of these effects of status upon communication for the manager are quite apparent. Since managers hold a position which in our society provides high status, they may find difficulty in communicating with workers with whom they have the greatest need for communication. They may communicate unnecessarily with peers simply because they are more comfortable in doing so. Managers should also be aware of the barrier which their status provides for getting information and opinions from lower-status people. Managers can often improve their communication with subordinates by reducing the perceived status differential between themselves and subordinates.

If we examine the market-research group in terms of status and communication, we find that the higher status of Sam in the group is a basis for his being the most frequent communicator and the most influential group member. He will be the most frequently listened to, agreed with, supported, and reinforced member of the group. In the brief communication samples recorded in the example, the tendency for the communication to be directed to Sam is also illustrated. In addition, the communication tends to remain within status levels, particularly during coffee and lunch breaks and other informal situations.

Role Relationships within the Group and Communication

Roles define the kinds of interaction that are prescribed for certain types of interpersonal relationships. Managers may play a number of roles concurrently. They are supervisors to their employees, subordinates to higher-level managers, colleagues to their professional club members, fathers to their children, and husbands to their wives. Each role requires a different set of behaviors and attitudes. The content and style of communication is strongly influenced by the individual's role. The nature of the communication to one's wife, daughter, and supervisor are clearly very different in nature. Sam, of the market-research group, served as supervisor to his team and subordinate to his boss, a colleague to managers of other departments, and a market analyst to key customers. His communication experiences in each situation were likely to be quite different.

The relative significance of the roles for an individual and the amount of time that is spent performing each vary widely. The role of a monk in a monastery is essentially a full-time role. By contrast, the role of a customer for the person at the drive-in bank window is very brief and of little significance in a person's life. A role may be clearly established, as that of the bride at her wedding, or it may be as flexible as that of a professor in defining how and what will be done in class, research, or university activities.

Distinctions should be made between the perceived role, expected role, and enacted role. The *perceived role* is the set of behaviors that the occupant of the position believes he or she should perform. The *expected role* is the set of behaviors that others believe he or she should perform. *Enacted role* is the actual set of performed behaviors. Obviously, these types of roles may be at considerable variance. The greater the variance between the three types of roles, the greater the stress upon the individual and the persons associated with the individual. This stress is called *role strain*. A difference between the perceived role and the enacted role reflects a barrier: either internal to the person performing the role, such as incompetency, or external to the person, such as lack of resources or support from others. Differences between the expected role and the enacted role produce interpersonal conflict which results in change or eviction of the occupant from the position.

Role conflict occurs when a person is required to enact two incompatible roles simultaneously. Recently, in New York City, a news reporter rushed to the scene of an automobile accident to find his own son was the victim. An insurance salesperson is encouraged to sell to friends, but in doing so establishes a conflict of roles which may place the salesperson in a highly stressed situation. In the disastrous Texas City fire, when oil refineries exploded and resulted in fires which endangered the entire city, police officers were faced with the question of whether they would enact the police officer role and help protect the community or give first attention to the needs of their families in the parent role. Only one person resolved the conflict in favor of the police officer role. This man did so in the knowledge that his family was visiting in another city and enactment of the parent role was not needed. Role conflicts, like forms of role strain, stem from a wide range of perceptual, environment, and behavioral elements. They are resolved either by altering the perceived role, the expected role, or the enacted role or by eliminating the behavioral constraints.

Role relationships, whether externally or internally determined, significantly influence communication. Each role will require a certain level of communication. Other communication which is not required emerges because of the circumstances in which the role occurs. The manager's role requires a large amount of communication and encourages even more. Certain routine, isolated jobs provide roles which require and permit little communication. The content of the communication is equally influenced by the role. Each role within a group has an information requirement and encourages the discussion of a definable range of topics.

Subgroups as Channels for Communication

Another aspect of social structure which influences the communication process is that of subgroup formation. Just as organizations are occasionally factionalized into groups, so groups are sometimes factionalized into subgroups. We usually think of subgroups as those factions or cliques which emerge spontaneously in the group. These are internal-system elements. However, subgroups can be external and required as well. A particular task may require that a subgroup be formed. For instance, two members of a research team may be sent to another laboratory to carry out a study that requires special equipment. A subgroup of design engineers may be assigned the task of selling the results of the work of the entire design team to a potential user.

Subgroups influence the channels of communication flow. The frequency of interaction among members of a subgroup is greater than that for nonmembers. Should special jargon be developed, barriers to communication from outside the subgroup may exist. For formal task-oriented subgroups, this communication is work-content-related. For cliques or factions most of the communication content will be oriented to the common needs, interests, or goals.

Interaction Relationships within the Group

Interaction relationships are the emergent, recurring interactions among group members. These relationships are significant aspects of the group process and are intimately tied to the communication process. Interaction relationships become established rather quickly. These relationships are influenced by the status and role structure in the work situation. For example, Keith and Betty have similar functions to perform. Sam has a related activity with the two of them, and so the social-interaction relationship tends to be directed among these three. Bryant and Dutch have closely coordinated functions and responsibilities. Consequently, they communicate frequently. The geographical location of the work stations for Bryant and Dutch facilitate their close interaction relationships. Sam communicates frequently with Bryant and Dutch because of his responsibility for coordination.

Social-Influence Patterns and Communication

The social-influence patterns relate closely to the other aspects of social structure. As the accepted, informal group leader as well as the formal leader, Sam has the greatest amount of social influence. Keith and Betty have greater influence over the activities of Bryant and Dutch than vice versa. Keith and Betty are collecting the information. Therefore, the rate of information collection and transmittal by Keith and Betty will determine to a large extent the work load and work output of Bryant and Dutch. The reverse is not the case. This arrangement, by which the higher-status persons are the influence initiators, is favorable for the communication process. An adverse communication situation results when low-status persons become the influence initiators.

We have seen that each of the elements of social structure relates closely to the communication process. Communication serves to influence the development of the social structure and it is significantly influenced by the social structure.

THE GOALS OF THE GROUP AND THE COMMUNICATION PROCESS

Group goals are the internal-oriented, emergent goals. We refer to the goals imposed upon the group from without (such as by higher management) as superordinate goals. While superordinate goals influence the group's own goals, the group goals hold the dynamic force for mobilizing group activity. Thus, the group goals are our primary concern here.

The Needs of Group Members

In terms of motivational structure, groups operate very similarly to individuals. In fact, the motivational forces at work within a group are a particular combination of the motivational forces at work within the individual members constituting the group. Like individuals, groups have needs and attentive goals. The needs of the group are more than the simple summation of the needs of the individuals within it. The very existence of the group brings additional needs and alters existing ones. Communication helps to establish and alter the needs. It also helps the group obtain the goals which will satisfy the needs. The group goals are not a simple composite of the goals for the individual members. Within the same group, one person will emphasize satisfaction of interpersonal needs while another person will be motivated primarily by the need for achievement or self-esteem. Other persons will be striving for security in group membership. Out of this complex array of needs, group goals emerge.

An Example of Group Needs and Goals

As a means of illustrating the composition of group goals, let us use the example of the market-research group described earlier. We shall assume that we have superior knowledge which allows us to know the nature of the goals of the individuals within the group (see Figure 15-2). First, examine the case of Sam. Sam's needs include the need for acceptance by the group and affiliation with the group. Sam also needs to achieve; he needs to be the leader of a successful group and to avoid failure. He needs the status and power of leadership. Thus his individual goals

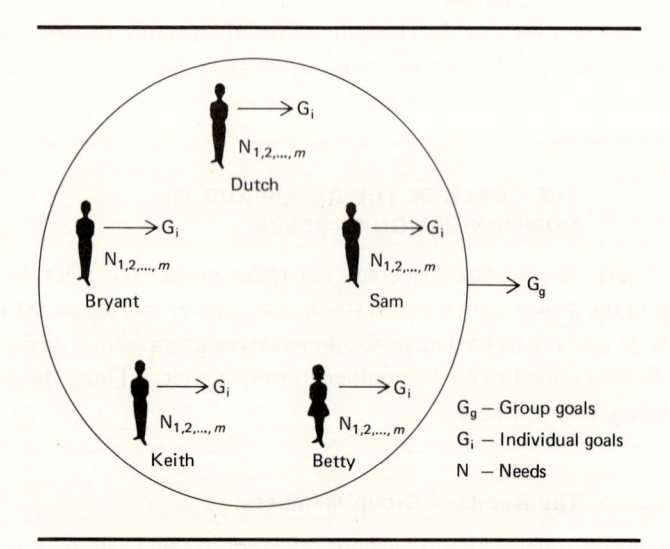

FIGURE 15-2 Group needs and goals.

include the continuity of the group, the success of the group, and a warm, close relationship with the group.

Betty has a number of needs which relate to group membership. Like Sam, Betty needs affiliation and close interpersonal relationships. Her need for security is not as strong as Sam's, but she does have a need for maintaining her position and for financial security for her family. Betty also has a strong need for achievement. She does not have the power drive that Sam has, but does desire to be recognized for her individual performance.

Being in his first job after graduation, Bryant has a very strong need for proving his ability at individual achievement. He feels less of a need for group achievement or being identified with a successful group but has a very strong security need as associated with being able to maintain his position and be accepted as an effective performer.

Obviously, we have simplified for brevity the needs of three of the group members. We have not attempted to identify all the possible needs of each member or to describe the complexity of each individual need. However, even this limited discussion should provide a framework for seeing how a group's goals emerge. The group goals may be written and clearly understood by all of its members; however, this is a rare situation. In most cases, at least a portion of the group goals are unexpressed or even subconscious. The uncommunicated goals are still highly significant and should not be ignored, because they are as important in determining group-member activity as are the goals that are well formulated.

Primary Group Goals

Group goals may be categorized as either achievement goals or maintenance goals. *Achievement goals* propel the group toward a desired target point of accomplishment. *Maintenance goals* are those which sustain the group, continue its existence, maintain the attraction of its members, and provide satisfaction for its members. Formulation of group goals occurs as we begin to consider our purpose for being and what we want to accomplish as a group. The goals include successful research regarding product Y, an effective planning of product Y, and fulfilling the group's responsibilities in the market-research area. In addition to these company-related goals, the group goals which are not in writing and may not be verbally expressed include continuity of the group and warm and cordial working relationships within the group.

Individual goals may be independent of these or may indeed be in conflict with these goals. Unless the individual sees enough opportunity to reach his or her goals to offset the conflicting goals, he or she will leave the group. However, individuals may find sufficient satisfaction of some of their needs to continue with the group even though many of their needs are being frustrated. This will lead to rather disgruntled and dissatisfied group members.

The process of establishing group goals is the focus of much communication early in the life of the group. As time progresses, the communication becomes directed toward evaluation of performance against the goals rather than their development. A number of approaches to management (especially the MBO approach) place strong emphasis upon the communication between the manager and the group members about their goals and their attainment.

GROUP COHESIVENESS AND THE COMMUNICATION PROCESS

Group cohesiveness refers to the degree to which the members desire to remain in the group. Cohesiveness is an internal-system factor. Members of highly cohesive groups are motivated to the continuance of the group, to advance the group, and to be active in the group. The highly cohesive group is close-knit, satisfied, and attractive to its members. Cohesiveness is closely connected to the maintenance goals.

We usually communicate more frequently in groups that are highly cohesive (Lott and Lott, 1961, and Moran, 1966). The quality of communication is also related to group cohesiveness. More highly cohesive groups engage in more objective problem-solving behavior and more open communication behaviors. The more highly cohesive groups are stronger in terms of both the quantity and the quality of interaction.

The content of the communication also appears to be influenced by cohesiveness. Groups whose cohesiveness is based upon task performance want to devote their discussion to completion of the task; groups whose cohesiveness is based upon member liking give more attention to pleasant conversation; and groups whose cohesiveness is based upon prestige are more cautious and avoid discussions which may endanger member status (Shaw and Shaw, 1962). Whatever the basis of cohesiveness, it seems clear that highly cohesive groups are more capable of affecting group and individual performance (including communication) than are the less cohesive groups (Seashore, 1954). The communication process allows the group to inform its members of its expectations. The discussion now turns to the matter of such group expectations or norms.

GROUP NORMS AND COMMUNICATION

A group norm is any standard of value or belief which is held by the members of a group. Norms are vital and viable forces influencing the behavior of members of the group. Groups have norms in most of the areas of their functioning. These areas include codes of dress, conduct, speech, choice of words, performance level, quality of performance, etc. Norms are similar to goals in that they are often not expressed verbally. They may not be a part of conscious awareness for group members. However, they are always communicated among the members of the group in one form or another. They may be communicated by way of example, grimace, smile, verbal criticism, or praise. The norms tend to be within the internal organizational system.

Not all group members are willing to conform to every norm. Those who choose not to follow group practice for a behavior are considered *deviants*. A group member who persists in disparate behavior will become ostracized or separated from other group members and is referred to as an *isolate*. Figure 15-3 depicts the behavior of a group of production workers in the classic Hawthorne studies (Roethlisberger and Dickson, 1939). In Figure 15-3, persons J.R. and B.J. performed at about normative output. Worker S.T. produced too much and was referred to as a "speed king" or a "rate buster." C.W. produced too low and was called a "chiseler."

Pressures for Conformity to Group Norms

The communication of disapproval of deviant behavior involves many forms of *group pressure*. Groups often take the form of a progression of increasingly more severe sanctions. The pressures are designed to bring the deviant into conformity with group norms. Early signs of deviancy are often met with gentle, jovial needling or with kind expressions of encouragement and correction. If the deviant behavior persists, the sanctions become more intense. Group members will directly attack the practice on rational grounds. If this fails, the deviant is faced with an emotional, usually hostile attack. In some situations the attack can involve

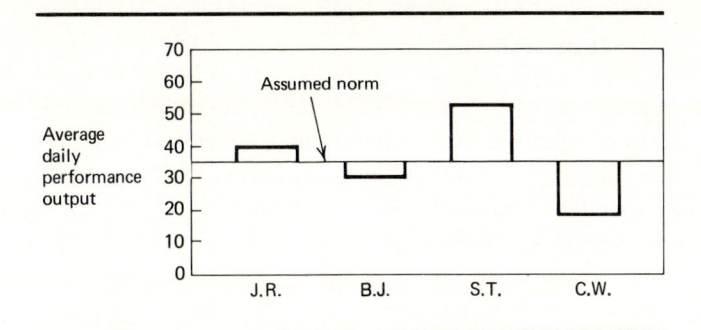

FIGURE 15-3 Example of behavior relating to a performance norm.

physical violence as well as verbal abuse. Should the deviant fail to yield under this pressure, the group will turn away and isolate the deviant member. Eventually, the sanctions may move to the form of expulsion from the group. Highly cohesive groups are able to exercise stronger pressures toward conformity to norms than are low cohesive groups. The more a person wishes to remain in the group, the greater is the potential for effective group sanctions. Consequently, we find greater conformity in behaviors of all types, including productivity, when the group is highly cohesive (Seashore, 1954).

Effects of Group Norms

In some situations the demand for conformity results in a mediocrity of action in which no person is allowed to excel or to be creative. However, this is not always the case; normative behavior is often an essential ingredient of effective group action. By having consistent group procedures, processes, and behaviors, we are able to reduce the amount of time required to perform a task. Without accepted norms each new group activity would require more communication in order to determine the role each person is to play and the behavior for each person. Normative jargon, speech patterns, and phrases allow rapid and accurate transfer of information within an established group. Group norms both influence and are influenced by communication. The form and content of communication within a group will be structured by the norms of the group. At the same time, all the norms of the group must be communicated among its members; otherwise, the norm does not exist.

If managers are not aware of the norms of their groups, they will be unable to effectively integrate the group and its processes (including communication) into the organizational scheme. The group norms can govern the occurrence, form, and content of the communication process itself.

SUMMARY

A number of group-process variables have been discussed which are significant in their impact upon organizational communication. These include group identity, social structure, group goals, cohesiveness, and norms. The general nature of such variables has been described and we have attempted to show the interrelationship of the various process variables and the communication process itself. The various process variables influence the internal-external context in which the communication process occurs. Thus, such variables affect the content, purpose, and quality of communication. Communication is frequently the means of establishing group-process variables. For example, in establishing its identity, the group discusses such things as its membership, location, and expectations. Group goals may also be developed through the discussion process.

The process of communication and the group-behavior process are closely intertwined in the dynamics of group functioning. Clear examples of this are seen in the effects of status and cohesiveness upon the freshness and openness of communication and in the effects of norms upon the sanctions communicated to the groups. Since the managerial role involves a good deal of functioning in groups, the manager should be aware of the group-process variables in their relationship to the communication process. The kinds of interactions between communication and group processes which influence managerial effectiveness were examined in this chapter. The group process which we described in this chapter provides a conceptual framework upon which the content of the remaining chapters of Part Three are built. The next chapter will deal with the communication networks in small groups.

IMPORTANT TERMS AND CONCEPTS

group identity, social structure, goals, cohesiveness, norms, location, time, membership, territorial space, value, expectations, role relationships, subgroups, interaction relationships, social-influence patterns, achieved status, ascribed status, deference, distributive justice, achievement goals, maintenance goals, group pressures, deviants, isolate.

REVIEW QUESTIONS

1. Using a small group used in a recent course exercise (for this course or some other), describe the nature of the group process in terms of group identity, social structure, group goals, group cohesiveness, and norms.

2. Contrast the group identity between your immediate family group and the group used in question 1 above.

3. What are the bases of achieved and ascribed status among the members of your class? What examples of deferential behavior have you observed? What would constitute distributive justice among the class members? Are there any evidences of lack of status congruence?

4. Describe your role as a student in your course in terms of perceived role, expected role, role strain, and role conflict.

5. What will occur when the achievement goals of a group are in conflict with its maintenance goals?

6. Discuss the relationship between conformity to group norms and group cohesiveness.
7. How does communication relate to (a) group identity, (b) status systems, (c) role relationships, (d) group goals, (e) group cohesiveness, (f) group norms?
8. Of what value is knowledge of communication as it relates to the group process for the manager of an organization?

INCIDENT: HENRY JAMES

On January 24, 1976, Henry James became supervisor of a newly formed maintenance crew for Bradco Drill Company.

His crew was assigned the responsibility for reducing the downtime and maintenance cost for the complex, automated drill presses which were the backbone of his company's production. Henry's crew consisted of three other employees: two were transferred from other maintenance operations and one was hired from a competitor in the area.

Henry was slow, methodical, but highly capable. He was viewed as a mastermind in tape-controlled machinery. His goal was to develop a group of highly capable personnel who could solve any problem which occurred.

Each crew member was assigned to a specific type of equipment. Henry worked closely with them to train them in the construction, operation, and maintenance of their equipment. The crew soon developed a deep respect for Henry. They enjoyed the challenge of repairing equipment that only a few people in the nation could repair. Within a year the preventive-maintenance program which they developed and the skilled repair and troubleshooting effort had reduced downtime by 30 percent and had cut maintenance costs by 25 percent.

Based upon their performance record, the crew was given a free hand to shut down equipment for preventive maintenance or repair at any time. Their advice to machine operators on changes that would lengthen the life of the equipment became respected and welcomed. The crew became a close-knit and effective work team.

1. What aspects of the group process are apparent within Henry's crew?
2. Why was the crew highly cohesive?
3. What would you predict would be the effects of the group-process variables upon communication for the crew?

EXERCISE 1: THE NATURE OF SOCIAL SYSTEMS AND GROUP PROCESSES

1. The class is divided into groups of six to eight members each. Each group assumes the role of the executive committee of General Motors. The executive committee has

met to set the goals of the corporation with respect to the response of the company to the need to conserve the nation's energy. These discussions last for fifteen minutes.

2. Each group discusses the communication with respect to the following questions regarding process variables:
   a. What is the group identity for your group?
   b. Was a social structure of the group apparent (status system, role relationships subgroups, and social-influence patterns)?
   c. How do you think the goals in this area relate to the broader goals of the board of directors for the corporation (superordinate goals) and to the needs and goals of the group members (individual needs and goals)?
   d. What are the norms for your group?
   e. Are there members of the group who appeared to talk to one or two others rather than to everyone in the group? Draw a diagram of the most frequently used flow of communication.

EXERCISE 2: OCCUPATIONAL PRESTIGE RANKING WORKSHEET

Instructions: Rank the following occupations according to the prestige which is attached to them in the United States. Place a 1 in front of the occupation which you feel to be most prestigious, etc., all the way to 15, least prestigious.

____ Author of novels

____ Newspaper columnist

____ Police officer

____ Banker

____ U.S. Supreme Court justice

____ Lawyer

____ Undertaker

____ State governor

____ Sociologist

____ Scientist

____ Public school teacher

____ Dentist

____ Psychologist

____ College professor

____ Physician

BIBLIOGRAPHY

Adams, J. S., and P. R. Jacobsen: *The Behavioral Manifestation of Cognitive Dissonance Reduction in a Work Situation* (New York: General Electric Co. Behavioral Research Service, 1963).

———, and W. B. Rosenbaum: "The Relationship of Worker Productivity to Cognitive Dissonance about Wage Inequities," *Journal of Applied Psychology,* vol. 46, pp. 161–164, 1962.

French, J. R. P., Jr.: "The Disruption and Cohesion of Groups," *Journal of Abnormal and Social Psychology,* vol. 36, pp. 361–377, 1941.

Lott, A. J., and B. E. Lott: "Group Cohesiveness, Communication Level, and Conformity." *Journal of Abnormal and Social Psychology,* vol. 62, pp. 408–412, 1961.

Moran, G.: "Dyadic Attraction and Orientational Consensus," *Journal of Personality and Social Psychology,* vol. 4, pp. 94–99, 1966.

Roethlisberger, F. J., and J. W. Dickson: *Management and the Worker* (Cambridge, Mass.: Harvard University Press, 1939).

Seashore, S. E.: *Group Cohesiveness in the Industrial Work Group* (Ann Arbor: The University of Michigan Press, 1954).

Shaw, M. E., and L. M. Shaw: "Some Effects of Sociometric Grouping upon Learning in a Second Grade Classroom," *Journal of Social Psychology,* vol. 57, pp. 453–458, 1962.

Thibaut, J. W., and H. H. Kelley: *The Social Psychology of Groups* (New York: John Wiley & Sons, Inc., 1959).

Whyte, W. F.: *Street Corner Society* (Chicago: The University of Chicago Press, 1943).

16

GROUP COMMUNICATION NETWORKS

Group communication networks are the connecting links between group members, but they also serve as interlocking subsystems of the external system itself. In this chapter we shall examine the various types of networks in terms of their determinants and their effects upon group functioning.

Suppose that you are a member of a small group formed to prepare a new layout for your work area. During the midst of the group discussion, you pause to notice the manner in which communication flows from person to person within the group. True, everyone in your group hears what each other person says (at least receives the signals), but if you will observe closely, you will notice that certain persons tend to talk frequently while others say little or nothing at all. If you watch the eyes, the gestures, and seating positions of your group members, you will also discover that each person favors one or two others as receivers of the messages. The phenomenon might become particularly noticeable if one person is assigned as the leader of the group.

THE NATURE OF COMMUNICATION NETWORKS

This directional pattern of communication within small groups is referred to as the network of communication. Such networks may be external (formal) or internal (informal) in their origin. Whether external or internal in nature, such networks constitute the building blocks of the organization through which information flows. In an informal discussion group, the exact network is difficult to determine. The network is emergent and rather imprecise. The formal network of communication which is described as an external system is much more easily plotted for a group. If the work layout and work flow formally specify the communication flow, it can be carefully defined and examined. We can much more easily record the interchange of communication. The chairman of the committee above or the manager of a formal group can often be clearly identified as the hub of such networks. We are not required to make inferences from nonverbal cues such as eye contact and gestures.

The network of communication in groups is far more complex than the channel of interpersonal communication. At the interpersonal level, we are merely concerned with whether communication is one way or two way and the media involved. In small groups the flow of communication among members may be not only one way or two way, but also between any number or combination of persons within the group. The media may include written, telephone, face-to-face, or nonverbal channels. Over a period of time, the flow of communication may be dense for one member and sparse for a less involved member. The network, which is the pattern of these exchanges within the group, may be fragmented by subgroups or may be evenly distributed. Subgroups are among the more complex problems in communication with which the manager must deal.

Examination of the communication networks can tell us much about the nature of the group and of the organization itself. The type of networks involved in a given situation tends to influence many group-process variables. By knowing the communication network, we can tell a good deal about the leadership, status, efficiency, member relationships, and member satisfaction of the group. The communication network is a basic determinant of the structure of the group. The network shows the way the members of the group are linked together. The consistent patterns of group relationships, authority, and status structure are closely tied to the network of communication within the group. Clearly, the manager must understand the intricacies of such networks if he or she is to effectively utilize them in completing the managerial process. We turn our discussion now to a closer examination of the nature of such networks.

TYPES OF COMMUNICATION NETWORKS

The types of communication networks which have received the greatest amount of theoretical and research attention are shown in Figure 16-1. The lines represent a flow of information between two positions. The arrows represent a unidirectional flow of information. The fact that the channel for communication flow is open for two-way interaction does not guarantee that the communication will actually flow in both directions. A person may choose not to send messages even though the network permits the person to do so.

GROUP COMMUNICATION NETWORKS 271

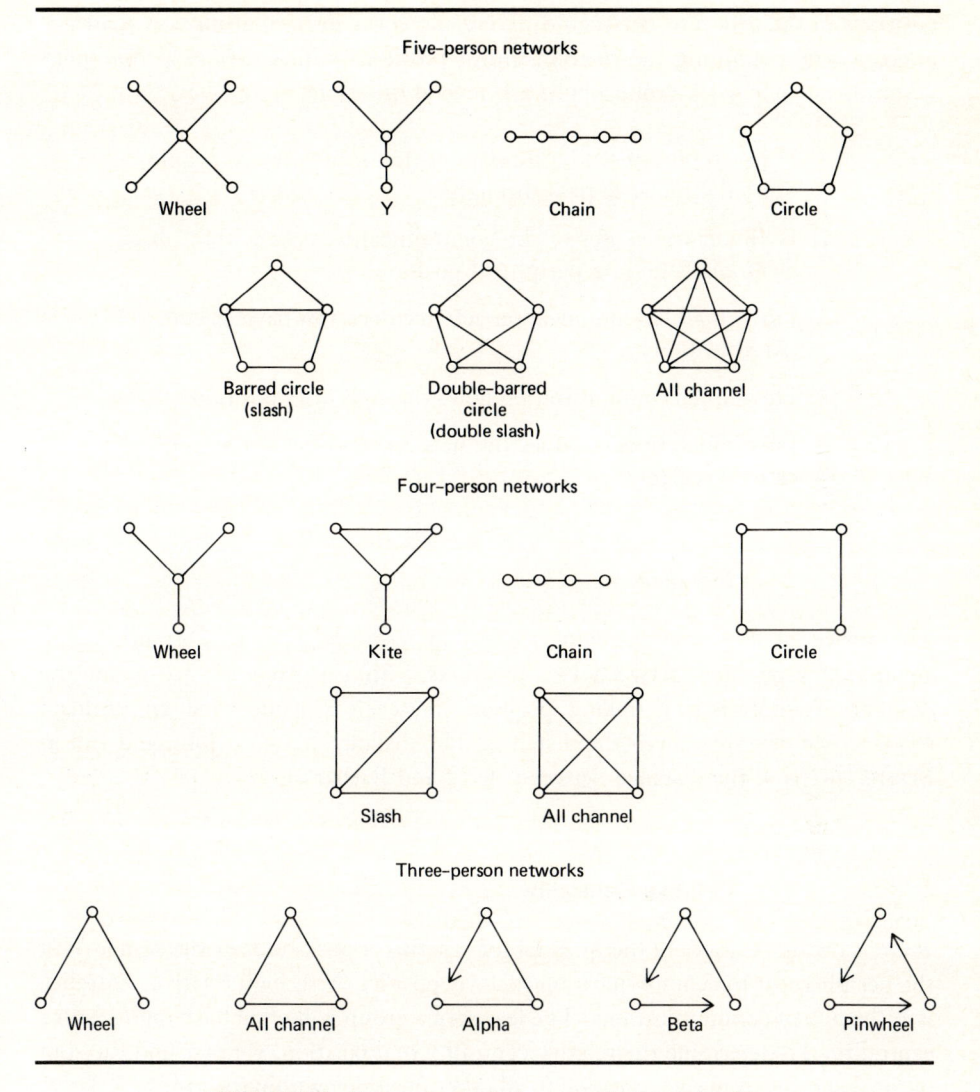

FIGURE 16-1 Frequently studied communication networks.

PROPERTIES OF COMMUNICATION NETWORKS

The various types of communication networks can be described in terms of a number of properties, i.e., distance, relative centrality, saturation, independence, and dispersion.[1] These properties may be used as a basis for comparison between

---

[1]Bavelas (1950) described several of these properties and developed measures for them.

positions in the group or between different networks for two groups. A manager interested in examining the relationship of positions which various people hold within his or her work group might ask several questions.

1. If Jim wants to send a message to John, how many people must the message pass through?
2. Is Jim at the center of the communication flow within his group or is he in a peripheral position?
3. How much communication activity does Jim have as compared to Betty?
4. How much communication flows through Jim's position?
5. How much freedom does Jim have in choosing a communication receiver?

Distance

The answer to the first question is given in terms of *distance*. Distance is the amount of separation between two positions within a group. If we count the number of intermediary linking positions between a sender and an ultimate receiver, we have measured the distance. The distance between John and Bill in Figure 16-2 is 4; the distance between Betty and Barbara is 2.

Relative Centrality

Relative centrality answers the question of whether a position is at the center or at the periphery of the communication flow. A position with high relative centrality is at the hub of communications. The leader of a group will often have high relative centrality. To determine the relative centrality of a position, we first find the sum of the distances from each position to all other positions within the group. Relative centrality for position *A* is the ratio of the sum of all the distances for all the positions to the sum of the distances for position *A*. For example, the relative

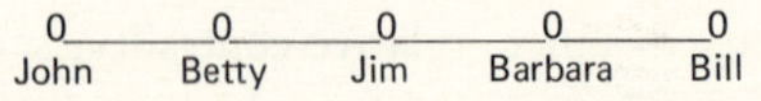

```
   0      0      0      0      0
 John   Betty   Jim  Barbara  Bill
```

FIGURE 16-2 Distances for the chain.

centrality for John in Figure 16-2 is 4 (40/10—the sum of the total distance for all five group members is 40; the sum of distances for John is 10). The relative centrality for Bill is the same as that for John. The relative centrality for Jim is 6.67 (40/6). You should calculate the relative centrality of a few positions in different kinds of networks to be sure you understand the concept. The relative centrality of a position has important implications for saturation, independence, and dispersion as we shall see in the following paragraphs.

Saturation

Saturation is the density of the communication activity for a position. Saturation tells us how active a position is within a group and how much communication flows through the position. Saturation for a position within a group is directly related to the relative centrality of the position. The most central position of Figure 16-2 is held by Jim, who also has the greatest level of saturation. The central position in a group that has a high level of information flow may reach the point of excessive saturation or communication overload. *Communication overload* occurs when a group member can no longer adequately process the load of communication which is received.

There are several responses to communication overload. These include: (1) omission—failing to process some of the information, (2) error—processing information incorrectly, (3) queueing—leveling the peak loads by delaying until a lull occurs, (4) filtering—separating out less significant and less relevant information, (5) approximation—categorizing input and using a blanket response, (6) employing multiple channels—altering the flow by introducing additional channels, (7) escaping—avoiding the information (Miller, 1960). Obviously, certain of these methods of responding to overload are more effective for the group than others. A response should be used which facilitates rather than retards achievement of group goals. The appropriateness of a response is determined by the task involved.

Suppose a group manager, Jenkins, is handling his daily in-basket. He may appropriately use omission for "junk" mail and "occupant"-type information by having his secretary discard this information. He may sort out less critical items to be handled on a date when he has more time available. He may filter out certain items that may be handled by a member of his staff. He may use a form letter to respond to a number of inquiries on a routine item. Jenkins may respond to a questionnaire by having several people complete certain portions of it. Finally, he may simply avoid information by casting an envelope into the trash unopened. Not all the information coming to him gets adequate attention, but if Jenkins is the typical manager he must use efficient methods of handling the mass of information which he must process or he will be inundated in a mound of paperwork.

Independence

Independence is the property of the network which indicates the degree of freedom that a group member has to choose a channel (Shaw, 1964). The greater number of available communication channels, the greater the independence of the person. For the circle network in Figure 16-1, each group member has an equal but limited degree of independence; each person can elect to send or receive a message from two others. The all-channel net allows each person to communicate with every other member, thus providing the maximum degree of independence. In Figure 16-2, John and Bill have no choice; they have the minimum possible level of independence. Betty, Jim, and Barbara each have two channels available. The greater the independence of a person, the more discretion is required and the greater the flexibility and adaptability of the group structure to changing demands. This flexibility and adaptability becomes more important as the task becomes more complex and changing. Think of the situations you have seen in organizations. You can probably identify many examples of the effects of independence, especially for supervisors and managers.

Dispersion

For the person who wishes to compare the flow of communication in one network with the flow for a different network, *dispersion* is a useful property. Dispersion is the sum of the distances for all the positions within a group. Suppose one wished to compare the dispersion of the wheel network with the Y network as shown in the five-person networks of Figure 16-1. The dispersion for the wheel is 32 and for the Y is 36. These dispersions indicate that the flow of communication for the wheel involves fewer links than for a Y network involving the same size group. As the number of links in the communication flow increases, the possibility of distortion and error is also increased. The all-channel network has the most favorable dispersion. The dispersion for a five-person all-channel network is 20. Now we shall examine the effects of the various networks.

EFFECTS OF THE NETWORKS OF COMMUNICATION

In working with small groups in his or her organization, the manager will find that the number of emergent relationships is influenced by the communication net-

```
┌─────────────────────────────────────────────────────────────┐
│  ┌───────────┐    ┌───────────┐    ┌───────────┐           │
│  │ Formal or │    │           │    │ Emergent or│           │
│  │ external  │    │ Leadership│    │ informal  │           │
│  │ group     │───▶│Problem-solving│─▶│ group    │           │
│  │communication│  │Group morale│   │communication│         │
│  │ network   │    │           │    │ network   │           │
│  └───────────┘    └───────────┘    └───────────┘           │
│        ▲                                 │                  │
│        └─────────────────────────────────┘                  │
└─────────────────────────────────────────────────────────────┘
```

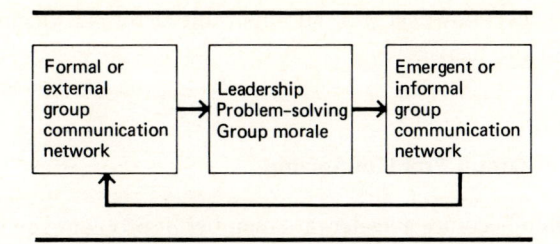

FIGURE 16-3 Interrelationship of effects.

works. We shall find that communication networks affect: (1) the emergence of leadership, (2) the effectiveness of group problem solving, and (3) group morale. In addition, each of these factors influences the nature of the emergent or informal networks. Each of these factors will be discussed below.

Emergence of Group Leadership

Communication networks have a strong impact upon the *emergence of leadership* within the group. If a person in the group is in a key communication-link position (a position with high relative centrality), the potential for influence is high, and consequently, the likelihood of that person becoming a leader is great. A communication network which funnels a large amount of information through a single position stimulates the emergence of leadership for the holder of that position. On the wheel net, the central person has a much higher centrality measure than that of the peripheral group members. In the circle and all-channel nets there is no central person; all members have an equal centrality measure. The frequency and the clarity for the emergence of a single leader are much greater in the wheel than for the circle or all-channel nets. According to research, the various networks rank as follows with respect to the highest to lowest likelihood for the emergence of a single, recognized leader: wheel, Y, chain, circle, and all channel. Neither the circle, slash, nor all-channel networks favor the clear emergence of a single leader (Leavitt, 1951; Shaw, 1954; Shaw and Rothschild, 1956; Hirota, 1953). Leadership functions tend to be shared among group members in groups with these networks.

It is not surprising for a central person in the communication flow to become the leader. He or she has access to information and the opportunity to coordinate the activities of the group. When a person in a peripheral position is singled out to receive more information and coordination opportunities than his or her position would normally afford, such a person is much more likely to become the group leader (Shaw, 1954). The information flow is only one of many determinants of leadership emergence; however, it is an important factor. Leadership is, of course, a key function of the manager.

Group Problem Solving

The manager often becomes a leader or a member of problem-solving groups. The effectiveness of a given communication network for *group problem solving* is dependent upon the type of problem involved. The effectiveness of a network in problem solving appears to depend upon the complexity of the problem involved. For simple tasks such as those requiring the group to discover or identify a symbol, letter, number, or color, the centralized networks (such as the wheel, chain, or Y) appear to be more efficient than the decentralized networks (such as the circle and all channel) (Leavitt, 1951; Shaw, 1954; and Bavelas, 1950).

For more complex problems such as arithmetic (e.g., application of arithmetic to solving a logistics problem), discussion problems, and human-relations problems, the decentralized networks have been found to be more effective (Davis and Hornseth, 1967; Gilchrist, Shaw, and Walker, 1954; Shaw, Rothschild and Strickland, 1957). For these complex problems, the relatively decentralized all-channel and circle groups are faster, exchange more ideas, and make fewer errors (Shaw, 1971). Most of the problems which the manager will typically face are complex. This leads to strong preference for the all-channel network for organizational problem solving. The research used as a basis for these conclusions was obtained in laboratory situations rather than in an operating organization. Burgess (1968a) has given evidence that the findings must be applied by the manager with much caution.

Effects of Formal Networks upon Informal Networks

Informal networks of communication often develop within the constraints imposed by formal communication networks. As we have seen elsewhere in this book, internal systems tend to emerge from formally prescribed frameworks. Two basic information networks usually emerge when the group is given freedom to develop these structures—the all channel and the wheel. The all-channel structure allows all group members to gain all available information and thus participate in solving a problem. The informal network which emerges tends to be in conformity to the formal communication network. The wheel structure is more likely to be established by groups with centralized formal communication networks. The all-channel structure is favored by formal networks with less centrality (Shaw, 1954, and Shaw and Rothschild, 1956).

Influence of Informal Networks upon Problem Solving

The influence of the emergent, informal network structure upon problem-solving effectiveness appears to be greater than the effects of the externally imposed communication network. In fact, the effects of the formal network upon problem solving tends to disappear when the group is given the time and opportunity to develop an efficient informal network structure within the constraints of the imposed formal network (Guetzkow and Simon, 1955; Lawson, 1964; Mulder, 1960; and Burgess, 1968a). This, of course, could be quite beneficial to the manager since an inherently bad design in the formal network might be offset by the emergent informal network.

Informal Networks and Communication Links

Efficient informal network structures are those which have a minimum of links among the members of the group. For each link, the process of selection, encoding, decoding, etc. must be repeated. Thus, with each additional link, the probability of semantic distortion and other communication problems is multiplied. Suppose the two groups of Figure 16-4 are required to determine the cause of a conflict between persons E and D. Person E is angry at D but is unwilling to tell D of the reason. In the informal network which has emerged, E will communicate with B, a close friend, but not to any other group member. A is the manager of the group and is attempting to bring about reconciliation. In Group I, A will only communicate openly with B about the problem. A's usual access to D is blocked by the interpersonal conflict. To reach D, A must communicate via B and C. In Group II, A handles the same problem by delegating the responsibility for the reconciliation to B. The slash network does not permit B to speak directly to D, but B can prevail upon C to assist in doing so. Obviously, Group II will be able to determine the cause of the problem and bring about reconciliation more rapidly than Group I simply because there is less linkage in the communication flow. The most efficient group is the one that organizes its informal network structure to minimize the number of links in the system (Guetzkow and Dill, 1957).

The all-channel network allows the greatest flexibility for establishing the

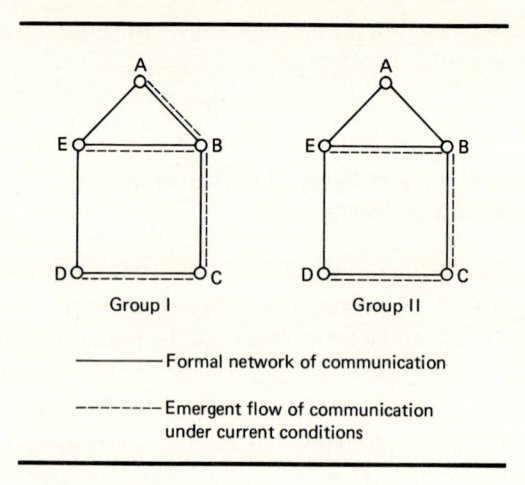

FIGURE 16-4 Operating structure for two slash networks.

optimum informal network structure, and therefore allows the most effective structure to emerge. However, when the wheel is the best network for a particular group task, formally structuring the group into the wheel network eliminates the loss of time in having it emerge informally.

We can find other explanations for the greater efficiency of the more decentralized formal and informal networks. The more decentralized system allows the participation in problem solving of a greater number of people—thus, a greater range of backgrounds, knowledge, and points of view is present. The highly centralized system, in funneling all the information through a single problem solver, tends to saturate the central person in communication exchange and leaves little time for thought about the problem. This fact becomes increasingly important as problems become more complex. In complex tasks the central person has demands other than communication which may overload him or her. Complex tasks often require greater concern for organizational decisions, handling irrelevant information, and analysis of data which increase the saturation for centralized systems. The decentralized networks provide more flexibility. An efficient group is able to develop an appropriate informal network for a particular problem and then change to meet new situations.

Effects of Networks upon Group Morale

Communication networks also have implications for *group morale*. Groups with decentralized communication networks have higher group morale (or group satisfaction) than do centralized networks. The satisfaction level of persons in peripheral group positions is lower than the level of those in central positions (Leavitt, 1951). The *higher independence* of the central position gratifies the need for autonomy which is one basis for higher satisfaction (see Figure 16-5). The order of the networks from lowest to highest in group satisfaction is wheel, chain, Y, circle, and all channel (Leavitt, 1951; Shaw, 1954; Shaw and Rothschild, 1956; Cohen, 1962; and Lawson, 1965). In many organizations the hierarchical structuring, work environment, manufacturing procedures, and the like tend to restrict the freedom of employees in their communication. Managers with highly rigid structures and procedures should recognize that they are suffering loss of morale due to lower independence.

FACTORS WHICH DETERMINE THE NATURE OF THE COMMUNICATION NETWORKS

In light of the effects of the communication network, managers need to be aware of the factors that determine which network will exist, so that they can establish the networks which will be most effective for their groups. Let us suppose that you are a manager who is about to structure a new work group. What factors will influence the type of network that your group will use? The all-channel network looks simple for group meetings, but is it? Suppose you call a group together to hold the first meeting and begin with a pep talk about how participation is expected; everyone should share any opinions. You then bring up the first item for discussion. A fellow sitting in the back row raises his hand, and you call on him. "I move that we follow plan *A*," he quickly states. Suddenly, you are in the midst of the use of the parliamentary method in which you serve as the communication gate and all the communication flows back and forth to you (you are using the wheel net). After fifteen minutes of the agony of stilted, formal jargon, you pull up short. "Wait a minute," you say, "this formal procedure is killing all the life and spontaneity of the discussion. No more motions; forget about my recognizing you. Just say whatever you wish, when you wish." At this point the atmosphere softens, and more of the group begins to enter into the discussion. However, you are attuned to the communication flow and you notice that persons sitting close to you talk much more than those in the back rows; and from your position, standing at the front of the room facing everyone else, you are inclined to do far more talking than any other person. Seeing this, you interrupt the discussion again, "Let's all move our chairs around so we can see one another. I'll sit down also." Now your chairs are in a circle. A few additional people enter the discussion. The only barriers remaining to the full and open communication that you desire are

	Low-morale groups		
	Wheel	Chain	Y
Mean satisfaction rating	5.4	5.8	6.8
Black dot represents low morale position			

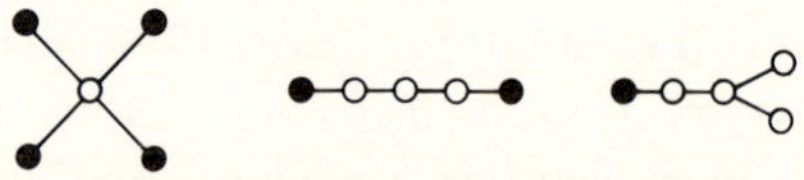

	High-morale groups		
	Circle	Slash	All-channel
Mean satisfaction	8.0	*	*
Black dot represents high morale position			

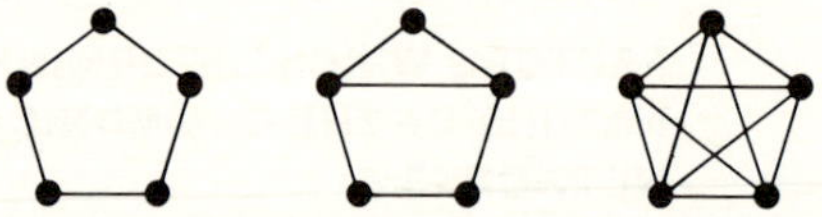

*Not included in Leavitt study.

FIGURE 16-5 The relationship of group morale to communication network. [*Source:* H. J. Leavitt, "Some Effects of Certain Communication Patterns on Group Performance," Journal of Abnormal and Social Psychology, *vol. 46, pp. 38–50, 1951.*]

found in the roles, status, perceptions, motives, and personalities of the group members. Some are dominant, others submissive; some are assertive, others are passive; some are personally independent, others are dependent; some are ascendant, others are timid. The high-status persons tend to talk more. Those who perceive themselves to be of low status or in less significant roles talk less.

Close examination by the manager will identify five factors which determine the type of communication network which should be established or which will emerge. These are (1) *task and functional* determinants (in the illustration above this is the group discussion), (2) *conventions and normative behaviors* (e.g., parliamentary method and informal discussion), (3) *environmental setting* (e.g., seating arrangement and distance), (4) *personal attributes* (e.g., motivation, perception, and emotion), and (5) *group-process variables* (e.g., roles, status, cohesiveness, and goals). (See Figure 16-6.) The formal, external-system variables among these are the formal aspects of the group-process variables. The informal, internal-system variables include emergent conventions and normative behaviors, personal attributes, and the more informal group-process variables.

Task and Functional Determinants

When the group task is primarily one of exchange of information and decision making in a group meeting, the channel options are quite varied. Normally, the all-channel network is in operation; but since not everyone speaks to everyone else, the network which emerges is often some modification of the all channel. In any group task, a person's need for information and the appropriate source of that information is dependent upon the action that the person is expected to perform. Frequently, a person receives more or less information than the role requires for effective and efficient functioning. Careful study of the role and the communication network will bring these imbalances to light. For example, the information requirements for employee morale may be somewhat greater than the requirements for task performance required of the external system. The individual may simply need to know "what is going on" in order to meet ego or security needs. If inefficiency does not occur, the person should be included in the information network.

Conventions and Norms as Determinants

The manager also should be aware of the set of *conventions* and *norms* of behavior which influence the network of communication. These recurring practices include the formality, or spontaneity of the deference behavior, emotional tone, forms of attention getting, and interaction-pattern norms. These norms allow group mem-

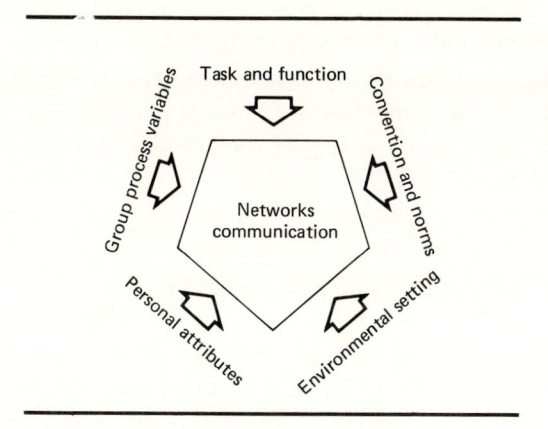

FIGURE 16-6 Determinants of the network of communication.

bers to know what to do. Therefore, members can avoid repeatedly discussing what should be done. Norms provide the security of knowing which communication behaviors and channels are accepted by the group. Norms can also hinder performance by producing needless conformity. The parliamentary method is an example of a level of norm behavior that is rarely desirable for a small group. It removes the openness and richness of direct dialogue that is usually desired in the small group.

Environmental Settings as Determinants

Important elements of the *environmental setting* include personal space, interaction distance, and seating arrangements. Personal space is the area surrounding one's body which is considered to be private. Intrusion into this space by another person causes emotions from mild discomfort to retaliatory action. For example, the personal space may become extremely small when a fellow is communicating with a beautiful blonde. The desired interpersonal distance varies with the relationship of the persons. A progression of preferred distances is found in an intimate family, which is closest, through acquaintances, to strangers (Little, 1965). A greater interpersonal distance is also preferred between high-status and low-status people than between people of equal status.

The seating arrangement that is used in a group meeting influences the communication network. When the seats are arranged in the shape of a circle, communication often flows between people sitting across from and facing one another rather than between people sitting in adjacent seats (Steinzor, 1950, and Hearn, 1957). The greater the distance between the seats of two people, the less friendly and talkative they are expected to be (Russo, 1967). A person seated at a position which encourages greater participation is likely to emerge as a leader (Howells and Becker, 1962). In addition, the manager through planning and organizing efforts determines the environmental setting of the group which in turn influences the flow of communication.

Personal Attributes as Determinants

Personal attributes of the group members influence the network. The intrapersonal factors of perception, motivation, and emotion and the interpersonal roles described in Transactional Analysis concepts were discussed earlier. Not only are these factors of significance for interpersonal communication, but they also influence the behavior of the people in small groups. Consequently, these factors are significant determinants of the emergent communication net. For example, a group consisting of people who all play the Adult role is more likely to use the all-channel network than a group whose members include a mix of people who play the Parent role and of people who play the Child role.

The communication net of the group is also influenced by the other *group-process variables*, such as group identity, status systems, cohesiveness, and goals. These were discussed in Chapter 15.

SUMMARY

Our discussion of communication networks has presented the types of networks and their properties. We discussed the effects of the various networks upon the emergence of leadership, group problem solving, and group morale. Then, we considered the individual, group, and environmental factors which determine the network to be employed.

A more centralized network encourages the emergence of a strong leadership role. The question of the effects of the networks upon problem solving is a moot one at this point; while some researchers say that the complexity of the problem is the deciding factor, others argue that the effects of complexity disappear with time in a group's life cycle. The informal network structure, rather than the more formal network, seems to have greater significance for performance. In general, the more decentralized networks are more favorable for morale than their counterparts.

The use of centralized networks, as contrasted to the decentralized networks, is facilitated when a small number of information sources are required by the tasks involved; when conventions and norms support the narrow spread of communication interchange; when the environmental setting forces communication through a central person; and when the attributes of the group members or of the group as a whole place one or a few people in more central positions.

Clearly, the communication network is a key variable in the behavior of the small group.

IMPORTANT TERMS AND CONCEPTS

communication networks, distance, relative centrality, saturation, independence, dispersion, emergence of leadership, group problem solving, informal networks, communication links, group morale, task and functional determinants, conventions and normative behaviors, environmental setting, personal attributes, group-process variables

REVIEW QUESTIONS

1. What is the significance of the communication networks to the organization manager?
2. Suppose you are the leader of a small group and you wish to make a decision about the kind of network your group should use. What factors would you wish to consider in arriving at your decision?
3. Which of the properties of communication networks do you view as most important for group functioning? Why?
4. Suppose you aspire to become the leader of a small group. How would you attempt to structure the network of your group in order to effect that result? What would be the effects of this network: (a) upon group effectiveness, and (b) upon group morale?
5. Discuss networks and operating structure in terms of the concepts of internal systems and external systems.

EXERCISE: INFORMATION FLOW WITHIN SMALL GROUPS

1. Divide the class into groups of five to six members. Select one member as a leader. Each group will be designated I, II, or III.

   Group I will sit with the leader (A) facing the other members.

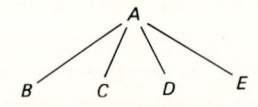

   B, C, D, and E are not permitted to communicate with anyone other than A during the exercise (see the lines above, which represent links).

   Group II will sit with the leader (C) in the middle of a chain.

   A —— B —— C —— D —— E

   Member communication is permitted only with the person to whom one is linked by a line (above).

   Group III will sit with all members facing one another.

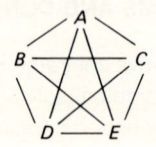

   Any member may communicate with any other member, or with the leader (A).

2. Each group member has a number of puzzle pieces distributed by the instructor. Each member (excluding the leader) is to assemble one jigsaw puzzle into the shape of a square. All puzzles will be the same size. No member is allowed to point out an error or to make a suggestion of a solution to another member. All messages must be in written form (no gestures or verbal comments are permitted). The transfer of pieces should also be restricted to these links.

3. The group to finish first wins. First-place, second-place, third-place, and fourth-place winners should be noted in a large class.

4. Discussion questions for each group:

   Redivide the groups before the discussion.
   a. How did you feel about your communication network?
   b. What were the problems that your group encountered?
   c. Was there a tendency for a pattern to emerge within the net that was assigned to your group?
   d. Which network appears to be most effective? Why?
   e. What was the impact of the network upon leadership?

BIBLIOGRAPHY

Bavelas, A.: "Communication Patterns in Task-oriented Groups," *Journal of the Acoustical Society of America,* vol. 22, pp. 725–730, 1950.

Burgess, R. L.: "Communication Networks: An Experimental Re-evaluation," *Journal of Experimental Social Psychology,* vol. 4, pp. 324–337, 1968a.

———: "An Experimental and Mathematical Analysis of Group Behavior within Restricted Networks," *Journal of Experimental Social Psychology,* vol. 4, pp. 338–349, 1968b.

Cohen, A. M.: "Changing Small Group Communication Networks," *Administrative Science Quarterly,* vol. 6, pp. 443–462, 1962.

Davis, J. H., and H. Hornseth: "Discussion Patterns and Work Problems," *Sociometry,* vol. 30, pp. 91–103, 1967.

Gilchrist, J. D., M. E. Shaw, and L. C. Walker: "Some Effects of Unequal Distribution of Information in a Wheel Group Structure," *Journal of Abnormal and Social Psychology,* vol. 49, pp. 554–556, 1954.

Guetzkow, H., and W. R. Dill: "Factors in the Organizational Development of Task-oriented Groups," *Sociometry,* vol. 20, pp. 175–204, 1957.

———, and H. A. Simon: "The Impact of Certain Communication Nets upon Organization and Performance in the Task-oriented Groups," *Management Science,* vol. 1, pp. 233–250, 1955.

Hearn, G.: "Leadership and the Spatial Factor in Small Groups," *Journal of Abnormal and Social Psychology,* vol. 54, pp. 269–272, 1957.

Hirota, K.: "Group Problem Solving and Communication," *Japanese Journal of Psychology,* vol. 24, pp. 176–177, 1953.

Howells, L. T., and S. W. Becker: "Seating Arrangement and Leadership Emergence," *Journal of Abnormal and Social Psychology,* vol. 64, pp. 148–150, 1962.

Lawson, E. D.: "Reinforced and Non-reinforced Four-Man Communication Nets," *Psychological Reports,* vol. 14, pp. 287–296, 1964.

———: "Change in Communication Nets, Performance and Morale," *Human Relations,* vol. 18, pp. 139–147, 1965.

Leavitt, H. J.: "Some Effects of Certain Communication Patterns on Group Performance," *Journal of Abnormal and Social Psychology,* vol. 46, pp. 38–50, 1951.

Little, K. B.: "Personal Space," *Journal of Experimental Social Psychology,* vol. 1, pp. 237–247, 1965.

Miller, J. G.: "Information Input, Overload and Psychopathology," *American Journal of Psychiatry,* vol. 116, pp. 695–704, 1960.

Mulder, M.: "Communication Structure, Decision Structure and Group Performance," *Sociometry,* vol. 22, pp. 367–386, 1960.

Russo, N. F.: "Connotations of Seating Arrangements," *Cornell Journal of Social Relations,* vol. 2, pp. 37–44, 1967.

Shaw, M. E.: "Some Effects of Problem Complexity upon Problem Solution Efficiency in Different Communication Nets," *Journal of Experimental Psychology,* vol. 48, pp. 211–217, 1954.

———: "Communication Networks," in L. Berkowitz (ed.), *Advances in Experimental Social Psychology* (New York: Academic Press, Inc., 1964).

———: *Group Dynamics: The Psychology of Small Group Behavior* (New York: McGraw-Hill Book Company, 1971).

———, and G. H. Rothschild: "Some Effects of Prolonged Experience in Communication Nets," *Journal of Applied Psychology,* vol. 40, 281–286, 1956.

———, ———, and J. F. Strickland: "Decision Processes in Communication Nets," *Journal of Abnormal and Social Psychology,* vol. 54, pp. 323–330, 1957.

Steinzor, B.: "The Spatial Factor in Face-to-Face Discussion Groups," *Journal of Abnormal and Social Psychology,* vol. 45, pp. 552–555, 1950.

17

GROUP COMMUNICATION AND PERFORMANCE

The purpose of this chapter is to examine the impact of communication upon group performance. The significance of communication for the group varies with the type of performance goals involved. Four categories of group performance are examined in the order of their dependence upon communication: from social interaction, to personal growth, to decision making, and finally, to defined production.

Group performance can be defined as either the output of individual members, or the composite outputs of the members of the group directed toward its goal (see Figure 17-1). The performance of a group is influenced by each element of the group process (goals, identity, norms, social structure, cohesiveness, leadership, etc.). The concern of this chapter is to consider the direct relationship between communication and group performance, avoiding insofar as possible the indirect effects of communication that occur as a result of the group-process variables. A number of communication factors appear to be of importance in influencing performance output. These factors include the type of communication, the relevance of the communication content to the task, the climate of acceptance and openness, the availability of information, the degree of agreement among group members, and feedback and communication networks. Since the effects of communication networks on group performance were discussed in detail in Chapter 16, they will not be considered here.

Groups differ markedly in the extent to which their performance depends on communication. Certain types of performance results depend very heavily upon communication; others do not. As will be shown, groups whose primary goals are social interaction, personal growth of members, or problem solving are highly

287

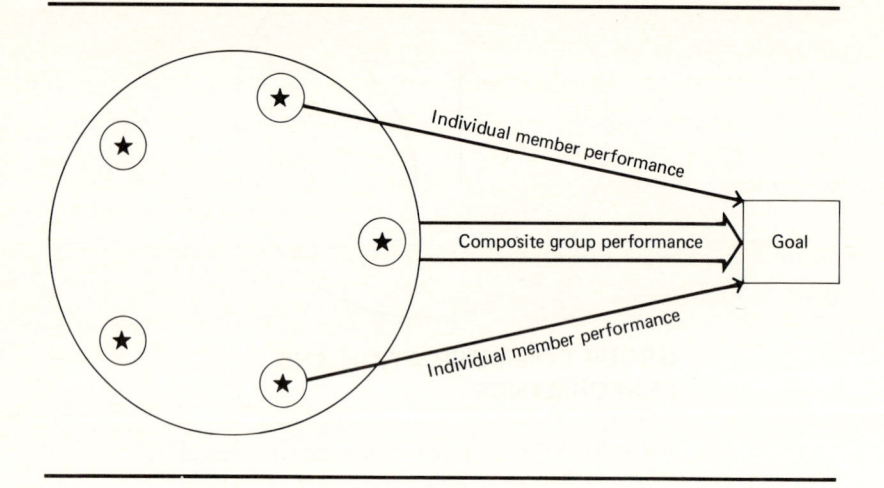

FIGURE 17-1 Communication and group performance.

dependent upon communication. On the other hand, groups involved in the production of tangible products are much less dependent on communication. The need for communication in defined, specified production is dependent upon the type of production process involved, types of tasks involved, and the demands of information flow. As we examine the performance of groups whose goals vary from that of social interaction, to personal growth, to decision making, and finally, to defined, routine production, we shall see a shift in the significance of communication from an almost total dependence upon communication behaviors to a level of minimal dependency. Similarly, we are moving from a type of group performance that is oriented toward the internal organizational system, to group performance that is oriented toward the external organizational system. Groups within an organization whose primary goals involve social interaction have far stronger emphasis on the internal system, and those oriented toward goals for specific products have greater external-system emphasis (see Figure 17-2). In the latter, the nature of the communication process itself tends to shift from an internal orientation to an external one.

COMMUNICATION IN GROUP SOCIAL INTERACTION

If you have been involved in church groups, social clubs, friendship groups, company parties, or bridge clubs, you have probably been a member of a group which meets for the express purpose of having members enjoy affiliation with one another and perhaps grow closer together as people. Improved cohesiveness and continuity are appropriate performance goals for most of these groups. Some form of communication is required for social interaction to occur. It is an essential process for the accomplishment of the goals of these groups. We often assess the effectiveness of our social interaction in such groups in terms of group satisfaction and enjoyment, member attraction and loyalty, or group maintenance and continuity.

Social-interaction groups typically receive little attention from the manager because they do not provide a direct link to his or her success in achieving group or organizational objectives. Yet many such groups exist within each organization, and they are often vital to the morale of the work force. Examples of social-interaction groups within organizations include the coffee groups, lunch groups, recreation teams, car pools, after-work friendship groups, parties, etc. Groups of this type often supply a needed bond to hold the work atmosphere in a cooperative, friendly state.

Dimensions Which Determine Group Attractiveness

Heslin and Dunphy (1964) performed an exhaustive survey of the literature and found three basic dimensions which seem to account for the satisfaction or attractiveness of small groups. The first of these dimensions is *status consensus*.

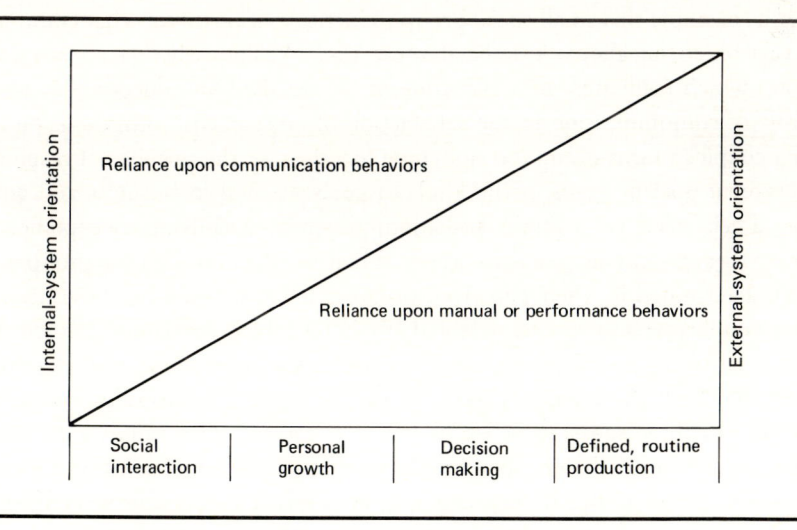

FIGURE 17-2 Orientation of group performance and communication.

Groups have the highest degree of member satisfaction if a consensus of opinion exists among the members of the group about their relative status. A second important determinant of member satisfaction is *progress toward the group goals*. Since members, in large part, belong to groups for the purpose of satisfaction of their personal needs through the attainment of the group goals, frustration will occur when the group is not progressing toward these goals. Conversely, gratification and member satisfaction occur with progress toward these goals. However, the key factor is the members' perception of progress or lack of progress rather than the actual degree of achievement. If the members perceive that there is progress toward the group goals, even when there is none, satisfaction will be high. The third dimension which contributes to group satisfaction is the *perceived freedom to participate*. Before examining these dimensions in more detail, let us look at a brief illustration of a social-interaction group.

Irene has decided that she would like to become better acquainted with two of her friends at work. She and her husband have invited the two women and their husbands to their home for dinner. The conversation is light and friendly as the couples arrive and greet one another before beginning the evening meal. As the evening unfolds, the conversation becomes less superficial and the relationship increases in warmth and openness. The discussion shifts from consideration of the weather, the day's events, and anecdotes about recent activities, to more personal interests, current problems and conflicts, and real-life concerns. After dinner, sitting around the hearth of a roaring fire on this cold December evening, the conversation becomes very warm and personal. By the end of the evening, the couples are sure that they have established friendships of lasting duration.

Let us examine this small social group to identify, if possible, what communication variables bring about close social interaction. We know that we are attracted to a group which facilitates the satisfaction of our needs. Our concern is to identify the role of communication in the satisfaction of one's needs within a group. The young couples in this group did not come together for the purpose of reaching an achievement goal in terms of the kinds of goals we find in business and government. Their need is to attain affiliation, warmth, friendship, acceptance, and security through interaction with others. Their satisfaction with the group will be largely determined by their perceived progress toward satisfying these needs.

Our couples possess several personal attributes which contribute to their developing a satisfying social interaction. A closer social interaction will develop for groups in which the members have similar backgrounds, attitudes, values, and interests. As the discussion of issues which involve certain values and attitudes occurs, an agreement based upon similarity of basic personal attributes increases the comfort of the group. If deep-running, intensely felt values are in conflict with one another, there is a strong tendency to disrupt the social interaction of a group. The need for security is also threatened by basic disagreement among group members. When one's basic values, interests, and attitudes are called into question, the feeling of security is threatened, whereas agreement on basic issues heightens the sense of security and support felt by the group members. Security needs are also supported in groups in which there is liking among the members of the group. Even in the case in which an individual is liked by other members, this security is threatened in a group in which there are other members who do not like one another (Festinger and Hutte, 1954).

Social Sensitivity of Groups

Both inclusion and security needs are gratified by the communication of acceptance. Group members who possess *social sensitivity* are disposed toward the expression of acceptance. Social sensitivity includes the social interaction factors of empathy, insight, social judgment, etc. Expressions of this type toward an individual group member enhance that member's feeling of acceptance and security, and in turn his or her feeling of satisfaction with the group (Pepitone and Wilpizeski, 1960). In groups in which there is a lack of security because of incompatibility, disagreement, or personal dislike, group members have a tendency to attempt to reestablish harmony within the group by increasing their social sensitivity. This lack of security tends to be accompanied by an increase in the social sensitivity of the members (Festinger and Hutte, 1954).

For maximum satisfaction, the group not only must place a high value on friendly and gentle interaction, but also must be open and frank in communication. If the friendly interaction makes the members of the group unwilling to mention the errors and the inappropriate behaviors of other members of the group, then the performance output of the group will tend to be low because of inadequate feedback. Dissatisfaction will occur as a consequence of this lack of performance (Riecken, 1952).

Freedom to Participate

The effects of the *freedom to participate* upon social interaction may be viewed from two points of reference: (1) the opportunity to participate, and (2) participation in accordance with expectations and status. A person feels satisfied with the social interaction of a group in which he or she has an opportunity to participate. Whether social interaction is occurring in a business group, a community club, or in your home, you do not like to be placed in a situation of listening to another group member dominate the conversation. The group experience is much more satisfying if there is a degree of balance in the amount of discussion among the members of the group (Heslin and Dunphy, 1964).

Democratic Leadership

Three factors seem to be critically important to the encouragement of participation in the group. First is the *democratic technique of leadership*. Democratic leadership allows members of the group autonomy in participation, which in turn produces a higher level of enthusiasm and enjoyment than is obtained from authoritarian leadership techniques. Likewise, *groups which are small* in number allow greater member participation. As the group increases from five to twelve members, there is a tendency for a concurrent decrease in member satisfaction (Hare, 1952). A *casual, relaxed atmosphere* also encourages participation among members. On the other hand, tension, hostility, and coolness discourage participation.

Opportunity to Participate

In most situations, the *opportunity to participate* is an important factor in determining one's satisfaction. However, in some group situations the different roles of the group members, or the different status levels of the group members, create differences in the expectations of members regarding the amount of the frequency with which they will communicate. In these circumstances, people will be quite happy to have very little participation if they perceive themselves to be of lower status or expertise than the participating members of the group. For example, in a heterogeneous group of top-level business executives and junior company managers, the high-status executives will be dissatisfied if they are unable to participate. On the other hand, the junior members of the group who are presumed to be less knowledgeable and of lower status will prefer less participation in the discussions. Since they expect to participate less, the junior members are more satisfied when this level of participation is realized (Berkowitz, 1953).

Suppose you are given the assignment to establish a group within your company which will possess the strongest possible social interaction and group satisfaction. In this unique assignment, you are not concerned with achievement goals or decision making. You are merely to establish a group that will have a good social affiliation and will improve the morale of its members. You begin by pulling together a group of individuals who are of about equal status, and you are sure that the group has a clear understanding and consensus about the status of the members. Since a group will be more satisfied if it has meaningful goals which are directly related to the needs of its members, you obtain permission from company executives to allow the group to work toward pertinent goals. You are careful to arrange the tasks to be performed so that there is full opportunity for steady progress toward the accomplishment of these goals. You choose members who are not only of about equal status, but also people who have a liking for one another and who are socially sensitive. You select a group leader who will encourage acceptance among members and establish an atmosphere in which mutual respect, support, friendship, warmth, empathy, openness, and frankness are the norms. Since the group is about equal in status and expertise, you establish the framework which will allow the members to participate about equally and with a relatively high frequency of interaction. Your group is made up of people who have similar backgrounds, values, attitudes, and interests, and who have a basic agreement of opinion on the topics that will be approached by the group. The group will be led by a democratic leader and, of course, will be kept to a small size of around six members. With these conditions established, you should indeed have a very well-satisfied group that is effective in meeting its social-interaction goals.

GROUPS ORIENTED TOWARD PERSONAL-GROWTH OBJECTIVES

We find a number of groups today which are specifically oriented toward the personal growth of the individual members. In business, government, churches, and social organizations, T-groups or *sensitivity training groups* and *Transactional Analysis* groups have become popular. *Group counseling* for personal and marriage problems is used quite frequently by family counseling centers and in private psychological practice.

In the mental health field, we find *group therapy* to continue to be a prominent technique. The performance objective which is sought by each of these types of groups is that of personal growth. In the case of sensitivity training, the desire is to help individuals to understand their social behavior more adequately—to be able to evaluate how they respond to others and how others respond to them, and consequently, to improve their ability to interact effectively.

Transactional Analysis is a process designed to help members of the group improve their ability to perceive and understand the behaviors of themselves and others. In essence, Transactional Analysis groups help their members to understand themselves in the Transactional Analysis (Parent-Adult-Child) concepts which were discussed earlier in Chapter 8. Psychological and family counseling groups are designed to help their members improve their personal adjustment, and their ability to handle problems of life, or to improve their family relationships.

Group therapy operates in a similar fashion, but at a more in-depth level—attempting to assist the group members in understanding and coping with deep-seated psychological problems.

Communication factors have a significant impact upon the degree of achievement of personal-growth objectives in the group. The basic performance activity of these groups, like that of the social-interaction group, is one of communication. The communication factors which influence social interaction operate with the personal-growth groups as well. Much has been written about the process of sensitivity training, and many managers today have been engaged in it. Some organizations have found sensitivity training so useful that they have involved their entire managerial staff in the process.

Sensitivity Training Groups

To fully appreciate the sensitivity training process, one needs to serve as a participant in a sensitivity training group. If you were a typical participant, you would travel to a resort retreat in a remote, scenic conference center where you would spend two weeks at the expense of your company. You would, no doubt, approach the center with a sense of bewilderment, since even the people you know who have participated in the process have found it difficult to really verbalize their experience. However, since most of them found it to be very interesting and worthwhile and since the company feels it worth the time from your busy schedule, you proceed with a great deal of anticipation that the two weeks are going to be quite beneficial.

You begin the first morning with a lecture which describes in general terms the sensitivity training and group process. In the afternoon you get together with your group, which you find to include your roommate and five or six other people. You look to the trainer for some direction about how to proceed, but he provides very little help. The group is immediately faced with an unusual and somewhat bewildering situation. You have come to the center with no idea about what you are expected to do. You are placed in a group in which you are going to spend a great deal of time during the next two weeks. Then you have almost no aid in developing a learning activity that will be of any value to you. Apparently, this same feeling is being expressed by others, because as time passes and people talk, the only beneficial thing that has been done is to make introductions and give life histories (which did not take a great deal of time). People are floundering. Anxiety begins to show itself in the form of hostility, particularly toward the trainer who is not at all helpful in getting you moving, then toward others who are trying to assume dominance of the group but whose efforts are unappreciated.

Next morning you hear a lecture on some of the concepts of understanding other people and gaining insight into the behavior of others, but it is not particularly helpful to you in knowing what you and your group are supposed to do. So, the rest of the morning, the afternoon, and the evening is spent in the same kind of aimless, anxious, and often hostile discussion-seeking structure for your group's activities.

During this time you notice that the trainer is taking a role. He often interjects a comment about someone's behavior, or the reaction of one person to another, the group atmosphere, degree of leveling with one another, and similar group-process activities. Gradually, it becomes apparent that his role is one of helping members of the group to see what is happening in their interaction process—to see how they respond to others and how others respond to them.

The group begins to settle down to a discussion of themselves, their feelings, who they are, where they are going, what they are doing, what their values are, what they like and dislike, how they feel, and what is happening. The feeling among participants shifts from one of anxiety and hostility to a gradually growing sense of empathy, appreciation, acceptance, and love. By the end of the two weeks, you know a good deal more about yourself and the way you respond to other members of the group. You leave very glad that you were able to participate, but still unable to communicate to others just exactly what happened.

Schein and Bennis (1965), in their book entitled *Personal and Organizational Change through Group Methods*, describe a number of prerequisite conditions to effective sensitivity training. These include a feedback to the individual members of how their behavior affects others in the group. Another significant contribution to the effectiveness of sensitivity training is the process of *unfreezing*. Unfreezing involves the establishment of an environment in which there is a desire to change one's social behavior. The climate created is one in which the ordinary expectations about group meetings do not hold true. An attempt is made to replace the customary way groups behave with one that is out of the ordinary. This involves removing familiar props and mechanisms which groups normally have, and establishing ambiguity in the situation. Since there is no task, the group is left to focus upon the process of group interaction. Another part of unfreezing is called *disconfirmation*, in which the sensitivity group members hear and receive cues about their own behavior which are inconsistent with their usual perceptions about themselves. These conditions create anxiety. However, psychological safety is established by creating a learning environment in which a person is allowed to make mistakes without the fear of reprisal. The condition of openness and heightened awareness of self and of others aids in moving the individual toward the goals of increased social sensitivity, changed attitudes, and greater interpersonal competence.

Group Counseling and Group Psychotherapy

Group counseling and group psychotherapy vary from sensitivity training in that counseling and psychotherapy groups meet with the intent of exploring problems within the lives of the group members and of examining their past and present behaviors both within and outside the group. In counseling and psychotherapy groups, an atmosphere of mutual respect and acceptance is created in an attempt to reduce the threat to the person, and to increase the comfort with which one expresses oneself openly and honestly. For most effective group therapy and group counseling, the members should be neither too heterogeneous nor too homogeneous. Group members who differ widely in age, intelligence, severity of illness, and so on, may be unable to relate and empathize with one another's problems; people who are too homogeneous are not able to benefit from a variety of perceptions and do not seem to have effective communication.

Transactional Analysis Groups

Like sensitivity training, Transactional Analysis groups are used extensively by organizations today in personal-development programs for managers. The intent of these development groups is to aid the manager in understanding and behaving in interpersonal relationships effectively.

Transactional Analysis is essentially a teaching and learning process by which individuals come to better understand their role transactions using the language of Transactional Analysis. In the initial meeting, the group discusses the treatment contract which is a statement of the mutual expectations of the members of the group. These expectations include the learning of the Transactional Analysis language and the elimination of the problems which are being experienced by group members. Transactional Analysis group members generally are encouraged to express the Adult role. Unlike group therapy, Transactional Analysis usually discourages the emotional impulses of the Child. The attempt is to keep the Adult in charge and to handle problems as they arise in an objective, forthright manner. A group exposes and confronts the games which Harris has described in his book *I'm OK, You're OK:* games such as "Husbands Are Stupid," "If It Weren't for You, I Could," "It's All for Him," and "Let's You and Him Fight." In Transactional Analysis the role of the therapist is that of a teacher-trainer and resource person with heavy emphasis on involvement. The therapist attempts to be aware of, and to point out, significant communications or signals in the group regarding roles or games that are being played.

COMMUNICATION IN THE GROUP DECISION-MAKING PROCESS

Group communication within organizations is more frequently directed toward group decision making than toward any other type of group objective. Groups are called upon to make decisions about a wide array of problem areas: setting goals and objectives, arriving at solutions to current problems, and effecting change. A good deal of difference of opinion has been expressed about how one should define the process of decision making to distinguish it from the process of problem solving. Here we shall use the terms interchangeably. The decision-making process involves four steps: first, definition of the problem; second, analysis of the problem; third, development of alternative solutions; and fourth, selection of a solution.

The complexity of each of these steps for a particular decision varies widely. The amount of attention given to each step depends largely upon the complexity and the potential consequences of the decision involved. Groups often are called upon to deal only with the fourth phase of the process, the selection of the solution. For example, the House Judiciary Committee, considering the articles of impeachment for President Nixon in July 1974, was presented with the case supporting these articles fully developed and analyzed by the Committee Chief Counsel, John Doar. Though the decision was certainly a complex and significant one, only the selection of the solution stage of the process was yet to be resolved.

Anatomy of a Business Decision

An interesting anatomy of a business decision was presented by Cyert, Simon, and Trow (1956), in which they presented a chronological narrative of a decision regarding the feasibility of using electronic data processing equipment in a medium-sized corporation. The narrative clearly points out the amount of effort, thought, and communication, both at the individual and group level, involved in the process of a complex and significant business decision. Place yourself in the position of the assistant controller, Ronald Middleton, who is assigned the task of arriving at alternatives and making recommendations with regard to the decision to institute a system of data processing involving electronic equipment.

> Ronald began the processing in July of 1971 (the dates are changed). To analyze the problem adequately, Ronald used three procedures to obtain information—letters to persons in established computer firms, discussions with persons in other companies who were experimenting with the use of electronic equipment in

accounting. In addition, he read literature about computer development. He communicated a summary of his insights to the controller through memoranda.

In the Spring of 1972, a computer company took the initiative to make a brief equipment application study. Based on the study, the computer company representative recommended that the company install electronic computing equipment. Ronald, the controller, and other executives concluded that it was necessary to gain outside help in evaluating electronic equipment needs. A consulting firm was retained in November of 1972 to do a study of electronic data processing needs of the company. They recommended positively for implemention of a computing system in February 1973.

The company decided to obtain a corroborative recommendation by a second consulting firm, and in July a contract with a second firm was signed. A committee headed by Ronald was established by the controller to aid the firm in making the decision. In the initial meeting between Ronald and the consulting firm's two staff members, an outline of the approach to the problem was discussed. Twenty-three information-gathering studies were designed. The studies involved the analysis of the volume of data processing transactions and information flow in obtaining data from the sales department and from the field staffs of the other departmental areas. Meanwhile, the consultants collected information regarding the method by which the information and accounting tasks were actually handled. On August 8, Ronald submitted a report to the controller stating the status of his work. On August 18, with the studies completed, consultants met with the company study committee to review the results of the studies.

On October 17, the consultants met with the company committee for a comparison of the current system and the proposed system. Ronald indicated to the consultants that the controller strongly favored decentralization of authority. The question was raised of the compatibility of this with electronic processing in general. The groups concluded that decentralization of purely clerical data processing operations was compatible with decentralization of responsibility and authority. On November 3, the consultants made a systematic presentation to the company's study committee summarizing their conclusions. The group decided that only two systems that had been considered would be worthy of final cost evaluation. In informal conversation, the controller indicated to Ronald that he felt that the consultants had placed too much emphasis on cost rather than organizational operations and management philosophies of decentralization. On January 28, 1974, Ronald prepared a final analysis of the electronic data system and the information processing system associated with it and discussed this with a group of sales department managers. A similar presentation was then made to the accounting department and subsequently to the top members of the manufacturing department in group sessions.

Two equipment companies were chosen to submit proposals; and on February 15, both companies presented their reports, each bringing a team of three or four men to present their recommendations orally. In conference with the controller, Ronald dictated the letter to his president requesting an authorization to proceed with the acquisition of the electronic equipment selected.

This letter was read to the management committee by the controller, and after questions and brief discussions, the management committee voted favorably on the recommendation. The controller informed Ronald of the decision when the meeting ended.

Obviously, organization decision making of this nature requires a variety of communication activities which would be absent in the case of a single individual making a decision alone. Numerous two-person interactions are recorded in this summarized anatomy of a decision-making process. Written communication is frequently used as well, generally taking the form of memoranda. The information-transmitting function is very efficient and involves a good deal of selection or filtering of information sources. In this complex decision process, checks were introduced in order to provide an independent information source. The company study committee, top-management departmental groups, and finally the management committee all are involved in group discussion and decision making on elements of the total decision process. The management committee makes the final decision between the two remaining alternatives.

In an involved decision-making process of this type, one should ask about the elements of communication within the group that can make the group most effective. What are the variables of communication that influence group success or failure? What are the effects of various types of communication content upon group effectiveness? By what means should one arrive at a final decision? How important is the communication of expert knowledge and information in the decision-making process? Should emotions be expressed or stifled? How much discussion should occur before a decision is reached? Does conflict within the group facilitate or retard the decision making and subsequent execution?

Problem Definition and Analysis

The *problem definition* phase of decision making is critical to the success of the process. Maier (1962) has shown that improved decision making can often be produced if the group moves away from conflict about the alternative to be chosen, and moves toward more careful assessment of what the problem actually is. Consensus on the phrasing of the problem is useful in avoiding a great deal of waste in the form of misdirected communication in later phases of decision making. The *analysis* phase involves collecting available information from existing records or individual experience, or from newly generated data, and evaluating or assessing the true nature of the problem from this information.

Development of Alternatives

The *development of alternatives* involves assembling, weighing, and arranging information. Creativity is important in each of the phases of the decision-making process, but it is perhaps most significant in the development of alternatives. An approach frequently used to stimulate creativity in groups is referred to as *group brainstorming*. Brainstorming is characterized by four basic rules: criticism is ruled out, freewheeling is welcomed, quantity is wanted, and combination of ideas and improvement of ideas are sought. This process of avoiding criticism of ideas as they are generated seems to produce a superior level of creative, alternative solutions to problems whether employed by groups or individuals. Researchers generally agree that when a short time limit is imposed, group brainstorming produces less quality and quantity of ideas than does individual brainstorming.

Two factors seem to have an inhibiting influence on group brainstorming. The first is a general tendency for people in brainstorming groups to be self-conscious or intimidated by the presence of others in the group. This inhibiting effect of the presence of others is increased when the people in the group see one or more other members as being experts in the brainstorming technique. To offset this effect, and to increase the freedom with which the members express their own ideas, it is important that each of the members of the group perceive the other members to be at about the same level of expertise as the member perceives himself or herself to be (Collaros and Anderson, 1969). The second inhibiting factor is homogeneity of personality among the members of the group. Groups in which members are basically homogeneous in personality tend to be less creative than groups which are heterogeneous. A variety of personalities within the group tends to stimulate expression. Groups made up of people who are basically similar in personality simply replicate members' ideas rather than stimulate additional creative ideas (Hoffman and Maier, 1961). Low productivity in brainstorming groups is sometimes the result of imposing a time limit. Groups which produce for longer work periods normally produce more under brainstorming conditions than does an individual. Groups continue to produce ideas indefinitely, whereas individuals taper off in their generation of ideas (Shaw, 1971).

Selection of the Solution

Selection of the solution often relies heavily upon group communication. The group goal in selecting the solution includes both the choice of the "best" alternative, and the choice of the alternative which will gain group acceptance.

Decision Schemes

Smoke and Zajonc (1962) identified seven *decision-making* schemes which are used by groups (see Table 17-1). Group acceptance is important to the execution of the decision. Indeed, it is the advantage of acceptance and commitment that leads many managers to rely on group decision when possible. All the decision schemes described are used in organizational groups. Unanimity (emerging from compro-

TABLE 17-1 Description of Several Decision Schemes

Decision schemes	Description
1. Dictatorship	The group decision is completely determined by the response of one individual within the group who may be a group leader, an expert, or an advisor.
2. Oligarchy	The group decision is completely determined by a vocal coalition of members within the group.
3. Unanimity	The group decision is the consensus decision of all members of the group.
4. Fixed	The group decision is based upon a predetermined, fixed number of favorable member responses.
5. Quorum	Group decision requires that at least a minimum number of usually one half or two thirds of the members agree with the specific decision.
6. Minimal quorum	The group decision requires only the agreement of one member of the group. If at least one member of the group prefers a given decision, that decision is chosen.
7. Independent	The group decision is independent of the decisions of the individual members and is determined by an external criterion. The probability of a given alternative being imposed by the external criterion is unchanged by any opinion or action of group members.

mise) and dictatorship are perhaps the most widely practiced schemes in private business.

Consensus versus Quorum Decisions

A study conducted by Barland (1959) examined the factors that cause group decisions to be more effective than individual decisions. He found that quorum decisions are less effective than consensus decisions; but here the quorum decision was a mathematically tallied decision with group members acting alone. He found that group members tend to develop a higher interest and ego involvement in the problems than would the same persons working alone. He also found that group members tend to find errors which might have gone unchecked in an individual setting. In addition, the greater number of viewpoints tended to increase the group's chances of making a good decision, and the challenge of private prejudices of one group member by another tended to bring about a greater objectivity.

Consensus decisions afford the greatest degree of acceptance by group members and therefore facilitate the execution of the decision. However, the time required to arrive at a consensus decision frequently prohibits its use.

Schemes Involving Participation

Unanimity, fixed, and quorum schemes depend most heavily upon participation in the selection of a solution. The value of having group members participate in decisions which affect them and which they must execute is widely recognized. Such participation leads to an improvement in both the morale of the group and the effectiveness with which the decision is implemented. Group discussion and decision making are particularly beneficial for the solution of complex problems. The group has a potential for a wider range of knowledge and experience to bring to the problem at hand. In addition, participation in decision making produces a better understanding on the part of the members of the group of the decision reached, and a deeper commitment to the execution of the decision. The level of participation is more equitable among group members where the status and organizational position of the group members are about equal. Frequently, a member of the group who is subordinate to another group member will be hesitant to contribute his or her point of view and will acquiesce to the view of the superior (Argyris, 1966).

Maier (1962) found that after problem-solving participation meetings, the telephone repairman performance record showed a 40 percent increase in repairs made, and an 80 percent reduction in the necessity of repeat calls. A classic study of the value of member participation in group decision making was reported by Coch and French (1948). The study was conducted in the plants of Harwood Manufacturing Company, whose declining profits necessitated the implementation of efficiencies in order to maintain solvency. Changes in the operations were introduced into the plant using three different decision models. The first model was a nonparticipation model which could be termed dictatorship in the terminology used in Table 17-1. Group members were told of the decision to change, and any questions they had were answered. In a second group, representatives were selected from the group members to work with management to develop the work methods and piece rates which would be involved in the change. The third approach involved total participation; all workers who were directly influenced by the change met with selected members of management, as a group, to make the decisions about the change. The results were striking. The group which was allowed total participation adapted to the change rapidly, and at the end of thirty days were producing about 15 percent better than their original standard. The nonparticipation group experienced a severe problem of low morale and turnover and a drop in production of approximately 20 percent—which did not recover by the end of thirty days. Grievances, restriction of production, and other forms of resistance were apparent with the nonparticipation group. This classic study became a foundation stone for the participative management approach advocated by many management and behavioral science theorists and researchers today.

The problem of communicating a decision to those who will carry it out is a significant one. The chances for communication failure in this activity are minimized by involving the executioners in the process of making the decision. The difficulty in group decision making is the tendency for members of the group to establish a preference and take a position early in the discussion. As the discussion continues, the individual goals become more and more oriented toward winning the argument rather than finding the best solution. As a consequence, the quality of the decision may be reduced.

Risk Taking

Risk taking is an important consideration in selecting the solution. Almost every decision of consequence involves a degree of risk or uncertainty about its effects upon the group members. Suppose you are a member of the executive committee of a small company. Your committee is to make a decision as to whether to enter a new product line or not. If the product line is a success, the company will expand rapidly. If it is a failure, the company will suffer a great deal of loss of profit due to the cost of producing and marketing the product. The more cautious decision is to stay with the slow but steady growth of existing products. You are neutral to the idea when the problem is presented to the committee. Given no more information than this, would you predict that you would shift your opinion toward the risky decision of marketing the new product line? Even though the question seems to be unanswerable, research has shown that the process of discussion of a problem in a group setting alone will tend to result in a shift toward a more risky decision—a "risky shift" (Marquis, 1962; Wallach, Kogan, and Bem, 1962; Kogan and Wallach, 1967).

Why does this "risky shift" occur? The most tenable answer seems to be that the act of risk taking is admired and valued by a large body of people (Wallach and Wing, 1968; Levinger and Schneider, 1969). In the socially potent small group, a person has a tendency to shift an opinion toward this socially valued decision in order to gain approval. A view held earlier that the "risky shift" occurred because of the opportunity to share with other members the dangers of failure has not stood the test of research (Wallach and Kogan, 1965). Not all groups will see a risky decision as more socially desirable. Members of such groups have a tendency toward a "cautious shift" as a result of discussion within the group (Stoner, 1967; Teger and Pruitt, 1967). The discussion does not have to be face to face. Communication by intercom of physically isolated persons also yields the "risky shift" (Kogan and Wallach, 1967).

The general admiration of people who make choices involving higher risk can be offset by the dangers of the results of the risky decision. If the cost to group members of making a risky decision is perceived to be greater than the value associated with being able to take risk, they will make a more cautious decision. Thus, group members will not shift toward risk to the extent that the personal consequence of failure becomes intolerable (Zajonc et al., 1968).

The process of group decision making is a complex one involving the full array of intrapersonal and communication factors. However, it is a valuable management tool both for improving the quality of decisions and for facilitating the execution of the decisions.

Communication Change in the Decision-Making Process

We shall now examine more closely the changes which occur in communication as we progress through the process of decision making. Bales's system of interaction analysis shown in Table 17-2 has been used by a number of researchers to tabulate and analyze the type of communication used by each person in group communication. The most significant types of statements during the problem-definition phase tend to be those providing orientation and sharing or asking for information. The activities devoted to making proposals, repetition, and evaluation increase as the analysis phase is encountered (Morris, 1970). Evaluation continues in prominence during the development-of-alternatives phase. Control becomes the most significant type of communication in the selection of the solution. As the amount of control exercised becomes more predominant, emotional reactions, both negative and positive, increase in frequency. At the very end of the decision-making process, the group moves toward agreement on the decision developed. The group tends to release in diffuse ways the tensions built up in its prior task efforts, thus repairing the damage done to its state of consensus and social integration and thereby releasing positive reactions. Thus, while both negative and positive reactions are stronger in the final phase of decision making, they are not developing

TABLE 17-2 The System of Categories Used in Observation and Major Relationships

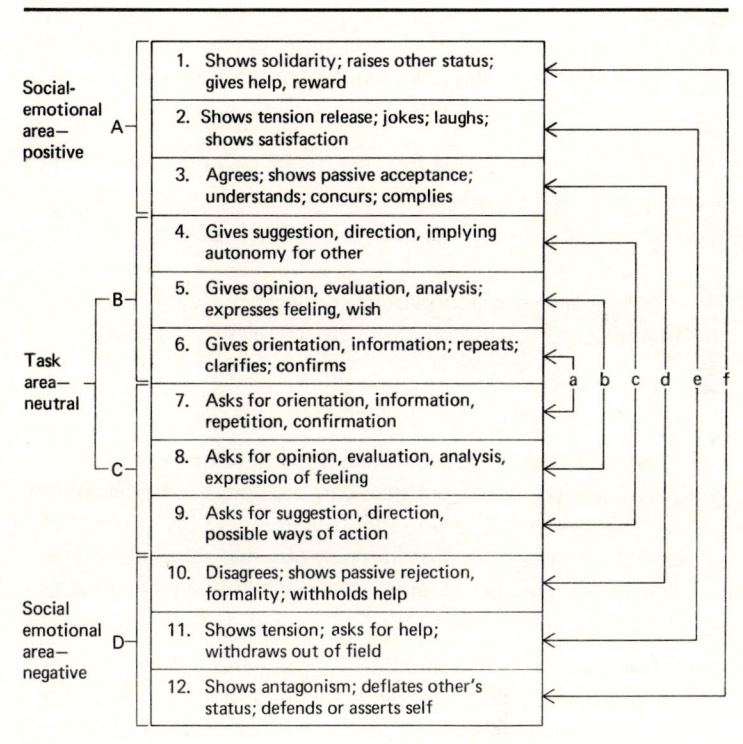

Social-emotional area—positive (A):
1. Shows solidarity; raises other status; gives help, reward
2. Shows tension release; jokes; laughs; shows satisfaction
3. Agrees; shows passive acceptance; understands; concurs; complies

Task area—neutral:

Attempted answers (B):
4. Gives suggestion, direction, implying autonomy for other
5. Gives opinion, evaluation, analysis; expresses feeling, wish
6. Gives orientation, information; repeats; clarifies; confirms

Questions (C):
7. Asks for orientation, information, repetition, confirmation
8. Asks for opinion, evaluation, analysis, expression of feeling
9. Asks for suggestion, direction, possible ways of action

Social emotional area—negative (D):
10. Disagrees; shows passive rejection, formality; withholds help
11. Shows tension; asks for help; withdraws out of field
12. Shows antagonism; deflates other's status; defends or asserts self

Key

a. Problems of communication
b. Problems of evaluation
c. Problems of control
d. Problems of decision
e. Problems of tension reduction
f. Problems of reintegration

A. Positive reactions
B. Attempted answers
C. Questions
D. Negative reactions

simultaneously; but rather, negative reactions emerge first in response to control communication, and then positive reactions emerge to bring about release of feelings and commitment to the decision (Bales and Strodtbeck, 1951).

Faust (1959) points out that this expression of negative emotions is an important factor in effective group problem solving. He contends that it is important to encourage the expression of negative emotions because they allow the release of tensions which otherwise would have hidden effects upon the quality of the decision made, as well as the commitment to the decision. When strong feelings are expressed, they can then be evaluated in a fashion similar to that used for other forms of communication. The disconcerting display of hostilities, even though unpleasant to the group, is more beneficial to the success of decision making than is controlled, unexpressed hostility which has a negative and more subtle effect upon the decision and its acceptance.

Key Implications of Communication Change in the Decision Process

Effective group decision making requires that the manager account for the communication needs in different phases of the decision process. Our discussion in this section suggests a number of implications which we list by way of summary:

1. The manager should assure that adequate time is given by the group to the discussion of the problem.
2. Care should be taken to collect all the needed information to adequately analyze the problem.
3. When sufficient time is available, the development of alternative solutions to a problem can be done most effectively by the process of group brainstorming. This process of group communication of ideas on possible solutions stimulates more and better alternatives when adequate time is available.
4. The manager should use a decision scheme which involves participation when time is available and task constraints permit. Participation by group members in a decision is especially beneficial when the group must implement the final decision.
5. The manager should be alert to the general tendency for people in a group discussion to shift their opinion toward a higher-risk choice in order to gain approval. Since this tendency for a "risky shift" becomes a factor in determining

a choice, time may well be spent in pointing out the danger of this phenomenon. Consciousness of the tendency by group members will help them to avoid its influence on their decisions. If the manager has a group whose members value cautious decisions (this is not as frequently the case), he or she should alert the group to the existence of this phenomenon.

6. The manager should use his or her knowledge of the changes in communication as the decision process continues to assure that proper attention is given to each phase. For example, if insufficient attention is being given to problem definition, the manager can encourage the group to give or ask for more orientation, to share or ask for more information. If insufficient attention is being given to problem analysis, then the manager may encourage additional proposals, more repetition of unexplored insights, and more careful evaluation of ideas. The manager may be more successful in encouraging adequate attention to problem definition by drawing out the kinds of communication approaches that support this phase, rather than by making a generalized request to "define the problem better," "analyze the problem more thoroughly," etc.

COMMUNICATION IN GROUPS ORIENTED TOWARD PRODUCTION OBJECTIVES

Defined or specified production often involves little or no internal-systems-oriented communication. The amount of external-system-oriented communication required varies widely with the type of production activity involved. Although the primary vehicle of operation for social interaction, personal growth, or decision making is communication, it is possible for production output to be accomplished with much less communication.

Communication in Group Production Planning

In this section we shall be concerned with the relationship between communication and production. As seen in Figure 17-3, several forms of communication relate to production output. Group planning prior to the actual performance of the production tasks involves group communication. The communication conducted during the execution of the production tasks may be either task-relevant or task-irrelevant.

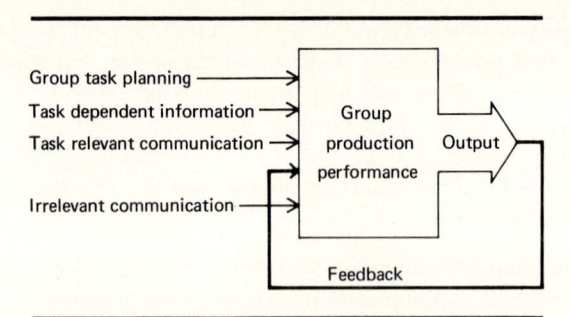

FIGURE 17-3 Communication influence upon production output.

We also find that certain types of group tasks are dependent upon communication for their execution. And finally, you may observe that feedback to the group regarding the results of its production is a significant and important form of communication.

Suppose you are a supervisor in an air-conditioning assembly plant chosen to lead a team in an experimental approach to the assembling of a home air-conditioning unit. You have the choice of using one of three approaches to *group task planning:* (1) your team can set aside time for planning the project prior to actually beginning to perform the task, (2) your team can begin the task and perform its planning functions simultaneously with the performance of the production task, or (3) your team can pursue the task with no planning. Which approach would you choose? In a simple eye-hand coordination task, Shure et al. (1962) provided these three alternative group planning conditions. They found that when there was planning by the group prior to beginning the performance of the task, the group's output was superior in that the least average time per trial and the lowest average amount of time for completion were required. In addition, Shure et al. found that the pretrial-planning group required the lowest average number of task messages and derived the most consistent pattern of organizational operation. The superiority of the preplanning task would no doubt be accentuated with a more complex operation such as that of an assembly task.

Task Relevancy of the Communication

Another question of importance to group production is that of the influence of the *task relevancy* of the communication. Does task-relevant communication have a facilitative or an inhibiting effect upon task performance? There is no generalized answer to this question. It appears that for some tasks, task-relevant information facilitates performance output. To illustrate, let us take the case of a radar control aerial interception task. Suppose that teams which are viewing activity on a radar scope are allowed to communicate with one another in order to offer assistance or to correct errors whenever it seems appropriate. Further, we shall establish two different conditions under which this task can be peformed: one, which we shall call "verbal," in which communication is necessary for the completion of the task, and another, which we shall call "verbal-visual," in which communication is not necessary.

Imagine for a moment that you are working in a team with two other participants and you are looking at three separate radar screens. Assume that there are two teams at work—one is required to exchange verbal information for the completion of the radar interception task, and the other may respond to visual cues alone, or supplement the visual information from the radar screen with communication. Which of these two groups would operate most effectively? According to research conducted by Williges, Johnston, and Briggs (1966), in which a simulation of a task similar to the one being considered here was established under research conditions, communication facilitated performance only when communication was essential to the completion of the task. Where an efficient visual information channel was available, verbal communication was not as efficient as the visual information channel.

When communication is permitted but not demanded by the task, verbal communication appears to be little more than an unnecessary and rather tempting luxury that has little positive impact upon team performance, even when the communication is relevant to the task being conducted (Johnston and Briggs, 1968). McConville and Hemphill (1966) have also reported research which indicates that communication within a group can have an inhibiting effect, even when the communication is relevant to the task. In light of the results of their study, in which problem analysis was a key aspect of the successful completion of the task, they concluded that the communication which was involved distracted group members from the analysis activities which were critical to successful completion. Under such conditions, where communication is distractive or will tend to create confusion, even task-relevant communication hinders performance. Obviously, communication that is irrelevant to the task will be detrimental to effective task performance if considered alone. However, the opportunity to communicate does have a positive effect on worker morale, particularly in the conduct of monotonous tasks.

Task Dependence on Communication

Clearly, when there is a *dependency* of one group member on the information supplied by one or more other group members, the impact of this communication on performance output is beyond question. In the operation of the production task, the team member is often dependent upon one or more other members of the team.

A worker on an assembly line may be required to clarify the production requirements with the supervisor, or it may be necessary to get information from both the supervisor and a parts-control specialist. As the degree of dependency upon the other team members increases, the amount of directive communication increases.

When two people within the group supply discrepant information, frustration and hostility often arise. When information is supplied by both a person and a physical source (such as a gauge or meter) and there is a discrepancy between the two, the degree of frustration and hostility is less than will be the case when two persons supply discrepant information. When discrepant directive information is supplied by a person and by a physical source, the differences will usually be resolved in favor of the physical source.

If there is a mutual dependency, so that not only is person A dependent upon the supervisor, but the supervisor is also dependent upon the information supplied by person A for the completion of a task, then both the supervisor and person A are less likely to place the blame and responsibility for problems upon one another (Raven and Shaw, 1970).

Feedback of Output Results

Feedback with regard to knowledge of results has positive effects upon performance output. Feedback allows a person to compare goals and expectations with the actual results of efforts. Knowledge of performance tends to increase motivation for future performance. The more specific the knowledge of performance, the more effect it will have upon future performance (Ammons, 1956).

Feedback regarding the individual performance of people working within the group is more beneficial than feedback regarding total group performance. Hardly any improvement can be expected as a result of feedback if the feedback does not provide the individual group members with an indication of how they are performing. Total-group performance feedback may be beneficial in providing positive motivation and in allowing group members to encourage one another; however, it has little value in correcting the errors that are performed by individual members of the group.

SUMMARY

The reliance of groups upon communication is largely determined by the type of tasks and performance goals involved. This chapter has compared the role of communication in groups which are highly dependent upon communication for goal achievement to those with low reliance upon communication. In order from most highly dependent upon communication to least dependent, the group performance goals were categorized as social interaction, personal growth, decision making, and defined production.

Social interaction is the goal for groups whose primary purpose is the building and maintenance of strong member interrelationships. Personal-growth groups are those intended to aid their members in individual personal development. Decision-making groups engage in a process of problem definition, analysis, development of alternatives, and selection of a solution as a means of attaining their goals. Production groups may or may not use communication as a tool in producing tangible products.

As we move from the more internal-system-related performance goals to the more external-system performance goals, we see a reduction in dependence upon communication. The group tasks which are benefited least by communication are those whose output is so well defined and routine that it can be performed without group planning, without group decision making, and without exchange of information. Most group activities require some amount of communication for their accomplishment.

IMPORTANT TERMS AND CONCEPTS

group social interaction, personal growth, decision making, routine production, status consensus, social sensitivity, freedom to participate, democratic leadership, opportunity to participate, sensitivity training groups, Transactional Analysis groups, group counseling, group therapy, group decision-making process, group brainstorming, decision schemes, risk taking, task relevancy, task dependence, feedback

REVIEW QUESTIONS

1. Why is communication more important for a group whose goal is personal growth than for one whose goal is production?

2. Describe a group of which you have been a member in which there was much satisfaction. Why was the satisfaction high?

3. Is it necessary to sacrifice productivity in order to obtain the highest level of group morale?

4. Suppose you have the assignment of establishing a work group that will have the highest morale possible within your company. Describe the ingredients you would attempt to build into the group.

5. Compare sensitivity training with Transactional Analysis groups.

6. Using the "anatomy of a business decision" discussed in this chapter, identify the four phases of decision making. What role does the small group play at each stage?

7. Suppose you were president of the company involved in the "anatomy of a business decision." Which of the decision schemes would you use? Why?

8. Your group is to make a decision for which the consequences are extremely significant for the future of your company and the livelihood of its employees. Caution is highly important. How would you avoid the "risky shift" phenomenon from bringing about an undesirably risky decision?

9. Discuss the relationship between communication and group performance in a defined production task.

EXERCISE 1: EASY MONEY GAME

Divide the class into groups of exactly eight persons each. Students not included in the groups are observers. The groups are divided into 4 pairs which are seated as follows:

```
            X X
        W         Y
        W         Y
            Z Z
```

Instructions: For ten successive rounds you and your partner will choose either a "star" or a "circle." The "payoff" for each round will be determined not only by your choice but by that of the other pairs in your cluster.

All 4 pairs choose star	Each pair loses $1,000.
3 pairs choose star	The 3 pairs get $1,000 each
1 pair chooses circle	The 1 pair loses $3,000.
2 pairs choose star	These 2 pairs get $2,000 each
2 pairs choose circle	These 2 pairs lose $2,000 each
1 pair chooses star	This pair gets $3,000.
3 pairs choose circle	These 3 pairs lose $1,000 each
All 4 pairs choose circle	Each pair wins $1,000.

Procedure: You are to confer with your partner on each round and make a *joint decision*. Before rounds 5, 8, and 10 you confer with the other pairs in your cluster.

Round	Strategy: Time allowed	Confer with	Your choice	$ Won	$ Lost	$ Balance	
1	2 mins.	partner					
2	1 min.	partner					
3	1 min.	partner					
4	1 min.	partner					
5	3 mins. +1 min.	cluster partner					Bonus round: payoff multiplied by 3
6	1 min.	partner					
7	1 min.	partner					
8	3 min. +1 min.	cluster partner					Bonus round: payoff multiplied by 5
9	1 min.	partner					
10	3 mins. +1 min.	cluster partner					Bonus round: payoff multiplied by 10

1. What was your experience during the game, and how did you feel about it?
2. What was the goal that you personally set for yourself? Was it to maximize your own payoff or to maximize the payoffs of the cluster? What were the effects of these goals?
3. What principles of group process did you find in your group?
4. What did the game show regarding follow-through on commitments as to gain for a small group?
5. What did your experience show about integration of goals?
6. Were there incidences of failure to implement consensus decisions, and if so, what were their effects?

EXERCISE 2: BRAINSTORMING

The instructor will give you directions for the brainstorming exercise. In preparation for the exercise, form into groups of five to six students each and carry out the following steps.

Step 1. Each member reads the following rules for brainstorming:

    A. The group should arrive at a consensus with regard to the definition of the problem prior to beginning brainstorming.

    B. All ideas are accepted. Everyone is encouraged to suggest any tentative solution however bizarre, outlandish, unrealistic, or foolish. No idea is excluded.

    C. Criticism is ruled out. No evaluation of comments or ideas is allowed during brainstorming.

    D. Quantity not quality is emphasized. Try to develop as many ideas as possible. Freewheeling is welcomed. One recorder should write the ideas as fast as possible, as each is verbalized.

Step 2. The instructor presents your brainstorming situation and problem. You will have three minutes to discuss and define the problem. You will begin the brainstorming process at a signal from the instructor.

Step 3. One-half of the groups in the class will work to list ideas as a unit, reporting ideas to the group as they occur; in the other half of the groups, the ideas for each person will be written down by the person. These latter groups are not permitted to share their ideas during step 3 with one another.

Step 4. Each of the groups counts the number of different ideas which they generated (i.e., different from other members of their own group). Most if not all of the discussion groups' ideas will be counted because the members heard one another's contributions as they were presented.

Step 5. Compare the number of ideas for the two approaches to brainstorming. List some of the ideas from each group on the chalkboard. Which approach yielded the greatest quantity and best quality of ideas?

BIBLIOGRAPHY

Ammons, R. B.: "Effects of Knowledge of Performance: A Survey and Tentative Theoretical Formulations," *Journal of General Psychology,* vol. 54, pp. 279–299, 1956.

Argyris, Chris: "Interpersonal Barriers to Decision Making," *Harvard Business Review,* vol. 44, no. 2, pp. 84–97, 1966.

Bales, R. F., and F. L. Strodtbeck: "Phases in Group Problem Solving," *Journal of Abnormal and Social Psychology,* vol. 46, pp. 485–495, 1951.

Barland, D. C.: "A Comparative Study of Individual and Majority and Group Judgment," *General and Abnormal Social Psychology,* vol. 58, no. 1, 1959.

Berkowitz, L.: "Sharing Leadership in Small Decision Making Groups," *Journal of Abnormal and Social Psychology,* vol. 48, pp. 231–238, 1953.

Coch, L., and J. R. P. French, Jr.: "Overcoming Resistance to Change," *Human Relations,* vol. 1, pp. 512–532, 1948.

Collaros, P. S., and L. R. Anderson: "Effect of Perceived Expertness on Creativity of Members of Brainstorming Groups," *Journal of Applied Psychology,* vol. 53, pp. 159–163, 1969.

Cyert, R. M., H. A. Simon, and D. B. Trow: "Observation of a Business Decision," *Journal of Business,* vol. 29, pp. 237–248, 1956.

Faust, W. L.: "Group versus Individual Problem Solving," *Journal of Abnormal and Social Psychology,* vol. 59, pp. 68–72, 1959.

Festinger, L., and H. A. Hutte: "An Experimental Investigation of the Effect of Unstable Interpersonal Relations in a Group," *Journal of Abnormal and Social Psychology,* vol. 49, pp. 513–522, 1954.

Hare, A. P.: "Interaction and Consensus in Different Sized Groups," *American Sociological Review,* vol. 17, pp. 261–267, 1952.

Heslin, R., and D. Dunphy: "Three Dimensions of Membership Satisfaction in Small Groups," *Human Relations,* vol. 17, pp. 99–112, 1964.

Hoffman, L. R., and N. R. F. Maier: "Quality and Acceptance of Problem Solutions by Members of Homogeneous and Heterogeneous Groups," *Journal of Abnormal and Social Psychology,* vol. 62, pp. 401–407, 1961.

Johnston, W. A., and G. Briggs: "Team Performance as a Function of Team Arrangement and Workload," *Journal of Applied Psychology,* vol. 52, pp. 87–93, 1968.

Kogan, N., and M. A. Wallach: "Effects of Physical Separation of Group Members on Risk Taking," *Human Relations,* vol. 20, pp. 41–48, 1967.

Levinger, G., and D. J. Schneider: "Test of the 'Risk Is a Value' Hypothesis," *Journal of Personality and Social Psychology,* vol. 11, pp. 165–169, 1969.

McConville, C. B., and J. K. Hemphill: "Some Effects of Communication Restraints on Problem Solving Behavior," *Journal of Social Psychology,* vol. 69, pp. 265–276, 1966.

Maier, N. R. F.: *Principles of Human Relations* (New York: Harper & Row, Publishers, Incorporated, 1962), pp. 225–228.

Marquis, D. G.: "Individual Responsibility and Group Decisions Involving Risk," *Industrial Management Review,* vol. 3, pp. 8–23, 1962.

Morris, E. G.: "The Changes in Group Interaction during Problem Solving," *Journal of Social Psychology,* vol. 81, pp. 151–165, 1970.

Pepitone, A., and C. Wilpizeski: "Some Consequences of Experimental Rejection," *Journal of Abnormal and Social Psychology,* vol. 60, pp. 359–364, 1960.

Raven, V. H., and J. I. Shaw: "Interdependence and Group Problem Solving in the Triad," *Journal of Personal and Social Psychology,* vol. 14, pp. 157–165, 1970.

Riecken, H.: "Some Problems of Consensus Development," *Rural Sociology,* vol. 17, pp. 245–252, 1952.

Schein, E. H., and W. G. Bennis: *Personal and Organizational Change through Group Methods: A Laboratory Approach* (New York: John Wiley & Sons, Inc., 1965).

Shaw, M. E.: *Group Dynamics: The Psychology of Small Group Behavior* (McGraw-Hill Book Company, 1971).

Shure, G. H., M. S. Roger, I. M. Larsen, and J. Tassone: "Group Planning and Task Effectiveness," *Sociometry,* vol. 25, pp. 263–282, 1962.

Smoke, W. H., and R. B. Zajonc: "On the Reliability of Group Judgment and Decisions," in J. H. Crisswell, H. Solomon and P. Suppes (eds.), *Mathematical Methods and Small Group Processes* (Stanford, Calif.: Stanford University Press, 1962), pp. 322–333.

Stoner, J. A. F.: "Risky and Cautious Shifts in Group Decisions: The Influence of Widely Held Values," working paper, Alfred P. Sloan School of Management, Massachusetts Institute of Technology, October 1967.

Teger, A. I., and D. G. Pruitt: "Components of Group Risk Taking," *Journal of Experimental and Social Psychology,* vol. 3, pp. 189–205, 1967.

Wallach, M. A., and N. Kogan: "The Roles of Information, Discussion and Consensus in Group Risk Taking," *Journal of Experimental Social Psychology,* vol. 1, pp. 1–19, 1965.

———, and D. J. Bem: "Group Influence on Individual Risk Taking," *Journal of Abnormal and Social Psychology,* vol. 65, pp. 75–86, 1962.

———, and C. W. Wing, Jr.: "Is Risk a Value?" *Journal of Personality and Social Psychology,* vol. 9, pp. 101–106, 1968.

Williges, R. C., W. A. Johnston, and G. E. Briggs: "The Role of Verbal Communication in Teamwork," *Journal of Applied Psychology,* vol. 50, pp. 473–478, 1966.

Zajonc, R. B., R. J. Wolosin, M. A. Wolosin, and S. J. Sherman: "Individual and Group Risk Taking in a Two Choice Situation," *Journal of Experimental Social Psychology,* vol. 4, pp. 89–106, 1968.

THE RELATIONSHIP OF LEADERSHIP BEHAVIOR WITH COMMUNICATION

This chapter discusses the dependency of leadership upon communication. It is designed to give an appreciation of the nature and styles of leadership, and the interaction of leadership styles with the situational variables and follower characteristics.

Leadership, broadly defined, is *"interpersonal influence, exercised in a situation and directed, through the communication process, toward the attainment of a specified goal or goals"* (Tannenbaum et al., 1961). This definition points out the close dependency of leadership upon communication. Leadership cannot occur without communication.

The determination of who is or will become the leader is not as straightforward or as well defined as we normally assume. Leadership may be designated as *attempted*, *successful*, or *effective* (Hemphill, 1958). *Attempted leadership* occurs when anyone in the group attempts to become the influencer and to affect the behavior of others through communication. Individuals are encouraged to attempt leadership by (1) rewards that are associated with the accomplishment of the group task, (2) expectations that the group task can be accomplished, (3) specific task characteristics as yet not clearly understood but which create requirements for someone to lead, and (4) personal acceptance by their fellow group members which comes about as a result of attempts to lead (Hemphill, 1961). We do not recognize a person as a leader unless he or she does, in fact, influence others. *Successful leadership* occurs when the would-be follower behaves in accordance with the desires of the leader. *Effective leadership* occurs when the followers' behaviors produce group goal attainment. Successful leadership may have a disastrous effect upon the attainment of group goals. The leader may influence the followers toward a path that will destroy either the group itself or its effectiveness. The effective leader not only influences the group, but also produces a favorable outcome.

COMPARISON OF THE EMERGENT AND THE FORMAL LEADERS

The person who performs the leadership functions but who is not designated by management as the formal leader is referred to as the *emergent leader* or *informal leader*. The emergent leader is, of course, a part of the internal system. Persons who emerge as leaders tend to be the ones who are able to understand and communicate their perception of the way the group operates and is organized. They assign to themselves the key role in the group. This assignment is then accepted by the other group members. These emergent leaders generally (although not in every group) possess a higher level of intelligence and are more ascendant than other group members. Apparently, the group recognizes the greater facility of the more intelligent person for making judgments, and for helping the group adapt to the demands of the environment in order to achieve the group's goals. Group members select the more intelligent person for leadership because they believe that this will facilitate goal achievement (Guetzkow, 1968). Persons who emerge as leaders also are more ascendant in personality makeup than are the other group members. Ascendance is an attribute of persons who seek leadership roles and who feel comfortable being in the limelight.

The best-liked members of a group are not necessarily the most influential. Friendship and leadership do not ordinarily overlap. The role of the leader frequently produces a separation from the members in a manner that often prevents the development of close personal relationships. The leader who is a close personal friend of group members is often unable to influence them effectively (Fiedler, 1967).

When the group is part of a larger organization, its management will usually designate a *formal leader* as a part of the external organizational system. The emergent leader has the potential for greater influence than does the formal leader. He or she is the choice of group members and is accepted as a member of the group by those being influenced. Thus, the emergent leader often is more powerful than the formal leader who fails to gain such acceptance. This important aspect of power and authority has long been recognized in the literature of management.[1]

---

[1]Such well-known works as C. I. Barnard, *The Functions of the Executive* (Cambridge, Mass.: Harvard University Press, 1938) and H. A. Simon, *Administrative Behavior*, 2d ed. (The Macmillan Company, New York, 1957) provide thorough treatments of the subject of authority.

A conflict often exists between the emergent leader and the assigned formal leader. This conflict is eliminated and the group is most effective in attaining the organizational goals when emergent leadership and the formal leadership are held by the same person. This occurs either when management chooses the emergent leader as the supervisor or when the group allows the formal leader to exercise strong influence. The group is most likely to make such allowances for an enlightened formal leader who is sensitive to the workings of small groups and accepts them as an important part of his or her organization.

THE COMMUNICATION-INFLUENCE FUNCTIONS OF THE LEADER

Broadly defined, the function of a leader is to influence the group toward fulfillment of two basic objectives:

1. Achievement of the group's goals
2. Maintenance and enhancement of the group itself

The goal-achievement functions involve stimulation of action toward group goals, planning for goal achievement, providing information, preventing irrelevant or inhibiting group action, and avoiding barriers to group goal attainment. The maintenance functions involve encouraging, harmonizing, and helping to release tension.

The goal-related functions of leaders differ depending upon the group task involved. When the task of the group is to rationally solve a problem, the leader more frequently "asks for information or facts" and coordinates information from each group member in order to obtain a solution. In a mechanical assembly task, "stimulation of effort" is the most appropriate leadership activity. For a group discussion task, the leader usually (1) "asks for expression of feeling or opinion," (2) "agrees or approves," (3) "gives general information," and (4) "disagrees or is skeptical" (Carter et al., 1950). In each case the leader's behavior logically relates to the task to be accomplished.

The leadership functions which support group maintenance are designed to build the cohesiveness and assure the continuity of the group and its membership. These functions are as important as the goal-related functions and require at least as much time and effort on the part of the leader. Direct communication acts on the part of the leader are also essential for these maintenance functions.

ANALYSIS OF LEADERSHIP INFLUENCE AND POWER

Interpersonal influence has been discussed in Chapter 12. Influence within a small group contains the same set of elements as that which occurs at the interpersonal level. We shall now extend our consideration of influence to consider the types of power used by leaders in small groups. French and Raven (1968) contend that leaders use five bases of power:

1. Reward power, based on P's (influencee) perception that O (influencer) has the ability to reward P

2. Coercive power, based on P's perception that O has the ability to punish P

3. Legitimate power, based on the perception by P that O has a legitimate right to prescribe behavior for P

4. Referent power, based on P's identification with O

5. Expert power, based on P's perception that O has some special knowledge or expertness

The influence of a leader is based upon the number and types of power available, and the strength of each. Influence may be gained by means of persuasion, or it may be attributed on the basis of the follower's perception of the leader.

THE PROCESS OF LEADERSHIP

The leadership model (Figure 18-1) reveals a process of communication and influence affecting the achievement of goals. In the discussion above, we have focused attention on the nature of leadership and the leader's emergence. At this point, we shall begin viewing the total process of leadership. As the model for this process suggests, the communication-influence behaviors of the leader are filtered and refracted by the situation, and then flow on to the followers, with a final impact upon their effectiveness in goal attainment.

The basis for leadership behavior is found in the personal characteristics of the leader. We categorize these characteristics into three areas: abilities, motivation, and physical structure. Abilities include the full range of perceptual skills, of general intelligence, and of several special aptitudes. Motivation refers to the energizers of behavior including needs, attitudes, and interests. Physical structure is the total set of bodily attributes of the person. These attributes establish a basis for behaviors of all forms. The specific communication-influence behaviors used depend upon the environmental situation, the follower, and the goals.

Leader characteristics	Mediating situational variables	Follower characteristics	Goal attainment
(internal influences)	(external influences)	(internal influences)	(external-internal)

Abilities
  Perceptual
  Intelligence
  Aptitude
 	
Motivation
  Needs
  Attitudes
  Interests
 	
Physical structure
	Social, cultural context
	
	Physical environment
	
	Organization
	  Structure
	  Management
	  Climate
	
	Group components
	
	Task variables
		Maturity
		
		Independence
		
		Motivation
		
		Perception
		
		Capability
			Organizational goals
			
			Group goals
			
			Leader goals
			
			Follower goals

Communication influence → Communication influence → Effective or ineffective →

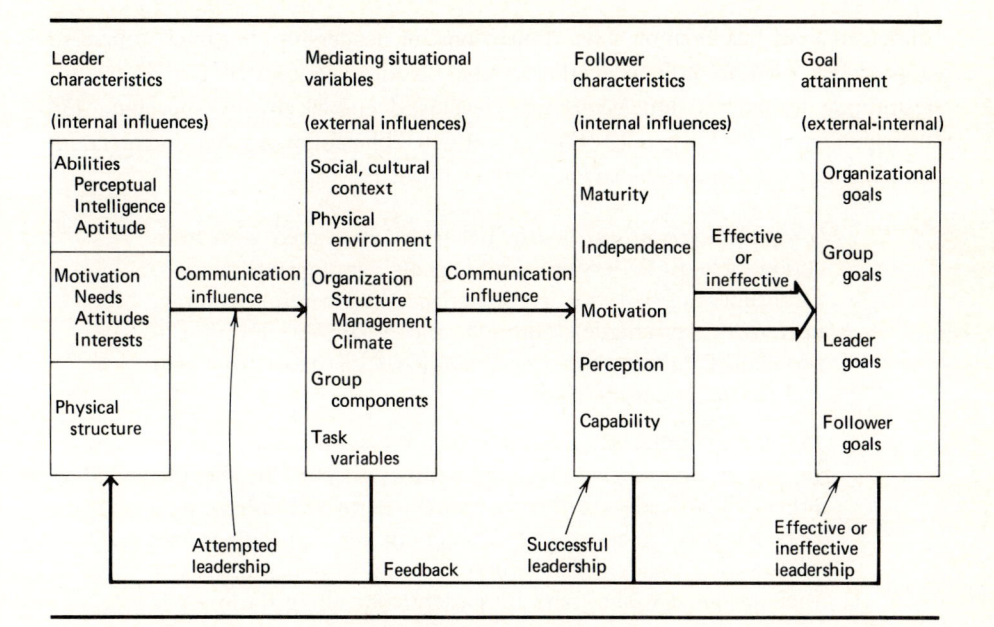

Attempted leadership · Feedback · Successful leadership · Effective or ineffective leadership

FIGURE 18-1 The process of leadership.

The behavior of the leader which emerges as a part of the internal system is encased in an array of variables from the external system. These variables include the social and cultural context; the structure, management, and climate of the organization; group factors; physical elements of the situation; and task variables. As these variables are different among leadership roles, the form of leader behavior must also change in order to achieve the desired goals. The behavior of the leader must also adapt to the type of followers in the group. For example, the type of leadership and communication used in influencing a group of assembly workers is normally quite different from that of the company president in working with the executive committee. The nature of the various types of goals which the leader, followers, group, and organization seek to achieve is a significant determinant of the nature of the behavior of the leader. The patterns of leader behavior which emerge out of this process are referred to as the *dimension of leadership*.

THE DIMENSIONS OF LEADERSHIP BEHAVIOR

In Chapter 9 we discussed a typology of six basic styles of communication. In the leadership role, we can observe these communication styles merging into recurring dimensions of leadership. The dimensions of leadership behavior represent approaches used to influence others. The broadest conceptual framework for examining leadership dimensions was developed empirically by surveying 136 managers from 85 companies (Wofford, 1970). The following five independent dimensions of leadership behavior were established:

Group Achievement and Order: Behaviors associated with team action, group leadership, group goals, and group success. Orderliness of behavior is emphasized, i.e., careful planning; neat work; systematic, thorough, and organized approach to problems (similar to the concepts of participative management and democratic leadership).

Personal Enhancement: Behaviors of leaders who enjoy the use of power and depend heavily upon authority in directing others. The leaders' efforts are directed toward enhancing a personal position above that of others by trying out their own ideas rather than those of others, by requiring compliance to their personal wishes, and by closely controlling the work of others in line with their personal judgments and decisions (similar to the concept of authoritarian and production-centered leadership).

Personal Interaction: Behaviors of leaders who desire close, personal, cordial relationships to subordinates. The leaders are informal, casual, and talkative. People led by the leaders readily become their friends (similar to the concepts of consideration and permissive and employee-centered management).

Dynamic Achievement: Behaviors of leaders who are forceful and active. The leaders spend a minimum of time in planning or in decision making, instead preferring to be on the firing line of activity. The leaders delegate authority to others to make decisions and then leave them alone to accomplish the desired results. The leaders have confidence in the people that are led and also have self-confidence.

Security and Maintenance: Behaviors of leaders who are highly secure and free from anxieties. The leaders do not worry about the work, about looking bad to others, or about their group doing poorly. The leaders take things as they come with little concern for the consequences of the future. The leaders do not pressure the people led and demand little of them.

The relationships between the leadership dimensions and communication styles are not fixed. Figure 18-2 shows the style of communication typically used by

Leadership dimension	Communication styles
Group achievement and order	Equalitarian and structuring
Personal enhancement	Controlling and structuring
Personal interaction	Equalitarian
Dynamic achievement	Dynamic
Security and maintenance	Relinquish and withdrawal

FIGURE 18-2 Relationship of leadership dimension and communication styles.

leaders strongly oriented toward each leadership dimension. Other styles may be used by these leaders; however, those shown in Figure 18-2 are most frequently used.

SITUATIONAL VARIABLES WHICH INFLUENCE LEADERSHIP EFFECTIVENESS

Once the dimensions of leadership behavior have been identified, the external situational effects become the focus of attention. How do the type of industry, company, and other environmental factors determine the effectiveness of each leadership dimension? The leadership environment plays a critical role in filtering and refracting communication and influence.[2] Suppose you are a leader in an organization in which the top-level managers make most of the decisions. They are not receptive to the ideas of lower-level people and supervise subordinates closely. Your work group is large and has little opportunity for interpersonal communication. Your group task is simple and has little flexibility. All the activities related to the task have been carefully engineered. Crises frequently occur in the work operations which call for a quick reaction.

One day you come to work and are surprised to learn that you have been assigned to another division of your company. You are to serve as director of basic research. You find what is to you a new work world. The new management team is open and flexible. Your participation and the contribution of your ideas are

---

[2]Korman (1966, p. 355) reviewed twenty-five studies on behavior and concluded that "there is very little evidence that leadership behavioral and/or attitudinal variation . . . are predictive of later effectiveness and/or satisfaction criteria. . . . What is needed, however, in future . . . studies is not just recognition of this factor of 'situational determinants' but rather a systematic conceptualization of situational variance as it might relate to leadership behavior." To date no widely accepted systematic formulation of situational elements has been developed.

	Group achievement and order	Personal enhancement	Personal interaction	Dynamic achievement	Security and maintenance
Organizational leadership climate	Company executives hold a democratic philosophy. Company executives use general supervision. Lower-level managers are able to exercise much influence upon higher managers	Company executives hold an authoritarian philosophy. Company executives use close supervision. Lower-level managers are not able to exercise much influence upon higher managers	Company managers have a high degree of job security. Company managers are people oriented	Company managers are aggressive. Company is in a stage of rapid growth and change. Managers have low job security	Company management is people-oriented. Company has reached a level of stability
Organizational structure	Organization is decentralized. Authority is delegated to lower levels	Organization is centralized. Decision-making authority is restricted to upper levels	Company is large and stable. Company is centralized	Company is fairly small but growing rapidly. Authority is decentralized with an atmosphere of giving the manager a chance to succeed or fail	Company is large. Organization is centralized

	Work group		
Work group is small There are frequent communication exchanges within the group The work situation supports the holding of group meetings	Work group is large Communication within group is infrequent	Work group is homogeneous in background Group members rarely meet as a unit because of the nature of the work Work structure and location reduce communication between group members	Work group is small	Work group may be large or small

	Tasks and work relationships		
Leader's work station is separated from that of his men Work tasks are flexible and subject to worker control Work is of a non-crisis nature Work to be performed is complex	Leader's work station is separated from that of his men Work tasks are structured Schedules, plans, and processes of work are simple Work crises occur frequently Performance effectiveness is difficult to measure	Tasks are structured Equipment is simple Work schedules are simple	Leader's work station is separated from that of his men Work tasks involve frequent crises Technical expertise of leader is not required	Schedules, plans, and processes of work are complex High technical knowledge is often required by the worker

FIGURE 18-3 Organizational environment for managerial behavior dimensions.

encouraged. You have a great deal of autonomy for operation. Your team of research engineers works closely together with frequent, open communication. The research tasks are highly flexible with very few crises occurring that require immediate definitive action to avoid great losses of resources or profits.

Would you use the same approach to leadership in the new job as you did in the previous one? No, not if you are an effective leader. Your styles of communication and your dimensions of leadership must change drastically in the new environment. In the first group, you would use structuring and controlling communication. Your leadership would be strongly oriented toward personal enhancement. Since the environment is unsupportive of open communication, the attempt to use high information sharing and feedback will only bring frustration to the group and to upper management. The existence of high stress calls for a stronger exercise of control. Crises or stress situations call for the emphasis of strong control communications and strong influence (Hamblin, 1958).

In the research group, your leadership orientation must shift to a strong emphasis upon equalitarian communication. Your leadership will be oriented toward group achievement and order, and personal interaction. Of course, it is not easy to make such behavioral changes. A rigid person who cannot adapt the leadership to the situation will be unable to succeed in a changing environment. Managers who are aware of the nature of such leadership and communicative behaviors are in a better position to adapt. Much research is required before we can accurately pinpoint the leadership dimension appropriate to every situation. Figure 18-3 identifies the current level of knowledge regarding the situational variables that are associated with each leadership dimension.

It can be seen from the above that the personal leader dimensions of the internal system interact significantly with the situational variables of the external system. Effective managers are aware of this interaction and attempt to adapt their leadership to the situation in which they operate.

THE IMPORTANCE OF THE FOLLOWER FOR LEADERSHIP COMMUNICATION

The dimensions of leadership have an impact upon the communication of followers. Leaders who inappropriately emphasize the controlling dimension bring about a higher resistance on the part of followers to sharing information with the leaders. The subordinate who feels pressured by the supervisor is not inclined to take complaints to the supervisor; as a result, the supervisor has less influence upon the worker's behavior (Likert, 1961). Workers are more willing to provide all types of information to supervisors who are high in personal interaction and low in control. The type of information is also important. As one might expect, subordinates are resistant to sharing information on an intimate, personal level with their boss (Wofford, Sims, and Calabro, 1975).

As our leadership process of Figure 18-1 emphasizes, followers are the object of the leader's influence and produce the group results. The followers are a dynamic component in the model. Each follower has a set of expectations and characteristics which determine his or her response to influence attempts.

An important follower characteristic is *maturity*. The leader's behavior must adapt to the changing maturity of the followers as they grow in ability and experience. Early in the life of a group, leader behavior should stress goal achievement and deemphasize group maintenance. As the work group becomes more experienced and capable, the leader can control the task performance less and emphasize group maintenance more (Hersey and Blanchard, 1972; Nakamura, 1958).

A follower characteristic related to maturity is *independence*. Independence is the willingness of group members to take action apart from the influence of others. Followers who are highly independent are not receptive to a strongly controlling communication style on the part of the leader. As independence increases among followers, the leader must exercise less and less control (Vroom and Mann, 1960).

Motivation is also important to the followers' reactions to their leaders. The follower who is strongly motivated to achievement is easily directed toward goal attainment. Group members who possess strong interpersonal needs strive for group maintenance. They may have little interest in expending effort toward goal achievement.

Managers should be aware of these characteristics of the followers in determining their leadership behavior. Effective performance results require a compatibility between follower characteristics and the approaches to influence and communication used by managers. To be effective, managers must develop a consistency and balance between their own behavior as leaders, the situational variables, and behavior of their followers. Our definition of leadership indicates that the communication-influence process of the leader is directed "toward the attainment of a specified goal or goals." As seen in Figure 18-1, leader communication attempts to influence the group toward attainment of organizational goals, group goals, followers' goals, and the leader's own personal goals. In this chapter we are primarily concerned with the attainment of group goals; however, some degree of attention must be given to goals at each level for the group to be effective over an extended period of time.

SUMMARY

Leadership is closely associated with communication. Without communication leadership cannot occur. We have identified three kinds of leadership: attempted, successful, and effective. The most significant type for the organization is effective leadership. Effective leadership involves the influence of followers toward goal attainment. Leaders who are assigned by higher authority within an organization are referred to as formal leaders; those who emerge as leaders out of the group are called informal or emergent leaders. The functions of leaders are basically oriented toward one of two objectives, i.e., group achievement or group maintenance. We have discussed five forms of power by which the leader may influence the members of his or her group toward these objectives.

Five basic dimensions of leadership were discussed, i.e., group achievement and order, personal enhancement, personal interaction, dynamic achievement, and security and maintenance. Each of these dimensions is associated with specific communication styles. The relationship between these dimensions and group effectiveness depends upon the situation in which the leadership is exercised and the compatibility between the followers' characteristics and the leader's behavior. Effective group performance requires a situation and type of follower which are compatible with the dimensions of the leader.

IMPORTANT TERMS AND CONCEPTS

attempted leadership, successful leadership, effective leadership, emergent leader, formal leader, communication-influence function, types of leadership power, leadership model, dimensions of leadership, situational variables, follower

REVIEW QUESTIONS

1. Imagine yourself as a leader in an organization in which all are using a one-way radio system. You can send messages to your subordinates but they cannot respond. What would be the effects upon your leadership behaviors and style?

2. If you are an effective leader, does this mean that you are of necessity a successful and attempted leader as well?

3. How would you characterize the differences between leadership functions oriented to the accomplishment of goals and functions oriented to group maintenance?

4. Identify the most likely type of leadership power used by each of the following:
    a. The police officer directing traffic
    b. The former United States President speaking on international policy
    c. The parent influencing the child to pick up toys
    d. The subordinate demanding a raise
    e. The lawyer advising a client
    f. The coach reprimanding a player

5. Compare the leadership style which you would use with a group of inexperienced assembly-line workers with that used with a group of corporate vice presidents.

INCIDENT 1: THE FRUSTRATED LEADER

Walt was elected captain of his high school football team for two consecutive years. His coach described him as a natural leader and largely responsible for the success of the team. In college, he was chosen the president of his fraternity and steered the group through two of their most active years. Everyone agrees that Walt is dynamic, decisive, tough-minded, demanding, and impatient with persons who are less well motivated than himself.

A good academic record along with his successful extracurricular activities landed Walt a good job in a small electronics plant. His enthusiasm and industriousness soon landed him a supervisory job.

He began having problems with his group almost immediately. He knew they were capable of much more than they were producing. He felt that this lack of performance resulted from lack of direction and encouragement. He worked with the group closely. He encouraged, cajoled, and finally threatened but to his dismay production was steadily declining.

INCIDENT 2: A CASE OF MISUNDERSTANDING[3]

In a department of a large industrial organization there were seven workers (four men and three women) engaged in testing and inspecting panels of electronic equipment. In this department one of the workers, Bing, was having trouble with his immediate supervisor, Hart, who had formerly been a worker in the department.

Had we been observers in this department we would have seen Bing carrying two or three panels at a time from the racks where they were stored to the bench where he inspected them together. For this activity we would have seen him charging double or triple setup time. We would have heard him occasionally singing at work. Also we would have seen him usually leaving his work position a few minutes early to go to lunch, and noticed that other employees sometimes accompanied him. And had we been present at one specific occasion, we would have heard Hart telling Bing that he disapproved of these activities and that he wanted Bing to stop doing them.

However, not being present to hear the actual verbal exchange that took place in this interaction, let us note what Bing and Hart each said to a personnel representative.

[3] Reprinted from MAN-IN-ORGANIZATION: ESSAYS OF F. J. ROETHLISBERGER. Cambridge, Mass.: The Belknap Press of Harvard University Press, 1968. Copyright © 1953 by the President and Fellows of Harvard College.

What Bing Said In talking about his practice of charging double or triple setup time for panels which he inspected all at one time, Bing said:

"This is a perfectly legal thing to do. We've always been doing it. Mr. Hart, the supervisor, has other ideas about it, though; he claims it's cheating the company. He came over to the bench a day or two ago and let me know just how he felt about the matter. Boy, did we go at it! It wasn't so much the fact that he called me down on it, but more the way in which he did it. He's a sarcastic bastard. I've never seen anyone like him. He's not content just to say in a manlike way what's on his mind, but he prefers to do it in a way that makes you want to crawl inside a crack on the floor. What a guy! I don't mind being called down by a supervisor, but I like to be treated like a man, and not humiliated like a school teacher does a naughty kid. He's been pulling this stuff ever since he's been a supervisor. I knew him when he was just one of us, but since he's been promoted, he's lost his friendly way and seems to be having some difficulty in knowing how to manage us employees. He's a changed man over what he used to be like when he was a worker on the bench with us several years ago.

"When he pulled this kind of stuff on me the other day, I got so damn mad I called in the union representative. I knew that the thing I was doing was permitted by the contract, but I was intent on making some trouble for Mr. Hart, just because he persists in this sarcastic way of handling me. I am about fed up with the whole damn situation. I'm trying every means I can to get myself transferred out of his group. If I don't succeed and I'm forced to stay on here, I'm going to screw him in every way I can. He's not going to pull this kind of kid stuff any longer on me. When the union representative questioned him on the case, he finally had to back down, because according to the contract an employee can use any time-saving method or device in order to speed up the process as long as the quality standards of the job are met.

"You see, he knows that I do professional singing on the outside. He hears me singing here on the job, and he hears the people talking about my career in music. I guess he figures I can be so cocky because I have another means of earning some money. Actually, the employees here enjoy having me sing while we work, but he thinks I'm disturbing them and causing them to 'goof off' from their work. Occasionally, I leave the job a few minutes early and go down to the washroom to wash up before lunch. Sometimes several others in the group will accompany me, and so Mr. Hart automatically thinks I'm the leader and usually bawls me out for the whole thing.

"So, you can see, I'm a marked man around here. He keeps watching me like a hawk. Naturally, this makes me very uncomfortable. That's why I'm sure a transfer would be the best thing. I've asked him for it, but he didn't give me any satisfaction at the time. While I remain here, I'm going to keep my nose clean, but whenever I get the chance, I'm going to slip it to him, but good."

What Hart Said Here, on the other hand, is what Hart told the personnel representative:

"Say, I think you should be in on this. My dear little friend Bing is heading himself into a showdown with me. Recently it was brought to my attention that Bing has been taking double and triple setup time for panels which he is actually inspecting at one time. In effect, that's cheating, and I've called him down on it several times before. A few days ago it was brought to my attention again, and so this time I really let him have it in no uncertain terms. He's been getting away with this for too long and I'm going to put an end to it once and for all. I know he didn't like my calling him on it because a few hours later he had the union representative breathing down my back. Well, anyway, I let them both know I'll not tolerate the practice any longer, and I let Bing know that if he continues to do this kind of thing, I'm going to take official action with my boss to have the guy fired or penalized somehow. This kind of thing has to be curbed. Actually, I'm inclined to think the guy's mentally deficient, because talking to him has actually no meaning to him whatsoever. I've tried just about every approach to jar some sense into that guy's head, and I've just about given it up as a bad deal.

"I don't know what it is about the guy, but I think he's harboring some deep feelings against me. For what, I don't know, because I've tried to handle that bird with kid gloves. But his whole attitude around here on the job is one of indifference, and he certainly isn't a good influence on the rest of my group. Frankly, I think he purposely tries to agitate them against me at times, too. It seems to me he may be suffering from illusions of grandeur, because all he does all day long is sit over there and croon his fool head off. Thinks he's a Frank Sinatra! No kidding! I understand he takes singing lessons and he's working with some of the local bands in the city. All of which is O.K. by me; but when his outside interests start interfering with his efficiency on the job, then I've got to start paying closer attention to the situation. For this reason I've been keeping my eye on that bird and if he steps out of line any more, he and I are going to part ways.

"You know there's an old saying, 'You can't make a purse out of a sow's ear.' The guy is simply unscrupulous. He feels no obligation to do a real day's work. Yet I know the guy can do a good job, because for a long time he did. But in recent months he's slipped, for some reason, and his whole attitude on the job has changed. Why, it's even getting to the point now where I think he's inducing other employees to 'goof off' a few minutes before the lunch whistle and go down to the washroom and clean up on company time. I've called him on it several times, but words just don't seem to make any lasting impression on him. Well, if he keeps it up much longer, he's going to find himself on the way out. He's asked me for a transfer, so I know he wants to go. But I didn't give him an answer when he asked me, because I was steaming mad at the time, and I may have told him to go somewhere else."

EXERCISE: COMMUNICATION AND LEADERSHIP

1. The class is divided into groups of five members. Each group selects a leader, three workers, and one observer.

2. Sets of tinker toys are distributed to each worker in the group.

3. The group will be asked to assemble units using the parts available. A plan for organizing the construction should be developed before the models are seen by the leader.

4. The leader receives the models from the instructor. The leader must set a unit production goal for the group for each model to be produced.
5. After the instructor says "begin," you will have twenty minutes of construction time. Record the goals and number of units produced by the team on Table 18-1. Units produced beyond the goal do not count. Two units are subtracted from the score for each unit short of the goal. Parts may not be exchanged among group members.

TABLE 18-1

Team	Model A			Model B			Total score
	Goal	Number produced	Score	Goal	Number produced	Score	
1							
2							
3							
4							
5							
6							
7							
8							
9							
10							

The observer should pay special note to assure the proper following of the instructions by group members and should review the questions below that will be discussed later.

Discussion led by the observer:

A. Describe the styles of the leaders. What leadership dimensions did they use?

B. What types of power and influence were employed?

C. What functions of leadership did they employ?

D. What situational factors were important for the group?

E. Which patterns of communication (Chapter 9) were used most frequently?

F. What characteristics of effective or ineffective followers were apparent?

BIBLIOGRAPHY

Carter, L., W. Haythorn, B. Shriver, and J. Lanzetta: "The Behavior of Leaders and Other Group Members," *Journal of Abnormal and Social Psychology,* vol. 46, pp. 589–595, 1950.

Fiedler, F. E.: *A Theory of Leadership Effectiveness* (New York: McGraw-Hill Book Company, 1967).

French, Jr., J. R. P., and B. Raven: "The Bases of Social Power," in D. Cartwright and A. Zander (eds.), *Group Dynamics: Research and Theory* (New York: Harper & Row, Publishers, Incorporated, 1968).

Guetzkow, H.: "Differentiation of Roles in Task-Oriented Groups," in D. Cartwright and A. Zander (eds.), *Group Dynamics: Research and Theory* (New York: Harper & Row, Publishers, Incorporated, 1968).

Hamblin, R. L.: "Leadership and Crises," *Sociometry,* vol. 21, pp. 322–335, 1958.

Hemphill, J. K.: "Administration as Problem-Solving," in A. W. Halpin (ed.), *Administration Theory in Education* (Chicago: Midwest Administration Center, 1958).

———: "Why People Attempt to Lead," in L. Petrullo and B. M. Bass (eds.), *Interpersonal Behavior* (New York: Holt, Rinehart and Winston, Inc., 1961).

Hersey, P., and K. H. Blanchard: *Management of Organizational Behavior* (Englewood Cliffs, N.J.: Prentice-Hall, Inc., 1972).

Korman, A. K.: "Consideration, Initiating Structure and Organizational Criteria: A Review," *Personal Psychology,* vol. 19, pp. 349–361, 1966.

Likert, R.: *New Patterns of Management* (New York: McGraw-Hill Book Company, 1961).

Nakamura, C. Y.: "Conformity and Problem Solving," *Journal of Abnormal and Social Psychology,* vol. 56, pp. 215–320, 1958.

Tannenbaum, R., I. R. Weschler, and F. Massarik: *Leadership and Organization: A Behavioral Science Approach* (New York: McGraw-Hill Book Company, 1961).

Vroom, V. H., and F. C. Mann: "Leader Authoritarianism and Employee Attitudes," *Personnel Psychology,* vol. 13, pp. 125–140, 1960.

Wofford, J. C.: "Factor Analysis of Managerial Behavior Variables," *Journal of Applied Psychology,* vol. 54, pp. 169–173, 1970.

———, A. Sims, and P. Calabro: "Leadership Styles and Follower Information Sharing," *Southern Management Journal,* vol. 1, 1975.

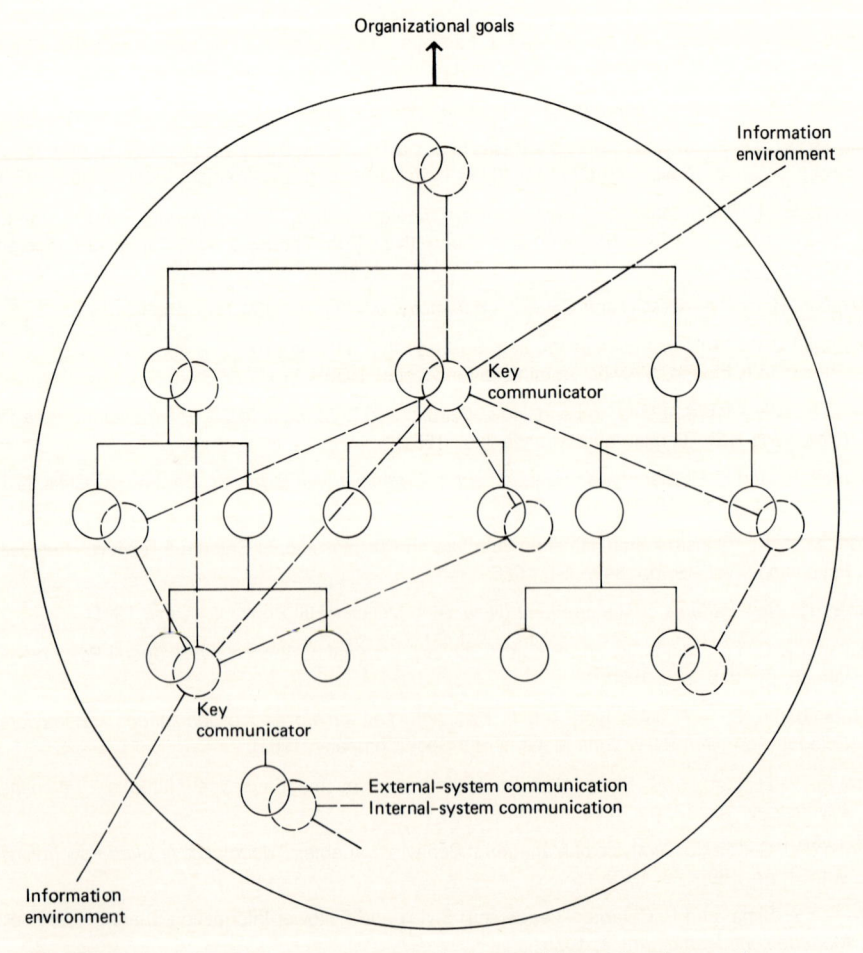

FIGURE 4 Organizational communication. The external-internal system overlay.

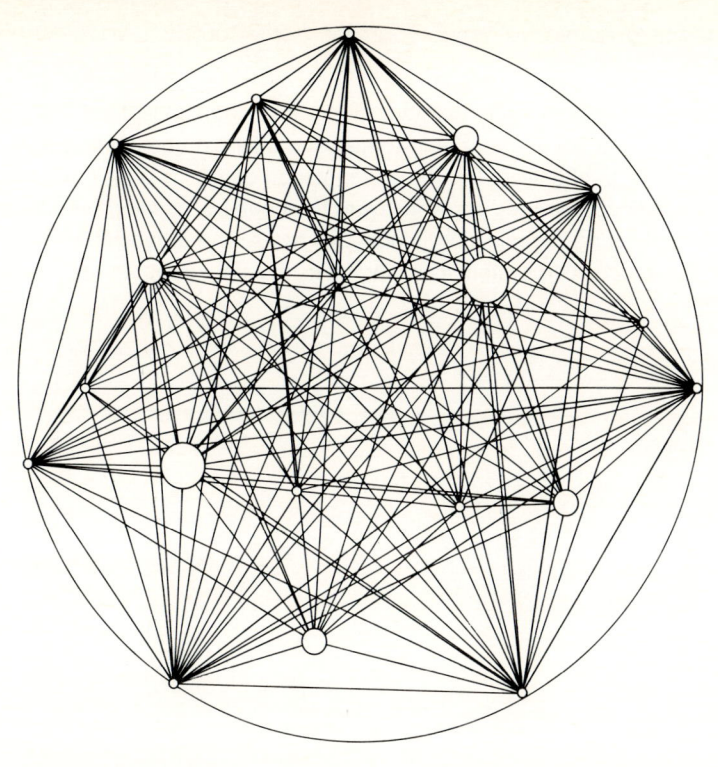

PART FOUR

MANAGING TOTAL ORGANIZATIONAL COMMUNICATION:
A Global Level of Analysis

In this final section the organizational level of analysis of the communication process is presented. Interpersonal, group, external, and internal considerations are blended into the organizational communication overlay. By understanding this complex mosaic of interrelated communications subsystems, the manager can effectively implement the communication process for his or her total organization. Chapter 19 will introduce the formal organization as an external system which is crucially dependent on its communication system to offset the effects of work subdivision. Some important external-systems difficulties which affect communication will be discussed in Chapter 20. Chapter 21 will treat the informal organization as an internal system which is highly dependent on face-to-face and other forms of personal communication. The informal communication system will be shown to have the potential to compensate for deficiencies in the formal system. The nature and flow of information in the informal system will be examined. Chapter 22 will deal with the managerial problem of integrating formal and informal communication such that the organization can effectively meet the information demands of its environment and situation. Chapter 23 provides an overview to the book by focusing on the role of the manager in facilitating organization information flows. The organization is viewed as an information-processing system involving interpersonal, group, formal, and informal subsystems.

19

FORMAL ORGANIZATIONS AND COMMUNICATION

Formal organizations are contrived to meet the needs of their environment in a rather programmed fashion. The formalization of such an external system includes the requirement for coordination and communication within the organization. The organization must have a functioning communication link to its environment. Communication and other forms of organization activity are interdependent.

We made the observation in Chapter 4 that formal organizations are essentially external systems which are planned to satisfy some environmental need and survive over time. External systems were seen to consist of a set of required activities, interactions, and sentiments that are logically considered appropriate to accomplish the organizational mission. External systems include all the behaviors necessary in view of the purpose which is to be accomplished, but, it is hoped, nothing more or less than this ideal. Such a system will arise from the recognition of some environmental need by individuals who are willing to associate to satisfy the need in return for an economic and/or psychological reward. In the paragraphs which follow, a fictitious example of an external system will be developed. We shall use the example to examine the nature and scope of the role of communication in implementing the formal organization.

NATURE OF COMMUNICATION WITHIN FORMAL ORGANIZATIONS

Suppose you lived at a time before the invention of the wheel. You are quite a student of human behavior and spend a considerable amount of time just observing the activities of your fellow humans. One day you are standing outside your cave and observe a neighbor, Neanderthal, struggling to move a heavy load of rocks on a primitive sled fashioned from tree branches which are tied together by vines. Being the good neighbor that you are, you offer to assist Neanderthal since he must move the load a considerable distance.

The task proves to be quite difficult since part of the route is uphill, and you and Neanderthal must take frequent rest stops. You might imagine that the conversation during the rest periods will focus to some extent on the task at hand. The two of you are in agreement that there ought to be an easier way to perform such a difficult task, and you begin to speculate as to what the alternatives might be. At this point, observers from an enlightened age such as our own would say that you and Neanderthal have recognized an environmental need.

Eventually, the recognition of this environmental need leads to some serious discussions between yourself and Neanderthal as to some realistic solutions to the problem. The two of you conclude that the transportation of heavy loads would be much easier if the frictional effects of heavy masses could be reduced. Perhaps if some sort of ovoid were inserted between the sled and the ground? How about a log? Why use the entire log? Sections of the log can be connected by a shaft which rotates.

At this point, you and Neanderthal have discovered the wheel, though you do not yet recognize it by that name. One thing is for sure, the two of you recognize that if these "ovoids" can be produced in quantity, neither of you will ever have to hunt your own food or build your own fires (assuming you knew how) again. With a good supply of ovoids, you'll be able to barter for all the goods and services you'll ever want.

Armed with the work-saving idea concerning the ovoid, you and Neanderthal set out enthusiastically to enlist the support of some other friendly cave dwellers. It is clear that if a larger number of individuals are involved, the venture can be much more productive. At this point, you and your primitive friends who agree to participate have decided to cooperate to form a primitive production system in order to satisfy the commonly perceived need. In essence, you have agreed to plan an external system or a formal organization.

We now wish to examine the nature of the formal organization more closely. We will look at the division of work and its effects, the tendency toward formalization, and the types of communication which are involved in the external system.

Division of Work in the Formal Organization

Once you and Neanderthal decided to involve some associates, an unavoidable commitment was made to divide the work up among participants. Let us examine just how this might have been done by using an external-systems form of analysis.

At the outset of Associated Ovoids, as the organization came to call itself, you and Neanderthal had informally agreed to the roles that each would play and had also defined some activities for your associates. Since Neanderthal was quite familiar with the nearby forest, he was to identify sufficient quantities of raw material which would meet manufacturing specifications. Cro-Magnon, who was quite handy with an axe, was to cut down the trees selected by Neanderthal and trim them for shipment. Piltdown, who was quite strong, was responsible for transportation of the logs to the site of the final production activity. Initially, it was agreed that you would serve as the sawyer who would make the finished ovoids from the logs by removing the bark and slicing them into sections.

After a supply of ovoids had been produced, you and Neanderthal (the founders of the organization) would then make contacts throughout the community seeking to barter the ovoids with individuals who needed them and who had something of value to trade. It was agreed that you would cover the northern territory and Neanderthal the southern territory. When the supply was exhausted, the cycle would repeat itself.

External System of Associated Ovoids. At this point, we can characterize our primitive external system as consisting of four individuals (you, Neanderthal, Cro-Magnon, and Piltdown) who are providing the necessary functions of raw materials procurement, shipping, production, and sales and distribution. Thus, the total work to be done by the organization has been subdivided among the various participants.

Looking more closely at the subdivision, we can identify some very specific activities, interactions, and sentiments which will be required of the participants if the association is to survive and fulfill the needs of the environment.[1] Within the procurement function, we find such activities as locating trees (Neanderthal), cutting and trimming trees (Cro-Magnon), and shipping (Piltdown). But since these three activities are performed by three different individuals, they must somehow be linked. Cro-Magnon must know which trees to cut.

Clearly, there is a required interaction between Neanderthal and Cro-Magnon, and in similar fashion there is a required interaction between Cro-Magnon and Piltdown so that the proper logs will be shipped at the appropriate time. It is important to note that such interactions are likely to occur as forms of interpersonal communication. Neanderthal will probably mark the trees he has selected in a particular way which has meaning for Cro-Magnon. Cro-Magnon and Piltdown are likely to agree on some specific method for identifying logs which are ready for shipment.

We have identified some specific activities and interactions in the procurement

---

[1] Activities, interactions, and sentiments were defined in Chapter 4 as the essential categories of behavior for all human systems, external and internal.

function of the external system, but what about sentiments? Sentiments are more abstract, but if we were there, we could probably observe the symptoms of certain sentiments. Even without being on the scene, we can identify sentiments which will be required as a minimum for the effectiveness of the external system. It should be clear that the attitudes of Neanderthal, Cro-Magnon, and Piltdown must be somewhat positive toward one another, the organization, and their specific jobs. If, for example, Cro-Magnon's attitude toward Piltdown, his job, or the organization becomes too negative, it will affect the manner in which he performs the required activities and interactions. The organization cannot tolerate a negative sentiment if it becomes too disruptive to the mission.

Turning from the procurement function to those of production and sales and distribution, we can make similar observations. Clearly you, as the only person engaged in the production function, must provide all the required activities in this functional area. It is you who will be slicing, trimming, and matching sets of ovoids. As for interactions, it is quite clear that the other functional areas will, of necessity, be involved. You must coordinate your activities with the activities of individuals in shipping and also those in sales and distribution (at least for the southern territory). Such coordination will involve cross-functional interaction. Were the production function subdivided further, the interactive relationships would obviously be even more complex.

With respect to sentiments, it should be clear that if you develop a very negative attitude toward Cro-Magnon in shipping, there will be problems. Suppose that over time the two of you begin to argue as to where he is to deposit incoming shipments. At first the disagreement is minor, but in time the situation reaches such a state that each of you is devoting energy and time to argument that could better be utilized in productive activities. Obviously, this will be disruptive of external-system operations and the production of ovoids will be unnecessarily impaired.

As for the sales and distribution function, we mentioned a subdivision of work between you and Neanderthal, the original partner. Your activities consist of locating prospects and making trades in the northern territory, and his activities are the same for the southern territory. The required interactions for sales and distribution would be those with the prospective customers. Additionally in the case of Neanderthal, his interactions would include those with you as a linkage between production and his share of sales and distribution.

It is interesting to note that the production-sales interaction for the northern territory is internal to yourself. No interaction is required between linked activities because there has been no division of work in that particular instance. The linked activities are performed by the same person, you. On the other hand, we might speculate that a form of interaction may well exist between the two sales territories.

There must be some agreement as to the boundary between the two sales areas, and/or interactions may be necessary if an unanticipated imbalance in sales occurs between the two territories. Perhaps the northern district experiences a low demand and the southern district an unusually high demand. In this case it may be necessary to use the surplus of ovoids in the north to make up the shortage in the south. It may even be necessary for you to go into the southern territory and help Neanderthal with the rush. It should be clear by now that the division into sales territories has resulted in a requirement for some specific interactions.

As was the case for the procurement function, there will be a need for positive sentiments in the sales and distribution function between yourself and Neanderthal. The external system requires such behavior if it is to achieve its goals of satisfying environmental needs and surviving. You and Neanderthal must find the work of sales to be reasonably satisfying, and the relationship between you and Neanderthal must be an agreeable one. Should you tire of being on the road constantly or having to be "friendly" with customers you secretly dislike, or should Neanderthal come to suspect that you have been stealing some of his customers, the success of the external system can be drastically impaired.

Flow of Work and Linked Activities. The external system of Associated Ovoids can be presented in the form of a flow diagram in order to make some important observations concerning the nature of human organizations. Figure 19-1 represents the organization as we have described it. In forming the external system for Associated Ovoids, we have clearly established a set of linked activities which must function in unison. The interactions are shown in a single direction because this represents the primary flow of work. In reality, there would be a need for interactions in the opposite direction also.

We are placing no particular weight or importance to any single set of behavioral elements. The activities serve important task functions; the interactions serve important linking functions; and positive sentiments are necessary if the system is to continue functioning over time. The important point for now is that the consequence of such a linked flow of activities is a need for coordination.

Subunit Interdependence. When the manager chooses to subdivide the totality of activities and interactions associated with some goal among two or more people, a very specific set of relationships is created. The resultant subdivided units become interdependent with respect to goal achievement. One subunit becomes dependent on another. Essentially, the interdependence results from the sequential nature of the system which is created. In the Associated Ovoids example, it can be seen that successive units in the sequence become dependent on standardized outputs from preceding units. Several dimensions of standardization are potentially of importance.

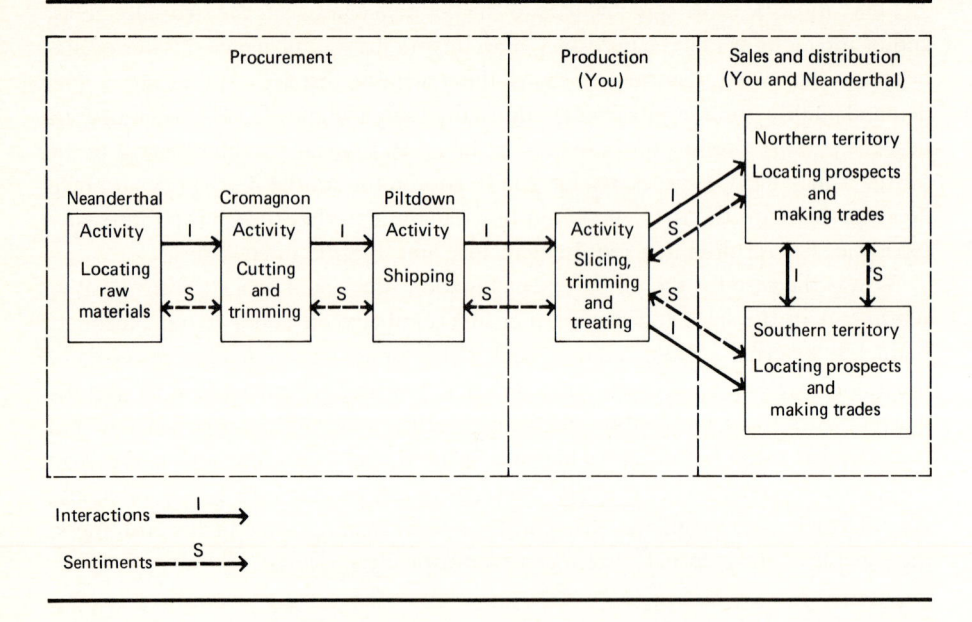

FIGURE 19-1 Flow of work in the external system.

Some common and important dimensions of standardization would be those of *form*, *content*, and *timing*. Examples of each can be found in the Associated Ovoids situation.

With reference to *form*, Neanderthal must be very careful that he selects only those trees which are of the appropriate size and shape. Should he select trees which are too large, too crooked, or too irregular in shape, the nonstandard output would have undesirable effects on subsequent operations. Cro-Magnon may be required to spend excessive time in his trimming activity in order to make the logs conform to the desired dimensions. Perhaps nonstandard sizes or shapes in the logs would also disrupt Piltdown's shipping activity. Finally, irregularities would undoubtedly impact on your ability to hew the proper-sized ovoids. At best the nonstandard size or form in the logs would slow up production because other individuals in the sequence would be required to perform nonstandard activities and interactions to compensate for the improper input.

In the case of *content*, a similar problem is encountered. However, in this case, there are clear communication overtones. Suppose Neanderthal fails to clearly mark the trees he has selected for procurement? Perhaps, even worse, he may use a nonstandard coding system. Again as before, such failures impair the effectiveness of subsequent operation. Other individuals involved in the flow of work expend additional energy and time to offset the difficulty. Should Neanderthal send an ambiguous or misleading message or perhaps send no message at all, the activities of Cro-Magnon, Piltdown, and yourself will clearly be disrupted.

The situation in the case of nonstandard *timing* is a similar one. Suppose Cro-Magnon spends a little too much time with the cave ladies during his lunch hour, and as a result, he is late in getting out the afternoon shipment of logs? The effect of the delay is to present a batch of logs for shipment at a nonstandard time. Again, the impact of the nonstandard output (in this case timing) will flow through and affect the actions of all others in the chain. The performance of Piltdown, yourself, and those in sales are disrupted, and even the ultimate consumer is affected.

Obviously, the seriousness of such deviations from standard or plan will be determined by the degree of interdependency of the units as well as the tolerance limits of the particular system. Should the deviations become severe enough, goal accomplishment for the total entity (as well as its subunits) will not be possible.

The relationship between division of work and subunit interdependence can be summarized as a simple graph such as the one in Figure 19-2. The graph is intended to express the essence of the relationship, but we do not mean to imply any particular precision. Indeed, the precise relationship for a specific system, if it were knowable at all, might be curvilinear rather than linear. Still, it can be stated generally that as the degree of work subdivision is increased, there is an increase in subunit interdependence. It is this interdependent relationship that we are attempting to express in the graph.

The Need for Coordination. The effects of dividing up work do not stop here. As organizational subunits become more highly interdependent (as the result of a high degree of work subdivision), the need for effective coordination becomes greater. The Associated Ovoids example involves three basic subunits—procurement,

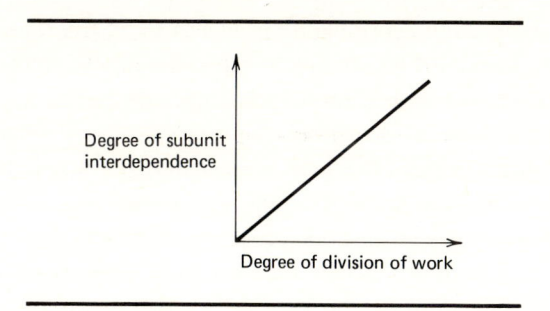

FIGURE 19-2 Division of work and subunit interdependence.

production, and sales. Should we change this system to one which involves eight subdivisions, each being more narrow and specialized, we increase substantially their interpendence and the consequent need for coordination among them.

Specialization, assuming the demand is sufficiently large, permits higher production volumes as certain economies and efficiencies are realized. Compared to jobs which are relatively broad in coverage, the more specialized ones will involve less loss of time in transferring from one set of activities to the next (setup time) and operator skill can be developed.

The problem is that the highly specialized activity standing alone has no value to the organization. Its value is that when specialized activities are effectively linked, the total product is produced more efficiently. The total operation, having been divided into parts, must be integrated into a meaningful whole. Otherwise there is no advantage or value in the initial separation. It is in this reintegration that coordination and communication become so important. Clearly the activities of the various specialists must be effectively integrated if satisfactory results are to be obtained. Higher levels of specialization result in greater interdependence and this in turn leads to the need for more coordination. These relationships can be expressed graphically after the fashion used previously. As was noted in the previous case, Figure 19-3 is intended to express a general relationship and not the precise parameters of the relationship. To reiterate briefly then, the greater the degree of work subdivision, the greater the degree of subunit interdependence; and the greater the degree of subunit interdependence, the greater the need for coordination.

Communication as an Element of Coordination

The important thing about coordination insofar as this book is concerned is that it involves communication. Litterer (1973) suggests that two basic elements are required if we are to provide coordination: communication and programs. Programs are essentially those formalized prescriptions for organizational behavior which we have characterized elsewhere as the external system. The requirements of the external system "program" the behavior of individual organization participants. Each individual has at least one program which identifies task elements for his or her position and indicates how they are to be performed. For given sets of circumstances and conditions, the external system programs the behavior of individuals in a coordinative fashion. The prescribed individual behaviors are designed to fit together as a meaningful whole. However, some jobs and situations are too complex and variable for one program or perhaps even many programs to

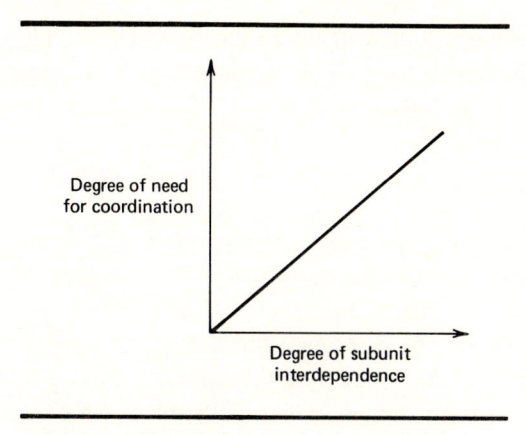

FIGURE 19-3 Subunit interdependence and the need for coordination.

suffice. It becomes necessary to adapt programs or perhaps develop new ones on an ad hoc basis to meet changing situations.

Programs alone are insufficient for providing coordination. The specific process of communication is also an important element. People who are performing linked activities must often communicate with one another. They must have information about the activities of others, and they must have information about the environment and overall organization goals. Much of the responsibility for such coordinative communication rests with management.

Management, Communication, and Coordination. Typically, as an integral part of the external structure, the managerial structure is provided to ensure that the external system does indeed perform as it was designed to. In the simplest sense, this aspect of the external system is a different sort of division of work. In this case, the work of coordinating rather than the work of production is subdivided.

Considering the Associated Ovoid case as an example, suppose that you and Neanderthal (as the founders and principal owners) decide that the company can be made more efficient by making certain changes which provide an additional element of coordination. It is decided that your production and sales duties in the northern territory are consuming too much of your time and that operations have grown to the extent that coordination between production and sales has suffered. Providing written procedures and other types of standard programs is no longer enough to ensure coordination. The company has a number of special-use ovoids now, and there is quite a variation in demand from one type to the next. The variety of products and demand have resulted in coordinative difficulties with respect to sales and production.

As part of the change in the organization, three new people are hired: one to replace you as the sawyer, a second to take on new activities of painting and treating the ovoids to increase their durability, and a third to perform testing and quality control.

In addition to expanding the work force, some further changes are necessary concerning your job. You are no longer to do the operative work such as production and sales; you are to be a manager. Neanderthal will assume responsibility for all sales in addition to his procurement activities. In your new role as a manager, it is your responsibility to plan the operations of Associated Ovoids and to make such decisions as are necessary to implement them.

In order to carry out these new responsibilities, authority has been given you over all others in the organization. Whereas the relationships expressed in Figure 19-1 were the result of a division of the operating work (the production of ovoids), Figure 19-4 reflects the effects of separating the coordinative work from that work which is more clearly of a production nature. The relationships reflected here are based on the assumption that it is your responsibility to provide coordination between the various functional subdivisions (procurement, shipping, production, testing and quality control, and sales). We might further comment that the coordinative work could conceivably be further subdivided at some later date.

Managers usually find that a major portion of their time on the job is spent in communication with others. Coordination involves the provision of needed information at various points in the system. In effect the division of work creates a set of linked activities which fit together to form the desired whole (production of a unit,

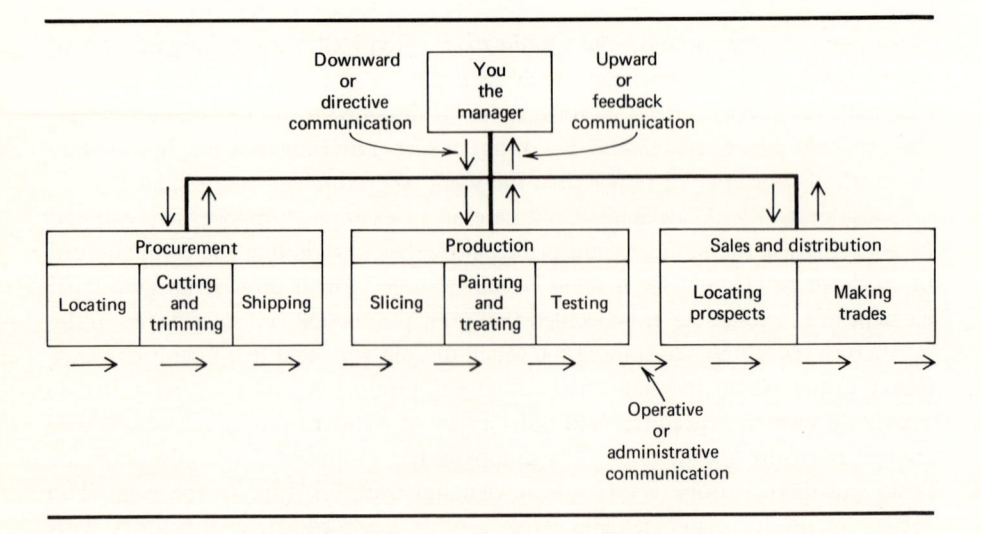

FIGURE 19-4 Dividing the coordinating work.

mission accomplishment, etc.). It becomes your responsibility to see that the proper relationships are maintained. The outputs from each function must be in a reasonably standard form and timed properly. The communication of information becomes critical to the coordinative effort.

In Figure 19-4, three major types of communication found in the formal organization have been represented. *Downward* or directive communication is represented by the arrows which point downward from the manager toward the operating employees. *Operative* or administrative communication is shown as flowing horizontally between functional subunits. *Upward* or feedback communication flows up the hierarchy from operating employees to the manager. Each of these types of communication will now be discussed.

Directive Communication. Much of the communication which occurs in the external system is of a *directive* nature and follows hierarchical patterns as it flows from manager to subordinate. Katz and Kahn (1966) have suggested that such downward communication has five basic purposes:

1. To provide specific task directives or *job instructions*.
2. To provide information which produces an understanding of the task and its relationship to other organizational tasks, thus providing a *job rationale*.
3. To provide information about organizational *procedures* and *practices*.
4. To provide *feedback* to the subordinate regarding his or her performance.
5. To provide information of an ideological character to inculcate a sense of mission and an *indoctrination of goals*.

It is clear that in providing directive communication to serve such purposes, the manager will be either facilitating programs or in some other fashion enhancing organizational coordination.

Referring back to the Associated Ovoids case, when you decided to take on the planning and decision-making responsibilities for the company, you also assumed the responsibility for directive communication to your subordinates. The flow of such directives would be vertical from you to your subordinates as seen in Figure 19-4. Directive communication can be either oral or written and will be aimed at accomplishing some coordinative purpose such as regulating the level of output, or controlling some other aspect of task behavior. Directive communication channels exist between each manager and his or her subordinates. In the case of large organizations having many managers, the directive communication networks can become rather complex.

To be sure you understand the nature of the directive channel, think for a moment about your own experiences with such communication. How often are you affected by such directives? In what form did they occur? Many who have served in the military recall the numerous written orders which were received daily from the various commanding officers. These orders were quite explicit in content and often reeked with the authority of the sender. Such orders were clearly related to the purposes of the external system (say, the Army). Some orders were of a standing nature and were in effect on a continuing basis for the operations governed. An example of such a standing written directive communication is the "General Orders" which apply to persons who are assigned to guard duty. Other directive communication might be issued on an ad hoc basis as warranted by the situation.

Again, directive communication may be written or oral, recurring or ad hoc. However, our experience is that written directives often receive the greatest attention. It is the written directive that we commonly associate with the external system. As you think about your own organizational experiences, you can probably think of many examples of written directives. Rules, regulations, policies, letters, memorandums, job descriptions, certificates, and an almost infinite number of documents direct our organizational lives. As for the matter of oral directives, surely you can identify numerous examples of this type also.

Operative Communication. Another significant type of communication which can be detected in the external system is of an *operative* nature. Such communication tends to flow in a horizontal direction because it is associated with the flow of work. Operative types of communication are perhaps the best examples of coordinative communications because they directly link the operative units of the organization.

Considering Figure 19-4 again, it is clear that the activities of locating trees (Neanderthal), cutting and trimming (Cro-Magnon), shipping (Piltdown), slicing, and painting and treating (the new employees) are closely linked. Suppose you, as the manager, decide that the appropriate coordinative information can best be provided by sending along a document from one of the activities to the next. It follows the work as it progresses from the forest through production and final delivery into the customer's hands. Such a document would be an operative communication and might contain such information as the quantity and type ordered, materials requirement, delivery dates, or other pertinent information. You have probably seen such documents in your own organization. Some examples should be work orders, routing slips, etc.

Of course, other kinds of operative communication may take place directly between individuals located along the flow of work. Such operative communication need not involve written communication but rather can be face-to-face interpersonal communication. Still, such communication is of an operative type. It is also clearly coordinative in that linked activities are facilitated. Interpersonal communication of the operative type can also function through the hierarchy. In the organization represented by Figure 19-4, operative information may be funneled up the hierarchy from procurement to the manager and then back down the hierarchy to production or sales. Obviously, if very much information must travel via these channels, we run the risk of overloading key positions.

Finally, as in the case with directive channels, we should mention that operative communication channels may be written or oral, recurring or ad hoc. However, the written or documented form of operative communication again tends to receive the most attention. The routing slip mentioned above is an example of such documentation. You have probably seen many other examples of such horizontally routed communication; for example, when you left your auto for service at the local dealership. Perhaps you instructed the service manager that you wanted your oil changed, the air conditioner charged, and a tune-up. The service manager indicated each of these operations on the service ticket which was attached to the car. Then, the car was moved successively from the lubrication area, to the air-conditioning servicing area, to the tune-up area. At each location, the service workers can determine from the service ticket what work is to be performed at their locations. The ticket remains with the auto as it moves from one functional operation to the next—in effect, a horizontal flow of information. As an operative communication, it helps ensure that the proper operations are performed, in the proper fashion, and at the proper time.

Upward Communication. Most formal organizations provide, to a degree, for the upward flow of information. In Figure 19-4, we have referred to this type of information as *feedback*. The provision of information regarding production and sales volume to top management is an example of upward communication. When a lower-level supervisor recommends to the plant manager that one of the production workers be promoted, this too is an upward communication. Should a lower-level manager or worker send a budget or purchase request to a higher level, this is also an upward communication.

Upward communication too may be written or oral, recurring or ad hoc. Again, the preponderance of attention seems focused on written or documented forms of upward communication. The manager tends to be concerned with the control function, and thus seeks information relevant to job performance at the lower levels. Numerous documents and reports must be completed on a periodic basis to satisfy the need. Production output data are necessary for production control and data concerning output quality are necessary for quality control. Data regarding sales, financial condition, and perhaps an infinite variety of other activities must also be provided for effective managerial control. The advance of computer technology has made it possible to present to the manager an almost overwhelming amount of data in documented form which can be used to control the organization.

There is, of course, the possibility of an upward flow of information via the interpersonal channels. Many managers rely on the "suggestion box" or the so-called "open door" to provide upward communication which supplements documented reports. There are some problems with such approaches. As we shall see in the next chapter, the suggestion box or the open door may not be a very rich channel. In truth, it is doubtful that many managers care about the upward interpersonal communication channel; they are too concerned about the downward channel or else they feel that the documented upward channel will tell them all they need to know. The research of Likert (1961) indicated that 80 percent of the managers surveyed felt that downward communication was the major communication problem.

Formalizing the External System and Its Communication

Specifying and Structuring. As Associated Ovoids operates over time, it would tend toward a very definite structural form. In the interest of ensuring that the desired activities, interactions, and sentiments are performed, management is likely to increasingly specify the detail and structure of the organization. Jobs of narrower scope will be defined so that individuals can specialize and develop their skill. Activities and interactions will be standardized and programs adopted for dealing with problems and situations which occur on a recurring basis. Much of the resulting external system will be formalized in writing. Communication systems will tend to be of the documented type. Such tendencies will be particularly noticeable as the organization grows in size and adds more employees.

As an example, the job of locating trees which meet the raw material specifications may become quite routinized. It may be that Neanderthal, who initially was pretty much left to his own devices in locating raw material, is eventually given explicit instructions as to how to go about his job. He may be given special job-related training. He may be given special tools and equipment for locating trees which have the desired qualities, and he may be required to follow rather detailed procedures in carrying out these activities. It may be that his activities will be focused on certain sections of the forest according to predetermined programs so that other sections may be left untouched to provide inventory for the future. He may be required to select only certain types of trees or to test for disease.

In general, Neanderthal's activities in the external system may be constrained in very explicit ways. Indeed, to a considerable extent, his job may be *formalized by providing rules, procedures,* and other instructions which are set forth on paper (perhaps more appropriately stone in Neanderthal's age). The other functional operations at Associated Ovoids can be similarly formalized. Can you see evidences of the same kind of specification and structuring in today's organization as we have been describing for Associated Ovoids? We think so. Think of the number of organizations which rely on rather detailed job descriptions, operating procedures, policies, organization charts, and perhaps you will agree. Indeed, much of what the external system is intended to be, can be and is stated on paper. Such written statements (it may take literally volumes to do so) become the "paper organization," and we often refer to it as the formal organization. Many writers have referred to the paper organization as the normative organization since it specifies what is normal or what "ought to be."

Documenting Communication. The formalization of the organization via such specification of structure carries over to the communication system. For many modern organizations, a substantial portion of the communication which occurs in the external system is of the documented or written type. Some researchers (Bodensteiner, 1970) have estimated that approximately 45 percent of all organizational communication is of the formal type (documented, written, or required by the external system). As was mentioned previously, it is certainly the documented communication which catches the attention of most of us when we try to describe organizational communication. We tend to think first of letters, memos, and written instructions. We often hear references to "red tape" when people talk of government bureaucracy and forms. We see all about us evidence that organizations in modern times are highly dependent on formal, documented communication channels.

There has also been a proliferation of computer usage, data banks, data transmission, business forms, inventory systems, and the like. Libraries are everywhere; the listing of new journals, bulletins, and other forms of written information are multiplying rapidly and threaten to swamp our ability to identify and retrieve the information needed for a given problem situation. Complex data and management information systems have been designed for many organizations in an effort to stay abreast of the need for information.

The Problem of Information Retrieval. Indeed, there is something of a paradox in that at the same time we have developed highly automated means for handling vast amounts of data, our knowledge base has also grown so rapidly that we still experience difficulty in bringing the needed information to bear on a given problem. Consequently, there has been a considerable effort to design computerized information-retrieval systems. It will probably not surprise the modern college students when we state that such systems have not solved the problem. Students discover with each term paper that despite the advances, a successful research effort still requires considerable leg work, time, and serendipity.

There are many other examples of the level of documentation which exists for modern organizations. Contractors to the federal government have been increasingly required to implement extensive and elaborate reporting and control systems either to bid on a possible contract or to administer the project once the contract has been awarded. The proposals alone for the project to develop the C-5A transport were said to weigh over 35 tons. Some 400 people and 132,000 worker-hours were needed just to read and evaluate the proposals (Davis, *Defense Industry Bulletin*, 1966, p. 3). It has been estimated that the number of managerial and engineering controls and techniques, together with the related paperwork, increased by a factor of 60 during the decade of the 1960s (Gerloff, 1973).

Organizations other than those engaged in government contracting also face a proliferation of formal documented communication. Indeed, it is often the case that the proliferation of documentation has resulted from managerial action. As was noted above, management often sees fit to formalize the external system by specifying standard methods and structures, often in writing. In doing so, management is providing downward or directive communication that is highly formalized. The following passage describes how the management of one company so formalized its operations and communication.

> In these instances, all action is designed to produce as much rayon as cheaply as possible, within the limits of the resources of the company and the requirements of the market. These are clearly defined in a programme. The normative character of everybody's work is quite explicit in the factory. The job of the "efficiency man" in the spinning room is to approximate the process of transforming raw viscose into yarn as closely as possible to complete effectiveness, in which no machine time and no material are lost. The other control operations mentioned have the purpose of keeping the process changes and the conditions affecting these changes within a range of limits, and close to a series of constants. There is, in fact, a collection of permitted tolerances ("limits and constants") set down for all stages, which are bound together in a book. This book was called the "Factory Bible" and was in the hands of every head of department. Most of the skilled work in the factory, and a good deal of the work of foremen and heads of departments, is the control of processes so they act according to the norms laid down in the "Factory Bible." [Burns and Stalker, 1961, pp. 80–81]

The "Factory Bible" in this situation is clearly a documented communication to the employees.

As another example of formal documentation, consider the Bell System. This company has set forth in a detailed fashion pertinent procedures, instructions, policies, regulations, and applicable limits or standards in an immense set of volumes known as the Bell System Practices or BSPs. These volumes cover every imaginable phase of the system's operations. There are BSPs which govern the procurement of right-of-way for the company's cable facilities. There are BSPs which specify how and when to perform maintenance on some piece of equipment at a remote repeater station. There are BSPs which govern relationships between the various associated companies that make up the system. There are BSPs which govern the operation of the huge fleet of vehicles. There are BSPs which assign control responsibilities for huge networks of private line services and for the telephone message network itself. Finally, of course, there are BSPs which cover the methods used in either of these networks. Such examples are only general ones; each facet of the company's operations is likely to have volumes of BSPs which cover its operations in specific detail, item by item and equipment by equipment.

Now obviously such a voluminous set of instructions has great value to the individual who works for the company. Whatever the job, whatever the problem at the moment, the worker can go to the office file of BSPs and find guidance as to how to handle the matter. Many other companies and governmental agencies, certainly most large ones, have sets of written communications that are similar to the Bell System's BSPs. We can usually find operating handbooks, administrative and policy manuals, and so on for any major organization.

Whatever the name, such material is essentially either a directive or operative type of communication. It is communication intended to specify and structure the external system in terms of the behavior expected of the organization's participants. If individuals will perform as prescribed by such communication, then the external system can accomplish its mission and satisfy the environmental need.

The Risk of Inflexibility. Highly specified and structured external systems such as we have been describing are aimed at making the behavior of participants stable and predictable. As we have seen, the role of management in such a system is largely of a coordinative and communicative nature. The observation of Burns and Stalker regarding such an organization may help make the point.

> The system of management within the factory was quite explicitly devised to keep production and production conditions stable. With this as the underlying principle, the system defined what information or instructions arrived at any one position in the hierarchy, what information or instructions

might leave it, and their destination. Such definition was a matter of fixed, clear, and precise routine. Similarly, each working position in the hierarchy had its authority, information, and technical competence specified once and for all. Moreover, since each position below the General Manager's in the hierarchy was specialized in all three features of authority, technique, and information, and nobody was empowered to act outside the defined limits, all departures from stable conditions were swiftly reported upwards, and, so far as the works were concerned, the General Manager existed as the fountainhead of all information about commercial and other conditions affecting the affairs of the factory (as against technique). [Burns and Stalker, 1961, p. 82]

It should be pointed out, however, that a high degree of specification concerning activities, interactions, sentiments, and communication does lead to a *type of inflexibility*. Indeed, the goal of such specification is to ensure that organization members conform to the role prescriptions as specified. The problem is somewhat analogous to baking a cake; one must follow the recipe. The recipe for Associated Ovoids consists of its organization charts, administrative procedures, and so on. Inflexibility or rigidity can result from the human tendency to rely on or conform to such rules and structure.

Now, we do not mean to make a sweeping statement to the effect that people always follow the rule; that is obviously not the case. But people *often do conform* to such requirements; cooperative behavior is rewarded. Further, it is generally the path of least resistance to conform to external-system requirements. Perhaps the reader can recall situations in which a rule was followed simply because that was the easiest thing to do. Some people take great comfort and security in the assumption that some specific order exists for a given organizational situation.

The following remark by a manager interviewed by Burns and Stalker (1961, p. 128) makes the point: "Well, when you start a new design or even a new series of an established model, there are certain steps you must go through to get a new production batch on the line." The statement was made in response to the interviewer's question as to why the manager felt that "things" were always going wrong in his company. The formal structure was a rather vague one. He rather clearly indicated that he would feel better if there could be more clear-cut lines of authority and responsibility, and a systematic way of doing things. Indeed, an attitude such as this is not inconsistent with the intent of organization structure as set forth at the beginning of this section. By providing structure and programs, we increase the predictability of our organizations. Thus, they may very well be rigid by design. In the case of one rather highly structured organization described by Burns and Stalker (1961, p. 83), management even attempted to restrict the efforts of the sales group to ensure that there would be no deviation in demand. In the following section, we turn to some further aspects of the external system.

MATCHING FORMAL ORGANIZATION AND COMMUNICATION TO ENVIRONMENT

For most organizations, then, a considerable effort is made to contrive a formal plan which will effectively accomplish the intended mission. Obviously, communication within the formal structure will be a crucial factor in organizational success. We now focus our attention on other factors which affect organization performance. Special attention will be given to the manner in which environmental constraints influence the organization plan and communication.

Requirements for Success

Most organizations, from Associated Ovoids to the Bell System, eventually reach a point at which the external system (required behavior) is rather clearly specified to its members via the formal communication system. In addition, most organizations come to be highly dependent on the formal communication system in accomplishing their day-to-day business. Disregarding differences in degree from one company to the next for the moment, let us consider some important questions about performance. When will the external system and its communication work? How well does it work? Logically, there is a rather simple answer to these questions. The success of the formal plan of the external system is dependent on three conditions: the adequacy of the plan, cooperative behavior by the participants, no significant changes occurring in the environment.

The Plan. If one thinks about it, the external system is a set of interrelated role prescriptions which have been contrived to meet a particular environmental need. We specify who does what, when they do it, and with whom it is done. We then communicate the plan to the participants who are to execute it. In a sense we have written a recipe, not for a cake, but for an organization. We are not being facetious when we say it will work if the recipe is correct. Does it include *all* the activities, interactions, and sentiments necessary to accomplish the mission? Has something important been left out? The cake will be a failure without flour; the organization will be a failure if some vital ingredient is omitted from the plans.

Role Behavior. A second requirement for success concerns *behavior*. Members of the organization must conform to their roles as prescribed by the external system.

It should be noted that communication is involved in at least two ways in this requirement. Part of the required behavior involves communication, and the prescribed behavior must be communicated to the affected individuals. The cake fails if the cook does not follow the recipe, and the organization can fail if its members do not perform their roles according to plan.

Effects of Change. Finally, a third logical requirement for the successful external system is that there be *no change in the environmental situation* once the external system has been planned and set. In planning the external system, certain assumptions are made about the environmental situations. Should the basis for our assumptions change or should the assumptions happen to be false ones to begin with, the plan cannot work. At Associated Ovoids we assumed a supply of trees. Suppose the supply is exhausted? Or worse yet, suppose the trees never existed—the region is a desert. In either case, the external system as originally conceived simply will not work.

You may have noticed that most baking recipes specify that the item be baked at a specific temperature for a specific period of time. If you follow the recipe instructions carefully, you will always be successful—or will you? What happens when the cook is baking the cake on a mountain top in Colorado? Many recipes assume the baking will be done in a location that is reasonably close to sea level. Drastic variations between the actual conditions and the assumed conditions must be accounted for or the plan will fail.

It should be clear that communication is closely linked with the successful satisfaction of all three conditions. The challenge of adequately planning the external system can be met only if the organization planners can accurately perceive the full information content of the relevant environment. Once the plan is complete, it must be adequately communicated to the members. Communication is also deeply involved in the implementation of the plan on a day-to-day basis. Finally, if the environment changes and there is a need for an adaptive response by the external system, the appropriate information must be channeled to the point where it is needed.

The formal communication system, no matter how detailed and carefully planned, is not always adequate to meet the demands of the organization. Written communication is slow, expensive, and frequently the least effective means for transmitting information. More specifically, formal communication systems are particularly cumbersome where unique, one-of-a-kind problem situations are encountered. The weakness is crucial where the organization's environment and circumstance necessitate an adaptive response. As has been noted earlier, some formal organizations are inflexible.

Menzel and Glock (1958) studied the flow of information among scientists and concluded that the formal communication system is most useful to scientists or engineers when they know precisely what they are looking for. Think of your own experiences in the library. If you know exactly what you are looking for, then the card catalog is all you need. But if you have a hunch, a vague notion, then you expect to use a trial-and-error approach until you find what you are looking for. This is why term papers can be so time-consuming and frustrating, but it is also the nature of many kinds of problem-solving behavior.

The topic is also not unrelated to the problem of organizational design—that is, the problem of planning the external system. If the environment is simple, easy to understand, unchanging, and we know precisely what we wish to accomplish, then the design of the external system will not be too difficult a task. We might mention, while the matter is fresh, that when faced with the more uncertain situation, whether it involves library research or organizational design, most of us seek our answers via the informal communication network. This is the conclusion of those who have investigated the problem. We will consider the matter further in a subsequent chapter. For now we turn to an important relationship between the formal organization and its environment.

Differentiation and Integration

It is clear from the remarks of the preceding section that each formal organization must be effectively matched to its particular environmental situation. It can be shown that the nature of the organization's environment determines the effectiveness of a particular organization plan. Environmental factors such as technology, stability, and certainty of information influence the character of operations and communication within the organization. The type of technology, the stability of the environment, and the certainty of information about the environment will necessitate a particular type and degree of work subdivision in the formal organization. As a result, organizations tend to differ with respect to two qualities: the need for differentiation and integration. The problems of organizational communication are inextricably involved with these twin facets of organizational design. Accordingly, we must treat differentiation and integration from a communication standpoint.

Differentiation has been defined (Dalton et al., 1970, p. 5) as "the differences in cognitive and emotional orientations among managers in different functional departments, and the differences in formal structure among these departments." The same writers describe *integration* as "the quality of the state of collaboration that exists among departments that are required to achieve unity of effort by the environment." All organizations possess each of these qualities, though the mix tends to vary from one organization to the next.

Differentiation. Differentiation can be explained using an example from the Associated Ovoids incident. Recall that a couple of new individuals have assumed responsibility for production and that Neanderthal is responsible for sales. If we were to interview the individuals involved in these functions, we would probably find that they had quite different goal orientations and that their functions would be structured quite differently.

Neanderthal is oriented to sales. He wishes to have a large inventory of all types of ovoids readily at hand. If the customer asks for an ovoid of unusual size or perhaps one that is pink with green polka dots, he wants it to be instantly available so that the sale can be made. In contrast, those in production prefer to maximize production efficiency. They wish to concentrate on a few product types and hold levels of production constant.

In terms of the degree of formalized structure associated with the jobs, the two functions would also be quite different. Neanderthal's job is probably rather loosely defined. He is not required to report to a specific location, and it is unlikely that he will be told just how to go about the job of selling. In contrast to a production operation, he is left pretty much to his own devices. He can determine his own programs and methods. The production jobs would be much more specifically structured and programmed. Deviation from prescribed plans is less likely to be tolerated. People are told rather precisely what to do and when to do it. The two functions are indeed differentiated.

If we were to examine positions in other functional areas, additional kinds of differentiation could be identified. For example, we might stretch things a bit and imagine that Associated Ovoids had a basic research group. In such a group, we would find that a research scientist would have a quite different orientation from those in the sales or production units. He would not be so concerned with ovoids, even if they involved new technologies. He would more likely be concerned with some far-out piece of research which he felt to be a significant contribution to his discipline. He would also be concerned that his professional peers throughout the world recognize his contribution to be of importance.

In contrast to either sales or production, the research function will be very loosely structured. Also, since the particular research is of a basic nature and not aimed at immediate application, the time frame of the research scientist is much longer. Progress here may be measured in terms of years or decades, whereas for sales and production it is measured by days, weeks, and months. From such examples, it can be seen that organizational subunits can become quite differentiated with respect to formalization of structure, personal orientation, and orientation to time.

Effects of the Environment. The organization's environment is an important determinant of how much differentiation is required for a given organization. Lawrence and Lorsch (1967) investigated ten different organizations and found that the degree of organizational differentiation involved for a given organization depended on the amount of certainty or uncertainty and diversity or homogeneity in its environment.

These investigators found that organizations tend to divide their environments into segments. For example, subsections were identified which were relevant to sales, production, and research, respectively. For some industries, information concerning how to meet environmental needs was relatively certain for each segment of the organization's environment. Lawrence and Lorsch described such an environment as being a homogeneous one. Conversely, the environments of other industries included a variety of information circumstances. For some segments of the diverse environment, one could be fairly certain about what the organization must do. But for other segments of the environment, information was very uncertain. This type of environment was described as being uncertain or diverse.

Effective or relatively successful organizations were found by Lawrence and Lorsch to have *properly matched* their *differentiation* to the *degree of diversity* present in their environments. Organizations facing an environment of high diversity must be highly differentiated to deal with such an environment. Organizations facing a stable and homogeneous environment can be of a much less differentiated nature. As an example, Lawrence and Lorsch (1967) found the plastic industry to be highly diverse and uncertain. The information environment of this industry involved fairly certain information with respect to production, but very uncertain information with respect to research. In contrast, the information environment of the container industry was stable and certain. Organizations in the plastic industry were found to be highly differentiated, while organizations in the container industry were not highly differentiated.

It can be shown that structural differentiation has clear ramifications for organizational communication. As each organization is differentiated to match its particular situational environment, its communication requirements are also differentiated. As an example, a department store which is part of a nationwide chain can satisfy the needs of its environment using only limited communication and coordination with headquarters or with stores in other regions. Each unit is relatively autonomous or decentralized with respect to decision making. Communication to headquarters may mostly deal with audit and performance-type data. In contrast, the refinery unit of a company which produces petroleum products may be under tight or highly centralized control from the headquarters unit. Refinery operations are highly interdependent with oil-field production, pipeline operations, and distribution. Extensive communication will be required in providing the planning and coordination needed to keep all units functioning together. Clearly, the impact of the environmental requirement for differentiation must be considered in planning the formal communication system.

Integration. The nature of the organization's environment also determines which issues become dominant from the competitive standpoint. The dominant competitive issues, in turn, influence the need for *integration* and the nature of its implementation. Is it most crucial to be innovative, to meet schedule and delivery, to meet costs, to make performance, or to be in style? Or is some other factor the crucial one in meeting competition? Obviously, each firm's environment is somewhat different, but the point is that the environment by affecting the dominant competitive issue *also determines* which *integration* patterns will be most important.

As an example, where innovation is the dominant competitive issue, the research department is likely to be the crucial pivotal point of integration. If the organization is to be effectively innovative, marketing information must be successfully integrated with research information. Such an integration will ensure that the resulting innovative ideas are consistent with the needs of the environment. In a similar fashion, there must be a successful integration of research and production information to ensure that innovative ideas are within the capabilities of the production system. In effect, where innovation is dominant, the research group is the focal point of the external system, but the information linkages must be such that there is a free and easy flow of information between the research group and the sales and production groups. Where the dominant competitive issue is different, say delivery or price, then another functional unit (perhaps production) is the appropriate focal point of the integrative pattern.

Successful organizations have been found to do a better job of satisfying the demands of their respective environments for both *differentiation* and *integration* than do less effective organizations. The specific mix and pattern of the two qualities varies with the nature of the environment which is involved. Dalton and his associates (1970, p. 9) noted that the concepts of differentiation and integration present the manager with something of a paradox. Successful organizations, in a given environment, tend to be characterized by both more differentiation and more integration than is the case for less successful organizations. However, the two qualities are antagonistic. Integration is more difficult to achieve between highly differentiated subunits. Differences in cognitive and emotional orientation which arise from differentiation tend to disrupt integration.

Finally, it should be emphasized that the necessary differentiation of organization subunits will also tend to interfere with communication. Differences in jargon, perception, and technical orientation are potential barriers to communication. Yet, it is largely through communication that the manager of the organization must accomplish integration. In a subsequent chapter, we shall see that alternative methods are available for achieving integration. For now, however, we turn to an overview of the role of communication in managing the formal organization.

MANAGING THE FORMAL ORGANIZATION THROUGH COMMUNICATION

It should be clear from the preceding discussion that managers of formal organizations often face a very complex set of problems. Management must somehow define an organization which can adequately satisfy complex environmental constraints and yet provide for the necessary flow of work and information. The organization must somehow cope with technological change and uncertainty and yet must maintain stable and productive relationships. The formal organization must be predictable but not inflexible. We must simultaneously achieve both differentiation and integration, two contradictory processes. How does the manager deal with such a problem? We noted in the first chapter that one cannot manage without communicating. We now wish to return to that point briefly.

Katz and Kahn (1966) observed that as one strolls from the factory to the office, a very conspicuous transformation occurs. In the shop, we experience the noise and commotion of people working with their hands and with machines. Heavy electric cables and pipes form a labyrinth. Machines, equipment, and production are emphasized. As we enter the office area, there is a very noticeable hush. Telephone lines replace electrical cables. Telephones, calculators, typewriters, and computer terminals replace the heavy, noisy factory machines. The contrast is immediately obvious; the emphasis now is on processing information. Katz and Kahn (1966, p. 223) state: "The closer one gets to the organizational center of control and decision-making, the more pronounced is the emphasis on information exchange."

It is clear from the observation that the manager's job is very deeply involved in communication. Davis (1972, p. 380) makes the point clear when he states that management of the organization can be achieved only through communication. He notes that even the manager's best plans are worthless unless they can be communicated to those who carry out the implementation. Thus, even the best-planned external system will fail if we fail to adequately communicate the plan to the organizational participants.

Davis (1972) characterizes communication as a bottleneck through which the management process must pass if it is to reach others in the organization. Figure 19-5 is an adaptation of Davis' "bottleneck" concept. The external system has been incorporated into the paradigm since that system is the culmination of the manage-

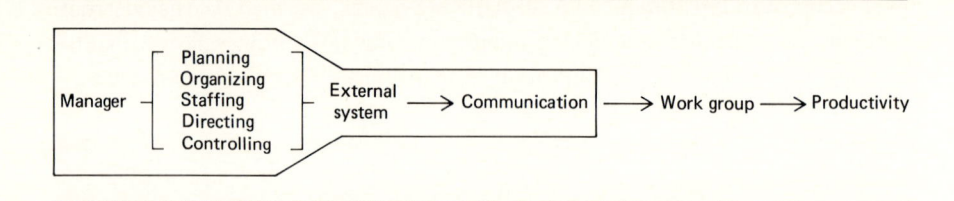

```
                  ┌ Planning   ┐
                  │ Organizing │
   Manager ──┤ Staffing   ├── External ──→ Communication ──→ Work group ──→ Productivity
                  │ Directing  │   system
                  └ Controlling┘
```

FIGURE 19-5 The bottleneck of communication. [*Adapted from Keith Davis*, Human Behavior at Work, *4th ed. (New York: McGraw-Hill Book Company, 1972), p. 380.*

ment process. It is the external system or formal organization which is the essence of the manager's expectations for her/his subordinates.

It should be clear from our discussion in this chapter that the manager faces a number of general problems in implementing the formal organization and its communication system. In the next chapter, some specific communication problems of the formal organization will be examined.

SUMMARY

The formal organization or external system is formed in response to the needs of the environment. The external system consists of a set of required activities linked via the appropriate interactions and facilitated by sentiments which are positively associated to the relationships of the system. Formal organizations with a high degree of division of work are characterized by a high degree of interdependence between the subdivided units. The greater degree of interdependence leads to a greater need for coordination.

Formal communication is critical to achieving the needed coordination, and the communication system provided is usually of a directive or operative nature and tends to be of a documented type. Upward communication is also provided. There are times when the formal, documented communication system is of questionable value. Sometimes the resulting structure and the natural human tendency to rely on it tend to lead to a degree of rigidity or inflexibility. The external system itself can function only if the plan is adequate, if people behave as required, and if there are no important changes in the environment.

It was seen that the environment of the organization requires that it differentiate and integrate, two antagonistic processes. The greater the diversity and uncertainty of the environment, the more differentiation and integration are required. But effective organizations were seen to be capable of accomplishing both.

Finally, the chapter was concluded by viewing communication as a bottleneck through which management of the formal organization is accomplished.

IMPORTANT TERMS AND CONCEPTS

differentiation, integration, specification of structure and rigidity, interdependence and division of work, coordination and interdependence, directive communication, operative communication, upward communication

REVIEW QUESTIONS

1. Under what conditions will the external system be effective? Discuss the relevant factors.
2. What determines the need for differentiation and integration in the external system?
3. What determines the certainty or uncertainty of the environment and how is the communication system affected by these factors?
4. How are successful formal organizations distinguished from the less successful ones?
5. The formal organization is sometimes seen as being somewhat inflexible. Discuss why this is so.
6. Discuss the consequences and implications of dividing work.
7. Why is the formal communication system viewed by some as a bottleneck?
8. Discuss the nature of downward, horizontal, and upward communication in the formal organization and give examples of each.

EXERCISE: AIRWAYS TOY MANUFACTURING CO., INC.

Your class will become Airways Toy Manufacturing Co., Inc. (ATMCI). You are to carry out three (3) basic assignments as a class. The first assignment is to be completed following the study of Chapters 19 and 20. The first assignment is to establish an organization and organization chart for ATMCI. You will assign members of your class to each position on the chart. The chart should show the formal communication flow by connecting the positions with a solid line which are required to have communication.

The second assignment for your class will be to operate ATMCI using only the formal communication lines shown on your organization chart.

The third assignment should be completed after the study of Chapter 21. You are now to operate ATMCI using both formal and informal communication channels. The statements listed below will aid you in completing each of the three assignments. Note particularly the rule in item 8.

1. ATMCI assembles paper airplanes.
2. Selling price per unit is: $10 Grade A
   $12 Grade B
   $14 Grade C
3. Cost of raw materials is negotiable.
4. Fixed cost of operation is $.5 per minute.
5. ATMCI has a production capacity of 1 unit of each grade per minute.
6. Purchase orders must be filled within 3 minutes.
7. Purchase orders will not exceed 20 units.
8. Each work function must be filled by a different person unless there are not enough people; i.e. accounting, quality control, market analysis, etc.
9. ATMCI has a union made up of your three producers. The union negotiates each 20 minutes. Present labor cost is $2 per unit. A minimum salary increase is $.5 per unit.
10. ATMCI must design grades and grade changes.
11. Inventory cost for finished products is $2 per unit.
12. Inventory cost for raw materials is $.5 per unit.
13. Other variable costs are $3 per unit. Overhead is $2 per unit.
14. Additional operating information will be added as operations progress, i.e., breakdowns, slowdowns, etc.
15. Instructor is customer and supplier.
16. Grade D (price $16) may be added as market demands and ATMCI desires.

Discussion Questions for the First Assignment: Upon completion of the first assignment the class should discuss the following questions:

1. How does the organization of ATMCI compare with traditional companies with which you are familiar?
2. Are there major functional areas of a traditional company that are not required for ATMCI?
3. Do you think that the lines of communication will carry all the required messages?
4. Will the communication flow smoothly and efficiently?

Discussion Session for the Second Assignment: Upon completion of the second assignment the class should discuss the following questions:

1. How well did the company operate using only formal communication?

2. Were there functional areas needed which were not planned?
3. Were there unanticipated activities?
4. Did you find dysfunctional consequences from your formal plan?
5. Did you find problems of distortion, filtering, or omission of communication?
6. How was conflict handled?

Discussion Questions for the Third Assignment: After completion of the third assignment the class should discuss the following questions:

1. Did ATMCI operate differently using informal channels? If so, how?
2. What advantages did you find? Disadvantages?
3. Did you find the informal communication to be richer than the formal?
4. Were there key communicators in the operation?
5. Were there differences in information-sharing norms for different units?
6. What did you learn from the operation of ATMCI?

BIBLIOGRAPHY

Bodensteiner, Wayne Dean: "Information Channel Utilization under Varying Research and Development Project Conditions: An Aspect of Inter-Organizational Communication Channel Usage," doctoral dissertation, The University of Texas at Austin, 1970.

Burns, Tom, and G. M. Stalker: *The Management of Innovation* (London: Tavistock Publications Ltd., 1961).

Dalton, G. W., Paul R. Lawrence, and Jay W. Lorsch: *Organizational Structure and Design* (Homewood, Ill.: Richard D. Irwin, Inc., and The Dorsey Press, 1970).

Davis, Keith: *Human Behavior at Work,* 4th ed. (New York: McGraw-Hill Book Company, 1972).

Davis, W. A.: "Management Systems for Package Procurement," *Defense Industry Bulletin,* vol. 2, p. 3, 1966.

Gerloff, Edwin A.: "Performance Control in Government R&D Projects: The Measurable Effects of Performing Required Management and Engineering Techniques," *IEEE Transactions on Engineering Management,* EM-20, pp. 6–14, February 1973.

Katz, Daniel, and Robert L. Kahn: *The Social Psychology of Organizations* (New York: John Wiley & Sons, Inc., 1966).

Lawrence, Paul R., and Jay W. Lorsch: *Organization and Environment Managing Differentiation and Integration* (Boston: Division of Research Graduate School of Business Administration, 1967).

Likert, Rensis: *New Patterns of Management* (New York: McGraw-Hill Book Company, 1961).

Litterer, Joseph A.: *The Analysis of Organizations,* 2d ed. (New York: John Wiley & Sons, Inc., 1973).

Menzel, Herbert, and C. Y. Glock: *The Flow of Information among Scientists* (New York: Columbia University Press, 1958).

20

MANAGEMENT AND COMMUNICATION PROBLEMS OF THE FORMAL ORGANIZATION

In this chapter we will see that the formal organization does not always function as it is intended to by its planners. It will be shown that the very nature of the formal organization portends certain kinds of problems and conflicts. In particular, there is some indication that the downward, upward, and horizontal flow of communication tends to be disrupted. Finally, we will look briefly at the manner in which the more effective organizations deal with such problems.

We have seen in the preceding chapter that three primary conditions must be satisfied if the formal organization is to function effectively. If the planner of the organization successfully maps all the necessary behaviors, if people follow the instructions, and if nothing changes, the organization will successfully accomplish its goals. In this chapter we shall examine more closely the problems which cause organization plans to go awry. We will discuss how plans can be inadequate and why people do not behave precisely as the organization requires. We will see that conflicts develop between people, between people and purpose, or between people over purpose. It will be shown that the problems involved often impair communication. The degree of environmental change and stability will be shown to affect both the plan and the people who attempt to implement the plan.

PROBLEMS, CONFLICTS, AND CONSEQUENCES OF FORMAL ORGANIZATION

Specifying the Plan

From the standpoint of organizational design, it is often difficult, if not impossible, to completely map or specify all the behaviors necessary to accomplish a complex task. Uncertainty regarding environmental circumstances prevents our drawing a truly complete plan of the organization. How can we plan specific behaviors in advance, which will deal with eventualities that are presently unknown to us? Some aspects of the organizational plan must be left open pending the availability of more complete information concerning the circumstances of the organizational situation. Much of the formal organization is of a control nature with respect to the communication that is involved. We seek to control the behavior of individuals in accordance with organizational plan. However, to provide such control before the problem has been adequately defined and evaluated is foolhardy. To do so commits one to a prescribed set of behaviors which may not match the situation as it ultimately materializes. We have already noted in the previous chapter that a certain rigidity or inflexibility results if individuals become too committed to a given plan.

Research results indicate that a rigid commitment to preconceived plans and tight control measures is particularly troublesome if the organization faces an uncertain and diverse environment. Indeed, such a rigid external system can experience great difficulty in achieving its intended goals. An investigation of 108 government-sponsored R&D projects (Gerloff, 1973) provided evidence that those projects with the lowest levels of control and specificity of formal plans tended to score highest on measures of global performance (technical, schedule, and cost performance combined). Those organizations which exercised high degrees of control and highly specified formal plans tended to have poor global performance if they were operating in highly uncertain and diverse environments. We would argue that an early commitment to the formal plan locks the organization unwisely to something which later proves to be undesirable. In preference to such a commitment, the organization (or more importantly its membership) should be left free to engage in problem-solving processes. Such flexibility would permit environmental uncertainties to be dealt with on an ad hoc basis. Thus as was noted in Chapter 17, the appropriate communication behaviors are of the orientation and evaluation nature. The situation varies from one organization to the next, but a given organization and its communication system must be left open and flexible in order to be responsive to an uncertain environment.

Dysfunctional Consequences of Formal Plans

Designing the external system to deal with an uncertain environment is not the only obstacle to a successful organization. There is still the problem of implementing the design. In the implementation of the formal plan we encounter some other problems which tend to affect communication. A number of undesirable consequences are the direct result of the necessary specification, differentiation, and division of work that we find in all formal organizations. We refer to these difficulties as the dysfunctional consequences of the effort to control behavior in the external system. It is not intended that the formal system have such undesirable effects, but sometimes it does.

The external system is obviously designed to constrain the behavior of organizational participants, but the results of the effort sometimes do not turn out as intended. People behave in a manner which is inconsistent with the intent of the plan. Various types of conflict occur and the flow of communication is disrupted. Such undesirable consequences will be specifically examined in the paragraphs which follow.

Conformity. It is possible that external-system requirements will unduly restrict individuality and innovation. Some individuals take great comfort in the formal structure and rules of the external system. The structure tends to become something that is "familiar" and "comforting," and they do not wish to see it change. Many of us even develop such a "sense of loyalty" to the rules and regulations of organizations that we resist efforts to change them. We refer to organizations where organization rules and policies become highly institutionalized as bureaucracies.

People in bureaucratic organizations become dependent on the "rules" and are reluctant to take individual initiative in dealing with a problem. Managers as well as others are affected. Blake and Mouton (1964) refer to a style of management as being withdrawn or "impoverished" if the manager tends to blame his or her actions and behavior on the "rules" or "policy." Such a manager is in effect saying, "I know it shouldn't be this way but the external system forces me to do this." Unswerving, absolute conformity to organization requirements can be particularly troublesome if the prescribed behavior is an inappropriate one because circumstances have changed.

The manner in which people in organizations communicate can be influenced by excessive dependency on the organization plan. People in bureaucratic organizations tend to rely almost totally on documented types of communication to get information that is relevant to their job performance. In the extreme case people can become so bogged down in a sea of "red tape," documents, and forms that little constructive business can be accomplished. Of course documented communication is not always dysfunctional, but then it is often not the richest form of communication either. We will see in the next chapter that face-to-face personal channels can be of great value to the formal organization.

Conflict. Another problem with the external system is the interpersonal conflict which may result from division of work. As was noted in the previous chapter, we simultaneously and unavoidably created differentiated organizational units when we divide up work to create formal organizational units. It is only to be expected that people in such differentiated units will have somewhat different goals and orientations. They see things differently, do things differently, and sometimes hold different values and norms. These perceptual and behavioral differences make interpersonal conflict almost inevitable.

As an example, organizational subunits may be in conflict with one another as they compete for scarce organizational resources. A conflict can result if one subunit seeks to maximize its own well-being at the expense of the others (suboptimization of organizational goals). The sales department wishes to have unlimited inventories of all types of products so that sales can be maximized. However, the production department is interested in stable production runs for a limited number of products. Each department in the organization tends to have its own special "axe" to grind. This is what division of work and differentiation are all about.

Problems occur when such conflict gets out of hand. Some conflict is natural and even desirable. However, we do not wish conflict to reach such a state that overall organizational goals cannot be achieved and coordination or integration is destroyed. In some organizations this is exactly what happens. A few organization subunits become so powerful that their purposes are accomplished at the expense of overall organizational purposes. From the standpoint of broader organizational goals, the dominance of a subunit is a means-ends reversal. An overall end or objective is sacrificed in favor of a means to that end.

Communication is involved in the problem of organizational conflict in two ways. Communication has potential for negating the disruptive effects of conflict, but conflict also has potential for negating communication. We will consider first the role of communication in reducing conflict.

We have all experienced conflict situations which resulted from a lack of understanding by those involved. In organizations, conflict can occur because individuals in one department are uninformed concerning the operation and importance of another department. We tend to distrust that which we do not understand, and this clearly can be a communication problem for the external system. It is imperative that the organizational communication system be capable of making people in each department or function aware of the role, scope, and value of other departments or functions.

Barriers to Communication. Communication, then, can be a conflict-reduction mechanism. Unfortunately the complementary statement is also true. Conflict is also a communication-reduction mechanism. The introduction of conflict to situations where the interpersonal relationship is negative and interpersonal competence is lacking will result in a number of barriers to communication. People in such situations tend to rely on emotions rather than facts and logic. They resort to evaluative statements, negative stereotypes, and otherwise belittling the adversary. There is little chance of getting to the reality of issues. Adult cannot talk to Adult, only Parent-Child types of relationships are possible.

We have seen many times in this book that relationships of this sort will set up barriers to communication. Interestingly enough, the separation of departments and functions in the formal organization can sometimes facilitate such undesirable consequences. The flow of the work process may not require much communication between departments. We have already noted in our discussion of the work of Homans that where people interact together over time, they tend to develop positive sentiments toward one another. Where such interaction does not take place, the positive sentiment is less likely to develop. Indeed, as was noted above, competition may develop.

In addition to conflict there are other barriers to communication in the formal organization. One is language. Recall that in the Associated Ovoids case work was initially divided roughly into raw materials procurement, production, and product sales and distribution. People who work in one of these functional areas, say procurement, are likely to develop a common orientation toward the company, its operations, and others in the company. Such a common frame of reference will enhance their ability to communicate with one another. They will tend to perceive things the same way. Further, they can develop a common jargon because they share a common technology and common problems.

However, as we enhance communication within a department through the development of a common language or jargon, we simultaneously create a communication barrier to the members of other units. They do not know the jargon. The very act of dividing some larger task into a number of smaller ones means that the individuals performing the narrower subdivided tasks will become more specialized. They develop a high degree of skill and knowledge concerning a narrower range of activities. The specialists of one unit tend to develop their own special languages or technical jargon. An outsider, someone from another department or function, will not be familiar with the coding system. The outsider cannot communicate with the insiders.

In making such a statement we do not mean to indict the use of jargon. It can and often does enhance the performance of the unit which uses it. We are simply making the observation that where such languages exist, there can be some degree of separation between organizational units. Indeed there is a need for the formal organization to constrain and restrict the flow of communication to some extent. Katz and Kahn (1966) observe that we must restrict information flows in order to move from an unorganized state to an organized state. It would be dysfunctional for the formal organization to provide for unlimited information flows to all its participants. Many people would be overwhelmed by it all. Information overload is always a distinct possibility.

Whether or not coding barriers unnecessarily impair organizational effectiveness and coordination will depend on the extent to which the organization's informal communication system is developed and utilized. The internal system has the capability of providing for necessary and desirable information flows on an ad hoc basis despite the existence of language barriers. The informal system can provide a backup to handle the overflow or perhaps can even be used to circumvent an unresponsive formal system. We will discuss such matters in later chapters.

Finally, it should be pointed out that the hierarchical nature of the external system is something of a barrier to effective communication. Communication which is evaluative, manipulative, or which implies superiority can lead to defensiveness in the receiver, and this sets up a barrier to the conveyance of meaning. Much communication in the external system is necessarily of a directive or control nature. Therefore, we must recognize that such communication is susceptible to defensiveness and the resulting communication barriers.

Again, whether or not such problems in the external system become unnecessarily disruptive to its operation will be dependent on how well the organization, its managers, and its rank-and-file members are able to offset the communication deficiencies in the external system. We will see in a later chapter that this problem too can be partly remedied. We turn our attention now to the specific problem of distortion in the formal communication system.

DISTORTION AND FILTERING IN THE FORMAL COMMUNICATION CHANNELS

It can be seen then that the formal organization faces something of a paradox. On the one hand communication must be constrained and restricted in a fashion beneficial for overall goal accomplishment. We use the external system to restrict communication as well as other forms of organizational behavior. On the other hand, the resulting barriers, conflict, and coding differences are sometimes too disruptive of needed communication. We will now briefly examine some of the research evidence which indicates specifically how downward, upward, and lateral communication is distorted and filtered.

Downward Communication

By now we should be able to accept the notion that effective downward communication is crucial to organization success. Managers must communicate to subordinates in order to effectively organize, direct, and coordinate the collective effort. Most managers also recognize the importance of being able to communicate down through the hierarchy and strive to make these important channels efficient.

Message Routing and Summarization. Recognizing that coding differences and information overload are potential threats to downward communication, some managers seek ways of countering such undesirable effects. Two methods of improving the efficiency of organizational information flows have been suggested by a number of authors (Vaidya et al., 1975, pp. 372–374): message routing and message summarization. Under the concept of message routing a limited number of individuals are the nodal points of communication links which carry the bulk of organizational messages. Though the research so far is incomplete, there is some evidence that message routing in a given organization is influenced by status and hierarchical relationships as well as how "good" a source of information a person is "perceived" to be.

The notion of message summarization is that communication can be improved by simplifying the message via the removal of components which are irrelevant or likely to produce noise at the receiver. Vaidya and her colleagues felt that senders sometimes tend to reduce message content in a fashion that causes the receiver to be either "positive" or "negative" about the message (Vaidya et al., 1975, pp. 372–374). This tendency, of course, can be dysfunctional. However, the authors felt that both message routing and message summarization were potentially beneficial to the organization. They observed that such processes can assist individuals in coping with the organization by minimizing the possibility of overload. It seems obvious that where performed properly, both message routing and summarizations can be useful to the manager in achieving downward (or for that matter upward) communication.

Unfortunately, as some writers have indicated, there is also the potential for distortion in either process. The effects of both message routing and message summarization can be dysfunctional. We sometimes route information to locations where it is not needed or is even damaging. In summarizing messages, we may remove important content or otherwise change the meaning in a fashion that is undesirable.

Message Distortion and Filtering. There is some evidence that message distortion, filtering, and perhaps even omission occurs as we attempt to communicate downward through the hierarchy. Brenner and Sigband (1973, pp. 323–324) found indications of such dysfunctional effects when they surveyed the opinions of over 500 executives and managers via personal interviews or questionnaires. The results of this research suggest that managers who are higher in a structured hierarchy tend to be better informed than those who are at a lower level. Individuals at higher levels seem to possess more of the information needed for their jobs than do individuals who are lower-level supervisors.

A lack of information at lower levels is, of course, not proof that distortion, filtering, or omission is occuring in the downward channel. However, the research of Brenner and Sigband found that 40 percent of the respondents had less than one-half of their assignments given them by their immediate supervisor. For 25 percent of the respondents, only one-fourth of their assignments came from the appropriate supervisor. Those respondents reporting that the bulk of their assignments came from the appropriate supervisor also indicated confidence that they were better informed. Respondents who received their job assignments from the supervisor felt they could perform their jobs better and provide better feedback to the supervisor.

It would appear, if this research is representative, that a substantial proportion of the organization's work force does not perceive that its activities are initiated directly via the vertical channel. It is, of course, possible that the jobs of many are so routine or so well known that little direction is needed. It is also possible that this is just a perception and not a fact at all. We will posit in the next chapter that the informal channels also play a role in communicating to people about their jobs. For now we turn to the question of accuracy in the formal, vertical channels.

Accuracy of the Vertical Channels. Formal organization participants depend, at least in part, on the hierarchical communication channels to keep them informed about their jobs and the company. How capable is the vertical channel for providing the needed information? Nichols (1962) found that the information content of messages was substantially reduced as one moves down through the hierarchy. It can be seen from Table 20-1 that a dramatic reduction in information content occurs as the message moves from the highest to the lowest levels of the organization. Perhaps the reduction is the result of an honest effort to summarize the message in the interest of improving communication efficiency. Such a well-intentioned motivation can have disastrous results should the "lost" information content be vital in the performance of an important job.

In many instances, downward filtering and distortion is not the result of conscious effort. Rather, the accuracy of downward communication is impaired by the perceptual distortions of managers along the chain. We have seen in many places in this book that communication must pass through the individual's perceptual lens. We must understand ourselves and how we feel about the job as well as others and how they feel about the job if we are to effectively communicate.

TABLE 20-1 Loss of Information Content through the Hierarchy

Level of hierarchy	Percentage of information received
Board	100
Vice president	63
General supervisors	56
Plant managers	40
General foremen	30
Workers	20

SOURCE: Ralph G. Nichols, "Listening Is Good Business," *Management of Personnel Quarterly*, p. 4, Winter 1962.

Consider the data from Likert which are shown in Table 20-2. These data clearly indicate a difference in perceptions of the job for individuals at different levels of the hierarchy. At each level, it appears that the manager does not understand the problems of her/his subordinates nearly as well as she/he might think. If this sort of difference is representative of many superior-subordinate relationships, then one should rightfully question the effectiveness of downward communication.[1]

As a matter of fact, there is some evidence that downward communication in organizations may not be as efficient as we would like it to be. We have already seen from the data of Table 20-1 that information content is lost as we move down through the hierarchy. Consider now the data of Table 20-3, which concerns the communication of information about job-related change. Data such as those in

[1] We can also question the effectiveness of upward communication for the same reason, but we will not do so until the next section.

TABLE 20-2 Perception of the Job at Different Levels

I. Of the men
    34% say their superior understands the men's problems well
II. But of the foremen
    95% say they understand the men's problems well
  Nevertheless, of these foremen
    51% say their general foreman understands the foremen's problems well
III. Of the general foremen
    90% say they understand the foremen's problems well
  But among these general foremen
    60% say their superior understands the general foremen's problems well

SOURCE: Rensis Likert, *New Patterns of Management* (New York: McGraw-Hill Book Company, 1961), p. 52.

TABLE 20-3 Communication to Subordinates Regarding Job Change, Perceptions of Superiors and Subordinates*

	Top staff says as to own behavior	Foremen say about top staff's behavior	Foremen say as to own behavior	Men say about foremen's behavior
Always tell subordinates in advance about changes which will affect them or their work	70% 100%	27% 63%	40% 92%	22% 47%
Nearly always tell subordinates	30%	36	52	25
More often than not tell	...	18	2	13
Occasionally tell	...	15	5	28
Seldom tell	...	4	1	12

*Data from unpublished studies by Floyd C. Mann of power plants in a public utility.
SOURCE: Rensis Likert, *New Patterns of Management* (New York: McGraw-Hill Book Company, 1961), p. 52.

Table 20-3 as well as the results of other research strongly suggest that managers are not always able to effectively communicate to subordinates using the formally prescribed channels. It can be seen from these data that managers at each level of the hierarchy are not communicating as well as they think they are. According to the subordinates, there is substantially less downward communication about change than the managers think. Results of this sort may be influenced by the manager's intentional effort to summarize messages or to route them only to locations at which they are needed. However, the nature of the research suggests that this is not the case. The managers actually thought they were communicating to subordinates using the formally prescribed channels. In any event, the evidence suggests a problem with downward communication exists. Yet, downward communication is vital to the accomplishment of the organization's mission. We shall discuss a remedy to the problem in the next chapter, but for now, we focus on formal upward communication.

Upward Communication

Bennis (1965) and a number of other authors have observed that communication upward tends to be distorted. Likert (1961, p. 47) commented that "upward communication, therefore, is at least as inadequate as downward communication and probably is less accurate because of the selective filtering of information which subordinates feed to their superiors." To the extent that subordinates do filter upward communication, it can be seen that the manager's control function will be adversely affected. The manager needs information about operations and operational problems if he or she is to make meaningful decisions. The very nature of the organization and superior-subordinate relationships sometimes prevents the needed upward flow of reliable information from occurring.

People sometimes do not feel free to discuss job-related problems with their superiors. The data of Table 20-4 reflect Likert's findings concerning this reluctance to communicate upward. It is only natural that one is reluctant to tell the boss about job-related problems. For example, subordinates may fear that in communicating upward they will convey a bad image of their own performance. In upward communication, we strive to put our best foot forward. Thus, we may withhold information which casts us in an unfavorable light. There are, however, other possible explanations for filtering and distorting upward communication.

Effects of Trust, Ascendancy, and Structure on Upward Communication. The results of some research suggest that several important influences may lead to the distortion of upward communication: the subordinate's trust in the superior; the subordinate's security level; the subordinate's ascendancy drive; and the influence of organizational structure on all three factors. Roberts and O'Reilly (1974) investigated the relationship between upward communication and three interpersonal variables: subordinate's trust in the superior; subordinate's perception of the degree to which the superior can influence his or her career; and the subordinate's aspiration for upward mobility in the organization.

The results of this study strongly supported the notion that trust in one's superior is related to the openness of upward communication. The impact of the superior's perceived influence on the subordinate's career was not clearly determined by Roberts and O'Reilly. Mobility aspirations also could not be generally associated with the distortion of upward communication. However, there was an indication that the upward-mobility factor influences the distortion of upward

TABLE 20-4 How Free Subordinates Feel to Discuss Job-related Matters with Superiors

	Top staff says about foremen	*Foremen say about themselves*	*Foremen say about the men*	*Men say about themselves*
Feel very free to discuss important things about the job with my superior	90%	67%	85%	51%
Feel fairly free	10	23	15	29
Not very free	...	10	...	14
Not at all free	...	...	...	6

SOURCE: Rensis Likert, *New Patterns of Management* (New York: McGraw-Hill Book Company, 1961), p. 47.

communication in some types of organizations. For example, there was some evidence that upward mobility may influence upward communication in highly structured organizations such as military units. The research of others seems to support this conclusion.

Athanassiades (1973) investigated the distortion of upward communication in two different types of organizations. One organization was a university faculty, an organization whose nonmanagerial members are relatively autonomous and free of supervision. The other organization was a police department, an organization which is heteronomous in that its nonmanagerial members are closely supervised. The research was designed to test the relationship between distortion of upward communication and certain personal and organizational factors. Personal factors included in the study were the subordinate's security level and ascendancy drive (aspiration for upward mobility). The degree of subordinate autonomy permitted by organizational structure was the major organizational factor studied.

The results of Anthanassiades's study suggest that the distortion of upward communication by subordinates is influenced by all three factors. In general, the degree of upward distortion is positively related to the subordinate's ascendance drive and his or her level of insecurity. Hierarchical structure and control are important situational or organizational factors which contribute to the character of security and ascendancy drives for different individuals.

As an example, bureaucratic organizations have a high degree of structure, rules, and regulations which reduce insecurity and stifle initiative. This can lead to a lower level of ascendancy for some individuals; thus this type of organization generates secure nonascenders. To the extent that organizations actually reach this state of affairs, we would expect to see very little upward distortion of communication. Secure nonascenders have no motivation to distort upward communication.

In another type of organization, we might find a high degree of work simplification and standardization. The resulting specialization and skill development in this circumstance tend to reinforce the self-confidence and security of subordinates, and again, we would expect less distortion of upward communication. Finally, still another type of organization can be characterized as having ambiguous and conflicting regulations and policies. This condition may encourage both the secure ascenders and the insecure ascenders to distort upward communication extensively. Faced with ambiguous and perhaps conflicting expectations from the external system, individuals respond defensively by distorting upward communication.

It should be clear from the preceding remarks that distortion of upward communication results from a particular blend or interaction of three types of variables: ascendancy, security, and structural factors. Athanassiades (1973, pp. 224–225) suggests that, under some conditions, distortion of upward communication is a mechanism by which the subordinate copes with the organization. To the extent that upward distortion permits the organization to effectively utilize those with strong ascendance drives or those who are highly insecure, it can be considered functional to the organization.

It can be argued that the "upward distorters" are the "misfits," the "black hats," or the "undesirables" of organizational life. As Athanassiades (1973, p. 225) observed, these individuals may feign loyalty to the boss "while stabbing him in the back," or they may assure him that "all is well" while clenching their fists in their pockets. Still Athanassiades argues, and perhaps rightfully so, that such individuals may truly be the adaptive, creative thinkers of organizational life. Be that as it may, there are other means for achieving adaptive responses and creativity in the organization. We shall discuss them in the next chapter.

Lateral Communication

Lateral or horizontal communication too is sometimes impaired within the formal organization. As we have seen, lateral communication is often vital in providing coordination between organization subdivisions. Interestingly enough, it is the formal organization hierarchy and the process of work subdivision which sometimes tends to disrupt horizontal communication.

Katz and Kahn (1966) comment that as organizations move toward a more authoritarian structure, the flow of horizontal information is controlled more closely. The top-level manager of an organization possesses information about each department and individual under his or her control, but department heads usually are familiar with only their own unit's operations. The possession of such information increases the power of the top-level manager and permits this manager to manipulate the affairs of those at lower levels. His or her powers, of course, include the potential to restrict horizontal communication between those at lower levels. An extreme example of hierarchically imposed restrictions on lateral communication is found in totalitarian forms of government. In this extreme case, lower-level participants can become almost totally dependent on information which is communicated via vertical channels.

Finally, before leaving the subject we should recall from our earlier discussion that work subdivision and specialization of task are also sources of potential impediment to horizontal communication. The development of functional specialization and differentiation increases the likelihood of special jargon and coding differences. Should the language differences become great enough, the flow of information across subunit boundaries will be reduced or perhaps completely prohibited.

HOW SUCCESSFUL ORGANIZATIONS PROVIDE COMMUNICATION AND DEAL WITH CONFLICT

Though the formal organization is highly dependent on communication, qualities are often present in the external system which are dysfunctional to the occurrence of communication. Uncertainty regarding the environment can prevent the development of an adequate plan for the organization and its communication system. Conformity and conflict are potential threats to effective operations and communication. The differentiation of organizational subdivisions creates barriers to communication. As we have seen, the flow of formal communication in all directions is impaired by a number of factors which can be either structural or interpersonal in nature. Where the disruption of formal communication is too great, integration and coordination will be difficult to achieve. In this final section we will discuss the general manner in which successful formal organizations respond to such dysfunctional consequences.

Overcoming Barriers to Communication and Achieving Integration

How do the more successful organizations manage to simultaneously provide for both differentiation and integration when the two qualities are opposed to one another? Dalton et al. (1970) suggest that two aspects of formal operations are crucial to the accomplishment: (1) the mechanisms used for achieving integration and (2) the behavioral style used to deal with intergroup conflict. Dalton and his colleagues observe that effective organizations tend to have more highly developed methods of integration. In some cases coordination can be achieved solely via hierarchical communication, formal plans, and controls such as are found in all external systems. Organizations can effectively integrate using this more normal approach when the environment is stable, certain, and homogeneous.

Organizations which face a more diverse and uncertain environment must rely on different methods for achieving integration if they are to be successful. The research of Dalton indicates that efficient organizations adapt to diverse or unstable environments by providing special integrating functions. In some cases specific individuals can be assigned the responsibility for performing the integrative function. In other circumstances groups or even entire departments must be used to perform integrative functions. As an example, project teams which cut across functional barriers may be assigned on an ad hoc basis to handle some special product or problem. Such a team may then be dissolved when it is no longer needed. An integrative team of this sort will be very beneficial to the flow of lateral communication as it applies to the assigned problem or project.

Table 20-5 from Dalton reflects the major differences in integrative styles and conflict management variables for successful organizations. It can be seen from this table that as the environment shifts from low to high diversity, the requirements for effective integration and conflict management change substantially.

Most of us think of all organizations as being similar to the container-industry model; that is, a high degree of reliance is placed on hierarchy, plans, and procedures to achieve integration and manage conflict. This is a dangerous assumption should our environment actually be an unstable or diverse one. An application of the "container model" in a highly uncertain environment is likely to result in an information overload for the hierarchical or formal communication system. Changes and problems in meeting the needs of the environment place great demands on the formal communication system. Simultaneously, the high levels of differentiation involved result in an increased potential for conflict and other barriers to communication.

Power, Influence, and Conflict Resolution

Power, Influence, and the Environment. A second factor which distinguishes effective organizations from ineffective ones is the behavioral style used in dealing with conflict. Obviously, the manner in which we resolve or do not resolve conflict will also affect our ability to provide integration. As has been discussed, a high level of differentiation is by nature a situation which results in differences in orientation. Differences in orientation are potential sources of disruptive conflict which must be controlled by the organization if it is to be successful. This is not to say we are to eliminate conflict. Rather, the notion is to control conflict by keeping it in a constructive mode which is not destructive to organizational communication, coordination, and productivity.

Power and influence are important variables which can be used by management in dealing with conflict. Communication of relevant situational information is a necessary prerequisite to the effective use of power and influence. Neither the manager nor an operating employee can effectively use formally assigned power and influence if he or she lacks task-relevant information. It can be seen from Table 20-5 that influence and power in effective organizations is concentrated at the organization level or function which possesses the relevant information for the particular situation.

If the functional department's environment is relatively certain, the necessary information can be obtained easily by the upper hierarchical levels. So in this case, effective organizations concentrate power and influence at the higher levels.

TABLE 20-5 Environmental Factors and Organizational Characteristics of Effective Organizations

				Integrative devices		Conflict-management variables	
Industry	Environment diversity	Actual differentiation	Actual integration	Type of integrative devices	Special integrating personnel as % of total management	Hierarchical influence	Unit having high influence
Plastics	High	High	High	Teams, roles, departments, hierarchy, plans, and procedures	22%*	Evenly distributed	Integrating unit
Foods	Moderate	Moderate	High	Roles, plans, hierarchy, procedures	17%*	Evenly distributed	Sales and research
Container	Low	Low	High	Hierarchy, plans, and procedures	0%*	Top high, bottom low	Sales

*This proportion was constant for the high and low performer within these industries.

SOURCE: G. W. Dalton, Paul R. Lawrence, and Jay W. Lorsch, *Organizational Structure and Design* (Homewood, Ill.: Richard D. Irwin, Inc., and The Dorsey Press, 1970), p. 13.

However, where the environment of the organization is relatively uncertain, relevant information is more likely to be available (if it is available at all) to managers who are at the lower levels of the hierarchy or in functional units. Thus, in the case of an environment which is relatively uncertain for all departments and functions, successful organizations tend to distribute power and influence more evenly across both higher and lower hierarchical levels.

As might be expected, those organization subunits which have access to information relevant to the dominant strategic variable tend to have the *most* power and influence in successful organizations. Thus, when we say power and influence are evenly distributed, we do not mean to imply there is an exact balance across all organizational subunits. The locus and distribution of influence and power relative to environmental uncertainty and diversity are shown in Table 20-5.

Conflict Resolution. It is of particular importance for our study of human communication to consider the nature of conflict resolution as it occurs in the more effective organizations. What sorts of people have the influence, and how do they approach conflict which naturally emerges from a high degree of differentiation? In effective organizations, the influence of those engaged in conflict resolution and integration is based on perceived competence. In the less effective organizations, influence is based purely on formal position or control over scarce resources. Thus for effective organizations, integration and conflict-resolution roles are assigned to those perceived to have the ability to perform effectively, regardless of their actual formal role.

In contrast, less effective organizations tend to rely on external-system requirements. Where an individual who is perceived by associates to be lacking in personal competence is assigned to a certain position, he or she will have only the formal power and influence of his or her office to achieve the needed integration and conflict resolution. Formalized powers are not always adequate in dealing with conflict, as we have already seen.

Indeed, when the approach to conflict resolution used by successful organizations is examined closely, there is a clear similarity to the approaches discussed earlier in this text. The ability to deal with conflict situations is more a function of interpersonal competence than it is of formalized power as assigned by the external system. According to Dalton and his colleagues (1970), effective organizations resolve conflict by: working directly with a problem until it is resolved; confronting conflict in preference to smoothing it over; and avoiding the use of force and raw power. Also, individuals who are engaged in integrating activities tend to have a more balanced orientation toward the groups they are integrating in the more effective organizations. In the less effective organization integrators tend to have one-sided orientations.

As an example, if an integrator were working at Associated Ovoids between production and sales, it would be important that he or she be able to understand and communicate with individuals in each of these functional areas. Someone whose background and orientation is strongly production and who tends to be rigid and unchanging will not function effectively to integrate and resolve conflict between the two subunits. This sort of person tends to see problems from a production viewpoint only.

In summary, we have suggested that the successful organization is one which is capable of relating to environmental uncertainties via the proper degree of differentiation, and then successfully integrating the differentiated subunits via effective communication and conflict resolution. It seems clear from what has been said that communication and conflict in the formal organization are influenced by both structural and behavioral variables. We shall take a closer look at the psychosocial aspects in the next chapter.

SUMMARY

We began the discussion of this chapter by noting certain deficiencies with the formal or external system. It is not possible to adequately specify a complete plan for the organization; there will be gaps. In addition, it was observed that the formal system often leads to certain dysfunctional consequences. The formal system may give rise to conformity, conflict, and communication barriers. Especially important are boundary and coding differences which are the natural result of work subdivision and specialization in the formal organization.

Data were presented which indicated that downward, upward, and lateral communication are impaired by the structural nature of the formal organization as well as certain personal factors. Message routing and message summarization are processes used by managers to increase the efficiency of information flow in formal organizations and to prevent information overload. Unfortunately, neither process is always effective. It was also shown that downward communication is distorted or filtered by the perceptions of managers and that managers are sometimes unaware of such problems.

Distortion and filtering of upward communication were seen to result from the subordinate's fear of leveling with the supervisor, the subordinate's trust in the supervisor, the subordinate's ascendancy drive, and perhaps the degree of autonomy given the subordinate. Lateral communication in the formal organization can be disrupted by coding differences between departments as well as hierarchically imposed restrictions.

Finally, we observed that successful organizations are distinguished from unsuccessful ones by their ability to achieve both differentiation and integration. In particular, effective organizations tend to provide special integrative measures and are more adept at overcoming conflict.

IMPORTANT TERMS AND CONCEPTS

dysfunctional consequences, bureaucratic organizations, coding differences, communication barriers, message routing, message summarization, ascendancy drive, security level, subordinate autonomy

REVIEW QUESTIONS

1. Discuss some of the significant problems which occur with the formal organization plan. What is the implication of these problems for communication?

2. Discuss the important factors which contribute to problems of distortion and filtering in downward communication. Give examples from your own experiences if possible.

3. Discuss message routing and message summarization as processes which improve the efficiency of information flow in the organization. Give examples of each process. How well do the processes work?

4. According to the research, what factors seem to cause distortion and filtering in the upward communication channel? Give examples of some of the kinds of problems which occur.

5. What kind of factors disrupt the lateral or horizontal flow of information? Give examples of the problem from your own experiences if possible.

6. How do successful organizations differ from unsuccessful ones in terms of methods for achieving integration and conflict resolution?

INCIDENT: BUROC (A)

A growing concern has been expressed regarding the efficiency of various governmental agencies. Despite an increased utilization of computers, documentation, and reports, and the detailed specification of external-system procedures, the performance of governmental agencies leaves something to be desired. Many feel that the source of such difficulties is the manner in which the highly specified and documented external organization affects operating-employee morale, perception of effectiveness in mission accomplishment, and the utilization of informal information channels.

An extensive investigation into one governmental agency with several hundred employees revealed the following situation. The responses on questionnaires as well as numerous personal interviews suggested that employee attitude in the agency was substantially less favorable than was the case for a national industry reference group. Figure 20-1 summarizes the results.

The agency represented by the data of Figure 20-1 is probably not very different from any of the myriad alphabet agencies that we see daily. We shall refer to it as BUROC. BUROC has approximately 1,000 employees who operate several administrative offices in the Southwestern part of the United States. The organization operates under a system that is not unlike that of the Civil Service or the United States military establishment. Job routines and procedures are highly documented and specified. Indeed, many of the key managers and other employees of BUROC would be quite comfortable in highly institutionalized situations such as might be found in Civil Service or the military.

Employees at BUROC frequently expressed dissatisfaction with working conditions and felt that their jobs were lacking in status and recognition. Many employees seemed

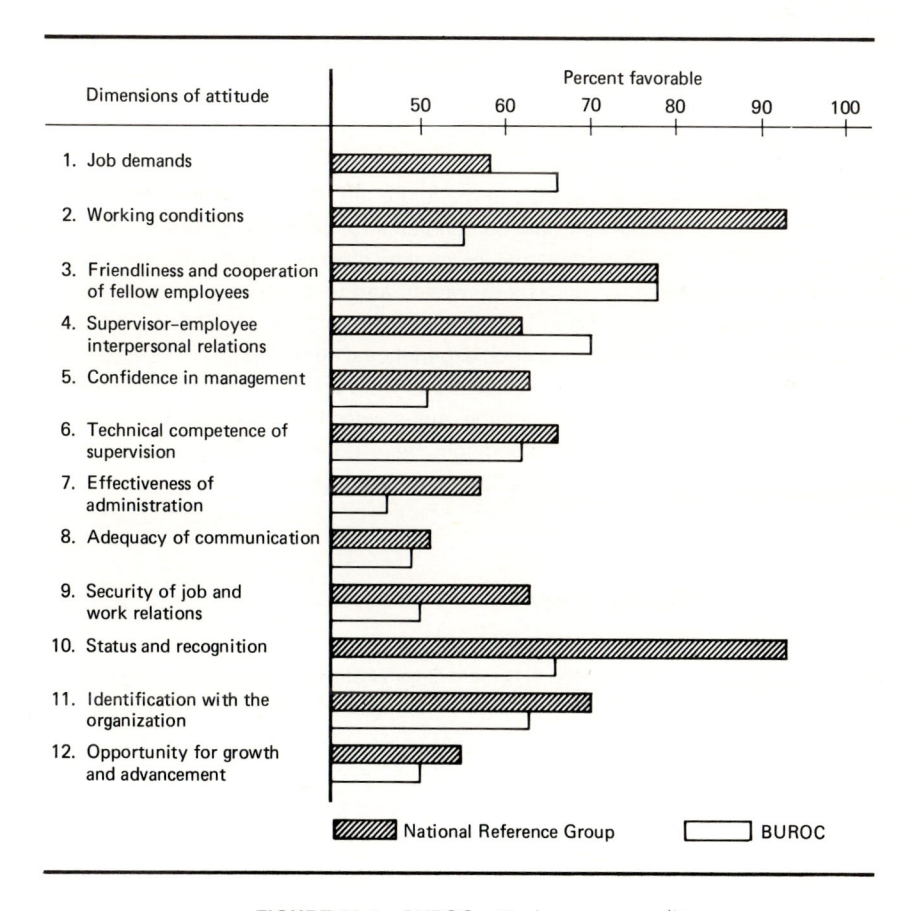

FIGURE 20-1 BUROC attitude survey results.

unaware of BUROC's overall mission. They tended to focus on the job routines, forms, and reports that were specifically associated with their own jobs.

A number of individuals commented that they had no confidence in the massive volume of reports and computer printouts associated with agency operations. Privately, they laughed at such documents and said they were meaningless because people adjusted the data inputs to give the desired impression. The comments of Herman Jackson and Laverne Patterson were typical for many of BUROC's employees.

Herman Jackson, who worked in quality control, stated that he was frequently required to spend considerable time compiling special reports for higher levels of the bureaucracy. He strongly believed the time could have been better devoted to tasks which were more relevant to the quality-control mission.

Laverne Patterson, an accountant, felt sure that her supervisor used external-system policy and regulation to justify his actions even though they were inconsistent with situational needs. To her, he was totally committed to external-system requirements. There could be no deviation.

Laverne encountered frequent situations in performing her job which required clarification data from specialists in other departments. She and other accountants had discovered that the most efficient way to deal with these problems was a telephone call to the individual specialist in the other department. When Laverne's supervisor learned of the practice, he became very upset.

He issued explicit instructions that, in the future, all data-clarification activities with specialists in other departments would be handled through formal channels. This meant, of course, that all requests for additional information must be referred through channels. He preferred that clarification requests be written and be processed through him.

The experiences of Herman and Laverne were not unusual for BUROC employees. Employee apathy often resulted from such experiences. People tended to "just go along" with the requirements of the external system and were unwilling to contribute their own creativity and interest to help it function more smoothly. Perhaps this is why the employees of BUROC felt working conditions were poor and offered little in the way recognition and status for individual effort (see Figure 20-1).

BIBLIOGRAPHY

Athanassiades, John C.: "The Distortion of Upward Communication in Hierarchical Organizations," *Academy of Management Journal,* vol. 16, pp. 207–225, June 1973.

Bennis, Warren G.: *Changing Organizations: Essays on the Development and Evolution of Human Organization* (New York: McGraw-Hill Book Company, 1965).

Blake, Robert R., and Jane S. Mouton: *The Managerial Grid* (Houston: Gulf Publishing Company, 1964).

Brenner, Marshall H., and Norman B. Sigband: "Organizational Communication: An Analysis Based on Empirical Data," *Academy of Management Journal,* vol. 16, pp. 323–325, June 1973.

Dalton, G. W., Paul R. Lawrence, and Jay W. Lorsch: *Organizational Structure and Design* (Homewood, Ill.: Richard D. Irwin, Inc., and The Dorsey Press, 1970).

Gerloff, Edwin A.: "Performance Control in Government R&D Projects: The Measurable Effects of Performing Required Management and Engineering Techniques," *IEEE Transactions on Engineering Management,* EM-20, pp. 6–14, February 1973.

Katz, Daniel, and Robert L. Kahn: *The Social Psychology of Organizations* (New York: John Wiley & Sons, Inc., 1966).

Likert, Rensis: *New Patterns of Management* (New York: McGraw-Hill Book Company, 1961).

Nichols, Ralph G.: "Listening Is Good Business," *Management of Personnel Quarterly,* p. 4, Winter 1962.

Roberts, Karlene H., and Charles A. O'Reilly, III: "Failures in Upward Communication in Organization: Three Possible Culprits," *Academy of Management Journal,* vol. 17, pp. 205–215, June 1974.

Vaidya, Christine, Russell F. Lloyd, and David L. Ford: "Organizational Information Flow Characteristics: A Selected Review and Suggestions for Future Research," *35th Annual Proceedings of the Academy of Management,* Arthur B. Bedeian et al. (eds.), New Orleans, La., August 10–13, 1975.

21

INFORMAL COMMUNICATION SYSTEMS AS COMPENSATORS

In this chapter we will discuss the nature of the informal communication system which emerges as one facet of the organization's internal system. It will be shown that this type of communication is widely used in the accomplishment of organizational work. Important considerations in the formation of the informal communication system will be examined. The operational aspects of managing the flow of information through the informal system will be discussed.

Our discussion in the preceding two chapters has focused on the communication process as it occurs in the formal organization. The organization is dependent on formal communication, and in turn, formal organization or external-system factors influence the communication process. Factors such as type of technology, degree of formalization, and degree of work subdivision tend to affect the implementation of the communication process. External-system variables can be viewed as a set of primary variables which simultaneously determine the need for and affect the implementation of communication for any organization. The effects of formal plans are sometimes dysfunctional: the formal communication system may not function as intended.

We now wish to turn our attention to internal-system factors which also influence communication. We have observed elsewhere in this book that the external system rarely stands alone. Internal-system factors frequently elaborate, color, or otherwise affect external-system behaviors. In particular, for our present purposes, the internal system is sometimes capable of responding to a problem when the external system cannot.

We have seen that it is often not possible to completely specify all behaviors required by the formal organization. Problems occur which are not accounted for in planning the external system. Under the proper conditions people confronted by such problems tend to supply the needed behaviors. They fill in the gaps of the formal system, so to speak. You have probably experienced this in your own work. Do your job description and other formalized communications which pertain to your job cover all contingencies? If you followed all formal communication to the letter, but did nothing else, could you effectively function? We think not.

A significant portion of the communication in any organization is not preplanned or contrived as part of the external system or formal organization. It simply "happens" as people do their jobs. We refer to this type of communication as informal communication because it is not preplanned or contrived as a part of the external system. Informal communication tends not to be written or documented. It most commonly is of the face-to-face or telephone variety. It need not involve authority in the formal sense of the word, and it is confined to no particular direction of flow. Informal communication merely "connects" people in the organization.

However, the fact that informal communication is so loosely defined and structured should not be taken as a weakness. Many of the messages flowing in the informal networks are as vital to getting the job done as are those which travel through the more formal networks. The manager who ignores the informal communication system has a very limited and misleading perspective of organizational communication. Such a manager may, indeed, be unaware of the richest form of communication.

A HIGH LEVEL OF USEFUL COMMUNICATION OCCURS IN THE INFORMAL SYSTEM

Activities in the formal system are systematic and preplanned, and communication tends to be authority-laden, planned, and documented. Informal or emergent system activities are ad hoc and spontaneous. Therefore, communication in the internal system is typically not planned or documented. It is of a face-to-face, interpersonal nature. People communicate to one another directly because the nature of their own psychology, situational circumstances, and their relationships with others cause them to "want to communicate," not because the organization "tells them to communicate."

Level of Informal Communication Activity

The work of a number of different researchers suggests that people in organizations tend to utilize the informal channels to a greater extent than the formal channels in performing their jobs. Table 21-1 from Bodensteiner's work summarizes the findings of several researchers. These data apply to scientists and engineers and perhaps to other kinds of professionals. We should not generalize too strongly to other kinds of organizations.

However, Borman et al. (1969) studied the historical practice of communication in business and observed that verbal communication is of growing importance. These authors stated that written communication has become the slowest and most expensive method of transmittting information. Although we have mentioned that such informal channels are spontaneous and ad hoc, it should not be inferred from this that they cannot have value to a rational system.

Powell and Goodin (1975) surveyed the research results of several other investigators and reported that people engaged in many kinds of managerial activities spend much of their time communicating orally. The results are given in Table 21-2. This kind of results suggests that the use of informal communication channels may be rather widespread in all kinds of organizations. Indeed, according to Powell and Goodin, the five executives surveyed by Mintzberg (1973) indicated a strong preference for verbal communication. They disliked mail and used it only for formal correspondence and lengthy documents. When possible these executives made use of telephones and informal meetings.

Usefulness of Informal Communication

One may be tempted to criticize such a high reliance on informal communication. It does not seem to be a very "organized" way of carrying out the managerial

TABLE 21-1 Four Studies Showing the Utilization of the Formal and Informal Communication Channels by Scientists and Engineers

Study	Sample	% Informal	% Formal
Menzel (1958)	77 scientists	55	45
Auerbach (1965)	1,375 scientists and engineers	55	45
Rosenbloom and Wolek (1967)	3,200 scientists and engineers	55	45
Graham and Wagner (1967)	326 managers of research and development projects	56	44
Arithmetic average of all data		55	45

SOURCE: W. D. Bodensteiner, "Information Channel Utilization under Varying Research and Development Project Conditions: An Aspect of Inter-Organizational Communication Channel Usage," doctoral dissertation, The University of Texas at Austin, 1970, p. 26.

TABLE 21-2 Percent of Time Spent in Oral Communication

Researcher(s)	Subjects	Percent of time in oral communication
Carlson	12 German executives	70
Stogdill and Shartle (cited by Dubin)	470 Navy officers	80
Kelly	10 middle managers	59.6
Burns	4 engineer executives	80
Sayles	First-line supervisors	50–80
Webber	Several levels of hierarchy	75+
Guest	Foremen	57
Lawler, Porter, and Tannenbaum	Middle managers	89
Stewart	Upper and middle managers	66
Mintzberg	5 executives	78

function. However, such a criticism fails to consider the problem of uncertainty. The best plan with which to face high levels of uncertainty is to remain flexible and use problem-solving approaches until environmental circumstances become more certain. Informal information systems can help us accomplish such an adaptation.

> The media for information transfer which emerge from the structure of the organization can be valid and effective mechanisms for meeting the needs of professionals. Although this sort of communication may appear to be haphazard and perhaps inefficient, it seems more useful to recognize that it may be the natural functioning of a highly sophisticated and well-structured social system. Provincialism is not a necessary result of reliance on local and informal sources. Whether or not it is the result will depend, in our opinion, upon the clarity and depth to which executives understand the many interrelated transfer systems which they manage and influence. [Rosenbloom and Wolek, 1970, p. 114]

The research of Davis (1953) provides a very specific example of how the informal flow of communication benefits the organization. Davis mapped the flow of information which occurred in one company with respect to a quality-control problem. The problem was first reported by a customer via a letter to the sales manager. Including the sales manager, fourteen people in the organization ultimately received messages about the problem. These individuals were located in several functional areas including sales, production, and engineering.

Now the problem-related messages could have been sent through the formal hierarchical channels, but this is not what happened. Davis pointed out that only three of the fourteen communications involved followed the chain of command. Only six of the messages sent were confined to the boundaries of the sales group.

It is not at all unusual for organizational participants to use the informal communication channel for work-related problems. People who face problems in organizations often turn to informal sources of information to solve them. Davis (1972) cautions, however, that managers may need to improve the flow of information through such channels. We will return to the matter of improvement shortly, but for now we turn to a discussion of some unique qualities which give informal channels their special advantage.

Multidirectional Maintenance Channels. Informal communication channels provide a convenient means for crossing the boundaries which exist between functional or even hierarchical units. We have seen that formal communication channels flow primarily either vertically along the hierarchical chain, or horizontally with the operative work. Informal channels are not restricted to any particular direction. However, we have also seen that differentiation and coding difficulties can prevent the flow of communication across the boundaries between units. The informal communication system has the capability for spanning such boundaries.

We saw from the quality-control problem described by Davis that eleven of the fourteen communications involved did not flow through the formal channels. Individuals relied on personal contacts. The informal channel is more or less "natural" in that it emerges to meet the needs of people. We can think of it as being multidirectional. It goes where the organizational participants wish it to. This may be vertical, horizontal, or diagonal insofar as organization structure is concerned. The network of informal channels is likely to be strongly influenced by the nature of social relationships that are extant in a given organization. The informal network is, in a sense, a composite overlay of the various group and social networks which exist in the organization. Properly cultivated, the informal channels can assist the manager in crossing boundaries between departments and in dealing with other problems.

Earlier in this book we observed that groups try to sustain themselves; they have maintenance goals. Organizations possess a similar quality; they tend to persist and survive. There is a great deal of communication activity in the informal system which is directed at sustaining the organization or one of its subdivisions. We can see this kind of communication activity in all organizations. If you think about this for organizations with which you have been associated, you can probably recall many examples of such maintenance-oriented communication.

There are repeated occasions in the organizational lives of all of us in which we utilize personal information sources to solve organizational problems. At coffee, you ask George and Joan about the solution to some problem you are experiencing because you know they have experienced similar difficulties. You value their advice. Because the informal information system is frequently used in this fashion, we refer to informal channels as *maintenance* channels. They can be and are used by the organization's members to help sustain the organization.

Active Channels. Informal channels can be distinguished from formal channels in terms of the degree of activeness or passiveness with which the participants are involved. Shapero (1974) discussed the role of communication in the management of innovation and made some important observations concerning the distinction between man-to-man communication and man-to-machine communication. His observations are repeated in Table 21-3. The value of the man-to-man system results from its potential for the active involvment of sender and receiver in a rich exchange of information.

> The extent to which the transmitter of a message is dependent on the active participation of the receiver can best be illustrated by what I call the "Good Soldier Schweik" defense. Imagine trying to transmit a set of complicated instructions to a person who absolutely does not respond, who shows no facial expression, and who never lets you know whether or not he understands what you have said. A reverse example would be a situation where I tell you, "I was driving my car when another car suddenly crossed my path. Quickly I put on my . . ." You would instinctively supply a word to help complete the message. [Shapero, 1974]

TABLE 21-3 Man-to-Man versus Man-to-Machine Information Systems

Man-to-Man	Man-to-Machine
Active two-way response	Passive one-way response
Two-way coding	One-way coding
Validation	No validation
Rich language	Nonrich language
Personally rewarding in several dimensions	One-dimensional reward

SOURCE: Albert Shapero, *Management of Innovation*, reprinted from 6th International TNO Conference: Organizing for Technological Innovation (Rotterdam, March 1 and 2, 1973). Reprinted in *Economics and Business*, no. 59, Bureau of Business Research, The University of Texas at Austin, 1974, p. 36.

Shapero's man-to-man relationship is the type of relationship found in the informal communication system. Man-to-machine relationships are the types of relationships we often find in the formal system. Examples would include man-computer printout, man-written instruction, or perhaps even man–controlling-style statement from the boss. The man-to-man relationship of the informal system is a rich, active, two-way relationship. It is clearly superior to the one-way man-machine relationship in which one party is a very passive "Good Soldier Schweik." The relationship between the individual and the formal, documented information system is no different from the man-machine system described by Shapero and suffers the same disadvantages.

You are asked to think of your own experiences with formal communication systems. Do you agree? Have you, for example, ever read the instruction booklet that accompanies your federal income-tax form, or perhaps the instruction booklet which tells you how to assemble the bicycle you purchased? Did you ever feel the need to call the Internal Revenue Service or the manufacturer of the bicycle for a clarification of their instructions? Most of us have—the formal system is often lacking in terms of its ability to adequately convey meaning. The informal system has the richness and flexibility that we need in such situations. Such advantages stem from the advantages of feedback, timing, and richness.

FACTORS AFFECTING THE FORMATION OF INFORMAL COMMUNICATION NETWORKS

Fiedler (1968) observed that when faced with crisis situations, the managers of business organizations would typically gather key people for joint consulting, problem-solving, and decision-making efforts. Such collaborative efforts were seen as deviations from the normal operation, and once the crisis had passed, there was a return to the routine and fairly well-structured activities of the external system. If these observations might be considered representative of the experiences of organizations in general, it can be argued that the internal system can provide a valuable supplement to the external system under certain circumstances. We would argue that this is the case and that the internal system is particularly an asset because it has the capability of enhancing the organization's information-processing capabilities.

In this section we will discuss some of the factors which influence people to use the interpersonal communication channels in solving organizational problems. We will discuss the prerequisites to the formation of an effective informal communication system, examine conditions governing the availability of the system, and briefly examine rumor as an example of such a system.

Considerations in Channel Choice and Channel Availability

Bodensteiner (1970) investigated the profile of communications between several organizations which were jointly engaged in two different research-and-development efforts. In total, seven different organizational entities (four on one project and three on the second project) were studied. For our purposes, the several organizations associated in a given project can be considered as a single organizational system composed of several subsystems.

Bodensteiner tabulated the frequency of usage for four types of channels between each pair of transacting organizations over extended time periods. Usage rate data were collected for face-to-face, telephone, telegraph-telegram, and written-correspondence channels. These data provided a communication profile which reflected the utilization of interpersonal communication channels between the members of pairs of organizations. Data were also collected which indicated project uncertainty and stress resulting from the occurrence of unanticipated difficulties and problems. These data were cataloged for weekly intervals throughout the extended time period covered by the research.

The major findings of the study were supportive of earlier research which had suggested that individuals rely on interpersonal channels. The findings also seem to support the contention of the present authors that the informal information system is an invaluable supplement to the external system. Specifically, it was concluded that: (1) the utilization of interpersonal communication channels is a function of project problems and the associated stress and uncertainty; and (2) individuals distinctly prefer the richer face-to-face and telephone channels to formal, documented channels when faced with problems, stress, and uncertainty. We shall defer discussion of the second point until a later section.

Choice of Informal Channels. Figure 21-1 reflects the frequency of utilization of the four types of interpersonal channels between two of the transacting organizations. It can be clearly seen that during times of stress and uncertainty, there is a sharp increase in the frequency with which the face-to-face and telephone channels are used. When problems occur and information is needed, people prefer face-to-face and telephone channels to the other types. The results were similarly dramatic for the other pairs of transacting organizations studied by Bodensteiner.

Face-to-face and telephone channels tend to be a more informal means of interpersonal communication. They are part of the internal system. Written correspondence and telegrams are formal or external in nature. Thus, the data of Figure 21-1 also suggest that when organizational problems occur, people rely on the informal channels for needed information. The availability of informal chan-

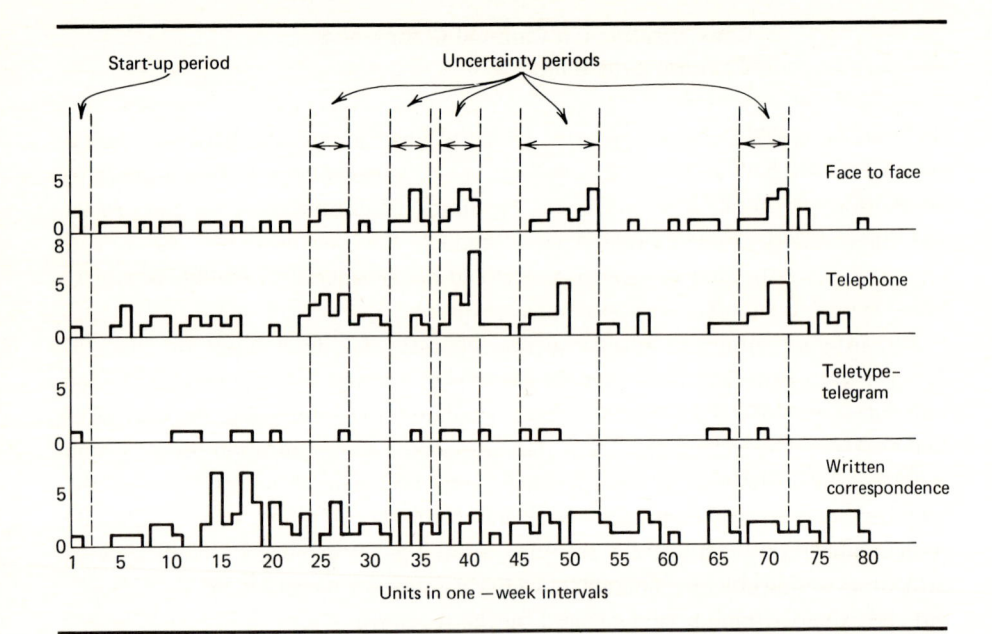

FIGURE 21-1 Frequency of channel utilization of transacting organizations A ↔ Aṁ. [Source: W. D. Bodensteiner, "Information Channel Utilization under Varying Research and Development Project Conditions: An Aspect of Inter-Organizational Communication Channel Usage," doctoral dissertation, The University of Texas at Austin, 1970, p. 117.]

nels to back up formal channels is not automatic. Certain conditions must be satisfied.

Availability of Formal and Informal Channels. Research on the grapevine, one type of informal channel, has generated somewhat conflicting evidence as to whether or not formal and informal communication channels complement one another (Guetzkow, 1965). Davis (1953, as cited by Guetzkow) concluded from his research into the grapevine that the two kinds of channels were either jointly active or jointly inactive. When formal channels are active, the grapevine is active. If the formal channel is inactive, the grapevine is inactive. Habbe (1952, as cited by Guetzkow), on the other hand, suggested that the grapevine thrives when formal channels are closed. The research of Bodensteiner suggests why we encounter such mixed results concerning the use of formal and informal communication.

In a given organization formal and informal communication can be jointly inactive, jointly active, or complementary. Which condition actually occurs can be influenced by the manager and other key individuals provided they recognize the need to maintain both kinds of communication channels in a state of readiness. As we have seen many times in this book, communication (in the sense of eliciting meaning) is a complex process involving emotion, perception, and motivation in addition to technological elements. We do not automatically communicate effectively with the mere transmission of the written word. Effective communication, whether formal or informal, requires time and practice. The manager and others must cultivate communication channels to be sure they will be "clear" and "available" when needed.

Communication systems cannot be turned on and off with the flick of a switch. A start-up period is required so that people may learn how to communicate with one another. Perhaps you have noticed that your favorite football team is off balance and awkward during the early season. It takes practice and playing time before the team members reach a state such that they can "read" one another. A valuable part of this learning period is the cultivation of effective communication channels between team members.

In a similar fashion the manager must devote time and effort in cultivating the communication channels of the organization. Start-up time is required. Communication channels do not exist because the manager says they do; they exist because people choose to use them. It can be seen from Figure 21-1 that both the formal and informal channels are used lightly during the early weeks of project life. This period might be viewed as a start-up period during which participants come to know one another. Later, when needed, the cultivated channel is more likely to be effective.

Factors Affecting the Start-up of Informal Channels. We have seen before that human systems tend to change and elaborate over extended periods of time. This is the basis for the emergence of the internal system. The informal communication system is no exception to the generalization. We cannot just plug people into some prearranged network, throw the switch, and expect it to work. Some period of time is required for interpersonal relationships, coding and filtering systems, jargon, informant contacts, and other features to be developed. Under the best of conditions, we can reach a state such that we are able to anticipate the reactions of our colleagues to circumstances and messages. Communication will be greatly improved. The time consumed as such aspects of the informal information systems are developed can be viewed as a type of setup cost. There is a similarity to the situation encountered in manufacturing operations where the work location must be set up before operations begin.

Because of such start-up costs, neither the formal nor the informal information system can be instantly available unless it has been operative for some suitable period of time. The data of Figure 21-1 suggest that some minimum, continuous rate of usage exists for all four types of interpersonal channels. Bodensteiner viewed such activity as "steady-state noise" which served the function of keeping the lines of communication open when they were not needed for major problems.

During "steady-state" periods and "start-up" periods, formal and informal systems can be "fine-tuned." Such periods can be used to ensure that there is an acceptable degree of compatibility between systems of coding and filtering and that distortions will be minimized.

Where interpersonal channels that cut across departmental boundaries are idle for long periods of time, the effects of differentiation will tend to prevent immediate reuse of the channels. Differentiated units tend to develop and elaborate their own internal informal information systems in the absence of any continuous interface with other units. It seems likely, then, that internally oriented coding and filtering systems will be unacceptably restrictive of inputs from external units. Katz and Kahn discuss such restrictions in the following statement.

> Individuals, groups, and organizations share a general characteristic which must be recognized as a major determinant of communication: the coding process. Any system which is the recipient of information, whether it be an individual or an organization, has a characteristic coding process, a limited set of coding categories to which it assimilates the information received. The nature of the system imposes omission, selection, refinement, elaboration, distortion, and transformation upon incoming communications. [Katz and Kahn, 1966, p. 227]

In our opinion, the effects of such barriers to communication can be partially offset by encouraging minimal levels of ongoing interaction and communication between units. Continuing interaction with people outside one's own unit helps to prevent excessively strong internal orientations. We keep the channels open.

During the periods of minimum activity, the informal system is not necessarily devoted to the communication of meaningless trivia. The communication involved can be directly related to the job at hand. For example, people can deal with minor matters of coordination, or new employees can be given information about the organization and their jobs. Also, there is an obvious social or psychological boost in that most people want to affiliate with others.

Before we leave the subject, it is suggested that you refer to your own organizational experiences. When you first entered a given organization, how did you find out about the job? Have you ever participated in the initiation of some new organization or subdivision of an organization? In either case, the informal, interpersonal channels probably played an important role. As a new employee, you probably felt lost at first. The helpless feeling gradually subsided as you began to meet people and to learn who to ask about what. But this all took time. Time is also required for those who are forming new organizations to develop the necessary informal nets.

Finally, the value of the informal system goes beyond its usefulness in crises or just getting started. It has the capability of supporting the formal system wherever and whenever support is required. As an example, Bodensteiner noted in his data that each time a monthly or quarterly report (formal, external-system communication) was due, there was a corresponding minor peak in the utilization of the interpersonal channels. His follow-up investigation and interview with project personnel confirmed his suspicions. When such formal reports were due, those involved found it necessary to consult with one another via the interpersonal channels to complete their reports.

The Need for Richer Channels

We stated in the preceding section that the informal communication system can complement the formal one under the proper circumstances. It is possible for the informal channels to compensate for inefficiencies in the formal channels. When and how does this fortuitous event take place? Where not prohibited by the arbitrary actions of management and faulty interpersonal relations, people will exercise their judgment and make a choice. Under the proper conditions they can and do choose to utilize the informal channels for solving organizational problems.

A second major finding of Bodensteiner's research was that individuals facing uncertainty and stress displayed a distinct preference for the richer face-to-face channels. The data of Table 21-4 reflect percentages of increase in channel utilization for four types of channels under varying conditions. Channel utilization levels for periods of certainty provide the base figures for these calculations, and the table is arranged to reflect changes by channel type for each separate uncertainty period as well as for all periods of uncertainty combined.

The results are startling. The preference for the richer face-to-face and telephone channels is clearly shown. When people in organizations encounter problems in doing their jobs, they seek information from other people in the organization via the informal information system. As can be seen in Table 21-4, there was some tendency for the utilization of the more formal written correspondence to drop off when problems occurred. Why do people prefer the informal information sources over the formal ones when they have a problem?

Advantages of Feedback and Timing. A number of factors help explain this kind of behavior; many have been discussed previously in this book. Richness and feedback are qualities possessed in heavy measure by the face-to-face channel. But such

TABLE 21-4 Percentage Increase in Utilization of Interpersonal Channels during Periods of Uncertainty

Sample	Transacting organizations		Channel	% Increase during individual periods of uncertainty					% Increase during combined period of uncertainty	Rank of channel according to greatest % increase
				1	2	3	4	5		
	A	A₁	F to F	322	271				299	1
			Tc	445	132				289	2
			T	165	31				98	3
			Wc	20	Neg				Neg	4
	A	A₂	F to F	857					857	1
			Tc	364					364	2
Project Alpha			T	200					200	3
			Wc	Neg					Neg	4
	A	A₃	F to F	809	1118				936	1
			Tc	733	1008				850	2
			T	Neg	Neg				Neg	3
			Wc	Neg	Neg				Neg	4
	A	Aₘ	F to F	317	317	495	288	376	348	1
			Tc	284	Neg	388	83	266	188	2
			T	39	39	178	111	11	78	3
			Wc	Neg	Neg	22	29	Neg	5	4

F to F = face to face
Tc = telephone conversation
T = teletype/telegram
Wc = written correspondence

SOURCE: W. D. Bodensteiner, "Information Channel Utilization under Varying Research and Development Project Conditions: An Aspect of Inter-Organizational Communication Channel Usage," doctoral dissertation, The University of Texas at Austin, 1970, p. 132.

qualities are successively degraded and diminished as we move toward the more formal, documented channels (see Table 3-1). Recall that the concept of richness included not only the technical capacity of the channel but also its ability to convey *meaning*. Why can the face-to-face channel, and to a lesser degree the telephone channel, more adequately convey meaning? There are many reasons, and perhaps it would serve as a good review if you were to list them. A few of the important advantages of face-to-face channels will be mentioned to emphasize our point concerning the value of the informal information system.

Certainly the major advantage of the richer face-to-face channels must stem from the nature of the feedback provided and the fact that a multiplicity of channels are involved. There is opportunity for visual contact, to detect body language as well as other forms of nonverbal expressions. All these channels are available for feedback purposes. The communicator can determine if his or her message is being received by making use of the information which is available as feedback. Further, there are advantages in terms of timing—the feedback is instantaneous. The communicator does not have to wait for return mail or until some formal report arrives to know if the message was received. One also can instantaneously make follow-up inquiries or provide such additional information as one deems necessary.

Selectivity of Use. Still another important point to be made about informal information systems in general is that there is always the possibility of selective utilization and choice of sources. One can use such channels or not use them, depending on whether or not one sees a need in a given situation. Likewise, one can choose from a number of possible sources of information depending on the needs of the situation. A caution is involved here. Remember that where the informal channels have remained too long idle and unused (perhaps a better word is "uncultivated"), they can grow stale. The coding and filtering systems between transmitter and receiver may not be adequately compatible.

It is for these and similar reasons that we all seek to use the more personal channels when we face problems. There may also be some psychological factors involved in such preferences. You have no doubt experienced many situations in which you found it comforting to consult with others about problems that you faced. Such behavior is most probable if there is reason to believe that the other person has experience in dealing with similar problems. In any event, we feel sure that as you inventory your own experiences, you will see there are numerous instances in which you tended to forego the more formal information sources in favor of the richer personal sources.

The data suggest that individuals in the organizations researched by Bodensteiner made similar trade-offs. There were definite gradations of increase and decrease in the utilization of interpersonal channels which correlated with uncertainty levels. The largest increases consistently occurred for the richer face-to-face and telephone channels. People relied on the informal channels when serious problems occurred. Data reflecting such an ebb and flow in the informal information system reinforce the notion of the informal system as a compensator.

Informal Information Systems as Organizational Slack. The informal information system is a form of organizational slack which can help meet unexpected needs or compensate for unforeseen circumstances. There will be differences from one organization to the next in terms of the ability of each to utilize the informal information system. There also will be differences in the need to use the informal information system depending on the circumstances encountered by a given organization. As will be shown in the next chapter, a very important factor will be the degree of uncertainty and stability of the environment.

In the case of the two projects investigated by Bodensteiner, the smaller project experienced a lower channel utilization rate over the total time frame of the study. However, it also experienced much sharper increases in the utilization of the face-to-face and telephone channels during periods of uncertainty. Beyond the influence exerted by stress and uncertainty and perhaps a history of successful experiences with the informal information system, there may be other explanations for variations in the informal system utilization rate from one organization to the next. One additional explanation of organizational differences with respect to using informal networks will be discussed in a later section as we review the flow of information as a two-step process. For now we turn to a brief examination of the grapevine as an example of how informal communication complements formal communication.

The Grapevine: A Case in Point

The well-known *grapevine* is an example of the informal communication system. The grapevine is a case in point which supports our contention that under the proper conditions, the emergent behavior of the internal system can support external-system goal accomplishment. Many people, including some managers, assume the grapevine is dysfunctional in nature, but this is not necessarily the case.

The word "grapevine" as generally used today refers to all informal communication. The term was originally used during the Civil War to characterize telegraph lines used by the military forces (Davis, 1972, p. 261). At that time, telegraph lines were strung from tree to tree in the fashion of a grapevine. Messages carried along these primitive communication channels were often distorted and garbled. Thus the grapevine had a negative connotation even at its inception.

The image of the grapevine is also impaired by the common tendency to associate rumor with the grapevine. Rumor is, of course, an undesirable form of message to send through any communication system. Rumors are not based on fact or evidence. They typically are the products of the prejudice, bad judgment, faulty perception, and emotion of those who transmit them. Davis (1972, p. 268) suggests that rumors thrive where ambiguous situations are of sufficient interest and importance to the participants. People are less likely to rumor about something which is of no interest to them.

Clearly, the manager must control rumor if he or she is to effectively utilize the grapevine for organizational purposes. Guetzkow (1965), citing the work of Caplow (1946–1947, p. 300), observed that the spread of rumors involves a form of behavior exchange. When one receives a rumor one is expected to: (1) supply the sender with another rumor in exchange; (2) render a validity judgment on the received rumor; or (3) perhaps supply some additional information which enhances the original story. Managers cannot directly interdict the grapevine and halt rumor. Since rumor arises from ambiguity of situation and the natural tendency of people to "fill in the gaps," managers can best negate rumor by attacking the source of the problem. They must seek to eliminate ambiguous organizational situations by supplying the needed information. In doing so, they must be aware of and cultivate the grapevine. They should make a positive effort to channel factual, useful information through the informal channels.

Assuming that rumor is controlled, research shows that the grapevine is a fine example of the manner in which people use informal communication systems to assist in the accomplishment of organizational work. The research of Bodensteiner (1970) indicates that people facing organizational problems need information and that they seek this information from the rich informal channels. Davis (1972, pp. 263–266) lists a number of features which suggest the grapevine fits this pattern and can be an asset to the organization:

1. The grapevine emerges to meet the needs of people.
2. The grapevine is relatively accurate.
3. The grapevine is rich and can be very fast.
4. The grapevine can cut across organizational boundaries.

Boundary Spanning. A point should be made about the grapevine, or the informal communication system in general, as a device for spanning boundaries. Informal communication systems are not purely democratic; not everyone gets and receives the same number of messages. Davis (1972, p. 264) observes that the grapevine network tends to take form as a cluster chain rather than as a straightforward chain. The difference between the two networks is shown in panels *a* and *b* of Figure 21-2. In panel *a* it can be seen that individuals at positions A, D, and E are very important. The individuals at positions A and E communicate to three other people and D links the two clusters together. D may very well span a boundary

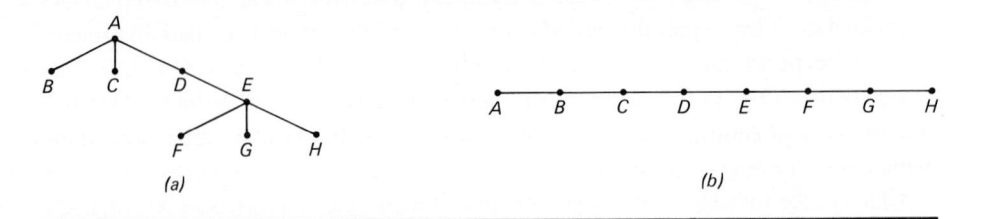

FIGURE 21-2 The grapevine as (a) a cluster chain and (b) a chain.

between two departments within a single organization or perhaps between two organizations. Gutezkow (1965, p. 563), in his review of the literature on rumor, also noted the existence of such "centers" of information flow.

It clearly is important for the manager to be acquainted with the nodal points of informal communication networks in the organization. The centers of the informal communication networks are logical places for the manager to input the factual information which is needed to accomplish organizational work and to offset rumor. As has been suggested previously in this book, the emergence of informal communication networks and their nodal points is influenced by both external and internal factors. Friendship, social and psychological factors, the flow of work, and other structural considerations all influence the networks which ultimately occur. In the next section, we will conclude the chapter by looking more closely at the flow of information through the informal networks.

OPERATIONAL CONSIDERATIONS: THE TWO-STEP FLOW OF INFORMAL COMMUNICATION

Should any doubt still exist as to the value of informal communication in complementing formal or hierarchical communication, consider the remark of Burns as cited in Gutezkow (1965):

> . . . the departmental manager might arrive back from a meeting with a crop of decisions affecting production. . . . This sort of occasion would be considerably disruptive, were it not for the existence of prior knowledge of varying specificity at the deputy's level, and at successive levels below him, that something was "in the wind," production commitments being lightened to accommodate the new situation when it arose.

> The "vertical" system would be virtually unworkable without the considerable flow of information laterally. [Burns, 1954, p. 92]

Informal lateral communication was found to be very valuable in the organizations investigated by Burns. It is important that the manager understand the important considerations involved in the flow of such information.

A growing body of literature spanning diverse disciplinary areas suggests that a two-step process is involved in the diffusion of information from one bounded entity to another. It seems likely that the notion of a two-step flow or process is equally applicable to the flow of information from environment into the organization and to the internal flow of information between organizational subdivisions. In the following paragraphs we wish to examine the nature of this process and why it is of value to the managers of organizations.

Moving Information across Boundaries

We observed in the previous chapter that organizations necessarily and intentionally involve certain restrictions and structural patterns which govern behavior. The restrictive nature of formal organizations applies to communication just as it does to other phases of the operation. Katz and Kahn note that:

> To move from an unorganized state to an organized state requires the introduction of constraints and restrictions to reduce diffuse and random communication to channels appropriate for the accomplishment of organizational objectives. [Katz and Kahn, 1966, p. 225]

As we have seen, organizations restrict the flow of information via the development of specialized coding systems. Such coding systems tend to impede the flow of communication across unit boundaries. Allen and Cohen (1969) build on the notion set forth by Katz and Kahn to theorize that a small number of persons can mediate the flow of information across boundaries if they are familiar with the code. Allen (1966), in contrasting the ease of internal information flows (where common codes are used) with the difficulty of external-internal information flows (noncommon codes), referred to such a filtering of information as *information impedance*.

In any event, the presence of such a filter or information impedance necessitates a special process if the system is to pass information across unit boundaries to those who need it, when they need it. A number of individuals writing in diverse disciplines have identified such a process. Many have referred to the process as a two-step information-flow process, and we shall do the same.

Two-step Process of Information Flow. As an example, Katz and Larzarfield (1955) referred to a two-step process in the literature of mass communication which involved: (1) the adoption of some new idea from the mass media by certain opinion leaders and (2) the subsequent acceptance of the new idea by the general public as they are influenced by the opinion leaders. We have all seen this process in operation in our day-to-day lives. The literature of social psychology provides another example of the same two-step flow. Lewin (1952), in discussing group decision and change, refers to those who are "technological gatekeepers." These key individuals seemed to be the nodal points of communication centers.

Allen (1967) determined that the two-step process also occurred in research laboratories, and he referred to those who linked the two phases of the process together as "technological gatekeepers." Holland (1970, 1972) researched information flows in two research-and-development organizations and a college engineering faculty, and concluded that the two-step process was present in these organizations also. He referred to the linking functionaries as "special communicators." Taylor (1973) determined that the two-step flow also existed in a large military in-house research-and-development laboratory and referred to the information mediators as "gatekeepers."

Many researchers then have identified the two-step flow of information. Figure 21-3 reflects the essence of the two-step flow of information and the key role played by the linking functionaries in the process. The terminology used varies from author to author, but the basic notion always seems to be the same. For many kinds of organizations we can identify a limited number of individuals who seem uniquely qualified to expedite the flow of necessary information across unit and subdivision boundaries. We shall look more closely at the qualities possessed by such key communicators in the next section, but first a brief discussion of why they are needed is in order.

As we have seen, the very nature of the external system creates boundaries which tend to interfere with the flow of communication. Also, there are occasions when even the most well-conceived formal system may fail to provide adequate information to some participants. Rarely, if ever, do the designers of the formal system assign the role of special communicator or gatekeeper to specific people so that they can deal with such unforeseen circumstances. Thus, where such functions are performed, they can best be characterized as part of the emergent informal organization. As such, the linking role and the two-step information flow are good examples of the manner in which the informal system supplements the formal system.

We would speculate that a partial reason for the integrative success of some of

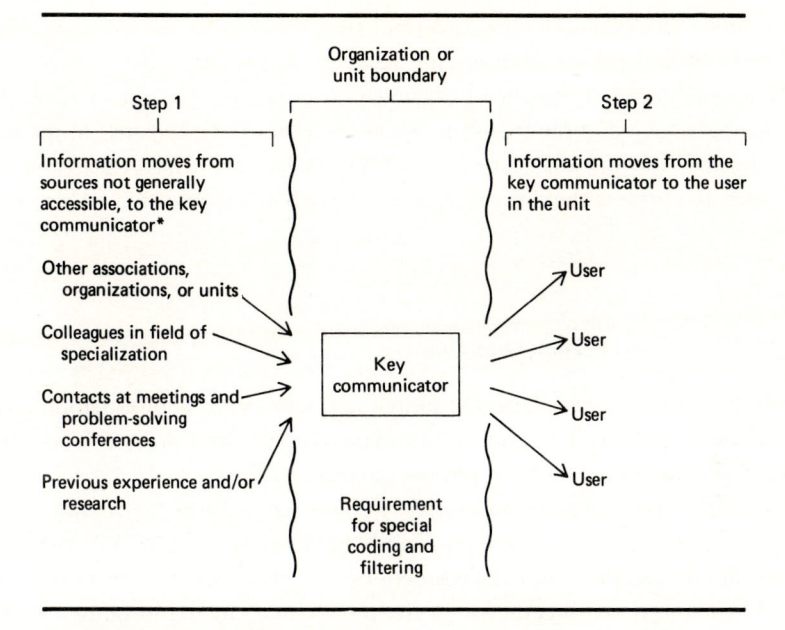

FIGURE 21-3 The general two-step information-flow process. [*Adapted from the notion expressed by Robert L. Taylor, "The Technological Gatekeeper: A Two-Step Flow Process for Scientific and Technical Communication," an unpublished report at the United States Air Force Academy, Colorado, 1974, p. 13.*]

*Such information may be from sources external to the organization or unit and thus involve a coding system not generally known, or it may be unavailable to the general membership for some other reason, such as inexperience. The point is that the information is available to only a limited number of individuals, the key communicators.

the organizations investigated by Lawrence and Lorsch (see Chapter 20) was the emergence and effective utilization of the two-step information flows. Such a flow permits people to rely on sources which are perceived to have the needed information instead of the source which may be arbitrarily (and erroneously) assigned by the external system. In some of the organizations investigated by Burns and Stalker, it was noted that:

> At lower levels in management the same free and frequent contact between individuals was maintained as prevailed between directors. . . . You go to the person who is most concerned with the problem in hand, whether foreman or director. . . . When Bill in the shop comes across something he doesn't understand, he can go straight to the design engineer or draftsman, and whatever it is is sorted out at that level. [Burns and Stalker, 1961, p. 91]

Gerstberger and Allen (1968) would refer to such behavior as the "law of least effort." By utilizing those with unique access to the needed information, time is saved and the accomplishment of organization goals is enhanced. Taylor (1974) sees the phenomenon of the two-step process as a necessary response to the failure of the formal information system. Such a process can utilize only a few key individuals to enhance the flow of information into an organization or between its subunits.

Key Communicators

We turn now to that special class of individuals who serve as information tenders and operate at the unit's boundaries to make the two-step process work. It has already been noted that such individuals have been called "gatekeepers," "opinion leaders," and "special communicators." To that list we may add: "innovators," "early adopters," "persuasive sources," and "influentials." Table 21-5 summarizes these additions together with their functions and characteristics as seen by Holland. When considered together with the research conducted in numerous R&D organizations (as described above), one can only conclude (as did Holland) that such individuals can be found in a broad range of social organizations.[1]

Who are these people? What distinguishes them from other people in the organization? Essentially, key communicators are people who possess or have access to a lot of information and who are frequently asked by their colleagues to share it. Obviously, they do not all tend the same gate; they specialize in the type of information they provide. But they do seem to share similar traits and characteristics. Some of these similarities can be seen in Table 21-5. Other similarities would be that such individuals are noticeably different from their colleagues in terms of (1) the frequency with which they are chosen as discussion partners and (2) the amount of information which they receive. Taylor (1974) and others see the key communicators as scoring well above the average of their colleagues on both criteria. Taylor defines a technological gatekeeper or key communicator as shown in Figure 21-4. Gatekeepers can be defined as those who are "stars" in terms of being the choice of others as a source of information and in terms of having a larger number of information contacts. Taylor found that the majority of people in the organizations he investigated could correctly identify the gatekeepers by name.

It should be clear from all this that our key communicators are individuals who are influential in the organization. They are perceived by other organizational

---

[1] As a convenience, we shall try to refer to such individuals as "key communicators" though at times it may be appropriate to use one of the other labels. In any event, we assume that all the labels refer to individuals who perform very similar communication roles.

TABLE 21-5 Key Communicators as Described by Three Different Sources

Source	Name	Function	Group role	Personal characteristics	
				Traits	*Outputs*
Mass communication literature	"Opinion Leader" "Influential"	Receiver and transmitter of outside information	Key man in communication network; "model" for other group members	Gregarious approachable, socially active	High competence; high experience; known by many people
Diffusion of innovation literature	"Innovator" "Early Adopter"	Sells group on innovation; attitude change; source of external information about innovations	Model group member; opinion leader; member of external cliques of earlier adopters	Younger than average; socially active	High status; wealthy; specialized
Psychology of persuasion and attitude change	"Persuasive Source"	An influential attitude changer	Opinion leader	Trustworthy; safe; dynamic	Competent; qualified; high status

SOURCE: W. E. Holland, "Intra- and Interorganizational Communications Behavior of Scientists and Engineers with High Information Potential," doctoral dissertation, The University of Texas at Austin, 1970, p. 58.

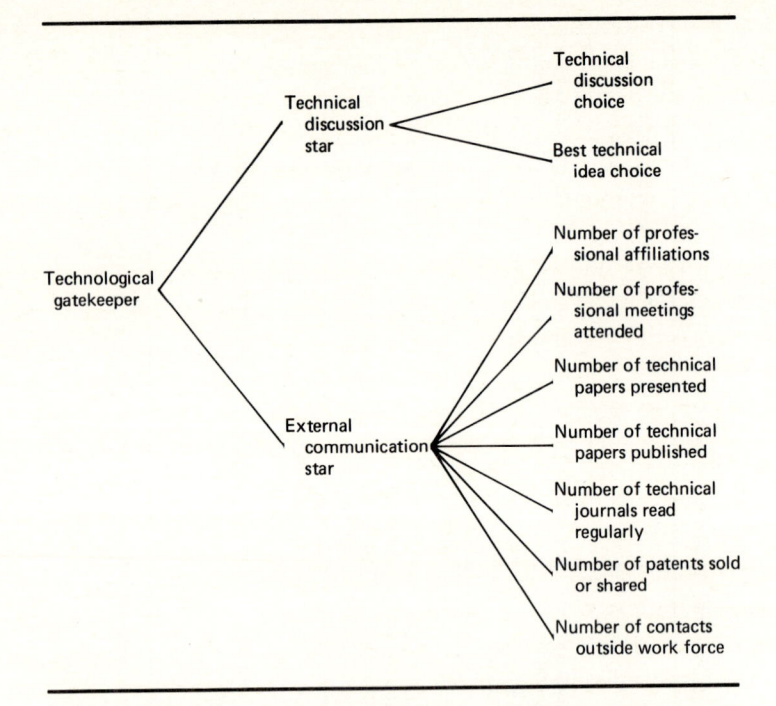

FIGURE 21-4 The technological gatekeeper: A definitional relationship. [*Source: Robert L. Taylor, "The Technological Gatekeeper: A Two-Step Flow Process for Scientific and Technical Communication," an unpublished report at the United States Air Force Academy, Colorado, 1974, p. 14.*]

members as being competent and trustworthy. As such, they play a key role in helping the successful organization to effectively integrate its efforts and minimize disruptive conflict.

Information Potential and Functions of Key Communicators

It can be seen from our remarks in the preceding section that whether or not a particular individual will become a key communicator is not fully self-determinable. Associates in the organization have a voice in the decision. In choosing a key communicator, people will be influenced by his or her potential as a source of information. When an individual is valued by colleagues as a source of information, we refer to the individual as having a high *information potential* (Holland, 1970). An individual with a high information potential will possess more information that is of better quality and will be more accessible to the members of the organization. There is some evidence that individuals with a high information potential are more credible and of higher status and technical competence than are others in the organization (Holland, 1970).

As might be expected, key communicators must possess multiple coding abilities. They can communicate across unit boundaries. People with high information potential are described by Holland as being dynamic and active. Such qualities are consistent with the notions expressed in earlier chapters concerning the dynamic style of communication and the dynamic dimension of leadership behavior. These are qualities we would desire to encourage in certain organizational situations.

We turn now to some of the functions in the organization which can be performed by the key communicator. Menzel (1964) observed that "certain individuals tend to act as nodal points of this sort of communication; they are the carriers of news from place to place, the recipients of correspondence and the host of visiting scientists." Key communicators are the prime receivers of information that is external to their own departments or units. Information from the environment or other departments is made available to those within the department of the key communicator as he or she consults with colleagues. The coding capabilities of the key communicator permit this person to function as a boundary spanner. Thus, the key communicators serve as receivers and transmitters of information across the boundaries which result from the division of work in the external system.

The nature and importance of the key communicator's function as a "mover" of information is frequently mentioned in the literature. Holland (1974), in a follow-up to his 1970 study of informal information flow, compiled the findings of ten different investigations into the function, role, and personal attributes of the key communicator. This investigation by Holland strongly reinforces the contention that key communicators can be differentiated from others in the organization by their information potential. Key communicators possess a substantially greater quantity of information and better-quality information than is the case for their colleagues. They are also much more accessible than their colleagues and, all things considered, are vital nodal points for the organization's informal information networks.

There is also some indication that some key communicators have special creative abilities and seem able to make idea associations that their colleagues cannot (Holland, 1970). Holland (1970, 1972, 1974) also noted that the key communicators tended to have much larger internal and external networks. As a result of his or her broader sources and contacts as well as the nature of the two-step information flow, it is possible for the key communicator to shift information from narrow vertically oriented flows to broader horizontal flows. Thus, the key communicator is in a position to enhance the flow of lateral communication.

Information-sharing Norms

Before closing the chapter, we turn briefly to the matter of organizational climate and some factors which may influence the ability of the organization to utilize the key communicator and the two-step information-flow process. A number of general factors seem capable of affecting the flow of information in the informal system. We have attempted to represent some of the more important ones in Figure 21-5. You are encouraged to give this some thought and see if you can add some of your own.

Level of informal information flow (or willingness to share information)

Driving forces tending to increase informal information flow → | ← Restraining forces tending to decrease informal information flow

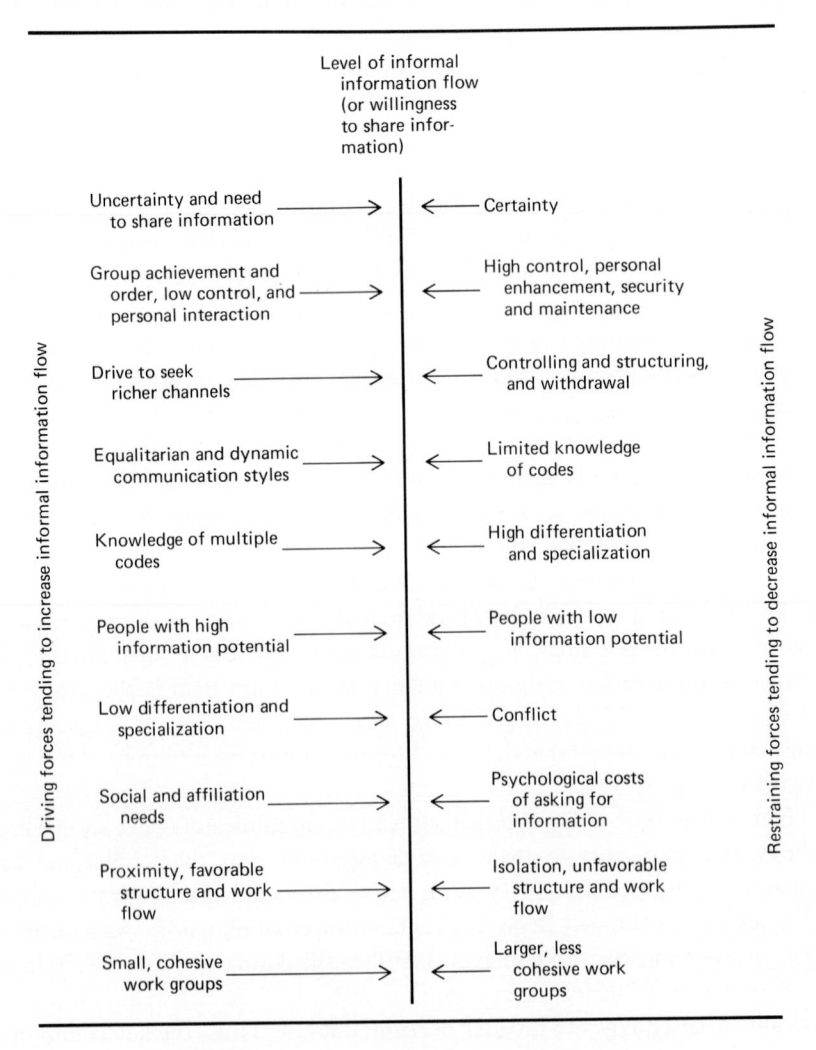

Driving forces	Restraining forces
Uncertainty and need to share information	Certainty
Group achievement and order, low control, and personal interaction	High control, personal enhancement, security and maintenance
Drive to seek richer channels	Controlling and structuring, and withdrawal
Equalitarian and dynamic communication styles	Limited knowledge of codes
Knowledge of multiple codes	High differentiation and specialization
People with high information potential	People with low information potential
Low differentiation and specialization	Conflict
Social and affiliation needs	Psychological costs of asking for information
Proximity, favorable structure and work flow	Isolation, unfavorable structure and work flow
Small, cohesive work groups	Larger, less cohesive work groups

FIGURE 21-5 Factors influencing information flow.

The notion of the diagram of Figure 21-5 is that a particular level of social activity tends to be the net result of sets of driving and restraining forces (Lewin, 1952). Driving forces tend to increase the level of the resultant, while the restraining forces tend to decrease the level of the resultant. It can be seen from this figure that many of the factors which influence informal information flow have been discussed throughout this book. As an example, a high degree of organizational differentiation is a structural factor which tends to restrict the flow of informal information. It would do so because of the coding barriers which exist for cross-unit communication.

Another example of forces which either increase or impede informal information flow is that managers who display relatively low levels of control and high levels of personal interaction are likely to exert a strong upward pressure on the level of informal information flow. If people are present who have high information potentials, then the flow is likely to be increased. Where there is a high degree of conflict, we would expect the flow of information in the informal system to be impaired. And so it would be with many other factors which have been discussed in this book.

We now wish to show how all these factors draw together and influence the quality of the organization's informal communication system. We remind the reader that the informal system can constitute a very large proportion of the total information system that is available—so it is important. Clearly, changes in any of the many factors will have an impact on the flow of informal information in the organization. Thus, it is important for each manager to be familiar with the extant forces for his or her organization so that they may be constructively used to improve informal information flows.

A manager trying to effectively utilize the factors and relationships expressed in Figure 21-5 is, in essence, concerned with improving the willingness of people in his or her organization to share organizationally relevant information. The willingness of organizational participants to share information can be thought of as an *information-sharing norm*. The manager should be aware of the information-sharing norm for his or her organization, and to the extent possible, the manager should work with the factors and relationships expressed in Figure 21-5 to improve it.

Dewhirst (1971), building on the work of Rosenbloom and Wolek, Litwin and Stringer, Allen, and others, investigated the matter of information-sharing norms among a group of scientists and engineers. He was specifically concerned with the effects of perceived information-sharing norms on the individual's behavior as an information user. An underlying factor which influences the information behavior of an individual is the psychological cost of asking others for information. To ask someone else is to concede that he or she "knows" and you "don't know." The circumstances may be such that some individuals are unwilling to ask. Their psychological makeup and the situational circumstances are such that if the information is not volunteered or available through the formal network, they will simply do without. Such individuals perceive that the organization has a low information-sharing norm, and they tend to rely solely on the formal system. But we have already seen that the formal system is incomplete.

Dewhirst argued that over time, the members of an organization do develop expectations based on what happens when they ask for information. Thus the organization does have, as part of its organizational climate, an information-sharing norm. As a result of his research, Dewhirst concluded that where the individuals in an organization perceive it to have high information-sharing norms, they will place greater reliance on the richer forms of interpersonal information channels. Where people perceive the organization to have low information-sharing norms, they tend to rely on the more formal and less personal channels.

Dewhirst further concluded that the manager is in a position to influence the information-sharing norms of the organization. The manager would do so by working with the factors and relationships expressed in Figure 21-5. We shall have a bit more to say about this in the final chapter when we discuss the role of the manager in managing the total organization information system.

SUMMARY

In this chapter we have shown that a high level of communication activity occurs in the informal communication system. Much of this activity is associated with achieving organizational purpose as people fill in the gaps of the formal plan by seeking and supplying information. Special advantages of the informal communication system include its multidirectional and boundry-spanning capabilities as well as its potential for actively involving both sender and receiver in a rich two-way exchange. Informal communication channels should not be viewed as haphazard or irrational. They can provide vitally needed slack and flexibility for dealing with unforeseen circumstances.

Evidence was presented which suggested that when people in organizations are faced with problems, stress, and uncertainty, they rely heavily on the informal channels for task-relevant information. Indeed they seem to make a trade-off in the sense that the utilization rates of informal channels increase while the utilization rates of the more formal channels decrease. Thus, the need of people for information is an important influence on the formation of informal networks. The informal system cannot easily be instantly turned on or off. The manager must strive for some minimal level of utilization in order to ensure the informal communication system will be ready when it is needed. We briefly reviewed some of the advantages that informal channels seem to possess in comparison to the formal channels. The grapevine was reviewed as an example of the informal communication system.

Informal information flow was described as a two-step process. Essentially the process was seen as a boundary-spanning device in that individuals familiar with the codes involved help mediate the flow of information across unit boundaries. These individuals were called "key communicators," and it was noted that they possess rather unique characteristics which distinguish them from their colleagues. Key communicators are a vital link in the informal system and are a key reason that this system can serve as a compensator for deficiencies of the formal system. Key communicators were described as having a high information potential, which means that their colleagues value them as sources of information.

Finally, whether or not such attributes can be effectively utilized in a given organization was seen as a function of its information-sharing norms. In the absence of high information-sharing norms, it was noted that organizational participants will rely mostly on the formal information system. This, of course, would effectively short-circuit the informal system and eliminate the opportunity to take advantage of its unique attributes. A number of factors which can enhance or impair the organization's information-sharing norms were briefly examined. It was noted that the manager will play a key role in determining whether or not such factors are effectively utilized. And thus, the manager determines whether or not high information norms will actually be present in a given organization.

IMPORTANT TERMS AND CONCEPTS

grapevine, rumor, key communicators, information-sharing norms, information potential, two-step information flow, information impedance

REVIEW QUESTIONS

1. Discuss from a communication point of view the role of the informal system in compensating for difficulties of the formal system.

2. What is meant by a "two-step information flow," and how is it related to the problem of unit and subdivision boundaries?

3. "We have no need for an informal information system in our organization. We have a completely computerized management information system which gives us everything we can possibly need." Suppose this statement were made by someone in your organization. Would you agree or disagree? Why?

4. Describe the concept of information-sharing norms. Discuss those factors which seem to influence the information-sharing norm of an organization. What are the effects of high or low information-sharing norms?

5. Inventory your own organizational experiences by thinking of a few recent critical incidents or problems. Tabulate your sources of problem-related information by informal and formal categories. Which sources were used most frequently? What are your own conclusions about the information-sharing norms of your organization?

6. In what ways are key communicators different from other people in the organization? What is their connection to the two-step information-flow process?

7. Discuss the major considerations involved if the manager is to successfully enhance the information-sharing norms of his or her organization.

8. Why do people in organizations rely on informal communication? Discuss.

9. A manager once ordered his subordinates to take action against the company grapevine. He wanted the grapevine eliminated and he particularly wished to stop "rumors" which had persisted for years. Comment on this situation.

INCIDENT: BUROC (B)

Leadership Influences on Formal and Informal Communication

This incident is based on data gathered during an in-depth investigation of interpersonal relations and communication at BUROC. See BUROC (A) for further details.

The attitude and behavioral patterns displayed by BUROC employees were by no means consistent throughout the organization. The employees of some departments seemed to display quite favorable attitudes and behavioral patterns. Informal communication in these departments was effective and often supported the organizational mission. Higher performance in selected offices seemed to result from at least two determinants: leadership style and organizational distance (physical and psychological) from the front office.

In those units which were geographically distant from the top manager's office, attitudes were noticeably more favorable toward BUROC than was the attitude at the headquarters office. Perhaps the difference in attitudes was because people in the distant offices were less subject to close control and daily contact with the top manager, his staff, and the related paperwork.

Another explanation of the favorable attitudes at distant offices could be found in the leadership styles of some key managers who were in charge of the distant offices. These managers tended to be more group-oriented and were inclined to control their subordinates less closely. People were free to use informal interpersonal communication channels as needed to perform their jobs. It is interesting to note that some of the remote departments were considered by knowledgeable people to be the best performers at BUROC in terms of mission accomplishment.

The following are random comments of various managers throughout BUROC regarding employee morale, attitude, and relationships with other departments.

Director of BUROC at Rockridge Headquarters:

> When I first came aboard, I sensed there was an attitude problem. It was evidenced by the lack of participation by employees in the payroll stock-purchase plan. Our people had no confidence in the organization and thus were unwilling to purchase its stock. I ordered the senior-level people on the headquarters staff to dedicate at least 6 percent of their income to stock purchases on a regular basis. In a very short while, stock purchases were up. I knew then that morale was improving and that attitudes were better. Purchases of stock went up dramatically.

Director of BUROC personnel at Rockridge Headquarters:

> I know we need to take more prompt action in personnel matters. Frankly, I wish we could do a lot better at this. I am afraid that no big improvement is likely. Many times the delay is caused by BUROC procedures which are unavoidable. I know of many cases in which individuals thought they were being given the runaround. They thought we were splitting hairs with them when we were actually doing our best to give an honest explanation of regulations. Where regulations are complicated, we attempt to simplify them and explain them in nontechnical language. If people don't understand, they should ask us to repeat it until they do understand.

A lower-level staff manager at Rockridge:

> Despite the efforts of the past year, no significant change or improvement has occurred. Some employees feel that management is something less than candid and that it hides behind rules and regulations. They feel it less than honest and slippery to bend the regulations when it suits management's purposes. Formal letters and certificates of award for high performance are often a sham. Some managers are just not close enough to the situation to understand who is doing what. I am tremendously overloaded and have contributed 800 hours of personal time in the past year to do my job. I don't want an award, I just want my boss to understand what's taking place.
>
> There is rarely an opportunity for liberal exchange of ideas. The boss really doesn't want my ideas. There are attempts but they usually result in a display of . . . "disinterest," "you're the expert," or "a reaction." Staff meetings are the same, "the less said, the better." It's listening only for us; the minutes of our meetings should support this observation.

Director of the Mudflats Field Office:

> I am not an expert technician or specialist. I do coordinate the efforts of specialists and technicians in my unit to make sure we achieve BUROC's mission. My people are the experts. I try to spend my time planning ahead. I avoid doing detailed operating-type work. I learned long ago that the formal organization is sometimes a roadblock to efficient communication and getting the job done. For example, there is a lack of clarity concerning the relationship between functional specialists at headquarters and here at the field office (see Figure 21-6). When should the quality

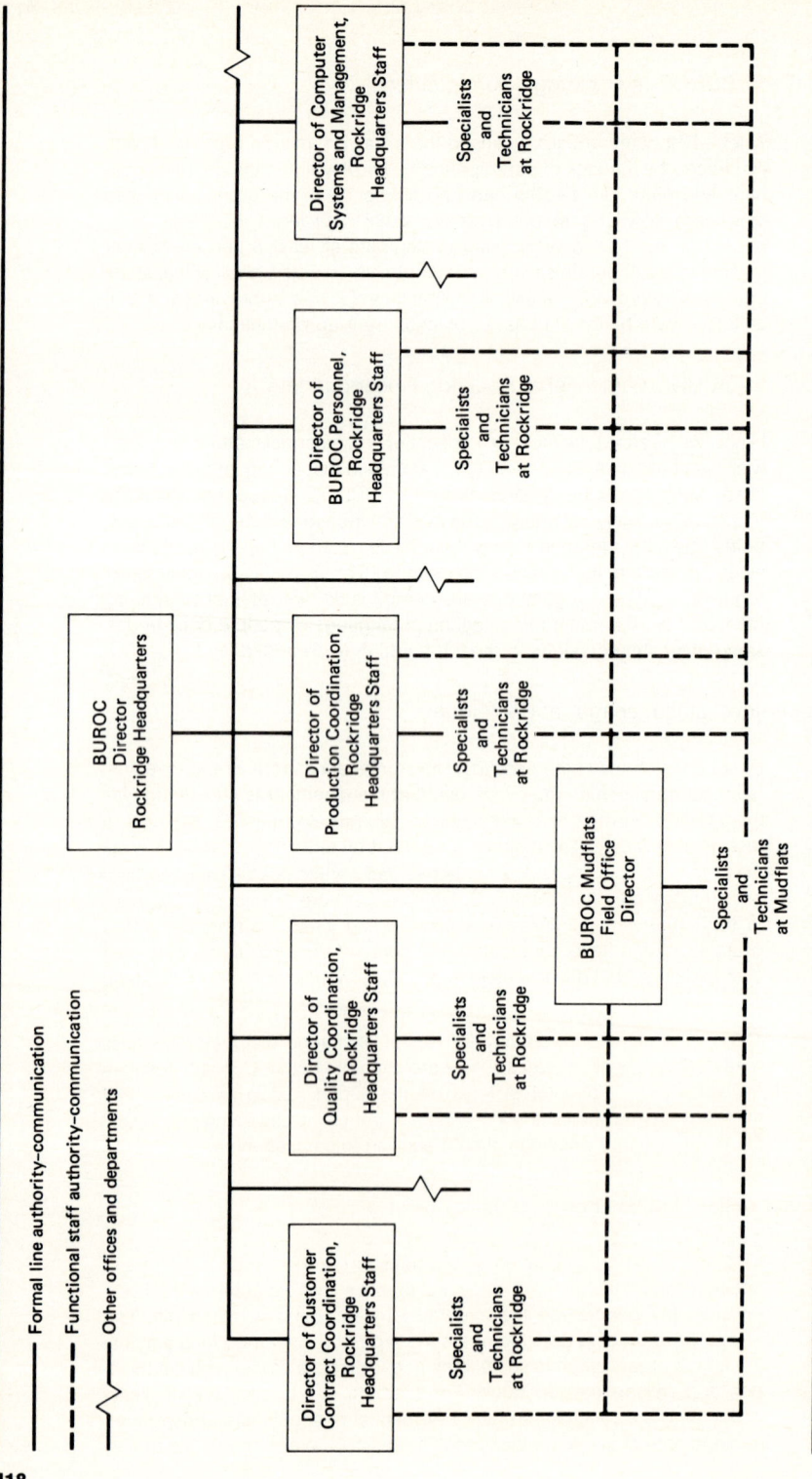

FIGURE 21-6 Partial organization chart for BUROC.

specialist at headquarters communicate directly with the quality specialist at the field office? In my experience, such roadblocks have not proven to be a serious problem. We have learned how to work around them and get the job done. We do experience some difficulty getting prompt attention from the personnel office.

With respect to our general relationship with headquarters, my first reaction is that there is too much in the way of regulation, red tape, and forms. It's difficult to get straight answers. The headquarters' staff may overreact to the director's wishes. I always check things out directly to get the story straight. The computer systems and management office is very large. I sometimes get the feeling that all they do is feed data into the computer so it can turn right around and tell them what they fed it. I tend to think that many of our technicians and specialists are adaptive, but the higher one goes in BUROC, the more we seem to be trying to structure things unnecessarily.

With respect to communication upward to headquarters, there are problems. When we pass a field office problem upward for assistance, the director's staff usually filters or distorts the situation. They don't really have rapport with him and can't go in and chat on a daily or informal basis. There is a gap between the director and his staff; they are reluctant to give him the bad news. The formal communication channel is very difficult to use.

The staff can really say no to a request without even consulting the director. He says they do not have the authority to make decisions. But they achieve the same effect by making the formal channels very difficult to use. For example, they may require the field office to conduct an extensive and costly study before requesting a change in price or packaging. Then the staff simply approves or disapproves. Why don't they do their own studies? Our resources are too limited for such extravagances.

Generally, morale is good at our field office. Our relationships are informal and we work as a team. Titles don't mean much here. We are honest with one another and have no secrets. Even when there had to be layoffs because of a drop in demand, we were very open. I worked closely with the people here and we decided just which jobs must go and under what conditions. I thought we handled the problem with much less difficulty and ill-feeling than did headquarters.

Our relationship with the personnel staff at headquarters is probably typical. Those guys up there don't discuss alternatives with us. They are unconcerned with getting the "right" person for a position. They just want to get the forms filled in properly. I might add that they don't even follow their own procedures. Most of them are too bogged down in paperwork to make a telephone call.

1. Which of these managers would you guess to have the most productive operation? Why?

2. For which of these managers would you prefer to work?

3. How would you expect each of these managers to score on the five dimensions of leadership behavior as discussed in Chapter 18?

4. What communication styles would tend to be used by each of these managers?

5. Compare BUROC headquarters at Rockridge and the Mudflats Field Office with respect to your expectations concerning the level of information sharing in each.

BIBLIOGRAPHY

Allen, T. J.: "Managing the Flow of Scientific and Technological Information," doctoral dissertation, Massachusetts Institute of Technology, Cambridge, Mass., 1966.

———: "Communications in the Research and Development Laboratory," *Technology Review*, vol. 70, pp. 31–37, October–November 1967.

———, and Stephen I. Cohen: "Information Flow in Two R&D Laboratories," *Administrative Science Quarterly*, vol. 14, pp. 12–19, 1969.

Bodensteiner, Wayne Dean: "Information Channel Utilization under Varying Research and Development Project Conditions: An Aspect of Inter-Organizational Communication Channel Usage," doctoral dissertation, The University of Texas at Austin, 1970.

Borman, E. G., W. S. Howell, R. G. Nichols, and G. L. Shapiro: *Interpersonal Communication in the Modern Organization* (Englewood Cliffs, N.J.: Prentice-Hall, Inc., 1969).

Burns, Tom: "The Directions of Activity and Communication in a Departmental Executive Group," *Human Relations*, vol. 7, pp. 73–97, 1954.

———, and G. M. Stalker: *The Management of Innovation* (London: Tavistock Publications Ltd., 1961).

Caplow, T.: "Rumors in War," *Social Forces*, vol. 25, pp. 298–302, 1946–1947.

Carlson, S.: *Executive Behavior* (Stockholm: Strombergs, 1951).

Davis, Keith: *Human Behavior at Work* (New York: McGraw-Hill Book Company, 1972).

———: "Management Communication and the Grapevine," *Harvard Business Review*, vol. 31, pp. 43–49, 1953.

Dewhirst, H. Dudley: "Influence of Perceived Information-Sharing Norms on Communication Channel Utilization," *Academy of Management Journal*, vol. 14, pp. 305–315, September 1971.

Dubin, Robert: "Business Behaviorally Viewed," in George B. Strother (ed.), *Social Science Approaches to Business Behavior* (Homewood, Ill.: Richard D. Irwin, Inc., 1962).

Fiedler, F.: "Personality and Situational Determinants of Leadership Effectiveness," in D. Cartwright and A. Zander (eds.), *Group Dynamics* (New York: Harper & Row, Publishers, Incorporated, 1968).

Gerstberger, P. G.: "The Preservation and Transfer of Technology in Research and Development Organizations," doctoral dissertation, Massachusetts Institute of Technology, Cambridge, Mass., 1971.

———, and Thomas J. Allen: "Criteria Used by Research and Development Engineers in the Selection of an Information Source," *Journal of Applied Psychology*, vol. 52, pp. 272–279, 1968.

Guest, R. H.: "Of Time and the Foreman," *Personnel Magazine*, pp. 478–486, May 1956.

Guetzkow, Harold: "Communication in Organizations," in James March (ed.), *Handbook of Organizations* (Chicago: Rand McNally & Company, 1965), pp. 534–573.

Habbe, S.: "Communicating with Employees," *Studies in Personnel Policy,* No. 129 (New York: National Industrial Conference Board, 1952).

Holland, Winford E.: "Intra- and Interorganizational Communications Behavior of Scientists and Engineers with High Information Potential," doctoral dissertation, The University of Texas at Austin, 1970.

———: "Characteristics of Individuals with High Information Potential in Government Research and Development Organizations," *IEEE Transactions on Engineering Management,* EM-19, pp. 38–44, May 1972.

———: "The Special Communicator and His Behavior in Research Organizations: A Key to the Management of Informal Technical Information Flow," *IEEE Transactions on Professional Communication,* PC-17, no. 314, September–December 1974.

Katz, Daniel, and Robert L. Kahn: *The Social Psychology of Organizations* (New York: John Wiley & Sons, Inc., 1966).

Katz, Elihu, and Paul Lazarfield: *Personal Influence: The Part Played by People in the Flow of Mass Communications* (Glenco, Ill.: The Free Press, 1955).

Kelly, Joe: "The Study of Executive Behavior by Activity Sampling," *Human Relations,* vol. 17, 1964.

Lawler, E. E., III, L. W. Porter, and A. Tannenbaum: "Managers' Attitudes toward Interaction Episodes," *Journal of Applied Psychology,* vol. 52, pp. 432–439, 1968.

Lewin, Kurt: "Group Decision and Social Change," in Guy E. Swanson et al. (ed.), *Readings in Social Psychology* (New York: Henry Holt and Company, Inc., 1952).

Menzel, H.: "The Information Needs of Current Scientific Research," *Library Quarterly,* vol. 34, 1964.

Mintzberg, Henry: *The Nature of Managerial Work* (New York: Harper & Row, Publishers, Incorporated, 1973).

Powell, James Donald, and Edward H. Goodin: "Organizational Communication: Are We Meeting the Need?" *35th Annual Proceedings of the Academy of Management,* Arthur G. Bedeian et al. (ed.), New Orleans, La., August 10–13 1975, pp. 390–392.

Rosenbloom, Richard, and Francis W. Wolek: *Technology, and Information, and Transfer: A Survey of Practice in Industrial Organizations* (Boston: Harvard University, Graduate School of Business Administration, Division of Research, 1970).

Sayles, Leonard R.: *Managerial Behavior* (New York: McGraw-Hill Book Company, 1964).

Shapero, Albert: *Management of Innovation,* reprinted from 6th International TNO Conference: Organizing for Technological Innovation (Rotterdam, March 1 and 2, 1973). Reprint in *Economics and Business,* no. 59, Bureau of Business Research, The University of Texas at Austin, 1974.

Stewart, R.: "Diary Keeping as a Training Tool for Managers," *The Journal of Management Studies,* vol. 5, pp. 295–303, October 1968.

Taylor, Robert L.: "A Study of the Effects of Security Classification Restrictions on Technical Communication," *IEEE Transactions on Professional Communications,* PC-16, pp. 194–199, December 1973.

———: "The Technological Gatekeeper: A Two-Step Flow Process for Scientific and Technical Communication," an unpublished report at the United States Air Force Academy, Colorado, 1974.

Weber, Ross A.: *Time and Management* (New York: Van Nostrand Reinhold Company, 1972).

THE EXTERNAL AND INTERNAL SYSTEM MIX AND APPROACHES TO ORGANIZATIONAL COMMUNICATION

In this chapter we will examine the manner in which two broad categories of factors affect an organization in terms of establishing the need for a particular blend of external and internal systems. The external-internal mix for a given organization, in turn, has implications for the nature of the organizational communication system. It will be shown that both environmental and interpersonal factors must be considered. Finally a number of possible approaches to organizational communication will be discussed.

Perhaps in some ways we have now completed a fully circular path in our discussion of organizational communication. Part One introduced both macro- and microviews of the topic. In Part Two a microlevel of analysis was involved as we discussed some of the important individual and interpersonal dimensions which are the heart of all human communication systems. In Part Three we progressed a bit more toward the macrolevel of analysis by building from the interpersonal foundations to the level of the small group and its processes. Finally, in closing Part Four we seek to move fully to the macrolevel of analysis by viewing the organization as an information-processing system which encompasses individual, group, structural, and environmental components.

In taking this final step, we have already seen that the organization is contrived by individuals to meet certain environmental needs. Contrived associations of humans involve a division of work and the need for integration and coordination. Organizational communication is vitally involved with the coordinative and integrative functions of management. It has also been noted that organizational communication, in the macro sense, includes formal and informal components. In this chapter we wish to continue our development of the macrolevel by examining the impact of particular external-internal system blends as they influence the character of organizational communication.

CONSIDERATIONS IN DETERMINING AN EXTERNAL-INTERNAL MIX

All organizations involve both external and internal components; the two categories do not represent an "either-or" dichotomy. Though it is convenient to separate the two for purposes of discussing the salient features of each, organizational reality is such that both systems are operative and must be dealt with. Managers will have no choice—they must deal with both the formal and informal aspects of their organizations. They may elect to concentrate on the external system, its rational plan, and the associated formal communication system. However, this will not prevent the internal system and the associated communication system from emerging.

Should the manager choose to disregard the informal system, this potentially rich and flexible means for communicating remains uncultivated and free to grow at random without regard to the mission and goals of the organization. From a communication standpoint, a substantial portion of the total information available for organizational purposes will be ignored. The organizational "unknown" is increased. Communication between the organization and its environment as well as among departments within the organization is impaired. It would be an infinitely better decision for the manager to accept the notion that the organization must seek to blend its internal and external components in a beneficial fashion.

Communication and the External-Internal Mix

Managers and others who plan and direct the organization should strive for an appropriate mix of the external and internal systems. A portion of organizational communication and behavior will be preplanned and required by the formal system. The balance of organizational communication and behavior will be permitted to emerge spontaneously as part of the informal system. Such emergent communication and behavior will provide a measure of flexibility and adaptation. The total of the behaviors present in the formal and informal systems should be sufficient for the organization to accomplish its goals. Ideally, communication and behavior in one system should complement communication and behavior in the other system.

Obviously, there will be variations in what constitutes an appropriate mix depending on the kind of organization with which we are dealing. The determining variables for the external-internal mix of a given organization can be roughly grouped into two broad categories: (1) those having to do with the certainty of the task and environment; and (2) those having to do with the nature of interpersonal relationships (particularly as they affect the organizational communication). One way of viewing the implications of these two classes of variables for the external-internal mix is represented in Figure 22-1.

We do not mean to imply with Figure 22-1 that the actual relationships would necessarily be linear as they are shown. But we do think that the general relationships expressed are representative of the situation faced by real organizations. Organizations facing a relatively certain task and environment and having an interpersonal-relations climate which is relatively unfavorable to the internal system can best implement an organization format which emphasizes the external system.

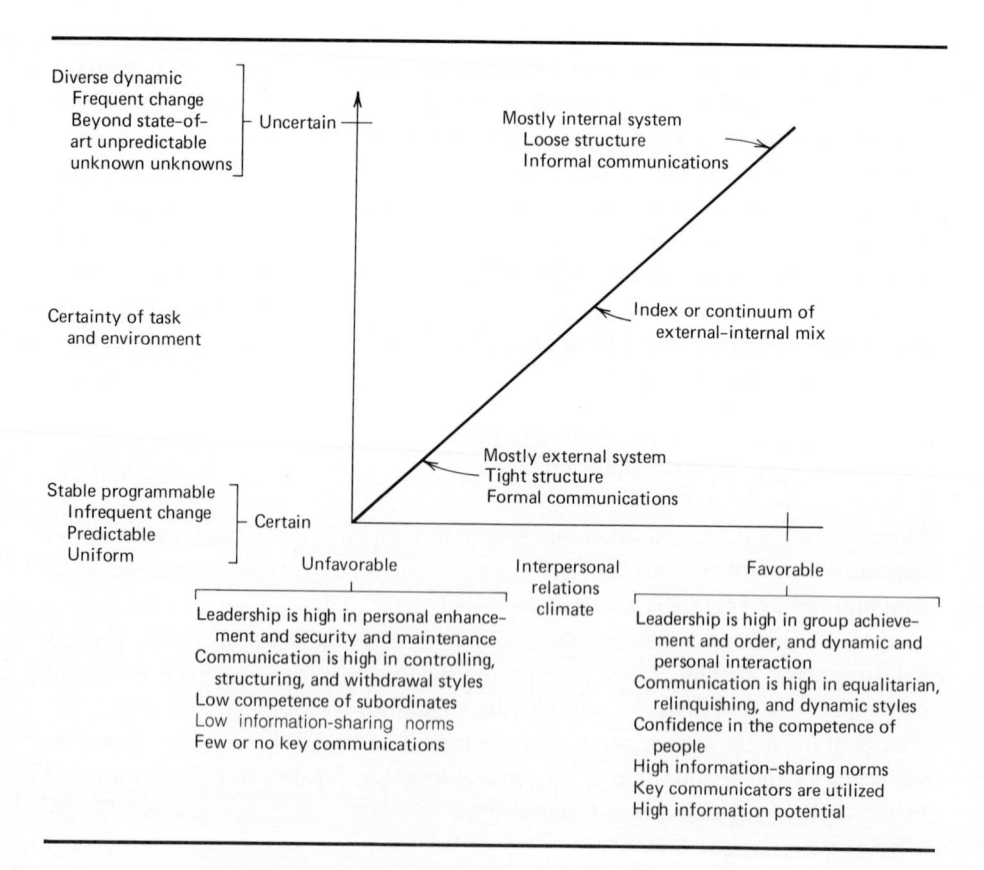

FIGURE 22-1 The determinants of external-internal systems mix.

This type of organization will have a relatively tight structure with little margin for deviation from requirements and will tend to emphasize the formal information system. Communication and coordination will be accomplished via the formal hierarchical or administrative systems. Individual activities and interactions will be explicitly spelled out as part of the organization plan.

However, even at this end of the continuum, there is still some minimum level of behavior that is clearly of an internal and informal nature. This informal phenomenon cannot be eliminated, and we would not want to eliminate the informal system even if we could. Limited informal communication and even the grapevine will persist. Davis (1972, p. 263) notes that "homicide will not work with the grapevine." Certain psychosocial as well as organizational values accrue in the informal system. At the opposite end of the external-internal mix continuum are those organizations which face uncertainty of task and environment and which possess an interpresonal-relations climate that is relatively favorable to the internal system. For this situation the internal system and the associated information system will be emphasized. At this end of the continuum we are not saying that an external system does not exist. Such a condition would be unlikely except perhaps for the smallest and simplest of organizations. However, the role and scope of the external system in organizational goal accomplishment will be considerably reduced from the organization described previously. In uncertain situations the organization is much less dependent on preplanned behavior, formal communication, and close control.

However, the emergent system and the informal information networks will be crucial in providing the organization with the flexibility it needs for dealing with the changing environment. Relative to the organization which lies at the other end of the external-internal continuum, the present one will be very loosely structured. Its membership will be working toward common goals, but beyond some very general constraints, they will not be given detailed instructions as to how they should do their jobs. Organization members will be oriented to overall goals, but will be relatively free to determine means to the desired ends. Much problem- and goal-related information will be needed. Richer face-to-face communication channels will be active.

Dealing with Certainty-Uncertainty

We will now examine the logic behind the relationships expressed in Figure 22-1 to see just how two organizations can be so different, and yet each be successful. The degree of certainty-uncertainty faced by the organization has been discussed in much of the literature as being an important influence on the design of organization structure. The certainty end of the continuum represents those organizational tasks and environments which are stable, predictable, and programmable. Change, to the extent it occurs, is slow and infrequent. Such an environment is of a uniformly static nature. If change occurs at all, it is slight and takes place gradually. The uncertainty end of the continuum represents those organizational tasks and environments which are much less stable and predictable. This situation is a dynamic one marked by such frequent and drastic change that many factors and relationships are simply not known. The technology involved or sought is beyond the state of the art and must be developed.

Perhaps examples of organizations which face the extremes of the continuum will help clarify the distinctions involved. Public utilities such as the local telephone or power company face an environment which has traditionally been stable and predictable (at least before the energy crisis). Except for the predictable growth in demand, these firms encounter about the same customers and problems year after year. Since problems can be pretty well anticipated, formal communication and behavior can be programmed to deal with them. However, a company under contract to develop and produce a passenger-carrying space shuttle system faces a quite different set of circumstances. The outcome of such an effort is quite unpredictable. Something is being attempted which has not been done before; all factors and circumstances cannot be anticipated. The task and environment faced by the first company is certain relative to the situation faced by the second company.

Information relative to the certainty-uncertainty of task and environment must be considered by managers as they establish the formal plan and structure of their organization. Should the manager place great emphasis on the formal structure when the task and environment are quite uncertain as in the second example, then the formal plan is likely to work poorly if it works at all. The organization will be locked to an inflexible plan and have difficulty adapting to change. Communication will be restricted instead of free-flowing.

As we have seen before, the manager makes certain assumptions about which activities, interactions, and sentiments will accomplish the intended goals and designs the external system accordingly. In effect, we predict which recipe will produce the cake, but in an uncertain environment this cannot be done accurately. Predictions and assumptions in an uncertain environment are subject to a high level of risk. How can one pick a technique or method in advance of knowing the problem to be faced?

Dealing with Interpersonal Relations

Along the other dimension of Figure 22-1, the interpersonal-relations continuum involves quite different variables. Here we are concerned with the impact of the many kinds of interpersonal and small-group behavioral factors which affect interpersonal competence and interpersonal relations. Though such factors have been isolated and discussed separately, we think a plausible argument can be made that their individual effects blend together in a sort of mosaic for the given total organization. Thus, many separate psychosocial factors are combined into a global or systemic effect that we can describe as an organizational interpersonal-relations climate.

In some organizations the dominant behavioral patterns will include: leadership dimensions which are oriented to group achievement and order, communication styles which are equalitarian, high information-sharing norms, confidence in the competence of people, etc. Many of the factors that are shown as driving forces in Figure 21-5 in the previous chapter could be included as variables which influence the favorable interpersonal-relations climate. Our point is simply that for an organization in which such behaviors are pervasive, the prevailing climate favors the development and utilization of the internal system. We are speaking in relative terms, of course; there are no absolutes in such matters.

We are confident that many people are capable of distinguishing the climate of the organization just described from one in which the dominant behavioral patterns are much less favorable. In some organizations we will find that leadership dimensions are oriented to personal enhancement or security and maintenance, communication styles are controlling or withdrawal, information-sharing norms are low, there is little confidence in the competence of people, etc. It clearly would be difficult to develop and utilize the internal system in such a climate. You are asked to think about this for a minute. Can you think of organizations in your own experience which were similar to these two? We think that many of you will be able to do so.

This class of variables which affect interpersonal climate present another complex problem with which the manager must grapple. A high degree of interpersonal competence will be required of the manager and others in dealing with such problems. The variables involved are of a behavioral nature. Interpersonal climate will be determined as specific personalities begin to interact in the external-system framework. Interpersonal climate is, in a sense, dependent on the internal system and can be influenced only indirectly by the manager. Indeed, it can be argued that the external-internal relationship is an inverse one. If the manager feels he or she is dealing with certainty and so specifies a highly formalized structure, then he or she must accept a truncated internal system. If on the other hand the designer views the task and environment as uncertain and chooses to emphasize the internal system, then the external system will be abbreviated. In this latter case the organization will be unstructured, people will be fairly free to determine how things should be done for themselves, and there will be a great deal of reliance placed on the informal information system. In the following section we will expand on these relationships by examining more closely the nature of mechanistic and organic organizations.

Mechanistic and Organic Organizations

Burns and Stalker (1961) characterized two general kinds of organizations which they called *mechanistic* and *organic* organizations. As a result of their investigation of a number of firms in different industries, these researchers concluded that the mechanistic type of organization was most suitable for stable conditions and that the organic type was most appropriate for changing conditions. In this section we wish to examine these two kinds of organizations with a view to understanding how they are linked to environmental circumstances and how they affect the character of organizational communication. In doing so we hope to lay a foundation for the subsequent chapter, which discusses the organization as an information-processing system.

Communication in Mechanistic Organizations. Mechanistic organizations are seen by Burns and Stalker (1961, p. 120) as involving a subdivision of overall organizational goals into task units or functions. A high degree of differentiation exists between such units and a high degree of specialization exists within subunits. Members are oriented to the technical *means* of the subunit task rather than the accomplishment of overall organizational goals or ends. There is a high degree of standardization of methods and individuals take pride in doing their jobs the "one best way."

Distinct styles of communication are present in the mechanistic organization. For example, interunit conflict which occurs at a given hierarchical level is resolved by the superior at the next higher level. Indeed, the entire structure of control, authority, and communication is of a hierarchical nature. Deviations from the hierarchical chains are not tolerated, and the substantive information of the organization tends to be located at the highest levels. Downward communication will obviously be a dominant element of organizational communication.

An admittedly extreme example of such a concentration of information is given by Burns and Stalker to make the point. The management in one company required that *all* correspondence with the company pass through the managing director, who then distributed it to the appropriate members of the organization. The managing director would then synthesize their replies into an appropriate response. Clearly such a restricted channel for the flow of information from the environment into the organization could quickly reach saturation. Overload will be a distinct possibility should the environment be subject to substantial rates of change.

It should be clear that, in the mechanistic organization, interaction patterns will tend to be of a vertical nature or between superior and subordinate. Operations and task behavior will be governed by instructions and decisions which are communicated from superior to subordinates. Loyalty to superiors and to the organization is required of all participants, and thus members tend to be oriented internally rather than toward outside associations. Members aspire for the status of position in the organization and for knowledge of its rules and procedures. Members of the mechanistic organization are not inclined to strive for some more general goal, or for excellence as judged by some external values or standards.

Communication in Organic Organizations. Organic organizations are in direct contrast to mechanistic organizations along each of these dimensions. Members are valued because they have a special knowledge or experience which can contribute to overall goal accomplishment rather than because they can do well in performing some specific task function. Of particular importance is the point that the individual's job is not rigidly specified, but rather it is continually adjusted and redefined through interaction with others. This is clearly a communicative behavior which permits the problem-solving approach to be used as unanticipated problems occur.

Since jobs are not rigidly defined, neither are responsibilities. People may not "pass the buck" by saying "that's not my responsibility." Problems cannot be passed up, down, or horizontally. Rather people acting as a team determine what behaviors are necessary to accomplish goals and solve problems. Members become committed to the organization beyond any superficial technical or legalistic requirement; they want to accomplish the goals of the organization.

Of particular interest to the study of organizational communication, omniscience is not assumed to rest just with the manager of the organization. In the organic organization, information relevant to goal accomplishment may reside anywhere in the information network. As a result, the structure is left flexible enough to permit an ad hoc center of information and control to emerge at the locus of the relevant information.

It should be clear that this characteristic is very similar to the notion of the key communicator which was discussed in the previous chapter. Lateral or horizontal communication networks tend to be developed, and individual communication is of a more consultative nature. This is in contrast with the command and directive nature of communication in the mechanistic organization. Individuals are committed to the organization's overall goals, but they wish to take pride that their organization is at the frontier of expansion and accomplishment compared to others in the field. Members aspire for recognition and accomplishment as measured against external values.

The Influence of Uncertainty and the Need to Process Information

As might be expected, mechanistic and organic forms of organizations represent the extremes of a continuum of organizational styles. In actual practice we would expect to find that many organizations would combine features of both types, but the major thrust of a given organization would tend to approximate one of the two. Burns and Stalker concluded that whether the dominant thrust would be mechanistic or organic would depend on the degree of stability or change associated with environmental circumstances. The particular mix can and does vary with the environmental circumstances.

In describing the experiences of actual companies in dealing with differing levels of environmental uncertainty and change, Burns and Stalker (1961, pp. 79–95) observed an increasing emphasis on the role of informal communication networks as more organic organizations emerged. Since they faced very stable environments, companies in the rayon industry were very mechanistic and relied on formal communication. Companies in the electrical switch-gear industry were confronted with a bit more change and instability but were able to meet their information-processing needs via committee meetings. Such meetings seem only one step removed from the more formalized means.

However, companies in the electronic industry were confronting a much less predictable environment and tended to resist detailed specification of the management task or the related communication activities. Companies in this industry were characterized as being organic. Managers in these companies were critical of the hierarchical communication system and displayed a definite reluctance to specify individual tasks and activities, communication or otherwise.

One manager, in revoking the notion of an organization chart (formalized hierarchical communication), indicated that he thought the idea of the organization chart was inapplicable in his concern and was a dangerous method of thinking about the work of industrial management (Burns and Stalker, 1961, p. 92). In organic organizations written communication was discouraged and personal interaction was considered essential in getting the job done. Since jobs were not rigidly defined, individuals were continually working with others in solving organizational problems as they emerged. Thus, in a sense, members were continually redefining their jobs based on the needs of the situation.

It should be clear that the organic type of organization will involve some degree of personal discomfort in that individuals are uncertain as to their specific roles. Still, individuals in such a company come to have a very good sense of the overall goals of the organization, and thus are in a position to judge what must be done to achieve them. Such an active role can produce its own psychological reward, and it does permit adaptive responses to changing circumstances. For organizations which face uncertainty, the vague but flexible organization and communication system may be the most rational system. It is our contention that this would be the case. We think the mechanistic-organic mix should be matched to the circumstances of the particular organization's environment. The achievement of such a match has implications for the organization's communication systems.

THE MECHANISTIC-ORGANIC MIX AND ORGANIZATIONAL INFORMATION NEEDS

It can be seen from the discussion of the preceding section that the effectiveness of a particular mechanistic-organic mix is at least partially determined by the nature of the organization's environment. The key factor in determining the appropriate proportions of mechanistic and organic qualities depends on the organization's information environment; that is, how much and what kind of information it must process. The organization is an information-processing medium and is linked to its environment by the flow of information.

Perhaps the impact of this information linkage to the environment can be best visualized by considering the relationships expressed in Figure 22-2. As the diversity and uncertainty of the organization's environment increase, increasing amounts of differentiation and integration are required if the organization is to be successful. Specifically, in the face of increasing environmental uncertainty, the organization and its integrating mechanisms must somehow process more informa-

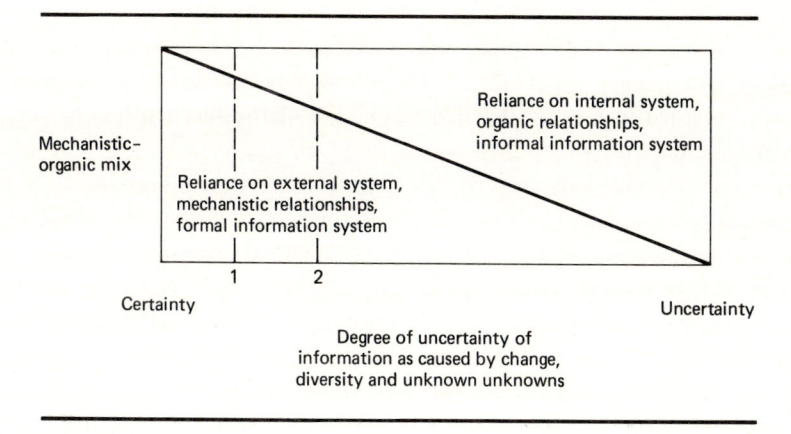

FIGURE 22-2 The mechanistic-organic mix and information demand of the environment.

tion. There are two general methods by which the organization can provide this additional information-processing capability. Additional information-processing capacity can be provided using either mechanistic or organic processes.

It can be seen then from Figure 22-2 that the mechanistic and organic aspects of an organization can complement one another with the particular mix being varied in accordance with the certainty-uncertainty of the information which is encountered. Now, there can be a problem with all this. Managers and others who design and plan organizations tend to focus on the mechanistic aspects of the organization in doing their planning. This is a natural tendency; most of us think first of organization charts, administrative manuals, and management information systems when we think of organizations.

However, as we have seen, there is another part of the organization which tends to emerge whether we consciously plan or design for it or not. This emergent aspect is a major component of the organic aspects of the organization, and its emergence will thus influence the mechanistic-organic mix. As an example, suppose that environmental circumstances are such that perpendicular number one (1) in Figure 22-2 represents the proper mechanistic-organic balance. However, interpersonal relationships in the company are such that the emergent organic effects are more on the order of that represented at perpendicular number two (2). It is not possible to say at which point the mismatch becomes a problem, but perceptive managers should be able to make some judgments about their own organizational situations if they understand that such relationships exist.

Further, it can be seen that whatever the particular mechanistic-organic proportions, it is desirable to obtain a favorable interface between the two. The mechanistic-organic interface is represented by the diagonal line in Figure 22-2. As has been noted elsewhere, we wish the two systems to be supportive of one another. In the next chapter, we will examine some factors which influence the mechanistic-organic proportion and the quality of the interface between the two systems, but for now, we turn to a more detailed discussion of the mechanistic and organic information alternatives.

Given that organizations must be able to process increasing amounts of information as the environment becomes less certain, we find that the designers or managers of organizations have a choice of two general means for doing so. They may choose to provide the needed information capacity via formalized (mechanistic or required) means or they may choose to use informal information flows (organic or emergent means). As we have seen, the choice will influence the character of organizational communication. Should management elect to supply information in a mechanistic fashion, organizational communication will be marked by formalized, documented, and directive communication. On the other hand, should the choice be for a more organic method of supplying information, organizational communication will be informal, free-flowing, and predominantly of a maintenance type. Several examples of each approach to organizational communication will be discussed in the following sections.[1]

Mechanistic Communication Approaches

Rules and Programs. At the lowest levels of uncertainty, rules and programs can suffice to provide the operating information needed by the organization. Where tasks and relationships are fairly predictable and unchanging, the rules and programs of the external system are adequate to permit the organization to function. Such an organization would be of a predominantly mechanistic nature; the behavior of participants would be largely determined by the information supplied via the formalized system. We might indicate the mechanistic-organic proportions of such an organization by a perpendicular such as that shown by one (1) in Figure 22-2. Organizations operating at this level of uncertainty can rely to a significant degree on programs for coordination and integration. Communication will be aimed at supplying needed programs and instructions to participants and at providing feedback regarding performance results.

Hierarchical Referral. Managers in an organization facing a slightly more uncertain circumstance may find it necessary to deviate somewhat from a strict reliance on rules and programs. Where an occasional and substantial change that is unpredictable occurs, rules and programs will be insufficient. Information concerning this change cannot be handled with routine rules and programs because it cannot be anticipated, but it can be referred to a higher level of the hierarchy as an exception. Such a referral process is less mechanistic than the previous example, but it still uses what is essentially the formal information system to deal with the problem. Problems are obviously referred through channels along the chain of command. This organization would probably fall slightly to the right of the first one on the scale of Figure 22-2; it would be somewhat more organic. This seems an appropriate adaptation, but problems can occur where the exceptions occur frequently enough to overload the hierarchical information system. The referral mechanism is a common one and is employed by many companies; it is sometimes called *management by exception.*

Goal Setting. Progressing a step beyond the previous examples, we might imagine an organization which is still substantially mechanistic but does provide for a bit

---

[1]The several approaches for meeting the organization's information-processing needs are discussed in depth by Galbraith (1969). The material in this section is based on the concepts expressed by this author.

more organic support of its information processes. Rather than program the behavior of operants in detail, some managers may *set goals* (not management by objectives) for subordinates, who would then be free to supply the appropriate behavior to accomplish the goals. This would obviously permit an added degree of organic behavior. Still, even in this case the dominant element of the organization would be its mechanistic aspects. The management would do extensive planning to ensure that the various subunit goals are effectively integrated. There still would be a substantial use of the formal information system for providing budget or other performance-related data to control subunit performance. Formal reports would be required to provide performance-type data to management. Such an organization might also make use of programs and referral as in the previous examples.

Again, as before, it is possible that in some environments, uncertainty may reach such a level that the goals and related plans are no longer valid. At the level of uncertainty which renders rules, programs, plans, and goals inadequate, the organization has two final categories of alternatives: (1) to seek some means for reducing the organization's need for information processing or (2) to further increase its capacity to process information. Each approach has its mechanistic and organic features. Mechanistic means for each approach will be discussed in this section and discussion of the organic aspects of each alternative will be reserved for the subsequent section.

Providing Slack. When the organization finds its information environment to be so uncertain that rules and programs, hierarchical referral, and goal setting are inadequate to provide the necessary coordination, it may then turn its efforts to reducing the need to process information. Under this alternative, managers and planners would begin to adjust targets and goals as the exceptions reach such a level that the hierarchical information system is overloaded. You may have seen examples of this in your own experiences with organizations.

Manufacturing organizations may quote delivery times of such length that there is only a very slight probability that unexpected problems will overload the company's information-processing capabilities. Other examples would be to increase budget targets or to provide buffer inventories. It should be clear that such methods have the effect of providing slack resources by extending limits or standards. Such a change does keep the information requirements within the limits of the organization's capacity. However, this occurs because the organization has redefined its tolerances so that an exception is less likely to occur.

Such an approach does have its costs. If budget targets are raised, then larger budgets are required. If delivery times are extended, customers may be lost, and buffer inventories do cost money. This is not to say that such alternatives should not be used. It will be necessary for management to consider the costs of the various information-processing alternatives before a choice is made.

Product Groups. Another approach that reduces the need for information processing is to restructure the organization into some sort of output-oriented grouping. For example, product groups might be organized. Each such unit would be designed such that it contained the necessary inputs and resources to achieve the required output. Using this strategy, one multiproduct organization involving the integration of numerous functional-skill inputs to simultaneously produce its several products would become several smaller organizations. Each smaller organization would have the necessary skill and resource inputs for its single-product output. Changes of this sort are clearly a modification of the external system. The work of the organization is divided according to different criteria than had previously been the case.

Several information-processing advantages may result from such a change. One advantage would be that the change eliminates cross-pressures caused as one information system seeks to meet the conflicting needs of several sets of customers as they compete for the output of a single set of resources. After the change, each customer or product is served by its own set of resources. Conflict is less likely to create a barrier to communication and coordination. Another possible advantage to this approach is that it generally leads to a reduced level of specialization because a given unit is confronted with lower demand levels. High levels of work subdivision and specialization are economic only for high levels of demand and production. The information consequence of reduced subdivision specialization is a lower level of interdependence and therefore a reduced need for coordination and communication. With the reduced level of specialization, we would also expect to find less differentiation and fewer barriers to communication. Coding differences would be less of a problem.

Finally, we should note that this strategy has its costs which must be considered before it is accepted in preference to any of the others which have been mentioned. There seem to be at least two significant costs for this particular strategy. One is the cost of duplicative resources. Similar skill resources will probably be needed in each of the product groups. This can be wasteful to the extent that a given skill can be only partially utilized in each unit because the demands are low. The effect is that a person with the appropriate skills may be assigned full time even though his or her skills are not gainfully employed on a full-time basis. Another cost of this strategy is that the advantages of specialization may be lost. We have seen that the loss of specialization can be a favorable circumstance, but it can also mean a loss of production efficiency where the demand levels actually justify specialization.

To reduce the organizational need for information processing by either creating slack resources or the creation of product groups still involves essentially mechanistic means. In the case of either strategy, we are relying on the external system and the formal communication system to provide the necessary information-handling capacity. If we were to place these last two strategies on Figure 22-2, the creation of slack resources would be similar to goal setting in terms of its mechanistic-organic proportions. Perhaps the use of product groups would involve a slightly greater emphasis on the organic aspects and therefore this strategy would be placed slightly to the right of the others in the figure.

Finally, the manager may decide that uncertain environmental situations can be dealt with by increasing the capacity of the organization to process information. Of the two specific alternatives involved here, one is quite mechanistic and will be discussed in this section and the other will be covered in the following section since it is of an organic nature.

Increasing Vertical Information Capacity. Some organizations respond to the need for greater information-processing capabilities by increasing their vertical information systems. Such an increase would obviously negate the possibility of overload. This step might be taken when it appears that previous plans, goals, and referral systems are no longer sufficient to prevent overload. As the problem becomes apparent, management might elect to implement periodic replanning to meet the needs of changing circumstances. However, more resources will be required to accomplish such planning. Examples of the kinds of additional resources required to handle the information load or replanning would be additional clerks, computer time, and computer hardware and software. Clearly, the use of computer facilities will involve some specific formalized languages, and all such changes amplify the mechanistic nature of the organization. The costs associated with this approach are the costs of the additional resources that are provided.

Whether or not investment of funds is justified will be determined by the nature of the information which the expanded vertical system must process. Galbraith (1969) observes that if the relevant data are formalized and quantifiable, the expanded vertical information system will work quite well. We noted earlier in this section that some organizations can be quite successful with a highly centralized structure and close control. The keys to such success are the effectiveness of the formal communication system and how well the structure of the organization matches the environmental situation. Perhaps you are familiar with companies which successfully employ centralized information-processing systems of this sort. However, we must offer the caveat that such systems may not be successful if the data to be processed are qualitative and vague. Under these uncertain circumstances it would be better to rely on the more organic mechanisms.

Organic Communication Approaches

There remains one other approach to the problem of providing a means for processing additional information in the uncertain environment. The final alternative is of a much more organic nature than any of the alternatives discussed previously, and it is capable of operating with qualitative and vague data inputs. The basic concept involves the facilitation of lateral relationships. Decisions are made at the locus of the problem where the information relevant to its solution is often found.

Usually this means that decision making is diffused into the lower hierarchical levels as opposed to being concentrated at higher levels via vertical information systems. Such an approach is one form of decentralization and can result in a somewhat horizontal expansion of the information system. Communication channels which operate horizontally and diagonally will be more fully developed and utilized under this alternative. In many cases lateral relationships can be improved without any formal reorganization or further development of the formal system. The manager simply gives subordinates more freedom with respect to the kinds of decisions they can make and the time period for which they are left to their own devices. The manager's methods of communication and control are much less mechanistic. In other cases, lateral relationships can be developed via formalized changes which would be of a mechanistic nature. However, the major thrust of our discussion in this section is aimed at the informal facilitation of lateral relationships since such an approach is more clearly organic.

Legitimizing Direct Lateral Contact. One way to expand lateral relationships is to legitimize *direct contact* between those who are experiencing a problem and those who possess the information which can solve it. As an example, in a certain class of problems, a direct contact between sales and engineering might prove more expeditious than some referral of information through the hierarchical system. If the engineers working on a new product need certain information about the needs of the customer, why can they not go directly to the salespeople who have the needed information?

According to Davis (1972), specialized functions and staff in some organizations develop a high rate of lateral communication activity. Though people in such positions are often formally assigned lateral communication activities, they tend to have little formal authority. People in these situations frequently find that effective interpersonal relations and interpersonal competence are the keys to success. They learn to use persuasion and interpersonal influence to expand lateral communication. Some organizations permit and encourage such contacts and others do not; our point is that the informal communication system has a rich potential to provide a valued service of this type. This is precisely the kind of service that the key communicators and others in the organic organization can provide.

In encouraging such linkages, the manager does run the risk of losing control of the organization. Under these circumstances, the manager may not be fully aware of all that is taking place. Still, as was noted in the previous chapter, people want to use these kinds of information relationships, and they can be a valuable asset in filling in the gaps of the formal system. It should be noted that the manager would experience great difficulty in formalizing such contacts. The manager may not be able to adequately anticipate the occurrence of problems, the nature of problems, or who might possess the information needed to solve them.

Providing Liaison. In those situations where the volume of such problem-related contacts across certain subunit boundaries becomes sufficiently large, the manager may elect to assign the responsibility for *liaison* between units to some individual. This, of course, would be a specialized function and can possibly be a formalized or mechanistic aspect of the organization. However, as was noted in Figure 20-5, the research of Dalton and his associates suggests that successful organizations provide integration via a variety of means. Some methods are definitely organic; others are mechanistic.

Beyond liaison, the manager may implement task forces or teams to bridge the boundaries between various separate specialties involved in a common problem. A *task force* is composed of representatives from the different units and is of a temporary nature. When the problem has been solved, the members of the task force return to their normal assignments. An example of a task force would be a group formed by using representatives from all departments in a university to oversee the implementation of a new computer system which is intended to serve the needs of all departments. Once the system is in operation such a task force could then be dissolved.

A similar group of representatives which exists on a *continuing* basis is called a *team*. One can find many examples of this method for enhancing the lateral flow of information. An admissions committee which reviews applications for certain programs of study at a university is one example. This team includes faculty members from the various fields of study, each of whom is concerned with ensuring that the selected candidates are qualified to study in his or her respective field. In a business organization we might see budget teams or product teams formed to deal with the problems of operating budgets or products which cut across departmental lines and require attention on a continuing basis.

Such teams can be formalized as a part of the mechanistic organization, as when the manager sees fit to establish a matrix form of organization. Matrix organizations are formed by assigning a team manager who has formal authority to integrate cross-functional efforts to the extent they affect the team's mission. Thus, those who are on the team have two superiors—one functional boss and one team boss. Such an approach is made in response to the need to provide formalized leadership and decision making that is of a lateral orientation.

Though such roles may be formally assigned to product managers, project managers, and others within the formal system, matrix-type relationships may also emerge in the informal system. Certain key individuals come to be recognized as sources of information, influence, and power. Others in the organization, perhaps even managers, recognize these key people as being uniquely qualified to provide integration for a given mission or product. They span boundaries and provide mission-relevant information to the various functional units.

This need not be a formal assignment at all; key people can function as informal leaders and boundary spanners simply because their colleagues accept them as such. Management can grease the skids by not interfering with this type of informal lateral communication. Artificial barriers and restrictions should not be needlessly inserted. Albaum (1964) observes that though such lateral communication is frequently relied on by management, it is sometimes inadequate. He suggests that lunchrooms, recreation rooms, and coffee hours can be arranged to benefit interaction across functional boundaries. We would add that sufficient thought given to the physical layout of plant and building can also be generally beneficial. Managers and architects sometimes seem to go to great lengths to provide physical barriers that deter human interaction and isolate people from one another.

Indeed, there are managers who chastize people for communicating with others outside their functional units. Managers of this type are very restrictive of direct lateral contacts and insist that their subordinates use the formal chain of command. There is a need for some restriction, of course, but we do feel there is a risk involved. Undue restriction on informal lateral communication creates the risk of interdepartmental isolation, conflict, and the many other types of dysfunctional consequences we have discussed before. The problem is an especially acute one should the organization face a diverse and uncertain environment.

SUMMARY

This chapter has been aimed at moving the reader toward a macrolevel of analysis by viewing organizational communication from a global perspective. The need for an external-internal system mix and its influence on organizational communication has been stressed.

The mechanistic-organic proportion for a given organization was seen to be a function of two general groups of factors. One such group includes those factors which tend to influence the uncertainty, diversity, and stability of the organization's environment and situation. In the face of higher levels of uncertainty, the organization should place a greater reliance on organic processes and the informal information system. Under more certain, homogeneous, and stable conditions, a greater reliance can be placed on mechanistic processes and the formal information system.

A second group of factors which affect the mechanistic-organic mix of a particular organization has to do with the determinants of the organization's interpersonal-relations climate. It is of particular importance that the manager and other key organizational personnel are capable of effective interpersonal relationships and enhancing the organization's information-sharing norm. The interpersonal factors will be particularly crucial for those organizations faced with uncertain environmental circumstances and the need to enhance organic modes.

Under predominantly mechanistic communication alternatives, organizational communication tends to be formal, documented, and hierarchical. The alternatives available to the manager in providing adequate flows of information include the use of rules and programs, hierarchical referral, goal setting, the provision of slack, the use of product groups, and the provision of additional vertical information capacity.

Under predominantly organic communication alternatives, organizational communication tends to be informal, ad hoc, and of a maintenance nature. The alternatives available to the manager for providing adequate information flows here include the legitimizing of informal lateral contacts and providing means for liaison between organizational units.

IMPORTANT TERMS AND CONCEPTS

mechanistic organizations, organic organizations, external-internal mix, mechanistic-organic mix, mechanistic information alternatives, organic information alternatives, rules and programs, hierarchical referral, goal setting, providing slack, product groups, vertical information capacity, legitimize lateral contact, providing liaison

REVIEW QUESTIONS

1. Discuss the concept of an external-internal system mix. What factors influence the mix and what is the implication for the nature of organizational communication?

2. What kinds of factors influence the certainty-uncertainty continuum faced by the organization? How will organizational communication be affected?

3. Discuss some possible communication strategies for dealing with differing levels of environmental and situational uncertainty.

4. Distinguish mechanistic communication systems from organic communication systems.

5. Consider some organization with which you are familiar. Where do you feel it is located on the uncertainty continuum of Figure 22-2? Is the mechanistic-organic mix of this organization a proper one? Why or why not?

6. Apply the concept of information-sharing norms (see Chapter 21) to the notion of organic organizations. With what factors must the manager work to achieve a successful organic approach to communication?

INCIDENT: A FAILURE TO COMMUNICATE?

The modern American automobile assembly plant is perhaps one of our best-known examples of management planning and "know-how." People in other nations have often admired our accomplishments in the manufacture of automobiles and have imported our technology and management systems for their own industries.

A crucial component of the complex American system is the highly sophisticated computerized information system which controls the flow of raw materials, component parts, and assembly operations. The system is capable of bringing together the precise combination of skills and parts to produce just the auto ordered by Sam Jones at the dealer's showroom in Mudflats, Texas, six weeks earlier. The accomplishment is all the more amazing when we realize that there are millions of Sam Joneses, each wanting something different. Each automobile involves thousands of parts and as many as 10 million autos are produced each year in the United States. The amount of data and information involved is overwhelming.

At the Rockridge assembly plant of a major American manufacturer something went wrong with the information system. This particular plant assembles two types of cars, the Eagle and the Cheetah, for the company's two major divisions. Though in final form the Eagle and Chettah appear to be quite different, each is actually constructed from the same basic body shell.

The basic body shell, the so-called "Z body," is assembled at Rockridge from Z body shell halves which are shipped by rail from the stamping plant. Chettah and Eagle Z body shell halves are distinguishable only by experts and differ mostly with respect to certain openings and attachment points. Two Z body halves are first placed in a jig which holds them in proper position for automatic welding, and the wedded halves then proceed down the line to be matched with chassis, fenders, doors, engine, drive-line, and other components which make them a Cheetah or an Eagle.

Both Eagles and Chettahs are moving along the same line in accordance with the plan set forth by the computerized information system. The plan tells each worker what must be done to each auto as it moves past his or her position on the line. One Eagle is a black four-door sedan, the next Cheetah is a bright-red hard top. One auto has air conditioning and myriad power options and the next is standard and void of options. If one were to consider all possible combinations and options for the two makes, the variety is almost limitless. Rarely will two identical autos move down the line.

Each worker along the line becomes wrapped up in his or her own operation. He or she tries to stay up with the steady pace of the line and may lose sight of what is taking place at other stations along the line. One tends to set a machine-like pace and just methodically "hang things on" as the auto moves down the line.

It is said that a peculiar thing happened at Rockridge one day. It seems that a Cheetah

Z body half was welded to an Eagle Z body half and the unit moved substantially far along the line before anybody noticed. Components were being added along the line and a hybrid Cheetah-Eagle was being constructed at Rockridge. A later check revealed that a programming error had initiated the problem. However, it is of interest to note that the auto was substantially completed before inspectors detected the error.

1. The problem of this incident might have been avoided had people at Rockridge been aware of the interplay of formal and informal information systems. Discuss.

2. The data of the management information system does not guarantee productivity and efficiency. Why?

3. Some managers would prefer that assembly-line workers not waste time in small talk. Why is this a dangerous practice?

BIBLIOGRAPHY

Albaum, Gerald: "Horizontal Information Flow: An Exploratory Study," *Academy of Management Journal,* vol. 7, pp. 21–33, March 1964.

Burns, Tom, and G. M. Stalker: *The Management of Information* (London: Tavistock Publications Ltd., 1961).

Davis, Keith: *Human Relations and Organizational Behavior,* 4th ed. (New York: McGraw-Hill Book Company, 1972).

Galbraith, J. R.: "Organizational Structure and Communications," a revised version of Sloan School of Management Working Paper No. 425–69, Massachusetts Institute of Technology, 1969. Reprinted in David A. Kolb, Irwin M. Rubin, and James McIntyre, *Organizational Psychology,* 2d ed. (Englewood Cliffs, N.Y.: Prentice-Hall, Inc., 1974).

23

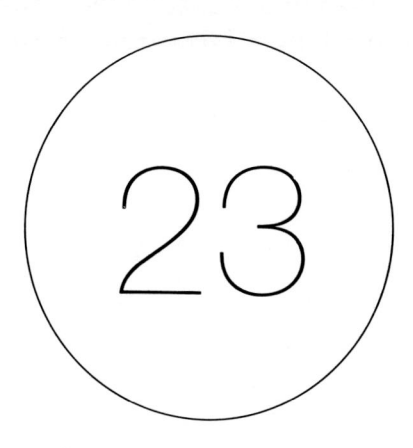

MANAGING ORGANIZATIONAL COMMUNICATION

In this chapter we will examine five major subsystems which seem to be operative for any fully developed organization and briefly discuss their information and communication needs. Whether or not the organizational communication system effectively meets such needs is determined by how well managers and other key individuals are able to implement both formal and informal information flows. Finally, the organization will be viewed as an information-processing system having communication links to its environment as well as internally between subunits.

It has been argued in the previous chapter that organizational communication, in the global sense, consists of both the formal and informal communication systems. It is the total of all documents, reports, written correspondence, computer printouts, manuals, charts, forms, and other contrived paraphernalia plus whatever interpersonal forms of job-related communication may emerge in a given organization. Such a global system not only is operative within the organization but also functions to link the organization and its environment. It is the function of management to manage this complex information network. As was noted by Banard (1938), "The first function of the executive is to develop and maintain a system of communications." Perhaps the magnitude of such an assignment can best be recognized by considering the range of activities that are involved for the typical organization.

ORGANIZATIONAL SUBSYSTEMS AND THEIR INFORMATION AND COMMUNICATION NEEDS

Katz and Kahn (1966) note that five significant subsystems are operative in most fully developed organizations: production, maintenance, boundary, adaptive, and managerial. Each subsystem will involve its own peculiar character of communication. The nature, function, and communication needs of each subsystem will be discussed in the following paragraphs.

Production Subsystem. The production subsystem is concerned with the efficient production of the organization's primary goods or services. The focus of this subsystem is the product or service which the organization supplies to its customers, and thus it is operative along the mainstream of the organization's means-ends chain. It is this function which often gives rise to the need for division of work, specialization, and the consequent need for communication and coordination.

The obvious information needs for this subsystem include information that is relevant to the choice of product or service, production quantities needed, production processes, coordination, etc. Much of this information can be provided via the formal communication system. Production-related organizational communication receives a great deal of attention in the day-to-day operations of the organization. Communication of this sort tends to be mechanistic in nature.

Maintenance Subsystem. The maintenance subsystem mediates between task demands and human needs to keep the production system functioning. Much of this subsystem is formalized by establishing procedures and systematic processes intended to assure that human behavior will be consistent with the needs of the production subsystem. Activities here would include recruiting, training and indoctrination, rewarding and sanctioning. Again, much of this function is provided via the formal communication system and this system can be quite mechanistic in nature. However, there is the risk that some managers may overlook the value of the internal system and the informal communication system as supplements to the external system in providing the needed maintenance for both production and human subsystems.

Boundary Subsystem. The boundary subsystems link the organization to its environment in two different ways, each of which involves significant levels of communication activity. One such linkage is production-oriented in that it provides the necessary inputs of materials and labor from the environment. Obviously, there will be significant information flows across organizational boundaries in connection with such inputs and outputs. Organizational communication for this subsystem can be purely mechanistic. However, as was noted previously, this can seriously restrict flexibility. Inflexibility is dangerous when the environment is uncertain. It should be noted that coding, filtering, and the availability of key communicators functioning as links in the two-step flow of information will be of great importance here.

A second boundary linkage is seen by Katz and Kahn as being of an institutional nature. This linkage is almost entirely of an informational character since it involves legitimatizing the organization to the rest of its environment. Two-way information flows will be required if the organization is to stay abreast of the laws and requirements of the social system in which it operates and, in turn, convince others in the social community that its continued existence is desirable. For some boundary applications, the approach to organizational communication should be organic in nature. In some situations, there is a need to be flexible and innovative and to use professional-caliber people in meeting the challenge of rapidly changing cultural norms and values.

Adaptive Subsystem. The fourth major subsystem is one which is oriented to ensuring that the organization will make adaptive responses to technological and economic changes in its environment. It should be clear that significant information flows will be involved in the successful implementation of this subsystem. The organization must have information which indicates that changes are necessary. Also, the process of researching, planning, and developing the actual adaptive responses will involve significant levels of communication behaviors. Adaptive responses to an uncertain environment are difficult to achieve with only the formal system and its associated mechanistic communication system. Here again, organic approaches may be desirable. Adequate preplanned mechanistic systems are not feasible for rapidly changing industries.

Managerial Subsystem. Finally, there is the managerial subsystem which is intended to oversee the activities of all other subsystems and minimize disruptive conflict while integrating diverse activities into a meaningful whole. The manager's job in doing so is essentially one of communication. As we have seen, upwards of 90 percent of the manager's time is consumed in communicating with others. If you have ever performed a managerial-type job, you have probably experienced this for yourself. We turn now to a further discussion of the managerial role and influence.

THE MANAGER'S INFLUENCE ON ORGANIZATIONAL COMMUNICATION

In carrying out his or her largely communicative role of integrating diverse functions, the manager has a choice of two general communication systems, formal and informal. Rather than make a choice between the two systems, we have seen that the manager strives to have the informal system effectively support the formal system. Whether or not such a supportive relationship is achieved is a function of the prevailing information-sharing norms of the organization. We have seen that a number of factors exist which influence the climate for interpersonal relations, and that a number of these factors are subject to some degree of control by the manager. Indeed, it can be argued that the interpersonal competence of managers influences that aspect of interpersonal relations that has been identified as the organization's information-sharing norms. Thus, whether or not the organization effectively utilizes its informal communication system will be significantly influenced by the interpersonal competence of its managers and other key people.

Managers and Restricted Organizational Communication

A number of authors have concluded that the interpersonal-relations climate and, in turn, organizational communication is significantly influenced by the manager. Barth (1971) investigated perceived communication problems and interpersonal-climate characteristics for a number of R&D groups and concluded that the quality of interpersonal relations was an important determinant of task-related information exchange. Jain investigated the effectiveness of hospital supervisory personnel in communicating and stated that:

> However, in order for the communication to be effective between the supervisor and his subordinates, it must be preceded by a climate of belief. This can be brought about by building employee confidence and trust in leadership. In other words, the supervisor must share information with his subordinates, consult with them on matters of mutual interest and settle their grievances promptly. [Jain, 1973]

Davis also recognized the key role played by management in establishing a climate which is favorable to organizational communication. He states that:

> If top managers establish sound information exchange with their associates and insist that their associates do likewise with

others, this spirit of information sharing tends to cover the whole institution. A successful communication program, therefore, depends on top management to initiate and spark it. [Davis, 1972, p. 385]

According to Davis (1972, p. 383), the result of some research suggests that productivity and performance is associated with the openness of communication between managers and their subordinates. We now wish to examine this important influence of the manager more closely.

In the following discussion, our main focus will be on the manager's influence on the willingness of organizational participants to share information via the informal communication system. Our discussion is restricted to managers as a matter of convenience. In reality, there are influential people who have an impact on the information-sharing norms of the organization but who are not managers. Included in this group would be the informal leaders of various small groups and the key communicators. We are interested in all those who significantly influence the flow of information in both the formal and informal communication systems.

An attitude of willingness to share information via the informal system results from a number of driving and restraining forces (see Figure 21-5). It seems clear that the manager can affect the level of such driving and restraining forces and, in turn, the willingness of organizational members to share information. As an example, managers can affect the degree to which their own behavior and the behavior of their subordinates are of a personal-enhancement or security and maintenance nature. Or, leaders of small groups can work to establish a climate which minimizes the psychological discomfort of asking for advice.

Management can also influence the willingness of people to share information by the manner in which it structures the organization and determines work flows. Does the manager deliberately attempt to discourage the formation of small groups? Does the manager insist that employees use only the formal hierarchical communication channels, that they avoid talking to one another? Perhaps you have experienced situations where supervisors reprimanded subordinates for directly consulting with the operatives of other units for job-relevant information.

One can argue (and this kind of supervisor usually does) that such action bypasses the chain of command. However, where such direct informal contact is efficient and gets the job done, why not encourage it? Direct informal contact reduces the likelihood of overloading the hierarchical channels with problems which can be handled directly by those closest to them. This is not to say that we should do away with formal hierarchical channels. We are simply saying they should not be used where they are inefficient.

Unfortunately, some managers and other key people in the organization tend to become "locked in" to the formal channels. They see the use of an informal channel in lieu of the formal channel as, at best, a violation of something sanctimonious. At worst, they feel a reliance on the informal channel will be interpreted by some as meaning that we are not "organized."

We think that there are circumstances where it is far better not to be organized. Why be committed to use a system that does not work or, at least, does not work very well? Unfortunately, there are people who do not share this viewpoint about the formal organization and its information system. They tend to rely almost totally on the formal information system and thus develop very restricted information relationships with others in the organization. In the next section we will examine the impact of restricted information relationships on organizational communication and suggest how the manager can deal with the problem.

Information Relationships and Organizational Communication

An individual's information relationship with others is one aspect of his or her interpersonal relations. The subject is examined now because the information relationships of managers and other key people are of vital importance in determining the information-sharing norms of the organization. The information-sharing norms, in turn, influence the character of organizational communication.

No doubt you have known people who "play it close to the vest" in their information relationships with others. They simply are not very revealing in their communication with others. Shapero's "good soldier Schweik" is this type of an individual. It would be very difficult to know what is really on his mind as you attempt to communicate with him. Have you ever encountered professors who seemed not to really level with you about the subject? Perhaps you felt they were holding something back. Perhaps you have known similar people in business organizations. Where an individual's information relationship with others tends to be dominated by an unwillingness to reveal his or her true thoughts to them, they respond by withholding information also. Should such behaviors become widespread, the organization cannot make effective use of its informal communication system. People are too cautious and guarded in dealing with one another and thus must depend on the formal communication system for information.

Johari Window of Organizational Communication. We have referred to the Johari window in our discussion of self-concept or perception of self. The Johari window (Luft, 1961), modified slightly, is also a useful model for analyzing the nature of the manager's information relationship with others in the organization. Used in this fashion, the window represents the openness of organizational communication. The necessary modifications have been incorporated in Figure 23-1. Essentially the paradigm involves four kinds of information: (1) that which is known to

```
                Feedback ──────────────▶
         ┌─────────────────┬─────────────────┐
    │    │ Arena of        │ Manager's       │
 Exposure│ effective       │ blindspot       │
    │    │ activity        │                 │
    │    │ Known to        │ Unknown         │
    │    │ manager         │ to              │
    │    │ and others      │ manager         │
    ▼    ├─────────────────┼─────────────────┤
         │ Manager's       │                 │
         │ facade          │ Unknown to      │
         │                 │ manager         │
         │ Unknown to      │ and others      │
         │ others          │                 │
         └─────────────────┴─────────────────┘
```

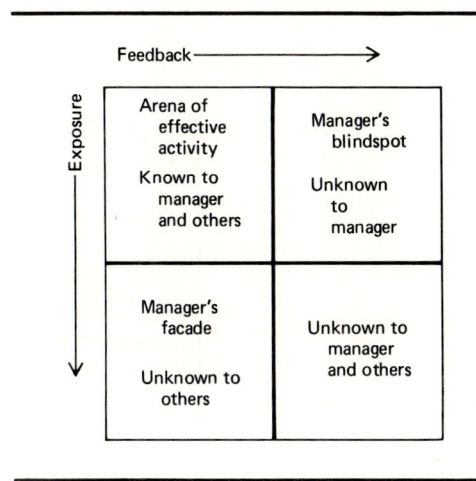

FIGURE 23-1 The manager's Johari window. [*After Joseph Luft, "The Johari Window," Human Relations Training News, vol. 5 (NTL Institute, Arlington, Va., 1961), pp. 6–7.*]

the manager and to others; (2) that which is known only to the manager; (3) that which is known only to others; and (4) that which is unknown to either the manager or others in the organization.

Where the manager and others combine bits of information which they possess separately, a potential for new ideas and relationships exists. The benefits of such interaction are not possible as long as the different bits of information remain separated and compartmentalized within the minds of individuals. A synergistic benefit can occur where people share information openly; this is why group problem-solving efforts can sometimes be more productive than individual efforts.

Enlarging the Window. The manager who truly wishes to minimize the disruptive effects of the organizational unknown must work to reduce the facade and the blindspot. In working to reduce unwanted additions to the organizational unknown, managers may utilize two kinds of communication behavior: (1) They must willingly supply relevant information to others via the process called *exposure*. (2) They must actively seek relevant information from others via the process called *feedback*.

Managers expose themselves in the information sense by being open in their dealings with others. They cannot be secretive or manipulative, and they must show confidence and trust in the abilities of others. The responsibility for establishing a climate of trust and confidence rests initially with the managers. It is the manager who sets the tone or climate of the information relationship for the organization. Where managers set an example of "facade building" by playing games with their subordinates, then the subordinates are likely to respond in kind.

```
                  Feedback ──────────►
          ┌─────────────────┬─────────────────┐
          │  Arena of       │  Manager's      │
   Exposure│  effective     │  blindspot      │
     │     │  activity       │                 │
     │     │                 │  Unknown        │
     ▼     │  Known to       │    to           │
          │  manager        │  manager        │
          │  and others     │                 │
          ├─────────────────┼─────────────────┤
          │                 │  Unknown        │
          │  Manager's facade│    to          │
          │                 │  manager        │
          │  Unknown to others│ and others   │
          └─────────────────┴─────────────────┘
```

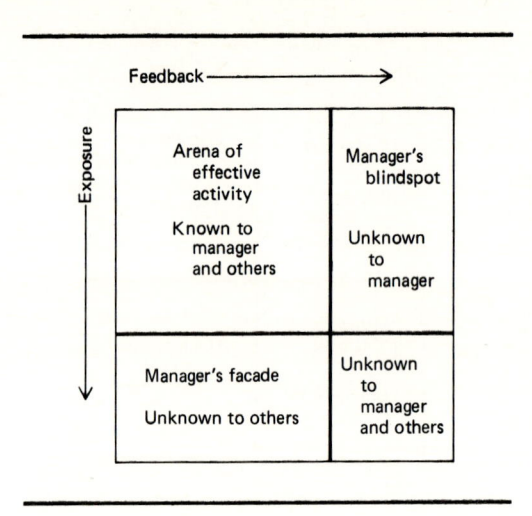

FIGURE 23-2 The manager's Johari window, an enlarged arena. [*After* Joseph Luft, "The Johari Window," *Human Relations Training News, vol. 5 (NTL Institute, Arlington, Va., 1961), pp. 6–7.*]

Subordinates will build facades and withhold information from the managers with the net effect being to enlarge the manager's blindspot and the organization's total unknown area.

Having established a climate of openness via the process of exposure, the manager can then begin to effectively solicit feedback. A supportive climate in which management values the opinions and competence of subordinates is more likely to produce the quality of feedback that is needed. Techniques such as active or nonevaluative listening will be useful in establishing the type of climate that enhances the occurrence of feedback.

A balanced use of exposure and feedback offers the potential for expanding the size of the arena of effective activity by a significant amount. Managers can simultaneously reduce their blindspots, their facades, and the total unknown of the organization by so opening the information relationship with others. The resulting enlarged arena might appear as is shown in Figure 23-2.[1] Experience suggests that it is possible to achieve an arena which is upwards of 80 percent of the total window area. Whatever size window is actually possible, we contend that the prevailing information relationships of managers and other key employees in a given organization tend to significantly influence the information-sharing norms of the organization.

[1] The *Personal Relations Survey*, which is designed to measure the respective dimensions of an individual's Johari window, is available from Teleometrics International of Conroe, Texas.

The Johari window expresses how freely people in the organization share information, and thus it indicates the extent to which organizational communication will include liberal or restricted use of the informal communication system. Organizations should seek to develop managers and other key people who: (1) utilize equalitarian communication patterns; (2) portray leadership behaviors that are dynamic, or involve personal interaction, or are high on group achievement and order; (3) avoid close control where possible; (4) seek the richer communication channels; and (5) make balanced use of exposure and feedback. To the extent this is possible, such organizations will tend to have Johari windows with large, productive arenas as is shown in Figure 23-2. Where managers exhibit such behaviors, substantial elements of organizational communication will be of an informal nature. The key role of the manager in achieving this type of an organizational communication system will be stressed in the next section.

The Manager's Influence on Information Sharing. We have seen that where managers and other key people in the organization display the appropriate leadership behaviors and communication styles, organizational communication will tend to involve significant levels of informal communication activity. Reliance on the informal communication system can occur only where the interpersonal-relations climate, especially the organization's information-sharing norms, supports the use of such channels. Figure 23-3 is designed to represent these important interrelationships.

The overall effect of such behavioral patterns by managers and other key participants will be that favorable information-sharing norms will be encouraged throughout the organization. Positive information relationships are as contagious as any other form of human behavior. An exchange mechanism is operative. People develop personal networks by exchanging information with one another. Ultimately, the various behavioral factors including leadership and communication styles affect the prevailing information-sharing norms as is shown in Figure 23-3.

Organizational information-sharing norms play a key role in achieving an adequate match between organizational communication and the organization's environmental circumstances. The prevailing information-sharing norms determine whether the organization can use *all* available information in dealing with uncertainty caused by unknowns and instabilities of the environment and situation. In Figure 23-4 we have attempted to represent the basic logic involved. It can be seen from this figure that uncertainty, diversity, and instability of the environment (technical, markets, economic) have an impact on the various task and situational variables. Ultimately, environmental effects flow through to determine the organization's need for information.

Formal and informal sources of information for dealing with the problem exist. If the prevailing information-sharing norms are low, then organizational participants will rely on the formal, documented communication system. Where prevail-

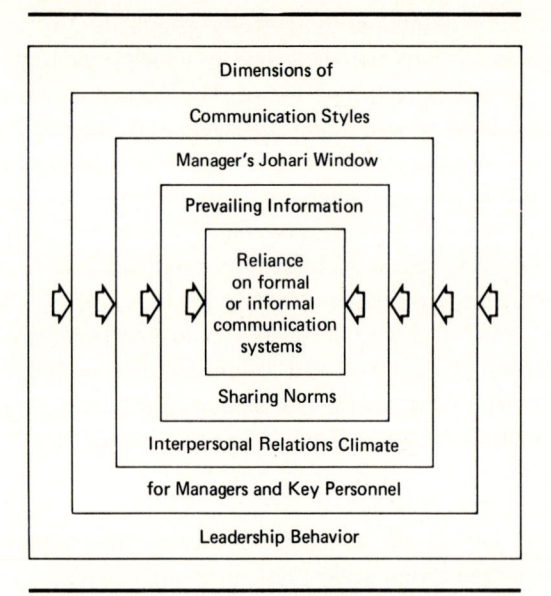

FIGURE 23-3 The manager's influence on organizational communication systems.

ing information-sharing norms are high, then organizational participants will rely to a greater extent on the informal communication system. It is important to note that the information relationships and styles of managers and other key people (as are shown in Figure 23-3) are important underlying determinants of this choice.

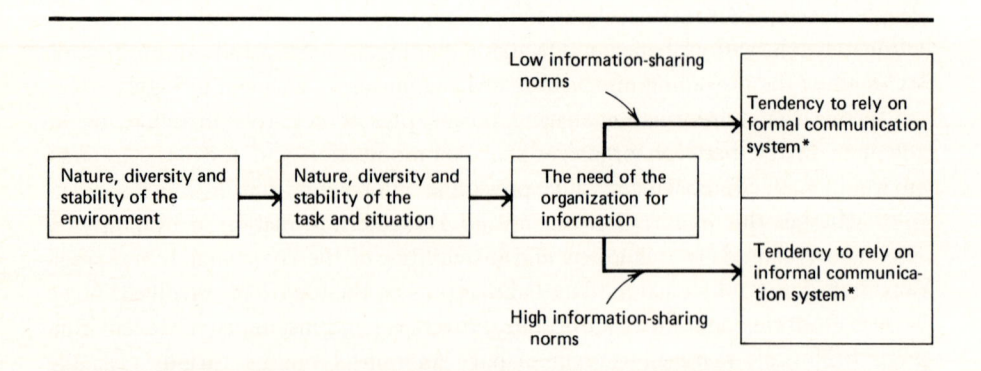

FIGURE 23-4 The influence of information-sharing norms on organizational communication systems.
*The organizational communication system consists of some mix of the formal and informal systems, but the balance between the two is dependent on the nature of the organization's information-sharing norms.

Finally, it should be noted that if the level of uncertainty is relatively high, formal communication is inadequate to the need. Consequently, it is very important that the manager strive to cultivate interpersonal relationships that will ensure that the informal communication system in his or her organization is primed and ready for service.

ORGANIZATIONS AS INFORMATION PROCESSORS

All organizations can be viewed as information processors. It was stressed in the preceding section that the manager is a key influence on the character of overall organizational communication. We now wish to stress that as the manager configures organizational communication into some specific blend of formal and informal systems, he or she also affects its ability to process information. Consideration should be given to the type of information which is being processed, its location, its availability, and how it is to be moved to the point of need. We turn the reader's attention now to these matters.

Information Knowns and Unknowns. We have seen elsewhere in this book that the organization is formed to meet some environmental need and thus is critically affected by the nature of its environment. Changes in environment affect the way the organization is structured, what it does, and how it does it. Essentially then, the organization is linked to its environment by a flow of information. Unfortunately, information circumstances vary from one organization to the next. Therefore, the character of organizational communication should also vary from one organization to the next.

The environment of any organization has three types of information: the known, the unknown, and the unknown unknowns. Obviously, we can be certain about the known. For some situations, we can know the market for our products, or we can know the technology for making our products, or we can know the costs involved in raw materials. On the other hand, in some environments we may not know some of the very same kinds of things. It may be known that there is a demand for a certain type of product. However, the technology which will provide us with such a product is not readily available. The product is beyond the state of the art; there are numerous unknowns. But this is not to say that we cannot have the product. We simply have to recognize the inadequacies of the information available and make adaptive responses.

One such adaptive response is to conduct the research and development needed to acquire the new product. Many formal organizations prescribe specialized subunits whose function is to deal with such unknowns. Such adaptive subsystems have been described in the previous section. They are part of the differentiation required if the organization is to meet environmental needs. An important point to be made here, however, is that the formation of such research units is a conscious response to a known uncertainty.

We know what we don't know and are compensating for it with the appropriate differentiation. This is a difficult thing to do for any organization. However, even more difficult is the circumstance in which we don't know something, and *we don't know we don't know it!* We refer to this circumstance as the unknown unknown; and if you think about it for a moment, perhaps you will understand why it can be critical.

Suppose you are faced with a situation in which it is critical that you perform very well on an examination in a statistics course (say you need an A). Some of the things you *know* are that: today is Friday; the test is scheduled for one week from Monday; a big football game is scheduled out of town this weekend; you have tickets; and the central limit theorem is to be covered on the test. There are some things you are aware of but about which you have insufficient information at this time: you do not understand the central limit theorem; you realize that some study will be required; but you do not know how much or of what type. These are the *unknowns* for your situation. Armed with this information about your environment, you begin to make plans.

You decide that the material to be covered by the test is not really that difficult and that several hours of intensive review of the text will be adequate. Since the test is more than a week off, you can delay this review until the following weekend. Also, by that time the statistics professor will have returned the homework paper you did on the central limit theorem and this can be used to enhance your preparation. It will provide an invaluable source of feedback. You feel this is a very sound plan indeed. It permits you to see the game, visit some out-of-town friends, and do a better job of preparing for the statistics exam.

Unfortunately, you, like many organizations, find out after making your plans that there were some things that you didn't know and didn't know you didn't know. The results are disastrous. The homework papers which are returned are useless except to reveal your total ignorance of the meaning and content of the central limit theorem. This information is, of course, of no direct value to your studies. Also, this feedback is ill-timed since the papers were not returned until the Friday prior to the test. Further, you have unexpected visitors on the Saturday prior to the test and are unable to study then. Well, you think, that's no problem, I'll just study on Sunday. I can still make it. But then the final unknown unknown strikes in the form of a twenty-four-hour virus which renders you incapable of any serious study throughout the day Sunday. To top it all off, your statistics professor doesn't give makeup exams and your team lost the football game. These are the *unknown unknowns* for your situation.

An Information-processing Continuum. It should be clear from the preceding example that the uncertainty of the environment has a critical impact on our ability to plan the formal organization. In a sense, the organization is an information-processing system which must derive mission-related information from the environment and process it in whatever manner is appropriate to organization effectiveness. The process is interpretive in nature as the organization seeks to determine "what to make" (the market) and "how to make it" (the technology). As we have seen, unknowns and unknown unknowns can impair the accuracy of our interpretation. Another aspect of information processing for the external system is, as we have seen, integrative (coordination and control), but this aspect of information processing is clearly in support of the interpretive aspect.

Some have argued that the organization itself is an interpretive continuum. At one extreme, managers and planners make judgments and form concepts as to what product or service is needed in a given environmental circumstance. At the opposite end of the continuum are specialists and technicians who make judgments and attempt to carry out the plan which has been refined at successive stages along the continuum. At each point along the continuum, individuals process information and make interpretations which progressively move from being concept- and idea-oriented to being product- and task-oriented. The interpretive continuum can be thought of as being subdivided among a number of specialists, each of whom relates to his or her portion of the idea continuum through his or her own perceptual lens and technical jargon.

Burns and Stalker (1961) liken the information-processing continuum to linguistics in the sense that the participants are all engaged in the conversion of an idea to reality. As an example, the scientist and engineer interpret the physical world to frame an idea using scientific and technical symbols as a means of communicating the idea. Those in manufacturing interpret the ideas of the scientist and engineer, and using their own technical jargon, take another step toward bringing the idea to fruition as a product. Perhaps the following quotation from Burns and Stalker will clarify the notion.

> In describing a concern in action as an interpretive process, it was intended to give prominence to the co-existence within the working community of a large variety of technical and specialist "languages"; those of the physicist and mathematician, of the cost accountant, of the draughtsman, the assembly room foreman, the salesman, the fitter; and equally to the way in which things and events may have a large variety of "special meanings" for these different people.
>
> The naming of different phases or aspects of the total interpretive process is itself a source of difficulty. The woman who

> comes in every afternoon to earn a few pounds a week soldering components onto a metal rack is doing a very difficult job, involving different technical knowledge and accomplishments, from that done by members of a design team who worked out the design of receiver equipment for a radar navigation system, of which the rack and components form a part. Yet in what she is doing, she is realizing the intentions of the designer; the *ways* in which she realizes those intentions have been devised by a production engineer, whose intentions she is also realizing. In fact the activities of both kinds of engineer, and of the designer, draughtsmen, planning engineers, methods engineers, and others who have preceded the assembly operative in the interpretive system are all directed at programming her activities. [Burns and Stalker, 1961, pp. 155–156]

It should be clear from this description that the interpretive process is subdivided among numerous organizational specialists in forming the external system. An interruption at any point, and there are numerous opportunities for this, will impair the organization's effectiveness as an interpretive information-processing system.

How well the interpretive process comes out for a given organization will, of course, be affected in a very important way by the effectiveness of the human communication system which is involved. It should be clear that how well the interpretive process is executed will be influenced by the capability of the system for providing rich channels of communication to deal with the presence of multiple meanings in an uncertain environment. Richer channels can be effectively utilized in a given organization provided key communicators can be strategically located at both its external boundary with the environment and within the organization at boundaries between units. These individuals will provide vital links along the information-processing continuum.

Links to the Environment. As we have seen, the organization can be viewed as an information-processing system which derives mission-relevant information from its environment and processes it as required for organizational effectiveness. Thus, an interpretive continuum extends from idea to end product or service and it can involve numerous interfaces between the organization and its information environment. At each interface point, individuals make interpretations as to the meaning of the information and take action based on their interpretations. The organization is not linked with its environment at just one or two points but has many linkages, formal and informal. Much of the environmental information exerts a pressure for organizational change and adaptation because participants in organizations, as a group, wish it to survive.

Managers of efficient organizations which face high rates of change and uncertainty seek to utilize both the formal and informal information linkages with the environment. We have seen that interpersonal competence and effective interpersonal relations are prerequisites to use of the informal communication system within the organization. We emphasize now that the requirement is an equally valid one for linking the organization to its environment.

Organizations can be linked to their environment via key communicators who serve as linking pins, but the quality of interpersonal relations with those outside the organization must be supportive of this. In an earlier chapter we discussed the research of Bodensteiner (1970) in which he found high levels of informal communication between separate organizations. Research of others has produced similar results.

Czepiel (1975) studied the diffusion of information concerning a major technological innovation in the steel industry and concluded it was a behavioral process. He found definite informal communication links between the various companies. Organizations tended to be clustered about the early adopters with respect to the diffusion of information regarding a particular innovation. Such networks were arranged so that a minimum number of links were involved to carry information regarding the innovation from an early adopter to a later adopter. Czepiel observed that "friendship" definitely smoothed the way in these networks.

It is obvious that informal communication links to the world outside the organization can be crucial where change is drastic and frequent. Enlightened managers will strive to cultivate such channels by using methods discussed at length throughout this book. Less perceptive managers may simply ignore or perhaps even attempt to close off the informal channels to the environment. In either case, they run the risk of stagnation and failure since the organization can adapt only via its formal communication system. Under some circumstances, formal links to the environment can be seriously overloaded.

Links within the Organization. Another aspect of the organization as an information-processing medium is operative within the boundaries of the organization. In this case the information processed is that which is relevant to the performance and coordination of tasks—tasks, incidentally, that have been defined as a result of the interpretive activity at a preceding stage of the continuum. Much of this information-processing activity is determined by the division of work, the consequent differentiation, and the need for integration.

Within the boundaries of organizations, we also find there are many linkages possible; both formal and informal types may exist. Information linkages within the organization can also be a source of pressure for organizational change. As an example, emergent behavior in the internal system may disrupt the operation of the external system; the relationship between the two systems is negative. A negative relationship between the two organizational systems will surely lead the manager to press for change.

Essentially, the manager finds that two kinds of communication links interconnect organizational units. Each type of link can be effective for processing information. However, to get the most out of each, the manager *must* deal with two subsets of the organization, the internal and external systems. Under the best of circumstances, the internal system can prove a valuable supplement to the external system. Under the worst circumstances, the internal system can disrupt the performance of the external system. In any event, whether they like it or not, managers do not get a choice of one or the other. They get both. The question is whether or not they are willing to work to have one augment the other.

We have seen that for some circumstances the manager can successfully preplan specific communication links for the organization. In other situations, it may be necessary to rely on people to supply the necessary communication links on an ad hoc basis. Again, whether the ad hoc response is favorable or not is a function of the quality of interpersonal relations in the organization. A key influence is the interpersonal competence of the manager as he or she seeks to facilitate the use of informal communication and key communicators as communication links between organizational units.

Likert (1961) suggested that a fundamental integrating principle in successful organizations centers on the process of leadership exhibited by managers. Effective managers are perceived by their subordinates as being supportive and as having influence with higher-level managers. Effective managers also cultivate in their subordinates a sense of personal worth and value to the organization. It is especially relevant to the current discussion to note that effective managers are often able to achieve such positive interpersonal relations by arranging the organization so that each participant is a member of one or more effectively functioning groups.

The managers themselves play a linking-pin role by holding simultaneous membership in groups at different levels of the hierarchy. Thus, a manager serves as a leader of a group at one level of the hierarchy and simultaneously as a subordinate member of a group at the next higher level. An environment of rich communication and close interaction can be achieved via groups which are so linked. An organization so structured and operated is an example of the beneficial blend of formal and informal processes that has been the topic of discussions throughout this book.

An Overview of Organizational Communication. In Figure 23-5 we have attempted to include some of the essential features of the organization as an information-processing medium. As we have seen, the manager can influence the capacity of the organization for processing both information from its environment and internal

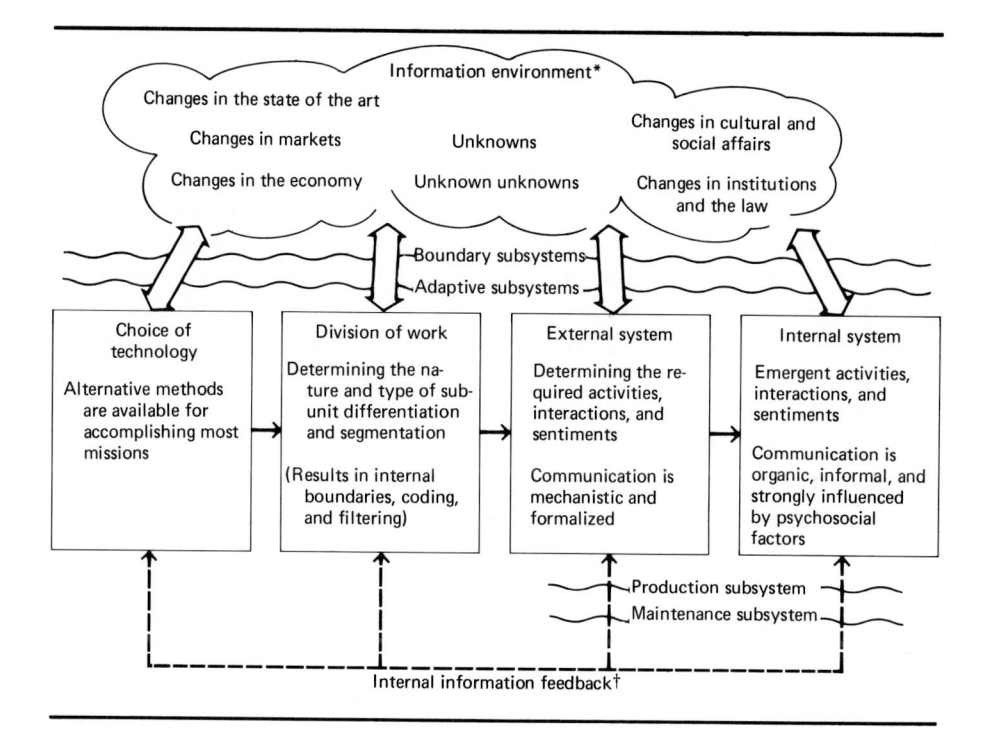

FIGURE 23-5 The organization as an information-processing system.

*For a given organization, the various aspects of the information environment may range from stable and certain to dynamic and uncertain. Thus, such information represents an external pressure for change, but it is also a constraint which determines the appropriateness of a given external-internal mix.

†Feedback may have a positive, negative, or neutral impact, but it is information that represents an internal potential for change.

coordinative information. A number of variables affecting organizational communication are under the manager's control. The manager must work with these variables if he or she is to enhance the organization's effectiveness as an information processor.

At the boundary of the organization the broad arrows represent the flow of information between the organization and its environment. Much of the information which flows across this boundary will be processed somewhere along the organization's interpretive continuum as individuals decide the implications of a change in the state of the art or a shift in the values of the social system. It seems clear that the organization's boundary and adaptive subsystems will make extensive use of these kinds of flows, but the fashion in which they do so depends on the organization's information-sharing climate as influenced by management and other key functionaries.

It may be that the climate is such that a given organization must rely primarily on its mechanistic processes and the formal communication system to provide the boundary and adaptive functions. Where this is the case, information must be processed through formal hierarchical channels connecting the external system to the environment. There is an obvious risk of information overload in such a situation.

Other organizations may establish a climate such that the internal system supplements the external system and thus information is also processed via the informal communication link to the environment. Indeed, there are many possible external-internal blends, as was pointed out in an earlier chapter. It is imperative that management determine the appropriate mix for the environmental and technological circumstances faced and then work to achieve the appropriate mix of formal and informal systems into the organizational communication system.

Within the boundary of the organization, there is a considerable flow of information that is primarily concerned with the performance and coordination of tasks. Some of this kind of information flow is required only infrequently. As an example, information used in making decisions about the basic technology and division of work is needed infrequently where the environment is stable. Suppose a manufacturing firm decides that it will fabricate its product using components supplied by other manufacturers? This decision sets the basic technology of that organization and determines the kind of work subdivision needed. Management can then recruit the necessary skills for its fabrication and assembly work and plan the necessary external system. Once these basic decisions have been made, choice of technology and division of work information will be processed relatively infrequently.

Of course, where the environment is subject to a high rate of change, then choice of technology and division of work information must be processed on a much more frequent basis. It should be clear that these decisions are linked in an important way to what is taking place in the boundary and adaptive subsystems. Still, it seems wise to stress technology and division of work as being connected with the external system because they determine the essential character of the external system.

The remaining significant information flows within the boundary of the organization are those associated with day-by-day task performance and coordination. These kinds of flows are of a continuous nature and are a major component of organizational communication. They occur almost entirely within and between the external and internal systems of the organization. The organization's production and maintenance subsystems will make extensive uses of such information flows. Production and maintenance information flows are shown as solid and broken (feedback) lines in Figure 23-5.

It should be emphasized that where managers and other key organizational participants choose not to develop the information-sharing norms of the organization, the flows which occur in the internal system will be truncated. Low information-sharing norms can lead to an almost total reliance on the formal sources of information. To the extent that some utilization of informal channels does occur under conditions of low information-sharing norms, such channels may be used in a way that is at cross-purposes with the goals of the organization and thus be dysfunctional.

The manager functions to integrate all these diverse information processes in such a way that the organization can achieve its mission. To accomplish this integrative role, the managerial information process must cut across many system and subsystem boundaries. It influences and is influenced by information events in the boundary subsystem, the adaptive subsystem, the production subsystem, and the maintenance subsystem. Because it overlays all other systems, it is management which will ultimately determine whether the organization is to develop as a rich and flexible information-processing system or one that is limited and inflexible.

SUMMARY

In this final chapter, we have attempted to develop an overview of organizational communication and the key role played by the manager in its implementation. Five key subsystems were seen to be operative in the fully developed organization. These were the production, maintenance, boundary, adaptive, and managerial subsystems. The communication needs of each subsystem were examined and suggestions were made as to whether such needs could be met via mechanistic or organic approaches.

A second major topic of this chapter was the key role of the manager in determining the nature of organizational communication. It was shown that managers influence the interpersonal climate of the organization and, as a consequence, the willingness of participants to share information. It is through this influence on the quality of interpersonal relations that the manager affects the character of organizational communication. People are unwilling to share information via the informal channels where this is an unacceptable form of behavior. It was shown that the Johari window can be used to represent the organization's prevailing information-sharing climate.

Finally, the organization was discussed as an information-processing medium. The nature of organizational knowns and unknowns were described and were shown to influence the organization's ability to process information. The organization was described as an interpretive continuum which is linked to and affected by the nature of its environment. The key role of the manager in achieving effective information links to the environment and among organization subdivisions was discussed. The efforts of management in providing effective linkages ultimately determines the nature of organizational communication.

IMPORTANT TERMS AND CONCEPTS

production subsystem, maintenance subsystem, boundary subsystem, adaptive subsystem, managerial subsystem, manager's Johari window, exposure and feedback, information processor, interpretive continuum

REVIEW QUESTIONS

1. What kinds of factors influence the certainty-uncertainty continuum faced by the organization? What are the implications of the certainty-uncertainty continuum for an organization's information-processing capacity?

2. Discuss some possible strategies for dealing with differing levels of environmental and situational uncertainty.

3. Discuss the manager's role as the manager of an information-processing system. What classes of variables must he or she work with?

4. How does the manager influence the information relationships of the organization?

5. Discuss the organization as an information-processing mechanism. Be sure to include all the significant information flows and subsystems.

6. What factors determine the character of organizational communication? Discuss.

BIBLIOGRAPHY

Banard, C.: *The Functions of the Executive* (Cambridge, Mass.: Harvard University Press, 1938).

Barth, Richard T.: "Intergroup Climate Characteristics, Perceived Communication Problems, and Unity of Effort Achieved by Task-Interdependent R&D Groups," *31st Annual Academy of Management Proceedings,* Atlanta, Ga., August 15–18, 1971.

Bodensteiner, Wayne Dean: "Information Channel Utilization under Varying Research and Development Project Conditions: An Aspect of Inter-Organizational Communication Channel Usage," doctoral dissertation, The University of Texas at Austin, 1970.

Burns, Tom, and G. M. Stalker: *The Management of Innovation* (London: Tavistock Publications Ltd., 1961).

Czepiel, John A.: "Patterns of Interorganizational Communications and the Diffusion of a Major Technological Innovation in a Competitive Industrial Community," *Academy of Management Journal,* vol. 18, pp. 6–23, March 1975.

Davis, Keith: *Human Behavior at Work* (New York: McGraw-Hill Book Company, 1972).

Hall, Jay, and Martha S. Williams: *Personnel Relations Survey* (Conroe, Tex.: Teleometrics International, 1967.

Jain, Harish C.: "Supervisory Communication and Performance in Urban Hospitals," *Journal of Communication,* vol. 23, pp. 103–117, March 1973.

Katz, Daniel, and Robert L. Kahn: *The Social Psychology of Organizations* (New York: John Wiley & Sons, Inc., 1966).

Likert, Rensis: *New Patterns of Management* (New York: McGraw-Hill Book Company, 1961).

Luft, Joseph: "The Johari Window," *Human Relations Training News,* p. 5, 1961.

INDEXES

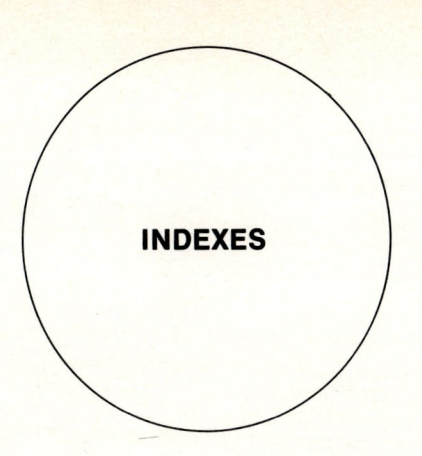

NAME INDEX

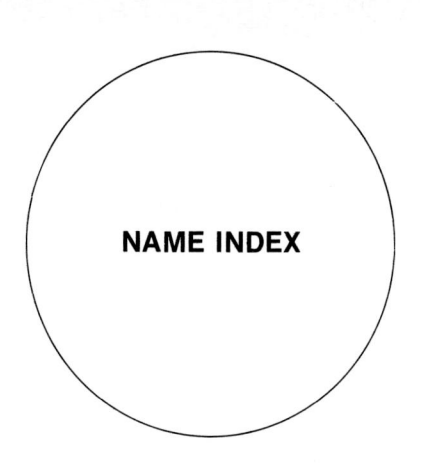

Adams, J. S., 255, 268
Albaum, Gerald, 439, 442
Albers, Henry, 14, 20
Allen, T. J., 405, 406, 408, 413, 420
Ammons, R. B., 310, 314
Anderson, L. R., 300, 315
Argyris, Chris, 85, 86, 97, 302, 314
Athanassiades, John C., 377, 378, 386

Bach, G., 112, 114, 119, 173, 182
Bales, R. F., 306, 314
Barland, D. C., 302, 314
Barnard, C. I., 318, 443, 462
Barth, Richard T., 446, 462
Bavelas, A., 271, 276, 285
Becker, S. W., 282, 286
Beller, R., 14, 21
Bem, D. J., 304, 316
Bennis, Warren G., 163, 166, 295, 315, 375, 386
Berkowitz, L., 292, 314
Berlo, David K., 23, 30, 32, 42
Berne, Eric, 99, 119, 137, 141, 146, 201, 206
Blake, Robert R., 5, 368, 386
Blanchard, K. H., 327, 333
Bodenstemer, Wayne Dean, 56, 60, 351, 365, 390, 395–397, 399, 403, 420, 457, 462
Borman, E. G., 191, 206, 390, 420
Bowers, D., 216, 229
Brehm, J., 210, 228
Brenner, Marshall H., 372, 373, 386
Briggs, G. E., 309, 315, 316
Burgess, R. L., 276, 285

Burns, Tom, 352–354, 365, 391, 404, 405, 407, 420, 428, 430, 442, 455, 456, 462
Byrne, D., 222, 228

Calabro, P., 327
Caplow, T., 403, 420
Carlson, S., 391, 420
Carter, L. W., 319, 333
Cartwright, D., 420
Christie, R., 223, 224, 228
Coch, L., 160, 166, 303, 315
Cohen, A. M., 279, 285
Cohen, Stephen I., 405, 420
Collaros, P. S., 300, 315
Coopersmith, Stanley, 124, 125, 131
Crowne, D., 102, 119
Cummins, R., 140, 143, 146
Cyert, R. M., 297, 315
Czepiel, John A., 457, 462

Dale, Ernest, 8, 20
Dalton, G. W., 357, 360, 365, 379–382, 387, 438
Davis, J. H., 276, 285
Davis, Keith, 361, 362, 365, 391, 392, 396, 402, 403, 420, 425, 437, 442, 447, 463
Davis, W. A., 352, 365
Dearborn, DeWitt C., 31, 42
Dewhirst, H. Dudley, 413, 414, 420
Dickson, W. J., 101, 104, 119, 263, 268
Dill, W. R., 277, 285
Dubin, Robert, 391, 420
Dunphy, D., 289, 292, 315

467

NAME INDEX

Ebbesen, E., 209, 229

Faust, W. L., 306, 315
Fayol, Henri, 8, 21
Feldenkries, Moshe, 187, 206
Festinger, L., 291, 316
Fiedler, F., 394, 420
Fiedler, F. E., 318, 333
Fleishman, E., 217, 229
Ford, David L., 372, 387
French, J. R. P., Jr., 160, 166, 168, 268, 303, 315, 320, 333

Galbraith, J. R., 433, 436, 442
Geis, F., 223, 224, 228
Gerloff, Edwin A., 352, 365, 367, 387
Gerstberger, P. G., 408, 420
Gilchrist, J. D., 276, 285
Glock, C. Y., 356, 365
Goodwin, Edward H., 390, 421
Guest, R. H., 391, 420
Guetzkow, Harold, 16, 277, 285, 318, 333, 396, 403, 404, 420

Habbe, S., 396, 421
Hall, Edward, 196, 206
Hall, Jay, 463
Hamblin, R. L., 158, 166, 326, 333
Hancy, W. V., 185, 206
Hare, A. P., 292, 315
Harris, T., 143, 146
Hastorf, Albert, 106, 119
Hearn, G., 282, 285
Hemphill, J. D., 158, 168
Hemphill, J. K., 309, 315, 317, 333
Hersey, P., 327, 333
Heslin, R., 289, 292, 315
Hicks, Herbert G., 14, 21
Higham, T. M., 7
Hirota, K., 275, 285
Hoffman, L. R., 300, 315
Holland, Winford E., 406, 408–411, 421
Hollander, E. P., 220, 229
Homans, George C., 70, 71, 73, 74, 81
Hornseth, H., 276, 285
Howell, R., 191, 206
Howells, L. T., 282, 285
Hutte, H. A., 291, 316

Jacobsen, P. R., 255, 268
Jain, Harish C., 446, 463
Johnston, W. A., 309, 315, 316
Jones, E. E., 172, 182

Kahn, Robert L., 347, 361, 365, 371, 378, 387, 398, 405, 421, 444, 445, 463
Katz, Daniel, 347, 361, 365, 371, 378, 387, 398, 405, 421, 444, 445, 463
Katz, Elihu, 406, 421
Kay, E., 158, 168
Kelley, H. H., 268
Kelly, Joe, 391, 421
Kelman, H. 172, 182
King, D., 143, 146
Kogan, N., 304, 315, 316
Kolb, David A., 442
Koontz, Harold, 8, 21
Korman, A. K., 323, 333

Laird, Dugan, 187, 206
Lanzetta, J., 319, 333
Larsen, I. M., 308, 315
Lawler, E. E., III, 391, 421
Lawrence, Paul R., 357, 359, 360, 365, 379–382, 387, 407
Lawson, E. D., 277, 285
Lazarfield, Paul, 406, 421
Leavitt, Harold J., 30, 42, 275, 276, 280, 285
Levinger, G., 304, 315
Lewin, Kurt, 213, 406, 413, 421
Likert, Rensis, 65, 68, 81, 159, 168, 248, 250, 326, 333, 350, 365, 374–376, 387, 458, 463
Litterer, Joseph A., 344, 365
Little, K. B., 282, 285
Lloyd, Russell R., 372, 387
Lorsch, J. W., 357, 359, 360, 365, 379–382, 387, 407
Lott, A. J., 262, 268
Lott, B. E., 262, 268
Lowen, Alexander, 92, 97
Luft, Joseph, 134, 136, 146, 448–450, 463

McClelland, David C., 99, 119
McConville, C. B., 309, 315
Machiavelli, Nicole, 223
McIntyre, James, 442
Maier, N. R. F., 300, 302, 315
Mann, F. C., 157, 158, 160, 168, 327, 333

March, James, 420
Marlowe, D., 102, 119
Marquis, D. G., 304, 315
Marrow, Alfred, 216, 229
Martin, N. H., 170, 182
Maslow, Abraham, 48, 60
Massarik, F., 317, 333
Massie, Joseph L., 8, 21
Mayman, M., 123, 131
Mehrabian, Albert, 196, 206
Melcher, Arlyn J., 14, 21
Mennenger, K., 123, 131
Menzel, Herbert, 356, 365, 411, 421
Miller, J. G., 273, 285
Miller, Merle, 239
Mintzberg, Henry, 390, 391, 421
Moran, G., 262, 268
Morris, E. G., 305, 315
Mouton, Jane S., 5, 368, 386
Mulder, M., 277, 285

Nakamura, C. Y., 327, 333
Naythorn, W., 319, 333
Newman, William H., 8, 21
Nichols, Ralph G., 186, 191, 206, 373–374, 387, 391, 420

O'Donnell, Cyril, 8, 21
O'Reilly, Charles A., III, 376, 387

Parker, T. C., 159, 168
Pelz, D. C., 170, 182
Pepitone, A., 291, 315
Polefka, Judith, 106, 119
Porter, Elias H., 6
Porter, L. W., 391, 421
Powell, James Donald, 390, 421
Pruitt, D. G., 304, 316
Pruysner, P., 123, 131

Raven, B., 320, 333
Raven, V. H., 310, 315
Reid, Peter C., 47, 60
Riecken, H., 291, 315
Roberts, Karlene H., 376, 387
Roethlisberger, F. J., 101, 104, 119, 149, 168, 263, 268, 329
Roger, M. S., 308, 315

Rokeach, Milton, 178, 182
Rosenbaum, W. G., 255, 268
Rosenbloom, Richard, 391, 413, 421
Rothschild, G. H., 275–277, 285
Rubin, Irwin M., 442
Russo, N. F., 282, 285

Sayles, Leonard R., 391, 421
Schein, Edgar H., 213, 214, 229, 295, 315
Schneider, D. J., 304, 315
Schneider, David, 106, 119
Schutz, William, 92, 97, 99, 103, 104, 119
Seashore, S. E., 216, 229, 262, 264, 268
Shannon, Claude E., 15n., 29n., 34, 36, 38n., 42, 46, 60
Shapero, Albert, 393, 394, 421, 448
Shapiro, G. L., 191, 206, 390, 420
Shaw, J. I., 310, 315
Shaw, L. M., 262, 268
Shaw, M. E., 156, 168, 262, 268, 274–277, 285, 286, 301, 315
Sheriff, Muzafer, 232, 241
Sherman, S. J., 304, 316
Shriver, B., 319, 333
Shure, G. H., 308, 315
Sigband, N. B., 14, 21, 372, 373, 386
Simon, Herbert A., 31, 42, 277, 285, 297, 315, 318
Sims, A., 327
Sims, J. H., 170, 182
Smoke, W. H., 301, 304, 316
Stalker, G. M., 352–354, 365, 407, 420, 428, 430, 442, 455, 456, 462
Steinzor, B., 282, 285
Stewart, R., 391, 421
Stodtbeck, F. L., 306, 314
Stoner, J. A. F., 304, 316
Strickland, J. F., 276, 285
Strother, George B., 420
Summer, Charles E., 8, 21
Swanson, Guy E., 421

Tannenbaum, A., 391, 421
Tannenbaum, R., 317, 333
Tassone, J., 308, 315
Taylor, Robert L., 406–408, 410, 421
Teger, A. I., 304, 316
Thayer, Lee, 8, 22, 42, 43, 60, 69, 81
Thibaut, J. W., 268

NAME INDEX

Timbers, E., 14, 21
Townsend, Robert, 152, 168
Trow, D. B., 297, 315

Vaidya, Christene, 372, 387
Vroom, V. H., 157, 158, 160, 168, 327, 333

Walker, L. C., 276, 285
Wallach, M. A., 304, 315
Walton, Richard, 232, 241
Warren, E. K., 8, 21
Weaver, Warren, 15*n*., 29*n*., 34, 36, 38*n*., 42, 46, 60
Webber, Ross A., 391, 421
Weschler, I. R., 317, 333

Whyte, William Foote, 5, 134, 146, 268
Wiener, Norbert, 15*n*.
Williams, Martha S., 463
Williges, R. C., 309, 316
Wilpizeski, C., 291, 315
Wing, C. W., Jr., 304, 316
Winter, D., 99, 119
Wofford, J. C., 159, 161, 168, 322, 327, 333
Wolck, Francis W., 391, 413, 421
Wolosin, M. A., 304, 316
Wolosin, R. J., 304, 316
Wyden, P., 112, 114, 119, 173, 182

Zajonc, R. B., 301, 304, 316
Zander, A., 420
Zimbardo, P., 209, 229

SUBJECT INDEX

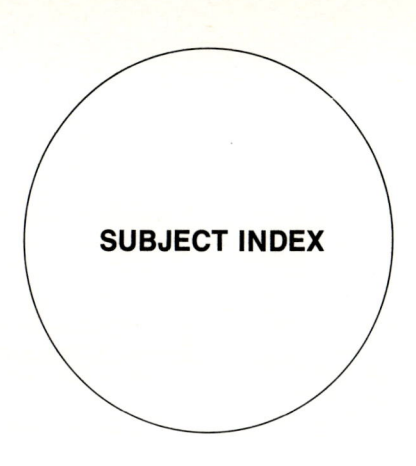

Acceptance, 125, 150, 195
Active listening, 450
   (*See also* Nondirective counseling)
Activities, as the traditional concern of management, 85–86, 89–90
Adaptive subsystem, 445, 459–461
   information needs of, 445
   nature of, 445
   need for flexible communication, 445
Adult ego state, 196, 209
Ambiguity (*see* Language; Perception; Semantic noise and distortion)
Anger, 112–114, 122
   (*See also* Emotions)
Anxiety, 121–123
Arena of Johari window, 136, 137, 154
Ascendancy and upward distortion, 376–378
Assumptive maps about organizations, 76–77
Authoritarian structure and horizontal communication, 379
Authority:
   challenge to, 170
   lines of, 151

Barriers to communication, 169–180, 370–371
Blindspot, 136, 137, 154, 449
   (*See also* Johari window)
Body language (*see* Nonverbal communication)
Bottleneck of communication, 361–362
Boundary subsystem, 444, 459–461
   boundary spanning needs, 445
   as an information link to environment, 445
   nature of, 444
   need for flexibility, 445
Brain storming, 300–301

Change process, 123, 124
Changing attitudes, 213–216
Channel capacities, matching with source, 37–38
Channel noise, 32–35
   definition of, 32
   identification of noise sources and correction, 33
   use of channel and language redundancy in compensating for, 33–34
Channels of communication, 15, 31, 258
   formal, 15
   informal, 15
   nonverbal, 15
   types of, 31
Child ego state, 209
Climate of openness, 447, 450
Climate of trust, 449
Close control leadership, 451
Coaching, as influence model, 208–209
Coalitions in organizational politics, 220–221
Coding, as a communication metering device, 38–39
Coercion, effects on interpersonal relations, 143
Cohesiveness in groups, 262
Communication process elements, 25–39
   channel, 31–32
   interdependency of, 38–39
   message, 26–27
   receiver-decoder, 35
   source-encoder, 25–26
Compliance in dealing with power, 172
Conflict, 173, 198, 230–241, 380–383
   emotional issues in, 232, 235
   resolving, 230–241, 380–383
   substantive issues in, 232
   theory, 232

471

SUBJECT INDEX

Conflict confrontation meeting, 232–236
  differentiation stage of, 233–234
  follow-up stage of, 236
  integration stage of, 234
Conformity, 172–173, 198, 263, 264
Constructive-destructive trust cycle, 184
Controling communication style, 149–150, 429
  (*See also* Styles of communication)
Coping mechanisms, 123, 124
Counseling, 208–209, 293
Criticism, effect on communication, 157–158

Decision making:
  alternative development, 300
  by groups, 297–307
  methods for, 301–302
  participative, 126, 156, 159, 170, 209, 210, 212
Decoder (*see* Communication process elements)
Defense mechanisms, 121, 122
  avoidance, 122
  projection, 122
  rationalization, 123
  regression, 122
  repression, 122
Defensive behavior, 176, 178–180, 211–212
Deference, 255
Democratic leadership, 292
Differentiation, 379, 380, 454, 457, 459
  definition of, 357
  effects on communication, 359–360
  examples of, 358–359
  in successful and unsuccessful organizations, 379–380
Dimensions of leadership behavior, 321–326, 427–447
  dynamic achievement, 322–323
  group achievement and order, 322–323
  personal enhancement, 322–323
  personal interaction, 322–323
  security and maintenance, 322, 323, 427–447
Direction of communication flow, 14–17
  downward communication, 14, 16–17
  feedback communication, 14–17
  forward communication, 14
  horizontal communication, 14–17
  (*See also* Formal organizational communication; Informal communication systems)
Disperson of communication, 274
Displaced aggression, 112
  (*See also* Emotions)
Distance of communication, 272

Distortion and filtering of formal communication, 69–70, 371–379
  accuracy of hierarchical channels, 373–375
  in lateral channel, 378–379
  message distortion and filtering, 372–373
  message routing and summarization, 372
  in upward channel, 375–378
Distributive justice, 255
Division of work, implications of, 337–347
  communication as an element of coordination, 344–347
  effects of standardization and specialization on, 342–343
  effects of subunit interdependence on, 341–342
  linked flow of activities, 341
Dogmatic communication, 177–180
Downward communication, 87, 372–375
  (*See also* Direction of communication flow)
Dynamic leadership, 451

Early adopters, 408–409
  (*See also* Key communicator)
Ego state:
  adult, 137–143, 153, 196, 209
  child, 137–143, 150, 153
  parent, 137–143, 150, 153
Emergent leadership, 220–221, 275
Emotions, effects on communication, 109–114, 193, 306
  anger, 112–114
  awareness of emotion, 110
  displaced aggression, 112
  effects of expressing anger, 113–114
  expression of emotion, 193, 306
  fear, 110–112
Encoder (*see* Communication process elements)
Equalitarian communication styles, 427, 451
Evaluative communication, 176–177
Exchange theory, 133–135
Exposure, 137, 154, 449, 451
  (*See also* Johari window)
External and internal systems in combination, 423, 425
  determining factors, 424–425
  effects on communication, 423–425
  as a management responsibility, 73–74, 89–90
External systems, 70–77, 148, 156, 163, 245–250, 270, 288–289, 337–344, 458, 459
  activities, interactions and sentiments, 72–74, 338–341
  an example of, 337–344

SUBJECT INDEX

External systems:
   interpersonal communication requirements of, 86–87
   nature and definition of, 70–71
   (*See also* Division of work; External systems communication)
External systems communication, 318, 344–350
   directive communication, 347–348
   operative communication, 250–251
   upward communication, 349–350
   (*See also* Direction of communication flow)

Facade of the Johari window, 136, 137, 154, 451
Facial expression, 196, 199, 209
Factions, as an influence tactic, 219, 221, 258
Failures in communication:
   interpersonal motives, effects of, 90–91
   interpersonal perception, effects of, 90–91
   interpersonal relationships, effects of, 89–90
   levels of the general communication problem, 36–37
      effectiveness problems, 36–37
      semantic problems, 36–37
      technical problems, 36–37
   (*See also* Barriers to communication)
Fear, 110–112, 189
   (*See also* Emotions)
Feedback, 49–51, 120, 133, 137, 154, 173, 178, 186–190, 310, 339–451, 459
   to counter effects of noise, 49
   to determine communication effects, 49
   and the face-to-face channel, 51
   influence of individual nature and psychology on, 49–50
   intrapersonal feedback, 187–189
Filtering (*see* Distortion and filtering)
Follower, effects on leadership, 326–327
Foot-in-the-door technique of influence, 221–222
Formal networks, 276
Formal organizational communication, 66–67, 156
   downward communication and the scalar chain, 66
   interrelated subtasks and coordinative horizontal communication, 67
   upward communication and managerial control, 66
   (*See also* External systems communication)
Functions:
   of leaders, 319
   of managers, 8–13

Games or transactions between people, 139, 141–145, 196–198
Gatekeeper, 406, 408
   (*See also* Key communicator)
Gateways to communication, 183–203
Goals:
   group goals, 259, 317–319
   individual goals, 61–65
   organizational goals, 61–65
   (*See also* Organizational goals and subgoals)
Grapevine, 67, 76, 402–404, 425
Group achievement and order, 427, 451
Group attractiveness, dimensions of, 289–291
Group decision-making schemes, 301–302
Group identity, 252–254
Group process variables, 251–283
Group structure, 242

Hawthorne studies, 104
Human communication, 43–44
   definition of, 43
   transmission of data, 44
   transmission of information, 44

Identification, as a change model, 214
Independence of communication networks, 274, 279, 327
Individual (human) communication, 16
Influence, 207–228, 319–321
Influence process, 207–210
Informal channels, factors influencing preference for, 394–402
   effects of problems and stress, 395–396
   feedback and timing advantages, 399–401
   informal communication as organizational slack, 402
   keeping channels open and ready for use, 396–399
   richness of informal channels, 399
   selectivity of use, 401–402
Informal communication networks, 276–277
Informal communication systems, 150, 388–
   as a backup to the formal system, 67–68, 390–392, 399
   distinguishing features of: active versus passive, 393–394
   distinguished from formal systems, 389
   multidirectional, 392–393
   frequency of use, 389–391
   purposes of informal communication of, 67
   (*See also* Grapevine)

Information impedance, 405
Information-sharing, 326, 446–453
Information-sharing norms, 412–414, 427, 446, 448, 451
Information theory, 15
Ingratiation, 172, 198
Initiating structure, 160
Innovators, 408–409
  (*See also* Key communicator)
Integration, 379, 380, 382, 457
  definition of, 357–358
  examples of, 360
  role of communication in dealing with, 360–

Interaction, as a concern of management, 85–86, 89–90
Interaction relationships in groups, 258
Internal systems, 71–77, 148, 156, 163, 245–250, 288–289, 318, 458, 459
  activities, interactions and sentiments, 72–74
  (*See also* External and internal systems in combination)
Interpersonal competence, 94–95, 120, 121, 127, 219, 427, 457, 458
  improving interpersonal competence, 92–95
    awareness of feeling, 92
    clarifying interpersonal motives, 93
    increasing accuracy of interpersonal perception, 93
    increasing self-awareness, 92
    self-disclosure of feelings, 92
    self-disclosure of interpersonal motives, 92
    lack of self-confidence, 94–95
    of the manager, 446–448
    norms against discussing interpersonal problems, 94
Interpersonal motives, 98–104, 133
  need for affection, 102–103
  need for control, 101–102
  need for inclusion, 99–101
Interpersonal relations climate, 141, 183–185, 425–428, 446, 457
  developing interpersonal trust, 184
  influence on use of formal and informal communication, 425–428
  interpersonal trust, 141, 183–185
  (*See also* Interpersonal competence)
Intrapersonal influences, 69–70
Intrapersonal variables, 120
Intrinsic and symbolic information sources, 48

Jargon, 174, 175, 370–371
Johari window, 133, 134, 136, 137, 448–452
  (*See also* Arena; Blindspot; Facade)

Key communicator, 407–412, 447, 456, 457
Knowns, 453–454
  (*See also* Organizations, as information processors)

Language, 173–175
  differences, 173
  specialized, 174
Language redundancy, 34–35
Lateral communication, 87, 378–379
  (*See also* Direction of communication flow)
Leader, 317–332
  emergent, 318
  formal, 318–319
  informal, 318–319
Leadership, 317–332
  attempted, 317, 321
  effective, 317, 321
  emergent, 318
  process, 320–321
  successful, 317, 321
Linking pin, 242, 245, 248, 458
Listening, 185–186
Love, 133

Machiavellian, 223–224
Maintenance subsystem, 444, 459–461
  information needs of, 444
  maintenance related communication, 444
  nature of, 444
Malicious obedience, 150
Management and communications, 8–15
  communication for controlling, 12–13
  communication for directing, 11–12
  communication for organizing, 10–11
  communication for planning, 9–10
  interdependence of, 14–15
Management by objective, 156, 175
Managerial subsystem, 445, 460, 461
  dependence on communication, 445
  nature of, 445
Manager's Johari window, 448–452
  influence on organizational information sharing, 446–448
  matching organizational communication to situational needs, 451–453
  use of exposure and feedback, 448–449

SUBJECT INDEX **475**

Managing through communication, 361–362
   (*See also* Bottleneck of communication)
Manipulate, 143, 210
Manipulative communication, 178–179
Maturity of followers, 327
Meaning (*see* Intrinsic and symbolic information sources)
Mechanistic and organic organizations, 428–431
   environmental stability and the need to process information, 430–431
   mechanistic communication, 428–429, 433–436
   organic communication, 429, 436–439
Message (*see* Communication process elements)
Message routing and summarization, 372
   (*See also* Distortion and filtering)
Model, 214
Modeling communication, 22, 208
   conveyor theory of communication, 23
   problems of, 22–23
   process model, 23–25
Motivation of followers, 327
Multiple meanings in information sources, 26–30
   effects of: selection of meaning, 28
   uncertainty of meaning, 28–29

National Training Laboratories, 190
Needs, 259–261
Networks of communication, 269–283
   determinates of, 279–283
   properties of, 271–274
   types of, 270–271
Nondirective counseling, 198–202
Nonevaluative listening, 450
   (*See also* Active listening)
Nonverbal communication, 192, 195–198
Norms, 262–264, 281

Ohio State leadership studies, 160
Openness, 120, 121, 150, 151, 171, 173, 183, 447, 450
Operating structure, 278
Opinion leader, 409
   (*See also* Key communicator)
Organization environment:
   effects on differentiation and integration, 379–383
   effects of uncertainty on formal and informal communication, 424–426

Organization goals and subgoals, 61–66
   communication as the cordinative or linking coordinative agent, 64–66
   means-ends chains and interdependency, 62–64
Organizational communication, 16–17, 458–461
   definition of, 16
   as a linking or binding agent, 16
   overview of, 458–461
   psychosocial influences on, 17
   structural influences on, 16–17
Organizational influences on communication, 69–70
Organizational performance:
   communication and conflict, 369–371
   conformity to plans, 368–369
   dysfunctional consequences, 368–371
   effects of conflict, 369
   flexible plans and communication, 367
   suboptimization of goals, 369
Organizational politics, 219
Organizations as information processors, 453–462
   formal and informal links to the environment, 456–457
   information linkages between units, 457–458
   interpreting the organization's environment, 455–456
   knowns, unknowns, and unknown unknowns, 453–454
Organizing, 151
Overload, 273

Paralanguage (*see* Nonverbal communication)
Participation:
   freedom to, 290–292
   opportunity for, 292
Perception, 104–109
   effects of receiver motivation, 105
   effects of stereotypes, 105
   faulty assumptions, 107
   influence on encoding and decoding, 30–31
   self-fulfilling prophecies, 105
   transmitter motivation and receiver perception, 104
Perception of organizations (*see* Assumptive maps)
Personal enhancement, 427, 447
Personal growth objectives, 293–296
Personal interaction leadership, 451
Persuasion, 320
Persuasive source, 408–409
   (*See also* Key communicator)

476 SUBJECT INDEX

Plans:
   effective formal: adequacy of plan, 375
      effects of environmental change, 356–357
      effects of role behavior, 355–356
   formal organization: conforming to plans, 354–355
      problem of inflexibility, 353–354
      problem of information retrieval, 351–352
      reliance on documented communication, 351
      specifying and structuring a normative plan, 350–351
Power, 169–173, 197, 198, 207, 214, 221
   coercive, 320
   differences, 169
   expert, 320
   and influence, distribution through organizations, 381–382
   legitimate, 320
   referent, 320
   reward, 320
   tactics, 170–171
Pressure, 159, 170, 263
Problem analysis, 300
   (*See also* Decision making)
Problem definition, 300
   (*See also* Decision making)
Problem solving, 276–277
   (*See also* Decision making)
Problems in communicating, 1–7
   differences in language and meaning, 4–5
   effects of psychological makeup, 5–6
   multiple messages, 4
   situational effects, 5–6
   (*See also* Failures in communication)
Process of communication, 317
   (*See also* Communication process elements)
Production planning, 307
Production subsystem, 444, 459–462
   information needs of, 444
   nature of, 444
   production related communication, 444
Proxemics (*see* Nonverbal communication)
Psychotherapy group, 296

Question, use of, in getting feedback, 192, 198, 199
   (*See also* Active listening; Nondirective counseling)

Receiver, 249
   (*See also* Communication process elements; Decoder)

Refreezing, 213, 215
Relative centrality, 272–273
Resistance to change, 160, 210–213
Resistance to communication, 140, 158–159
Respect in developing self-confidence, 125
Restricting information flows to avoid overload, 370–371
Reward:
   of feedback, 193
   use of, in influencing, 207
Reward value, 133
Richness of communication, 51–57, 153, 451–456
   a comparison of formal and informal channels, 54–57
   definition of, 52
   the influence of message timing, 53–54
   use of rich communication channels, 451, 456
Risk taking, 303–304
Risky shift, 304
Role:
   enacted, 257
   expected, 257
   perceived, 257
Role conflict, 257
Role relationships, 257–258
Role strain, 257
Rumor, 402–403

Saturation, 273
Scanning of information for change, 214–215
Security and maintenance leadership, 427, 447
   (*See also* Dimensions of leadership behavior)
Self-confidence, 120–121, 123–127, 143
   developing, 124
   lack of, 120
Self-disclosure, 173
Self-esteem, 126, 128, 152, 195, 217
Semantic noise and distortion:
   multiple meanings at transmitter and receiver, 47–48
   nature of, and effects on human communication, 46–47
   semantic problems, 36–37
Sender, 249
   (*See also* Communication process elements; Encoder)
Sensitivity group, 293–295
Sentiment, 85–86, 89–90, 148
   (*See also* External and internal systems; External systems; Internal systems)
Shaping of behavior, 207–208, 210
Signals and symbols, relationship of, 25
Situational variables, 323–325

SUBJECT INDEX **477**

Social influence patterns, 259
Social sensitivity, 291
Social structure, 254
Solution, selection of, 301
  (*See also* Decision making)
Special communicator, 406, 408
  (*See also* Key communicator)
Specialization, 173, 174
  (*See also* Division of work)
Status, 133, 172, 173, 197, 198, 254–256
  achieved, 254
  ascribed, 254
Status consensus, 289–290
Structure and upward distortion, 376–378
Structuring communication, 140, 150–152
Styles of communication, 147–164, 321, 323, 326
  controlling, 148–150, 153–159
  dynamic, 148, 151–153, 156
  equalitarian, 148, 150, 153–157, 159–160
  relinquish, 148, 152–156, 161–162
  structuring, 148, 150–151, 153–156, 160–161
  withdrawal, 148, 153–156, 162–163
Subgroups, 220
Superior-subordinate relationship, 120, 139, 140
Superiority implying communication, 178–179

T-group, 293–295
Task relevance, 308–309
Technical problems in communication, 36–37
Technological gatekeeper, 406, 410
  (*See also* Key communicator)
Technological influences on communication, 69–70

Transactional analysis, 133, 137, 150, 153, 217, 230, 282, 293, 296
  adult, 217, 230, 283, 293, 296
  child, 217, 230, 283, 293, 296
  parent, 217, 293
Trust, 183–185
  climate of, 449
  effect on upward distortion, 376–378
Two-step information flows, 404–412
  boundary spanning, 403–408
  gatekeepers, key communicators, and opinion leaders, 406–410
  information potential, 410–412
Two-way communication, 153
  (*See also* Feedback)

Uncertainty (*see* Organization environment; Organizations as information processors)
Unfreezing, 195, 213, 216, 295
Unknown, 453–454
  (*See also* Organizations as information processors)
Unknown area, 136, 137, 154
  (*See also* Johari window)
Upward communication, 87, 375–378
  in bureaucracies, 377
  (*See also* Direction of communication flow; Formal organizational communication)

Withdrawal communication style, 427
  (*See also* Styles of communication)